THE COLLECTED LETTERS OF
JOSEPH CONRAD

GENERAL EDITOR
LAURENCE DAVIES

FOUNDING GENERAL EDITOR
FREDERICK R. KARL (1927–2004)

CONSULTING EDITOR
HANS van MARLE (1922–2001)

VOLUME 8

THE COLLECTED LETTERS
OF JOSEPH CONRAD

VOLUME 8

1923–1924

EDITED BY

LAURENCE DAVIES

AND

GENE M. MOORE

CAMBRIDGE
UNIVERSITY PRESS

CAMBRIDGE UNIVERSITY PRESS
Cambridge, New York, Melbourne, Madrid, Cape Town, Singapore, São Paulo

Cambridge University Press
The Edinburgh Building, Cambridge CB2 8RU, UK

Published in the United States of America by Cambridge University Press, New York

www.cambridge.org
Information on this title: www.cambridge.org/9780521561976

First published 2008

Printed in the United Kingdom at the University Press, Cambridge

A catalogue record for this publication is available from the British Library

ISBN 978-0-521-56197-6 hardback

This volume is dedicated to
Cedric Watts, colleague, mentor,
scholar, and dear friend.

CONTENTS

PLATES

Between pages 152 and 153

These images appear by kind permission of: Corbis Images Ltd (1, 4a); British Library Newspapers (2); Library of Congress, Prints & Photographs Division (3); Princeton University Library Department of Rare Books and Special Collections, Frank N. and Nelson Doubleday Collection (4b); the Hallowes Family and Mr David Miller (5a and b); Special Collections, Baker-Berry Library, Dartmouth College (6a); Estate of Jacob Epstein / Tate Picture Library (6b); Henry W. and Albert A. Berg Collection, The New York Public Library, Astor, Lenox, and Tilden Foundations (7, 8).

ACKNOWLEDGMENTS

The editors are grateful to holders of manuscripts, listed separately, for their co-operation.

Special thanks are due to Dr J. H. Stape, Mr Owen Knowles, and the late Hans van Marle, whose gracious help and wise counsel greatly facilitated work on this volume.

The editors are grateful to the following individuals for answering inquiries or otherwise facilitating their work: Professor Richard Ambrosini, Dr Olga Amsterdamska, Ms Wanda Bachmann, Dr Katherine Baxter, Professor David Benyon, M. Charles Bost (fils), Dr Grażyna Branny, Ms Laura Braunstein (Baker-Berry Library, Dartmouth College, NH), Dr Keith Carabine, Ms Rachel Corkill, Mr Phil Cronenwett (Rauner Special Collections Library, Dartmouth College), Mr Stephen Crook (Berg Collection, New York Public Library), Professor Mario Curreli, Ms Kate and Mr Tom Delaney, Dr Krystina Dietrich, Dr Stephen Donovan, Dr Linda Dryden, Dr Roger Eaton, Mr Simon Edsor (Director, The Fine Art Society, London), Ms Jill and Mr Aubrey Essery, M. Alexandre Fachard, Mr Steve Forbes, Mr Andrew Gaub (Lilly Library, Indiana University), Dr Rick Gekoski, Mr Israel Gewirz (Curator, Berg Collection, New York Public Library), Dr Robert Goldman, Ms Susan Guerrero, Ms Sarah Hartwell (Rauner Special Collections Library, Dartmouth College), Mrs Nina Hayward, Professor James Heffernan, Professor Virginia Jewiss, Professor Neill R. Joy, Ms Bonnie Kirchstein (Director, Forbes Collection, New York), Professor John Kopper, Ms Wendy Lamb, Dr Claes Lindskog, Mr Eric Lupfer (Humanities Research Center, University of Texas at Austin), Dr Donald Mackenzie, Professor Claude Maisonnat, Dr Rob and Ms Kirstie Maslen, Ms Patricia McCaldin (Forbes Collection, London), Mr David Miller, Ms Mary Modeen, Professor Paul Moravec, Professor Zdzisław Najder, Professor Josianne Paccaud-Huguet, Ms Pamela Painter, Ms Véronique Pauly, Dr Marcin Piechota, Mr Ben Primer (Rare Books and Special Collections, Princeton University Library), Professor John Rassias, Professor Sid Reid, Dr Hazel Rowley, Ms Naomi Saito (Beinecke Rare Book and Manuscript Library, Yale University), Dr Allan H. Simmons, Dr Helen Smith, Dr Mariuccia G. R. Sprenger, Professor Ray Stevens, Ms Elizabeth Sudduth (Special Collections, University of South Carolina), Dr George Talbot, Mr Robert Voltz (Special Collections, Williams College),

Professor Andrea White, the late John Ll. Williams, Captain A. D. Wood, Ms Joanne van der Woude, and Professor Melissa Zeiger.

Volume Six of this edition was dedicated to 'the doyen of French Conradians', Sylvère Monod, who died in August 2006. As well as mourning the loss of a kind and brilliant man, we are deeply grateful for the continuing support he gave to this edition, even in the final months of his illness when he gallantly undertook research on Charles Chassé.

The dedication of Volume Eight to Cedric Watts is a small but heartfelt tribute to a great scholar and teacher.

HOLDERS OF LETTERS

Arkansas	Special Collections Division, University of Arkansas Libraries, Fayetteville
Berg	Berg Collection: New York Public Library, Astor, Lenox, Tilden Foundations
BL	The British Library
Bodley	Bodleian Library, Oxford University
Boston	Boston Public Library, Massachusetts
Bryn Mawr	College Archives, Bryn Mawr College, Bryn Mawr, Pennsylvania
BU	The Howard Gotlieb Archival Research Center at Boston University
Clifford	Mr Hugo Clifford-Holmes
Colgate	Special Collections, Colgate University Library, Hamilton, New York
Congress	Manuscript Division, Library of Congress, Washington, DC
Conrad	The late Philip Conrad
Dartmouth	Rauner Special Collections Library, Dartmouth College, Hanover, New Hampshire
Davies	Mrs Helen Davies
Delaware	Special Collections, University of Delaware Library, Newark
Doheny	Estelle Doheny Collection (now dispersed)
Doucet	Bibliothèque littéraire Jacques Doucet, Paris
Duke	William R. Perkins Library, Duke University, Durham, North Carolina
Emory	Special Collections, Woodruff Library, Emory University, Atlanta, Georgia
Favre	M. Pierre Favre
Fitzwilliam	Fitzwilliam Museum, Cambridge
Forbes	Forbes Collection, New York and London
Harvard	Houghton Library, Harvard University, Cambridge, Massachusetts
Haverford	James P. Magill Library, Haverford College, Haverford, Pennsylvania

Wellington	The Honourable Company of Master Mariners, HQS *Wellington*, London
Williams	Chapin Library, Williams College, Williamstown, Massachusetts
Wright	Mrs Purd B. Wright III
Yale	Beinecke Rare Book and Manuscript Library, Yale University, New Haven, Connecticut
Yenter	Mr Charles E. Yenter

PUBLISHED SOURCES OF LETTERS

Books cited without place of publication originated in London.

Adams	Elbridge L. Adams, *Joseph Conrad: The Man* / John Sheridan Zelie, *A Burial in Kent*. New York: William Edwin Rudge, 1925
Candler	Edmund Candler, *Youth and the East: An Unconventional Autobiography*. 2nd edn. Edinburgh: Blackwood, 1932
Carabine and Stape	Keith Carabine and J. H. Stape, 'Family Letters: Conrad to a Sister-in-law and Jessie Conrad on Conrad's Death', *The Conradian*, 30.1 (Spring 2005), 127–31
Conrad (John)	*Joseph Conrad: Times Remembered*. Cambridge University Press, 1981
Curle	Richard Curle, ed., *Letters: Joseph Conrad to Richard Curle*. New York: Crosby Gaige, 1928
Curreli	Mario Curreli, *Cecchi e Conrad: tre lettere inedite*. Viareggio: Pezzini, 1999
CWW	Norman Sherry, *Conrad's Western World*. Cambridge University Press, 1971
Fletcher	Chris Fletcher, *Joseph Conrad*. The British Library Writers' Lives. British Library, 1999
Ford	Ford Madox Ford, *Joseph Conrad: A Personal Remembrance*. Duckworth, 1924
G.	Edward Garnett, ed., *Letters from Joseph Conrad, 1895–1924*. Nonesuch Press, 1928
Głos	Bruno Winawer, ed., 'Listy Conrada', *Głos Prawdy*, 1926, no. 114
Gullason	Thomas A. Gullason, 'The Letters of Stephen Crane: Additions and Corrections', *American Literature*, 41.1 (1996), 104–6
Hunter	Allan G. Hunter, 'Letters from Conrad, 2', *Notes and Queries*, 230 (December 1985), 500–5
J-A	G. Jean-Aubry, ed., *Joseph Conrad: Life & Letters*. 2 vols. Garden City, NY: Doubleday, Page, 1927

JCLW	Jessie Conrad, ed., *Joseph Conrad's Letters to His Wife*. Privately printed, 1927
Jessie Conrad	Jessie Conrad, *Joseph Conrad and His Circle*. Jarrold's, 1935
Keating	George T. Keating, comp., *A Conrad Memorial Library: The Collection of George T. Keating*. Garden City, NY: Doubleday, Doran, 1929
Knowles	Owen Knowles, ed., 'Conrad and David Bone: Some Unpublished Letters', *The Conradian*, 11 (1986), 116–35
Knowles and Miskin	Owen Knowles and G. W. S. Miskin, eds., 'Unpublished Conrad Letters: The H. Q. S. *Wellington* Collection', *Notes and Queries*, 230 (September 1985), 370–6
Knowles and Stape	Owen Knowles and J. H. Stape, 'Conrad and Hamlin Garland: A Correspondence Recovered', *The Conradian*, 31.2 (Autumn 2006), 62–78
Krzyżanowski	Ludwik Krzyżanowski, ed., 'Joseph Conrad: Some Polish Documents', *Polish Review*, 3.1–2 (1958), 59–85 (See also: Ludwik Krzyżanowski, ed., 'Joseph Conrad: Some Polish Documents', in Ludwik Krzyżanowski, ed., *Joseph Conrad: Centennial Essays*. New York: Polish Institute of Arts and Sciences in America, 1960, 111–43)
L. fr.	G. Jean-Aubry, ed., *Lettres françaises*. Paris: Gallimard, 1929
Landfall	David Bone, *Landfall at Sunset: The Life of a Contented Sailor*. Duckworth, 1955.
Letters	*The Collected Letters of Joseph Conrad*, gen. ed. Laurence Davies. 9 vols. Cambridge University Press, 1983–2007
Listy	Zdzisław Najder, ed., Halina Carroll-Najder, trans., *Joseph Conrad: Listy*. Warsaw: Państwowy Instytut Wydawniczy, 1968
Marrot	H. V. Marrot, *The Life and Letters of John Galsworthy*. Heinemann, 1935
Maxwell (1923)	Perriton Maxwell, ed., 'What They Thought of Santa Claus', *Collier's Weekly*, 15 December 1923, p. 10

Maxwell (1924)   Perriton Maxwell, 'A First Meeting with Joseph Conrad', *New York Herald Tribune*, 21 August 1924, sec. 10, p. 1

Meynell   Viola Meynell, ed., *Friends of a Lifetime: Letters to Sydney Carlyle Cockerell*. Cape, 1940

Morley   Christopher Morley, 'The Folder', *Saturday Review of Literature*, 21 May 1927, 845

Mursia (1972)   Ugo Mursia, 'The True "Discoverer" of Joseph Conrad's Literary Talent and Other Notes on Conradian Biography, with Three Unpublished Letters', *Conradiana*, 4.2 (1972), 5–22

Mursia (1980)   Ugo Mursia, 'Arte e vita in una lettera inedita di Conrad', *Nuova Rivista Europea*, 17 (1980), 49–50

Mursia (1983)   Ugo Mursia, *Scritti Conradiani*, ed. Mario Curreli. Milan: Mursia, 1983

Najder   Zdzisław Najder, ed., Halina Carroll-Najder, trans., *Conrad's Polish Background: Letters to and from Polish Friends*. Oxford University Press, 1964

Najder (1969)   Zdzisław Najder, ed., 'Nieznany List Josepha Conrada do Karoli Zagórskiej', *Twórczość*, 1969, no. 8, 106–7

Najder (1970)   Zdzisław Najder, ed., 'Joseph Conrad: A Selection of Unknown Letters', *Polish Perspectives* (Warsaw), 13 (1970), no. 2, 31–45

Najder (1983)   Zdzisław Najder, ed., Halina Carroll-Najder, trans., *Conrad under Familial Eyes*. Cambridge University Press, 1983

NRF   G. Jean-Aubry, ed., 'Lettres françaises de Joseph Conrad', *Nouvelle Revue Française*, 135 (1 December 1924), 108–16

Phelps   William Lyon Phelps, *Autobiography with Letters*. New York: Oxford University Press, 1939

Pion   'Listy Conrada-Korzeniowskiego do Karola Zagórskiego i Anieli Zagórskiej', *Pion*, 15 December 1934, 6

Randall   Dale B. J. Randall, ed., *Joseph Conrad and Warrington Dawson: The Record of a Friendship*. Durham, NC: Duke University Press, 1968

Randall (1969)   Dale B. J. Randall, 'Conrad Interviews, No. 1:
                        Perriton Maxwell', *Conradiana*, 2.1 (1969–70),
                        17–22
Ray   Martin Ray, ed., *Joseph Conrad: Interviews and
                        Recollections*. Macmillan, 1990
Ruch   *Ruch Literacki*, 1927, no. 5, 142–3
Rude (1974)   Donald W. Rude, 'Conrad as Editor: The
                        Preparation of *The Shorter Tales*', in Wolodymyr T.
                        Zyla and Wendell M. Aycock, eds., *Joseph Conrad:
                        Theory and World Fiction*. Lubbock: Texas Tech
                        University, 1974, 189–96
Rude (1986)   Donald W. Rude, 'Joseph Conrad Letters,
                        Typescripts, and Proofs in the Texas Tech
                        Conrad Collection', *The Conradian*, 11 (1986),
                        136–54
Rude (1988)   Donald W. Rude, 'Two Unpublished Joseph
                        Conrad Letters in the Texas Tech University
                        Conrad Collection', *Conradiana*, 20 (1988),
                        159–62
Rude and Neeper   Donald W. Rude and L. Layne Neeper, 'An
                        Unpublished Letter from Conrad to Richard
                        Curle in the Texas Tech Library', *The Conradian*,
                        12 (1987), 78–9
Stape (1988)   J. H. Stape, 'Conrad on the Russian Revolution:
                        An Unpublished Letter', *Notes and Queries*, 233
                        (1988), 335–6
Stape (1989)   J. H. Stape, 'Conrad and J. St Loe Strachey: A
                        Correspondence Recovered', *Conradiana*, 21
                        (1989), 231–40
Stevens   Ray Stevens, 'Conrad, Gilbert Grosvenor, *The
                        National Geographic Magazine*, and "Geography
                        and Some Explorers"', *Conradiana*, 23 (1991),
                        197–202
t. r.   Ford Madox Ford, 'Communications', *transatlantic
                        review*, 1.1 (January 1924), 98–9; facsimile [of 23
                        October 1923] to Conrad, 2.2 (September 1924),
                        326
Visiak   E. H. Visiak, *The Mirror of Conrad*. Werner Laurie,
                        1955

Watts   C. T. Watts, ed., *Joseph Conrad's Letters to R. B.*
                         Cunninghame Graham. Cambridge University Press,
                         1969
Wise   Thomas J. Wise, *A Conrad Library: A Catalogue of*
                         Printed Books, Manuscripts and Autograph Letters by
                         Joseph Conrad. Privately printed, 1928

OTHER FREQUENTLY CITED WORKS

Conrad, Borys   Borys Conrad, *My Father: Joseph Conrad*. Calder & Boyars, 1970

Documents   Gene M. Moore, Allan H. Simmons, and J. H. Stape, eds., *Conrad Between the Lines: Documents in a Life*. Amsterdam: Rodopi, 2000

Moore   Gene M. Moore, 'Conrad Items in the Dent Archive in North Carolina', *Notes and Queries*, 43 (December 1996), 438–9

Morey   John Hope Morey, 'Joseph Conrad and Ford Madox Ford: A Study in Collaboration'. Ph.D. dissertation, Cornell University, 1960

Najder (1978)   Zdzisław Najder, ed., *Congo Diary and Other Uncollected Pieces*. Garden City: Doubleday, 1978

Saunders   Max Saunders, *Ford Madox Ford: A Dual Life*. 2 vols. Oxford: Oxford University Press, 1996

Sherry   Norman Sherry, ed., *Conrad: The Critical Heritage*. Routledge & Kegan Paul, 1973

Stape and Knowles   J. H. Stape and Owen Knowles, eds., *A Portrait in Letters: Correspondence to and about Conrad*. Amsterdam: Rodopi, 1996

Unless otherwise noted, citations of Conrad's work are from the Kent Edition, published by Doubleday, Page, in twenty-six volumes (Garden City, NY, 1925).

CHRONOLOGY, 1923–1924

Unless otherwise stated, dates are for book publication in Britain rather than the United States; dates and locations for essays in periodicals record only the first appearance.

January–March 1923	Returned to work on *Suspense*, suspended during the writing of *The Rover*.
February 1923	Jessie Conrad's *A Handbook of Cookery for a Small House*, with a preface by her husband, published by Heinemann.
8 March 1923	Thomas Beer and Alfred Knopf visited Oswalds.
13 March 1923	Finished 'Part Three' of *Suspense*.
15 March 1923	Declined an honorary degree from Cambridge University.
23 March 1923	Finished preface for Thomas Beer's biography of Stephen Crane.
16 April 1923	Visited Fountaine Hope in Colchester.
17 April 1923	Addressed the National Life-Boat Association at the Aeolian Hall in London, followed by a *soirée* at the home of Mme Alvar.
21 April 1923	Left Glasgow in the *Tuscania* for a promotional tour in America. Wrote 'Ocean Travel' during the voyage.
1 May 1923	Arrived in New York to stay with his American publisher, F. N. Doubleday, at Effendi Hill in Oyster Bay, Long Island.
7 May 1923	'Mass interview' with nineteen journalists at Effendi Hill.
9 May 1923	Lunched with Colonel Edward House and met Ignacy Paderewski.
10 May 1923	Lectured on 'Author and Cinematograph' and read from *Victory* before 200 guests at the Park Avenue home of Mrs Arthur Curtiss James.
15 May 1923	'Ocean Travel' published in the *London Evening News*.

15–24 May 1923	Toured New England with the Doubledays, visiting Yale and Harvard universities, staying with Annabel and William Phelps in New Haven, Margery and Elbridge Adams in the Berkshires.
2 June 1923	Departed from New York in the *Majestic*, accompanied by the Doubledays.
9 June 1923	Arrived back in England.
mid-June 1923	Unable to write because of a severe attack of gout.
July 1923	Resumed work on *Suspense*, plagued by ill health.
1 July 1923	Finished 'Christmas Day at Sea'.
15 July 1923	First meeting with Borys Conrad and his wife after learning that they had married in September 1922.
29 August 1923	Finished '*The Torrens*: A Personal Tribute'.
September–December 1923	*The Rover* serialised in the *Pictorial Review*
12–15 September 1923	The Conrads visited Le Havre to arrange John's stay with the Bost family, which began in mid-October.
26 September 1923	A defective stove forced the Conrads to relocate to London for five days.
October–December 1923	Conrad 'laid up for days and days' with gout and other ailments.
12 November 1923	Finished 'Geography and Some Explorers'.
3 December 1923	*The Rover* published by T. Fisher Unwin on Conrad's sixty-sixth birthday.
24 December 1923	'Christmas Day at Sea' published in the *Daily Mail*.
25 December 1923	Christmas visitors at Oswalds included Jean-Aubry and the Muirhead Bone family.
11 January 1924	Conrad's grandson, Philip James, was born.
February–March 1924	His health somewhat improved, Conrad resumed work on *Suspense*.
March 1924	Sat for the sculptor Jacob Epstein.
March–May 1924	Negotiated with Ford Madox Ford over the rights to their collaborated works.
5 May 1924	Finished Preface to *The Shorter Tales of Joseph Conrad*.
5–8 May 1924	Sir Hugh Clifford visited Oswalds.
14 May 1924	Finished Preface to *The Nature of a Crime*.
27 May 1924	Declined offer of a knighthood from the Prime Minister, Ramsay MacDonald.

June–July 1924	Conrad plagued by bronchitis.
11 June 1924	Invited to luncheon at the Polish Legation, London.
13 June 1924	Jessie Conrad underwent knee surgery, followed by six weeks of recovery in St George's Nursing Home, Canterbury.
July 1924	Worried about finances; began 'Legends' for the *Daily Mail*.
24 July 1924	Jessie Conrad returned from St George's Nursing Home.
3 August 1924	Conrad died of a heart attack at about 8.30 a.m., aged 66.
7 August 1924	Funeral and burial in Canterbury Cemetery.

INTRODUCTION TO VOLUME EIGHT

The company at Oswalds on Christmas Day 1923 included G. Jean-Aubry, the painter Muirhead Bone, the writer Gertrude Bone, and their two sons. John Conrad was home from France for the holidays, Jessie Conrad, suffering from an as yet undiagnosed bone infection, knew only that her leg 'felt sick' (to the Galsworthys, 15 June 1924), and Joseph Conrad had been bedridden for most of December. As he described events for Frank and Florence Doubleday: 'It wasn't a rowdy revel, the major part of the company drinking water steadily, but there were mince pies and a certain affectation of cheerfulness. Your munificent presents were displayed, and John was playing tunes (whether sacred or profane, I am not sure) on the heavenly gong' (7 January 1924).

Looking back a year or two later, Gertrude Bone took a gentler view of this stoically domestic scene, gentler yet acutely observant:

> It was Christmas day at Conrad's house and his last Christmas Day, it transpired, though the shadow was not then upon us. Muirhead, the boys, Jean Aubry & Jessie & I sat around the fire, a soft wet mist drawing the curtain from outside the windows of the salon. Conrad, less than anyone I have ever met, had the home-making faculty. He, the voyager, sought his home here and there in the mind of a friend. No furniture contained him for long. Seated on the other side of the fireplace from myself, he addressed me across it, his face winning & sweet.[1]

She was writing 'to amuse' Edward Garnett, telling him how the conversation turned towards him, how both she and Conrad admired him and yet confessed to being frightened of him. Garnett, a resolute pacifist, was intimidating, so physically large and shaggy, so magisterial in his literary judgments, so – as Conrad put it on that misty day – 'distinguished-looking'. His distinction, indeed, must have been vividly in Conrad's mind that day, for, at the start of the month, Garnett had sent him one of those sympathetic but disconcertingly specific critiques, this time of *The Rover*, that had so often greeted Conrad's latest work. Conrad was moved by it, and exhilarated:

> The generosity of your criticism, my dear Edward, is great enough to put heart into a dead man. As I have not claimed to be more than only half-dead for the last month, I feel, after reading your letter, like a man with wings . . . My absolute belief in your sincerity in questions of literary art has relieved me of that load of weary doubt

[1] Carolyn Heilbrun, *The Garnett Family* (Allen & Unwin, 1961), p. 65, n. 1.

which I have not been able to shake off before . . . Your very prejudices are genuinely
personal and, in a manner of speaking, can be thoroughly trusted.   (4 December)

This trust in Garnett meant that Conrad, too, wrote more openly about his
problems as an author than he could to any prying journalist, or would-be
novelist, or academic with a case to make: 'That scene would have checked
the movement and damaged the conception of Catherine. It would have
been, and it would have looked, a thing "inserted". I was feeling a little bit
heart-sick then, too, and anxious also to demonstrate to myself as soon as
possible that I could finish a piece of work. So I let it go' (*ibid.*).

Ever since their first meeting in 1894, the frightening aspect notwithstanding, Garnett's mind had been one of those where Conrad found a home.
Not the only mind, and not the only spiritual home. He no more required
ideological like-mindedness in his friends than he required ideological consistency in himself. Comforting Ted Sanderson, who felt unworthy to marry
Helen Watson, he wrote 'When we pray: "Lead us not into temptation" we
pray really for the strenght* and courage to resist the evil; for in the belief
of God's Sacrifice and Pity we must work our own salvation' (28 October
1896).[1] Writing at an earlier Christmastide to Garnett, who railed against all
orthodoxies, he brushed aside 'the Bethle[h]em legend . . . that nobody – not
a single Bishop of them – believes in' (22 December 1902; *Letters*, 2, pp. 468–9).
In both cases, though, and with other confidantes and confidants, he knew
someone to whom he could listen as well as talk, someone with whom he was
at home, or, as Gide or Jean-Aubry might have put it, *comme chez soi*.

One way or another, most of the principal happenings in the last year and
a half of Conrad's life touched on the idea of home. Even his experience
of transatlantic crossings, for instance, made him think that 'Formerly a
man setting out on a sea voyage broke away from shore conditions and
found in the ship a new kind of home', whereas the modern liner's comfort,
regularity and speed had turned it into 'a more or less luxurious prison'.[2] His
separations from Jessie Conrad, caused by illness or the visit to the United
States, interrupted their domestic intimacy even though the often tender
correspondence between them provides an enduring demonstration of that
intimacy's strength:

I miss you more and more. As a matter of fact I am on the edge of worrying tho' I
suppose there is no reason for it. It seems ages since I left you in that bedroom in the
hotel.   (30 April 1923)

---

[1] This letter will appear in Volume 9. For the use of asterisks, see 'Editorial Procedures'.
[2] 'Ocean Travel' (originally published as 'My Hotel in Mid-Atlantic'), *Last Essays* (New York:
Doubleday, 1926), pp. 35–6.

I am with you in spirit all the time. I hear each beat of the engines and picture you
to myself very vividly.   (from Jessie Conrad, 23 April)

Yesterday my heart was made glad by the sight of your handwriting. I felt better
at once and by the virtue of Your dear letter I was made to feel fit for the great
dinner-party.   (6 May)

Everything is now ready for dear old John tomorrow. I shall miss him desperately, to
have you all away has never happened before.   (from Jessie Conrad, 26 April)

Don't imagine my dearest that the delights of this country make me forget my home –
which is where you are; and indeed is nothing to me but *You*, You alone wherever you
may be.   ([24 May])

A pervasive longing for the familiar dampened his curiosity and curbed his
old exuberance and wit. A few days after his arrival, he confided his sensations
to Borys: 'All this is not unpleasant but it is not exactly enjoyable. Not from
any fault in the people, but simply because I have lost my power of enjoyment
in strange surroundings and in novel conditions' (6 May).

This letter ends: 'My blessings and a paternal hug to you my dearest son
Yours J. C.' The next day he wrote to John, 'I think of you with affection and
confidence. Your devoted father JC'. In October, John went to stay with the
family of Pastor Bost, the aim being to improve his French. Although he had
already been to boarding school, his absence in France was harder to bear,
Normandy being more difficult to reach than Tonbridge: 'John left home on
Friday for Havre. It will be an experience for him. We shall see. Meantime
we feel bereaved. No child in the house' (to John Galsworthy, 14 October). At
least John's absence was in a good cause, but it compounded the loss brought
about by Borys's secret marriage in September 1922. Conrad was staggered
to hear of it when he came back from the United States, nine months after
the event. Jessie Conrad had known on the very eve of his departure but
spared him the news till he returned. Both of them tried hard to regain
their equilibrium, for, as Conrad observed, 'Marrying is not a crime and one
can not cast out one's son for that. I believe that this particular marriage is
foolish and inconsiderate. I shall not conceal my opinion when I write. My
confidence is shaken but I will not *assume* the worst' (to Eric S. Pinker, 11 June).
Nevertheless, this realignment, and the revelation of the subterfuge that lay
behind – with its implication that Borys had not had confidence in them –
shook the household. Not until the birth of a grandson in January 1924 was
there much in the situation to cheer the family or distract Mrs Conrad from
the miserable condition of her leg:

Jessie bears up very well. She puts in time, upstairs where she is confined, in making
hats and coats for Mʳ Philip J. Conrad who, as far as I have been able to judge, seems

a very decent sort of person indeed. I believe Jessie thinks so too – at any rate she has
been talking of inviting him down here soon.   (to F. N. Doubleday, 28 January)

In the last years of his life, Conrad saw *The Rover* published and struggled in
vain to finish *Suspense*. What we have of the latter poses a critical challenge.
Do the four existing parts constitute a nearly completed whole, or do they
constitute one substantial, nearly completed portion, but only a portion, of
the 'big piece of work – the biggest since "Western Eyes"' (to Eric S. Pinker,
23 March 1923), the novel with 'weight and body enough in what is coming'
promised to Pinker on 3 February 1924 – or do they lack even that sort of
completeness? There is no agreement on these questions.[1] One might take
Conrad at his word, but this is the word of an exhausted man who has
set a mark he cannot reach. One might extrapolate from what is there, as
if finishing a partial building whose plans have gone astray by duplicating
rhythms and extending curves in the 'spirit' of the original, but doing that piles
one questionable authority upon another. One might simply be contented
with a gnomic 'What we have is what we have.' Among much else, what we
do have is the motif of exile.

   All through Conrad's fiction, home and exile go contrapuntally together.
Whatever brings them there, nearly every character in *Almayer's Folly* is an
incomer to Sambir. In *Suspense*, the London émigrés are scandalised when
the Marquis 'leaves the disagreeable lodgings in a squalid street for a little
house in Chiswick', this being 'an abominable apostasy from the faith in a
triumphal return of the old order of things in a month or two' (p. 34). Miss
Aglae, the descendant of uprooted Africans, has herself been doubly exiled,
first from the Antilles, then from France. In Genoa, Adèle lives in a palace
which has 'to Cosmo's eye the air of a sumptuous prison' (p. 80) and has
'had not a moment's peace' since she left the idyllic refuge of the Lathams'
house in Yorkshire (p. 82). The brief restoration of the monarchy allows the
Marquis, who has 'always remained a Frenchman' (p. 101), and his family to
return to France, only to be sent away again, this time to Turin as ambassador
to the Kingdom of Sardinia, with the prospect of London at some later date.
Everyone in the novel as it stands – travellers, émigrés, diplomats, sailors, and
stay-at-homes – lives in the 'uneasy suspense' (p. 106) created by Napoleon,
the most formidable of exiles.

   Not without cause, Conrad detected a 'note of disappointment' in the
critical reception of *The Rover*, though the reason he offered, that 'many

---

[1] The day before he died, Conrad told Curle 'that he saw about six different lines of treatment
    which might be followed in *Suspense*': *The Last Twelve Years of Joseph Conrad* (Garden City:
    Doubleday, 1928), p. 203.

people . . . took that book for the long-talked-of Mediterranean novel' (to Pinker, 3 February 1924), ignores the considerable number of reviewers who compared it to prior achievements rather than future possibilities. Those who were not disappointed dwelt upon its epic quality, especially as shown by Peyrol's final voyage in Chapter 16. In Greek terms, it belongs among the *nostoi*, the epic tales of homecoming, the most famous of these being the return of Odysseus, and the most harrowing, the return of Agamemnon. This particular homecoming begins in Chapter 1, with the 'rumble' of the anchor-cable, the interrogation at the Port Office, and the sunset journey into the Giens Peninsula, where the present landscape merges with Peyrol's memories of the cartwheel tracks, the barren stones, the indigo sea, his mother shaking olives from the trees. Yet this is a frustrated *nostos*; instead of the signs of constancy that greet Odysseus – the aged dog, the marriage bed, the tree, Penelope herself – there are the quill-drivers at the Port Office, the venomous captain who despises Brothers of the Coast, and, all too soon, Citizen Scevola, the master of Escampobar, 'hunter of the ci-devants and priests, purveyor of the guillotine, in short a blood-drinker' (p. 26). The Gang of Virtue is in charge.

As Conrad apparently believed, it was taking charge of the United Kingdom. Nine days after Ramsay MacDonald became the country's first ever Labour Prime Minister, Conrad wrote to Bruno Winawer about his offer to adapt *The Rover* for the stage: 'I do not think that the Labour Government would forbid the play on the ground that being both Poles we are "horrid aristocrats" and enemies of the virtuous Bolsheviks' (31 January 1924). No doubt Conrad was joking, but the acrid aftertaste of his remark is one of many hints that he felt less than at home in post-war Britain, with its strikes, its shifting mores, and its antagonistic politics. For instance, several of the letters to Richard Curle praise his columns in the *Daily Mail*, unsigned, or written as 'John Blunt': 'Blunt is great. Really you are very good in that column' (5 October 1923). In the most recent piece, Curle had deplored 'an idiotic class-hatred . . . profoundly un-English, appealing neither to the English kindliness nor to the English commonsense'. England was loosening its grip on Conrad. Sometimes he thought of southern France, lower taxes, and a warmer climate.

According to Jessie Conrad, her husband had 'a cherished dream to return to Poland to end his days', and she was willing to go with him.[1] Given her

---

[1] *Joseph Conrad and His Circle* (New York: Dutton, 1935), p. 263. She notes that Curle would not accept the idea of Conrad's wanting to go back to Poland. An account by his distant cousin Irena Rakowska, who visited him in July 1924, reinforces Jessie Conrad's version: Najder (1983), pp. 271–2.

infirmity and her ignorance of the language, it would have been an extraordinary sacrifice. And where could they have gone? Central and eastern Ukraine, including the family heartland of Podolia, were now in Bolshevik hands. Poland (which included much of western Ukraine) was no longer at war with what was now the Soviet Union, but the threat of future wars and instability lingered on.

If he could not travel far, he could still travel in his adopted county. The tendency to chafe that Gertrude Bone so shrewdly noticed made Conrad desperate to leave Oswalds, to move to some other part of Kent and take another lease. The house was expensive to maintain, and furnished at 'Mama Grace' Willard's insistence in an over-formal, costly manner that had begun to feel oppressive. With Jessie Conrad still in the nursing home and Miss Hallowes, his secretary, on holiday, he wrote to Auguste Gilbert de Voisins, an exotic aristocrat who had been nearly everywhere, 'je suis seul à me morfondre, dans cette horrible boite que nous espérons quitter en septembre' (11 July 1924).

Irritating though this handsome building with extensive gardens may have been, it was the scene of much good cheer and hospitality, much quiet talking well into the night. During the last years of Conrad's life, the principal companions in these talks were G. Jean-Aubry and Richard Curle. Jessie Conrad, too, was very fond of them both: of Curle for his attentiveness to her husband's interests and his eventful social life; of Jean-Aubry for his solicitude to her, his charm, and his willingness to take a hand at bezique. They also ranked among Conrad's most frequent correspondents. Although based in London, where he edited *The Chesterian*, a wide-ranging magazine put out by a firm of instrument makers but far from being a mere in-house publication, Jean-Aubry spent a great deal of time on the Continent, where he kept up a vigorous programme of lectures on literature and music. Among his favourite topics was Conrad, and, in terms of Conrad's French reception, these lectures spread the word of Conrad's excellence to every corner of France, strengthening the effect of the translations he arranged or carried through himself, and the articles in literary magazines. Conrad's letters to Jean-Aubry are often relaxed and jovial. Planning the visit to Le Havre, for example, to meet the Bost family, an introduction arranged by Jean-Aubry's mother, Conrad wrote:

Trouve-t-on du Bordeaux a l'Hotel de Bordeaux?
    Voulez-Vous dejeuner avec nous le 12. Disons a midi. Avec du Bordeaux.
    M et Mme Bost ne trouveront pas mauvais que ma femme vienne les voir avec moi? Elle veut voir où son oisillon sera niché.   (7 September 1923)

Jean-Aubry kept him *au courant* with contemporary writers: 'Ne m'envoyez pas du Proust (que je vous ai demandé) car les volumes sont arrivés cette après-midi. Mais les vers de Valéry et tel autre œuvre que je dois lire. Oui!' ([26 February 1923]). Now that the correspondence with Gide had dwindled (only two letters to him and two from him survive from 1923 and 1924), Jean-Aubry was Conrad's chief informant on matters French, not to mention his link to the artistic distinction of Louise Harding's salon in Holland Park.

When Conrad set off for his ocean crossing, Richard Curle travelled as far as Glasgow with him and escorted him on board. The first letter to Jessie Conrad from the *Tuscania* epitomises their feelings about Curle. The summary is poignant, for Borys had been unwilling (or, as his father thought, too busy) to see him off in London. 'Dick has been marvellously attentive – could not have looked better after me if he had been our son' (21 April). Moreover, this was a 'son' who could help his father out with literary matters. Curle was adept at putting him in touch with editors, dealers, and collectors, and arranging lucrative projects such as the appearance of the Preface to *Into the East* as a pamphlet before Curle's book had even been published: 'a most welcome windfal[l] which I owe to your ingenious friendship' (6 January 1923). Minding Conrad's financial interests went along with guarding the story of his life and literary reputation – a little too doggedly, some might say, but, subject to correction, Conrad evidently wanted him to persist in his course. That was particularly the case with 'The History of Mr Conrad's Books', an essay written for the *Times Literary Supplement*, reprinted in part by the *New York Times*. (It is typical of Conrad's generosity that, when the American newspaper was slow to pay Curle, he should ask Doubleday to deduct the fee from his own royalties and send it on without a word about its source.) Conrad's letters to Curle of 14 and 17 July 1923 make much of this chance to set the record straight: 'My point of view is that this is an opportunity, if not unique then not likely to occur again in my lifetime' (14 July). Because the American press had been making so much of Conrad as the salt-caked master mariner rather than the professional author of nearly thirty years' standing, he wanted to insist that 'I may have been a seaman, but I am a writer of prose' (*ibid.*). In truth, the real history of his work was artistic, not biographical, a narrative of experiment too mercurial to confine: 'As a matter of fact the thought for effects . . . (often at the cost of mere directness of narrative) can be detected in my unconventional grouping and perspective, which are purely temperamental and wherein almost all my "art" consists' (*ibid.*). Conrad's attitude here is a matter of nuance; warning Curle against taking him literally, he still hopes Curle will pay attention to the spirit of his

words. Conrad is suggesting, rather than dictating, the artistic legacy whose
executor the younger man will be:

My dearest fellow, I can not, (I would never dream!) tell you what to publish and what
not to publish . . . I always come back to my first statement that this is an opportunity
that will never be renewed in my life-time for the judgment of a man who certainly
knows my work best and not less certainly is known for my closest intimate, but before
all is the best friend my work has ever had.   (*ibid.*)

All this of course short, and even crude if you like. You do know how to write pregnant
sentences.   (17 July)

Conrad uses the same arguments about artistry and the pitfalls of biography
in his general correspondence with critics, journalists, teachers, and scholars.
He praises Ruth Matilda Stauffer for her attention to technique (to Ernst P.
Bendz, 7 March 1923). He holds up the King's Treasuries edition of 'Youth'
and 'Gaspar Ruiz' as a model of educating school-age readers (to Doubleday,
10 July 1923). He reminds Henry S. Canby that not even 'Youth' or *The Nigger
of the 'Narcissus'* is simply a sea-story: 'In the "Nigger" I give the psychology
of a group of men and render certain aspects of nature. But the problem that
faces them is not a problem of the sea, it is merely a problem that has arisen
on board a ship' (7 April 1924). Nevertheless, he talked and wrote to Curle as
a familiar, only slightly distanced by the difference in age, a great deal more
by the difference of talent and achievement, yet still in effect his designated
spokesman. To disseminate the idea that the life might stand in the way of
the work, Conrad relied on a man who would claim their intimacy as one of
his strongest qualifications for the role.

   In the past, Conrad had readily hinted to literary acquaintances that works
like *The Shadow-Line* and *The Arrow of Gold* embodied a great deal of personal
experience. What made him so conscious that the legend of his life might
distort the understanding of his books was his visit to the United States, where
he came abruptly into contact with overwhelming celebrity. His picture had
never been on the front page of a newspaper (few serious English papers even
had one), but his arrival in New York made him the lead story, and the face of
the man in a bowler hat, his eyes deep-set, his eyebrows black and heavy, his
beard elegantly grizzled, peered from every news-stand. Before his journey,
he expressed his anxieties to Elbridge L. Adams, an American lawyer and
booklover whom he had known since 1916, when they spent an afternoon
drive heatedly debating ends, means, and individual liberty. Having survived
the experience without rancour, Conrad was able to confide in him: 'What
frightens me most is the fact that people on your side won't be able to
understand how the commonest social exertion may on any given day be
too much for me, and take my shrinking for ungraciousness, or laziness, or

lack of appreciation, or any other repulsive trait of character' (22 January 1923).

Another admirer was Christopher Morley, a poet, novelist, and literary journalist who tried to make the best of Prohibition in venerable bars and chop-houses where he and his circle could find barely legal shandygaff and cider. Conrad had not yet met him, but liked the advance publicity he had been writing for Doubleday, and saw him as, potentially, a reassuring presence: 'I do hope that I will find you within reach of my arm for that hand-grip which may be made to mean much more than any amount of blackened paper' (5 February 1923). In dealing with his visit, Conrad could also muster considerable powers of restraint and charm: 'you need not be uneasy about the safety of American pressmen. I am going to leave my revolver at home. If I have to show them my teeth (artificial) it will only be in an agreeable smile' (to John Galsworthy, 14 April). The reality, however, taxed his powers: not only the onslaught of reporters and photographers on the wharf, or the 'Polish deputation men and women (some of these quite pretty)' who 'rushed me on the wharf and thrust enormous nosegays into my hands' (to Jessie Conrad, 4 May), but a formidable array of the great and would-be good all eager to have him in their drawing-rooms, or at their dinner-tables, or hear him read and briefly talk at the Curtiss James mansion on Park Avenue: 'One hour and a quarter with an ovation at the end . . . people fought for invitations' (to Curle, 11 May). The impresarios of this spectacle were the Doubledays, who seem to have managed the whole visit with a judicious balance of consideration for their guest and acknowledgment that their lion-in-residence was greatly in demand. From the time of the visit onwards, the tone of the correspondence reflects the warming of an often cautious and sometimes testy professional relationship into open affection:

D'day insists on sending you a message in every week-end cable they dispatch to Europe. It is very nice of him and I am pleased to think you will hear of me pretty often . . . Mrs Dou'day has just knocked at the door of my bedroom (next to the billiard-room) to say good-night (she had been out) and ask me to remember her to you. She is really very good and tries to make me feel at home.   (*ibid.*)

Give Effendi a slap on the back from me. The hearty kind you know. He is great – that's settled!   (to Florence Doubleday, 15 July)

Thank you for all your nice letters. I hope I am not making myself a nuisance to you and partners with my comments, questions, and suggestions. Don't imagine I am *insisting* on anything I may propose. The decision rests with the House.
(to F. N. Doubleday, [27 August])

This was not the way that Conrad usually wrote to publishers, much less about them.

Conrad's other warm professional relationship was with Eric Pinker. The day *The Rover* was published in Britain, he wrote to him: 'My thoughts were very much with poor J. B. this morning . . . And I am touched to think that now he is gone from us the connection is not broken, since he left me on going away the friendship of his son which has been such a support to me both in my public work and in my private life, for nearly two years now' (3 December). With the son, Conrad had soon settled into an easy candour. He took him into his confidence about Borys and his marriage, the extent of Jessie Conrad's suffering, and his own 'flabbiness of heart', a literal and a figurative diagnosis: 'All the other powers of my ego are similarly affected – intellect, the power of kicking – of getting into a rage – of making jokes' (8 November). Even so, this letter has its own wry wit, and Conrad is not so sunk in misery as to forget to ask after Pinker's wife, Margit, who was going through a difficult pregnancy. Conrad's being sorry for himself almost never stopped his being sorry for the troubles of his intimates.

The bulk of the correspondence with Eric Pinker concerns business matters, but here, too, there is a frankness that recalls Conrad's dealings with his father, J. B. Thus the discussions over Thomas Beer's invitation to preface his biography of Crane turn not simply on the lavish fee offered but on its ethical snags and the possible squandering of his own energies: 'Personally I don't want to behave like a ghoul, feeding on the memory of a departed friend . . . In Beer's case the man is thrusting the amount on me without the slightest suggestion on our part (I take it). The real question is whether I can afford in the present circumstances to throw away the offered sum' (9 March 1923). He returned to such questions after finishing his 8,300 words: 'So strictly speaking I would have done better for myself *morally* and financially if I had stuck to my novel' (23 March). Conrad relied on Pinker's discretion and good sense (this was well before his disgrace in the USA, where he was jailed for peculating clients' funds), not least in dealings with Ford Madox Ford. Long ago they had been collaborators, but the sultry emotional climate of Ford's time at the *English Review* and the collapse of his marriage soured what had been a gleeful friendship. For a while it sweetened again amid the intensities and dangers of the war, but once more Conrad had come to see him as an egotistical pest, 'the swelled-headed creature who seems to imagine that he will sweep all Europe and devastate Great Britain with an eventual collected edition of his own works' (to Pinker, 1 May 1924). At issue were the book-form edition of *The Nature of a Crime*, Ford's plans for the *transatlantic review*, and the question, ever an irritant to Conrad but more fretsome now that collected editions were appearing, of how to present – and how to allocate the royalties from – their co-authorship of two novels. Whatever the rights and wrongs of the prolonged and stiffly polite exchanges between Conrad and Ford, Conrad's agent indubitably earned the title of 'My dear (long suffering) Eric' (15 February 1924).

Conrad's abhorrence of being framed as a maritime writer did not mean that he had in any way renounced his seafaring past. The letter to the Owners and Ship's Company of the *Tusitala* (2 June 1923) ends 'in all confidence and affection'. Nostalgia for life at sea and a keen interest in anything to do with ships feature in many letters, among them those to Lieutenant Blanchenay (8 April 1924) about an embarrassing anachronism (anachronistic by only a few years) in the opening paragraph of *The Rover*; to John C. Niven ([5 December 1923]) about old times in the *Vidar*; to Mrs Ffooks (4 April 1923) about improvements to lifeboats and the history of the *Lady Jocelyn*; to Captain Phillips (12 January 1924) about Captain Cope's ill-luck aboard the *Torrens* and the unnervingly mechanical routines of ocean liners ('But I remained cold, completely cold before all those things which make the position of a ship's officer almost an indoor occupation'); and to his host in one of those liners, the amiable and bookish Captain David Bone:

> I confess that as soon as that project of a visit to the US came up for consideration I formed the intention to stow myself away on board the ship you commanded. In my time the stowaways (to Sydney) were kindly treated. But as I see from your letter that you are disposed to treat me kindly in any case I'll try to get a ticket in the usual way and let "romance" go by the board.   (17 February 1923)

In the unfamiliar role of passenger, Conrad found himself better equipped than the captain's brother Muirhead Bone: 'Our cabin steward is an amiable old fraud. He has taken Muirhead in completely – but I have talked straight to him this morning at 7 a.m. and we are now on terms of a strict understanding as to service and tips' (to Jessie Conrad, 22 April 1923).

The correspondence offers other glimpses of Conrad's past. He was worried about the health of his oldest and one of his closest English friends, Fountaine Hope, who had suffered a stroke, and corresponded with Hope's son, who was named after Conrad (9 March 1924). A letter to Amelia Ward (24 May 1924) recalls the days of lodging with her family in the north-east London suburb of Stoke Newington. Another, to Jessie Conrad's sister Dolly Moor (31 January 1924), who was living in Zululand, remembers carrying her to bed as a child: 'Generally you would be fast asleep and as insensible as a stone, but, of course much more pleasant to carry.'

As in previous volumes, the letters to and from the Zagórska sisters kept up an important connection with his relatives, all the more because Aniela had been busy with translating his work and assembling the first Polish collected edition. Stefan Pomarański sent him the precious gift of poems in the hand of Apollo Korzeniowski (28 June 1924). The translator Kate Żuk-Skarszewska, the literary historian Roman Dyboski, and two of the most important contemporary authors, Bruno Winawer (who proposed a stage version of *The Rover*) and Stefan Żeromski (who wrote a 'wonderful preface' to *Almayer's Folly*: 25 March 1923) sent him news of contemporary Polish writing. Conrad was well aware that, troubled and often threatened as the new Poland was, its renewed independence had brought fresh life to all the arts.

Then, as ever, there were those whose relation to Conrad over the years exemplified Gertrude Bone's description of 'the voyager' who 'sought his home here and there in the mind of a friend': Cunninghame Graham and Hugh Clifford, for example. We have only two letters from this period to Graham and three to Clifford, but many passing references in letters to others to remind us that these men of widely differing views each had a temperament, a knowledge of life, an energy, and an authority that exhilarated Conrad. 'I don't remember such a great pleasure for years than that your letter in praise of Gaspar Ruiz has given me . . . to receive such a testimony to its general truth (of impression) *from You*, is the most gratifying thing that has happened to me in my career – of letters' (to Graham, 30 March 1923). Graham would have known exactly the pull of experience outside the literary sphere signified by that dash. The same alert familiarity prompts this response to Clifford's *Address to the Legislative Council of Nigeria*: 'Yes my dear friend! – I haven't missed either the romance or the spirituality of high endeavour in Your report' (30 March 1924); or this farewell after a period of home leave: 'Au revoir then my dear friend. I hope kind Heaven will look after you – I mean our Heaven which knows not the Gods of the Wilderness' (22 August 1923). Whole histories of colonial thought and feeling lie packed in these remarks, and they are among the several tangled clues this volume offers to Conrad's sense of Africa (see, for instance, the letter to Galsworthy about his play *The Forest*, 8 June 1924). Yet whatever Conrad or Clifford may have meant by 'the Gods of the Wilderness' or, at least in Conrad's case, by 'Heaven', their understanding was mutual, and they knew a dialect of their own.

The same experience of a language shared pervades the letters to Rothenstein, Galsworthy, Gardiner, Walpole, and Garnett. It is there as well in Conrad's response to the news of Lady Colvin's mortal illness (when neither he nor Jessie Conrad was well enough to travel to London), shot through with regret for something now impossible:

What adds to my desolation is the awful feeling of not being able to show in any way the profound affection I have for you both, dear Lady Colvin and for dear Colvin whose friendship is the greatest reward and the most precious gift that the gods have given me . . . I feel and Jessie feels with me, that we ought to be nearer – to have always been nearer – to You both. (8 July 1924)

Only one late letter to Sir Robert Jones survives, but it begins 'Dearest and best of friends' (19 April 1923), suggesting that he too belonged in this group of intimates, almost all men, but otherwise so various by temperament, by vocation, and by understanding of the world.

A letter to a schoolgirl on the verge of her teens broadens – and lightens – the picture of Conrad's making himself at home with other minds. Veronica, daughter of Ralph and Iris Wedgwood, wanted to compare notes about Corsica, where the Conrads had spent nine weeks in 1921. Conrad replied with a hectic series of tall stories. A driver abandons his horse and trap to climb a mimosa tree, leaving the Conrads 'within about three inches from the edge of a dreadful precipice'. All Conrad's bribes and blandishments fail to get the driver down:

The mimosa shook and cracked most pathetically. The horses dozed. The precipice yawned (they always do), and I admired the Corsican scenery but wished myself back in England – on Romney Marsh for preference. Yes, Corsica is a lovely island, but dangerous – because of its drivers who are a public terror; and thus worse than the vendettas which are private affairs. Did Cook's people show you a vendetta? I haven't seen one but I saw a bandit. He was quite tame. He took a cigarette from my hand most delicately. (31 March 1923)

Now that Veronica is 'taking' her mother to Constantinople, she will be stepping into a world of '18th century tales' but Conrad has devised an elaborate plan to rescue her. This is a letter for someone young enough to take tall tales a little seriously yet old enough to laugh at their conventions – someone not dissimilar to Conrad. It ends, 'and please, my dear, keep a little corner of your heart for your old and frivolous friend'.

When Conrad sent Arnold Bennett a copy of *The Rover*, he wrote a letter to go with it in a firm and elegant hand unaffected by the gout-pained tremble that marked so much of his recent correspondence. Bennett had long admired his fiction, and Conrad always remembered his enthusiasm for *Nostromo*. 'I feel (why conceal it?) that twilight lies already on these pages. Perhaps it is not unfitting that the man who for twenty years or more gave to my work so many proofs of his appreciation should now accept this book from my hand' (5 December 1923). Not long before, he had described himself to Walpole as a 'crocky, groggy tottery, staggery, shuddery shivery, seedy, gouty . . . wretch' (19 November). An atmosphere of death foretold envelops Conrad's final months. The last two novels are often read as farewells. Peyrol's homecoming, the offering up of his life in the French cause, and the epigraph from Spenser in *The Rover*, the dialogue between Attilio and Cosmo on the last page of *Suspense* – these, it would appear, belong to the twilight. Yet, as we have seen, though Peyrol comes home to a familiar landscape, its inhabitants and its mores are not familiar; as Charles Chassé pointed out in his review for the *Figaro, supplément littéraire*, his death is one of a long chain of Conradian suicides; the moving words that promise 'Sleep after toyle, port after stormie seas' are spoken in *The Faerie Queene* by Despair; as published, the final paragraphs of *Suspense* were far from the last to be written.

To borrow Cedric Watts's term, Conrad's work is janiform; the appropriate sculptural analogy might not even be the Roman god who faces both ways but the many faces of a Hindu deity. In this, his life – and death – accorded with his work. The man who had dismissed 'the Bethle[h]em legend' was buried in consecrated ground according to the rites of the Roman Catholic Church. In itself this fact is not surprising; although no frequenter of rituals or ceremonies, Conrad had a sense of the ceremonious, the done thing. Concerned with family morale and the after-life of reputation, he may have made a Pascalian wager, not so much on faith as on observance. More illuminating, though, than such a guess is his reply to Gordon Gardiner, who had asked him to join a club restricted to communicants of the Church of England; in the religious sense, Canterbury was not as near to him as Rome: 'though dogma sits lightly on me I have never renounced that form of Christian religion' (8 October 1923). As his letter firmly but courteously pointed out, he was born to the religion of his Polish kin. His grave bears a misspelled version of his Polish name and the two comforting yet potentially deceptive lines from Spenser. Was he, as some Polish-American scholars like to put it, 'always sailing toward Poland'? Was he, as Cunninghame Graham's memorial tribute suggests, buried in the right place, 'his sails all duly furled, ropes flemished down, and with the anchor holding truly in the kind Kentish earth'?[1] Was he at heart an exile, a hybrid, a *peregrinus*, divorced by circumstance from any hope of either being at home or coming home? Was he, to return to Gertrude Bone's observations, only at home in, and with, the minds of others – his wife, his family, certain friends, even certain casual acquaintances who knew a thing or two about the world? It is hard to imagine him invoking Wordsworth's 'inward eye / Which is the bliss of solitude'. In his home and for his work, Conrad wanted tranquillity but also

---

[1] Written for the *Saturday Review*, 16 August 1924, pp. 162–3, and known variously as 'Inveni Portum' and 'Inveni Portam': 'I Have Found Port' or 'I Have Found the Door' – the uncertainty seems apt.

company. Few authors in the twentieth century have written so much about solitude, both the forces that create it and the experience itself, but unlike Beckett, or Kafka, or Pirandello, Conrad also writes at length about the joy (and sometimes the awkwardness or horror) of recognising kindred beings.

If we think of *The Rover* as a *nostos* imagined by a man who had been a 'young Ulysses' in Marseilles, we might remember, if only in passing, that Ulysses was not only a mariner and hero but a survivor and the prince of tricksters who, in some versions of the story, is not content to live in Ithaca. Was Conrad an ever-resourceful survivor, whether as the follower of 'a few very simple ideas . . . notably . . . the idea of Fidelity',[1] or as somebody who, like Keats's Shakespeare, could live with contradiction, 'capable of being in uncertainties, Mysteries, doubts, without any irritable reaching after fact & reason'? It is fitting that an enigmatic author should be buried with an enigmatic epitaph. In his Author's Note to *The Shadow-Line*, disparaging the 'supernatural' (by which he may simply mean the uncanny as opposed to the religious), Conrad writes that, 'The world of the living contains enough marvels and mysteries as it is.' Among these marvels and mysteries are his life and works, not least as they appear in his letters.

Laurence Davies
University of Glasgow

---

[1] 'A Familiar Preface', *Some Reminiscences* (1912).

CONRAD'S CORRESPONDENTS
1923–1924

A dagger after a name marks a tentative ascription.

Elbridge L(apham) ADAMS (1866–1934) attended Williams College and practised law first in Rochester, New York, and then after 1906 in New York City. He first met Conrad in England in 1916. During Conrad's tour of New England, he spent two days as the Adamses' guest at Green River Farm, their country home near Great Barrington in western Massachusetts. An ardent bibliophile, in 1931 Adams purchased and published the correspondence between George Bernard Shaw and Ellen Terry.

J(ohn) A. ALLEN (b. 1855) was a London publisher with offices at 16 Grenville Street, near Russell Square, Bloomsbury. In 1925 Allen reprinted a series of articles by Lord Darling from the London *Evening News* on crime, insanity, and murder, and in 1926, Kipling's speech 'The Art of Fiction' from *The Times*. After 1926 the firm specialised in equestrian literature.

Mme ALVAR: see HARDING

Frédéric-Ferdinand AUBRY (b. 1860) was G. Jean-Aubry's father.

Jean-Frédéric-Émile AUBRY (1882–1950) wrote as G., Georges, or Gérard Jean-Aubry. Born in Le Havre, he became a friend of many composers, including Debussy and Ravel; both Falla and Roussel wrote settings of his poems. He first met Conrad in 1918, became a close friend, and worked to promote Conrad's reputation with *Joseph Conrad in the Congo* (1926), *Joseph Conrad: Life & Letters* (1927), *Lettres françaises* (1929), *The Sea Dreamer: A Definitive Biography* (1947; trans. 1957), and numerous French translations of Conrad's works. From 1919 to 1930, he lived in London, editing *The Chesterian*, a magazine published by a firm of musical instrument makers.

Thérèse AUBRY (née Contant) and her husband, Frédéric-Ferdinand Aubry, were the parents of Conrad's friend Jean-Aubry. They lived at various addresses in Le Havre and had a country house at nearby Fontenay (Montivilliers). She helped arrange for Conrad's son John to stay with the family of Pasteur Bost in order to improve his French.

An anarchist and secularist, Ambrose G(eorge) Barker (1862–1932) was keenly interested in the history of English dissidence. He wrote a history of the Walthamstow Working Men's Club and Institute, and built up a notable collection of works by and about Tom Paine; later (1938), he published a biography of Henry Hetherington, a leading Chartist, publisher of radical newspapers, and opponent of censorship.

Lt-Col. Matthew Gerald Edward Bell (1871–1927) was the owner of Bourne Park, Bishopsbourne, and thus the Conrads' landlord at Oswalds. He had served in India and Somalia.

Ernst Paulus Bendz (1880–1966) graduated from Lund University in 1914 with a dissertation on Oscar Wilde, and taught in Gothenburg. He often travelled to England and France, and published many articles and reviews in Sweden and Finland. His thirteen books in Swedish include studies of Alfred de Vigny, Paul Valéry, André Gide, François Mauriac, and Henri de Montherlant.

(Enoch) Arnold Bennett (1867–1931) is best remembered for novels such as *The Old Wives' Tale* and the Clayhanger trilogy, set in the 'Five Towns' of Staffordshire where he spent his youth. After a decade in Paris, Bennett returned to England in 1912 and served during the First World War as Director of Propaganda for the War Ministry. In 1918 he refused a knighthood. He was a longstanding admirer of Conrad's work and reviewed it perceptively.

'Lieutenant de vaisseau' Blanchenay, as Jean-Aubry calls him, was presumably the same person as the more junior 'enseigne de vaisseau' who had translated Pietro Gribaudi's study of Genoa as *Le Port de Gênes, les voies d'accès des Alpes*; later published in book form (Paris, n. d.), it first appeared in the *Revue Maritime* for October 1910. Tentatively, he may be identified as Pierre-Frédéric Blanchenay (1884–1958), born in Tebessa, Algeria, to a military family with connections in Toulon.

Trained as a lawyer, the Valencia-born writer and political activist Vicente Blasco Ibáñez (1867–1928) edited a radical republican journal, *El Pueblo*, and was imprisoned many times over for his anti-royalist activities; he went into voluntary exile in 1923. His internationally famous novels *Los cuatro jinetes del Apocalipsis* (1916, trans. as *The Four Horsemen of the Apocalypse*, 1918), a rendering of the First World War, and *Sangre y arena* (1908, trans. as *Blood and Sand*, 1913), a story of bull-fighting, became immensely popular films. His other novels include *Cañas y barro* (1902, trans. as *Reeds and Mud*, 1928) and *Mare Nostrum* (1918).

Captain David William BONE (1874–1959; knighted 1946), the brother of Muirhead and James Bone, first went to sea in 1890. He served with the Anchor Line after 1899, eventually becoming Commodore, and commanded troop ships in both World Wars. He was captain of the *Tuscania*, in which Conrad sailed to New York. Although discouraged by Conrad from 'leaving the ship' to become a writer, he produced numerous sea tales and nautical memoirs, among them *The Brassbounder* (1910).

Actress, director, and playwright, Louise BURLEIGH (1890–1960) staged twenty-four plays while a senior at Radcliffe College. An energetic proponent of the Little Theater movement, she published *The Community Theatre in Theory and Practice* (1917) and moved in 1919 to Richmond, Virginia, to direct the Richmond Little Theater League. In 1928 she married Conrad's acquaintance, the pianist and composer John Powell (*q. v.*).

A Yale graduate, Henry S(eidel) CANBY (1878–1961) edited the *New York Evening Post Literary Review* before founding the *Saturday Review of Literature* in 1924 and organising the Book-of-the-Month Club two years later. A Yale professor after 1922, Canby influenced American literary tastes for decades. His many publications include an autobiography and studies in nineteenth-century American literature. Among the items in his collection *Definitions* (New York: Harcourt, 1922) is an article reprinted from the *Evening Post*, 'Conrad and Melville' (pp. 257–68), one of the first to bring these authors together. He wrote introductions to *Within the Tides* for Doubleday's Memorial Edition (1925) and *Under Western Eyes* for Keating's *A Conrad Memorial Library* (1929).

A teacher, traveller, and author, Edmund CANDLER (1874–1926) read classics at Cambridge, then taught in Indian schools and colleges from 1896 to 1903. From 1906 to 1914 he was Principal of Mohindra College in Patiala. He was for many years a prolific correspondent and travel writer for *Outlook*, *Blackwood's*, and the *Allahabad Pioneer*. Grievously wounded in Tibet in 1904, he recovered to become the official correspondent with the Indian Expeditionary Force in Mesopotamia in 1917, recording his experiences in *The Long Road to Baghdad* (2 vols., 1919). He was also a roving reporter for *The Times* in the Transcaucasian republics in 1918–19. After the war he retired to the French Basque country.

A Florentine living in Rome, the scholar and critic Emilio Martino Gaetano CECCHI (1884–1966) was instrumental in introducing the works of Conrad and other English and American authors to Italian readers; one highly influential work was his *Storia della letteratura inglese nel secolo XIX* (1915). A prolific author of essays, travel narratives, and studies in art history, and co-founder of the Roman literary review *La Ronda*, Cecchi became one of the foremost Italian critics of the first half of the twentieth century. Most of his essays on Conrad were reprinted in *Scrittori inglesi e americani* (Lanciano: Carabba, 1935).

Charles CHASSÉ (1883–1965), a French writer on English literature and modern art, took a particular interest in the work of Gauguin and the Fauvists. He was Director of the Paris School of New York University, and in 1922 published *Les Sources d'Ubu roi*, a study of Alfred Jarry's iconoclastic play. He wrote two books on Brittany and studies of Mallarmé and the Nabis; among the authors he translated were Sir Thomas Browne, Izaak Walton, Sir Walter Scott, Gordon Craig, George Bernard Shaw, and H. G. Wells.

Samuel Claggatt CHEW (1888–1960), a graduate of Johns Hopkins University, taught English literature at Bryn Mawr College from 1914 to 1954. The author of several books and some 3,000 book reviews, in 1925 he was awarded first prize in the *Saturday Review of Literature* contest to suggest an ending for Conrad's *Suspense*.

American-born, George Herbert CLARKE (1873–1953) was educated in Canada and taught at various universities in the USA. From 1925 until his retirement in 1943, he was Professor of English and head of the English Department at Queen's University in Ontario. The *Sewanee Review*, which he edited from 1920 to 1925, featured his essay on Conrad in July 1922. He reviewed *The Rover* and *Suspense* for the same journal.

Harald Leofurn CLARKE (1874–1942) was an apprentice on Conrad's first voyage in the *Torrens* in 1891–2. He eventually earned a master's certificate and was Harbour Master of Suva, in the British colony of Fiji, where he died.

Born into an aristocratic West Country Roman Catholic family, the Cliffords of Chudleigh, Sir Hugh Charles CLIFFORD (1866–1941; knighted 1909) went out to Singapore in 1883 to begin a career as a colonial administrator. He was serving as British Resident in Pahang, Malaya, when he wrote one of the earliest general appreciations of Conrad's work for the *Singapore Free Press*. Later, he was appointed to the governorships of Labuan and North Borneo, the Gold Coast, Nigeria, Ceylon, and the Straits Settlements. He published many volumes of short stories and sketches set chiefly in East Asia, and the novel *The Downfall of the Gods* (1911), whose background is the decline of the Khmer empire; collaborated on a Malay dictionary; and produced a Malay translation of the colonial penal code. His restless energy and independent mind were a frequent irritation to the Colonial Office.

After a brief career as a coal merchant, Sydney Carlyle COCKERELL (1867–1962; knighted 1934) became secretary to William Morris and the Kelmscott Press. Director of the Fitzwilliam Museum, Cambridge, from 1908 to 1937, he was widely connected in artistic circles and counted among his literary friends not only Conrad but Wilfrid Scawen Blunt and Thomas Hardy.

Frances, Lady COLVIN (née Fetherstonhaugh, 1839–1924), made a living as an essayist after she separated from her first husband, the Revd A. H. Sitwell. She married Sidney Colvin in 1903, and they became close friends with Conrad, as they had been with Stevenson.

Sir Sidney COLVIN (1845–1927; knighted 1911) was among Conrad's closest literary friends. Conrad loved to read English poetry with him. Colvin had been Slade Professor of Fine Arts at Cambridge and Director of the Fitzwilliam Museum; from 1884 to 1912, he was Keeper of Prints and Drawings at the British Museum. Among his literary works were editions of Stevenson's letters and biographies of Walter Savage Landor and John Keats.

Alfred Borys Leo CONRAD (1898–1978), Conrad's elder son, was educated at private schools and in the training-ship HMS *Worcester*. Gassed and shell-shocked during the war, he found employment with the Daimler Company in Manchester and London. His secret marriage in September 1922 strained relations with his parents, but the birth of a grandson in 1924 helped to reconcile them.

Jessie Emmeline CONRAD (née George, 1873–1936), the second of nine children, met her future husband in 1894 when she was working as a typist and living with her widowed mother. The Conrads married in March 1896. An accident in 1904 exacerbated a previous knee injury, leaving her lame and in pain for the rest of her life despite a series of operations in 1917–24. In addition to a cookery book (1923) and a signed limited edition of her correspondence with her husband (1927), she published two accounts of their life together: *Joseph Conrad as I Knew Him* (1926) and *Joseph Conrad and His Circle* (1935).

(Madeline) Joan CONRAD (née King, 1894–1981) met Borys Conrad during the war. They married secretly in 1922, but Conrad knew nothing of the marriage until his return from America in June 1923. Jessie Conrad, in particular, was hostile to it and to her daughter-in-law: 'Apart from the secrecy, which was not necessary, it was a most disastrous marriage from every point. To begin with she is not even of a good working class, in fact she belongs nowhere. Both Conrad and and* I tried to make the best of it' (Jessie Conrad to Warrington Dawson, 18 May 1926, MS Duke). They were officially separated in 1933, after a three-year estrangement (Jessie Conrad to Walter Tittle [1935], MS Texas).

John Alexander CONRAD (1906–82), Conrad's younger son, spent much of 1923 and 1924 away from home at boarding school in Tonbridge or learning French in Le Havre. He later made a career as an architect, and became executor of the Conrad estate in 1944. His memoir, *Joseph Conrad: Times Remembered* (1981), provides details of the Conrads' domestic life.

F(rederic) G(eorge) COOPER (1876–1966) served in the war as a transport officer and was appointed Lieutenant Commander in 1915, leaving the service as Commander in 1921. His articles on Conrad, whom he had met, appeared in the *Nautical Magazine* (1921), *Blue Peter* (1929), *Mariner's Mirror* (1940), and *Annual Dogwatch* (1953).

The actor, director, theorist, and playwright Jacques COPEAU (1879–1949) was one of the most important figures in modern French theatre. Together with André Gide and others, he founded the *Nouvelle Revue Française* in 1909 and in 1913 launched the innovative Théâtre du Vieux-Colombier, whose acting school he directed from 1921 to 1925. He adapted Dostoevsky's *The Brothers Karamazov* for the stage, and played the part of Mikulin in Marc Allégret's 1936 film version of *Under Western Eyes*.

Edith F(leming) CRANE (1886–1962) was Stephen Crane's niece, the daughter of his older brother Edmund Brian Crane (1857–1922) and Mary L. Fleming. She lived in Port Jervis, New York, where her grandfather had been a Methodist minister.

Born in Scotland, Richard Henry Parnell CURLE (1883–1968) left Wellington College in 1901 and established himself as an author and journalist in London. His friendship with Conrad began with an article published in 1912, which he elaborated into the first full-length appreciation of Conrad's work, *Joseph Conrad: A Study* (1914). A prolific writer, Curle also published three volumes of short stories, along with accounts of his travels in Burma and Malaya, including *Into the East* (1923), to which Conrad contributed a preface. From 1919 to 1928, Curle wrote a regular column for the *Daily Mail* under the pseudonym 'John Blunt', as well as unsigned articles 'from Our Special Correspondent'. A close friend of the Conrad family, he published an account of Conrad's final days (1928) and a volume of their correspondence (1928). He arranged for the publication of Conrad's last novel, *Suspense* (1925), and served with Ralph Wedgwood as executor of Conrad's estate until 1944. Curle married Cordelia Fisher (1879–1970) in 1912; they were divorced in 1923. Charles, their son, always known as Adam (1916–2006), devoted his life to the theory and practice of pacifism.

The Texas-born journalist and author Clare Ogden Davis (1892–1970) was a police reporter before her marriage to John Burton Davis, with whom she collaborated on seven novels under the pen name Lawrence Saunders. Her interview on 24 July would have been the last granted by Conrad, but there is no record of its publication.

Author, editor, and translator, Henry-Durand Davray (1873–1944) was an active promoter of Anglo-French cultural friendship. As editor of the Collection d'auteurs étrangers for the *Mercure de France*, he translated novels by Conrad, Arnold Bennett, Rudyard Kipling, George Meredith, and H. G. Wells.

Major Ernest Dawson (1884–1960) was introduced to Conrad by W. H. Henley and H. G. Wells. He served in Burma as a magistrate and an officer in the Rangoon Volunteer Rifles, and contributed reminiscences and stories of Burma and Australia to *Blackwood's Magazine*. He lived in Rye, East Sussex, but he spent long periods of his retirement on the Continent. His brother A. J. Dawson was also among Conrad's friends.

(Francis) Warrington Dawson (1878–1962) came from a family of former plantation owners in Charleston, South Carolina. He wrote prolifically – fiction, essays, newspaper stories – and covered strikes, wars, peace conferences, and French politics. To quote Randall, 'he had a special taste and talent for conversing with the great and near-great' (p. 4). In 1909, while on a safari in East Africa with Theodore Roosevelt, he met Conrad's old friends the Sandersons, and when Dawson came to England in May 1910 to report the funeral of Edward VII, he carried an introduction to Conrad, to whom he introduced his fellow Southerner, the composer John Powell, in 1912. Subject after 1915 to attacks of psychosomatic blindness and paralysis, Dawson became increasingly confined to his apartment in Versailles.

Hugh Railton DENT (1874–1938), J. M. Dent's eldest son, spent his professional life in the family publishing house, J. M. Dent & Sons. He joined the firm in 1909 and took over its management after his father's death in 1926.

Joseph Mallaby DENT (1849–1926) was apprenticed to a printer at the age of thirteen, and set up in business as a London bookbinder in 1872. He turned to publishing in 1888, achieving success with popularly priced series such as the Temple Classics, the Temple Shakespeare, and Everyman's Library. In Conrad's lifetime, Dent published *'Twixt Land and Sea* (1912), *Within the Tides* (1915), *The Shadow-Line* (1917), *The Rescue* (1920), *Notes on Life and Letters* (1921), and most of the Uniform Edition. The rest of that edition appeared posthumously, as did the first publication of *Suspense* (1925) and *Last Essays* (1926).

Florence DOUBLEDAY (née Van Wyck, 1866–1946), married F. N. Doubleday, who was a widower, in 1918. She was active in civic, political, and cultural affairs in and around New York. Her memoir, *Episodes in the Life of a Publisher's Wife*, appeared in 1937.

Brooklyn-born, Frank Nelson DOUBLEDAY (1862–1934) began his publishing career at Charles Scribner's Sons in 1877. He joined forces with S. S. McClure from 1897 to 1900, before entering into partnership with Walter Hines Page. After 1921, Doubleday also owned a controlling interest in the firm of William Heinemann. Encouraged initially by Alfred A. Knopf, Doubleday took a closer and more personal interest in Conrad after 1912, and shared in Conrad's rise to popular fame and fortune following the American publication of *Chance*, Conrad's first commercial success. Doubleday hosted and organised Conrad's American tour; Conrad stayed with the Doubledays at Effendi Hill, their estate on Oyster Bay, Long Island, and they travelled with him on his return voyage.

The Polish literary historian Roman DYBOSKI (1883–1945) lectured at King's College, University of London, and helped to define the literary traditions of the reconstituted Polish state. His *Periods of Polish Literary History* (1923) and *Modern Polish Literature* (1924) were published in London by Oxford University Press. Dyboski also published studies of Shakespeare, Milton, and Byron, and became Professor of Comparative Literature at the Jagiellonian University, Cracow. His wartime experiences were recorded in *Seven Years in Russia and Siberia (1915–1921)*.

H(enrietta) Maud FFOOKS (née Standen) was born in 1858 in Hoshungabad, India, where her father was serving as an officer in the Madras Native Infantry. Around 1865, she was photographed by the Revd C. L. Dodgson ('Lewis Carroll') and became his lifelong friend; she sold her collection of letters and presentation copies from him in 1933. Educated in Dresden, she spoke fluent German, and, as a young woman, worked as a governess in Russia. In 1891, she married (Edward) Archdall Ffooks (1859–1932), a solicitor, Clerk of the Peace, and County Clerk of Dorset. They lived in Dorchester and had a holiday house in Bridport, where Mrs Ffooks took an interest in the Lifeboat Service.

Fiskes abound in the USA, but, given the milieu in which Conrad found himself, there is a strong possibility that the Miss Fiske he had met was Katherine C(ushman) FISKE,[†] who lived with her parents at 898 Park Avenue. Her mother, Marione Cushman Fiske (d. 1947), was active in good causes, especially the welfare of delinquent girls and women; her father, Haley Fiske (d. 1929), was the President of the Metropolitan Life Insurance Co. and, as his membership of the Grolier Club signified, a booklover. They had married in 1887. Miss Fiske, who had long been active in New York society and bred Pekinese dogs, married an Episcopalian priest, the Revd Emmons P. Burrill, in 1938.

Ford Madox FORD (né Hueffer, 1873–1939) wrote some eighty novels and memoirs in the course of a long and varied career in England, France, and the United States. He was also a poet and an inspired editor, who created two remarkable magazines, the *English Review* and the *transatlantic review*. His collaborations with Conrad included *The Inheritors* (1901), *Romance* (1903), and *The Nature of a Crime* (1909). Conrad and Ford quarrelled in 1909; by the end of 1911, a rapprochement had begun, but the friendship never regained its earlier closeness. After serving in the First World War, Ford changed his surname from Hueffer and, after a brief period as a smallholder in the south of England, settled in France, where he split his time between Paris and Provence. It was in Paris that he founded and edited the *transatlantic review*, though it only ran from January 1924 to January 1925, it is the most significant of all Modernist periodicals in English. In his later years, he taught at Olivet College, Michigan, and became the mentor of such American writers as Robert Lowell, Peter Taylor, and Robie Macauley.

Alice-Maude-Marguerite GACHET, also known as Alice Mary Gachet de la Fournière (1884?–1960), was a niece of Conrad's 'aunt' Marguerite Porad-owska (née Gachet). Her mother was English, and she made her début on the London stage in 1922. An actress and director, she was for many years on the staff of the Royal Academy of Dramatic Art.

Ada Nemesis GALSWORTHY (née Ada Pearson, 1864–1956) was adopted by Ernest Cooper, a Norwich doctor. As a teenager she studied the piano in Dresden; later, she composed songs. Conrad wrote a Preface for her transla-tions from Maupassant, *Yvette and Other Stories* (1904). Although involved with John Galsworthy, she had been unhappily married to his cousin Arthur until 1904, when the death of John, Senior, eased the threat of family sanctions and she and John Galsworthy were able to marry. The Galsworthys had houses in Hampstead and Devonshire, but, for the sake of her health, they often wintered overseas.

John GALSWORTHY (1867–1933) met Conrad in the *Torrens* in 1893. His early work, some of it under the pseudonym of John Sinjohn, was tentative, but in 1932 he won a Nobel prize (an honour denied his friend) for his fiction and his plays. Like his fictional Forsytes, his family was well supplied with money, and he helped Conrad with many gifts and loans as well as constant encouragement.

An Aberdonian, Major Theodore James Gordon GARDINER (1874–1937), though troubled by ill health, had been a civil servant in South Africa, a tea planter in Ceylon, and a student at Harvard. After the war, in which he was involved in spy-hunting and the surveillance of enemy aliens, he worked as an arbitrator of industrial disputes and as Secretary of the National Club, London, a Christian society dedicated to improving 'the moral and social condition of the people'. His posthumous *Notes of a Prison Visitor* (1938) records his experiences of befriending convicts; he also published novels, and at his death was at work on a study of Napoleon. The friendship with Conrad began during the latter's visits to Scotland in 1916 and strengthened over the years.

The critic, playwright, and satirist Edward William GARNETT (1868–1937) was the most influential publisher's reader of his generation. His wife Con-stance translated Russian literature, and their home, The Cearne, was a meeting-place for writers, artists, anarchists, socialists, and Russian refugees. Many other young writers benefited from Garnett's generosity, among them

Robert Frost, D. H. Lawrence, Dorothy Richardson, and Edward Thomas. Garnett staunchly supported Conrad from the very beginning of his career, and Conrad often consulted him on matters of style or tone. Although Conrad disapproved of Garnett's pacifism and Russophilia, they remained close and loyal friends. In 1928 Garnett published a selection of his letters from Conrad.

Of all the literary friends of Conrad's later years, the French writer André-Paul-Guillaume GIDE (1869–1951) was among the most distinguished and artistically remarkable. A born-again pagan and a recidivist puritan, his strengths lay in intimate autobiography and ironic fiction. Among his works are *Les Nourritures terrestres* (1897), *L'Immoraliste* (1902), *La Porte étroite* (1909), *Les Caves du Vatican* (1914), and *Les Faux-monnayeurs* (1926). He first met Conrad in July 1911, translated *Typhoon*, directed the other translations of Conrad's work into French, and dedicated *Voyage au Congo* (1928) to Conrad's memory.

The son of a French officer and a Greek princess, Taglioni's grandson, and Hérédia's son-in-law, Comte Auguste GILBERT DE VOISINS (1877–1939) enjoyed a large fortune that enabled him to collect and travel as he pleased; he featured as a rider in Buffalo Bill's circus and made two expeditions to remote parts of China. He also wrote poetry and fiction and translated some of Robert Browning's poems; Conrad owned four of his books, including *Le Bar de la Fourche* (1909), a novel about prospecting for gold in California.

Overcoming ill-health and family tensions, Ellen Anderson Gholson GLAS-GOW (1873–1945), who lived in Richmond, Virginia, wrote poetry, stories, and some twenty novels, the best-known being *Barren Ground* (1925). Set in the Upper South, her work often dealt with women struggling to be independent, and took issue with the sentimental fictions of her time and place. Her visit to the Conrads at Capel House in June 1914, with her travelling companion Louise Collier Willcox, was recorded in photographs taken by her fellow Southerner Warrington Dawson, who had arranged the introduction (Randall, pp. 84–6).

Harold GOODBURN (1891–1966) came from Liverpool. A schoolmaster whose chief subjects were chemistry and biology, he held posts in Dorset, Argentina, and Brazil before moving to the King's School, Canterbury, where he taught science from 1919 to 1945. He then taught in the Midlands before retiring to Canterbury. In *More Wrestling than Dancing: An Autobiography* (1990), David Moreau recalls him as the eccentric 'Captain Burnwell'. John Conrad went to Mr Goodburn for private tuition in mathematics.

Robert Bontine Cunninghame GRAHAM (1852–1936) began a lasting friend-ship with Conrad in 1897, the result of a letter praising 'An Outpost of Progress'. Among the consequences was the help he gave Conrad with the cultural and political background to *Nostromo*. A socialist and (according to some) rightful King of Scotland, Graham worked and travelled widely in the Americas. He drew on his experiences in many volumes of tales, sketches, and essays and also in his travel narratives, such as *Mogreb-el-Acksa: A Journey in Morocco* (1898), and his unorthodox histories of Latin America, such as *A Vanished Arcadia: Being Some Account of the Jesuits in Paraguay* (1901). From 1886 to 1892 he represented North-West Lanarkshire in Parliament; he spent more than a month in gaol for his part in the Bloody Sunday demonstration of 1887. He became the first President of the Scottish Labour Party in 1888 and President of the Scottish Home Rule Association in 1920.

Herbert John Clifford GRIERSON (1866–1960; knighted 1936) was Professor of English Literature at Aberdeen University from 1894 to 1915, and then Professor of Rhetoric and English Literature at the University of Edinburgh, where he became Rector in 1936. His many publications include editions of the poetry of John Donne, the Metaphysical poets, and the letters (in twelve volumes) of Sir Walter Scott.

Gilbert Hovey GROSVENOR (1875–1966) was born in Istanbul. Upon gradu-ating from Amherst College, he was invited by his father-in-law, the inventor Alexander Graham Bell, to join the National Geographic Society as editor of its magazine. He held this post from 1899 to 1954.

John Alexander HAMMERTON (1871–1949; knighted 1932) was the editor and publisher of *Geography*. An energetic and prolific editor, Hammerton spe-cialised in the subject of war: from 1914 to 1919 he edited *The War Illustrated*, a lavishly pictorial weekly, and later produced other popular and encyclopaedic works, among them the *Harmsworth History of the World* (8 vols., 1907–9), *The Great War* (13 vols., 1914–19), *Peoples of All Nations* (7 vols., 1922), *Wonders of the Past* (4 vols., 1923), *The Masterpiece Library of Short Stories* (20 vols., *c*. 1925), and *Outline of Great Books* (1936).

The Swedish soprano Louise ('Loulette') Victoria Alvar Woods HARDING (née Beckman, 1883–1965) performed as 'Louise Alvar' and toured with Mau-rice Ravel, among others. She and her husband, a wealthy English barrister, held a literary and musical salon at their house in Holland Park, Kensington.

She was a close friend of Jean-Aubry, and her circle included Manuel de Falla, Camille Saint-Saëns, T. S. Eliot, Hugo von Hofmannsthal, and Paul Valéry.

HODGSON & Co. was a long-established London auction house in Chancery Lane, offering literary MSS and fine books. Conrad sold copies of the privately printed limited edition pamphlets through the firm, and after his death they sold his library and papers for Jessie Conrad. Its principal was John Edmund Hodgson (1875–1952), an authority on the history of British aviation.

The Hon. Michael James HOLLAND (1870–1956) was a Kentish neighbour and a keen book collector. Until the end of 1913, he lived at Smeeth Hill, near Aldington. In his earlier years he had travelled in South Africa and British Columbia; his experiences there were recollected in *Verse* (1937). During the First World War, he won the Military Cross while serving as a captain in King Edward's Horse.

Conrad HOPE (1890–1963), named in honour of Conrad, was the youngest child of Fountaine Hope. A motor engineer, he was the director of Candor Motors in Colchester.

(George) Fountaine (Weare) HOPE (né Hopps, 1854–1930) was one of the first friends Conrad made in England. A *Conway* boy who later served in the *Duke of Sutherland*, Hope became a 'Director of Companies' and invited Conrad to cruise the Thames estuary in his yawl, the *Nellie*; Conrad drew upon these cruises in *Chance* and *Heart of Darkness*. Hope left a memoir entitled 'Friend of Conrad' (see *Documents*, pp. 1–56).

American-born, Margaret HUGHES (née Kelly, 1893/4–1980) lost her first husband, Lt James Jackson Porter, in the Meuse-Argonne offensive of the First World War. She married John Chambers Hughes (1891–1971) in 1923. As a resident of Paris, during the Second World War she did volunteer service to aid French prisoners of war in Meaux, and recorded her experiences in *Les Lauriers sont coupés . . .* (1941). She was thrice decorated by the French government for her services to the country, and died aged eighty-six in Manhattan.

The educator and author Robert Maynard HUTCHINS (1899–1977) was named Secretary of the Yale Corporation upon graduating from Yale in

1921. He completed a law degree in 1925, became Dean of the Yale Law School at the age of twenty-eight, and from 1929 to 1951 was President of the University of Chicago. From 1943 to 1974, he chaired the editorial board of the *Encyclopaedia Britannica*. In his emphasis on Great Books and his dislike of over-specialisation, Hutchins had a long-lasting influence on American higher education. His challenge to the cult of college sports had less effect.

G. JEAN-AUBRY: see AUBRY, Jean-Frédéric-Émile

A leading British orthopaedic surgeon, Sir Robert Armstrong JONES (1858–1933; knighted 1917, baronetcy 1926) came from North Wales, and practised in Liverpool, where he was consulting surgeon to all the major hospitals. He was also a consultant at St Thomas's Hospital, London, and a member of the War Office's Medical Advisory Board. During the war, he held the rank of Major-General and took on the immense task of organising reconstructive surgery at home and in the field. From 1921 to 1924, he served as President of the British Orthopaedic Association, and was frequently honoured overseas. His monographs and textbooks on the surgery of joints, military orthopaedics, and general orthopaedics were widely used. The professional relationship that began in 1917 with the care of Jessie Conrad developed into a warm personal friendship.

New-York-born George T(homas) KEATING (1892–1976) amassed a rich collection of Conradiana from various sales as well as from Thomas J. Wise. He donated his collection, catalogued in *A Conrad Memorial Library: The Collection of George T. Keating* (1929), to Yale University in 1938. Keating worked his way up from errand-boy to the head of Moore and Munger, a New York firm dealing in paper and clay products, eventually retiring to California. He also collected operatic recordings and music manuscripts, the American author James Branch Cabell, and materials about war, diplomacy, and the Spanish conquest of the New World.

While still an undergraduate, Alfred A(braham) KNOPF (1892–1984) had corresponded with the Galsworthys and visited them in Devon. On graduating from Columbia University in 1912, he went to work at Doubleday, Page, where he was responsible for orchestrating the highly successful publicity campaign for *Chance*. In 1915, he began his own firm. With his wife, Blanche Wolf Knopf, he built up an extraordinary list that included, over the years, Wallace Stevens, Willa Cather, Dashiell Hammett, Langston Hughes,

Thomas Mann, Jean-Paul Sartre, Simone de Beauvoir, Albert Camus, Yukio Mishima, Doris Lessing, and Toni Morrison.

T(homas) Werner LAURIE (1866–1944) had worked for T. Fisher Unwin before establishing his own publishing house in 1904. Conrad remained wary of involvement with Laurie, but had accepted his offer to publish a limited edition of *The Secret Agent* in its stage version.

Donald Collins LEECH (1899–1961) took a BA (Hons) at King's College, London, in 1921 and taught English at the King George V School, Southport. He eventually published five books on secondary-school English and preparing for the GCE (General Certificate of Education).

Bertram Arthur LEVINSON (*c.* 1877–1961) was a lawyer who recalled that, while reading *A Personal Record* in 1923, he came upon a report of a current case involving the collision of the *James Westoll* with another ship in the Channel, and wrote to tell Conrad of this news.

The Right Honourable James Ramsay MACDONALD (1866–1937), the illegitimate son of Scottish farm labourer and a maid-servant, became the first Labour Prime Minister of the United Kingdom in 1924, after more than twenty years as a national official of the party. His first term lasted for only nine months, but he served again as Prime Minister from 1929 to 1935, this time as the head of a 'National' or coalition government.

Born in New Zealand to Scottish parents, Lewis Rose MACLEOD (1875–1941) began his journalistic career in New South Wales. In 1905 he moved to South Africa, where he became editor of the *Johannesburg Sunday Times*. From 1916 to 1924 he was literary editor of the London *Daily Mail*, where several of Conrad's essays first appeared. Macleod returned to Johannesburg in 1924 to edit the *Rand Daily Mail*.

George MANSFIELD (b. 1869), from Essex, made his first voyage as assistant butcher in the *Torrens* from London to Adelaide in 1891–2. At the request of Captain W. H. Cope, Conrad, who was first mate, wrote to Mansfield offering him a berth for the return voyage as an ordinary seaman at wages of £1 per month.

As 'Archibald Marshall', Arthur Hammond MARSHALL (1866–1934) wrote a multitude of novels and critical essays. A partner in the short-lived publishing house of Alston Rivers, he worked with Ford Madox Ford, and was employed for a time on the *Daily Mail*.

The editor and author Perriton MAXWELL (1866–1947) worked for many New York newspapers and periodicals including the *World*, *Metropolitan Magazine*, *Cosmopolitan*, *Saturday Evening Post*, and *Vogue*. In April 1912, when Maxwell was editing *Nash's Magazine* in London, Conrad had offered him a commentary on the sinking of the *Titanic*; Maxwell's New York newspaper rejected the offer, and the essay appeared in the *English Review* (Ray, pp. 66–70).

The Revd Henry Simpson McCLELLAND (1882–1961) was Rector of Trinity Congregational Church in Glasgow from 1915 until his retirement in 1956. During his ministry he invited many well-known figures, chiefly authors, to address the Trinity Literary Society, and sometimes also to take part in one of the Sunday services. He gave his recreation in *Who's Who* as 'travel in search of trouble', and at times lived as a tramp in London and Glasgow to learn the needs of the destitute. He described what he saw in 'I Became Down and Out That I Might Know the Brethren', *Nash's and Pall Mall Magazine*, October 1926.

An Irish-born author and adventurer, Captain Francis McCULLAGH (1874–1956) was fluent in five languages. As a reporter for the *New York Herald*, he rode with the Cossacks in the Russo-Japanese War of 1904–5 and was captured by the Japanese. During the First World War he served in the Dardanelles campaign as a lieutenant in the Royal Irish Fusiliers, and then involved himself with cloak-and-dagger intrigues in Serbia and Macedonia. Captured in Siberia after the fall of Omsk, McCullagh spent two years as a prisoner of the Bolsheviks in Moscow, an experience he described in *A Prisoner of the Reds* (1921). An ardent Catholic and anti-Bolshevik, McCullagh later wrote books denouncing *Red Mexico* (1928) and praising the deeds of the Nationalist armies in *In Franco's Spain* (1937).

METHUEN & Co., the London publishing house founded in 1889 by Algernon Methuen (1856–1924), brought out *The Mirror of the Sea*, *The Secret Agent*, *A Set of Six*, *Under Western Eyes*, *Chance*, and *Victory*. Although text-books were the company's mainstay, its other authors included Kipling, Stevenson, and Maeterlinck.

Mary St Lawrence, Lady MILLAIS (née Hope-Vere of the Marquesses of Linlithgow, 1861–1948, widowed 1897), a Scotswoman, lived in Ashford with her son Sir John Everett Millais (the artist's grandson), Conrad's sometime chess partner. She was a close friend of Jessie Conrad, and served in her later years as a Justice of the Peace.

Allan Noble MONKHOUSE (1858–1936) was the dramatic and literary critic of the *Manchester Guardian* from 1902 until his retirement in 1932. A dramatist and novelist in his own right, he developed extensive contacts in the literary and theatrical worlds, and several of his plays were produced at Annie Horniman's Gaiety Theatre. His works include *Books and Plays* (1894), *Four Tragedies* (1913), and *Essays of Today and Yesterday* (1926).

Alice Dora ('Dolly') MOOR (née George, 1884–1949) was one of Jessie Conrad's younger sisters. Joseph Conrad helped to pay for her education at the Bernardine Convent in Slough, Middlesex. In 1910 she married John Harold Harwar (born 1882), who was killed in action near Cambrai on 23 November 1917. She then married (George) Harold Moor in London and emigrated to South Africa, where her husband worked as a sugar refiner. They lived in Zululand, not far from Durban.

A jovial Rhodes Scholar and prolific essayist and poet, Christopher Darlington MORLEY (1890–1957) produced some fifty books while working as an editor for various publishers and journals including Doubleday, Page and the *Saturday Review of Literature*. His novels include *Parnassus on Wheels* and *The Haunted Bookshop*. He was an ardent fan of the Sherlock Holmes stories, an indefatigable admirer of Conrad, and a ubiquitous member of the New York literary scene. His account of Conrad's arrival in New York, which appeared in instalments in the *New York Evening Post* during May 1923, was collected as *Conrad and the Reporters* (1923).

John Campbell NIVEN (1853–1926) was second engineer in the *Vidar* in 1887, when Conrad was serving as first mate. There is a lively fictional portrait of him as 'John Nieven', a 'sturdy young Scot' and a 'fierce misogynist' in *The Shadow-Line* (p. 6).

Wilfred George PARTINGTON (1888–1955) worked in London and Birmingham before joining the *Bombay Gazette* in 1912. After serving in the First World War, he edited the *Bookman's Journal and Print Collector* until 1931. His books include an anthology in praise of tobacco (1924), works on Sir Walter Scott, and, with Hugh Walpole, *Famous Stories of Five Centuries* (1934). A book collector and bibliographer, he was instrumental in documenting and exposing

Thomas J. Wise's forgery of literary rarities. He issued a privately printed edition of Conrad's *Laughing Anne* in 1923.

Edmund Courtenay PEARCE (1870–1936) was Master of Corpus Christi College, Cambridge, before serving as Vice-Chancellor from 1921 to 1924; he was Bishop of Derby from 1927 until his death.

Annabel PHELPS (née Hubbard, 1864–1939) married William Lyon Phelps in 1892.

William Lyon PHELPS (1865–1943), Professor of English at Yale University from 1892 to 1933, was well known as a prolific scholar and resourceful teacher, renowned for his courses on Tennyson and Browning ('T and B'). He attended Conrad's reading in New York, and invited Conrad and the Doubledays to visit Yale and stay overnight at the Phelpses' home in New Haven.

Captain Arthur W(aller) PHILLIPS (1861 – *c*. 1932) was born in Kent and educated in Weimar (during the Franco-Prussian War) and at Tonbridge School. In 1877 he joined the training-ship HMS *Worcester* at Greenhithe, but was persuaded by his mother to enter a City office. After a couple of years, he escaped and became apprenticed to Captain H. R. Angel, master and principal owner of the *Torrens*. Phillips later served as master of a steamer on the Great Salt Lake, Utah. He remained in America twenty-two years and was a pioneer in opening up Wyoming Territory.

Upon leaving Westminster School, Eric Seabrooke PINKER (1891–1973) went to work in his father's literary agency. During the war, he was awarded the Military Cross for bravery under fire. When J. B. Pinker died in 1922, 'Mr Eric' became the firm's senior partner and thus Conrad's principal agent. He later became a literary agent in New York.

(James) Ralph PINKER (1900–59), Eric's younger brother, was a frequent visitor at Spring Grove in the summer of 1919 while taking a course in Wye. He eventually joined his brother in the family firm, managing it alone after Eric Pinker emigrated to America.

A Polish archivist and historian, Stefan POMARAŃSKI (1893–1944) was later an editor and biographer of Marshal Józef Piłsudski (1867–1935). In June 1924, he presented Conrad with the original MS of 'some youthful poems' by Apollo Korzeniowski, with the request that it be returned some day to one of the Polish libraries.

Mrs James J. PORTER: see Margaret HUGHES

Margaret PORTER: see Margaret HUGHES

Introduced to Conrad by Warrington Dawson, the pianist and composer John POWELL (1882–1963) played for Conrad at Capel House, Oswalds, and Effendi Hill. His *Rhapsodie Nègre* (1918) was a musical tribute to *Heart of Darkness*. At the time of Conrad's American tour, Powell was an active sponsor of what became Virginia's Racial Integrity Act of 1924 prohibiting interracial marriage. In 1928, he married Louise Burleigh (*q. v.*).

Louis-Marie-Émile ROCHÉ (1903–89) was a minor French poet who later made a career as a diplomat, serving as French attaché to Warsaw (1931), Brussels (1932), Vienna (1934), London (1937), and Dublin (1940), and after the war as Ambassador to Australia (1952–5) and Lebanon (1956–60). He published two further volumes of poetry: *Si proche et si lointaine* (1946) and *Le Solitaire de Castille* (1949).

Walter Barnstaple RODD (1884–1965) lived in Roseville, New South Wales.

The son of a Yorkshire wool merchant, William ROTHENSTEIN (1872–1945; knighted 1931) studied art under Degas and Whistler, and held his first exhibition in Paris at the age of nineteen. During the First World War he was the official artist of the British Fifth Army and the Canadian Army of Occupation. He was admired above all for his portraits, whether graphics, paintings, or drawings. Thanks to an introduction from Cunninghame Graham, the Conrads had been friendly with him, his wife Alice, and their family, since 1903 when Conrad sat for the first of several portraits. They were now living in the Cotswolds.

In 1911, Marie Florence SALTUS (née Giles, 1873–1960) became the third wife of the author and theosophist Edgar Evertson Saltus (1858–1921), an admirer of Schopenhauer, Balzac, Flaubert, and Barbey d'Aurevilly, whose works include fiction, poetry, philosophical speculations such as *The Philosophy of Disenchantment* (1885), and vivid, impressionistic historical narratives such as *Imperial Purple* (1892), *The Lovers of the World* (3 vols., *c.* 1895), and *The Imperial Orgy: An Account of the Tsars* (1920). Among Marie Saltus's publications was a biography, *Edgar Saltus, the Man* (1925); *Poppies and Mandragora* (1926) is a joint collection of their poems.

After an education at Uppingham and Oxford, Frank SAVERY (1883–1965) entered the British foreign service, posted first to Munich and then Bern. Consul to the Polish Republic after 1919, he became Consul-General in 1939; during the Second World War, he was Counsellor in the diplomatic mission to the Polish Government in Exile. He was well known as a collector of porcelain and ancient bronzes.

(R.) Townley SEARLE was the owner of the First Edition Bookshop at 99 Wardour Street, London. In 1923 Searle published *The Flying Horse* as a literary and book-collector's magazine edited (and largely written) by T. W. H. Crosland, who died the following year. Later, Searle wrote a book on Chinese cookery (1932), compiled a bibliography of Gilbert and Sullivan (1931), and edited and illustrated a selection of Gilbert's ballads and his farce *A Colossal Idea*.

Henry SOTHERAN & Co. can claim to be the oldest antiquarian bookshop in the world. Founded in York in 1761, the firm moved to London in 1815. In Conrad's day, the firm's premises were at 42 Piccadilly, dealing in books and literary MSS, and sometimes publishing titles under its own imprint.

Evelyn John St Loe STRACHEY (1860–1927) was editor and proprietor of the *Spectator* from 1897 to 1925. A cousin of Lytton Strachey and grandson of John Addington Symonds, the Oxford-educated Strachey was an ardent promoter of Anglo-American friendship. Under his management, the Conservative *Spectator* became the most influential English weekly in the colonies and the United States. Strachey wrote several books, including a historical novel, *The Madonna of the Barricades* (1925). In 1897, while editor of the *Cornhill Magazine*, he published Conrad's story 'The Lagoon'.

Julian Leonard STREET (1879–1947) was a prolific author of novels, stories, autobiographical works, film scripts, and books about French foods and wines. He was a close friend of Booth Tarkington, with whom he wrote *The Country Cousin* (1921).

Frank Arthur SWINNERTON (1884–1982), a publisher's reader for Chatto & Windus, was a chronicler of English literary life, reviewer, and novelist; among his novels were *The Merry Heart* (1909) and *Nocturne* (1917). Though

London-born, he felt a great affinity for the Kentish countryside and wrote on other authors who loved the land in *The Georgian Literary Scene* (1935). As 'Simon Pure', he had a regular column in the New York *Bookman*, bringing the latest news from literary London. He reviewed Conrad sympathetically and sent him condolences after the ill-starred production of *The Secret Agent*.

Nora Mary Dorothea TATTERSALL (née Beatson, 1867–1942) and her husband Major John Cecil de Veel Tattersall, whom she married in 1909, were acquaintances of the Conrads living at Charlton Place, Bishopsbourne.

Robert de TRAZ (1884–1951) was born in Paris to a family of Swiss hoteliers. He began his literary career with *L'Homme dans le rang* (1913), a memoir of his life in the Swiss army. A passionate francophile, he became a war correspondent for the *Journal de Genève*, reporting from Verdun and the Argonne. His novel *Fiançailles* (1922) was 'crowned' by *Le Figaro* and awarded the Schiller Prize in Switzerland; his short stories appeared in the *Revue de Paris* and the *Mercure de France*. He edited the *Revue de Genève*, a significant international journal, from 1920 to 1930 – the whole of its run. In the *Revue*, he published translations of 'The Partner', 'The Tale', 'The Brute', and 'Freya of the Seven Isles', and his 'compte-rendu' of *Within the Tides*.

The *TUSITALA*, a square-rigged sailing ship, Greenock-built in 1883, was owned by the 'Three Hours for Lunch Club', a New York syndicate whose members included James A. Farrell and Christopher Morley. The name *Tusitala*, a homage to Robert Louis Stevenson, was the fourth she had carried.

T(homas) Fisher UNWIN (1848–1935) published *Almayer's Folly*, *An Outcast of the Islands*, and *Tales of Unrest* at the beginning of Conrad's career, *The Arrow of Gold* and *The Rover* towards its end, and *Tales of Hearsay* posthumously. Neither his business practices nor his adherence to the Liberal party endeared him to Conrad.

Arthur Turner VANCE (1872–1930) was editor of the *Pictorial Review*. From 1900 to 1907 he had edited the *Ladies' Home Journal* and *Woman's Home Companion*.

E. H. VISIAK was the pseudonym of Edward Harold Physick (1878–1972), a poet, novelist, and Milton scholar. He worked as a telegraph office clerk and schoolteacher before winning a Civil List pension to pursue his scholarly interests, producing a series of notes on Conrad in *Notes & Queries* in 1939–40, followed by *The Mirror of Conrad* (1955).

The actor, director, bibliophile, and scholar Allan WADE (1881–1958) made his début in 1904 and worked for Harley Granville-Barker from 1906 to 1915. A producer for the Stage Society and a founder of the Phoenix Society (1919), he also assembled a large library of Modernist writers. His numerous publications include a bibliography of W. B. Yeats (1951) and editions of Henry James's dramatic criticism (1948) and Yeats's letters (1954), along with translations of plays by Jean Giraudoux and Jean Cocteau.

Hugh Seymour WALPOLE (1884–1942; knighted 1937) was born in New Zealand, but his parents soon returned to England, where his father became Bishop of Durham. As a young man, he admired and was admired by Henry James. As a novelist, Walpole first met recognition with *Mr Perrin and Mr Traill* (1911) and *The Duchess of Wrexe* (1914). In *The Dark Forest* (1916), he drew on his experience of working as an orderly with the Russian Red Cross, for which he was invested with the Order of Saint George for bravery under fire. Before meeting Conrad, who was to treat him as a protégé, Walpole had already published his critical appreciation, *Joseph Conrad* (1916; revised edition, 1924). Among his more recent novels were *Jeremy* (1919) and *The Cathedral* (1922).

Amelia WARD (1862–1929) was one of the eight children (four sons and four daughters) of William Ward, Conrad's landlord at 6 Dynevor Road, Stoke Newington. When Conrad and his friend Adolf Krieger were lodging with the family, she was nineteen and working as a machinist. Her younger brother William worked as an assistant storekeeper at the London Sailors' Home, where Conrad had often stayed between voyages. The Wards had lived in Gibraltar and South Africa, and after some years in England emigrated to Australia.

Christopher Lewis WARD (1868–1943) had been a successful Delaware lawyer and businessman before he took up literature at the urging of his cousin, Henry S(eidel) Canby, the editor of the *Saturday Review of Literature*. He published novels, plays, short stories, and poetry in addition to several historical works about the American Revolution.

Lorna Maclaren WATSON (1912–97; Mrs Frank H. Ralph Allen after 1943) was the daughter of Frederick William Watson (1885–1935) and his wife Hilda (née Jones, 1888–1954), and the granddaughter of the Scottish 'Kailyard' novelist 'Ian Maclaren' (the Revd John Watson, 1850–1907) and Sir Robert Jones, Jessie Conrad's surgeon.

(Cicely) Veronica WEDGWOOD (1910–97; Dame Veronica, 1968) was the daughter of Conrad's friends Ralph and Iris Wedgwood. After reading history at Oxford, she devoted her grasp of recondite detail, ability to see through dense thickets of political intrigue, and narrative flair to writing, lecturing, and broadcasting on historical topics, especially the great conflicts of the seventeenth century. As C. V. Wedgwood, she published biographies of *Strafford* (1935), *Cromwell* (1939), and *William the Silent* (1944), several studies of the struggle between King and Parliament, and a masterly survey of *The Thirty Years War* (1938). In 1969, she became the third British woman to be awarded the Order of Merit.

Edgar Huidekoper WELLS (1875–1938) was an English instructor and Acting Dean at Harvard College before the First World War, when he served in England as Deputy Commissioner for the American Red Cross. After the war, he settled in New York and in 1921 founded E. H. Wells & Co., a bookshop at 602 Madison Avenue specialising in rare books and first editions.

W(alter) C. WICKEN was Pinker's office manager, whose duties included handling the firm's day-to-day finances.

Catherine Livingston WILLARD (1898–1954; Mrs William Edwin Barry 1925–31; Mrs Ralph Bellamy 1931–45) spent her childhood in Cincinnati, Ohio, and her teenage years in England and France. After a theatrical training at the Comédie Française in Paris, she made her début in 1915 with F. R. Benson's travelling company as Katharina in *The Taming of the Shrew*, and went on to play in Shakespeare at the Old Vic, where her roles included Hermione, Beatrice, Gertrude, Chorus (in *Henry V*), Olivia, and Lady Macbeth. She also took on roles by Congreve and Ibsen. Conrad had been intrigued by the thought of her playing Lena in *Victory*. She had returned to America in 1921. At the time of Conrad's tour there, she was a member of the Henry Jewett Company in Boston, where she took some eighty-six roles at the Copley Theatre. Thereafter, she spent twenty-five years as a leading lady on Broadway.

Grace Robinson WILLARD (1879–1933) was Catherine Willard's mother. A clergyman's daughter, she grew up in Cincinnati, Ohio. Her first métier was that of journalist and book-reviewer. While working in Europe as a foreign correspondent, her interests turned to interior design; she was a frequent visitor at Capel House and advised the Conrads on the furnishings and décor at Oswalds.

The Polish dramatist and fiction writer Bruno WINAWER (1883–1944) sent his play *Księga Hioba* (*The Book of Job*) to Conrad hoping he would find an English translator. Conrad took up the challenge himself and did a translation that was hawked about to London producers without success. Winawer, in turn, translated Conrad's dramatisation of *The Secret Agent* into Polish with Aniela Zagórska.

Thomas J(ames) WISE (1859–1937) collected – and fabricated – literary rarities. Having prospered as a dealer in lavender and other essential oils, he built up a considerable collection of books and manuscripts, many of which are now in the British Library's Ashley Collection, and enjoyed a steady reputation as a bibliophile and bibliographer. Meanwhile he was forging and selling at high prices unique early editions of Wordsworth, Shelley, Tennyson, Charlotte Brontë, George Eliot, Swinburne, and the Brownings, all hitherto unknown to scholarship. In order to improve his own collection of Jacobean plays, he was also helping himself to leaves from copies in the British Museum. His career as a forger was not exposed until three years before his death, and his career as a literary thief and vandal came to light long after. In 1918, he began to purchase manuscripts and typescripts from Conrad, and in 1920 overtook John Quinn as principal purchaser. As Conrad's first bibliographer, he published *A Bibliography of the Writings of Joseph Conrad* (1920) and *A Conrad Library: A Catalogue of Printed Books, Manuscripts and Autograph Letters by Joseph Conrad* (1928). He also printed twenty limited-edition pamphlets of Conrad's occasional writings between December 1918 and January 1920.

Aniela ZAGÓRSKA (1881–1943) was a granddaughter of Conrad's maternal cousin Karol Zagórski (d. 1898) and an early admirer of his work. After a lapse of fifteen years, Conrad's friendship with his cousins was renewed during his visit to Poland in 1914, and she became his most important Polish editor and translator. With her sister Karola, she held the Russian and Polish translation rights to Conrad's work. She supervised the first Polish collected edition, for which she translated *Almayer's Folly*, *Lord Jim*, and *The Mirror of the Sea*.

Karola ZAGÓRSKA (c. 1885–1955), Aniela's younger sister, spent six months at Oswalds in 1920, after which Conrad supported her with a regular allowance of £10 per month. A professional singer, she lived in Italy and later in the United States, where she sang in opera.

The son of an impoverished *szlachta* (gentry) family, the Polish novelist Stefan ŻEROMSKI (1864–1925) began his literary career while working as an assistant librarian at a Polish museum in Switzerland. After living in Italy and Paris, he returned to Poland in 1912 and lived in Zakopane, where he met Conrad in 1914. After the war he settled in Warsaw, where he was granted quarters in the Royal Castle, but kept his cottage in the spa town of Nałęczów. He was a founder of the Academy of Literature and the Polish branch of PEN. His novels include *Ludzie bezdomni* (*Homeless People*, 1900), *Popioły* (1904, trans. as *Ashes*, 1928), set during the Napoleonic Wars, and *Wierna rzeka* (1912, trans. as *The Faithful River*, 1943), set during the insurrection of 1863. In 1926, he was shortlisted for the Nobel Prize.

Kate ŻUK-SKARSZEWSKA (née Hadley, 1868–1950) was the English wife of a Polish journalist and novelist, Jan Tadeusz Żuk-Skarszewski (1858–1933), whom she married in Brighton in 1897. She accompanied him on his return to Poland, where in 1899 he contributed to the debate about the emigration of Polish talent and was cited approvingly by Eliza Orzeszkowa, the novelist who attacked Conrad as an émigré traitor. Żuk-Skarszewska lived for many years in Cracow, where she translated a wide variety of texts from Polish into English and became acquainted with the Zagórska sisters.

EDITORIAL PROCEDURES

Hoping to balance the comfort of the reader against the requirements of the scholar, we have adopted the following conventions:

1. The texts stay faithful to Conrad's spelling, accentuation, and punctuation, but letters missing from within words are frequently supplied in square brackets. Abbreviated proper names, such as 'B' for Borys or 'FND' for F. N. Doubleday, are left as they are if the reference is quite clear. Rather than use *sic*, we mark words that might be taken as misprints with an asterisk. If they appear in *Chambers English Dictionary* or the *OED* in the sense intended, unusual (but typically Conradian) spellings such as 'negociation' and 'inclose' are not marked. In general, we neither restore nor mark missing or misplaced apostrophes, nor do we star lower-case days of the week or adjectives of nationality, like 'russian' or 'american', which reflect the influence of French and Polish.

2. Where necessary to the sense, missing words are also supplied in brackets. When we expand abbreviated words, we remove the punctuation Conrad uses to mark the shortening; thus 'Hein:' becomes 'Hein[emann]', 'D'day' becomes 'D[ouble]day', 'B.' becomes 'B[orys]'. Contracted words not marked with a period (e.g. 'D. P & Co') normally stay as they are. Gaps in the text, such as those caused by damage to the MS or omissions by copyists, appear thus: [. . .]. [?] marks a doubtful reading.

3. Again when sense dictates, commas, full stops, and question marks are tacitly provided, and quotation marks completed; words apparently repeated by accident have been deleted. A list of these silent emendations can be found at the end of the volume. Typing errors in letters dictated by Conrad appear in a separate list; unless of particular interest, any errors in letters to Conrad quoted in the footnotes are corrected without further ado. Since spelling and punctuation on telegrams was entirely at the mercy of telegraph clerks, we emend without flagging, but, in the interest of preserving the inimitable texture of telegraphic language, keep such emendations to a minimum.

4. Especially when writing pronouns such as 'You', Conrad used capitals more profusely than other English writers of his time. We preserve his usage,

but distinguishing between upper and lower case must often be a matter of judgment rather than certainty. The same is true of locating paragraph breaks. Rather than mark the shift in title from upper to lower case made while the first issue was in press, we call Ford's magazine *transatlantic review* throughout.

5. For the letters in French we observe the same conventions, but use square brackets and asterisks more sparingly. Conrad's erratic accentuation we leave as it is, except in texts from *L. fr.*, where some presumed misprints or misreadings have been altered.

6. For the convenience of those who do not read the letters in sequence, information in footnotes may appear more than once.

7. American readers should note that Conrad used the British system of abbreviating dates; thus 3.6 would mean 3 June, not 6 March.

8. The Nonesuch rather than the less reliable Bobbs-Merrill edition of the letters to Garnett provides the copy-text when no manuscript is available. In the same circumstances, we use the American rather than the British edition of the letters to Curle because the former is less likely to censor names.

9. This edition collects all available letters, but only the more interesting telegrams; references to some others appear in the notes.

10. The heading TS/MS denotes a typed letter in which passages other than the salutation or farewell are handwritten.

11. In the provenance headings for letters to Bruno Winawer and Aniela and Karola Zagórska, the description 'MS copy' or 'TS copy' indicates a transcription or translation of Conrad's now lost original. Where letters to these persons were translated by them from Polish into French, only an English translation is provided.

12. In the provenance headings, letters that have appeared only in microfilmed dissertations, as disjointed fragments in books or articles, or only in translation are described as unpublished. Letters appearing in a fuller but still incomplete form are described as published in part. The provenance headings are not meant to be complete lists of appearances in print; in general, reprints and translations of letters already published in English are only cited when they offer fresh commentary or context, as in editions by Najder, Watts, and Knowles.

For a discussion of Oswalds stationery, see *Letters*, 6, p. lvii, and 7, pp. lxiv–lxv.

1923

To G. Jean-Aubry
Text MS Yale; Unpublished

[letterhead: Oswalds]
1. Jan. 23

Très cher Jean.[1]

Enfin nous allons vous voir!

Venez D[iman]che pour lunch. C'est entendu. Il n'y aura personne ici cette fin de semaine. Moi aussi j'ai de[s] choses a vous dire.

Je suis bien fâché de savoir que Vous avez du Vs mettre au lit en arrivant. Faites pas d'imprudence mon cher aprésant* que Vs êtes levé. Le temps est traître.

Il faut qu'on soit bête a la "Revue"![2] pour envoyer la lettre a Londres.

J'ai eu une lettre amicale de Gide.

Je Vous embrasse de tout mon coeur

Votre

Conrad

My very dear Jean.

We are going to see you at last!

Come on Sunday for lunch. That's settled. No one will be here this weekend. I also have things to tell you.

I'm quite annoyed to hear that you had to take to bed on your arrival.

Do be careful, my dear fellow, now that you are up and about again. Time is a betrayer.

They must be stupid at the *Revue* to have sent the letter to London.

I've had a friendly letter from Gide.

I embrace you with all my heart

Your

Conrad

---

[1] Jean-Frédéric-Émile Aubry (1882–1950) wrote as G., Georges, or Gérard Jean-Aubry. Born in Le Havre, he became a friend of many composers, including Debussy and Ravel; both Falla and Roussel wrote settings of his poems. He first met Conrad in 1918, became a close friend, and worked to promote Conrad's reputation with *Joseph Conrad in the Congo* (1926), *Joseph Conrad: Life & Letters* (1927), *Lettres françaises* (1929), *The Sea Dreamer: A Definitive Biography* (1947; trans. 1957), and numerous French translations of Conrad's works. From 1919 to 1930, he lived in London, editing *The Chesterian*, a magazine published by a firm of musical instrument makers.

[2] The *Nouvelle Revue Française*.

3

To Harald Leofurn Clarke

Text MS photocopy BL RP 2313 (iii)[1]

[letterhead: Oswalds]
2.1.'23

My dear Mr Clarke.[2]

Of course! We must have been shipmates on my first voyage in the Torrens. I made one other in her, when Cottar* was again 2^d mate and Jones the senior app[renti]ce.[3]

I have the best recollection of the ship's company (on that first voyage) as a whole. But as to individuals I must confess that my memory has grown dim and confused. These are old times – just 30 years ago.

Nevertheless, pray believe, I was very glad to hear from you. I am touched to learn that I have been remembered by an old shipmate for so many years, and I thank you for the kind thought which has prompted you to write to me.

With all best wishes for your health and prosperity in the new year I remain dear Mr Clarke,

very faithfully yours

Joseph Conrad.

---

[1] The original was tipped into a copy of *Notes on Life and Letters* auctioned by Christie's (London) on 5 May 1982 as lot 96.

[2] Harald Leofurn Clarke (1874–1942) was an apprentice on Conrad's first voyage in the *Torrens* in 1891–2. He eventually earned a master's certificate and was Harbour Master of Suva, in the British colony of Fiji, where he died.

[3] Leonard Edmund Cotter (b. 1869) was second mate on both of Conrad's voyages in the *Torrens*; he married in 1896 and was drowned on service on 1 January 1919. William Jones (b. 1873) served as an apprentice in the *Torrens* for three voyages; at age sixteen he had been indentured for four years to Henry R. Angel, the master and principal owner, who left the ship before Conrad signed on as first mate.

To Richard Curle
Text MS Indiana; Curle 107

[Oswalds]
Tuesday. 2.1.23

Dearest Dick.[1]

We were glad to get Your note. I do hope all your worries will be "downed" for good soon.[2]

Can you advise me how I could get hold of the N° of New Review for Sept[er] 1897? Would advertising in the literary press be the only way – and if so what papers? I think that if I could make up my set of the New Review containing the *Nigger* serial I could sell it for a few pounds. As it is the 4 nos I have are valueless, I fear.[3]

B[orys] was here last Sunday for a few hours. He was notified of a rise in his salary, amounting to £85, from Jan 1st (£100 less 15%).[4] He thinks it is very good after only 4½ months service. – I had an optimistic letter from Eric about the prospects of *The Rover* being out *next* autumn. – Le Figaro has asked Aubry for an article on Joseph Conrad at an early date: Boom in J. C. in France.[5]

Our dear love to you

Ever yours

J. C.

---

[1] Born in Scotland, Richard Henry Parnell Curle (1883–1968) left Wellington College in 1901 and established himself as an author and journalist in London. His friendship with Conrad began with an article published in 1912, which he elaborated into the first full-length appreciation of Conrad's work, *Joseph Conrad: A Study* (1914). A prolific writer, Curle also published three volumes of short stories, along with accounts of his travels in Burma and Malaya, including *Into the East* (1923), to which Conrad contributed a Preface. From 1919 to 1928 he wrote a regular column for the *Daily Mail* under the pseudonym 'John Blunt', as well as unsigned articles 'from our special correspondent'. A close friend of the Conrad family, Curle published an account of Conrad's final days (1928) and a volume of their correspondence (1928). He arranged for the publication of Conrad's last novel, *Suspense* (1925), and served with Ralph Wedgwood as executor of Conrad's estate until 1944.

[2] Curle's divorce from Cordelia Curle (née Fisher, 1879–1970) was granted in February; they had been married since 1912. Curle seems to have had at least partial custody of their son, Adam. 'Downed' in the sense of *done away with* is a metaphor from aerial combat in the First World War.

[3] *The Nigger of the 'Narcissus'* was serialised in the *New Review* from August to December 1897.

[4] Borys had been working in Manchester since August for the trading department of Daimler Motors, Ltd. The 15 per cent reduction in salary was imposed by the company because of the economic depression in 1922 (*Letters*, 7, p. 508).

[5] Jean-Aubry's article, 'Joseph Conrad et la France', appeared in *Le Figaro* on 21 April.

To Eric S. Pinker
Text TS/MS Berg; Unpublished

[letterhead: Oswalds]
Jan. 3rd. 1922. [1923]¹

Dearest Eric.²

Thank you for your letter answering divers points of mine and containing a ray of light on "The Rover" situation.³ May it not be extinguished by the poisonous breath of the well-known "nigger in the fence" who has been the curse of my existence for years.⁴ However, I reckon *your own* luck will come in now to keep him out of our joint affairs.

I am glad you share my views as to W. Laurie.⁵ I am much distressed by the advertisement he proposes to put forth. He has sent me a copy which I enclose here for you to see. Could there be anything more contemptibly unworthy of that play? It's hardly worth while to touch such bosh. But I have just touched it. Perhaps you could give another touch. But I don't want you to bother about it. The last line is just damned cheek. Will you answer W. L.?

As to a portrait, he could reproduce one of Arbuthnot's photographs.⁶ There are eight negatives to select from.

I know you will be pleased to hear that I have made a quick recovery and am getting on with the novel⁷ – if not exactly like a "house a-fire" – quite well enough to begin cheerfully the year under the new scheme of economy.

---

¹ Conrad's secretary typed 1922, but 1923 is indicated by the agreement with Laurie and other references.

² Upon leaving Westminster School, Eric Seabrooke Pinker (1891–1973) went to work in his father's literary agency. During the war, he was awarded the Military Cross for bravery under fire. When J. B. Pinker died in 1922, 'Mr Eric' became the firm's senior partner and thus Conrad's principal agent. He later became a literary agent in New York.

³ American book publication of *The Rover* was brought forward at Conrad's request to allow for the novel's serialisation in the *Pictorial Review*. The 'situation' required complicated negotiations, and F. N. Doubleday had kept Eric Pinker abreast of developments by cable (F. N. Doubleday to J. M. Dent, 10 January 1923, TS Berg).

⁴ T. Fisher Unwin, Conrad's first publisher, had insisted on publishing certain new works by Conrad as a condition for releasing others for the collected editions of Dent and Doubleday. To secure copyright, Doubleday had to ask Arthur T. Vance to bring forward the planned serialisation of *The Rover*. See the letter to him of 6 February. The American slang phrase 'nigger in the fence' (as an alternative to 'woodpile') began appearing in print during the American Civil War, when it featured in various song lyrics; it also occurs in Bret Harte's *A Phyllis of the Sierras* (1888) and became popular with English journalists and politicians.

⁵ T(homas) Werner Laurie (1866–1944) was going to publish a limited edition of Conrad's *The Secret Agent* as dramatised in the four-act version (see *Letters*, 7, pp. 628–34).

⁶ Conrad had been photographed by Malcolm Arbuthnot (1877–1967), a society photographer and also a painter in oils and watercolour, in July 1919 (see *Letters*, 6, p. 449).

⁷ *Suspense.*

In this connection, dear Eric, I understood that Miss Seale's* salary for Dec. fell under the old scheme. As she has not had it I have paid it to her to-day; but, my dear fellow, I cannot spare it from my cash in hand. Would you send it to me? She leaves us in Jan. but whether she goes or stays she is eliminated as far as the office is concerned from this year's expenditure, with B[orys] and K[arola] and half of Mrs G[eorge] together with other reductions.[1] Don't think me grasping, but my income is reduced this year by £1600, at least, while the conditions of living cannot be reduced as quickly as the expenditure must be.[2] We are making efforts to find a tenant for Bell at the half-year or sooner.[3] There are some prospects.

I have thought of various things which it would take too long to write about. I would take it as very friendly of You if You would come down to see me any day before the 15 prox – let us say. Coming up to town unsettles me considerably and I want to absorb myself completely in the novel. It would ease my mind to see you. But of course I *could* come up if you couldn't spare the time.

B. came down last Sund. He has got a rise of £85 (100 less 15%) as from Jan[y] 1[st]. He was notified *not* to make permanent arrangements to live in M[anche]ster, and instructed to get rid of his Surrey Scien[tif]ic C[o] shares as D'lair's* employees are not supposed to be interested in undertakings of that kind (wireless).[4] This, in conjunction with the knowledge he has of his name being on the Gen[l] Man[ager]'s list for special jobs, makes him think that he may be put on to the wireless-fitting dept for cars and 'planes of the company. Changes will take place in Febr[y], but whatever they are they cannot mean for him to be fired out.[5] So far good, and I am relieved.

Affect[ionate]ly yours

J. Conrad

---

[1] Audrey (Etheldreda Maude Victoria) Seal, Jessie Conrad's nurse-companion (1887–1966), remained in service, and continued to tend her after Conrad's death. She was born in Wrotham, Kent, and married Charles Roberts Vinten (born 1900), the Conrads' chauffeur, on 24 September 1923. Conrad had been helping to support Borys since his return from the front. Since 1919, he had being sending monthly cheques to his cousin Karola Zagórska, who was recovering from ill health in Milan (*Letters*, 7, p. 21); she had gone there to study singing. He had been sending quarterly cheques to his widowed mother-in-law, Jane George (née Nash Sex, 1847–1925), since 1917 (*Letters*, 6, p. 102).

[2] MS from this point.

[3] Lt-Col. Matthew Gerald Edward Bell (1871–1927) was the owner of Bourne Park, Canterbury, and thus Conrad's landlord. Conrad was hoping to leave 'Oswalds' for a less expensive house.

[4] On Borys's involvement with the ill-fated Surrey Scientific Company, see *Letters*, 7, pp. 498–9, to Messrs Hammond Clark & Daman. Borys had been employed in the sales office of the Daimler Company since the previous August.

[5] In connection with jobs, *to fire out* appeared earlier than *to fire*: the *OED*'s earliest example dates from 1885 and comes from a newspaper in Dakota Territory.

To Richard Curle
Text MS Indiana; Curle 108

[Oswalds]
6. Jan 23

Dearest Dick.

Many thanks for the cheque for £60 received to-day – the product of the pamphlet and a most welcome windfal[l] which I owe to your ingenious friendship.[1] The hard times are beginning with a vengeance – but as long as I can go on with the novel I will not be dismayed. I wish I were feeling better in myself – but I am going on since the first so far unchecked.

Jessie sends her love.

I would be happy to hear some good news from You.

Ever Yours

J. Conrad

To Borys Conrad
Text MS Conrad; Unpublished

[Oswalds]
14. Jan. 23.

Dearest Boy.[2]

I send you my blessing and my loving wishes of every happiness for your birthday.[3] I congratulate you also on this occasion on the position you have obtained by your own efforts and which I hope and believe you will preserve and improve by your work and abilities. I want you to know that I appreciate these traits of your character on which I found my confidence for the future when in the nature of things You will be left to take care of your Mother and guide and assist your brother.[4] Whatever happens keep a warm corner in your heart for me, now and ever, in return for the love I bear You. Think tenderly of my shortcomings and believe in the constancy of my thoughts of You.

Your father.

J. C

---

[1] Conrad's Preface to Curle's *Into the East: Notes on Burma and Malaya* (Macmillan, 1923) had been published as a pamphlet (see *Letters*, 7, p. 597). It was reprinted in *Last Essays* under the title 'Travel'.

[2] Alfred Borys Leo Conrad (1898–1978), Conrad's elder son, was educated at private schools and in the training-ship HMS *Worcester*. Gassed and shell-shocked during the war, he found employment with the Daimler Company in Manchester and London. His secret marriage in September 1922 strained relations with his parents, but the birth of a grandson in 1924 helped to reconcile them.

[3] Borys would be twenty-five on 15 January.

[4] Conrad's younger son John was sixteen at the time and in boarding school at Tonbridge.

To Eric S. Pinker

Text MS KSC; Unpublished

[letterhead: Oswalds]

14.1.23

Dearest Eric.

Herewith John's school acc^t. He returns on Friday.[1]

I expect to see Goodburn tomorrow and find out from him whether the transfer of John to King's School would be a possible operation.[2] If it is to be done it ought to be done with the least possible delay.

Yrs affect^{ly}

J. Conrad

I send you an Am[erican] newsp[a]per cutting written by Morley.[3] Please return.

To Aniela Zagórska

Text MS copy Yale;[4] Najder 286

Oswalds,

19.1.23.

My dear Aniela,[5]

Thank you for your letter. I am overjoyed that your excellent interpretation of *Almayer* has met with such a great success among people whose opinion counts.

I shall be writing to Mr. Żeromski, as soon as I have completed the third part of my long novel.[6] As to the translation of "Wszystko i nic" by Mr. Żeromski,

---

[1] To Tonbridge School.

[2] Harold Goodburn (1891–1966) taught science at The King's School, Canterbury, one of the oldest schools in England; it also had the attraction of being closer to Oswalds than Tonbridge was. For the first extant letter to him, see [30 January]. In the event, the school had a long waiting-list and no place could be found for John.

[3] Christopher Darlington Morley (1890–1957), a prolific New York journalist, poet, and man-about-town, was one of Conrad's most enthusiastic supporters. He apparently enclosed the cutting with an inscribed copy of *Shandygaff* (1918), a collection of newspaper essays, which he forwarded to Conrad through Elbridge L. Adams; see Conrad's letter to Morley of 5 February. The cutting, which has not been identified, mentioned Conrad's planned American visit.

[4] Zagórska's French translation: the Polish original was lost in the Warsaw Uprising of 1944.

[5] Aniela Zagórska (1881–1943) was a granddaughter of Conrad's maternal cousin Karol Zagórski (d. 1898) and an early admirer of his work. After a lapse of fifteen years, Conrad's friendship with his cousins was renewed during his visit to Poland in 1914, and she became his most important Polish editor and translator. With her sister Karola, she held the Russian and Polish translation rights to Conrad's work. She supervised the first Polish collected edition, for which she translated *Almayer's Folly*, *Lord Jim*, and *The Mirror of the Sea*.

[6] *Suspense.*

I find the idea of sending the manuscript to our Legation absurd![1] What have they been doing with the manuscript for a whole year? I must know all the details before I get involved. Perhaps they've sent the manuscript to various publishers? That would be fatal, because it's obvious that it has been turned down. And going around with a rejected manuscript is a bad affair. I would try to place it somewhere if Mr. Żeromski would instruct our Legation to send me the manuscript *with a little note*.[2] But I must warn you that the "magazines" do not print translations, and the more serious "reviews" do not accept novels or short stories. At present there is nothing here comparable to the *Revue des deux Mondes* or *Revue de Paris*.

I must finish now since my hand hurts me. I shall write to you soon.

I kiss you a thousand times and so does Jessie, and likewise John. In half an hour I am taking him to the station; he is returning to school.

Your faithful

Konrad.

To Eric S. Pinker
Text MS KSC; Unpublished

[Oswalds]
Sat. 20.1.23

Dearest Eric

Thanks very much for your letter of two days ago. John left us on Friday. The King's School (Canterbury) being full, with a long waiting list, the moving of John is out of question.

I have only to hope for the best.

I am hard at work. Miss H[allowes] has been laid up for 3 days.[3] Bad luck.

I quite agree with you as to the factual value of the press-cutting. The thing is decent in intention however; and, of course, the information could only have come from D[ouble]day.[4]

Always affectly yrs

J Conrad.

---

[1] The British Legation in Warsaw. Stefan Żeromski (1864–1925) was at this time the most prominent Polish man of letters. His *All and Nothing* (1919) is a lengthy historical novel of events leading up to the Polish Insurrection of 1830.

[2] Najder's text leaves '*avec une petite note*' ('with a little note') in French.

[3] Albeit with many interruptions, Conrad's secretary, Lilian Mary Hallowes (1870–1950), had worked for him since 1904. In 1917, he began dictating his works to her as she typed.

[4] The article was written by Christopher Morley, who had heard from Conrad's American publisher, Frank Nelson Doubleday, that Conrad was planning a visit to the USA.

To Julian Street
Text MS Williams;[1] Unpublished

[letterhead: Oswalds]
20.1.23

Dear M[r] Street.[2]

I ought to have thanked You before for your kind and friendly letter. The assurance of Your sympathetic appreciation of my work is a very fine birthday present.[3] I wish I had deserved it better. But an honest man can only give what is in him, and I accept your generous words without misgivings.

I have read your delightful and "penetrating" (I write the word deliberately) *Japan*.[4] I have the book. I was looking into it again only the other day. Pray do send me your *Roosevelt* and don't forget to write your name and mine on the fly-leaf.[5]

With warm good wishes for years of good work and happiness I am

very Cordially Yours

Joseph Conrad.

To Kate Żuk-Skarszewska
Text Krzyżanowski; Najder 286

[Oswalds]
20. I. 1923

Dear Mrs Skarszewska,[6]

It was very good of you to write. I had no idea I owed the pleasure of receiving those examples of Polish art to your husband. I was intensely delighted. The cover[7] arrived all right by last night's post.

Many, many thanks.

---

[1] Conrad included a handwritten note 'For M[r] Julian Street. For insertion in his copy of the Rescue': 'This is the only work to which I played truant. I stuck all these people in the shallows and abandonned* them for twenty years. (Laid aside 1898. Taken up 1918) Joseph Conrad.'

[2] Julian Leonard Street (1879–1947) was a prolific author of novels, stories, autobiographical works, film scripts, and books about French foods and wines. A Princeton resident, he was a close friend of Booth Tarkington, with whom he wrote *The Country Cousin* (1921).

[3] Conrad had turned sixty-five on 3 December.

[4] *Mysterious Japan* (Garden City and Toronto: Doubleday, Page, 1921).

[5] *The Most Interesting American* (New York: Century, 1915), a biography of Theodore Roosevelt.

[6] Kate Żuk-Skarszewska (née Hadley, 1868–1950) was the English wife of a Polish journalist and novelist, Jan Tadeusz Żuk-Skarszewski (1858–1933), whom she married in Brighton in 1897. She accompanied him on his return to Poland, where in 1899 he contributed to the debate about the emigration of Polish talent and was cited approvingly by Eliza Orzeszkowa, the novelist who attacked Conrad as an émigré traitor. Żuk-Skarszewska lived for many years in Cracow, where she translated a wide variety of texts from Polish into English and became acquainted with the Zagórska sisters.

[7] Envelope or package? Conrad was writing to her in English.

Will you please give my warm regards to your husband and tell him I have just finished reading the *Rumak*[1] with the greatest possible interest. I think it's simply wonderful in its sustained power and its charm of expression.

I am just now desperately busy with a novel which I must finish by a given date;[2] and as ill-luck would have it, my secretary is laid up, so that I must attend myself to that part of my correspondence of which she relieves me generally. I haven't been able as yet to find time to begin *Pustka*.[3]

Believe me, dear Mrs Skarszewska, with the greatest regard,

Very faithfully

Joseph Conrad.

To Elbridge L. Adams

Text J-A, 2, 293 (in part); Adams 29 (in part)[4]

Oswalds.

Jan. 22nd, 1923.[5]

My dear Adams,[6]

Your registered article arrived this morning and I put everything aside to welcome it with all the regard and care due to this proof of your solid friendship for us.[7]

I have just read it carefully once and am writing this to (first of all) give you my warm thanks for the pervading sympathy of this sketch of our personal relations. The man who would not be satisfied with it would have to be a very cantankerous, conceited, crooked-minded and objectionable brute. Seriously, my dear Adams, I am touched by the genuineness of sentiment which informs this survey of our intercourse. I am not alluding here to facts,

---

[1] Tadeusz Żuk-Skarszewski, *Rumak Światowida: karykatura wczorajsza* (*Światowid's Steed: A Caricature of Yesterday*), published in Cracow in 1919.

[2] *Suspense*, which Conrad was trying to finish before his departure for America.

[3] *Desert*, another novel by Żuk-Skarszewski, published in Cracow in 1918.

[4] Jean-Aubry's ellipsis after 'one' in the third paragraph may be misplaced; Adams's text is supplied from 'right note' to 'the best that is in me'.

[5] In his reply, Adams confirmed receipt of a second (unlocated) letter from Conrad dated 24 January; see Stape and Knowles, p. 199.

[6] Elbridge L(apham) Adams (1866–1934) attended Williams College and practised law first in Rochester, New York, and then after 1906 in New York City. He first met Conrad in England in 1916. During Conrad's tour of New England, he spent two days as the Adamses' guest at Green River Farm, their country home near Great Barrington in western Massachusetts. An ardent bibliophile, in 1931 Adams purchased and published the correspondence between George Bernard Shaw and Ellen Terry.

[7] Adams's article, 'Joseph Conrad – The Man', appeared in the *Outlook* (New York), 18 April 1923, pp. 708–12, and was reprinted under the same title as a handsome octavo volume (vi + 74 pp.) with a Muirhead Bone portrait etching as a frontispiece (New York: William Edwin Rudge, 1925).

which are correct but which might have been expressed accurately in many other forms of words, but to that something intangible, proceeding from the spirit, which makes your form specially welcome to me.

I have not yet touched the text so I cannot allude here precisely to certain corrections which I am going to make. Some of them will bear mainly on the minor details of matters of fact; just a few words changed. One will deal with a whole paragraph. It is very short and relates to the remarks I made to you about Wells, Belloc and Chesterton.[1] I think it could very well come out, as it is a very general statement, dealing mainly with Wells from a critical point of view, and certainly not expressing all my view of Wells, which in many respects is quite appreciative. There is also the passage dealing more or less with my material position, which I should like to tone down, as what one says to a friend for whom one has a particular regard need not be repeated quite so openly to the world at large. You may think that I am too particular in that respect. It is, no doubt, a weakness of mine to cling to my prejudices in favour of privacy. If, in a sense, it may be a weakness, it is a harmless one.

[. . .][2] Morley's article is perfectly charming and I cannot but be grateful to him for striking the right note.[3] What is most vexing is to think that after all the thing may not come off, as you know my health is very uncertain, and the months of March and April are a critical time for me in that respect. So the least said about it the better.

I am hard at work at a novel and am feeling fairly well, but the uncertainty of which I have spoken prevents me indulging in hopes. Even my "good" health is a very poor and precarious thing. What frightens me most is the fact

[1] Adams cut this passage. Virtually nothing is known about Conrad's opinion of Hilaire Belloc (1870–1953) and G(ilbert) K(eith) Chesterton (1874–1936), although he did once complain about 'that preposterous Papist Belloc' (*Letters*, 4, p. 486). For over ten years, starting from an enthusiastic review of *An Outcast* in 1896, his relations with Wells were moulded by friendship and mutual admiration. See, for example, *Letters*, 1, p. 282, and the dedication of *The Secret Agent*, or Chapter 7 of Wells's *When the Sleeper Wakes* (1899), where 'The Heart of Darkness' appears in a collection of 'post Victorian authors'. As time went by, however, Conrad came to think of Wells as too much the preacher and too little an artist.

[2] The following passage cited by Adams apparently corresponds either with this ellipsis in Jean-Aubry's text or with the unlocated letter of 24 January. It concerns the proposed visit to the USA: 'I beg you, my dear friend, do not plan engagements for me. Apart from the general uncertainty of human purposes, I do really believe that I may not be equal to it. Consider the effect of such novel experience on a man of my age, whose life has been hard and whose nervous system was always highly strung up, and the emotional side untried and unblunted, while the sensibilities have been exacerbated by many years of creative work in almost complete solitude, and don't be annoyed with me. If I had not been what I am it is very probably I would not have produced the writings that are before the public and contain the best that is in me . . .' (Adams 29).

[3] Morley had often praised Conrad, but the article in question here has not been identified; see, further, Conrad's letter to Morley of 5 February.

that people on your side won't be able to understand how the commonest social exertion may on any given day be too much for me, and take my shrinking for ungraciousness, or laziness, or lack of appreciation, or any other repulsive trait of character.

I have just finished annotating and modifying – as you have permitted me to do. You may think I have been too meticulous in the alterations suggested. My view is that this first personal sketch by a friend of mine will become an authority. People will refer to it in the future. This accounts for my care to get the shades of my meaning established in your recollections, which are wonderfully accurate in the main. As to alterations on pp. 20 & 21, I tried to tone down all references to my age. Must give no opportunity to seize on what may have been a pessimistic moment in our talk. The world is very stupid and one must be careful. I must finish here to catch the mail.

With our united love to you both and the chicks.

P.S. Thanks for the press-cuttings. The accident on board that ship was an extraordinary one.[1] I have had a 50-foot spar on deck getting adrift in a gale and it was terrifying enough to tackle it in the dark.

To Louise Burleigh
Text MS Virginia; Unpublished

[letterhead: Oswalds]
25. Jan. 23.

Dear Mrs Burleigh.[2]

I hasten to catch the post, Your letter having reached me only this evening.

I have no doubt the performance will be a truly artistic thing under your direction.[3] As to the points of dialogue you mention – well, the audience

---

[1] A reference to Conrad's letter to the *London Mercury* of December 1921, reprinted in *Last Essays* as 'The Loss of the *Dalgonar*'. He was commenting on W. A. H. Mull's narrative 'A True Story: Loss and Record of the Wreck of the Ship *Dalgonar* of Liverpool', published in the September issue (4, pp. 482–8). On 9 October 1913, outward bound from Callao, the *Dalgonar* lost two sails in a bad squall; like the *Narcissus*, the vessel was thrown on her beam-ends, with the main and mizzen topsail yards in the water. Captain Isbister was washed overboard and drowned. The crew managed to cut away all the masts, but the main mast fouled the ship. On the 10th, the French barque *Loire* stood by, but could not rescue the survivors until the 14th.

[2] Actress, director, and playwright, Louise Burleigh (1890–1960) staged twenty-four plays while a senior at Radcliff College. An energetic proponent of the Little Theater movement, she published *The Community Theatre in Theory and Practice* (1917) and moved in 1919 to Richmond, Virginia, to direct the Richmond Little Theater League. In 1928 she married Conrad's acquaintance, the pianist and composer John Powell (1882–1963).

[3] Louise Burleigh was evidently directing an American production of Conrad's one-act play *One Day More* (1905).

will laugh if it wants to. I did not mean Hagberds: "From impatience" to be comic – and it did not seem so when the play was performed here.[1]

In great hurry not to miss this week's packet, I remain Your most faithful & obedient servant

Joseph Conrad

To Harold Goodburn

Text MS Davies; Unpublished

[Oswalds]

Tuesday. [30 January 1923][2]

Dear Mʳ Goodburn.[3]

Thanks for Your inquiries about John. He hasn't said much to us. I haven't been out or I would have called on You to thank you for all the trouble you have taken with the boy. Our best regards

Sincerely Your[s]

J. Conrad

To Eric S. Pinker

Text TS/MS Berg; Unpublished

[letterhead: Oswalds]

Jan. 31st. 1923.

Dearest Eric

Thank you for your letter and its news. I am glad my Guardian article has been published in America.[4]

In the matter of "Gaspar Ruiz" I must remind you that that work was done on commission for Lasky Players. Father and I collaborated on terms

---

[1] In the play, adapted from Conrad's story 'To-morrow', Captain Hagberd waits sixteen years for his son to return, then fails to recognise him. The line 'From impatience' is not Hagberd's, but Bessie Carvil's reply to the son's question about the cause of his mother's death. Conrad was present when the play was first performed in London in June 1905.

[2] Date added in pencil on the original, perhaps taken from a postmark. Conrad had met Goodburn on Monday 15 January to enquire about a place for John at The King's School, and Goodburn was evidently worried that John would be disappointed at not being admitted.

[3] Harold Goodburn (1891–1966) came from Liverpool. A schoolmaster whose chief subjects were chemistry and biology, he held posts in Dorset, Argentina, and Brazil before moving to the King's School, Canterbury, where he taught science from 1919 to 1945. He then taught in the Midlands before retiring to Canterbury. In *More Wrestling than Dancing: An Autobiography* (1990), David Moreau recalls him as the eccentric 'Captain Burnwell'. John Conrad went to Mr Goodburn for private tuition in mathematics.

[4] Conrad's 'Outside Literature' first appeared under the title of 'Notices to Mariners' in the *Manchester Guardian Weekly* on 4 December 1922 (vol. 7, no. 23, 453), and as 'Outside Literature' in the *Bookman* (New York) in February 1923 (vol. 56, pp. 680–2). It was reprinted in *Last Essays*.

of equal shares.[1] Our method was that we sat at the same table, and Father held the pen while I with the book before me suggested the wording depicting the episodes from the film point of view. We discussed each scene, and after settling it I spoke the description and Father wrote down the agreed text.[2] From those pages (which I have) in his handwriting Miss H. made one typed copy. That typed copy was sent to the office and from it was made one copy or more, (I don't know) which of course was delivered to the Lasky Players; and my idea is that having paid a sum down for the writing of the scenario they naturally kept the typescript.

The question may arise, my dear Eric, whether Lasky have still any lien on that thing. The amount they paid for the writing was, I believe, 1500 dollars.

All I have got here are the pages in Father's handwriting, which I asked him to present to me. From those certainly a copy could be made; but it would not be so good as the one which was taken from Miss H's type, which of course had many corrections made in pen and ink. Miss H's type, as far as I remember, is now in the possession of Mr Wise.[3] I propose, therefore, if you can not find a clean copy in the office and if, in your opinion, our hands are free to deal with the scenario, that I should write to Wise and ask him to lend me Miss H's copy, from which another clean one could be made for present use.

Will you drop me a line – or wire on receipt of this (if time presses) so that I may write to Wise at once.

Ever affectionately Yours
J. Conrad.

To Eric S. Pinker
Text MS Berg; Unpublished

[letterhead: Oswalds]
[January 1923][4]

Dearest Eric.

As to that application: we must regard the fact that this is not for an ant[h]ology but for a book of *literary criticism* by Miss W. A. Bone.[5] A critic

---

[1] The 'film-play' *Gaspar the Strong Man* was drafted in September–October 1921 during a holiday in Deal, but never filmed. For the collaboration with Conrad's agent and friend J. B. Pinker, see *Letters*, 7, pp. 163, 188, 193. For the negotiations with Famous Players-Lasky, see p. 278.

[2] The surviving MS (Yale) shows no sign of Pinker's hand.

[3] Thomas J. Wise had replaced John Quinn as the principal buyer of Conrad's MSS in 1918. For Wise's circumstances, see the letter to him of 1 March.

[4] Date added in pencil on the original.

[5] Woutrina Agatha Bone (1872–1958), a lecturer in education at the University of Sheffield; the daughter of an Anglo-Dutch family, she was no relation of the Scottish Bones. The book

may quote – in fact they all do that – (Freeman, Lynd and several others here[1]) – in the course of his study of an author. It is a different thing from fabricating a book merely with pieces of other men's brains. I do not think we can ask for payment: – in case of the two men I have mentionned* above, it would be unthinkable. The trouble is that I do not know anything about Miss B, her standing, her capacity and so on. Nether have I heard before of the firm. But we must assume, I suppose, that it is a genuine piece of work.

Ever Yrs

J. C.

To Frank Savery

Text MS Private collection; Mursia (1972) 12 and facsimile 21

[letterhead: Oswalds]

[late January–February 1923][2]

My dear Sir.[3]

Many thanks for your letter and the parcel which arrived safely yesterday. Need that dear Angela have troubled you? [4] I feel a certain compunction; but all the same I am glad of this opportunity to thank the writer of the preface to the German translation of *Western Eyes*.[5] Friends able to judge have pronounced it a most sympathetic piece of work and an excellent introduction to a new public. The little German I knew in 1874, when I left St Anne's School (in Cracow),[6] soon evaporated into the sea-air of the next 20 years.

mentioned here is *Children's Stories, and How to Tell Them* (Christophers, 1923). In the chapter on 'Picture Making', she quotes the passage from 'Youth' where the shipwrecked crew wake up in a Sumatran harbour. She had written children's stories herself, such as *Pippa's Holiday* (1904).

[1] John Freeman's essay on Conrad appeared in *The Moderns: Essays in Literary Criticism* (Robert Scott, 1916); Robert Lynd had written on Conrad for the *New Statesman* and *Publisher's Weekly* and in *Old and New Masters* (London: Unwin; New York: Scribner's, 1919).

[2] Dated by Conrad's letter to Zagórska of 19 January.

[3] After an education at Uppingham and Oxford, Frank Savery (1883–1965) entered the British foreign service, posted first to Munich and then Bern. Consul to the Polish Republic after 1919, he became Consul-General in 1939; during the Second World War, he was Counsellor in the diplomatic mission to the Polish Government in Exile. He was well known as a collector of porcelain and ancient bronzes.

[4] On 19 January, Conrad had complained to Aniela Zagórska about an MS that had been sent to the British Legation in Warsaw, and Savery had apparently fowarded the 'parcel' to Conrad following her enquiry.

[5] *Mit den Augen des Westens*, translated by Ernst Wolfgang Günter (Ernst W. Freissler) (Munich: A. Langen, [c. 1913]).

[6] Conrad's claim to have attended the city's most prestigious school has not been documented; see Zdzisław Najder, *Joseph Conrad: A Chronicle* (New Brunswick, NJ: Rutgers University Press, 1983), p. 505, n. 96. It is possible that he took classes there without being formally enrolled.

Pray believe in my sincere appreciation of the friendly thoughts which had prompted your letter. It was a great pleasure to read it.

Kind regards

Very sincerely yours

Joseph Conrad.

To Richard Curle

Text MS Indiana; Curle 109

[Oswalds]

Friday. [2 February 1923][1]

Dearest Dick

I was glad to see from Your letter to Jessie that You are all right and that you started working at your novel.[2] This is great news.

When are you coming down here? Will next week end suit (I mean from Friday to Sund. morning). I miss your company.

I am working – but nothing like the rate I ought to keep up to make things look better. And yet I am hard at it all the time. Can't talk about it on paper. No doubt the anxiety itself prevents me in a way to reach my best. I find life rather a trial just now. I am a little worried about B's health – and the more so because he is doing well otherwise.

Ever Yrs

J. C.

To Wilfred G. Partington

Text MS Williams; Unpublished

[letterhead: Oswalds]

Sunday. [4 February 1923][3]

Dear Sir.[4]

Will you come on Wednesday to lunch? There is a train from Vic[toria] arrives in Canterbury at 12.30. I am afraid you will have to taxi from there as there is no connection to B[ishops]bourne. You could return by the 4.3.

---

[1] Dated by Curle.

[2] Curle's first novel, *The One and the Other* (1928), was a tale of marital unhappiness set in London, with flashbacks to Malaya and Central America.

[3] Dated by Conrad's note to Partington of 8 February.

[4] Wilfred George Partington (1888–1955) worked in London and Birmingham before joining the *Bombay Gazette* in 1912. After serving in the First World War, he edited the *Bookman's Journal and Print Collector* until 1931. His books include an anthology in praise of tobacco (1924), works on Sir Walter Scott, and, with Hugh Walpole, *Famous Stories of Five Centuries* (1934). A book collector and bibliographer, he was instrumental in documenting and exposing Thomas J. Wise's forgery of literary rarities. He issued a privately printed edition of Conrad's *Laughing Anne* in 1923.

Will you drop us a pc on receipt of this.
Pardon this hasty scrawl.
                                          Sincerely Yours
                                                              J. Conrad.

To Eric S. Pinker
Text MS Berg; Unpublished

                                                              [Oswalds]
                                          Sunday. [4 February? 1923][1]
Dear Eric,
  Herewith the *M[anchest]er Guard[ian]* cheque.[2]
  Thanks for your last. We are expecting you for lunch on Wednesday next.
Very good of you to come. With our love
                                          Yours
                                                              J. C.

Re Ins[uran]ce forms.
  I have never filled that form. It was done at the office which also paid the
prem[ium]. So I return the serv[an]ts ins^{ce} form signed, and perhaps your
people will put in the figures like last year. They must have a record.
  Will you use the £10.10 which will come from M'er Guardian (Eng^{sh} rights
which I reserved for myself) to pay this ins^{ce}. If the cheque comes to me I will
send it on to you. It's about time I was paid, I think.

To F. N. Doubleday
Text TS/MS Princeton; J-A, 2, 294

                                                [letterhead: Oswalds]
                                                       Feb. 5th. 1923
Dear Mr Doubleday.[3]
  Your letters of the 18th and 25th, together with the excellent photo-
graph in which I recognised the features of my old and valued friend

---

[1] Possibly 28 January, but the reference to the *Manchester Guardian* seems to follow Conrad's
  remark in the letter to Pinker of 31 January.
[2] Apparently for 'Outside Literature', which appeared in the *Manchester Guardian Weekly* as
  'Notices to Mariners' on 4 December 1922.
[3] Brooklyn-born, Frank Nelson Doubleday (1862–1934) began his publishing career at Charles
  Scribner's Sons in 1877. He joined forces with S. S. McClure from 1897 to 1900, before entering into partnership with Walter Hines Page. After 1921, Doubleday also owned a controlling
  interest in the firm of William Heinemann. Encouraged initially by Alfred A. Knopf, Doubleday took a closer and more personal interest in Conrad after 1912, and shared in Conrad's
  rise to popular fame and fortune following the American publication of *Chance*, Conrad's
  first commercial success. Doubleday hosted and organised Conrad's American tour; Conrad
  stayed with the Doubledays at Effendi Hill, their estate on Oyster Bay, Long Island, and they
  travelled with him on his return voyage.

Sheik Abu-Kitâb (Father of the Books), arrived this evening to gladden my heart and delightfully interrupt my toil over the TS pages of the novel.

I am extremely gratified to hear that it has interested and pleased you, as far as it goes, in the part in your possession, for later on the interest increases with the development of the dramatic situation. I send you my warmest thanks for the labour and time you have expended over the "Rover" tangle.[1] This is a Rescue indeed. *Your* Rescue; and I hope that unlike Lingard it won't turn to dust and ashes[2] and end in disillusion. And, quoting the words of Mrs Travers, all I can say is that you are "the most generous of men".[3] On the other hand, unlike Mrs Travers, I am sure you will not turn your back on me after accomplishing the noble feat. I haven't heard yet from Eric, so that your news had all the force of the unexpected relief from suspense.

I say no more here because I want to dispatch this by to-night's mail to be sure it will catch the Wednesday packet. Your other author Mrs C[4] joins me in sincerest regards.

Yours Gratefully

J. Conrad

PS I will certainly write to Mr Vance as soon as your news is confirmed, through Eric to whom, I understand, you are going to cable to that effect.[5]

---

[1] In a letter to J. M. Dent dated 10 January 1923, Doubleday confirmed that 'This has not been an easy matter and I have spent a great deal of time on it' (Dent Archive, University of North Carolina). Doubleday had agreed to cover the expenses incurred by bringing forward the serialisation of *The Rover* in the *Pictorial Review*.

[2] Cf. 'ashes to ashes, dust to dust' from the Service for the Burial of the Dead in the Anglican Book of Common Prayer, and the words of Abraham in the Hebrew Bible: 'Behold now, I have taken upon me to speak unto the Lord, which am but dust and ashes' (Genesis 18.27).

[3] These words are spoken not by Mrs Travers but by Tom Lingard, who tells her (in Ch. 6 of the final part of *The Rescue*): 'You are the most generous of women.'

[4] Doubleday was also the American publisher of Jessie Conrad's *A Handbook of Cookery for a Small House*, which came out in 1923.

[5] See Conrad's letter to Vance of [6 February].

To Christopher Morley

Text MS Texas; Unpublished

[letterhead: Oswalds]
5. Febr. 1923

My dear Morley.[1]

Just a few lines to thank you for the friendly inscription on the copy of *Shandygaff* sent me by Adams.[2]

A month before he sent me a press-cutting from which I saw that F.N.D. had taken upon himself to let the cat out of the bag much sooner than I expected.[3] But reading your words so full of kindness and understanding (no favourite son could have done it better) I perceived that F. N. D. knew what he was doing when he made you the first recipient of the news. I hope he had given you the messages for you I gave him every time I met him here.

The truth is that event is on the knees of the Gods[4] – a notably insecure place. Last time I made up my mind to come over they could think of nothing but starting a world war. They have no sense of proportion. It was squashing a fly with a steam-hammer. And they are careless. This time, as likely as not, they will let some 'no account' nigger get into the fence – which would be even a worse fate. But if they are good enough to leave me alone I do hope that I will find you within reach of my arm for that hand-grip which may be made to mean much more than any amount of blackened paper. Meantime rest assured of my warm regard and my affectionate gratitude

Yours

J. Conrad.

---

[1] A jovial Rhodes Scholar and prolific essayist and poet, Christopher Darlington Morley (1890–1957) produced some fifty books while working as an editor for various publishers and journals including Doubleday, Page and the *Saturday Review of Literature*. His novels include *Parnassus on Wheels* and *The Haunted Bookshop*. He was a Sherlock Holmes enthusiast, an indefatigable admirer of Conrad, and a ubiquitous member of the New York literary scene. His account of Conrad's arrival in New York, which appeared in instalments in the *New York Evening Post* during May 1923, was collected as *Conrad and the Reporters* (1923).

[2] Essays in the collection *Shandygaff* (Garden City: Doubleday, 1918) praise Conrad alongside Kipling and William McFee. Morley recalls that 'There were five volumes of Conrad in the officers' cabins on the *Lusitania* when she went down, God rest her. I know, because I put them there' (p. 177).

[3] By announcing Conrad's visit to America.

[4] Although 'lap' has become the more familiar site, 'in' or 'on the knees of the Gods' occurs at least as far back as George Chapman's *The Whole Works of Homer* (1616).

To Marie Saltus

Text TS Private collection; Unpublished

[letterhead: Oswalds]
Feb. 5th. 1923.

Dear Mrs Saltus.[1]

Pray pardon the delay in answering your letter. I beg to offer my sympathetic condolences on the heavy loss you have sustained, and of which I was not aware.[2]

I am acquainted with some of the books of the late Professor, but I am now overwhelmed with work delayed by a long period of inability. I would, however, lay it aside if it were not for the conviction that neither my early training, nor the course of my later life, nor yet the little ability I may have in imaginative literature, fit me mentally for the honour you do me by your proposal to write an introduction to one of your husband's books.

Pray accept with my regrets the expression of my profound respect.

Your most obedient servant

Joseph Conrad

To G. Jean-Aubry

Text MS Yale; *L. fr.* 180–1

[Oswalds]
6.2.23.

Cher Jean.

Merci de Votre bonne lettre.[3] Je suis heureux de Vous savoir là.[4] Quand pourrez-vous venir nous voir?

Je me suis fait envoyer le Fortnightly. Je viens de finir Votre Sainte-Beuve.[5] Mon cher! C'est une admirable éxposition analytique de l'homme lui même.

---

[1] In 1911, Marie Florence Saltus (née Giles, 1873–1960) became the third wife of the author and theosophist Edgar Evertson Saltus (1858–1921), an admirer of Schopenhauer, Balzac, Flaubert, and Barbey d'Aurevilly whose works include fiction, poetry, philosophical speculations such as *The Philosophy of Disenchantment* (1885), and vivid, impressionistic historical narratives such as *Imperial Purple* (1892), *The Lovers of the World* (3 vols., *c.* 1895), and *The Imperial Orgy: An Account of the Tsars* (1920). Among Marie Saltus's publications was a biography, *Edgar Saltus, the Man* (1925); *Poppies and Mandragora* (1926) is a joint collection of their poems.

[2] Saltus had died on 31 July 1921.

[3] Of 4 February (MS Yale). Among other pieces of news, it announces his plan to give a series of lectures on Conrad's work at the Théâtre du Vieux-Colombier in Paris.

[4] After spending the Christmas holidays with his family in Le Havre, and making a successful lecture tour of France, Jean-Aubry was now back in London.

[5] An essay on the critic and literary historian Charles-Augustin Sainte-Beuve (1804–69), *Fortnightly Review*, NS 113 (January–June 1923), 265–74.

Je n'ai jamais rien lu de ce genre qui me fit le même effet de vision pén[é]trante
jointe a une forme parfaite.

Mes félicitations très cher ami.

Je Vous embrasse

Votre

Conrad

PS Jessie sends her love.

Merci pour le "Corresp[on]d[an]t" avec article corrigé.[1] Chic.

– C'est une faute d'impression. La phrase: "La famille Caporali etc etc" aurait
du être: "Les familles Caporali etc etc". (Remarque générale de l'auteur)

Le comm^{dt} est excusable.

Dear Jean.

Thank you for your good letter. I'm happy to know you are there. When
can you come to see us?

I've had the *Fortnightly* sent to me. I've just finished your Sainte-Beuve. My
dear fellow! It's an admirable analytic exposition of the man himself. I've
never read anything of this kind that gave me the same sense of penetrating
vision coupled with formal perfection.

My congratulations, dear friend.

I embrace you

Your

Conrad

PS Jessie sends her love.

Thanks for the *Correspondant* with the corrected article. Chic!

– It's a misprint. The phrase "The Caporali family etc, etc" should have
been "The Caporali families etc, etc." (General remark by the author)

The commandant is excusable.

---

[1] Jean-Aubry had published a translation of the *Tremolino* episode, Chs. 40–45 of *The Mirror of
the Sea*, in *Le Correspondant* of 25 January. His letter of 4 February and his notes in *L. fr.* explain
the circumstances. Since the editor was pleased with this fragment and had asked for more,
Jean-Aubry wanted to turn next to 'Initiation'. Meanwhile, a 'Commandant' who had read
the translation wrote to Jean-Aubry pointing out that the reference in Ch. 42 to the Caporalis
(from whom Dominique Cervoni claimed descent) should be in the plural. Whether the sailor-
reader knew that Conrad's original has 'families', not 'family', or was well-versed in Corsican
genealogy, Jean-Aubry does not say.

To Eric S. Pinker

Text TS/MS Berg; Unpublished

[letterhead: Oswalds]
Feb. 6th. 1923.
10. AM.

Dearest Eric.

Thanks for yours of yesterday. I enclose here Doubleday's letter which I got last night and which I answered at once with warm acknowledgements of the service he has rendered to us.

I am writing to Vance to-day and I regret that it will miss the Wednesday's packet. However not much time would have been lost.

In regard to Fisher Unwin I can only say in writing what I have told you before in conversation: that I will endorse any attitude you will find necessary to take in this matter, (in which my opinion is that we can not be made responsible) or close it in the way of the best possible compromise. In connection with this I agree with you that the publication of Uniform Edition may safely be begun at once if Dent is anxious to do so. My point of view is that F. U. is bound to come in, at one time or another, out of regard for his own interests, seeing that the unfortunately high price of that edition will protect his cheaper issues. That is why I still hope that you will be able to save The Suspense from his clutches. The surrender of that book will be an altogether immeasurable compensation for whatever expense the delay of The Rover may have caused him. I don't believe he could prove quite £50. And as to the argument that the sales will suffer, it is absurd and no court would entertain it as The Rover is not a topical book but a work of art which people who read Conrad would buy for the sake of its literary value as readily in 1924 as in 1923.

As to the work all I can say is that I am devoting all my energies and thoughts to it during the day and part of the night also; for I am sorry to say I have not been sleeping very well lately – a new thing for me. I grudge the time it takes me to dictate this and so I close now without touching on any other matter.

Always affectly yours

J. Conrad

I have signed 500 cop⁵ of *S. Agent* for W. Laurie.[1] He will have the rest this week.

---

[1] In all, Conrad had to sign a thousand copies of the four-act play for Laurie's deluxe edition.

To Arthur T. Vance
Text TS Princeton;[1] Unpublished

[Oswalds]
[6 February 1923][2]

for F. N. D.
copy of pen-and-ink letter to Mr Vance

Dear Mr Vance,[3]

I have received last night a letter from my very good friend Mr Doubleday advising me that you have consented to arrange for "The Rover"'s appearance serially this year.

I know enough of the work and responsibilities attached to the direction of an important periodical like "Pictorial Review" to understand that this arrangement goes far beyond a mere manifestation of courtesy or good-nature such as a stranger might offer, but takes rank with the sort of service one could only expect from a personal friend. It is with that feeling that I am sending you my sincere thanks for your action which has saved me a lot of inconvenience and worry in carrying through certain projects of mine connected with the publication of my works in a popular edition here.

So your kindness, as you see, has a far-reaching effect and I beg you to believe my gratitude is commensurate with it.

With cordial regards,

Very sincerely yours,

JOSEPH CONRAD.

To F. N. Doubleday
Text TS/MS Princeton; Unpublished

[letterhead: Oswalds]
Feb. 8th. 1923.

Dear Mʳ Doubleday.

Your letter confirming the good news foreshadowed in the preceding one arrived yesterday. I have devoted to-day to a last look at the galley proofs of "The Rover", and they are going to America in the same ship with this letter. They are very much corrected and the corrections are very important from a literary point of view. Of course in galley-form those corrections will not

---

[1] Enclosed with Conrad's letter to Doubleday of 8 February.
[2] Dated by Conrad's letter to Pinker of 6 February, which also refers to the arrival of Doubleday's letter 'last night'.
[3] Arthur Turner Vance (1872–1930) was editor of the *Pictorial Review*. From 1900 to 1907 he had edited the *Ladies' Home Journal and Woman's Home Companion*.

be difficult to make (numerous as they are) and I am extremely anxious they should all be carried out, because it has been always my ambition to make the text of American editions absolutely flawless if possible. Generally the pressure of time has prevented me from doing that thoroughly. In the case of this work, however, there will be time, I am glad to think. It would be a great kindness if your printing department would pull off for me a set of corrected galleys, to be set up from, here, so that the English edition should conform exactly to the American, which, in this case, would be the standard one. I would also be glad if the "Pictorial Review" were given corrected galleys to set up the serial from. I want to appear at my best before its numerous readers.

I enclose here a typed copy of my letter to Mr Vance which of course I wrote in pen and ink.[1]

I am profoundly touched by the warm interest you took in this affair of mine and your inspiring exertions in straig[h]tening it out, hopeless as it looked. Will you please give my respectful regards to the Ladies and remember me cordially to Mr Nelson.[2]

Always, Dear Mr Doubleday, most sincerely yours

Joseph Conrad

To Wilfred G. Partington

Text MS Williams; Unpublished

[letterhead: Oswalds]

8. 2. 23.

Dear Mr Partington

We were sorry to hear of Your bad cold. I hope it is nothing serious; but it was prudent and very considerate of you to give up your visit here.[3]

In the hope of hearing soon of Your complete recovery I am always

faithfully Yours

J. Conrad.

---

[1] As if to a friend rather than a man of business – a form of flattery or politeness.

[2] The 'Ladies' included Doubleday's wife Florence and his daughter-in-law Martha Nicholson Doubleday, known as 'Patty'. She was the wife of 'Mr Nelson' (1890–1949), a son from Doubleday's first marriage, who entered publishing via the magazine trade, joined his father's firm as a junior partner in 1918, and became president in 1928.

[3] Partington visited Conrad later in the month; see Conrad's letter to Pinker of 21 February.

To H.-D. Davray
Text TS copy Yale;[1] Unpublished

Oswalds
Feb. 12th. 1923.

Dear Davray,[2]

Thank you very much for the invitation and I assure you that I am grieved not to be able to come to the dinner and meet M. Chevalley;[3] but a most horrible cough keeps me confined to the house, and I do not think it would be prudent for me to come up to town.

faithfully yours

J. Conrad

To Aniela Zagórska
Text MS copy Yale;[4] Najder 287

Oswalds,
Feb. 12th 1923.

My dearest,

I return you the proof of "Il Conde."[5] I dictate this letter because I want to post it to-night to you. The translation of Mr. L. Piwinski is really very good. I have made several suggestions as to the rendering of the English text and proposed a few emendations as to Polish. As to that last you will have a look and judge of them yourself. I think, my dear, that you can safely let him do the whole of "Set of Six" if it is convenient to you.

I have read "Almayer's Folly" with great attention. The only suggestion I can make relates to the very last line where Abdulla recites the attributes of Allah.

Could it be expressed in Polish with capital letters as below?

. . . szeptem imię Allaha. Łaskawego! Miłosiernego![6]

---

[1] A typed copy prepared for Jean-Aubry from an original TS letter now lost.

[2] Author, editor, and translator, Henry-Durand Davray (1873–1944) was an active promoter of Anglo-French cultural friendship. As editor of the Collection d'auteurs étrangers for the *Mercure de France*, he translated novels by Conrad, Arnold Bennett, Rudyard Kipling, George Meredith, and H. G. Wells.

[3] A diplomat by profession, Abel Chevalley (1868–1933) was also a poet, critic, and translator. He translated the Tudor novelist and balladeer Thomas Deloney into French, and with his wife Marguerite, compiled the *Oxford Concise French Dictionary*. He wrote widely, producing books, for example, on Queen Victoria and on Egyptian steles.

[4] Zagórska's MS transcription of the original TS, most of which was written in English.

[5] For a Polish translation of *A Set of Six* (Warsaw, 1924).

[6] *Fantazja Almajera* (Warsaw, 1923), Zagórska's translation of *Almayer's Folly*, was the first volume of Conrad's *Selected Works* in Polish, with an introduction by Stefan Żeromski. The last words in the original are: 'breathed out piously the name of Allah! The Merciful! The Compassionate!'

My point is that Abdulla recites the well-known formula mechanically; and if that effect can be conveyed into Polish, too, the impression would be more accurate. But perhaps it may seem to you disagreeable in sight or sound; in which case please leave it as it is. It is quite faithful enough.

Thank you for the press cuttings and the very interesting illustrated paper. I think that the criticisms of the work are intelligent and just and I am very touched by the warmth of appreciation. As to the translation every word in praise of it is *more* than deserved. I admire it immensely and am most grateful to you.[1]

I take comfort that there are people who can appreciate the value of your translation. It is a triumph, my Aniela! – I am working with a feeling of genuine despair.

A thousand kisses

your

Konrad.

To Eric S. Pinker

Text MS Berg; Unpublished

[Oswalds]

[13 February 1923][2]

Dearest Eric.

Thanks for You[r] definite news of peace being concluded with F. U[nwin]. Another historical episode closed – on which I congratulate you. For You did well in getting the serial contract – F. N. D. did well by, apparently, revolutionising a whole year's arrangements of the Pic^t Rev: and Vance too showed some courage. So did you in facing F. U. during the blackest hours, while old Dent displayed some virtue too. A curious (and satisfactory) episode, on the whole. Many thanks.

We have here a *correct* text to give Unwin when the time comes.[3] But we may get revised galleys from U.S. before that. Do you want the correct type-text in your office in case there may be an opening for an English serial?

Affectly Yours

J. Conrad

PS Yesterday I comp[lete]^d and posted signed sheets to W. Laurie.

---

[1] The remainder of the letter was in Polish.   [2] Date added by Miss Hallowes.
[3] Of *The Rover*, published by Unwin on 3 December 1923.

To G. Jean-Aubry
Text MS Yale; Unpublished

[letterhead: Oswalds]
Jan. 14th. [14 February] 1923.[1]

Mon cher Jean.

Merci de Votre bonne lettre. Nous Vous attendons donc pour le week-end de la semaine prochaine. Je viens d'écrire a Ridgeway au sujet de Jean.[2] Aussitôt reponse reçue je vais écrire a M. Bost.[3] C'est évidemment ce qu'il faut a tous les points de vue. Mme Votre Mère a été bien bonne de s'en occuper.

Au revoir

Ever yours

J. Conrad

My dear Jean.

Thank you for your good letter. We shall expect you for the week-end after next.

---

[1] This is clearly a response to a letter from Jean-Aubry dated '10 fev. 1923' (MS Yale). In it, Jean-Aubry expresses his delight that Conrad admires the article on Sainte-Beuve, an admiration expressed in Conrad's letter of 6 February. Moreover, Conrad's letter of 20 February continues the agenda of the present one, as if they were written a few days, rather than several weeks, apart. Thus it is Conrad rather than Jean-Aubry who has his dating wrong. Although the rest of the letter is in MS, Conrad's date is typed, with a handwritten '14' obscuring the original number. In a frugal moment, perhaps, Conrad may have taken up a sheet discarded by Miss Hallowes and remembered to change the day but not the month.

[2] See Conrad's letter of 10 November 1922 (*Letters*, 7, p. 578). The Revd Neville and Agnes Ridgeway, Ted Sanderson's brother-in-law and sister, were John Conrad's housemaster and housemistress at Tonbridge School. They took a particular interest in John for Conrad's sake, Conrad having been friendly with 'Miss Agnes' since the mid-1890s.

[3] Charles Bost (1871–1943) was a pastor of the Eglise Réformée de France in Le Havre, the author of many scholarly articles on the history of French Protestantism, and a notable lecturer on this subject all over Protestant France and Switzerland. He published the two-volume study *Les Prédicants protestants des Cévennes et du Bas-Languedoc: 1684–1700* in 1912; it was 'crowned' by the Académie Française in 1913. His most recent book was *Les Martyres d'Aigues-Mortes* (1922). Following the example of his son Pierre, he began to write plays in 1924, mostly on historical and religious themes. In his letter of the 10th (MS Yale), Jean-Aubry describes him as 'un pasteur protestant libéral, très intelligent et sympathique'. Jean-Aubry's mother, Thérèse Aubry, had arranged for Conrad's son John to improve his French by staying with Bost's large family. Jean-Aubry wrote that Le Havre 'ne serait pas "a bad spot" pour John: il n'y serait pas absolument dépaysé, et mes parents pourraient également s'en occuper, si nécessaire'. To supplement the family income, the Bosts often took young men and women boarders.

I've just written to Ridgeway about John. As soon as I hear from him I shall write to Monsieur Bost. It's clearly what's needed from all points of view. It was very good of your mother to help with this.

Until next time

Yours truly,

J. Conrad

To Captain David Bone
Text MS Sprott; *Landfall* 155; Knowles

[letterhead: Oswalds]

17. 2. 23.

My dear Capt Bone.[1]

I was very glad to receive your friendly letter.[2] I confess that as soon as that project of a visit to the US came up for consideration I formed the intention to stow myself away on board the ship you commanded. In my time the stowaways (to Sydney) were kindly treated. But as I see from your letter that you are disposed to treat me kindly in any case I'll try to get a ticket in the usual way and let "romance" go by the board.

Seriously my dear Bone I am very grateful to you for the suggestion. The matter however is not quite certain. There is always the possibility of a gout attack knocking me out; and I am sorry to say that there may be the possibility of another operation on my poor wife's knee. I should not like to be away. This is the only reason why I haven't yet rushed to secure my passage in the *Tuscania*.[3] Your brother is a great artist. I don't know his work as well as I ought to do – but enough to base my great regard and admiration for it on something more than a superficial impression.

Warm regards.

Most cordially Yours

Joseph Conrad.

---

[1] Captain David William Bone (1874–1959; knighted 1946), the brother of Muirhead and James Bone, first went to sea in 1890. He served with the Anchor Line after 1899, eventually becoming Commodore, and commanded troop ships in both World Wars. He was captain of the *Tuscania*, in which Conrad sailed to New York. Although discouraged by Conrad from 'leaving the ship' to become a writer, he produced numerous sea tales and nautical memoirs, among them *The Brassbounder* (1910).

[2] Of 13 February; see Stape and Knowles, p. 201.

[3] A vessel of 16,991 tons, built for the Anchor Line in 1922 at the Govan yards, Glasgow; an earlier ship of that name had been torpedoed and sunk in 1915.

To H. J. C. Grierson
Text MS NLS; MS draft Berg; Morley[1]

[letterhead: Oswalds]
18 Febr. 1923.

Dear Sir.[2]

I am very much indebted to you for the friendly thought of writing to me unofficially about the intention of the Senate Committee of your University.[3]

An obscure feeling, taking its origin, perhaps, in an abiding consciousness of the inward consistency of a life which, at this day, may, in truth, be said to have been lived already, compels me to decline the offer of an academic degree.

As I know that you will not suspect me of brutish insensibility, or of some objectionable form of stupidity, I venture to hope that you will find an occasion to convey to the Committee of the Senate of Your illustrious University my deep sense of the intended honour and the expression of my most respectful gratitude.

Pray accept, my dear Sir, my thanks for your personal communication and believe me, with the greatest regard, always
very faithfully Yours
Joseph Conrad.

To G. Jean-Aubry
Text MS Yale; Unpublished

[letterhead: Oswalds]
20.2.23
6. pm

Mon très cher.

Ridgeway etait absent au chevet de sa mère[4] qui est très malade de sorte que je viens de recevoir sa reponse il y'a dix minutes seulement.

---

[1] Following a catalogue by Edgar H. Wells and Company (New York) recording the sale of this and two other letters concerning honorary doctorates, Morley erroneously identified the addressee as the 'Vice Chancellor of Oxford University'.

[2] Herbert John Clifford Grierson (1866–1960; knighted 1936) was Professor of English Literature at Aberdeen University from 1894 to 1915, and then Professor of Rhetoric and English Literature at the University of Edinburgh, where he became Rector in 1936. His many publications include editions of the poetry of John Donne, the Metaphysical poets, and the letters (in twelve volumes) of Sir Walter Scott.

[3] The University of Edinburgh.

[4] Pauline Josephine Ridgeway (née Newall, 1841–1923), born in Poona, India, was the widow of the Bishop of Salisbury. She died in April.

Je me hâte de Vous dire que le head-master a recommandé "proprio motu"[1] a Ridgeway de faire travailler Jean a la mathematique ces vacances-ci. Il faut suivre ce conseil. Mon cher je ne peux pas trouver V[o]tre lettre avec l'adresse de Mme Bost. Voulez Vous écrire pour moi un petit mot?

    Pardonnez moi En toute hate

Votre

Conrad

My very dear fellow.

Ridgeway was away at the bedside of his mother, who is very ill, so I received his reply just ten minutes ago.

I hasten to tell you that the headmaster has recommended *proprio motu* for Ridgeway to have John work on maths during this vacation. This advice must be followed. My dear fellow, I can't find your letter with Mme Bost's address. Would you write a brief note for me?

    Forgive me.

        In great haste

Your

Conrad

To Eric S. Pinker

Text TS/MS Berg; Unpublished

[Oswalds]
Feb. 21st. 1923.

Dearest Eric.

I begin by telling you that the conjunctions of the stars point towards us having an interview and I propose to accomplish this destiny next Monday, for a varied talk with you; so that after we have settled the things I have in my mind I can, so to speak, stop my ears and shut my eyes against everything for another thirty days' work at the novel.

Meantime I enclose you three letters, of which Adams' contains a material fact, apart from speculative views. The article of which he speaks and which I revised deals with his personal impressions of J. C. It is the first thing of that kind written by an unliterary man and it will be certainly reproduced largely all over the States. Its publication will fall in with the scheme of the projected visit.

The other letters also speak for themselves, and whatever reflections they suggest to you, you will communicate to me on Monday.

---

[1] 'Of his own accord'. The Headmaster was H. N. P. Sloman.

Partington ("Bookman"[1]) has just gone away after a short visit, the object of which I discovered to be a proposal to print the play, "Laughing Anne", in the same form as Drinkwater's, Masefield's and Walter de la Mare's things: Limited Edition on vellum, beautiful print and binding. But you must have seen those things. He offered 12/6 per copy, on a 150 Edition, which amounts precisely to £93.15.0. He blurted out the conditions unasked or else I would have declined to listen to them, but I referred him to you, saying that I would let you know of his visit. As I calculated in my head that his offer was very little less pro-rata than what we get from Laurie, I took upon myself to say that I did not apprehend that there would be any difficulties.[2] That of course may mean anything and does not, of course, tie your hands at all; but that little man is very sympathetic to me and, after all, that money is a windfall (outside all our estimates of incomings for the next twelve months) and to tell you the truth, my dear, I have been worrying my head off about the surgeon's bill that will fall due at the end of March, anything between £40 and £50. I was just thinking of selling the two Collected Editions I have had as a present.[3] But since this turns up I propose you should let me meet the doctor from the proceeds; and the balance might help towards the first outlay of the American journey. Pay for the ticket anyway; for I don't suppose that Bone would consent to sign me on even as a boatswain's yeoman, though I believe I would be quite competent. Bone's proposal would mean, of course, a passage on the bridge and would be quite interesting for me. Three weeks in May would be enough in America. Anyhow I am sure the Doubledays will have enough of me after three weeks in their house. I promise to make myself sufficiently objectionable to make them glad to see my back at the end of that time.

This being a sufficient hint for you as to my state of mind I reserve a lot of other weighty matters for Monday. I will be at the office about 12.30, unless I hear from you that the day, or the time, or both, are inconvenient.

Ever affectly Yours

J. Conrad

PS. I am afraid I did not acknowledge Your letter advising paym[t]. I am sorry.

---

[1] He edited the *Bookman's Journal and Print Collector*, not the *Bookman*.

[2] *Laughing Anne, a play* was published as a 66-page booklet by the *Bookman's Journal* office in 1923 (Vine Books, no. 4) in a limited edition of 200 numbered copies signed by Conrad.

[3] Conrad had been receiving volumes in the Heinemann and Doubleday collected editions since 1921 (*Letters*, 7, pp. 286–90). He was often anxious about expenses, but there is no evidence of his having sold any sets.

Jessie sends her love. I am sorry to say there is another set-back with that limb, causing pain and worry. She will have to see Sir Robert end March[1] – if not sooner.

I send You (in this envelope) the material part of a long letter from B. He joined to it (as an evidence of his having been confirmed in his new appt^ent I suppose) a letter from his first direct chief now the Co's manager in London.[2] Perhaps you will glance at it at your leisure.

To Eric S. Pinker
Text MS Berg; Unpublished

[Oswalds]
Tuesday [February 1923][3]

My dear Eric.

It may be that Evans and Bayard*[4] are right as to the illustrations of M[irror] of the S[ea].[5] They must decide as to the "full page". I should like to have some say as to the head and tail pieces. The idea is to have each *subject* begin on a new page; the "sections" in each subject being numbered I. II III etc. not "run on" as they are in the existing editions; the pages being set so that each *subject* beginning and ending at half-pages can have its own head and tail piece. (Black and white.)

This is only a suggestion. The great thing is to make the book like art-production – atmospheric – not a shop article. But the house can be trusted for that.

As to Dent: – yes, certainly.

Affectly Yours

J. C.

---

[1] The distinguished orthopaedic surgeon Sir Robert Jones had been treating her since 1917.
[2] The appointment was as manager of Daimler's new depot in Manchester.
[3] Dated '2/23'in pencil. February Tuesdays were the 1st, 8th, 15th, and 22nd.
[4] Charles ('Charlie') Seddon Evans (1883–1944) and Theodore Byard (1871?–1931) were Heine-mann employees who became managers after the firm's acquisition by Doubleday in 1921. An illustrated edition of *The Mirror of the Sea* had long been under discussion, but nothing came of the project; see Conrad's letter to Pinker of 21 March.
[5] In November 1921, William Rothenstein showed Conrad photographs of paintings and draw-ings by the marine artist and sailor (Herbert Barnard) John Everett (1876–1949). His work made a deep impression on Conrad, who began discussions with J. B. Pinker and Heine-mann's about a possible de luxe edition of *The Mirror* that would in effect be a collaboration between writer and artist. See *Letters*, 7, pp. 372–3, 380–2, and *passim*. Everett sold little of his work during his lifetime and bequeathed well over 2,000 paintings, graphics, drawings, and photographs to the National Maritime Museum.

To G. Jean-Aubry

Text L. fr. 181

[26 February 1923.][1]

Très cher,

Ne m'envoyez pas du Proust (que je vous ai demandé) car les volumes sont arrivés cette après-midi.[2] Mais les vers de Valéry et tel autre œuvre que je dois lire.[3] Oui!

Vous embrasse.

My dear fellow,

Don't send me the Proust (which I asked you for) since the volumes arrived this afternoon. But Valéry's poems and any other work I should read. Yes!

I embrace you.

To Thomas J. Wise

Text MS BL Ashley 2953; Unpublished

[letterhead: Oswalds]
1st Mch. 1923.

Dear Mr Wise.[4]

I had lately a visit from Mr Partington who told me you were looking well when he saw you last. I hope your health is good and everything else is exactly as you wish it.

---

[1] Date from Jean-Aubry.

[2] Jean-Aubry identifies them as Proust's *Sodome et Gomorrhe* (1921–2).

[3] Jean-Aubry brought Paul Valéry (1871–1945) to Oswalds in November 1922; see *Letters*, 7, pp. 557, 611. He had just published the last of his major collections of poetry, *Charmes ou poèmes*, which includes 'Le Cimetière marin'. His earlier volumes included *La Jeune Parque* (1917) and *Album de vers anciens* (1920). The reference to 'tel autre œuvre' may be to Valéry's prose or to the work of another author.

[4] Thomas J(ames) Wise (1859–1937) collected – and fabricated – literary rarities. Having prospered as a dealer in lavender and other essential oils, he built up a considerable collection of books and manuscripts, many of which are now in the British Library's Ashley Collection, and enjoyed a steady reputation as a bibliophile and bibliographer. Meanwhile he was forging and selling at high prices unique early editions of Wordsworth, Shelley, Tennyson, Charlotte Brontë, George Eliot, Swinburne, and the Brownings, all hitherto unknown to scholarship. In order to improve his own collection of Jacobean plays, he was also helping himself to pages from copies in the British Museum. His career as a forger was not exposed until three years before his death, when his career as a literary thief and vandal came to light long after. In 1918, he began to purchase MSS and TSS from Conrad, and in 1920 overtook John Quinn as principal purchaser. As Conrad's first bibliographer, he published *A Bibliography of the Writings of Joseph Conrad* (1920) and *A Conrad Library: A Catalogue of Printed Books, Manuscripts and Autograph Letters by Joseph Conrad* (1928). He also printed twenty limited-edition pamphlets of Conrad's occasional writings between December 1918 and January 1920.

I am very hard at work at my novel – and have done quite a lot to it lately.[1] The Rover will begin to come out as serial (in US) in Sept^{er} (Pictorial Review) and be ready for book-form in December.

I don't know whether you know I am contemplating a visit to America, and may start for N. York about 15 Ap. returning about end May.

It would be very nice if you came to see us here. We are leaving this house definitely in Sept^{er}. We could have a talk on various matters. My wife suggests a visit next Sunday; but really you can name your day up to the 20th of this month. There is a train on Sund^y from Vic[toria] arriving Canterbury about 12.24; I would come to meet you. You could be back in town at 7.13. Will you drop us a line? With our united kind regards

always sincerely yours

J. Conrad.

PS Have you heard of the L^d E^{dn} of S. Agent (play) by W. Laurie? I'll have a copy for you of course. Also a copy of "Anne" which Parting[t]^{on} is going to do. Only 150 cop^s.

To Ernst P. Bendz

Text TS/MS Private collection; Unpublished

[letterhead: Oswalds]
March 7th. 1923.

Dear Dr Ben[d]z[2]

Thank you very much for the copy of the pamphlet on myself and my work.[3] I need not tell you that I have perused it with great attention and no small appreciation.

I have the more reason to be grateful to you for this remarkable, and in so many ways generous, recognition of my work because I have heard, from a friend who has visited Sweden last year,[4] that I am regarded in that country as literarily a sort of Jack London. I don't mean to depreciate in the least the talent of the late Jack London, who wrote to me in a most friendly way many years ago at the very beginning, I think, of his literary career, and

---

[1] *Suspense.*

[2] Ernst Paulus Bendz (1880–1966) graduated from Lund University in 1914 with a dissertation on Oscar Wilde, and taught in Gothenburg. He often travelled to England and France, and published many articles and reviews in Sweden and Finland. His thirteen books in Swedish include studies of Alfred de Vigny, Paul Valéry, André Gide, François Mauriac, and Henri de Montherlant.

[3] Bendz's *Joseph Conrad: An Appreciation* (Gothenburg: Gumpert; New York: H. W. Wilson, 1923; rpt New York: Haskell House, 1971).

[4] Jean-Aubry (see *Letters*, 7, p. 405).

with whom I used to exchange messages through friends afterwards;[1] but the fact remains that temperamentally, mentally, and as a prose writer, I am a different person. I sympathised much with the warm and direct talent of Jack London, and was sorry to hear of his death – but, after all, one doesn't like to be taken for what one is not. For one thing, for instance, I am much less of a good humanitarian than Jack London;[2] but I think that I am not taking too much on myself in saying that I am a good European, not exactly in the superficial, cosmopolitan sense, but in the blood and bone as it were, and as the result of a long heredity.

Apart from the natural gratification one finds in meeting with such admirably expressed sympathy, I followed your analysis with no little curiosity. It is interesting to learn about one's self from a judge for whose attainments one can not but have a sincere respect. I will confess to you frankly that I do not know much about my own work. I can not defend myself from the suspicion that you make perhaps too much of its merits, while I see with profound satisfaction that you never question its absolute sincerity, both in its qualities and in its defects.

I will take the liberty to point out that Nostromo has never been intended for the hero of the Tale of the Seaboard. Silver is the pivot of the moral and material events, affecting the lives of everybody in the tale. That this was my deliberate purpose there can be no doubt. I struck the first note of my intention in the unusual form which I gave to the title of the First Part, by calling it "The Silver of the Mine", and by telling the story of the enchanted treasure on Azuera, which, strictly speaking, has nothing to do with the rest of the novel. The word "silver" occurs almost at the very beginning of the story proper, and I took care to introduce it in the very last paragraph, which would perhaps have been better without the phrase which contains that key-word. Some of my critics have perceived my intention; the last of them being Miss Ruth Stauffer in her little study of my Romantic-Realism, published in Boston in 1922.[3]

---

[1] Conrad's memory is faulty here. The American novelist Jack London (1876–1916) wrote to Conrad only at the very end of his career, on 4 June 1915, to say that he had been 'swept . . . off his feet' by *Victory* (Stape and Knowles, p. 100). Comparisons between these none-too-similar authors began by noting that they both wrote adventure stories and had been to sea.

[2] Ten weeks later, talking to the Yale professor William Lyon Phelps about H. G. Wells, Conrad said 'I love humanity but I know it is unimprovable' (Phelps, p. 754).

[3] Ruth Mathilda Stauffer's MA. thesis (University of California, 1919) was published as *Joseph Conrad: His Romantic-Realism* (Boston: Four Seas, 1922). She draws attention to the silver motif (p. 39), discusses the characters of *Nostromo* as slowly assembled mosaics (pp. 45–7), and argues that his sweeping yet meticulously detailed imagination of an entire country is the greatest of all his achievements (pp. 66–7).

I am only too acutely aware of my lapses of style, but, in one or two instances which you give, the construction of the speech is shaped on purpose to characterise the person; as for instance when Therese speaks, all through "The Arrow of Gold".[1]

It is very obvious that I don't possess the English language in an exceptional way; but that is no reason to doubt my sincerity when I say that it has possessed and even shaped my thoughts. Idiomatically I am never at fault, and it is absolutely true that if I had not written in English I would not have written at all.

Pray dear Dr Ben[d]z accept my renewed thanks and believe me, with the greatest regard

very sincerely Yours

Joseph Conrad.

To Hugh Dent

Text TS/MS Berg; Unpublished

[letterhead: Oswalds]

March 7th. 1923.

My dear Mr Dent.[2]

I am glad to hear that you got home safely, and I hope that Mrs Dent and yourself are fit and well.[3]

I need not tell you how glad I am that the "Rover" tangle has been cleared; which means, of course, that the long novel will appear with your imprint.[4] It won't of course be very soon, but it is perhaps just as well, as it will benefit by any success "The Rover" may have.

As to the device for the side of the binding (Uniform Edition) I send you here the impress on sealing-wax, just to show you what sort of thing it is.[5] It is too small to be engraved from for the die. To tell you the truth I don't know whether it is advisable to do that. Possibly I did throw out the idea but it must have been half-heartedly. A man may put his arms on the binding

---

[1] Sometimes revealing his own slippery grasp of English idiom, Bendz examines Conrad's supposed solecisms, all the while insisting that they do not matter very much. Indeed, Bendz claims, Conrad's idiosyncratic language is one of his strengths (pp. 95–9).

[2] Hugh Railton Dent (1874–1938), J. M. Dent's eldest son, spent his professional life in the family publishing house, J. M. Dent & Sons. He joined the firm in 1909 and took over its management after his father's death in 1926.

[3] Dent had been in America and in Toronto on business, arriving in New York on 2 February.

[4] The 'tangle' concerning *The Rover* is recorded in letters to J. M. Dent from F. N. Doubleday (10 January 1923) and from Eric Pinker (11 January 1923) held in the Dent Archive, University of North Carolina, Chapel Hill; see also Conrad's letter to Arthur T. Vance of [6 February 1923]. The 'long novel' mentioned here is *Suspense*, published by Dent in 1925.

[5] An impression of Conrad's signet ring, which bore a family crest; see the letter to Aniela Zagórska of the same date.

of the books in his library, but I don't think it is quite appropriate for books offered to the public. I admit it has been done, but mostly on biographical books, and these were the arms of the subject of the biography, not of the author. The more I think of it the more I shrink from the idea.

Will you consider whether a plain side will not do? Should that not please you, then the best suggestion I can make is (don't be surprised) – an Hour-glass.[1] That idea is not so stupid as it may seem to you at first sight. An hour-glass by itself is a comely object and it falls in with my humour just now. It is inoffensive, suggestive, unpretentious, and symbolic enough, almost, to please anybody. Will you ask the Chief[2] and stand my friend in this affair?

And in connection with the Edition I should not like it to be called "The Standard Edition" – to which the Chief seems inclined. First of all it's all very well for historians and scientific men to have their Standard Editions. Secondly, it would not be true, since it is being printed from American plates. Thirdly, it's a name that can be used later for some cheaper, more popular edition. What it is exactly is the: First Uniform Edition; because the previous one was a Limited Edition. Then why not call it Uniform?

I expect very soon to be in town, in preparation for my American journey and look forward to seeing you then.

Kindest regards from us both

Your[s] sincerely

Joseph Conrad.

PS Salutations to the Chief.

To T. Werner Laurie
Text TS SIU; Unpublished

[letterhead: Oswalds]
March 7th. 1923.

Dear Mr Werner Laurie[3]

I would give with the greatest pleasure my consent for the staging of "The Secret Agent" by the Leeds Art Theatre if I were certain that my agreement with Benrimo permits me to do so.[4]

---

[1] The firm took Conrad's suggestion; a winged hour-glass is embossed on the covers of volumes in the Uniform Edition.

[2] Conrad's affectionate nickname for Hugh's father, Joseph Mallaby Dent (1849–1926), the founder and bearded patriarch of the publishing firm.

[3] T(homas) Werner Laurie (1866–1944) had worked for T. Fisher Unwin before establishing his own publishing house in 1904. Conrad remained wary of involvement with Laurie, but had accepted his offer to publish a limited edition of *The Secret Agent* in its stage version.

[4] The American-born actor and director J. Harry Benrimo (1874–1942) produced *The Secret Agent* at the Ambassadors Theatre in November 1922. For the agreement, see *Documents*, pp. 226–7.

I have sent your nephew's letter to Eric Pinker, asking him to ascertain how I stand with regard to that agreement, and to write to you direct.[1]

The corrected proofs of the play have been sent to you on Monday. It will be in every respect a very nice edition.

I see that our agreement gives me five complimentary copies. I wonder if you would consent to pull off three more which I would like very much to send to Poland. One to Mr Żeromski, the most distinguished Polish novelist of the present time; and the others to two girls, my distant cousins,[2] people who are not likely to be subscribers. Of the other five Edward Garnett will get one, and the others I will keep for myself and my family.

Believe me very faithfully Yours
Joseph Conrad.

P.S. Of course I mean to pay for the manufacturing cost of the three extra copies, should you consent to pull them off for me.

To Eric S. Pinker
Text TS Berg;[3] Unpublished

Oswalds.
March 7th. 1923.

My dear Eric

1) Your letter was very interesting. The fact of the matter is that I have never been in any correspondence with Mr Beer;[4] neither have I given any promise some years ago to write an introduction to a biography.

"Some years ago" there was no man in America who would have dreamt of writing a biography of Crane and no publisher who would have thought of a complete edition.

The first I heard of Mr Beer was in a letter from Hamlin Garland[5] "July/22" enclosing a letter from Mr Beer to himself, not to me. From this I learned that there was such a person and that that person was writing a biography of Stephen Crane. The trouble was that some schweinhund having seen in the papers that Beer was writing a biography of Crane tried to blackmail Beer by threatening to publish some correspondence relating to

---

[1] Laurie's nephew was L. B. Ramsden; see the following letter from Conrad to Pinker.

[2] Aniela and Karola Zagórska. For Stefan Żeromski, see the letter to him of 25 March.

[3] Conrad wrote the section numbers in the margin.

[4] The American author and biographer Thomas Beer (1889–1940) wanted Conrad to write a Preface for his biography of Stephen Crane.

[5] Hamlin Garland (1860–1940), an American author best known for the stories in *Main-Travelled Roads* (1891) and his autobiographical *A Son of the Middle Border* (1917).

Mrs Crane[1] unless Beer bought those letters from him for a considerable sum.

I send you Garland's letter and my reply, from which you will see the nature of the information sought. Of course I am disposed to do an introduction for the price you mention, but as a matter of fact I have very little material for that and it will take some spinning to make it go to 3000 words. I suppose Knopf[2] knows what he is doing, though when I saw him last he did not seem to be very enthusiastic about Crane; I mean as a business proposition.

What strikes me most is the fact that my name seems to be worth something with the American public since such a sum is offered to me for what can not be a very profound piece of work.

I will be very glad to attempt it, as you suggest. As a matter of fact this is rather a good time, or at least not an unfavourable time, to lay the novel aside for a few days, as I have just finished with the third part altogether and would be glad of a change of work before plunging deep into the fourth.[3]

2) I enclose here copies of the letters received this morning.[4] I think that an overture from that quarter ought to be considered, though it may not mean much in the way of money. I am sorry J. Aubry is away lecturing in France, on me amongst other people. He is also writing an introduction to the serial publication of a "Gaspar Ruiz" in the Revue Franco-Americaine.[5] The South Americans on its staff profess themselves delighted with the story. Aubry has also arranged for a series of three lectures at the Theatre de* Vieux Colombier[6] in the autumn of this year. He will be back before the end of

---

[1] Cora Crane (née Cora Howarth Stewart, alias Cora Taylor, 1863–1910) was Crane's common-law wife; she had an unconventional history, including a stint as madam of a brothel in Jacksonville, Florida, the Hotel de Dream.

[2] Alfred A(braham) Knopf (1892–1984), whose publicity campaign had been largely responsible for the success of *Chance* in America. His own firm was publishing Beer's biography, *Stephen Crane: A Study in American Letters* (1923).

[3] At this stage in the composition of *Suspense*, the 'third part' consisted of three chapters: the first two chapters of Part III, plus a chapter describing Cosmo's escape from Genoa that Conrad later rechristened Part IV. The 'fourth' part envisioned here describes reactions in Genoa to Cosmo's disappearance and was published as the novel's penultimate chapter (Part III, Chapter 3). See Gene M. Moore, 'How Unfinished Is *Suspense?*' in Mario Curreli, ed., *The Ugo Mursia Memorial Lectures, Second Series* (Pisa: Edizioni ETS, 2005), pp. 237–43.

[4] As part of his plan to publish a Spanish edition of Conrad's novels, the novelist Vicente Blasco Ibáñez had approached R. B. Cunninghame Graham and his close friend Elizabeth 'Toppie' Dummett. Conrad was forwarding excerpts from letters they had written on his behalf. For more on Ibáñez and his plans, see his letter to Conrad of 10 March (Stape and Knowles, pp. 202–6) and Conrad's letter of the 21st.

[5] Philippe Neel's translation ran in the *Revue de l'Amérique Latine* from April to July.

[6] Founded in 1913 by Jacques Copeau, Louis Jouvet, and a group of friends including Gaston Gallimard and André Gide, the Théâtre du Vieux-Colombier in Paris became one of the most important centres of French drama. The lectures were to be on Conrad (Jean-Aubry to Conrad, 4 February, MS Yale).

March, however, and we will be able to ask his opinion of Ibanez' publishing house. I think A. well qualified to be an Adviser on Spanish Affairs.[1]

3) I enclose for you also a communication from Laurie, together with a letter from his nephew, L. B. Ramsden, of the Leeds Art Theatre. I am disposed to give him the right of performance (I suppose three of them) if I am at liberty to do so.[2] Will you write to Laurie direct in that sense, after ascertaining whether our agreement with Benrimo permits it. And anyway perhaps Benrimo would give his consent. I am writing to-day to Laurie saying that he will hear from you very soon.

I hope you don't think I give you a lot of unprofitable trouble, but I feel that all my business should officially go through you, even in matters of that sort.

Ever affectly Yours

J. Conrad.

PS Your wire to hand. It suits me to see Beer this week as I could not begin to write before having a talk with him.[3]

To Aniela Zagórska

Text MS copy Yale;[4] *Ruch*; Najder 288; *Listy* 443

[letterhead: Oswalds]

7. 3. 23.

My dear Anielcia,

Thank you for Slowacki's[5] letters, which I have not yet begun to read. I have no time at the moment. My work progresses very slowly. I spend entire days sitting at my desk and by evening I feel so tired that I no longer understand what I am reading.

The beautifully bound copy of Almayer has also reached me and I kiss you tenderly for the pleasure it has given me.

---

[1] Jean-Aubry had many contacts in Spain, including the composer Manuel de Falla (1876–1946).

[2] L. B. Ramsden's production of *The Secret Agent* opened at the Leeds Art Theatre on 12 November 1923 and ran for four nights (see Conrad to Curle, 2 November).

[3] Conrad wired Pinker later the same day: 'Let Beer take the 10.40 Vic[toria] to Canterbury tomorrow car will meet please wire me today if all three intend to come am disposed to do my best in the matter writing' (telegram, Berg).

[4] A French translation in the hand of Aniela Zagórska. Text from Najder's translation of the Polish; the original was published in *Ruch* in 1927 and destroyed in the 1944 uprising.

[5] Juliusz Słowacki (1809–49), Romantic poet and revolutionary who lived in exile following the Polish Insurrection of 1830 against Russian rule. Various collections of his letters had appeared, including the two volumes of *Listy* (Lwów, 1883) and the *Korespondencya* with his mother and other relatives (Warsaw, 1910). A new collection, edited by Zdzisław Londoński, would appear in 1924.

Could you, *ma chère amie*, send me a drawing of the Nalecz coat of arms? I need an emblem for the binding of the new edition of my works. Here I have only a little seal from which it is difficult to make a copy.[1] This edition will start publication in May.

Is there a Polish armorial less detailed than Niesiecki,[2] and less expensive? If so, could you perhaps send me a copy and I will reimburse you. What matters is only that the drawings should be clear and precise.

I close with a brotherly embrace.

Always your

Konrad.

Sorry for all the bother I am giving you.

To Eric S. Pinker

Text TS/MS Berg; Unpublished

Oswalds.
March 9th. 1923.

Dearest Eric.

Thanks for your letter with returned enclosures.

The interview was very much like such interviews generally are, lots of talk about Crane, from which I learned things not previously known to me, as for instance that Crane mentioned me in his correspondence with certain people in America – and so on. Upon the whole very satisfactory; and B[eer] produced on me and everybody else in the house a very good impression. Incidentally one was able to gather that B. himself, the son of a very successful lawyer,[3] is a man of means, so that there can be no scruple in accepting the amount which Knopf, quite justifiably, thinks uneconomical.

Personally I don't want to behave like a ghoul, feeding on the memory of a departed friend. All I wanted to say about him I said in the two pages and a half published in the Mercury, for which I got the usual fee.[4] There was no

---

[1] For the Nałęcz arms and the family's place in the Korzeniowski lineage, see *Letters*, 2, pp. 244–5.

[2] The standard four-volume work, published 1728–43 by Kasper Niesiecki, was available in many abridgments and editions.

[3] In the sixth generation of his family to enter the law, Thomas Beer was the son of William Collins Beer, a corporate attorney in Council Bluffs, Iowa.

[4] Originally written for Peter Somerville, editor of *The Englishman*, who was making an unsuccessful attempt to resuscitate his defunct journal after the war, 'Stephen Crane: A Note without Dates' appeared in the inaugural issue of the *London Mercury* in December 1919 and was reprinted in the New York *Bookman* in February 1920. It was collected in *Notes on Life and Letters*. Conrad had received £10 from the *London Mercury* (see *Letters*, 7, p. 8).

reason for making a present to the Mercury. In Beer's case the man is thrusting the amount on me without the slightest suggestion on our part (I take it). The real question is whether I can afford in the present circumstances to throw away the offered sum. That and nothing else is the question, as far as I am concerned. I would not be exploiting my friendship with Crane. Whether the transaction is worth while for Beer, that is his own affair. From what he told me of my reputation in America (as being the man who understood Crane best) it is clear that he thinks that it is worth while. Therefore I told him that I would take the matter in hand at once, without waiting to see what his biography was like, trusting that his work would be the right thing,[1] just as much as he trusted me to produce the right thing also. I told him that I would bring the MS over with me to the U.S. or (alternatively) that I would deliver it to him in June. All this he agreed to.

Of course I intend to do it at once; anything between 3000 to 4500 words – which of course will take some doing. Beer seemed more than satisfied with the suggested length. His textual words were that he "hoped for four or five pages." I have jotted already some ideas for the groundwork of the thing which must be more personal than critical; but in point of fact will have to contain some references to Crane's literary and creative characteristics.

In this connection I want to ask you what would be your feeling if I took into my confidence Edward Garnett (not as to the amount offered or anything of the kind) as to the proposed Preface, for which, of course, I would tell him I was being paid, and asked him to jot me down some of the facts, opinions and views as known and entertained by him about S.C. to be used by me, either with or without the mention of his name, for which I would offer him, say a cheque for twenty or twenty-five pounds. The transaction would be strictly between ourselves. Edward's position is no secret to anyone and it's obvious that the money would be quite useful to him.[2]

Will you, my dear Eric, look at it all round, and tell me without reserve how the idea strikes you. If you see the slightest objection I will drop it, because I

---

[1] Scholarly editors of Crane's correspondence have discredited Beer's biography as scattershot, and marred by the use of faked letters; see Stanley Wertheim and Paul Sorrentino, 'Thomas Beer: The Clay Feet of Stephen Crane Biography', *American Literary Realism*, 22 (Spring 1990), 2–16.

[2] Garnett's work as a publisher's reader was never especially lucrative, and he was contributing to the expense of two households, the country house which he shared with his wife, and a flat in Chelsea which he shared with his lover, Nellie Heath. He now worked for Jonathan Cape, and had recently negotiated an annual salary of £300: George Jefferson, *Edward Garnett* (Cape, 1982), pp. 193–5.

can do without E.G. and E.G. as we all know, is a ticklish person to deal with. He may, metaphorically, give me a kick; but I wouldn't mind that very much. Once having accepted B.'s offer I really would like to give him as much as possible for his money.

The real importance of Beer's proposal, to my view, is that it secures the material conditions of my journey to the States, without encroaching on the incomings of the year (as we have figured them) even in case of the most complete non-success, either on account of health or for any other reason. I would propose that you should credit me with £200, which would leave from this transaction £200 to cover your commission, £40; interest on the above credit £10; also the commission on roughly £100 from Partington, and interest on that credit together, say £25; leaving £125 or thereabouts as an unexpected addition to the receipts of the year as we estimated them. A clear gain, after providing for the American journey. I present this transaction to you in this shape, though of course in practice it will be thrown into our general account.

On my own side I reckon like this: Cr. from Partington and Beer, £293. Dt. To return-passage, with expenses, £100; doctor's account end March, £50; fitting out, about £40; leaving me for pocket expenses, £103 – which is fairly safe. For contingencies of the unforeseen kind there is a *certain £100* awaiting me on the other side (for signatures) as arranged by E. Adams.

So that we may say that if anything at all in the way of dollars is made during that trip it would be credited in full to my account; and if nothing is obtained (except some moral advantage) well then, the year's budget will in no way be affected by failure.

Jessie sends her love.

Ever affectly Yours

J. Conrad

PS Of course I would settle with Edward out [of] my credits.

Pardon me pursuing you to your home with a business letter. But I am anxious to hear as soon as possible about the "Edward" idea from Your point of view.[1]

---

[1] This paragraph was added to the opening of the letter as a handwritten PS.

To Edward Garnett

Text G. 321

[letterhead: Oswalds]
March 10th, 1923.

Dearest Edward,[1]

I was just preparing to write to you – but certainly not to the Maison Basque.[2] I didn't know you were a Basque; and had any right to date your letters from your national habitation. Life is full of surprises!

One of them certainly was Mr. Beer, who had communicated with me through dear old Hamlin Garland some time last July or August. I was under the impression I had told you something about it; but truth to say I attached no importance whatever to the episode which had something to do with a batch of Mrs. Crane's letters. Anyway I knew that there was such a person, and that a biography of Crane was in contemplation. About a week ago I heard from Eric Pinker that Beer and Knopf wanted to see me. They came here last Thursday and Beer did mention to me that he had had a talk with you. Your good letter arrived on Friday morning, after their visit.

Its object was to ask me to write an introduction for the aforesaid biography. God knows I don't want to play the ghoul, feeding on the memory of my friends; . . . that trip is not going to be a lecturing tour but simply a visit to Doubleday at his home in Oyster Bay, for three weeks or so. As I can't suppose that Doubleday intends to keep me shut up in his cellar for all that time I fully expect to be let in for some at least semi-public appearances. . . .[3] But the less I think of it the better, or I may die of funk before I put foot on that distant shore. They begin already to talk about it. David Bone heard of it in New York and very kindly asked me to come over with him. Muirhead[4]

---

[1] The critic, playwright, and satirist Edward William Garnett (1868–1937) was the most influential publisher's reader of his generation. His wife Constance translated Russian literature, and their home, The Cearne, was a meeting-place for writers, artists, anarchists, socialists, and Russian refugees. Many other young writers benefited from Garnett's generosity, among them Robert Frost, D. H. Lawrence, T. E. Lawrence, Dorothy Richardson, Sean O'Faolain, and Edward Thomas. Garnett staunchly supported Conrad from the very beginning of his career, and Conrad often consulted him on matters of style or tone. Although Conrad disapproved of Garnett's pacifism and Russophilia, they remained close and loyal friends. In 1928 Garnett published a selection of his letters from Conrad.

[2] The restaurant in Dover Street, Piccadilly, where Garnett had lunched with Beer on 7 March. After lunch, Garnett wrote to Conrad on Maison Basque stationery, suggesting that he invite Beer to Oswalds. Garnett, who thought highly of Crane's fiction, had written to Conrad on 7 March suggesting that he invite Beer to Oswalds on the 8th or 9th (Stape and Knowles, p. 202).

[3] The American edition of Garnett's letters (Indianapolis: Bobbs-Merrill, 1928) has no ellipsis following this sentence (p. 290).

[4] Muirhead Bone (1876–1953; knighted 1937), the brother of Captain David and the journalist James Bone, was famous for his etchings and drypoint engravings. He often collaborated with his wife, Gertrude, who wrote essays, fiction, poetry, and travel books. On the voyage in the *Tuscania*, he shared a suite with Conrad and drew several portraits of him. See 'An

will be there too, and we have got to join on April 21st, in Glasgow – but I haven't yet got my ticket. That I should want a ticket in order to go on board a ship on a foreign voyage seems to me the most absurd thing in the world. Anyway the whole thing doesn't bear thinking about, and that is why I didn't tell you of it before. There would have been an awful finality about it. And now there is; though I don't quite believe yet that it will ever come off. Of course, I will have to come to London before I go, and we will have a long talk. That confounded Introduction, which I haven't begun yet, is worrying me.

Jessie suggests that if I asked you nicely you would perhaps come down to see us for a couple of days before the end of this month, at any time convenient to you. Well, I am asking you nicely now; and I am sure that, (as Mr. Ratsch would say), "the amiability of your character and the elevation of your sentiments will induce you to visit the house of the departing."[1]

I am no end pleased at David's book going so strong.[2] Did you see the review in the (American) Bookman?[3] Give him my greeting and congratulations.

Mrs. C. sends her love.

Ever yours

J. Conrad.

To Richard Curle
Text MS Indiana; Curle 110[4]

[Oswalds]

12 Mch '23

Dearest Dick.

Pardon this scrap of paper. It is only to send you my congratulations on reaching the mature age of 40 – and to thank you for the copy of the special

---

Artist's Impression', first published in the *Manchester Guardian Weekly* (8 August 1924), in Ray, pp. 164–7.

[1] A reference to Ivan Turgenev's story 'An Unhappy Girl' (1846), which Constance Garnett had translated in 1899 for the volume *The Jew and Other Stories*. The hyper-punctilious Mr Ratsch is a 'professor of . . . various subjects'.

[2] *Lady into Fox*, by Garnett's son David (1892–1981), a fantastic story about a woman abruptly turned into a vixen, her confused identity and the perplexities of her husband, was his greatest commercial and literary success, winning the Hawthornden Prize. It had been published by Chatto and Windus the previous November, with woodcut illustrations by Garnett's wife, Ray (Rachel Alice, née Marshall).

[3] The New York *Bookman* carried a regular 'Londoner' column by 'Simon Pure' (the novelist and man of letters Frank Swinnerton). In the February 1923 issue, Swinnerton commended Conrad's stage version of *The Secret Agent* and David Garnett's novel, praising the latter as a 'queer work' and a 'remarkable *tour de force*' (56, p. 738).

[4] A fold-out facsimile of this letter was the frontispiece to the English edition of Conrad's letters to Curle, *Conrad to a Friend: 150 Selected Letters from Joseph Conrad to Richard Curle* (Sampson Low, 1928).

edition[1] received to-d[a]y. I like the appearance very much. I hope the book will meet with the recognition it deserves.

I have begun to-day an introduction to a forthcoming biography of Crane by a man called Beer. He and Knopf came here on Thurs: last on that business – which is in truth a marvellously good business for me. I want to give him about 3500 words. It will take some doing, tho'.

I am sorry no end to see from Jessie's letter that you cannot come over with me into the Land of the Mohicans.[2] I have a short note from F.N.D. (from the Bahamas). The letter in which I announced your possible arrival with me had not reached him yet when he wrote. He must have it now. He intends to be back long before the date of the voyage of the New Columbus (without Pinzon!!?[3])

Can't get up any enthusiasm for it. More details when we meet – which will have to be soon.

Ever Yrs

J. Conrad.

To F. N. Doubleday
Text TS/MS Princeton; J-A, 2, 296

[letterhead: Oswalds]
March 13th. 1923.

My Dear Mr Doubleday.

Thanks for your good letter of Feb. 25th. A few days before it reached me I had heard from Mr Everitt[4] and I knew you had gone in search of warmth and sunshine at the Bahamas. I saw them for the first and last time in 1875 when beating through the Florida Channel in the ship Mont-Blanc on the first voyage of my sea-life. At that time Nassau was not a winter resort and stagnation and poverty lay over the whole group which seemed very much out of the world.

I will now proceed to report to you on the situation.

---

[1] Curle's footnote: 'A copy of the large paper edition of *Into the East*'.

[2] Conrad's boyhood reading included James Fenimore Cooper's *Leatherstocking Tales*, which closes with *The Last of the Mohicans* (1826). He also liked Cooper's maritime novels, and wrote about them in 'Tales of the Sea' (*Notes on Life and Letters*).

[3] Columbus's trusted lieutenant, Vicente Yáñez Pinzón (1463–1514), captain of the *Niña*, one of the three ships on Columbus's first voyage to the West Indies.

[4] Samuel A(lexander) Everitt (1871–1953), usually known as Sam, had long worked for Doubleday; he became the company's Treasurer and Executive Vice-President, retiring in 1930.

I have finished Part Three of the novel,[1] having been able to slow down the pace after the success of your intervention in the matter of "The Rover". I was glad to do that because I was feeling strained by working against time; and I am persuaded that it wouldn't have been worth while to keep it up when the necessity for it was gone. Of course the novel will be finished, say, by September or October of this year and, as I suppose you will agree with me that "The Rover" must be given a year's run in book-form, there would be time to serialise "The Suspense" and issue it as a book in the autumn of '24.

A gentleman called Beer has asked me to write an introduction to a life of Stephen Crane, which I think he is going to publish some time this year. I decided to do it for him and have begun this very day. It makes a change and upon the whole I am glad of being able to talk a little to the world at large about Crane, whose particular gifts I admired and for whom both my wife and myself had a great affection. Directly this is finished, say, in five or six days, I shall return to the novel and do as much as I can up to about a week before sailing.

In regard to various circumstances of the domestic order I have concluded[2] to start from Glasgow on Ap. 21st. by the "Tuscania", which David Bone is commanding now. It will make a great difference to me, to cross over with a friend. The "Tuscania" will be returning on June 7th, which would give me a clear month (of May) in the United States.

It seems an awfully long time to inflict myself on the kindness of Mrs Doubleday and yourself. I hope you will not regret your friendly impulse to make me free of your home for such a long time. Your optimistic view of the prospects of this visit cheers me up immensely. I assure you I do not look on my visit as a dollar-raiding expedition. And indeed if I never made any I would not feel disappointed.

It has occurred to me, dear Mr Doubleday, that I ought to tell you of the offers I had by the Universities of Oxford, Edinburgh, Liverpool and Durham, of an honorary degree, which I have declined. This is between ourselves. I only would like to point out that this would debar me from accepting a similar offer from any other quarter. Refusing such an honour is the most disagre[e]able thing in the world, but I am perfectly determined to have nothing to do with any Academic distinction.

---

[1] The original 'Part III' of *Suspense*, comprising Chs. 1 and 2 of Part III of the published novel and the original third chapter that was later renamed 'Part IV'.

[2] A Gallicism, from *conclure*, 'to decide'.

I hope to hear from you once more before I leave England. I am sending this letter to Garden City,[1] assuming that you will be returning soon there. Pray give my duty to Mrs Doubleday.

Always sincerely yrs—

Joseph Conrad

To Captain David Bone

Text TS/MS Sprott; *Landfall* 156; Knowles

[letterhead: Oswalds]

March 14th. 1923.

My dear Capt Bone.

As I imagine you will be home in a day or two I drop you a few lines to tell you that I intend to apply for my ticket (return) on Monday next, as I will be in town that day. I think I will get to Glasgow on the 20th Ap. as I should like to call on James Lithgow (Russell & Co.) whose acquaintance I made in 1917 and who was my eldest boy's Battery-major for some two years in France.[2]

I have had, last weekend, from my old friend, Major G. Gardiner,[3] a light thrown on you from an unexpected side, which Gardiner appreciated very much at the time of trouble. I will tell you about it when we meet. G. G. is a friend of Henderson's,[4] but he said to me that since I am going with you (on your suggestion) there is no need to recommend me specially. Would you, my dear Captain Bone, use your influence to have my name kept out of the passengers' list – if such a thing is published. I am going over quietly to stay with F. N. Doubleday for a month or so and he has agreed that it would be better for me to slip past the reporters.[5] He has promised to be with his car at the wharf on your ship's arrival.

I look forward immensely to the passage with you and Mr Muirhead Bone. What gave me immense pleasure is that you should have written first to me just as I was preparing to write to you. What delayed me for a day was a doubt

---

[1] On Long Island, the home of Doubleday's Country Life Press.

[2] James Lithgow (1883–1952; 1st baronet of Ormsary 1925) was Chairman of Lithgow's, one of the great Clydeside shipyards. Wounded on the Somme and awarded the Military Cross, he had dined with the Conrads in London before Borys returned to the front; he was Borys's commanding officer in the Royal Army Service Corps (see Conrad (Borys), pp. 125–7).

[3] They had made friends during Conrad's visit to Scottish naval bases in 1916, when Gordon Gardiner was his military escort. For his career as a writer, soldier, arbitrator, and philanthropist, see the letter to him of 29 July.

[4] A member of the Glasgow shipbuilding family, owners of the Anchor Line until 1911, when Cunard became the majority shareholder. The company kept its public identity as Anchor Line (Henderson Brothers) and members of the family still served on the board.

[5] In the event, a large crowd of newspaper reporters and photographers greeted Conrad on his arrival in New York.

as to the name of the ship, so that I could not look up the departures, and also a vague idea that you were perhaps on the Mediterranean service. Last December Doubleday told me of having met you at Gibraltar in command of the Berengaria.[1]

I intend after getting my dunnage together to sit close at home up to the 17th, working at my novel. On that day I will attend the National Life-Boat Institution Meeting, it being the centenary. After that I will allow myself two more days to say good-bye to various people, before starting on my voyage of discovery; for N. America will be as novel a sight to me as it was to Cabot[2] a few centuries ago.

Always sincerely yours

Joseph Conrad

To Eric S. Pinker

Text MS Berg; Unpublished

[Oswalds]

Wed^y [14 March 1923][3]

My dear Eric.

Of course I made no sign to G. H., and I will not do so – as I feel you are right in your advice.[4]

Will Monday be convenient to you for a talk with me? I think I ought to take my return ticket soon. Also order the clothes. Having done these things I want to have one more go at the novel – feel my grip on it before putting it by for nearly 2 months. I can not say that I feel sure I will be able to bring the "Crane" with me for you to take to U.S. and complete the transaction. But I'll bring it with me in the Tuscania. There's no doubt of getting the number of words – but I am afraid of falling into drivel.

Au revoir

Ever yours

J. C.

---

[1] At 52,226 tons, one of the largest liners in the world. Formerly the Hamburg-Amerika Line's *Imperator*, she was impounded under the war reparations programme; Cunard acquired her in 1921.

[2] The Italian-born explorer John Cabot (1461–98) sailed from Bristol in 1497 and is often credited with discovering the 'New Founde Landes' off North America; that he had been preceded by Beothuks, Basques, and Vikings does not lessen the novelty and danger of his voyage.

[3] Dated by Conrad's PS mentioning the offer from Cambridge University.

[4] About G. H. Clarke? See Conrad's dismissive letter to him of 9 August 1923.

I am going to second the Resolution at the meeting of the Nat. Lifeboat Inst. on the 17 Ap. Beatty[1] in the chair. To-day have received offer of Hon. Degree from Cambridge University. That makes the fifth.[2]

To Elbridge L. Adams
Text TS unlocated;[3] Adams 30 (in part)

[Oswalds]
[15 March 1923][4]

[. . .] I can now tell you that short of buying the ticket, which I will do next Monday, I have made my arrangements to arrive at New York by the Tuscania, leaving Glasgow on April 21st. Pray don't mention this fact, because I want to keep the exact day of arrival dark. I imagine it will be the first or second of May. I will ask the Company to keep my name out of the passenger list and Doubleday has promised to be at the wharf to meet me and whisk me away. I take your own view of the visit to your side. I always shrank from considering it as a dollar-gathering expedition. I assure you that half of its significance would be gone for me if I were not to spend a day at least under your roof. Pray give my affectionate remembrance to Mrs. Adams.

To Eric S. Pinker
Text TS Berg; J-A, 2, 298

Oswalds.
March 15th. 1923

Dearest Eric.

I have received this morning a letter from Ibañez, in a* most extraordinary jargon of French I have ever read in my life.[5] The gist of it is that a letter to you has been written care of Grant Richards;[6] since, apparently, that is the only address in the whole city of London that Ibañez knows. I imagine you

---

[1] Admiral David Beatty (1871–1936; 1st Earl Beatty, 1919), a veteran of river battles in the Sudan campaign and the Boxer Rebellion, had served with distinction during the war. He was Commander of the Grand Fleet, and later Admiral and First Sea Lord. Sir William Hillary founded the Royal National Institution for the Preservation of Life from Shipwreck in 1824; in 1854, it became the Royal National Lifeboat Institution or RNLI. The RNLI maintains lifeboat stations around the coasts of Britain and the Isle of Man. In its centennial year, it was launching an appeal for extra funds. Najder gives two versions of the speech, the first one Conrad ever gave, in Najder (1978), pp. 109–12. See also Conrad's Preface to *Britain's Life-Boats* (1923), by his friend A. J. Dawson (*ibid.*, pp. 107–8).

[2] In his letter to Doubleday of 13 March, Conrad identified the other four universities as Oxford, Edinburgh, Liverpool, and Durham.

[3] Formerly in the Estelle Doheny Collection, now dispersed.

[4] Dated by the reference to buying the ticket.

[5] See Stape and Knowles, p. 202.   [6] The publisher and novelist (1872–1948).

would either get it to-day or you have had it already. By the time we meet I will have mastered the Ibañez language sufficiently to translate it for you. Unless I hear from you to the contrary I shall raid the office on Monday at the usual hour.

Affct^ly Yrs

J. Conrad

To the Vice-Chancellor, Cambridge University
Text MS Fitzwilliam; MS draft Berg; Morley

[letterhead: Oswalds]
15 Mch 23

Dear Sir[1]

With all possible deference I beg to be permitted to decline the offer contained in your letter.

I hope you will accept and communicate to the Council of the Senate of your illustrious University my grateful sense of the proferred* distinction and the expression of my profound respect.

Believe me

very faithfully Yours

Joseph Conrad

To Vicente Blasco Ibáñez
Text TS/MS draft Yale; *L. fr.* 182

[letterhead: Oswalds]
Mars 21st. 1923.

V. Blasco Ibanez.[2]

Cher et illustre Confrère,

Je vous remercie de votre aimable et intéressante lettre dont la lecture m'a fait le plus grand plaisir.

---

[1] Before serving as Vice-Chancellor from 1921 to 1924, Edmund Courtenay Pearce (1870–1936) was Master of Corpus Christi College, Cambridge; he was Bishop of Derby from 1927 until his death.

[2] Trained as a lawyer, the Valencia-born writer and political activist Vicente Blasco Ibáñez (1867–1928) edited a radical republican journal, *El Pueblo*, and was imprisoned many times over for his anti-royalist activities; he went into voluntary exile in 1923. His internationally famous novels *Los cuatro jinetes del Apocalipsis* (1916, trans. as *The Four Horsemen of the Apocalypse*, 1918), a rendering of the First World War, and *Sangre y arena* (1908, trans. as *Blood and Sand*, 1913), a story of bull-fighting, became immensely popular films. His other novels include *Cañas y barro* (1902, trans. as *Reeds and Mud*, 1928) and *Mare Nostrum* (1918).

Je suis très heureux de savoir que Vous Vous intéréssez a mon oeuvre. Je désire vivement me présenter au public espagnol sous Vos auspices. C'est un honneur auquel je ne m'attendais pas. Je Vous assure que je l'apprecie profondement.

Mon agent M. Eric Pinker a reçu la lettre de la Maison Prometeo.[1] Sans doute il n'y aura aucune difficulte a nous entendre; seulement comme Pinker part pour les Etats Unis après-demain il a prié la Maison Prometeo de lui permettre de reprendre les négociations a son retour, au commencement du mois de Mai prochain. Je pense que ca vaut mieux car, comme cela, la correspondence, une fois commencée, ne sera pas interrompue.

Moi-même je pars dans une quinzaine faire une petite visite a des amis a New York. E. Pinker sera de retour ici avant moi et s'addressera tout de suite a la Maison Prometeo. Il a mes pleins-pouvoirs, et il n'aura pas besoin de ma presence ici pour conclure un contrat definitif.

J. C.

Dear and Illustrious Colleague,

Thank you for your friendly and interesting letter which I have read with the greatest pleasure.

I am very glad to know of your interest in my work. I wish ardently to be presented to the Spanish public under your auspices. This is an unexpected honour. I assure you that I appreciate it deeply.

My agent Mr Eric Pinker has received the letter from Maison Prometeo. No doubt there will be no difficulty in reaching an agreement, but since Pinker leaves for the United States the day after tomorrow, he has asked Maison Prometeo to allow him to resume negotiations on his return at the beginning of May. I think this is better, since in this way the correspondence, once begun, will not be interrupted.

I myself leave in a fortnight to pay a brief visit to friends in New York. E. Pinker will be back here before me and will contact Maison Prometeo immediately. He has my full authorisation and will not require my presence here to conclude a final agreement.

J. C.

---

[1] Editorial Prometeo, a Barcelona publishing house.

To Eric S. Pinker

Text TS/MS Berg; Unpublished

Oswalds.

March 21st. 1923

Dearest Eric.

Thank you for communicating to me Everitt's letter. As to its subject matter, really there is not much to give him. There is a pretty bad photograph or two of myself in the North Sea in 1916[1] and I may send it out to him, but as you may imagine I don't care much for that sort of thing.

I went to your people and gave my orders. Thank you very much for the introductions.

Please tell me whether Tuesday morning would be enough time for you to get a fully corrected Crane introduction to take over with you. And if I post it on Monday had I better send it to your private address or to the office. I hope, however, that you may get it before, say on Monday.

As we said good-bye I don't think I will come up to town next week. If it isn't too much to ask you while you are so much rushed would you please mention to me whether the plan of the Illus. Ed. of the "Mirror" still holds good for this year.

Affectly Yrs

J. Conrad

PS Re Crane intr[on]. You may tell Beer that he may cut out what may not appear suitable. I'll be glad to answer any communication from him on that subject.

You'll remember no doubt my wish to pub[li]sh eventually say 25 copies. Privately for the Author. of that Intrd[on]. I don't think he can object but it will be better to ask him, perhaps.

Will you tell F. N. D. that the *Tuscania* will be 8–9 days on the passage. The Anchor (or Cunard) office[2] will give him the exact day if he asks them.

We may just get sight of each other on the other side. But should you be leaving before do please[3] leave a letter for me with F. N. D. with whatever news or good advice You think will [be] useful to me for my guidance during my visit.

Yrs

J. C.

---

[1] Presumably Samuel A. Everitt was gathering publicity materials in advance of Conrad's visit. Photographs of Conrad in the 'Q'-ship HMS *Ready* in November 1916 were published in J. G. Sutherland's *At Sea with Joseph Conrad* (1922). The originals are at Yale.

[2] Now owned by Cunard, the Anchor Line had been sailing the Glasgow – Moville – New York route since 1856.

[3] Either 'before [I] do, please' or 'before, do please'?

To Richard Curle

Text MS Indiana; Curle III (in part)[1]

22. 3. 23
Oswalds.

Dearest Dick

Herewith the £2 with thanks.

I hope things are going as well as possible with you. I am just finishing the Crane Introduction and my head is simply buzzing with the strain.

Best wishes for the book's career begun yesterday – wasn't it?[2]

Ever Yours

J. Conrad

To Eric S. Pinker

Text TS/MS Berg; Unpublished

Oswalds.
March 22. 1923

Dearest Eric

I drop you the news here that the Crane introduction is finished. It will be over 7000 words, mostly twaddle! But at any rate I will be giving good weight of paper to Beer for his money. Seriously I think it's quite good enough.

And Edward is coming to-morrow!!

He has been preceded by a letter in which he instructs me what and how to write about Crane.[3] Therefore he will be told that the MS is no longer in the house, because I will have it put out into the garage. I will make all the corrections on Saturday and post it registered to your office. I am sincerely glad I have pulled it off before your date of sailing.

John is coming home on Monday and will be going back to school on the *20th April*. You will, my dear Eric, advise me of the credit being opened in both sums of £400 and of £93, less £50 on one sum and £25 on the other to cover commission due and possible interest. This will leave £312 to be credited to me, for the expenses of the American journey. As the doctor's bill (about £50) has also to come out of it you will see that it won't be too much. Will you kindly undertake to give a hint to Doubleday about the American degrees. I have had this morning a letter from Yale with that very offer, which

---

[1] With no mention of the loan.

[2] Curle's *Into the East: Notes on Burma and Malaya* (Macmillan) had just appeared, with a Preface by Conrad.

[3] Insisting on the quality of Crane's style, 'perfection at its finest'; Garnett had 'tried to rub into those blasted Americans that Crane was a master, & do you know that my essay on Crane . . . was rejected in turn by the half a dozen American quarters I tried' (Stape and Knowles, pp. 206–7).

of course I am declining with infinite civilities. A word or two dropped in the right place might prevent this sort of thing coming from other quarters.

I am retaining my return passage in the "Tuscania" on June 2nd. But I think I could change for the Carolina on the 9th should it turn out advisable to have another week.[1]

I'll write to you on the 17th Ap. (Tuesday) to catch the Wed: mail ship just to remind you that I am coming over. Give my best regards and wishes of pleasant passage to your wife.[2]

Affectly Yrs

J. Conrad

PS I will enclose on Sat something for Everitt you could give if You think advisable.

To Eric S. Pinker

Text MS Berg; Unpublished

Oswalds.

23 Mch '23[3]

"For your *leisure*."

My dear Eric.

Excuse this paper – the only kind I have handy. I'll confess to you that I am very sorry you communicated to K[nopf][4] my request *re* the introduction (now ready). Let us agree to treat each other's com[municati]ons as confid[enti]al – unless, of course, under some exceptional pressure of circumstances. You know very well that had you expressed your dislike of the mission, I would have accepted it without remonstrance. Your advice is always welcome (even when we differ) because it is the only one which is above suspicion, for me. As to other people it is not so. That man will talk. There is no bond of secrecy on him; and I have the disagreeable impression that I may be represented as unconscionably greedy. Moreover what has he to do with it? Is he B[eer]'s keeper? I didn't like his attitude. Our attitude to the transaction was influenced by its timeliness – and the terms were good.

---

[1] Conrad left New York on 2 June in the *Majestic*.

[2] Margit Vibege Watney (née Dietrichson, 1893), was born in Copenhagen; they married in 1921 and divorced in March 1927.

[3] The '3' is written right over the '2', but the final reference to Yale's offer confirms the 23rd as the proper date.

[4] Alfred A. Knopf had accompanied Thomas Beer to Oswalds on 8 March. The terms of Conrad's agreement with Beer for an introduction to Beer's biography of Stephen Crane were divulged by Pinker to Knopf, who apparently thought them exorbitant.

That's agreed. But one does not like to have this intruded on one's notice too much – by a third party, at that! I suspect M[r] J. C. is pretty good too. Now what are the facts:

You know that from the first I intended to give M[r] B something important for his money. Well I am giving him 8300 words (not counting the quoted letter), his plain request having been for 3 or 4 pages (I suppose 8vo). I have worked under a certain stress. I did not want to get out of touch with the novel.[1] I was and am anxious about it. My reputation hangs on its quality. It is a big piece of work – the biggest since "Western Eyes". The mental disturbance c[a]n not be put into the balance – for that sort of thing is not in my way – it's hack-work. And the stuff (if it is good) is barred now from the 'suite' to the Personal Record, which I have had long in my mind.[2] I had said lately in the Mercury all I wanted to say about Crane. I've told something of this to M[r] B and would have said more if the other had not been there. Those are the facts. Now for some figures, which we cannot tell at large to everybody but which ought to close the beak (to a certain extent) of M[r] K.

8.000w. for £400 that is £50 per thousand. I have been paid as much as £250 for 2400 words. (Tradition). It was written in answer to a special request[3] – as in the case with M[r] B. No Am[can] rights were reserved and I did the pamphlet (or rather Wise did) without dreaming of asking permission. – I have repeatedly been paid £100 for 12 – 1300 words. by The Times; and several times £50 per column by the D[ai]ly. Mail (1100 – 1200 words) *as a matter of course*. All was pamphleted either by Shorter or Wise without any scruple. Those things are recorded in your office. Even as early as 1904 the D. Mail paid me £30 per column (three articles out of Mirror of the Sea).[4] That is not recorded as I negotiated personally. Those are evidences of my standing. Now as to hard cash: I contend that I dropped my proper work from which I get my reputation, artistic satisfaction and general recognition, to do a piece of writing of the kind for which I do not care and using material which I intended to use for a purely literary purpose in the future, – for no specially high remuneration. For B pays me no more for his special call than I can get (taking it all round) for my creative work. You yourself have done it for me, The Rover is just under 80.000 words. You have obtained (certain money)

---

[1] *Suspense*, imagined here as more ambitious than *Chance* or *Victory*.

[2] Conrad had mentioned a second volume of reminiscences as early as 1908; he may have meant 'Prince Roman' to be a part of this volume, but nothing else came of it (*Letters*, 4, pp. 153, 159).

[3] Lord Northcliffe gave him 250 guineas (£262 10s) for 'Tradition', which appeared in the *Daily Mail* on 3 March 1918; when Conrad agreed to write this essay, he did not know how extraordinarily large the payment would be (*Letters*, 6, pp. 191–3).

[4] See *Letters*, 3, pp. 116, 120–1.

£4000 for it = £50 per thousand (all sources) and every likelihood of more to come from a moderate success – not mentionning* the value of continued royalties in the future. (Rescue touched 50. Arrow brought nearly that by this time). So strictly speaking I would have done better for myself *morally* and financially if I had stuck to my novel. If you hear anybody exclaiming at the enormity of the fee you may safely say that. Of course I was glad to get it. I don't depreciate, far from it, the unasked offer of M^r B who is a good fellow and behaved with perfect decency and good-feeling. Since K knows and has taken on himself to treat it as mere rapacity I must ask you to tell M^r B from me that I *intended* to ask his permission to print 20 private copies in order to distribute them as follows: –

In US. To C. Morley. Mencken. Miss R. Stauffer. Prof. Chew. G. H. Clarke; (who all have been writing about me).[1] Doubleday. Keating. Adams. Quinn.[2] as is only natural this piece of writing being about an American of genius and my intimate friend.

In England. To Garnett. Wise. Curle.

In Sweden. To Prof. Ben[d]z.

In France. To A. Gide. Aubry. –

But [as to] that I have given up the idea – unless he feels inclined to have 10 extra sheets pulled off, while printing his book, for distribution to Americans alone – or *at least* to the first five named above.

I also beg him to give me the assurance that there will not be any difficulties raised by himself *or his publisher*[3] as to the inclusion of the Introduction in a posthumous vol: of coll^{ed} pieces; and that I would be glad if he wrote me a letter to that effect.

You may tell him with my regards that if he has any observations to make or wishes specially to have some point touched upon I will be ready to meet his wishes, when I come over.

Always my dear Eric

affctly Yours

J. Conrad

[1] H. L. Mencken (1880–1956) first came to Conrad's attention in 1913 (*Letters*, 5, pp. 292–3, 304); for his reaction to Mencken's most recent article on him, see *Letters*, 7, pp. 614–15. For Samuel C. Chew, see the letter to him of 31 May; for G. H. Clarke, see the letter of 9 August.

[2] George T(homas) Keating (1892–1976) was a New York businessman and avid book collector; his impressive Conrad collection is now in the Beinecke Rare Book and Manuscript Library at Yale. The New York lawyer, collector, and patron of the arts John Quinn (1870–1924) had purchased almost all Conrad's prewar MSS and TSS.

[3] Knopf.

Please note. The Yale University requests its communication to be treated as Confidential. Therefore please do no[t] tell D'day of it and generally no one in the US.

To Edward Garnett

Text G. 323

[letterhead: Oswalds]

[25 March 1923][1]

Dearest Edward.

Your wire was a great blow. It was good of you to write from the bed of sickness. We are so sorry. I could not leave for U.S. without seeing you but you will be mended long before the date which is 20th April. I hope your 'flu if very disabling will not be very serious. Should you shake it off soon perhaps a couple of days here would do you no harm. I will be leaving this [house] on the 16th.

Jessie sends her love. She is again very lame and somewhat depressed.

The Crane article for Beer is gone. It's just personal gossip, not critical – not even literary. Our first day together and so on. I have asked Miss H. to take a copy of the passages in which I mention you which I'll send you in my next letter.

Ever affect[ly] yours

Joseph Conrad.

To Julian Street

Text MS Williams; Unpublished

[letterhead: Oswalds]

25 Mch '23

My dear Mr Street.

Just a line to thank You for Your Roosevelt book[2] and to tell you that apart from its very interesting subject it is an admirable little thing of its kind.

Cordially Yours

J. Conrad.

---

[1] In the Bobbs-Merrill edition of the letters to Garnett and in the sale catalogue of Garnett's letters from Conrad and Hudson (New York: American Art Association, 24 & 25 April 1928), the date is bracketed, as if taken from a postmark. Garnett had written from his sickbed on the 23rd (Stape and Knowles, p. 207).

[2] Street had sent Conrad a copy of his biography of Theodore Roosevelt, *The Most Interesting American* (New York: Century, 1915).

To Karola Zagórska

Text MS Warsaw 2889; Najder (1969); Najder (1983)[1]

[letterhead: Oswalds]
[25 March 1923][2]

My dear Karolka,[3]

Ci-inclus[4] chéque for 952,50 lire for April.

I am unbelievably tired. I have had a lot of work this month and there is still some to be done before I go to the United States. I am sailing there with my old friend, Captain Bone, on the *Tuscania*, returning probably by the same ship about 10 June.[5]

To tell the truth the journey does not appeal to me. But it has to be. Everybody tells me that it will be very advantageous for my business affairs. So it is a kind of duty envers ma petite famille.[6]

Poor Jessie is again troubled by her knee. How long her cheerfulness will stand up to it, I really do not know. She asks me to give you her love. So does Jan.[7] He has just gone outside and I can see him through the window running in the garden with our little dog. It is the son of the old Hadji and rather like his daddy. Hadji has aged a lot and can only walk in a dignified manner. So do I, as a matter of fact. My health is fair. America will put it to the test. There is one thing I like the Americans for: they are friendly towards Poland. I have friends over there whom I have never even seen. I wonder how they look. I know in advance what they will be saying.

We have not seen Borys since Christmas. He is working, is in good form and doing quite well as far as I can make out.

We shall be here until September. Then – all depends on God's will. Probably 3–4 months in London and in the winter somewhere in the south of France. After that I do not know and it is not really worth thinking about.

You will hear once again from me, from England – in April. Then Jessie will be writing.

A hundred hugs

Always yours

Konrad

---

[1] Translation from Najder (1983) with minor alterations.

[2] Obviously March, and most probably the 25th, a Sunday. On that day, now that he had sent off his introduction for Thomas Beer and settled affairs with Pinker, Conrad took up his personal correspondence, writing several letters by hand; he also mentions his wife's low spirits and ailing knee to Garnett.

[3] Karola Zagórska (*c.* 1885–1955), Aniela's younger sister, spent six months at Oswalds in 1920, after which Conrad supported her with a regular allowance of £10 per month. A professional singer, she lived in Italy and later in the United States, where she sang in opera.

[4] 'Herewith'. At the current rate of exchange, the cheque was worth about £10.

[5] Conrad returned to Southampton in the *Majestic*, arriving on 9 June.

[6] 'Towards my little family'.   [7] Conrad's younger son, John.

To Stefan Żeromski

Text J-A, 2, 298–9 with facsimile; Najder 289[1]

[letterhead: Oswalds]
25. March 23.

Dear Sir,[2]

I am sending you my book Notes on Life & Letters. I would never have taken the liberty of doing so, had not Aniela Zagórska written to me recently that you wished to have it. The book consists of articles – chiefly contributions to newspapers, written during the course of many years.

Immediately after reading your wonderful preface to Almayer's Folly I asked Aniela to convey to you my gratitude for the great favour you have done me. I confess that I cannot find words to describe my profound emotion when I read this appreciation from my country, voiced by you, dear Sir – the greatest master of its literature.

Please accept, dear Sir, my most sincere thanks for the time, thought, and work you have devoted to me and for the sympathetic assessment that disclosed a compatriot in the author.

With all my gratitude, believe me dear Sir, to be always your faithful servant.

J. K. Korzeniowski.

PS The book will be posted separately tomorrow.

To Thomas J. Wise

Text TS/MS BL Ashley 2953; Wise 50; Fletcher 114

[letterhead: Oswalds]
March 26th. 1923.

Dear Mr Wise.

I have finished my Crane article which consists of 62 pages of *manuscript*, containing 8351 words, besides the title-page and the signature.

---

[1] Translation from Najder.

[2] The son of an impoverished *szlachta* (gentry) family, the Polish novelist Stefan Żeromski (1864–1925) began his literary career while working as an assistant librarian at a Polish museum in Switzerland. After living in Italy and Paris, he returned to Poland in 1912 and lived in Zakopane, where he met Conrad in 1914. After the war he settled in Warsaw, where he was granted quarters in the Royal Castle, but kept his cottage in the spa town of Nałęczów. He was a founder of the Academy of Literature and the Polish branch of PEN. His novels include *Ludzie bezdomni* (*Homeless People*, 1900), *Popioły* (1904, trans. as *Ashes*, 1928), set during the Napoleonic Wars, and *Wierna rzeka*, (1912, trans. as *The Faithful River*, 1943), set during the insurrection of 1863. In 1926, he was shortlisted for the Nobel Prize.

Considering it relates to an American author about whose memory there will be a certain stir made, I think I could get for it $600 from Janvier.[1] I wouldn't think of taking it to America without asking you whether you would care to have [it] for, say, £110.[2] I have not been in communication with anybody in America about it, my intention being, unless you like to acquire it, to take it with me to the U.S.

I know there will be inquiries for it and I expect to be bitterly reproached for having left it in England.[3]

I am not going over there on a dollar-hunting expedition; and, though Messrs Doubleday may make arrangements for a few semi-private lectures, there can't possibly be much in it. Very likely nothing at all. So I have been making arrangements to meet my expences* and have reckoned on this MS to complete the minimum sum with which I can venture on that journey. I need not tell you that whether you secure this or not I shall not engage myself over there for any more MS. In fact whatever happens I will ask you to treat this matter as strictly between ourselves for a time.

Kindest regards.

Sincerely Yours

J. Conrad

PS Should you like to have the text of the letter (from Crane to me) alluded to in the MS, I will copy it in my own hand (it is very short) and join it to the MS.

To Thomas J. Wise

Text MS Virginia; Unpublished

[letterhead: Oswalds]
29. 3. 23

My dear Mr Wise.

Herewith the MS with the copy of Crane's letter.[4] I am also sending You the last letter from Keating, I received two or three days ago. He never said he had acquired a *MS*. From the first he seemed to claim having acquired a "first draft." But it is obvious that he has a copy of some sort.

Thanks very much for the cheque. I hope to start writing again a little. This attempt has been successful. I took about ten days. I suppose I am the slowest writer on earth.

---

[1] About £128 at the prevailing rate of exchange. After careers as a Baltimore lawyer and a photographer, Meredith Janvier (1872–1936) became a rare book dealer and collector.
[2] Wise purchased the MS immediately; his bank draft for £110 is dated 27 March.
[3] MS from this point.
[4] The purchase on 29 March is confirmed by Miss Hallowes's notebook (*Documents*, p. 217).

I find a* have a lot to do before leaving. The galley-proofs of The Rover (revise) have arrived and we are hard at it making the final correction[s].

My wife joins me in kind regards.

Very sincerely Yours

Joseph Conrad

PS I am ready to sign to* copy of Romance. Send me a note of what you would like me [to write] on the fly above my signature.

To R. B. Cunninghame Graham

Text MS Dartmouth; J-A, 2, 299; Watts 196

[letterhead: Oswalds]

30 Mch 23.

Ex[celentísi]mo Don Roberto, my dear friend.[1]

I don't remember such a great pleasure for years than that your letter in praise of Gaspar Ruiz has given me.[2] That story was written about 1905 and published in book form in 1908. I thought you had seen it a long time ago; and to receive such a testimony to its general truth (of impression) *from You*, is the most gratifying thing that has happened to me in my career – of letters. But it is a longish story and you may not be so pleased with "la suite."

Still, even if no more than those few opening pages secure you[r] commendation it is something to be proud of. I can't however let you read it in French (in slow instalments, at that)[3] and I am writing to Methuen to send me the vol: (Set of Six) which I will inscribe and forward to You. G.R. is the first story in it.

---

[1] Robert Bontine Cunninghame Graham (1852–1936) began a lasting friendship with Conrad in 1897, the result of a letter praising 'An Outpost of Progress'. Among the consequences was the help he gave Conrad with the cultural and political background to *Nostromo*. A socialist and (according to some) rightful King of Scotland, Graham worked and travelled widely in the Americas. He drew on his experiences in many volumes of tales, sketches, and essays and also in his travel narratives, such as *Mogreb-el-Acksa: A Journey in Morocco* (1898), and his unorthodox histories of Latin America, such as *A Vanished Arcadia: Being Some Account of the Jesuits in Paraguay* (1901). From 1886 to 1892 he represented North-West Lanarkshire in Parliament; he spent more than a month in gaol for his part in the Bloody Sunday demonstration of 1887. He became the first President of the Scottish Labour Party in 1888 and President of the Scottish Home Rule Association in 1920.

[2] For the full letter, see Stape and Knowles, p. 208. It opens: 'Querido mio Amigo. How? & why? & wherefore have I never seen your splendid story of Gaspar Ruiz before?' The narrative reminded him of his own experiences in Latin America: 'I remember one young man having his throat cut, much in that way, for he was quite innocent . . . All my congratulations on the insight, the local colour, & the marvellous air of South America, you have imparted to the tale.'

[3] Graham had just seen the first instalment in the *Revue de l'Amérique Latine*, as translated by Philippe Neel (1882–1941), a Parisian doctor and Anglophile whose translations Conrad usually found congenial.

I found the seed of it in Capt Basil Hall RN. "Journal of the years 1820–21–22"; a work of which you may have heard. Hall was a friend of Gen: San Martin.[1] The original of G. Ruiz is a man called Benavides, a free-lance on the southern frontier of Chile during the wars of the revolution. Hall gives him a page or two – mostly hearsay. I had to invent all his story, find the motives for his change of sides – and the scenery of the tale. And now the very writing of it seems like the memory of a dream!

I was about to write to you to tell you that I had a letter from Ibañez (which I answered at once) and also from his publishing house.[2] As Pinker is gone to the US[3] and I am going on the 21st I asked both Ibañez and the publishing house to let us take up the negociation early in June when Pinker will be back. I also expect to be back by the 10th of that month. Mine is not a dollar hunting expedition. I am going to stay with Doubleday at Oyster Bay and see a few people. You'll hear from me in a few days as to my movements. We must meet if at all possible before I leave. Jessie sends her love.

Ever Yours

J. Conrad

To Veronica Wedgwood

Text MS Private collection; J-A, 2, 300

[letterhead: Oswalds]
31. Mch. 23.

My dear Veronica[4]

What a traveller you are – and, incidentally what a nice person, to write me such an interesting letter! Yes. Ajaccio is all right and Corsica is lovely and

---

[1] The full title of Hall's work is *Extracts from a Journal, Written on the Coasts of Chili, Peru, and Mexico, in the Years 1820, 1821, 1822* (1824). For a fuller discussion of his work, see Watts, pp. 197–8. General José Francisco de San Martín y Matorras (1778–1850) commanded insurgent armies in three South American wars of independence, first in Argentina (his homeland), then in Chile, and Peru. His principal ally in Chile was Bernardo O'Higgins; they fought their campaigns there in 1817–18.

[2] Graham had told Conrad how keen Ibáñez was to publish him.

[3] Pinker and his wife had left Southampton in the *Olympic* on 29 March and arrived in New York on 4 April. He was among those greeting Conrad at the dock on 1 May.

[4] (Cicely) Veronica Wedgwood (1910–97; became Dame Veronica Wedgwood, 1968) was the daughter of Conrad's friends Ralph and Iris Wedgwood (for her parents, see the notes to the letter to Pinker of 9 April). After reading history at Oxford, she applied her grasp of recondite detail, ability to see through dense thickets of political intrigue, and narrative flair to writing, lecturing, and broadcasting on historical topics, especially the great conflicts of the seventeenth century. As C. V. Wedgwood, she wrote biographies of *Strafford* (1935), *Cromwell* (1939), and *William the Silent* (1944), several studies of the struggle between King and Parliament, and a masterly survey of *The Thirty Years War* (1938). In 1969, she became the third British woman to be awarded the Order of Merit. At the time of this letter, she was twelve years old.

I have admired it – for three months on end;[1] which is a sufficient tribute, I think. I, too, have been oppressed, buried under, smothered and choked by the mimosas thrown into the carriage by a driver – by many drivers. They *will* do it. They are all mad – you know. One of them, once, left his horses and trap (where my wife and I were sitting) within about three inches from the edge of a dreadful precipice in order to climb a mimosa tree. He sat there for (I think) one hour, like a sort of devastating bird, showering broken branches on the ground below. Neither my prayers nor my threats could induce him to come back to his horses. I offered him at last all the money I had in my pocket, my watch and chain, any sum that I (a stranger) could borrow in Corsica (which is a poor country). He remained deaf. He did not think the offer good enough I suppose. The mimosa shook and cracked most pathetically. The horses dozed. The precipice yawned (they always do), and I admired the Corsican scenery but wished myself back in England – on Romney Marsh for preference.[2] Yes, Corsica is a lovely island, but dangerous – because of its drivers who are a public terror; and thus worse than the vendettas which are private affairs. Did Cook's people show you a vendetta? I haven't seen one but I saw a bandit. He was quite tame. He took a cigarette from my hand most delicately.

Directly I heard you were taking your Mother to Constantinople I began to think what I should do if the Turks captured you as they always have done in the 18th century tales. I would have had to go (of course with your Father's permission) to rescue you from the hands of the Infidels. So I formed a plan. An excellent plan – but I can not tell you of it now. It is not because I am lazy but because I am going to America in three weeks' time and the plan would take several months to describe properly.

Give my love to your Mother and your Father; and please, my dear, keep a little corner in your heart for your old and frivolous friend

Joseph Conrad.

---

[1] The Conrads spent nine weeks in Corsica in the spring of 1921.
[2] Where everything is tranquil, green, and flat. Pent Farm, the Conrads' first home in Kent, stands on higher ground close by the Marsh.

To J. M. Dent

Text TS/MS Berg; Unpublished

[letterhead: Oswalds]
April 2nd. 1923.

My dear Mr Dent.[1]

Thank you for sending me the drawing you had made of the coat of arms. It is surprising how near your artist came to the real thing while working from that small impression. All the same it was not correct enough for reproduction. The one I send to you, drawn by my boy John, under my direction is what the thing should look like. As you see the knot in the shield is not made with a rope as your man was justified in thinking, but with a handkerchief. The woman in the crest does not wear a hat (though I admit that on the impression of the seal she looks as if she did) but has her eyes bandaged. The points of the crown have in my son's design the correct shape.

You may therefore use it safely as you intend to do – unless I receive in time the Polish heraldry book which I asked my cousin in Warsaw to send me. I made John draw the enclosed at once, as I did not know how soon the first vol is to come out.

My wife sends her love. Pray give my friendliest regards to M^r & Mrs Hugh.[2]

Yours Cordially

J. Conrad.

PS I will try to run in to shake hands with you both before I leave.

To F. N. Doubleday

Text TS/MS Princeton; J-A, 2, 301

[letterhead: Oswalds]
April 2nd. 1923.

My dear Mr Doubleday.

You would have heard from D. Bone that my passage is engaged for the 21st. I am looking forward very much to my visit to the country where I have so many good friends to my work.

[1] Joseph Mallaby Dent (1849–1926) was apprenticed to a printer at the age of thirteen, and set up in business as a London bookbinder in 1872. He turned to publishing in 1888, achieving success with popularly priced series such as the Temple Classics, the Temple Shakespeare, and Everyman's Library. In Conrad's lifetime, Dent published *'Twixt Land and Sea* (1912), *Within the Tides* (1915), *The Shadow-Line* (1917), *The Rescue* (1920), *Notes on Life and Letters* (1921), and most of the Uniform Edition. The rest of that edition appeared posthumously, as did the first publication of *Suspense* (1925) and *Last Essays* (1926).

[2] Hugh Dent's wife was Letitia Edith (née Garnham, 1880–1952).

In consequence of dear C. Morley's article I have had a few letters from various parts of the U.S. of the most kind character, and mainly from private persons. I have had also a letter from the Professor of Sclavonic Literature at the University of Columbia, begging me for a formal visit there.[1] I intend to answer him by next Saturday's mail, saying that knowing nothing about Sclavonic Literature (or, in truth, of any other) I can't consent to do that; but that I would be glad to meet the students of his department in an informal manner. I could do no less, as the Professor is a very distinguished man and a brother-in-law of the President of the Polish Academy of Letters in Cracow. A downright refusal would be heard of over there and probably produce a false impression.

I do not know whether I have told you that I have given an interview to the "Philadelphia Ledger" on a cable request from there. A very nice and sympathetic young man came to see me here and we had a long talk. I don't know what he made of it because the number containing the interview was not sent to me.

May I ask you, dear Mr Doubleday, to send a set of my works (in buckram) to Major Gordon Gardiner, 12 Queen Anne's Gate, London, S.W. He is a great friend of mine and is one of the voluntary Visitors of H.M.'s Prisons. The set is destined for one of the prisons where short term prisoners (up to two years) are detained.

Eric Pinker will be able to tell you more about me, though I have confided no "important messages" to him. A few days before his departure I was asked to write an introduction for a biography of Stephen Crane, which has been written by Mr Thomas Beer. I was pleased to pay my little tribute to the memory of my first American friend, for whom I had a great affection. Notwithstanding the difference of our ages Crane and I were very intimate. That introduction is not at all literary but purely personal, giving a sketch of our relations.

I was much cheered up by receiving a set of corrected galleys of "The Rover" for my English publisher. I made a few minor corrections, of which Miss Hallowes has made an abstract. She is sending it by the same mail to Mrs Robins,[2] with the request they should be applied to the American edition. It has been always my ambition to make the American and English texts identical, word for word; and I think that in this book I will attain it.

---

[1] Professor Wojciech Zygmunt Morawski-Nawench.
[2] Doubleday's secretary, Lillian Robins.

Will you please remember me to the Ladies and give my friendly greeting to Mr Nelson.

Believe always, with great regard

sincerely Yours

Joseph Conrad.

To G. Jean-Aubry

Text MS Yale; *L. fr.* 183

Mardi

[3 April 1923]¹

Très Cher Jean.

Reçu Votre lettre avec joie.

Nous VS attendons pour lunch le samedi.

R. Am Latine m'a envoyé le numéro avec votre préface² dont je VS remercie de tout mon coeur.

Oui! Le moment de la découverte de l'Am[éri]que approche.

Je Vous embrasse.

Jessie sends her love.

Ever yours

Conrad.

My very dear Jean,

Your letter joyfully received.

We shall expect you for lunch on Saturday.

R. Am Latine has sent me the number with your preface, for which I thank you with all my heart.

Yes! the moment approaches to discover America.

I embrace you.

Jessie sends her love.

Ever yours

Conrad.

---

¹ Date written by Jean-Aubry on MS. Conrad left Oswalds on the 16th *en route* to America, so the 7th and 14th were the only possible Saturdays for a visit.

² Jean-Aubry's 'Joseph Conrad et l'Amérique Latine', prefaced the first instalment of 'Gaspar Ruiz' in the April issue of the *Revue d'Amérique Latine*, 4, 290–9.

To H. Maud Ffooks

Text MS Bryn Mawr; Unpublished

[letterhead: Oswalds]

4. Ap. 23

Dear Mrs Ffooks[1]

Pardon this short note. I am exceedingly busy on the eve of my departure on a short visit to the U.S.

It was very kind to send me the pamphlet about the Keel Rail. It is of course an excellen[t] invention.[2] I heard of it vaguely before. The letters from the seamen you have been good enough to send me are very interesting.

I regret I can not tell you about the ship *Lady Melville*.[3] I imagine she must have lived on the seas long before my time. The only *Lady* I was personally acquainted with in my sea-life was the *Lady Jocelyn*.[4] I suppose the *Lady Melville* must have been a regular East Indiaman.

My speaking at the N[ational] L[ife] B[oat] meeting will be limited to seconding a resolution in as few words as possible. As I have never spoken to a roomful of people in my life I am feeling extremely frightened at the prospect.

Believe me, dear Mrs Ffooks,

Your very faithful and obedient servant

Joseph Conrad.

To Ellen Glasgow

Text MS Virginia; Randall 210

[letterhead: Oswalds]

4. Ap. '23

My dear Ellen Glasgow[5]

Let me address you like this in affectionate remembrance of our meeting at Capel House, and because of our fellowship in the Craft. Thank you for

---

[1] H(enrietta) Maud Ffooks (née Standen) was born in 1858 in Hoshungabad, India, where her father was serving as an officer in the Madras Native Infantry. Around 1865, she was photographed by the Revd C. L. Dodgson ('Lewis Carroll') and became his lifelong friend; she sold her collection of letters and presentation copies from him in 1933. Educated in Dresden, she spoke fluent German, and, as a young woman, worked as a governess in Russia. In 1891, she married (Edward) Archdall Ffooks (1859–1932), a solicitor, Clerk of the Peace, and County Clerk of Dorset. They lived in Dorchester and had a holiday house in Bridport, where Mrs Ffooks took an interest in the Lifeboat Service.

[2] In this case, probably a device for launching the new generation of motor-lifeboats down steep slipways.

[3] A 1,200-ton ship of the East India Company in service from 1813 to 1832.

[4] A full-rigged vessel of 2,242 tons, built in 1852 and relegated in 1889 to service as a floating cold-store in the London Docks, she belonged to the Shaw-Savill line. Although designed as a fast steamer for the Indian mail service, she carried troops to the Crimean and Second Maori Wars, and then became an emigrant ship on the New Zealand route.

[5] Overcoming ill health and family tensions, Ellen Anderson Gholson Glasgow (1873–1945), who lived in Richmond, Virginia, wrote poetry, stories, and some twenty novels, the

your charming letter which has touched us both deeply. Poor Mrs C (as we all call her) is in no state to travel. She was much better last year but now there came a sort of relapse – renewed inflammation of the deeper tissues in the limb which has been operated upon so many times. She just can move about the house – and no more. I am most reluctant to leave her; but I have accepted Mr & Mrs Doubleday's invitation to spend 3 weeks with them at Oyster Bay and I could not think of drawing back now.

I fear my dear and unforgettable friend that it will be impossible for me to come as far as Richmond – this time. I have had two very bad years and now feel as tho' I were made of brown paper. It is not the sort of thing that gives me much confidence for travelling. No doubt Mr D. has made a few engagements for me; but I will have to keep very quiet for the most part. I wish I could borrow for a month one hundre[d]th part of our Hugh's spirits and vitality.[1] But such a transaction is impossible in this imperfect world. Pray pardon me and believe me always your faithful and affect^{te} friend admirer and servant

Joseph Conrad.

PS Jessie will be writing and sending you a few photographs of us all in a day or two.

To Louise Alvar Harding
Text MS Morgan; *L. fr.* 183

[letterhead: Oswalds]
4. Ap. '23

Chère Madame et Amie,[2]

Merci mille fois de Votre bonne lettre et de Votre aimable invitation. Je ne saurais Vous exprimer combien je regrette de ne pouvoir pas l'accepter. Je serais retenu ici jusqu'au 17ème du mois par le travail. J'espère que Vous me permettrez [de] venir vous saluer le soir de ce jour.

---

best-known being *Barren Ground* (1925). Set in the Upper South, her work often dealt with women struggling to be independent, and took issue with the sentimental fictions of her time and place. Her visit to the Conrads at Capel House in June 1914, with her travelling companion Louise Collier Willcox, was recorded in photographs taken by her fellow Southerner Warrington Dawson, who had arranged the introduction (Randall, pp. 84–6).

[1] Conrad's friend Hugh Walpole had lectured widely in the USA and had met Ellen Glasgow on one of his tours.

[2] The Swedish soprano Louise ('Loulette') Victoria Alvar Woods Harding (née Beckman, 1883–1965) performed as 'Louise Alvar' and toured with Maurice Ravel, among others. She and her husband, a wealthy English barrister, held a literary and musical salon in their home at 14 Holland Park, Kensington. She was a close friend of Jean-Aubry, and her circle included Manuel de Falla, Camille Saint-Saëns, T. S. Eliot, Hugo von Hofmannsthal, and Paul Valéry.

Voulez Vous me faire la grâce d'exprimer a M Ravel mes vifs regrets de manquer cette occasion de le voir.[1]

Ma femme Vous remercie de Votre bon souvenir et Vous envoit mille amitiés. Veuillez me croire chère Madame toujours
Votre très devoué serviteur et ami
Joseph Conrad.

PS My regards to Mr Harding and our dear love to the children.[2]

Dear Madam and Friend,

Many thanks for your good letter and friendly invitation. I cannot tell you how much I regret being unable to accept it. My work keeps me here until the 17th. I hope you will allow me to come and greet you on the evening of that day.

Would you please do me the favour of expressing to M. Ravel my keen regret at missing this opportunity of seeing him.

My wife thanks you for remembering her and sends you most cordial greetings. Please believe me, dear Madam, always
your very devoted servant and friend
Joseph Conrad.

To W. C. Wicken

Text MS Berg; Unpublished

[letterhead: Oswalds]
5. Ap. 23.

Dear M[r] Wicken.[3]

I am sending you the Am: corrected galleys for F. Unwin to set up the Rover from. They had better reach him through the office. If I remember rightly he had asked M[r] Eric to have the text delivered to him as early in the year as possible. You know he can not publish till next Dec[er].

John will be going back to school on the 27 inst. I will send you his acc[t] (as arranged with Mr Eric) in a few days.
Yours faithfully

J. Conrad

---

[1] Conrad liked Maurice Ravel (1875–1937), whom he had first met at a *soirée* in Holland Park the previous July, when the composer had conducted a private performance of his work (see *Letters*, 7, p. 611). He was present when Conrad visited Mrs Harding on the evening of the 17th, after his speech to the Royal National Lifeboat Institution.

[2] Charles Copeley Harding, Sigrid, and Charlie.

[3] W(alter) C. Wicken was Pinker's office manager, whose duties included handling the firm's day-to-day finances.

To Bruno Winawer
Text Głos; Najder 290[1]

[letterhead: Oswalds]
6. Ap. 23.

Dear Winawer,[2]

Please accept my, unfortunately, belated thanks for your letters, newspaper cuttings, and news of our "Agent".[3] Your Comedie du Laboratoire[4] is perfect. "Très chic" – as French painters used to say of their pictures. This formula expressed the highest praise. Why are you hesitant about sending me your "Inżynier"?[5] To tell the truth for once (a novelist has to lie constantly, from morning till night – and for money) you must know que j'aime beaucoup vos écritures de toutes sortes. You know what? – if you will send it addressed to Curzon Hotel, Curzon Street, London – I shall take it with me to America – comme compagnon de voyage. I shall be in London from the 16th till the 19th. On the 20th I leave for Glasgow and sail from there on the 21st in the S.S. *Tuscania* whose captain is David Bone, an old acquaintance of mine. I return on the 10th of June. There you have my timetable. As for my programme in the United States – it will be a private visit to my publisher, Mr. Doubleday. He has a house at Oyster Bay and there I shall stay with the exception of a few visits to people with whom I have been in correspondence for years, or who came to see us in England. Voilà tout. Even so, I don't feel very much like going.

With a hearty handshake.

Bien à vous

J. Conrad.

To F. N. Doubleday
Text TS Princeton; Unpublished

[letterhead: Oswalds]
April 9th. 1923.

My dear Mr Doubleday.

Just a word to acknowledge your kind letter and to send my warm thanks to Mrs Doubleday for her charming message.

---

[1] Translation from Najder with minor alterations; phrases in French are as in the original.
[2] The Polish dramatist and fiction writer Bruno Winawer (1883–1944) sent his play *Księga Hioba* (*The Book of Job*) to Conrad hoping he would find an English translator. Conrad took up the challenge himself and did a translation that was hawked about to London producers without success. Winawer, in turn, translated Conrad's dramatisation of *The Secret Agent* into Polish with Aniela Zagórska.
[3] Winawer's translation of Conrad's play *The Secret Agent* opened at the Teatr Bagatela in Cracow on 23 March.
[4] *Roztwór profesora Pytla* (*Professor Pytel's Solution*), staged in Warsaw, 1921, and published in 1922.
[5] *R. H., Inżynier* (*R. H., Engineer*), a comedy performed in 1923 and published in Lwów the year after.

I don't know whether I told you that in order to test myself, both as to nerve and as to voice-production, I accepted the invitation to speak in support of a resolution at the National Life-Boat Institution's 99th Annual Meeting. The Aeolian Hall holds 250 people, if not more;[1] and, considering that this is the first time I speak in public, the other test will be good too. As it is a sort of favour that was asked of me it doesn't matter if I faint or burst into tears – in which case the account of the scene will be sent to you by cable. Otherwise, my dear Mr Doubleday, this will be the last communication you will receive from me before I have the pleasure of taking you by the hand on American soil.

From the above you will see that I am fairly well in health though, perhaps, I am suffering from fright. But that's nothing. Fright has never stopped me from taking risks.

I am under the impression that you consented that my first talk should be to the Garden City staff and workers. Anyway, on that assumption, I have sketched it for myself on a particular line, which, with the change of a few words, would do equally well anywhere else.

Always most sincerely Yours

Joseph Conrad

To Eric S. Pinker

Text TS/MS Berg; J-A, 2, 302 (in part)

[letterhead: Oswalds]
April 9th. 1923.

Dearest Eric.

It seems ages since you left and I begin to feel rather anxious to get away.[2] I have prepared a five-minute speech for the Life-Boats[3] and have sketched out the outlines of a lecture, or rather of a familiar talk, on the (apparently) extravagant lines: of the imaginative literary art being based fundamentally on scenic motion, like a cinema; with this addition that for certain purposes the artist is a much more subtle and complicated machine than a camera, and with a wider range, if in the visual effects less precise – and so on, and so on, for an hour; with a mixture of jocularity and intense seriousness, (which *may* do). I intend to try it on the Garden City people (as Doubleday promised me) with illustrative bits of reading from "Victory".[4]

I have another one in my head which I may begin here and finish on board. Another one will suggest itself in due course, no doubt, and, for all I expect to do, those 3 ought to be enough.

---

[1] Located at 135 New Bond Street, the hall was normally a venue for classical music.
[2] Pinker and his wife were in America.   [3] Wise bought the MS on 16 April.
[4] For the text of this speech, see Arnold T. Schwab, 'Conrad's American Speeches and His Reading from *Victory*', *Modern Philology*, 62 (May 1965), pp. 345-7.

(Don't imagine that I am going to be impertinent to the cinemas; on the contrary, I shall butter them up).

The date-table is as follows: This week at home, with a lunch or two out and a guest or two here. Squaring up my correspondence. Packing . . . and generally fussing.

Monday, 16th. I shall leave here early via London for Colchester to see my old friend Hope[1] who is recovering from a stroke. Back in Curzon Hotel at 7.

On the 17th, Mrs C. arrives at 12 o'cl. and we will have Ralph[2] to lunch. Life Boat Institution at 3 o'cl. After dinner I must pay a visit to Mrs Harding, where I will meet Ravel, the French composer, who has come over to conduct one of his works at the Queen's Hall.[3] We got rather thick together last time he was here.

On the 18th, various small matters in the morning. At one, your mother and Oenone are coming up to lunch.[4] I did ask your mother which day of three would be most convenient to her for us to go down to say good-bye, but she very kindly offered to come to London, so as to see Mrs. C., who, I am sorry to say, is anything but improving. In the afternoon, see Garnett, by appt. and at five o'clock a few people will call in to tea.

The 19th, I lunch with a man called Gardiner to meet a man in the Diplomatic Service, and in the afternoon I will call on Mrs Dummett and Mrs Wedgwood, hoping to see Wedgwood himself. That sort of thing is due to one's executor.[5] In the evening it is just possible that Sir Robert will pay his professional call on Jessie.[6]

---

[1] (George) Fountaine (Weare) Hope (né Hopps, 1854–1930) was Conrad's oldest English friend, and served as a model for the 'Director of Companies' in *Heart of Darkness*. For Hope's memoirs of Conrad, see *Documents*, pp. 1–56.

[2] Eric's younger brother.

[3] On the 14th, he shared the rostrum with Sir Henry Wood; Ravel conducted 'La valse' and the 'Ma mère l'oie' suite to the great delight of orchestra and audience.

[4] Mary Elizabeth Pinker (née Seabrooke, 1862–1945) and Eric's sister (Mary) Oenone (1903–79).

[5] Conrad had signed his will on 8 August 1922, appointing Richard Curle and Ralph Wedgwood executors of his estate (*Documents*, pp. 244–51). Ralph Lewis Wedgwood (1874–1956; baronetcy 1942) came from the celebrated family of potters but devoted his career to railway administration. He spent the war years in France organising docks and railways; from 1916 to 1919, as Director of Docks, he held the rank of brigadier-general. Between 1921 and 1939, as Chief General Manager of London and Northeastern Railway, he encouraged technical daring and imaginative design. His interests in literature and music were also well developed, and his cousin Ralph Vaughan Williams dedicated several pieces to him. Along with his wife, he was also the dedicatee of *Within the Tides* (1915). Iris Veronica Wedgwood (née Pawson, 1886–1982) was a writer. In the 1920s she published several novels (*The Iron Age, The Fairway, The Livelong Day, Perilous Seas*), and in the 1930s, topographical studies (*Northumberland and Durham, Fenland Rivers*). The friendship with Conrad began in 1914, when Curle gave him an introduction to the Wedgwoods. For a letter to their daughter Veronica, the future historian, see 31 March 1923.

[6] Thomas J. Wise invited him for the evening of the 19th, but Conrad declined the invitation (19 April, telegram BL).

If not, then he will do so on the 20th – I trust in the morning, because I will leave for Glasgow at 12.30 p.m. in any case. I intend to spend the night in Glasgow before going on board. Dick has offered to come with me and see me off. He has been acting as Daily Mail special commissioner[1] for the last month and has his time free now for a few days. I am rather glad of having him.

Borys turned up yesterday here for a few hours. He is now acting manager of the Manchester depot, which is being enlarged and altered. It is not likely he will be able to run up to Glasgow. As a matter of fact I told him that I won't take it badly if he doesn't turn up; as he really has his hands full, and Saturday is the pay-day for all the workmen and employees and a heavy day for him. He told me he never is done with the accounts and the rest of it till six in the afternoon. He has invented a labour-saving device, (he brought me a photograph of it in action) which the Daimler company has adopted and paid him a hundred pounds for. He took the money for the patent, as it is not a thing that would be used in hundreds of thousands but only in very big garages and repairing workshops. I think he was wise in that. As to his patent aluminium piston, it has passed the workshop tests of the Daimler Co. perfectly, and is now at the end of its five-thousand-miles test in a car, which the general manager of Daimlers, Mr Percy Martin,[2] is using himself. The test ends this week and the Board Meeting which will decide will sit on the 16th. B is suffering from a slight inventor's fever in consequence. This is a more profitable matter. He was told that he will be given £750 down for it, and $2\frac{1}{2}$% royalties *if passed*. His health is better, but the nose hemorrhages continue and his eyes looked a little bit inflamed when he was here.

So far I will be able to go away without worrying. I hope you had my telephone message on Tuesday before you left. It struck me after posting my long letter,[3] that it was not fair to commission you to ask a favour, after all. I can do that myself. As to the other matter: reserving inclusion in some possible future volume, that was eminently a matter for you to treat of. The long letter was mainly meant to suggest to you a line of argument towards people who may say that I have been overpaid; the basis of it being that I am entitled to be remunerated for my time on the highest scale my time can earn.

I was duly advised of the opened credit to the amount of £312, which is in fact what I had asked you for. But I fear that I will have more expenses before leaving than I reckoned on, as for instance bringing my wife to London to

---

[1] Special correspondent: see the letter to him of 12 April.
[2] Born in Columbus, Ohio, Martin began with Daimler in 1896 as manager of their Coventry works. He was managing director of the company from 1906 to 1929 and retired in 1934.
[3] Of 23 March.

see Sir R. Jones, and a little travelling on my own account; so please, my dear
Eric, when you get paid by Beer leave me a further £50 with Doubleday. I
want to pay two visits on my own, not long, but involving some travelling,
and I should like to feel that I have everything that I may need. As we have set
aside both the Beer and the Partington proceeds for this journey, (amounting
in gross to £493) and as of that you have credited me with £312, I reckon that
even with the £50 you leave behind for me in America (together £362) there
will be enough to pay both commissions and any other charges there may
be; and even then leave a few pounds surplus.

I am anxious as to how your wife stood the passage and the American
"high-time". Of course I won't expect a letter from you, you will be much
too busy for private correspondence, but I do hope I shall have a glimpse of
you both before you start for home.

My health is at least as good as when you left. The only thing I couldn't
stand would be "pace". I must go slow.

Jessie joins me in love to you both.

Always affectly yours

J. Conrad.

To Richard Curle
Text MS Indiana; Curle 112

[Oswalds]

10 Ap. '23

Dearest Dick

As I see from your letter to Jessie that you mean if you can to see me
off at Glesga¹ I write to ask if you would have any objection to start from
Sᵗ Pancras at 9.50 A.M. on Friday. arr: Glas: 7.5 pm. I propose the Midland
as the food on that line is eatable – but on the N. Western it is *not*.²

Of course if it is too early for you we might start at 12.15 arr: G. 9.25.

You are a dear fellow to stand by me so nobly. Methinks we might travel 3ᵈ
on Midland and in fact spend most of our time in the restaurant car. What
do you say?

Ever Yours

J. Conrad.

B. came for a few hours last Sunday. Everything's very satisʳʸ with him. Will
you come to the Curzon on the 16ᵗʰ at 7.30 and dine?

---

¹ A Scots name for Glasgow, as often used by Cunninghame Graham.
² Curle leaves out the judgment on the London and Northwestern Railway's cuisine; the Midland had pioneeered the use of proper dining-cars.

To W. C. Wicken

Text TS Berg; Unpublished

Oswalds.
April 10th. 1923.

Dear Mr Wicken.

Thanks for your letter enclosing copy of the communication from Gallimard.[1] I see, he seems to demand this "concession" apparently only for "Victory".[2] I have heard from independent sources that they are really making special efforts to bring forward my work before the French public and to augment its sales. A series of three lectures has been arranged for the autumn in Paris and others in the provinces. Upon the whole, then, I should think that it may be just as well to accede to his request; though of course I see that it may open the way to further proposals of that kind. But with those we could deal as they arise.

Would you like me to write to him on the matter on those lines, or do you prefer to deal with his letter from the office?

faithfully Yours

J. Conrad.

To Aniela Zagórska

Text MS copy Yale;[3] *Pion* 1934; Najder 290

[Oswalds]
11. 4. 23.

My dearest Aniela,

I know that you are not angry with me, but I also know that it is simply a crime not to have written you for so long. But I must tell you that I had a lot of unexpected work; among other things, I have written a preface for the biography of my friend Stephen Crane who died young in 1900 – some 30000 words,[4] which was for me a rather large undertaking. I had also the revision of the English and American texts of my Rover (which will be published towards the end of the year), as well as checking and correcting the

---

[1] The French literary publishing house established in 1911 by Gaston Gallimard (1881–1975).

[2] The 'concession' probably involved royalties, since Gallimard was involved at this time in a dispute with Philippe Neel, who had been asked to revise Isabelle Rivière's translation of *Victory* and was upset to learn that royalties were to be divided between the two translators; see Walter Putnam, 'A Translator's Correspondence: Philippe Neel to Joseph Conrad', *The Conradian*, 24.1 (Spring 1999), 59–91.

[3] Zagórska's translation into French; the Polish original, published in *Pion*, was destroyed in 1944. English translation from Najder.

[4] Evidently a transcription error, since Conrad had planned to write some 3,000 words and by his own count produced 8300 (to Pinker, 23 March).

first two volumes of the "uniform edition" of my works, which will appear in May. At present I tire quickly – and when I am tired I am without conscience and feel no pangs of remorse. A nice cousin you have! A thousand thanks for the two booklets of the armorial which arrived just in time. John copied everything necessary and I could return them to you if you need them. In any case I kiss your hands for your kindness and your efforts.

Mr Winawer has written me that the Secret Agent was performed in Cracow and – received politely, I understand. I'm afraid that your work (yours and that of Mr Winawer) will be lost. That will teach me not to poke my nose where I shouldn't. And I think I am doing exactly that in preparing to leave for America. But it's of course for the sake of my wife and children – to improve the state of my affairs. I leave on the 21st of this month and will return the 15th of June.

We all thank you for the Easter mass on our behalf – for your steadfast friendship and for remembering us. Do not doubt, dearest cousin and friend, our warmest feelings towards you.[1] You are daily in my thoughts and I am ever your (alas! now old and sick) but faithful and devoted

Konrad.

To Captain David Bone

Text TS/MS Sprott; Knowles

[letterhead: Oswalds]
April 12th. 1923.

My dear Bone.

It was very good of you to think of writing to me from Moville and still kinder to invite me to spend a day with you in Helensburgh.[2] I can't tell you how sorry I am that the thing is quite impossible, as all my days up to Friday morning are filled up. I would have probably managed to break through but you will understand if I say that I wanted to be there when Sir Robert Jones sees my wife professionally, and as things are settled now it can not be before Friday morning. That is the major reason for which I need not make excuses – but I am main sorry.

Should I hear at the last moment that Sir Robert must put off his visit till the afternoon I will then try to catch the ten o'clock train on the Midland and arrive at St. Enoch[3] a little after seven. If Sir Robert keeps to his time I

---

[1] This sentence is missing from Zagórska's French copy.
[2] On their way to the USA, Anchor Line ships moored off the tiny port of Moville, on Lough Foyle, County Donegal, taking on mail from the North of Ireland and dispatching mail from passengers. Helensburgh is the resort west of Glasgow where Captain Bone lived.
[3] St Enoch Station in central Glasgow, now demolished.

won't be able to get away till 12.15 and in that case won't arrive at St. Enoch until half past nine in the evening, dragging my luggage with me, just a cabin trunk and a gladstone bag. They haven't filled in the number of my cabin, so the luggage labels can not bear it. I see the luggage labels direct it to be forwarded to York Hill Wharf, Glasgow. I suppose it will be time to do that from St. Enoch in the morning.

It would be very kind of you if you could direct my movements by a few words to the St. Enoch Hotel. I have an idea that sometimes your ships don't start from the Yorkhill Quay, but from somewhere down the river.[1] If it is to be from Yorkhill I suppose it is just simply a matter of coming alongside with my cabin luggage. Perhaps you will tell me what time I had better be on board.

I have had a letter from your brother James. He had an idea I should write some correspondence for the Manchester Guardian which could be published with your brother Muirhead's drawings.[2] I feel very much honoured by the suggested association; but I had to tell James that I can't write that sort of thing. It isn't in me at all; and I certainly would not like to produce rubbish to be associated with Muirhead's art. Moreover I made up my mind to have nothing to do with scribbling for six weeks at least. I have been at it so hard for the last six months that I am quite sick of it.[3] As you will no doubt have M. with you, will you please give him my regards and mention this matter as I should be very unhappy if he were to misunderstand my attitude.

Warmest regards.

Always yours

Joseph Conrad.

To Richard Curle

Text MS Indiana; Curle 113

[letterhead: Oswalds]

12 Ap. '23

Dearest Dick.

I was just about to write to you specially on the Dole articles.[4] They are wonderfully the right thing: matter, tone, attitude, interest. They are in fact so

---

[1] Yorkhill Quay was less than two miles from the city centre; although it was capacious, passengers on the largest ocean-going ships had to travel downriver to Greenock by tender.

[2] Bone's brother James (1872–1962) was the London editor of the *Manchester Guardian*. The previous November, Conrad had agreed to Bone's request for an article entitled 'Notices to Mariners', reprinted in *Last Essays* as 'Outside Literature' (see *Letters*, 7, p. 580).

[3] Despite uncertain health and many interruptions, Conrad had been trying to finish *Suspense*, and had completed the original 'Part III' by March.

[4] Under the by-line 'Our Special Correspondent', Curle's four articles on 'Scandals of the Dole' appeared in the *Daily Mail* from 9 to 12 April. A world-wide economic slump and an awkward readjustment to peace-time conditions in Britain meant that jobs were scarce, especially in the heavy industries. Dependent on workers' and employers' contributions, the

easy and interesting that I (being myself in the "trade") am not a bit surprised at you feeling tired. Only real concentration could have produced such all round excellence.

Jessie is lost in admiration.

I'll tell you more of my feelings when we meet on Monday.

Sorry my dear fellow that I cannot toe the line on Wednesday. Absolutely impossible. Indeed I regret it very much.[1]

3 lines in your letter have taken a certain worry out of the back of my head. I did not know how much there was of it till the relief was felt about thirty minutes ago.

Ever Yours

J. Conrad.

To John Galsworthy

Text MS Forbes; J-A, 2, 304 (in part)[2]

[letterhead: Oswalds]
14. Ap. 1923.

My dearest Jack.[3]

Thanks for your good letter. I am glad to hear that poor Ada had been able to face the journey.[4] I think the way she bears up is really wonderful. Nothing can change her. As I sat there talking with her it seemed to me that time had stood still from way back in pre-war days. It was very good of her

national insurance scheme set up in 1911 and extended to the whole population in 1920 had run short of money and in any case only covered brief periods out of work. In response, the Liberal–Conservative coalition of the day had introduced a system of means-tested payments to the long-term unemployed, funded out of tax revenues; generally known as the Dole, this system was disliked either for its grudging paucity and reliance on busybody administrators or for its fraying effect on moral fibre and the public purse. The *Mail* took the latter position, and so, unsurprisingly, did its Special Correspondent. In the words of a sub-editor, Curle found the idea 'extremely unpopular with everybody save officials and slackers. It demoralises men out of work, and even those in work. In fact, vast masses of people are beginning to look at The Dole as a means of livelihood which renders work – or even looking for work – unnecessary. In this way, our Special Correspondent points out, we are driving a wedge of Socialism into the social structure and destroying the foundations of individual effort' (9 April, p. 9). Curle was particularly upset by the 'scandal', as he put it, of women who refused to take jobs as domestic servants (10 April, p. 9). He returned to this strange reluctance later in the year: see Conrad's letter to him of 20 September.

[1] Curle's note: 'I had wanted him to meet a friend of mine.'

[2] Jean-Aubry omits the passage about Ada Galsworthy's stoicism.

[3] John Galsworthy (1867–1933) met Conrad in the *Torrens* in 1893. His early work, some of it under the pseudonym John Sinjohn, was tentative, but in 1932 he won a Nobel prize (an honour denied his friend) for his fiction and his plays. Like his fictional Forsytes, his family was well supplied with money, and he helped Conrad with many gifts and loans as well as constant encouragement.

[4] She had gone to Littlehampton, on the south coast, to convalescence after a winter of ill health, made worse by persistent rheumatism.

to let me come for indeed I could see she had suffered much, though from
her manner and conversation no stranger could have guessed that there was
anything the matter. It was a severe disappointment not to see you before I
go. I thought of running down to Littlehampton – but Fate steps in there.
You will understand when I tell you that I have to give up all next Monday
to a journey to Colchester to see poor Hope (you remember him?) who a
little time ago had some kind of stroke. His wife[1] has just written to me to say
that he can be seen now and that he expects I would come down. We knew
each other ever since 1880! I dread the visit a little as his speech is affected,
his son[2] tells me, tho' apparently not his mind.

Jessie will come up to town on Wed^y to see me off, as it were, but mainly
to be seen by the good, unwearied Sir Robert. She is again very lame and in
pain. I'll be off on Friday morning with no very light heart though what you
say of the news you had from Eric cheers me up a bit. I hope that journey
will not turn out a fool's errand. As to sneaking in quietly into the U. S., there
is no hope of that. Muirhead Bone is going in the same ship (his brother
commands her) and of course James Bone (of the Man: Guardian) knows
all about it and has been talking. I have had quite a few wires from various
papers, already. The fat is in the fire. But you need not be uneasy about the
safety of American pressmen. I am going to leave my revolver at home. If I
have to show them my teeth (artificial) it will only be in an agreeable smile.
And as to what may come after I leave it to Chance and the inspiration of the
moment. I, absolutely, can not think about it now. Our dear love to you both.
It would be a hypocritical affectation on my part to ask you to keep me in
your mind. I know You will do that. That is one of the certitudes of my life.

Ever Yours

J. Conrad

To Ralph Pinker
Text MS Berg; Unpublished

[Oswalds]
15.4.23.

Dear Ralph.[3]

Will you lunch with us at the Curzon Hotel on Tuesday (the 17th).
Mrs C with John and Audrey will arrive at one o'clock – so we will make a
little family party like old times.

---

[1] Frances Ellen Hope (née Mayer, 1854–1941).
[2] Conrad Hope (1890–1963), named in honour of Conrad, was a director of Candor Motors in
Colchester.
[3] (James) Ralph Pinker (1900–59), Eric's younger brother, was a frequent visitor at Spring Grove
in the summer of 1919 while taking a course in Wye. He eventually joined his brother in the
family firm, managing it alone after Eric Pinker emigrated to the USA.

I will be in the lounge soon after 12.30 and we may snatch a cocktail before all these respectable persons arrive.

Yours

J. C.

To Sir Robert Jones

Text J-A, 2, 304

Hotel Curzon,
Curzon Street,
Mayfair, London, W.
Thursday 19. 4. '23

Dearest and best of friends,[1]

I am so sorry not to see you before I sail. You will forgive me; but the fact is I have been hard at it almost to the last moment doing a special bit of work which is to pay part of the expenses of this trip.

Scribbling has become utterly distasteful to me. As to this voyage, I start on it without enthusiasm, not because I doubt getting a good reception in the U.S. and probably deriving a certain benefit materially from the visit, but simply because I do not feel quite fit for it – in myself. However, everybody tells me that I look very well – so it may be imagination on my part.

It is an immense comfort to me to think that you will see Jessie the day after my departure. I think she will miss me – and I know that I shall feel like a lost sheep without her. I believe there are many people ready to take care of me on the other side, but no number of them could make up for her absence.

Always your grateful and affectionate friend.

---

[1] A leading British orthopaedic surgeon, Sir Robert Armstrong Jones (1858–1933; knighted 1917, baronetcy 1926) came from North Wales, and practised in Liverpool, where he was consulting surgeon to all the major hospitals. He was also a consultant at St Thomas's Hospital, London, and a member of the War Office's Medical Advisory Board. During the war, he held the rank of Major-General and took on the immense task of organising reconstructive surgery at home and in the field. From 1921 to 1924, he served as President of the British Orthopaedic Association, and was frequently honoured overseas. His monographs and textbooks on the surgery of joints, military orthopaedics, and general orthopaedics were widely used. The professional relationship that began in 1917 with the care of Jessie Conrad developed into a warm personal friendship.

To Jessie Conrad

Text MS Yale; *JCLW* 59

5pm. 21st Ap. 1923
Tuscania.

My dearest and best Kitty.[1]

I am writing this in my cabin on my own bit of paper, in great anxiety as to the news your wire to Moville may bring me and feeling most remorseful at having left you in a state of suffering.

I was met in Glasgow by Muirhead Bone, who has just done for you that pencil "note" of a bit of the coast we have passed about ½ an hour ago. With him was John Bone[2] and the editor of the Glas: Ev^g news – an old friend – A. Munro.[3] I gave them a dinner (excellent) at the hotel. Dick has been marvellously attentive – could not have looked better after me if he had been our son. Capt B[one] is delightfully friendly. The Ship is fine. Weather very clear, a little cold, with an easterly breeze.

You may rest assured I'll be well looked after. But I won't tell you I'll have a pleasant trip. I'll miss you too much. I will do my best to make the visit a success – for all your sakes. B sent me a cheery wire this morning. Dick promised to wire you on getting ashore and write you on Sunday.

My breathing is better today and the cough quite tolerable. I wish I could see You and hear your voice. Thanks no end for the beautiful packing. I found everything to my hand. You are a treasure. I will keep this letter open on the chance of being able to add two words or so on receipt of Your wire. – It has been hard to part with dear John at the station. Give him a kiss from me.

Your own Boy.

---

[1] Jessie Emmeline Conrad (née George, 1873–1936), the second of nine children, met her future husband in 1894 when she was working as a typist and living with her widowed mother. The Conrads married in March 1896. An accident in 1904 exacerbated a previous knee injury, leaving her lame and in pain for the rest of her life despite a series of operations in 1917–24. In addition to a cookery book (1923) and a signed limited edition of her correspondence with her husband (1927), she published two accounts of their life together: *Joseph Conrad as I Knew Him* (1926) and *Joseph Conrad and His Circle* (1935).

[2] Perhaps an error for James Bone (1872–1962), London editor of the *Manchester Guardian*, the elder brother of David and Muirhead. Curle's *Last Twelve Years of Joseph Conrad* (Garden City: Doubleday, 1928, p. 161) refers to the presence at a farewell dinner at the St Enoch Hotel of John Bone, a Glasgow printer, but he was not one of the Bone brothers.

[3] Although Conrad distinctly wrote 'A.', this can only be the poet, critic, and novelist Neil Munro (1864–1930), who edited the *Glasgow Evening News* from 1918 to 1927.

To Jessie Conrad

Text MS Yale; *JCLW* 61; J-A, 2, 305

[letterhead: Anchor Line, T.S.S. Tuscania]

22. 4. 23.

My dearest Chica.

I begin now the letter that will be sent to you as soon as we arrive in N. York.

It is 10 o'clock AM. I have just had breakfast with Cap[t] Bone and Muirhead. M's and my cabin communicate and we are great chums. Our cabin steward is an amiable old fraud. He has taken Muirhead in completely – but I have talked straight to him this morning at 7 a.m. and we are now on terms of a strict understanding as to service and tips.

Yesterday at Moville it was blowing half-a-gale. Your wire and another from D[r] Reid[1] reached me only about 8 pm. Thank you for yours my dearest and you please thank R[obert] for his to me containing the confident hope that this new treatment will do you good. May it be so! my dear poor Jess.

I must confess that I slept well on my first night on board, in a very narrow bunk. My first thought on waking was for you and I was glad you had John with you and the prospect of a friendly visit from the Rustons before you.[2]

Yesterday I sent you a message by wireless and now (Tuesday 10.30 AM) I am wondering whether you have had it the same day. Capt Bone franked it for me – so this news was really a present from him to you.

In the 2[d] & 3[d] class there are 800 passengers not including the swarm of children. But in the first class we are only 48 all told (seven kids); so all these rooms – lounge, drawing room, smoking room, writing room look absolutely empty. I am writing this in the smoking room where there are only two persons beside myself. A M[r] & Mrs Bell.[3] Can't get away from Bells, it seems.[4] Last night it rained, and, at about midnight, it came on thick enough for the foghorn to be blown at intervals till 1.30 when it cleared. Water smooth. Wind east. Ship making only 11 knots, since 7 o'clock, as the

---

[1] After graduating from Cambridge, (Edwin) Douglas Ian Whitehead Reid (1883–1930) qualified as a surgeon and radiologist in 1909. He was senior surgeon at the Kent and Canterbury Hospital and medical adviser at St George's House nursing home, also in Canterbury. The wire announced a plan to try electrical treatments on Mrs Conrad's knee (Jessie to Joseph Conrad, MS Yale, 23 April).

[2] Curle's sister Muriel was married to Lt-Col. Joseph Seward Ruston. They lived in Lincolnshire.

[3] Charles and Margaret Bell of Glasgow. He was a 'garment dyer'.

[4] Colonel Matthew Bell was Conrad's landlord at Oswalds.

starboard engine has been stopped on account of some small trouble. I know that but the passengers don't. I guess we won't be in till Tuesday next.

29. Ap. 9pm

I am afraid my dearest that this letter will not be so long as I intended. 2 days ago I had the bad luck to hit my little finger (the deformed one). This started a lot of pain which extended to the wrist and made me feel quite seedy. It is much better to-day. On the 27th the temperature dropped from 63° (in the Gulf stream) to 51°. That sudden change gave me a touch of lumbago so I have been sitting in my cabin with a hot-water bottle against the small of my back.

30th 10. AM.

Much better every way this morning. Have just come up from breakfast. Ship was rolling a good deal last night. Expect to see the Nantucket light ship about noon and at about 11 this evening we will anchor at the quarantine station for the night. The custom house will be on board at 6.30 am. and we shall be moored at the jetty by 10 o'clock. I have had a radio from D'day yesterday. He and Eric will meet me with the car and we shall proceed either to Garden City or to Oyster Bay.

Thank Audrey with my love for the accessible way the medicines were packed. I have used a little belladonna, one bandage and a good few cachets.[1] I am feeling almost chirpy – but I confess that all this expedition seems to me a ghastly nuisance.

However I may change my opinion before long.

In an hour or so I shall go to the Capt's room, drink beef tea with him and discuss the situation. In the afternoon the packing will have to be done. Several people Owen Wister, Old Bok,[2] C. Morley have sent me messages of welcome. It does not give me any particular pleasure but I admit that it is very good of them.

I miss you more and more. As a matter of fact I am on the edge of worrying tho' I suppose there is no reason for it. It seems ages since I left you in that bedroom in the hotel. When I think of it I have a funny sensation under the breastbone.

And those boys! I hope John has been a comfort to you while at home and has gone back to school with good resolutions. Send him my paternal love. B. too haunts me rather. I would write to him but there is really nothing to

---

[1] Pills coated with gelatin or paste to disguise their flavour.

[2] Dutch-born, Edward William Bok (1863–1930) rose from Western Union office boy to editor of the *Ladies' Home Journal*, a post he held from 1889 to 1919. His autobiography, *The Americanization of Edward Bok* (1921), won a Pulitzer prize. The American novelist Owen Wister (1860–1938) is best known for Westerns such as *The Virginian* (1902).

say of actual interest. I wonder how his patent piston turned out. Let him know You have heard from me and tell him he is very near my heart – in which your dear image dwells constantly commanding all my thoughts and all my love.

Your ever devoted husband

J. C.

PS This letter will be sent direct on board the Aquitania which will be leaving to morrow (Tuesday) at noon from the jetty at which we will moor at ten o'clock.

To Richard Curle

Text MS Texas;[1] Curle 114

[*Tuscania*]
29. Ap. 23.

Dearest Dick.

It's the best I can do. It is very poor, but I trust you will be able to make something of it. I can not look these pages over.[2] We will be at the jetty on Tuesday 10 AM and I shall try to send them across to the outgoing mailboat which will leave at noon.

I have had a bad wrist (left) which hindered me in this work. It is distinctly better today tho' still painful. I have had a radio from Doubleday. The passage was good and M. Bone has been looking after me like a good fellow. Can't say I feel very bright. No need to tell Jessie that. You are very much in my thoughts and I feel I would give anything to have you by. Pardon me for not saying any more.

Ever yours

J. Conrad.

To Jessie Conrad

Text MS Yale; *JCLW* 75; J-A, 2, 307

[letterhead: Effendi Hill]
4. 5. 23

My dearest Chica.

You know from D'day's cable of my safe arrival not only in New York but in this very place. I will not attempt to describe to you my landing, because it is indescribable. To be aimed at by forty cameras held by forty men that look as if they came out of the slums is a nerve-shattering experience. Even

---

[1] Written on the last page of the MS of 'Ocean Travel'.

[2] 'My Hotel in Mid-Atlantic' appeared in the London *Evening News* for 15 May 1923, and was reprinted in *Last Essays* under the title 'Ocean Travel'.

D'day looked exhausted after we had escaped from that mob – and the other mob of journalists.[1]

Then a Polish deputation men and women (some of these quite pretty) rushed me on the wharf and thrust enormous nosegays into my hands. Eric nobly carried two of them. Mrs D'day took charge of another. I went along like a man in a dream and took refuge in D's car.

Imagine, my dear! Powell was there too![2] Mrs D. asked him to call, and he dined here yesterday and then played Beethoven and Chopin. Between whiles we talked of you. In fact you have been very much to the fore in everybody's conversation.

To-morrow Friday I go to the Garden City in the morning. In the evening there is a dinner-party for J. W. Davies* (late ambassad[r] to England) and Col. House[3] to meet me. In an hour or so I expect Eric to arrive here for a quiet talk. From what I have seen he seems to be in good form. Certainly our prospects here are excellent – on the face of them. My reception by the press was quite remarkable in its friendliness. — But I am feeling distinctly home sick. It comes over me strongly as I sit writing these words.

D'day insists on sending you a message in every week-end cable they dispatch to Europe. It is very nice of him and I am pleased to think you will hear of me pretty often. As to writing to you long reports of the daily proceedings it is not to be thought of. It must be left till my return when I'll tell you the whole wondrous tale.

I do long for the sight of Your handwriting. Mrs Dou'day has just knocked at the door of my bedroom (next to the billiard-room) to say good-night (she had been out) and ask me to remember her to you. She is really very good and tries to make me feel at home. The house is charming – large – luxurious; and the garden quite pretty in the American way.

I close this by depositing many kisses on Your dear face.

Your devoted husband.

J. C.

---

[1] All the tabloids splashed his picture across the front page. For a more sedate account of his arrival, see the *Herald*'s report in Ray, pp. 175–7.

[2] John Powell, the pianist and composer.

[3] John W(illiam) Davis (1873–1955), a lawyer and Congressman from West Virginia, was US Ambassador to the Court of St James's from 1918 to 1921. He was a Democratic hopeful in the 1920 election, and in 1922 declined the offer of a seat on the Supreme Court. In 1924 he ran unsuccessfully against Calvin Coolidge for the US presidency. Texas-born, Edward Mandell House (1858–1938) became President Woodrow Wilson's closest adviser, and helped to draft both the Treaty of Versailles and the Covenant of the League of Nations. In 1911 he published a dystopian novel about an American dictator entitled *Philip Dru: Administrator*. He was an honorary colonel in the Texas Rangers, and liked to use his title.

Give my love to Audrey. Remember me to all the domestic staff of our faithful retainers.

PS. Tenderest love and hugs to the children – quite as if they were still little.

To Borys Conrad
Text MS Yale; *JCLW* 83

[letterhead: Effendi Hill]
Sund. 6. 5. 23

My dearest Boy.

I have been thinking of you and your affairs all the way across and since my arrival here.

The passage was good; but travelling by sea is a silly business anyhow. The landing was a dreadful experience. Cameras, journalists, deputations. C. Morley stood nobly by me (from 7 am to 12.30 pm) but I felt all broken up in the evening. Even Doubleday looked haggard as we got into his car at last.

I have had a great reception by the press – something unprecedented in fact. I have seen a good many "smart" and important people, of whom Col. House was the most interesting and Mrs Curtis[s] James the most "smart."[1] I am going to lecture in her drawing room on Thursday next. Next week we are going to motor by easy stages to Boston.

All this is not unpleasant but it is not exactly enjoyable. Not from any fault in the people, but simply because I have lost my power of enjoyment in strange surroundings and in novel conditions.

The people are overwhelmingly kindly. They are also very human in the conventional sense of the word. They have also amazing intuitions. All this very curious, very attractive. As to the kindness of the Doubledays really there are no words to tell you of it adequately. M^r D'day has the greatest hopes of splendid material results from this visit. This does not mean lecturing, even in an informal sense. My attitude of a private visitor has produced an excellent effect. My daily mail is enormous! In an hour a dozen editors from various parts of U.S. are coming in here for a friendly chat. It will [be] some professors turn later in the week.

My blessings and a paternal hug to you my dearest son

Yours

J. C.

---

[1] Mrs Curtiss James (née Harriet Eddy Parsons, 1868–1941) was married to Arthur Curtiss James (1867–1941), one of the wealthiest men in America. He was the last of the great railroad tycoons, a financier and philanthropist, as well as an avid yachtsman and Commodore of the New York Yacht Club. Their mansion (1914–59) occupied the northwest corner of Park Avenue and 69th Street.

To Jessie Conrad
Text MS Yale; *JCLW* 79; J-A, 2, 308

[letterhead: Effendi Hill]
6. 5. '23

My dearest Chica.

Yesterday my heart was made glad by the sight of your handwriting.[1] I felt better at once and by the virtue of Your dear letter I was made to feel fit for the great dinner-party – Col. House & Mrs. H., J W Davis the ex ambassador and lady[2] – Judge Harriman and his wife (great railway people)[3] and a few others.

To-day (Sunday) we lunched at the Long Island Club. I have just got back and am going to have an hour's rest before we start for the Davis' home for afternoon tea.

Then a quiet evening here.

The *Tuscania* has been taken off the route. In consequence I've asked F. N. D. to engage my passage in one of the smaller Cunard ships for Southampton. I will let you know her name in my next letter. I am timed to arrive (in S.) on the 12th of June.

A Mrs Safford is leaving for England on the 15th. She will be in Canterbury about the 28 with her daughter (about 12) and has volunteered to come and see you if you have no objection.[4] She is really a nice woman so please receive

---

[1] Jessie Conrad reprinted her letters to her husband in *JCLW*; the MSS are now at Yale. As well as writing long, affectionate messages to him spiced with her characteristic humour, she was keeping up with his general correspondence: 'You can picture me every morning sitting up in bed writing letters. I am answering each letter as it comes so as not to be overwhelmed by them. There have been several modest requests that if folks brought over in their car their collection of first editions you should add to their value by signing them' (26 April).

[2] House had married Loulie Hunter in 1881; they had two daughters. Davis married his second wife, Ellen G. Basell, in 1912.

[3] Understandably confused by this welter of glamour, power, and hospitality, Conrad turned at least two people into one. By the time he died in 1909, E. H. Harriman controlled, among others, the Union Pacific, Southern Pacific and Illinois Central Railroads, and the Wells Fargo Express Company. His widow, the philanthropist Mary Williamson Averell (1851–1932), then took over the greater part of the family empire. After the First World War, her son William Averell Harriman (1891–1986), the future diplomat and Presidential candidate, set up a private bank to manage and expand their holdings; he was soon joined by his younger brother Roland, who had served in the war as a naval pilot. William had married Kitty Lanier Lawrence in 1915. The only judge in the Harriman circle was a Texan, Robert Scott Lovett (1860–1932), General Counsel, later Chairman of the Union Pacific, whose son Robert Abercrombie Lovett had been at Yale with Roland.

[4] Passenger lists of arrivals at Ellis Island show that Ray J. Safford, aged fifty-six, his wife May, aged forty-three, and their daughter Cornessia, aged thirteen, returned to New York in the SS *Finland* on 6 September 1923, having sailed from Cherbourg. They lived at 226 Central Park West. Cornessia, also known as Cornelia, died in 2004.

her in Your nice way. She wants to tell you all about me; and as she will be one of the guests of Mrs Curtis[s] James where I am to lecture on Thursday next (10th) she will be able to describe the ordeal to you.

There will be practically no lecturing. The press has been magnificent. Doubleday is delighted and foretells great financial results from this visit. Everybody most amiable. Tomorrow some editors (16) from various parts of the U.S. are coming here to have a talk with me. Mrs. D'day (who is looking to my comfort admirably) is going to give them some tea. We all expect great results from this meeting. I am made to feel I am a considerable person.

On Tuesday morning we all go to the flat in N. York.[1] I lunch at the Century Club 1 o'clock.[2] At 3 I go to Mrs Curtis[s] James to see her drawing-room and try my voice there in the presence of Mrs C. J.'s secretary. At 8 dinner at Mrs Martin. Quiet party. On Wed. lunch at Col. House's to meet Paderewski.[3] Afterward I go to the East India House,[4] a sort of Museum and am to drive about N. Y. streets. Return here, to dine and sleep. Go up to town again on Thursday after lunch here. Call on Mrs Adams[5] in town about 4. Then rest in the flat till 9 pm when we all go to Mrs C. James where my audience will be about 50 women and men. Supper at 11. Sleep in the flat and return here on Friday morning for a quiet week-end. There! I can not tell you any more now.

There is not a moment when You are not in my thoughts. I long to be back. I have heard nothing from B. Oh my dearest I do miss You.

Ever your own

J. C.

---

[1] The Doubledays' flat at 52 West 58th Street.

[2] The Century Association was founded in 1846 by a group that included the landscape painter Asher B. Durand and the poet William Cullen Bryant. Eventually, those who fostered as well as those who practised the arts became eligible for membership. Since 1891, the Association has occupied a building designed by McKim, Mead, and White at 7 West 43rd Street.

[3] House was influential in shaping American policy towards Poland, and had introduced Paderewski to President Wilson in 1914. Ignacy Paderewski (1860–1941) gained an international reputation as a virtuoso pianist in the late 1880s. During the First World War, Paderewski was a member of the Polish National Committee; he was living in Switzerland at the time, and returned there after serving as the first Prime Minister and Foreign Minister of the new Polish government from January to November 1919. He had now resumed his career as a pianist.

[4] India House, 1 Hanover Square, near Wall Street, has been a private club since 1914, with a fine collection of maritime art. As described in his *Plum Pudding* (1921), it was a favourite resort of Christopher Morley and fellow members of the Three Hours for Lunch Club.

[5] Probably Elbridge L. Adams's wife, Margery.

To John Conrad

Text Conrad (John) facsimile 217

[letterhead: Effendi Hill]

7. 5. 23.

6. pm.

My dearest John.[1]

You[r] letter (and mothers) have been delayed and have just arrived.

The packet sails tomorrow and I have only just time to thank you and send you my dear love. I think of you with affection and confidence.

Your devoted father

JC

PS. Tell Mother You heard from me.

To Robert Maynard Hutchins

Text MS Yale; Unpublished

[letterhead: Effendi Hill]

7. 5. 23.

My dear Mr Hutchins.[2]

Many thanks for your more than friendly letter. Mr Doubleday is arranging our car journey to Boston so as to include New Haven. He will write to you shortly.

As to addressing an audience great or small! Well you can't teach new tricks to an old dog – and especially a sea-dog. I can yet talk with people – and even with young people; but talk *to* people is a trick I have never learned, and I shrink from performing it. But I will do my best to express my deep sense of the honour the University does me by taking notice of me at all.

Very Cordially Yours

Joseph Conrad.

---

[1] John Alexander Conrad (1906–82), Conrad's younger son, spent much of 1923 and 1924 away from home at boarding school in Tonbridge or learning French in Le Havre. He later made a career as an architect, and became executor of the Conrad estate in 1944. His memoir, *Joseph Conrad: Times Remembered* (1981), provides details of the Conrads' domestic life.

[2] The educator and author Robert Maynard Hutchins (1899–1977) was named Secretary of the Yale Corporation upon graduating from Yale in 1921. He completed a law degree in 1925, became Dean of the Yale Law School at the age of twenty-eight, and from 1929 to 1951 was President of the University of Chicago. From 1943 to 1974, he chaired the editorial board of the *Encyclopaedia Britannica*. In his emphasis on Great Books and his dislike of over-specialisation, Hutchins had a long-lasting influence on American higher education. His challenge to the cult of college sports had less effect.

To Catherine Willard

Text MS Wright; Unpublished

[letterhead: Effendi Hill]
8. May. 1923.
Tuesday

My dear Catherine.[1]

Just a word to tell you that I am coming to Boston next week, on a tour arranged by my dear friends and hosts in this country M^r & Mrs Doubleday. I will let you know more when the dates are fixed. But it is certain that we will see each other before long.

Thank you for your letter. Please thank from me Mama Grace[2] for hers, with my love. In haste ever

your affectionate old friend

J. Conrad

To Jessie Conrad

Text MS Yale; *JCLW* 91; J-A, 2, 309

[Effendi Hill][3]
11 May 1923
New York.

Darling own Jess.

Thanks for your letters which are arriving regularly. The news of the offer to direct the cooking dept of a magazine has excited me greatly.[4] I don't see why it should come to nothing if you feel like accepting it. I am sure you would do it very well.

I am writing you on this card because there is nothing else in D's flat where we slept last night; and if I waited till we get back to Oyster Bay I would miss

---

[1] Catherine Livingston Willard (1898–1954; Mrs William Edwin Barry 1925–31; Mrs Ralph Bellamy 1931–45) spent her childhood in Cincinnati, Ohio, and her teenage years in England and France. After a theatrical training in Paris, at the Comédie Française, she made her début in 1915 with F. R. Benson's travelling company as Katharina in *The Taming of the Shrew*, and went on to play in Shakespeare at the Old Vic, where her roles included Hermione, Beatrice, Gertrude, Chorus (in *Henry V*), Olivia, and Lady Macbeth. She also took on roles by Congreve and Ibsen. Conrad had been intrigued by the thought of her playing Lena in *Victory*. She had returned to America in 1921. At the time of Conrad's tour there, she was a member of the Henry Jewett Company in Boston, where she took some eighty-six roles at the Copley Theatre. After that, she spent twenty-five years as a leading lady on Broadway.

[2] Her mother, Grace Robinson Willard (1879–1933). See the letter to her of 25 October 1923. The birthdates given for the Willards come from their passports, as presented for inspection at Ellis Island.

[3] Written on an Effendi Hill note-card whose letterhead Conrad crossed out.

[4] 'There was also an offer to me from a big London magazine to take on the whole cookery side of the magazine and to write two articles a month' (23 April).

to-morrow's packet. And besides, dearest girl, I feel at this moment (10.30 am) perfectly flat, effect of reaction after last evening – which ended only after midnight – at Mrs Curtis[s] James. I may tell you at once that it was a most brilliant affair, and I would have given anything for you to have been there, seen all that crowd and all that splendour, the very top of the basket of the fashionable and literary circles. All last week there was desperate fighting and plotting in the N York Society to get invitations. I had the lucky inspiration to refuse to accept any payment; and, my dear, I had a perfect success. I gave a talk and pieces of reading out of Victory. After the applause from the audience which stood up when I appeared had ceased I had a moment of positive anguish. Then I took out the watch you had given me and laid it on the table, made one mighty effort and began to speak. That watch was the greatest comfort to me. Something of you. I timed myself by it all along. I began at 9.45 and ended exactly at 11. There was a most attentive silence, som[e] laughs and at the end when I read the chapter of Lena's death audible snuffling. Then handshaking with 200 people. It was a great experience. – On Tuesday we start for a tour towards Boston. They are calling me to go and see Vance. I must end.

Love to You best of darlings.

Your devoted

J. C.

PS. Thank Audrey for her message. My love to her. Tell the boys.

(had a cheery letter from B. nothing positive)

To Richard Curle
Text MS Indiana; J-A, 2, 310; Curle 115

[letterhead: Effendi Hill]
11. 5. 23

Dearest Dick.

Am awfully rushed or else lying prostrate to recover – but in either case in no writing mood. But I must drop you a line to say that the evening at Mrs Curtis[s] James was a most fashionable affair – and what's more a real success. I gave a talk and readings from *Victory*. One hour and a quarter with an ovation at the end. They were most attentive. Laughs at proper places and snuffles at the last when I read the whole chapter of Lena's death. It was a great social function and people fought for invitations. I made it clearly understood from the first that I was not doing this sort of thing for money. This gave my visit to US a particular character about which the press spoke out. Generally my reception in the papers was wonderful. F. N. D. himself is impressed.

My love to You.

J. Conrad

PS Leaving on motor tour New Eng<u>d</u> & Boston on the 15. About 10 days. Rem'ber me to the Wedgwoods.

To Eric S. Pinker

Text MS Berg; J-A, 2, 311

[letterhead: Effendi Hill]
11. 5. 23.

Dearest Eric

Just a word to say that my talk and reading from Victory at Mrs Curtis[s] James' was a complete success. I think I acted in accordance with your feeling, by declining all payment. This is the "note" of my visit here. It is greatly appreciated. The affair was very splendid and I only wished your wife and You had been there. She would have been amused and you would have been pleased.

I bear in mind all You have said and Govern myself accordingly. We must have a long talk, the first thing on my return.

My love to you both to R[alph] and to the ladies at Burys Court.[1]

Ever affectly Yours
J. Conrad.

PS Great comfort to me to think you are home. I do hope you are well.

Starting for Boston & N. Eng^d ten days tour on the 15th. Going to see Vance to-day.

To Jessie Conrad

Text MS Yale; *JCLW* 95; J-A, 2, 311

[letterhead: Effendi Hill]
14. 5. 23.

My dearest, best of Girls.

Since the evening at Mrs. C. James I have been leading a very quiet life here. Some visitors mostly journalists did come. Very nice fellows. Morley

---

[1] The home, near Reigate, Surrey, of Pinker's mother, Mary Elizabeth (née Seabrooke, 1862–1945) and sister (Mary) Oenone (1903–79).

too showed up for one afternoon and signed for us the little book of verse.[1]
He is really a good fellow.

Thanks for your cable saying "Bobby[2] satisfied, Love" which came over
the phone wire from Garden City on Sat: morning. As days go on I am
missing you more and more – tho' indeed I could not have been looked after
better by a brother and sister than I am by F. N. D. and Mrs Doubleday
whom I am now calling Florence – by request. She sends her love.

The greatest news I have to send you is that these good people have made
up their minds to see me actually home themselves. It is arranged therefore
that we start on the 2[d] June by the White Star boat for Southampton where
we arrive on the 8th or 9th. (I wish it was to-morrow!)

As a matter of fact to-morrow we start on a motor tour across New England
states as far as Boston, where I will just get a sight of Catherine and Mama
Grace.[3] Then on the return trip I shall spend two nights and the day between
with the Adams's and sign that set of books.[4] From the 25th inst to the 2[d]
June I shall keep quiet here.

This is the programme as far as I know it. Don't be disturbed by the
shaky handwriting. My wrist is slightly powerless but it is getting better – and
indeed it was never very bad; and for the rest I feel tolerable. The cough has
left me almost completely which is a distinct gain. I keep perfectly "dry"[5] –
drinking tea (excellent) and also water with my meals with, occasionally, a
glass of good cider.

Well – no more at present my dearest Chica. I must write a few words to
Eric and to Aubry. Send my love to Dick, and hugs to the boys. I don't know
whether I'll have time to write to them by this boat.

No – I can't say I *regret* coming over here but the fact is I am growing
anxious to get home.

You will be prepared to entertain the D'ays perhaps for one night at
Oswalds. I will tell you more of this later. Give my love to Audrey and
regards to Mr & Mrs W[hitehead] Reid.

Your ever most devoted Boy.

J. C.

PS Remembrances to the staff.

---

[1] Morley's most recent volume of poetry was *Translations from the Chinese* (New York: Doran,
1922), a collection of free verse.

[2] Sir Robert Jones.

[3] Conrad saw them in Boston on the 19th.

[4] The Adamses' country house, Green River Farm, was in the Berkshires, near Great
Barrington, Massachusetts. The inscriptions in Adams's Conrad collection were published
as 'Bibliographical Notes' in his *Joseph Conrad: The Man* (1925).

[5] Coming to terms with Prohibition.

To G. Jean-Aubry

Text MS Yale; *NRF* 114–15; J-A, 2, 310 with facsimile

14.5.23.
Effendi Hill. Oyster Bay.
N.Y.

Mon très cher Jean.

Merci mille fois de Votre bonne lettre. J'ai reçu tout le paquet et je suis infiniment touché par les offres de mes amis français de me procurer l'œuvre de Garneray.[1] Votre Article dans le Figaro[2] est tout ce qu'il y a de plus sympat[h]ique. Merci mon bon.

J'ai vu hier M. Beckman.[3] J'ai passé deux heures avec lui. J'aime ce garçon là. Nous nous entend[o]ns parfaitement. Il m'est très sympathique. Je Vous prie dites cela a Mme Alvar en lui présentant mes hommages affectueux et mes souhaits de bon voyage.

Jeudi soir a 9.30 j'ai causé et lu quelques extraits de Victory devant une audience très brilliante* dans le grand hall de la maison de Mme Curtiss James. Près de deux cent personnes – le dessus du panier comme lettres et "society". On se battait pour avoir les invitations – on me dit. Eh bien, mon cher, presque sans preparation ça a été un succès. On a ri, on a reniflé dans les mouchoirs (mort de Lena) on a beaucoup applaudi. J'ai fermé le livre a onze heures moins le quart et il y a eu un moment de silence avant la tempête qui m'a assez emotion[n]é moi-même. Souper a minuit.

Ma reception par la presse a été excellente. Tout ce qu'il y a de plus amical – a la manière américaine bien entendu. J'ai plu au[x] journalistes – c'est un fait. Un courrier énorme tous les jours. Doubleday enchanté.

Je reviens par Southampton ou* j'espère debarquer le 8 ou le 9 Juin. Demain nous partons pour Boston – un petit tour en auto de dix jours.

Voilà tout mon cher. Je suis content de penser que VS avez vu Jessie.

Je VS embrasse de tout mon coeur.

Votre vieux

Conrad.

My very dear Jean,

Many thanks for your good letter. I've received the whole package and I am infinitely touched by the offers from my French friends to find me

---

[1] *Récits, aventures et combats. Souvenirs de ma vie maritime* (1853), which, according to Jean-Aubry, Conrad 'had read with enthusiasm as a child and wanted to reread'. Its author, Louis Garneray (1783–1857), was both a sailor and a painter.

[2] 'Joseph Conrad et la France', *Le Figaro, Supplément littéraire*, 211 (21 April 1923), 1.

[3] Louise Alvar Harding's brother Robert lived in the USA, as did her father, Ernst Johan Beckman; Conrad's tone suggests that he met the younger man.

Garneray's work. Your article in the Figaro could not be kinder. Thanks, my good fellow.

I saw Mr Beckman yesterday. I spent two hours with him. I do like that fellow. We understand each other perfectly. He is very likeable. Pray tell that to Mme Alvar with my affectionate greetings and best wishes for her journey.

Thursday evening at 9.30 I spoke, and read a few extracts from Victory before a very brilliant audience in the grand hall of the house of Mrs. Curtiss James. About two hundred people – the top of the basket of the literary and fashionable circles. They were fighting for invitations – so I'm told. Ah well, my dear fellow, I've been a success almost without any preparation. They laughed, they snuffled into their handkerchiefs (Lena's death), there was much applause. I closed the book at a quarter to eleven and there was a moment of silence before the tempest, which I also found quite moving. Dinner at midnight.

My reception by the press has been excellent. Everything most friendly – in the American way, of course. The journalists like me – it's a fact. Piles of mail every day. Doubleday delighted.

I return by Southampton where I hope to arrive the 8th or 9th of June. Tomorrow we leave for Boston – a little motor tour for ten days.

That's everything, my dear fellow. I am happy to think that you have seen Jessie.

I embrace you with all my heart.

Your old

Conrad.

To Eric S. Pinker
Text MS Berg; Unpublished

[letterhead: Effendi Hill]
14. 5. 23.

Dearest Eric.

It is settled (suddenly) that F. N. D. and Mrs D are coming over with me in the White Star boat leaving here on the 2 June. They intend to stay a fortnight in England.

Therefore you will have a talk with F. N. D. In these circumstances I need not report fully to you now the talk I had with him since you left. It is the same story of periodic payments at agreed dates – the whole scheme of which he will embody in a memorandum which he will give you – but each transaction is to be carried separately by an exchange of letters in order to save taxation. You know what that means: a series of sales. He insists that the whole will amount to no less than 4,000 p. year. (That is apart from serial rights). Meantime he's endeavouring to place second serials – and so on. He's very buoyant. Well – good luck to him.

I shall see Brand[t]¹ before I leave. This is arranged.

We start to-morrow for Boston and other places. 10 days' tour.

My general impression is that F. N. D.'s proposals are made in perfect good faith but that he is tenacious in his views and plans. It is impossible for me to raise a controversy in present conditions. We must manage to see each other somehow before he talks to you which he intends (very much) to do.

I am very anxious to get home and *go to work*. That is the only thing that matters, really. Give my love to your wife.

Ever Yours

J. Conrad.

To Annabel Phelps

Text MS Yale; Phelps 754

[letterhead: Hotel Kimball, Springfield, Massachusetts]

16. 5. 23

Dear Mrs Phelps²

I do not know how to express to you my deep sense of your charming hospitality and friendly kindness.³ Pray take the will for the deed and believe that I am saying no more than the bare truth when I assure you I have found an unforgettable impression under your roof.

Will you kindly convey to the Professor my affectionate regards and allow me to subscribe myself

your very grateful and most faithful servant

Joseph Conrad

¹ The New York literary agent Carl Brandt (1888–1957), of Brandt & Kirkpatrick.
² Annabel Phelps (née Hubbard, 1864–1939) married William Lyon Phelps (1865–1943) in 1892. After a tour of the Yale campus and interviews by several students, Conrad spent the night of 15 May at their home, 110 Whitney Avenue, New Haven.
³ For an account of Conrad's visit to Yale, see Phelps and also Dale B. J. Randall, 'Conrad Interviews, No. 4: Edward K. Titus, Jr', in *Conradiana*, 3.1 (1970–1), 75–9. Of an earlier meeting with Conrad, a family dinner at Effendi Hill, Phelps wrote 'he was not only affable; he was affectionate' (Phelps, p. 753).

To Jessie Conrad

Text MS Yale; *JCLW* 103; J-A, 2, 312

[letterhead: The Copley-Plaza, Boston]
Friday 18 May '23

Dearest Jess.

I am writing this in the hope to catch the mail-boat leaving N York to-morrow (Sat); but I shall send You a night-radio message tomorrow which you will get on Monday next.

Here I send you only my devoted love and the assurance that I am standing the motor tour very well so far. Before leaving, last Tuesday, I received a letter from You (7th May, I think) and was delighted with the sight of your dear handwriting. Send my dear love to Borys and to John. My thoughts are constantly with you all. In the midst of new scenes my mind remains fixed on your dear person at Oswalds.

On Monday (21st) we leave here and on Tuesday morning I will be with the Adams's in the country and stay there till Thurs: morn^g. He will have the set there for me to sign. On Friday ev^g we will be back at Effendi Hill – where I shall stay quietly till my departure on the 2d. Doubledays are coming over with me. We shall have to entertain them one night at least.

Give my special love to Audrey and remembrances to the "faithful retainers."

Ever your devoted husband

JC

To Richard Curle

Text MS Indiana; Curle 116

[letterhead: The Copley-Plaza, Boston]
18. 5. 23.

Dearest Dick

Just a line to tell you that I continue to be entertained in a princely fashion by the D's. The articles on J.C. continue to appear all friendly and in some sort respectful.[1] D'y offers to guarantee £4000 p.y. for 3 years – (and as much more as possible) apart from serial-proceeds. I will tell you all the details when we meet

The D's are coming over to see me home. We leave on the Second June and ought to reach South'on on the 9th (Majestic.[2])

---

[1] For examples of his reception in the Boston press, see Ray, pp. 181–90 (citation on p. 181, n. 1, should be *Boston Evening Transcript*).

[2] At 56,551 tons, the largest ship afloat. Originally the *Bismarck* but acquired unfinished as a war reparation, she made her maiden voyage in 1922 as a member of the White Star Fleet under the command of Commodore Sir Bertram Hayes. Conrad made his voyage in her as one of 800 first-class passengers (*New York Times*, 3 June, p. S5).

I hope my dear fellow You are keeping well and have no worries on your mind.[1] In the midst of New England my thoughts are fixed on *England* (tout court) where my affections for my family and my friends dwell immovably.

We must meet very soon after my return. I would like [you] to come while I entertain the Doubledays. But of all that more anon.

My love to You

Yrs

J. Conrad.

To Eric S. Pinker

Text MS Berg; Unpublished

[letterhead: The Copley-Plaza, Boston]
[18 or 19 May 1923][2]

Dearest Eric.

This is a damnable pen. I am being entertained in a sort of princely fashion by the D's. Just before leaving he showed me his letter to you which you will have read by the time this reaches you.

As there are no conditions and he offers to guarantee £4000 (or more) p. y. for 3 years there can be no objection to our acceptance. The only thing that worries him are serials – but he made no verbal objections to anything we may like to do. He made only one request of which I'll tell you when we see each other. Brand[t] has promised to come to Oyster Bay (on D's invitation) after our return there. Lorimer[3] has been ill at home for a fortnight. The last letter from his secretary stated: that he would be pleased to come to Effendi Hill in order to meet me. I hope he will be well enough. Vance is a nice friendly person. The weather is magnificent. We dine to-morrow with Mrs. Page[4] (the Ed^{or} of Atlan[t]ic M[onth]ly[5] will be there) and we leave here on Sunday. I expect to reach South[hampt]on on the 9th.

---

[1] Curle had divorced Cordelia Fisher the previous year after ten years of marriage.

[2] Dated by context: the dinner with Mrs Page was actually on Sunday the 20th, and Conrad left Boston the following day.

[3] George Horace Lorimer (1867–1937), an astute judge of popular American tastes in literature, became editor of the *Saturday Evening Post* in 1899.

[4] Willa Alice Page (née Wilson), the widow of the journalist and diplomat Walter Hines Page (1855–1918). He had edited the *Atlantic Monthly* in 1898–9 and then was Doubleday's partner and editor of the *World's Work* until his appointment as Ambassador to the Court of St James's in 1913. As Ambassador, Page was a strong advocate of American entry into the First World War.

[5] Ellery Sedgwick (1872–1960) edited the *Atlantic Monthly* from 1909 to 1938. In 1916, he had asked Conrad to write an article about Poland; Conrad declined, while praising the magazine in his courtliest manner (*Letters*, 5, pp. 669–70).

Perhaps you could arrange to run down to Oswalds for a talk on the 10th. I will have to ask the D's down almost at once and should like to have a talk with you before their visit.

Give my love to Your wife.

Ever affectly Yours

J. Conrad.

To Jessie Conrad

Text MS Yale; *JCLW* 111; J-A, 2, 313

[Effendi Hill]

[24 May 1923][1]

My very own dear Jess.

I am more touched than upset (tho' I've been a little) by your letter of the 14 where you seem to be a little angry with me for not writing to you.[2] My dearest girl, that wretched Tuscania did not get here till Tuesday, too late to catch the mail leaving that very day. Therefore my first letter to you did not leave till next Saturday the 5th of May. Therefore it is possible you did not get my first letter when you wrote on the 14th. I did ask D'day to mention I had missed the mail when cabling you my arrival. I have written five letters in all – of course apart from cable-letters of which one more goes to you to-day. Don't imagine my dearest that the delights of this country make me forget my home – which is where you are; and indeed is nothing to me but *You*, You alone wherever you may be. Consider dear Chica that I am in a strange country on Long Island where I do not know where the nearest P office is – miles off probably; that the postal arrangements are very primitive and that I am at the mercy of people around me. The Garden City is 15 miles from here. During our tour it was just the same, and You know the hotels have no letter boxes and I am not the sort of person that can rush out at the last minute and post a letter. I have been looked after like an infant, I must say but I have been also helpless like an infant in a way. I have also had an enormous amount of correspondence which had to be attended to, if this visit is to do any good. The Garden City staff dealt with some of it. F. N. D. also took some off my hands, but what had to be left to me was an immense pile every day.

---

[1] Date added in Jean-Aubry's hand; Conrad returned to Effendi Hill from his New England tour on the 24th and wrote another letter and a telegram to Jessie the same day.

[2] This one has not survived, but the letter of the 17th begins 'I am looking forward with great impatience to your next letter. I am so anxious to hear how your lecture went off.' At that point, she had had the letter of 6 May, alerting her to the Saffords' visit.

I can't give you the slightest idea how impatient I am to get back to you. I think of nothing else. The time seems interminable – and yet the visit is a success.

When I arrived I was not feeling well. Now I do – as long as I have not to exert myself. Upon the whole I have improved in health; but what it really amounts to I cannot say, and, truth to say, I am not much concerned. What I am concerned about is your poor leg – your treatment, your prospects of final cure.

Saw in Boston (last Saturday) Mama Grace and Cath. Both are looking well, both are sick of America, both send you their warmest love. On Sunday dinner party (12) at Mrs Loring (ex-Miss Page).[1] She has turned out a charming woman. She and Mrs Page send you their affectionate regards. I assure you that you are not forgotten. So do the Adams's with whom I stayed two nights and a day (Tuesday).[2] Talked much of You. The baby really charming and loves its doll.

I must confess that I am heartily sick of all this infinite kindness. It is overwhelming simply. And yet it must be acknowledged the D'ays have actually planned coming over for no other purpose but to see me safely home! Of course they will make a stay but of no more than a fortnight. My dear you must prepare yourself to entertain them for 2 nights and the day between which will very likely be Tuesday the 12th or Wednesday the 13. So dearest make preparations to get some extra help and arrange for them to have the spare room and B's room and generally the use of that end of the house with the bathroom. Of course I have fixed no date positively. I said it must depend on how I find you. I hope to be with you dearest on Sat 9th for lunch – unless the ship is late. She may be as she has to call at Cherbourg and may be delayed there. We will talk all these matters over. How awfully far off it seems yet!! Oh! My dear I am Your, in heart and soul, most devoted "Boy."

JC

My love to Audrey. Tell the boys of my return and give them severe hugs from me. Kind regards to the faithful staff.

---

[1] Katherine Alice Loring was Walter Hines Page's only daughter. A Bryn Mawr graduate, she married Charles G. Loring (b. 1881) in 1915 in London, where her father was serving as US Ambassador. As a gesture of gratitude from King George V, the wedding was held in the Chapel Royal in St James's Palace.

[2] John Sheridan Zelie's account of one of these evenings is reprinted in Ray, pp. 191–7.

To Jessie Conrad

Text MS cablegram draft Princeton; Unpublished

[Garden City]
[24 May 1923]¹

Conrad. Bridge. Kent.

Dearest Jessie. Have sent five letters up to now. One more will be posted to-day. All well. Leaving with Mr & Mrs Effendi on Saturday 2 June in Majestic. Hope reach Southampton Friday 8 June late evening and be home on Saturday. Write no more here after receiving this but drop me a line to the R[oyal] a[utomobile] c[lub]. on the seventh and I will wire train. Dear love.

To Jessie Conrad

Text MS Yale; *JCLW* 105

[letterhead: Effendi Hill]
24. 5. 23. Friday. 4 pm.

My dearest Girl.

I wrote and despatched a cable *and* a letter to you this morning, the latter to catch to-morrow's ship. I am scrawling this in the hope it will be in time too. If not the Tuesday ship will take it over. I enclose here one of the batch of the letters of thanks received by Mʳ & Mrs Curtiss James for the lecture I delivered in their ball-room to some 200 invited guests.

Others are much the same. This is one of the shortest.

I long to be on the sea on the way to You – and the passage will seem long – very long! I fear some delay in Cherbourg but I do hope to lunch with you on Saturday the 9th.

Hugs and kisses for my Chica.

Ever hers

J. C.

To Borys Conrad

Text MS draft Haverford; Unpublished

[Garden City]
[25? May 1923]²

Conrad care Daimler Cᵒ Rusholme. Manchester

Drop me a line to the Curzon where I will be on the 9th telling me if any chance seeing you at Oswalds to meet Doubledays 13th and 14th next. Dear love

JC

¹ Dated by the following letter.
² Written on the same ruled paper as the other draft telegrams of the 24th and 25th.

To Eric S. Pinker
Text MS draft Princeton; Marconigram Berg; Unpublished

[Garden City]

[25 May 1923]¹

Bookishly London

Returned from delightful tour in New England feeling well. Leave here on the second by Majestic and expect arrive London late on the eight[h]. Drop me a line to the R[oyal] a[utomobile] c[lub]. Please remind bank to send ten pounds to Italy before end of this month.² Affectionately Yours. Conrad.

To John Powell
Text MS Virginia; Randall 211

[letterhead: Effendi Hill]

[28 May 1923]³

My dear Powell⁴

I take the first quiet moment since our return from the New England tour to drop you a line. I found here a letter from my wife who asks me to give you her "very special love", and hopes that she will see you next year in England.

I join in that message and in that hope with all my heart. You are one of our "precious friendships" and you know that they are not many. I was made happy by seeing and hearing you this time – and I am grateful to you for giving me the opportunity.

And now, my dear fellow – Good-bye! May success attend all your activities and give you the happiness your great gift and your warm heart deserve.

Always your old friend

Joseph Conrad.

---

¹ Text from MS. Sent at the overnight rate, the Marconigram was received in London on the morning of the 26th. The MS draft of another telegram to Pinker is at Emory, tipped into a copy of *Youth*. Conrad probably wrote it in early June, just before embarking. 'Bookishly. London. Arrive Curzon some time Saturday intending to go home with Jessie on Sunday. D's visit to Oswalds fixed for 13th & 14th. Fix our meeting without disturbing your weekend arrangements. Could run up on London if necessary. Yours. J. C.'

² For Karola Zagórska's monthly allowance.

³ Date from postmark.

⁴ Introduced to Conrad by Warrington Dawson, the pianist and composer John Powell (1882–1963) played for Conrad at Capel House, Oswalds, and Effendi Hill. His *Rhapsodie Nègre* (1918) was a musical tribute to *Heart of Darkness*. At the time of Conrad's American tour, Powell was an active sponsor of Virginia's Racial Integrity Act of 1924 prohibiting interracial marriage. In 1928, he married Louise Burleigh (*q.v.*).

To Elbridge L. Adams

Text J-A, 2, 314; Adams 33 (in part)[1]

Effendi Hill, New York
31 May '23

My dear Adams,

Your good letter in the name of you both reached me yesterday. I am ashamed of not having written to you and your dear wife before. I put it off from day to day in the hope of finding a really "free" moment in which I could attempt to express to you my gratitude for your gift of warm friendship and charming hospitality. But that hope must be given up. Even now I am oppressed by the prospect of a dozen or more of letters to write – and by the packing which has to be done to-day.

So a short word of "thanks" must do; and I put into its accent all the depth of sincerity which it can carry in its six letters. May the blessings of peace and contentment attend the life of comparative retirement which you intend to lead, and extend to your posterity of which Ann is such a lovely and lovable representative. I beg Margery[2] to give her a kiss from me.

I shall try to give Jessie some idea of your delightful home and its rural surroundings.

If you ever have photos taken of your abode please send them to us for our American album. We shall look forward to important good news from you before long. I must ask you to send me a copy of the pamphlet when it appears, signed by you, for deposition in the "family archives," so that my descendants should have this record of our friendship and of your view of me, and transmit it to their posterity.

I am going away with a strong impression of American large-heartedness and generosity. I have not for a moment felt like a stranger in this great country about the future of which no sensible man would dare to speculate. But no sensible man would doubt its significance in the history of mankind. I am proud to have had from it an unexpected warmth of public recognition and the gift of precious private friendships. I kiss Margery's hands and grasp both yours in farewell and recommend myself and all mine to your kind and unfailing memory.

Your affectionate and grateful friend
Joseph Conrad.

---

[1] Adams omits the first sentence, but supplies the farewell and signature missing from Jean-Aubry.

[2] Margery Lee (née Stetson) was Adams's second wife; his first wife died in 1914.

To Samuel C. Chew

Text MS Bryn Mawr; Unpublished

[letterhead: Effendi Hill]
31 May '23

My dear Professor.[1]

Pardon this belated acknowledgment of your kind and valued letter.

My stay here was time-tabled and arranged for me with such exactness that I had no hope of being able to break through it. I can't tell you how sorry I am at not seeing you both. It was simply impossible to arrange; but I am deeply grateful to you and your dear wife for your invitation.

I have just had a letter from Jessie sending her love to you both. My greatest regret is that I cannot deliver this message personally to You. I am leaving for home on the 2[d] carrying off with me memories and impressions of much that is great and of everything that is kind. Pray keep us in your friendly memory as we shall always do You.

Believe me always your faithful friend
Joseph Conrad

To Edgar H. Wells

Text MS Bryn Mawr; Unpublished

[letterhead: Effendi Hill]
31. 5. '23

Dear M[r] Wells.[2]

I could not find the time to deliver to you the letter of introduction from our friend Gardiner. Where I am unpardonable is in not having thanked you before this for putting me up for the privileges of the Harvard Club.[3] I assure You I feel very penitent. I can say no more.

All arrangements were made for me and I could not very well break through them. I regret very much not having seen you. I hope that when you come over on our side that "truly good man" G. G.[4] will manage (with his

---

[1] Samuel Claggatt Chew (1888–1960), a graduate of Johns Hopkins University, taught English literature at Bryn Mawr College from 1914 to 1954. The author of several books and some 3,000 book reviews, in 1925 he was awarded first prize in the *Saturday Review of Literature* contest to suggest an ending for Conrad's *Suspense*.

[2] Edgar Huidekoper Wells (1875–1938) was an English instructor and Acting Dean at Harvard College before the First World War, when he served in England as Deputy Commissioner for the American Red Cross. After the war, he settled in New York and in 1921 founded E. H. Wells & Co., a bookshop at 602 Madison Avenue specialising in first editions and other rarities.

[3] Whose substantial premises are at 27 West 44th Street.

[4] Gordon Gardiner had studied at Harvard before the war.

usual efficiency) to bring us together. Till that happy event comes to pass I
hope you will charitably believe in my most friendly sentiments.

Yours

Joseph Conrad.

PS I am leaving on the 2^d with a strong sense of having had a great experience
of an enlightening and moving kind in human achiev[e]ment and human
kindness.

To Katherine C. Fiske†

Text MS Private collection; Unpublished

[letterhead: Effendi Hill]
1. June 1923.

My dear Miss Fiske.[1]

Your present and your charming little note have given me the greatest
pleasure. I shall use the one at the proper season and treasure the other at all
seasons as a touching memento of the last evening of my travels in America.

Pray give my most respectful regards to your Mother, remember me to M^r
Partridge[2] and believe me always most faithfully

Yours

J. Conrad

To William Lyon Phelps

Text MS Yale; Phelps 754

[letterhead: Effendi Hill]
1st June '23

My dear Professor.[3]

Accept my warmest thanks for the more than friendly terms of Your letter.
I had in your house an unforgettably kind and charming reception and you

---

[1] Fiskes abound in the USA, but, given the milieu in which Conrad found himself, there is
a strong possibility that this Miss Fiske was Katherine C(ushman) Fiske, who lived with her
parents at 898 Park Avenue. Her mother, Marione Cushman Fiske (d. 1947), was active in
good causes, especially the welfare of delinquent girls and women; her father, Haley Fiske
(d. 1929), was the President of the Metropolitan Life Insurance Co. and, as his membership of
the Grolier Club signified, a booklover. They had married in 1887. Miss Fiske, who had long
been active in New York society and bred Pekinese dogs, married an Episcopalian priest, the
Revd Emmons P. Burrill, in 1938.

[2] Another circumstantial identification: Theodore Dwight Partridge, an accomplished amateur
sailor, lived with his father, the obstetrician and conservationist Edward L. Partridge, at 19
Fifth Avenue.

[3] William Lyon Phelps (1865–1943), Professor of English at Yale University from 1892 to 1933,
was well known as a prolific scholar and resourceful teacher, renowned for his courses on
Tennyson and Browning ('T and B'). He attended Conrad's reading in New York, and invited
Conrad and the Doubledays to visit Yale and stay overnight at the Phelpses' home in New
Haven.

gave me an impression of Yale Coll: which shall be treasured. I commend myself to Mrs Phelps' and your memory as

your affectionate friend

J. Conrad

To Margaret Porter
Text MS Morgan; Unpublished

[letterhead: Effendi Hill]

1923. 1st May. [June] 10pm.

My dear Mrs Porter[1]

As you may guess by the hour (noted above) this is the last letter I write from this hospitable house, whence I am carrying away so many pleasant and touching memories.

Not the least of them is the experience of some delightful moments (all too short) in your company and of your graciously thoughtful kindness in inviting me with Florence & Effendi to dine at your flat on *that* evening.

I can't tell you how much I appreciated the sympathetic insight which prompted you to offer that refuge to my troubled spirit. I can only thank you with all my heart, and venture to hope that you will keep a little place in your memory for

your very grateful and most faithful servant

Joseph Conrad.

PS My love to your enchanting little girl[2] to whom I have lost my heart.

To Edward Garnett[3]
Text Telegram Indiana; Unpublished

[New York]

[2 June 1923][4]

Garnett 19 Pond Place Chelsea London

Sending you my love ahead of my arrival on Saturday next will write

Conrad

---

[1] Margaret Porter (née Kelly, 1893/4–1980) lost her first husband, Lt James Jackson Porter, in the Meuse-Argonne offensive of the First World War. She married John Chambers Hughes (1891–1971) in 1923. (For a letter to her under her new name, see [7 January 1924].) Living in Paris during the Second World War, she volunteered to help French prisoners of war in Meaux, and recorded her experiences in *Les Lauriers sont coupés* . . . (1941). She was thrice decorated by the French government for her services to the country, and died aged eighty-six in Manhattan.

[2] Mrs Porter's daughter Jamie.

[3] Garnett replied on 11 June, two days after Conrad's arrival in Southampton. His letter ends: 'I shall hope to hear from your lips an account of all you did & suffered' (Stape and Knowles, p. 210).

[4] Cabled from New York, received in London at 6.25 pm on that day.

To the Owners and Ship's Company of the *Tusitala*

Text MS SCI; Unpublished[1]

[letterhead: Effendi Hill]
2[d]. June. 1923.

On leaving this hospitable country where the cream is excellent and the milk of human kindness apparently never ceases to flow I assume an ancient mariner's privilege of sending to the Owners and the Ships-Company of the *Tusitala*[2] my brotherly good wishes for fair winds and clear skies on all their voyages. And may they be many!

And I would recommend to them to watch the weather, to keep the halliards clear for running, to remember that "any fool can carry on but only the wise man knows how to shorten sail in time" . . . and so on, in the manner of Ancient Mariners all the world over. But the vital truth of sea-life is to be found in the ancient saying that it is "the stout hearts that make the ship safe".

Having been brought up on it I pass it on to them in all confidence and affection.

Joseph Conrad.

To Eric S. Pinker

Text MS Berg; Unpublished

[letterhead: Oswalds]
Monday 11. 6. 23.

Dearest Eric.

I have been thinking over all you have told me about the possible inconveniences of forming a fund on the American side under what we may call the "F. N. D.'s scheme."

---

[1] Written at the suggestion of Christopher Morley, who published a description of the ship's departure, 'Outward Bound', in the New York *Evening Post* for 11 August 1923. James A. Farrell, having just relinquished ownership of the *Tusitala*, donated this letter to the Seamen's Church Institute, New York, in 1938. Farrell (1862–1943) had been President of the US Steel Corp. and was the founder of a shipping line plying between Africa and the USA. On his orders, a facsimile of the letter was framed and posted in the chart-room of every Farrell Lines ship (information from Captain A. D. Wood), and it has had a lasting popularity among sailors, especially in the USA.

[2] An iron-hulled sailing ship of 1,684 gross tons, the *Tusitala* was the last ship built by Robert Steele & Co. in Greenock, Scotland, where she was launched as the *Inveruglas* in 1883. Sold to the Sierra Shipping Company in 1886 and renamed the *Sierra Lucena*, she was resold in 1904 to a Norwegian group and renamed *Sophie*. After the First World War, she hauled coal between the United States and Europe. In 1923 she was purchased by the Three Hours for Lunch Club, a New York syndicate of artists and writers, and become the *Tusitala* (*Storyteller*), the name his neighbours in Samoa gave to Robert Louis Stevenson; Morley, the syndicate's leading light, read Conrad's letter at the renaming ceremony. After a further decade of service trading with Brazil and Hawai'i under the ownership of James A. Farrell, the *Tusitala* became a training ship berthed at St Petersburg, Florida, in 1939, and was broken up in Mobile, Alabama, in 1947. For Berenice Abbott's photograph of her, see: www.mcny.org/collections/abbott/a256.htm.

It is clear to me that I can not expose my executors to any trouble with the Revenue officials. It would not be fair to them. It has occurred to me too that it would affect you more seriously – I mean the disclosure consequent upon my death. They could always say with perfect truth that they did not know what I was doing with my money. You of course, as my agent, could not say that; and, even if the Revenue people did not regard it as an "attempt to defraud" I think that you ought not to be mixed up in any transaction that is questionable in the slightest degree. In your position, with the affairs of so many authors in your hands, all your dealings must be above the merest shadow of suspicion in every respect and in regard to *all* the parties. That consideration is decisive. But that does not mean that the "F. N. D. scheme" must be totally rejected.

A)[1] On the contrary: from the point of view of an interest-bearing investment it may be desirable. You will talk it over with him. But I think that the only course open to us is to declare the whole of Am: earnings, pay inc: tax on it (as we would have had to do if it came over here to be capitalized) and leave the surplus with F. N. D. at interest – with the condition that it should be paid up at my death, and the proviso that I should be at liberty to draw on it, in case of need, during my life. This stipulation is reasonable since if I had it invested in stock here I could always either sell or pledge my holding in case of need.

Will you consider the above and negotiate in that sense if you are in agreement with me as far as the point A is concerned.

B) Coming now to the yearly amount of £4000 which F. N. D. says he can and will pay (apart from serial rights) you made a remark (which stuck in my mind) questioning its sufficiency. On reckoning it up I start with the deduction of 400 comm[issi]^{om} which leaves 3600 net. Assuming the scale as from Jany 1st Jessie gets 730. I get (180 to my acct p. month) 2160. John 150. rent 250. Mrs George 50. (*I pay Karola, Miss Hallowes & Miss Seale*[*] *out of my acct*) Together 3337. Let us say in round figures 3340, leaving for contingencies 260.

And the first fact that stares me in the face is that (for this year at least) the doctors will have 200 at least out of that; an expenditure which I can not meet out of my acct. To talk of savings in these conditions is futile. One must have a margin. I can't spring unprovided-for demands on you – even if you had a margin from English-book and (possible)-serial rights. But we assume that the English rights will just pay inc-tax on the total income, and no more.

Till now I have to a great extent met the contingencies by booklets and the sale of MS. But that source is dried up now. We must therefore stipulate for more from FND who as a matter of fact is well disposed now and I believe

---

[1] Conrad added the alphabetical section breaks in the margin.

is quite ready to help in making my mind easy. The prospects of The Rover are good enough to warrant me asking him for 2500 doll: more – at any rate for this year and the next – or anyhow for the next 24 months, under his "periodic payments" scheme. This will help with the doctors and enable me to do what I want to do in another direction.

C) It is this. Marrying is not a crime and one can not cast out one's son for that. I believe that this particular marriage is foolish and inconsiderate.[1] I shall not conceal my opinion when I write. My confidence is shaken but I will not *assume* the worst. He may all the same make good with Daimlers, where he seems to be liked. He has asked me for nothing and even told me last Mch that he needed not the reduced allowance I was making him out of my acct. I on my side am not anxious to see his wife but I want to recognise his married status in some way – or else it would be a complete break. In order to avoid this I want you to arrange that F.N.D should deduct from each quarterly pay^t (on the increased scale) $250 and send it direct to him. My reason for this is to diminish my "apparent income". In the same way I wonder whether it would not be useful that F.N.D should deduct and pay your comm^{on} direct to you. That is if you don't object and if it does not damage you in any way. To reduce even by $600 the part of inc. liable to super tax[2] would be a consideration.

FND is coming to-morrow. Please wire me if you had a talk with him yet as you may see each other in the morning.

Ever affectly yours

J Conrad.

To Eric S. Pinker
Text MS Berg; Unpublished

[letterhead: Oswalds]
14. 6. 23.

Dearest Eric.

I have to-day a painful wrist, but must send you a word of thanks for your good and wise letter.

To ease the refusal you may tell Effendi that my executors (to whose wishes I must defer in some measure) would prefer me to have all the estate in this

---

[1] Borys Conrad had kept secret his marriage to (Madeline) Joan King on 2 September 1922. Jessie Conrad learned about it at the Hotel Curzon the evening before Conrad left for Glasgow, on his way to the United States, but Conrad was not told until after his return. Mrs Conrad described her predicament and the intense anxiety it fomented in *Joseph Conrad and His Circle* (New York: Dutton, 1935), pp. 242–58.

[2] About 90,000 Britons were liable to super tax, an extra levy payable on incomes over £2,000 per annum; rates started at 1s 6d on the first £500, and rose to a maximum of 6s in the pound. Rates had been much higher during the First World War.

country. I can't very well make things difficult for a man like Wedgwood, who is full of business. This is only an additional argument.

D. will then pay over whatever is earned, and we shall see what we can save. I suppose we will be able to pay (F. N. D.) the first $250 (say £50) to B in July. I much app[recia]te the sympathetic manner in which you recognise my point of view. The more this affair is looked into the less satisfactory it appears.

F. N. D. and wife have just left. He will see you again of course. I have hinted to him the objection to his "saving" scheme. He is quite reasonable. You will settle that definitely.

Thanks for everything You have done and arranged. D. has a scheme for paying B direct which is worth listening to.

I will certainly write for *Delineator*.[1] Glad to do it, as I have bought some small presents (it had to be done) for Mrs D and Mrs Nelson[2] in Hythe yesterday. I want to give a cigar case to F. N. D. As you are often near Pic[c]adilly perhaps you could get something good in stout leather with his initials stamped on. Pardon all the trouble I am giving you.

Our love.

Yours

J. Conrad

To F. N. Doubleday

Text Telegram Princeton; Unpublished

[Oswalds]

[18 June 1923][3]

Doubleday Brownotel Ldn

My love and best wishes to you both and affectionate messages to Patty and Nelson Sorry impossible to come up have had a bad time but feeling better today Signed pages will be mailed as soon as completed which I hope will manage in a fortnights time Hope you will be able accept Curles invitation to lunch and meet Mrs Wedgwood then Curle commissioned write front article Times Literary Supplement on my uniform edition which could perhaps be held over for publication in America till first volumes Concord edition ready Am grieved not to see you again here

Yours Ever

Conrad

---

[1] *The Delineator*, a New York publication, took 'Christmas Day at Sea' for the December issue (p. 10). It is collected in *Last Essays*.

[2] Martha Nicholson Doubleday, known as 'Patty'.

[3] Handed in at the Post Office in Bridge, near Bishopsbourne, date-stamped on receipt at the Piccadilly office.

To Eric S. Pinker
Text Telegram Berg; Unpublished

[Oswalds]
[18 June 1923][1]

Bookishly London

I have been laid up will you please hand over cigar case Doubleday as my coming up is out of question for a week or so

Yours

Conrad

To F. N. Doubleday
Text Telegram Princeton; Unpublished

[Oswalds]
[19 June 1923][2]

Doubleday Brownotel London

Hope to hear from Florence and you by tomorrow mornings post Trust F not overtired yesterday Despatched to your address box containing old glass for P[atty] and N[elson] my love to them Have asked Eric hand you the promised cigar case Ask you both to give suitable messages to all kind acquaintances and good friends particularly in Garden City Feeling better and anxious to begin my writing intend to keep up my end

our love

J. C.

To F. N. Doubleday
Text TS[3] Princeton; Unpublished

[letterhead: Oswalds]
June 21st. 1923.

My dear Effendi,

I am trying to imagine Florence and you on board and feel for some reason or other as if I had deserted you. But now and then I also feel as if I had been

---

[1] Handed in at the Bridge Post Office, date-stamped on receipt in London.

[2] Handed in at the Bridge Post Office, date-stamped on receipt at the Piccadilly office.

[3] The first letter since 12 April typed by Miss Hallowes from Conrad's dictation. On 21 June she wrote to Jean-Aubry on Conrad's behalf (MS Yale), passing on a copy of *The Amenities of Literature* (1841) by the great scholar of forgotten literature Isaac Disraeli (1766–1848): 'Dear M[r] Aubry. M[r] Conrad has asked me to send you this book to look at. He is unable to write to you himself as he is still suffering very much from the gout in his right hand. He has been, however, able to dictate each day, so the story makes progress. Yours sincerely, L. M. Hallowes'. The following day she wrote to J. M. Dent in a similar vein: 'Dear Mr Dent, Mr Conrad asks me to send you a line to say that he hoped to have called to see you on his

left behind. However I know though you two are gone you will never desert me.

I am feeling better to-day and feel with the greater bitterness my disappointment at having missed seeing you once more before you left.

Lamentations are useless and moreover if I indulge in them I may miss the packet, so I will tell you at once without further groans, that I am glad you like the cigar case and that I want to thank you for your friendly attitude towards Curle, who is very sensible to it. I just had a note from him giving me an idea of your conversation.

We have just received page proofs of "The Rover" from Fisher Unwin, in duplicate, page 1 to 96 so far. If you like to set up from that text, which will receive my own attention, the duplicate set is very much at your service if you include the words "forward Rover" in a weekend cable you may be sending to Eric. Otherwise I shall keep it here. You will find enclosed here dedication, jacket motto, and the title-page motto of "The Rover", all clearly typed. As to signatures for the special edition I have not been able to hold the pen yet, but I have good hopes of completing the signatures by the end of this month. It will be the first use I will make of my right hand when the bandages are off.

I kiss the hands of the Lady Commander of The New England Exploring Expedition, which of course marks an epoch in history (my own anyhow) and is one of the most successful undertakings of the sort ever attempted by mankind. You and I who have humbly shared in its hardships and dangers will always proudly remember it.

You shall hear from me soon, for it is not news that I will want to send you but the expression of our warm affection for you both.[1]

Yours ever gratefully,

J. Conrad

P. S. Borys's address for the first payment will be:

B. Conrad, C/o Messrs The Daimlers' Company,
Rusholme, Manchester, Eng.

---

return from America, but unfortunately he has had an attack of gout since his arrival here, and has not been able even to write any letters. He hopes, as soon as he is better, to come up to town and to see you, then. Would you be good enough to send him a copy of the School Edition of "Youth" & "Gaspar Ruiz"? Mr. Conrad sends his greetings and regards to you and the whole firm. He has welcomed with great interest the first volumes of the Hour-glass Edition. Yours sincerely, L. M. Hallowes' (TS UNC).

[1] Jessie Conrad wrote them an affectionate letter on the 25th. Its chief news is about her husband's severe attack of gout (MS Princeton).

For dedication page of "The Rover"

To G. JEAN AUBRY
In friendship
this tale of the last days of a
French Brother of the Coast
- - - . . . - - -
"They were of all nations, Frenchmen, Englishmen,
Dutchmen, Spaniards, and even Blackamoors, but
they were all brothers."[1]
. . . .
Motto for title page of "The Rover"
Sleep after toyle, port after stormie seas,
Ease after warre, death after life, does greatly please.
Spenser.[2]

To Eric S. Pinker
Text TS Berg; Unpublished

[letterhead: Oswalds]
June 21st. 1923.

My dear Eric,

I replied to your letter by wire under the impression that to-day was
Friday.[3] Thank you very much for getting this thing through. I will do the
article within the next fortnight.[4]

I had a friendly letter from FND. He is really a very good fellow. Thank
you for getting for me the cigar case, which he describes as "lovely". Did
you give him an address to send B. the first quarter of the agreed sum? B.
expects, as far as I can make out, to be shifted to London next month.

---

[1] Although close in spirit to several passages in *The Rover* describing the Brotherhood of the
Coast, this quotation did not come from the novel, nor was it used as an epigraph. These
are the words of an old Breton talking to Conrad about the sailors he had known around
the Indian Ocean. Conrad quoted him in an interview at Effendi Hill with James Walter
Smith published in the *Boston Evening Transcript*, 12 May 1923, p. 2 (reprinted in Ray, pp. 181–7,
misattributed to *Evening Telegraph*).

[2] *The Faerie Queene*, Book I, Canto 9, 40. These are the words of Despair, who tries to seduce the
Red Cross Knight into killing himself. They are also inscribed on Conrad's gravestone.

[3] 21 June was a Thursday.

[4] The draft of 'Christmas Day at Sea' was finished by 1 July.

B's last letter says that he has been laid up for more than a week at an hotel in Blackpool with flu and a very bad throat. He was there on business with Shepherd, the sales manager of Daimlers, and their respective wives were there too. Shepherd left some days before and B. had to stay on by doctor's orders till yesterday, when he was taken home in a car, feeling still very shaky. Letter not depressed at all and containing the news of both of them having received an invitation to stay with the Shepherds for a weekend in July. I mention it to you as a symptom.

Before his letter arrived I had written to him informing him of the payments arranged for the next twelve months in recognition of his new status as I had been telling you. I said in my letter "you may look upon it as a wedding present". I made no statement about the future, but I expressed forcibly my opinion as to his personal history for the last two years, adding that the only good point[s] were his sincere endeavours to find something to do and his apparent success in his present berth which I hoped he would keep.

The position about his patent piston is obscure. What upset him about a month ago was to discover by taking (in the usual course of business) to pieces the engine of one of the cars in his Manchester depot that his piston was being apparently fitted in without his knowledge. Upon which he told Shepherd that he would send in his resignation. S. told him to reconsider his intention and shortly afterwards he got notified of a rise of salary and got the promise of a berth as Shepherd's assistant in London. Meantime he had made enquiries and discovered that in the absence of a formal agreement a Company can make use of any improvements designed by their employees. I am afraid that it is so – at least in practice. As far as I know there has been no test case fought out in courts to the end on that point.

My arm is still pretty bad, but, as you may have surmised, Miss H. is back, and things will begin to move. Of course I am disappointed at this beastly fit. It was pretty severe too, but I am not cast down. I am very pleased at this bit of work you have put in my way, and the price you have got for it. The situation not being desperate in point of time, if any more of that sort of thing turns up don't discourage the applicants. From the nature of things there will be days while I am finishing the "Suspense" in which I could do a little occasional work like that. It would be an easy way to get a little more money. And as to the prices I think you share my opinion that the figures are not so much for the stuff actually delivered but in proportion to the reputation earned by nearly thirty years of literary work.

Always, my dear E. affectionately yours,

JOSEPH CONRAD +his mark

To Borys Conrad

Text TS Conrad; Unpublished

[letterhead: Oswalds]
June 23rd. 1923.

Dearest B.

I can't use my right hand yet and so I only acknowledge your letter by these few words in type. The phrase "lack of confidence"[1] was not applied precisely to you but to the future. Let us replace it by the word "uneasiness." And that is only natural if you look at the matter all round. But we don't want to talk about it now. Our anxiety is about your health. Please let us be informed of your progress and of your plans, for it seems to me now a matter of doubt whether you will be able to take up your new post in London at the end of this month. Mother will be writing to you tomorrow, so I won't say any more here except that I wish I too were not disabled at this juncture.

Ever your affectionate father,

J. C.[2]

To Richard Curle

Text TS Indiana; Curle 117

[letterhead: Oswalds]
June 25th. 1923.

My dear Dick,

Thank you very much for all the trouble and thought you give to the success of the Hour-glass Edition.[3] To tell you the truth, the Richmond idea of giving a history of the books does not strike me as brilliant, as from its very nature it must be a second-hand thing, and, moreover, as those books are not depending upon any ideas their genesis can not be made to appear important.[4] Prefaces are in the light of personal confessions which can only interest somebody acquainted with the books, and it was on that assumption that they were written.

---

[1] The present whereabouts of the previous letter to Borys, mentioned in the letter to Eric Pinker of 21 June and quoted here by Conrad, is unknown. While on display at a conference in Marseilles in 1990, the MS vanished in suspicious circumstances.

[2] In this and the following letters, Conrad's initials show the effects of severe gout. A PS in Jessie Conrad's hand reads: 'I had wired you to Daimlers to-day pre-paid. Perhaps you haven't received it yet. I will write to you to-morrow. This is only to bring you my love. Your loving Mum'.

[3] The Uniform Edition published by Dent; see Conrad's letter to Hugh R. Dent of 7 March.

[4] Bruce Richmond, editor of the *Times Literary Supplement* (*TLS*), published Curle's article 'The History of Mr. Conrad's Books' on 30 August (p. 570). Conrad gave it a close reading; for his comments, see the letter to Curle of 14 July and *Documents*, pp. 185–204.

If you could say what sort of fiction mine is from the point of view of story-telling and hint at some characteristics, that, perhaps, would arouse curiosity. I am telling you what is in my mind but I can have no possible objection to anything you wish to do. I am very sure that even on the historical side you will do something excellent and infinitely helpful.

By all means, my dear, do try to infuse some spirit of enterprise into Dent. All your suggestions have my authority behind them. You may say that.

I don't know how to thank you for your unwearied friendship. Whatever you do will be well done.

Ever yours,

J. C.

To Eric S. Pinker

Text TS Berg; Unpublished

[letterhead: Oswalds]
June 25th. 1923.

My dear Eric,

The enclosed wire speaks for itself. As a matter of fact, from reports received about Borys's health we expected the necessity for him to have a change. Of course I have enough money in the bank to anticipate Doubleday's remittance, which after all strictly speaking is due on the 1st; but I am not able to write out a cheque yet, having been recommended not to use the right hand before it has thoroughly recovered. And to tell you the truth, even if I could I would rather avoid a cheque for Borys to go through my bank. Will you then be kind enough to let him have the money now, at 9 Glenthorne Grove, Brooklands, Cheshire, and I will write you a cheque this week.

We need not communicate with Doubleday at all, as I will tell Borys that he can repay me with the endorsed draft when it reaches him.

On Friday evening I had a sort of relapse, but now a decided improvement, both as to the pain and general feeling, has taken place. All I have been able to do till now is to correct Fisher Unwin's proofs with Miss H's help.[1]

Ever affectionately yours,

J. C.

---

[1] Of *The Rover*. This same day Miss Hallowes typed the following letter to Jean-Aubry on Conrad's behalf (Yale): 'Dear Mr Aubry, Mr Conrad has been laid up with a bad wrist and is still in bed, and so asks me to send you his love and thanks for your letter. He wants me to tell you that – luckily as it has turned out – he has had no invitation from the Embassy, which of course it would have been impossible for him to accept. He will write to you directly he is able to do so. Yours sincerely, L. M. Hallowes'.

To Eric S. Pinker
Text TS Berg; Unpublished

[letterhead: Oswalds]
June 27th. 1923.

My dear Eric,

Thanks for all you have done. I am decidedly on the mend and have the hand out of cotton-wool for the first time to-day, but must not use it yet. Re the Fine Edition.[1] I enclose here the last letter written by Miss H. to Fisher Unwin on the matter and his reply to the same. Mr. J. C. objects definitely to the Fine Edition in England, for reasons which he will not state at length here but which have some weight, both sentimentally and practically. Therefore that matter is decided – against.

I do not think F U can do it against our wishes, as there is nothing of the kind stipulated in any contract.

No more at present except to tell you that I am proceeding as fast as I can with correcting proofs for Unwin, which will establish the final text, a duplicate of which may be sent to America any time now, as far as the first half of the book is concerned. The "first instalment" proof of the serial arrived two days ago. It bears date of September number and an editorial note states that the tale will be completed in four instalments, which makes the last one December.[2]

Ever affectionately yours,

J. C.

To F. N. Doubleday [?][3]
Text MS draft telegram Berg;[4] Unpublished

Canterbury [Oswalds]
[Summer? 1923][5]

Telegram forgery. I never wired Doubleday on any subject whatever and did not give the editions a single thought since your visit here. The thing is absurd

---

[1] Unwin's rights to Conrad's work continued to complicate arrangements for collected editions with Dent in England and Doubleday in America. Unwin was publishing *The Rover*, and five other titles were included in Unwin's 'Adelphi Library': *Tales of Unrest, Almayer's Folly, An Outcast of the Islands, The Arrow of Gold,* and the posthumous *Tales of Hearsay.*

[2] *The Rover* was serialised in the *Pictorial Review* from September to December 1923.

[3] The mention of 'your visit here' points to either F. N. Doubleday or his son Nelson, as does the farewell 'Love from all'; since Conrad could be irascible even with his friends, the tetchiness of the last sentence does not stand in the way of these ascriptions.

[4] A transcription, not in Conrad's hand, of what may be a draft or the telegram itself.

[5] The Doubledays visited the Conrads in June 1923. Discussion of the collected editions, chiefly the Concord, ebbed and flowed during the summer, but there were periods in mid-July and the first three weeks in August, when the subject does not feature in the Doubleday correspondence and may not have been to the fore in Conrad's mind.

on the face of it. Pray set up enquiry about office of origin date and other circumstances of this stupid hoax. You must credit me if not with decency then at least with Sanity.

Love from all

Conrad

To Eric S. Pinker

Text TS Berg; Unpublished

Oswalds.

July 2nd. 1923.

Dearest Eric

I am just dropping you a line to tell you that I am still alive and at any rate beginning to kick.

I will be posting to you the "Christmas at Sea" article to-morrow afternoon. It has got to be put into shape and re-typed. It is about 800 words, but those people will be at liberty to cut it down to suit their space.

All the corrected proofs of "The Rover" have been sent to F. U. on Saturday. Have you heard from Effendi whether he would like to set up on his side from the corrected proofs? That of course would make the two texts identical. In a letter which he must have had by the mail-boat following his departure I asked him to say yes or no in a cable letter to your office.

Jessie has asked me about Mrs George's allowance, which she generally gets by cheque from you. It is provided for in the budget.

I don't send you a cheque for the £50 which you have been good enough to send to Borys, because, as usual, I have more bills to settle than I anticipated. I could do it; but it would leave me stranded for a time; and, anyhow, you will be able to settle the thing automatically on the 15th next. Do you agree?

The signed sheets for Sp. edition of "The Rover" in America[1] are going by this Wed. packet.

I may not be a man of my word, but I am an honest sort of chap, and therefore I ask you to debit my account with £5 com[mission] on the article bespoken to measure by the Evening News which appeared some time in May.[2]

Ever affcly Yours

J. C.

---

[1] Limited to 377 numbered copies and a few more for presentation, this US edition was published on 30 November; the regular US edition appeared the next day, and the first English edition on 3 December.

[2] Written on board the *Tuscania*, 'Ocean Travel' appeared in the London *Evening News* (15 May 1923), p. 4, under the title 'My Hotel in Mid-Atlantic'. Conrad took £50 for it, and owed Pinker a commission of 10 per cent.

To Eric S. Pinker
Text MS Berg; Unpublished

[Oswalds]

[3 July 1923][1]

Dearest Eric.

Voilà. Good measure just over 1000 w.

I suppose (if free to do so) you might manage to place in this country also.[2]

Ever Yrs

JC

To Aniela Zagórska
Text MS copy Yale;[3] Najder 291

Oswalds,

3. 7. 23.

Dear Aniela,

Please forgive me, but just think that immediately upon my return from America I began to suffer from gout in my right arm. I couldn't write and I didn't want to dictate [. . .][4] Thank you for the copies of the "Nigger." I like the translation and I am certain that it was a very difficult affair.[5] But what gives me the greatest pleasure is the translation of the preface; your work has succeeded admirably – a true gift of your faithful and inestimable friendship and your support. I kiss your hands and embrace you with true gratitude.

I shall not write more as it is still difficult for me. Jessie sends her love.

Yours with all my heart

Konrad.

---

[1] Dated by the previous letter. The MS of 'Christmas Day at Sea' is dated '1st July '23'.
[2] In Britain, 'Christmas Day at Sea' appeared in the Christmas Eve issue of the *Daily Mail* (p. 4).
[3] Zagórska's French translation of the original, which was destroyed in 1944.
[4] When translating, Zagórska evidently cut some of the Polish text.
[5] *Murzyn z załogi "Narcyza"* (Warsaw: Ignis, 1923), Jan Lemański's translation of *The Nigger of the 'Narcissus'*. Conrad was less enthusiastic about it in the letter to Winawer of 9 September. It was vol. III of Zagórska's edition of the selected works, but the second to be published.

To J. St Loe Strachey

Text TS Lords; Stape (1989), 233

[letterhead: Oswalds]
July 4th. 1923.

Dear Mr Strachey[1]

Two or three days after my return from America I had the misfortune to get a bad wrist (gout), but I hoped for a prompt improvement – I ought to have known better – and put off acknowledging your most welcome letter until I could do so in pen and ink. I hope you have not misunderstood the delay. Its cause is nothing more reprehensible than sheer, senseless optimism.

It was my great luck and privilege to be able to withdraw from the muddle of merely superficial new impressions to commune quietly with your orderly and consistent pages which were as welcome as the voice of an old friend heard in a foreign land.[2] Apart from that, and the interest of the subject matter, a fundamental sympathy with the feelings disclosed, the opinions expressed in their steadfast sincerity and the touching dignity of many passages, made the closing of the book at the end resemble a parting from a friend for whom one has the greatest esteem and, allow me to say, affection. I am very glad to hear that you are preparing another book.

It is very kind of you to suggest that I should write something for the "Spectator".[3] My impressions of America, thin as they are, are not clarified yet. There is still a cloud of preconceived notions, a priori conclusions, perhaps prejudices, floating about, unsettled, after the short contact with things as they are. And frankly I must confess to you that I do not know *what* they really are. As in speaking to you I would be ashamed of being anything less than honest I will not conceal that I am not as confident as to the future as you seem to be. Certainly, I have been impressed by the possibilities concealed in that enormous, vague and unfenced piece of ground. And suppose that vast (more or less kinsmen's, I admit) plantation turned out to be, morally and politically, nothing but a bed of nettles, ungraspable by its nature and terrifying by its size!

---

[1] Evelyn John St Loe Strachey (1860–1927) was editor and proprietor of the *Spectator* from 1897 to 1925. A cousin of Lytton Strachey and grandson of John Addington Symonds, the Oxford-educated Strachey was an ardent promoter of Anglo-American friendship. Under his management, the *Spectator* became the most influential English weekly in the colonies and the United States. Strachey wrote several books, including a historical novel, *The Madonna of the Barricades* (1925). In 1897, while editor of the *Cornhill Magazine*, he published Conrad's story 'The Lagoon'.

[2] Strachey's *The Adventure of Living: A Subjective Autobiography* (Hodder and Stoughton, 1922).

[3] In a letter dated 13 June, Strachey had invited Conrad 'to write something for the *Spectator* upon some point in America that struck him' (Stape and Knowles, pp. 210–12).

All this entre nous. Of course I may be utterly wrong, I may be even absurd, but you must forgive an old European (who by the strongest possible affinity of heart and mind is also a good Englishman) for unveiling to you the innermost trend of his thought on this, in any case, momentous problem. Au fond, I am in sympathy with your views. The coalescence of which you think is probably unavoidable, but my attitude towards it is not that of hope but really of resignation . . . It occurs to me that if I can't help going on like that I had better stop.

Please give my cordial greetings to your son, with the acknowledgments due from a slow but industrious author to an appreciative "reader of his works."[1] And, by the way, speaking of a very different sort, there are on my table fifteen letters (American) all from readers of my works – everyone of them asking for an autograph. And I can't write them! The most I can hope for is to be able to sign this letter, (which it is about time I did) with the assurance of the greatest regard and grateful thanks for your friendly communication.

Cordially yours

Joseph Conrad

To F. N. Doubleday
Text MS draft Yale; Unpublished

[Oswalds]

[6? July 1923][2]

Doubleday Garden City

Rover proof left on the fourth. Hope to hear by next post good news from you. Our love to you both. May and Cornelia[3] left here to day for Paris all well

Your affon^te

Jessie & Joseph

---

[1] The idea for a *Spectator* article had come from Strachey's son, Evelyn John St Loe Strachey (1901–63), described by his father as 'a very ardent admirer' of Conrad. The younger Strachey had just forsaken the Conservative *Spectator* for the Independent Labour Party's *New Leader*; in 1924, he ran for Parliament as a Labour candidate.

[2] Conrad wrote this draft message on a Marconigram from Doubleday which reached London on 6 July at 8.03 am; it reads: 'Letter received many thanks forward Rover.' Thus the date would be the 6th or not long after.

[3] Safford.

To G. Jean-Aubry

Text TS Yale; J-A, 2, 315

Oswalds,
Bishopsbourne,
Kent.
July 7th. [1923][1]

Mon très cher.

I must dictate this, for writing is still very difficult. And I dictate it in English because it is easier to dictate. You will forgive me.

I quite imagine how busy you must be in Paris. C'est dans votre caractère. I never remember you otherwise but with your hands full. It was very good of you to find time for your most welcome letter. I can't imagine how the tale of a visit to Paris had got about. I would certainly like to go there but it is out of the question for the present.

I have done nothing but a short and insignificant article for an Am. paper, and I certainly do not feel very happy just now.

Please, my dear Jean, come to see us as soon as you can after your return to London, which will be, I reckon, about the 20th of this month. I hope meantime to get hold of "The Suspense" again and be in a better frame of mind.

Jessie sends you her love.

Je vs embrasse

Votre vieux

Conrad

To Edward Garnett

Text MS Indiana; Unpublished

[letterhead: Oswalds]
7. 7. 23

Dearest Edward.

I was laid up with a bad wrist but can now write – in this fashion.[2]

Drop us a line to say when You think You will be able to spare us a day, *at least*, here.

Our love to You.

Ever Yours

J. Conrad

---

[1] Allusions to *Suspense*, 'Christmas Day at Sea', and gout suggest the year.
[2] In a hand not so much feeble as awkward and unusually large.

To Eric S. Pinker
Text MS Berg; Unpublished

[letterhead: Oswalds]
9. 7. 23.

Dearest Eric.

I will come up on Thursday unless I hear to the contrary.

I think it would be only civil to ask A. Page[1] to lunch. I suppose You have no insuperable objection to R A C.

I will be in Your office about 12.30 and we could pick him up on the way – that is if he attends at H[einemann]'s office[2] – about 1 o'clock.

I have plunged into Suspense. Well there is only that to think of and stick to.

Should you hear from the D. Mail about *Xmas at Sea* (of which McLeod[3] knows) I suppose we could accept £50. – But that's for You to say.

Ever affectly Yours

J. Conrad.

Give my love to Ralph.

To F. N. Doubleday
Text TS/MS Princeton; Rude (1974) (in part)

Oswalds
Bishopsbourne
Kent.
July 10th. 1923.

My dear Effendi,

This day, very fine and hot, began happily with the receipt of your most welcome letters from the "Olympic" and from Garden City.

I have followed you day by day in my thoughts across the ocean, and now my spirit is haunting Effendi Hill – though of course you are unable to see it. But I assure you it is there all the time. Meantime the body of J. C. after having been in bed for some days has, for this week past, been for the

---

[1] Arthur W(ilson) Page (1883–1960), the son of Walter Hines Page (Doubleday's partner and American Ambassador to Great Britain from 1913 to 1918), began working for Doubleday in 1905, eventually becoming vice-president of the magazine department and succeeding his father as editor of the *World's Work*. He later joined the telephone company AT&T as a vice-president and public-relations specialist, and served as a consultant to several American presidents. Conrad had dined with Page's mother and sister in Boston during his American tour.

[2] 'Attends' is a Gallicism. Doubleday held a controlling interest in William Heinemann & Co.

[3] Lewis Rose Macleod (1875–1941) was literary editor of the London *Daily Mail*, 1916–24.

most part sitting close at its literary table and attempting to get hold of the "Suspense" in an effective and practical way.

I have been much cheered by your good letter and the sight of the Concord Edition advertisement. It is an excellent conception and brings the reality of the new edition vividly before my eyes. I can see a mile-long row of volumes in cases vanishing at one end and growing at the other for years and years. My belief in the Concord Edition is absolute and indestructible. There is an atmosphere of good luck and good-will about it which no other scheme seems to have had in the same degree. When my thoughts go back to that morning when, in the soft light filtered through young foliage into the room beyond the billiard-room, we agreed on the name, and you explained to me the form and get-up of that edition – you and I alone, with the protecting personality of Florence hovering in the near background – I grow tenderly (and cheerfully) sentimental. I beg you both to believe that I am speaking seriously.[1]

I suppose I am right in taking it that "The Rover" will appear (to the general public) in two shapes only. That is: The Deep Sea and The Concord.

As to the *de luxe* copies of "Rover" it is a very great satisfaction to me to know that you and your experts' opinion is so positive as to its success at the higher price. You would have received by this time the signed sheets. I completed the signatures as soon as the improvement in the state of my wrist allowed me to do. I am very glad I did it because afterwards it got worse again for a time. However now the bandages are off and we will call this episode closed.

Curle was here this last weekend and very full of his talk with you. You have made his conquest. Both he and Eric appreciate very much your readiness to help towards a success on this side. As to what you say of your visit to the Dent family I must confess I expected to hear something of the kind. The immovability of the people on this side is exasperating, and hopeless too. Thank you very much for your friendly action.

Since we are talking of Dent, I am reminded to send you by the same mail with this a copy of Dent's School Edition composed of "Youth" and "Gaspar Ruiz". You will see that I gave him an Author's Note for it of an explanatory nature, and that the book has been furnished with a set of rather

---

[1] The Concord Edition has a frontispiece to each volume; most are photographs of scenes relevant to Conrad's life and work, others are facsimiles of documents. Before sailing home, Conrad told a journalist 'That he selected this name . . . because of the peculiar connotation the word has with American and British ideals and because of the beautiful sound of the word itself', *New York Times*, 3 June, p. S5. Americans would also associate the name with the village in Massachusetts, the War of Independence, Hawthorne, and the Transcendentalists. Signifying this New England *pietas*, the emblem of the Minute Man, a citizen soldier with his plough and rifle, appears on the half-title; for Conrad's reactions, see the letter to Doubleday of 6 December.

intelligently conceived questions.[1] I call your attention to this feature in view of your plans for getting my works read in schools. My feeling is that scholastic editions should be differentiated and given a particular appearance. If you really think of exploiting that line (and in view of acquainting the younger generation with my prose it would be worth doing) I am ready to furnish you with explanatory notes of the kind I prepared for Dent. As to the catechism at the end intended to assist and guide the teachers I wouldn't know how to compose it. In the case of this one I am really impressed by the skill and judgment displayed in arousing and guiding literary appreciation in the mind of a school boy or girl. Even if the child did not attempt to answer the questions they are bound to make him think. We could find here a competent man to do the work for a small fee. Now, I may be wrong, but it seems to me that a school series advertised as containing author's remarks and a syllabus of that kind (proving that a really educative production is meant) would attract attention. I am not thinking of myself only. I suggest that educational "selected" editions of a few American authors would be a new and worthy series for the Garden City Press to put forth.

Pardon me taking this liberty.

Thank you very much for the remittance to B which you advise me of. He has been laid up with influenza and generally I am a little worried about the situation.

I am glad, my dear friend, that you like the cigar case and that Keatings cigars lasted you for the voyage. Good little man, that. And by the bye: could you print a few extra copies of *de luxe* Rover for presents? I would like to give K one; and there are Mrs. C. James and Mrs. Morrow.[2] But perhaps you don't approve of presentation copies of that kind? If so I take it all back.

I am writing to dear Florence by this packet.

Our love to you both.

Ever your old

J. Conrad.

---

[1] Miss Hallowes had written to J. M. Dent on 22 June asking for a copy. A small volume, designed to slip into a pocket or school satchel, it was published in 1920 in the series The King's Treasuries of Literature, whose general editor was the academic and man of letters Sir Arthur Quiller-Couch. The stories are followed by the Author's Note (pp. 165–8), a 'Conrad Catechism', drawn up by Dr Richard Wilson and 'approved by the author in the spring of 1920' (pp. 171–8), and a brief essay by Guy N. Pocock (pp. 181–9).

[2] Probably the poet and educator Elizabeth Reeve Cutter Morrow (1873–1955), who became the first woman President of Smith College in 1939. In 1903, she had married Dwight Whitney Morrow, a banker and politician who served in France as General Pershing's chief civilian aide.

My kindest regards to S Everitt, Mr Russell and all your "band of brothers".[1]
I have had a charming letter from Mrs Patty[2] to whom I am writing.

To [?]

Text Mursia (1980) facsimile; Mursia (1983), 145 and facsimile 113

Oswalds
Bishopsbourne,
Kent.
July 10th. 1923.

My dear Sir,[3]
I have just read your friendly and interesting letter.

Without referring to the book from which you quote (I refrain on purpose)
I don't think there can be any difficulty in us understanding each other. What
I meant to say, exactly, was that the mastery of art and also of life consists in
the imaginative rendering (or view) of one's own experience (with, of course,
all its mental and emotional associations); and this, if I understand your letter
rightly, is what we both have been doing in our writing.

I am afraid that you may find this answer unsatisfactory, but I assure you
that whatever I may have written in the book you quote, this was all I meant
to say.[4]

With my best wishes for your success in our damnable trade,
Believe me

very sincerely Yours
J. Conrad.

To Richard Curle

Text TS/MS Indiana; J-A, 2, 316; Curle 118

[letterhead: Oswalds]
July 14th. 1923.

My dearest Dick
I am returning you the article[5] with two corrections as to matters of fact
and one of style.

---

[1] Shakespeare's *Henry V*, 4.3.60: 'We few, we happy few, we band of brothers'.
[2] Doubleday's daughter-in-law, Martha.   [3] Unidentified.
[4] Mursia suggested that the unknown correspondent might have been referring to Conrad's
essay 'Books', which opened *Notes on Life and Letters*, at this time Conrad's latest volume.
[5] Curle's 'The History of Mr. Conrad's Books' was a general survey of Conrad's canon, meant
also to publicise Dent's Uniform Edition. Curle took Conrad's suggestions. The draft (TS
Virginia) shows MS revisions in the hands of Conrad and Miss Hallowes (*Documents*, pp. 185–
204).

As it stands I can have nothing against it. As to my feelings that is a different matter; and I think that, looking at the intimate character of our friendship and trusting to the indulgence of your affection, I may disclose them to you without reserve.

My point of view is that this is an opportunity, if not unique then not likely to occur again in my lifetime. I was in hopes that on a general survey it could also be made an opportunity for me to get freed from that infernal tale of ships, and that obsession of my sea life which has about as much bearing on my literary existence, on my quality as a writer, as the enumeration of drawing-rooms which Thackeray frequented could have had on his gift as a great novelist.[1] After all, I may have been a seaman, but I am a writer of prose. Indeed, the nature of my writing runs the risk of being obscured by the nature of my material. I admit it is natural; but only the appreciation of a special personal intelligence can counteract the superficial appreciation of the inferior intelligence of the mass of readers and critics. Even Doubleday was considerably disturbed by that characteristic as evidenced in press notices in America, where such headings as "Spinner of sea-yarns – master-mariner – seaman writer" and so forth predominated. I must admit that the letter-press had less emphasis than the headings; but that was simply because they didn't know the facts. That the connection of my ships with my writings stands, with my concurrence I admit, recorded in your book[2] is of course a fact. But that was biographical matter, not literary. And where it stands it can do no harm. Undue prominence has been given to it since, and yet you know yourself very well that in the body of my work barely one-tenth is what may be called sea stuff, and even of that, the bulk, that is "Nigger" and "Mirror", has a very special purpose which I emphasise myself in my Prefaces.

Of course there are seamen in [a] good many of my books. That doesn't make them sea stories any more than the existence of de Barral in "Chance" (and he occupies there as much space as Captain Anthony) makes that novel a story about the financial world. I do wish that all those ships of mine were given a rest, but I am afraid that when the Americans get hold of them they will never never never get a rest.

The summarising of Prefaces, though you do it extremely well, has got this disadvantage that it doesn't give their atmosphere, and indeed it can not give their atmosphere, simply because those pages are an intensely personal expression, much more so than all the rest of my writing, with the exception of the "Personal Record" perhaps. A question of policy arises there: whether it is a good thing to give people the bones, as it were. It may destroy their

---

[1] Twenty years earlier, he had asked: 'Is not Thackeray's penny worth of mediocre fact drowned in an ocean of twaddle?' (*Letters*, 2, p. 418).

[2] Curle's *Joseph Conrad: A Study* (1914).

curiosity for the dish. I am aware, my dear Richard, that while talking over with you the forthcoming article, I used the word historical in connection with my fiction, or with my method, or something of the sort. I expressed myself badly, for I certainly had not in my mind the history of the books. What I was thinking at the time was a phrase in a long article in the Seccolo*.[1] The critic remarked that there was no difference in method or character between my fiction and my professedly autobiographical matter, as evidenced in the "Personal Record". He concluded that my fiction was not historical of course but had an authentic quality of development and style which in its ultimate effect resembled historical perspective.

My own impression is that what he really meant was that my manner of telling, perfectly devoid of familiarity as between author and reader, aimed essentially at the intimacy of a personal communication, without any thought for other effects. As a matter of fact the thought for effects is there all the same, (often at the cost of mere directness of narrative) and can be detected in my unconventional grouping and perspective, which are purely temperamental and wherein almost all my "art" consists. That, I suspect, has been the difficulty the critics felt in classifying it as romantic or realistic. Whereas, as a matter of fact, it is fluid, depending on grouping (sequence) which shifts, and on the changing lights giving varied effects of perspective.

It is in those matters gradually, but never completely, mastered that the history of my books really consists. Of course the plastic matter of this grouping and of those lights has its importance, since without it the actuality of that grouping and that lighting could not be made evident any more than Marconi's electric waves could be made evident without the sending-out and receiving instruments. In other words, without mankind my art, an infinitesimal thing, could not exist.

All this, my dear fellow, has apparently no reference to your article, but truly enough is extracted from me by a consideration of your article. My dearest fellow, I can not, (I would never dream!) tell you what to publish and what not to publish; but as far as America is concerned I am a little bit alarmed, for the reasons stated above. I would take the privilege of our friendship to point out to you too that things written for a friend in a copy of a book, in a particular mood and in the assurance of not being misunderstood, look somewhat different in cold print.[2] And then I wonder whether, quoting

---

[1] Untraced. There were at least two daily papers of this name: *Il Secolo XIX* of Genoa and *Il Secolo* of Milan. Emilio Cecchi (see the letter to him of 21 November) wrote on Conrad for the latter, but this piece does not appear in any edition of his collected literary journalism.

[2] Conrad's inscriptions to Curle were privately printed in 1925 in a limited edition of 100 copies as *Notes by Joseph Conrad Written in a Set of His First Editions in the Possession of Richard Curle*, with a preface by Jessie Conrad.

me as an authority on myself, is a discreet thing to do. I always come back to my first statement that this is an opportunity that will never be renewed in my life-time for the judgment of a man who certainly knows my work best and not less certainly is known for my closest intimate, but before all is the best friend my work has ever had.

Jessie and I are very delighted at your having met B in that friendly manner, and by your good impression as to his health and his optimistic mood. I went up yesterday in the hope and indeed for the purpose of bringing about a personal interview. That's why I did not tell you of my coming. I was somewhat affected by the heat and bolted home by the 4.20. My wrist has got achey again or else I would have written in pen and ink, and I trust expressed myself better.

    Our love to you,

Ever Yours

J. Conrad.

To Florence Doubleday

Text J-A, 2, 319

15. 7. '23, Oswalds.

The Oswaldians,
a serial[1]
(not for the press)

My dear Florence,[2]

I missed a mail in my answer to your delightful postscript in F. N. D.'s letter because it went too much against the grain to communicate with you by dictation.

I am trying to forget the distance that separates me from you and F. N. D. It is too many miles and too many days not to depress one somewhat. When I think that it will be more than a week before you read this I feel like a man separated from his friends by an enormous and bottomless chasm and trying to shout across. Very poor comfort that, even if you are sure that your voice will carry so far. The futility of shouting as a means of expressing one's deeper sentiments, such as affection, for instance, comes home to one appallingly. However I must begin my shouting before my heart fails me.

---

[1] Named, perhaps, with a smile towards Howard Talbot and Lionel Monckton's musical comedy *The Arcadians*, a gently satirical story of worldly metropolitans and innocents from the far side of the world. First staged in 1909 (London) and New York (1910), it was popular all through the First World War and beyond, and made into a film in 1927.

[2] Florence Doubleday (née Van Wyck, 1866–1946), married F. N. Doubleday, who was a widower, in 1918. She was active in civic, political, and cultural affairs in and around New York. Her memoir, *Episodes in the Life of a Publisher's Wife*, appeared in 1937.

Imprimis: the Safford women came, conquered – and went. Of course everything that's nice goes too soon. They were both perfectly delightful – mother and child. We got all extremely chummy together in no time, in the warm whiff of the Effendi Hill atmosphere they brought with them, and in the evocation of certain (invisible) personalities: R. F. & F.,[1] P[atty] & N[elson] round whom our talk revolved. In the afternoon Miss Hallowes took them over to Canterbury for a visit to the Cathedral. I don't know what their appreciation of Gothic architecture may be but I know that they were very much amused by the verger who took them round. He, I believe, was Gothic too. In the evening we talked late. Later still (at one o'clock in the morning) I detected a flow of lively murmurs in Jessie's bedroom. I put in just a little ferocity into the polite tone of my remark (through the closed door) that it was time for travellers to be in bed. Then a great silence fell on Oswalds and my conscience found peace. Cornelia had the sense to retire at 9. She is a dear. On parting we fell into each other's arms; and I must say that tho' Mrs. Safford is just right as she is I regretted she could not go back to her twelfth year for a moment and be hugged too before being helped into the car. I helped her in "frigidly" (that is in comparison with my feelings); the saturnine Charles[2] pressed the throttle . . .

We had charming letters from both of them from Paris . . . (To be continued.)

Jessie's love to you both. Give Effendi a slap on the back from me. The hearty kind you know. He is great – that's settled! I kiss your hands and am always your most faithful friend and devoted servant.

To Lorna Watson

Text J-A, 2, 318

Oswalds,

15. 7. '23

My dear Lorna,[3]

You will think I have neglected you heartlessly in your trouble. No, my dear. My sympathy was with you every day, but I had some trouble of my own of the mind (not broken bones) that prevented me using the pen.

Did the heat worry you much? Perhaps you have a nice airy room? I have to tell you that here the very gardens (we have three) felt hot and stuffy.[4]

[1] Unidentified.   [2] Vinten, also known as 'Long Charlie'.
[3] Lorna Maclaren Watson (1912–97; Mrs Frank H. Ralph Allen after 1943) was the daughter of Frederick William Watson (1885–1935) and his wife Hilda (née Jones, 1888–1954), and the granddaughter of Sir Robert Jones and the Scottish 'Kailyard' novelist 'Ian Maclaren' (the Revd John Watson, 1850–1907). She was eleven years old when Conrad wrote this letter.
[4] The weather had been humid, and, by the standards of the period, abnormally hot; on Wednesday the 11th, the temperature in London had reached 89° F (32° C).

My chauffeur's puppy would not play: Mrs. Conrad's chickens did nothing but stand in the shade and yawn: the flowers drooped their heads and no bird would touch a crumb on the lawn. And some of them were very good crumbs too. At 2 P.M. on Thursday last I watched from my chair a wagtail crossing our so-called tennis-court. He could hardly put one foot before the other; he was positively dragging his tail after him. I suppose no such sight was ever seen since the creation of wagtails. I could not bear it. I closed my eyes; and when I opened them (3 hours afterwards) the wagtail was not to be seen anywhere. I wish I knew what became of him.

What a tragic mystery.

I hope, my dear, your father and mother will bring you and your sisters here when you are well. It would be nice to see you running as if nothing had ever been the matter. Give my dear love to your Grandfather but don't tell him the story of the wagtail. He may not believe it – and that would hurt my feelings.

Your affectionate old friend.

To Richard Curle

Text TS Indiana; J-A, 2, 320 (in part); Curle 119 (in part)[1]

Oswalds.
July 17th. 1923.

Dearest Dick.

Thank you very much for your letter. I am afraid that my mind being very full of your article at this, what I consider as critical, period in the fate of my works, I absolutely forgot to thank you for the successful negociation with the Daily Mail;[2] though I meant to do it and, as a matter of fact, have been under the impression that I had done it. Eric had a letter from Macleod and the thing is settled. Thank you ever so much. The money, I think, from both sides won't be available till the end of the year, which is all right; for Eric will advance me the amount for doctors' bills (nearly £80 for the last quarter) and also in Sept. for the current quarter which probably will not be quite so much. This is a bad time for me because I have to pay local taxes for the half year, (some £35) and dressmakers' bill for about the same amount.

B. and his wife came here for the day last Sunday, by previous arrangement. It appears that there was a certain amount of trepidation on the other side – what about, God only knows. Neither Jessie nor I are of the sort to ask their son and daughter-in-law to come only to have their heads bitten off.

---

[1] Jean-Aubry and Curle leave no mention of the 'private affair' of Borys Conrad's visit; they also omit the visit from 'Bartimeus' and prune the remarks about national habits of reading.

[2] Placing 'Christmas Day at Sea'.

Anyway B's nervousness induced him to pass through Tonbridge and collect John to act as a buffer, or mascot, or whatever it was. But John too was very anxious. So when the car drew up at the door we beheld him sitting at the back looking about forty years old and frightfully responsible. Nothing could have resembled less a boy who has an unexpected day's leave from school. After all, I daresay, it helped over the first awkwardness. I behaved exactly as I would have done to any lady sitting at my right hand at lunch; the wife of a good air of dignity, but of course with the *two* boys in the house she could not have looked grumpy even if she had tried. The domestic play culminated in a sort of tableau about 4 o'clock, of Jessie sitting on a chair in the middle of the bowling-green with all the family squatting on the grass in a semi-circle in front of her. It must have been very impressive. I wish you had seen it. Then there was a sort of faint commotion in the direction of the house and who should appear on the scene but Bartimeus, of all people in the world![1] It appears that his wife and kids have been away for a month, and he was feeling lonely in the barracks in Chatham, so he came to see us, entirely unheralded. The poor fellow had lost his mother less than a month ago. We welcomed him duly and the rest of the day was very much like any Sunday on which there is "company" here. All the "company" left together at eight o'clock, B. giving our guest a lift as far as Sittingbourne. I will just add that the car contained also a large bunch of flowers and a garden hat, in a paper bag, from Jessie's private store of hats, and leave you to draw your own conclusions.

B. seized a moment to interview his mother and myself separately. I suppose he was less incoherent with her than with me, but it was all clear enough. I never saw him look less like a man who has something on his mind as when he said good-bye. John looked like a schoolboy again, and Mrs B. C. like the wife of a friend who feels pleased with her reception. Even poor Bartimeus looked brighter as he sat at the back completely over-shadowed by John. I have the impression that B's position with Daimlers is fairly secure. He reckons on an income of £500 a year, as from July 1st; which, he assures me, is sufficient. I too think it would be sufficient, if there were a ready-fitted home. That will be the difficulty; but after all he has £200 promised from me

---

[1] 'Bartimeus' was the pen-name of Lewis Anselm(o) da Costa Ricci (1886–1967). Born in London to a Portuguese family, he grew up in South Wales. His many volumes of stories and memoirs such as *Naval Occasions* (1914) and *The Navy Eternal* (1918) drew on his career as a cadet in *Britannia* and a naval officer. Eventually he rose to the rank of Paymaster Lt-Commander and became the royal family's first press-officer; by then, he had anglicised his name to Ritchie. For his letter to Conrad of 29 December 1923, see Stape and Knowles, p. 233.

in the course of the next twelve months. I can do no more. He had the first quarter from Doubleday a few days ago.

I tell you all this because I want you to know that this worry is off my mind. But that is a private affair. I am afraid, my dear, that you think that I am unduly worrying about the affair of publicity for my uniform edition here; but you understand that the moment is perhaps critical. It may fix my position with the buying public. I have always tried to counteract the danger of precise classification, either in the realm of exoti[ci]sm or of the sea; and in the course of years here and there I have had helpful paragraphs and articles in that sense. But they never amounted to much. Neither were my protests very effective. Truly I made no special efforts. But the situation now is worth the trouble of special handling. I don't mean on the point of literary appreciation, but simply of *classification.* You know how the public mind fastens on externals, on mere facts, such, for instance, as ships and voyages, without paying attention to any deeper significance they may have. If Richmond really wants this, you ought certainly to send it to him.[1] But I should have thought that his public is rather select and, in a sense, literary. It certainly will draw attention to the Edition, but the question is in which way? I have visited many foreign places and have been on board many ships. But so has the author of "Captain Kettle" of whom it used to be frequently stated that he "made a point of covering ten thousand miles of new ground every year."[2] The bulk of my last letter to you, my dear Dick, was not so much a suggestion as a sort of thinking aloud, for which I feel called to apologise, mainly on the ground that you knew all that before, and indeed had thought all that out for yourself. But if I may make a suggestion, what do you think of this? – Suppose you opened by a couple of short paragraphs of general observation on authors and their material, how they transform it from particular to general, and appeal to universal emotions by the temperamental handling of personal experience. You might also say that not everybody can do that, and then you might say "look at Conrad, whose new edition is coming out. It is a case in point.[3] His prefaces are now for the first time made accessible

[1] Bruce Richmond, of the *TLS.*

[2] The Captain Kettle books were among many works by the prolific adventure novelist C(harles) J(ohn) Cutcliffe Hyne (1865–1944).

[3] Curle's essay, as revised, begins: 'The material facts on which great novels are founded and the places in which they are enacted are of no vital importance because the supreme art of the novelist consists in transmuting the particular into the general. His appeal, in other words, is to universal emotions through the temperamental handling of universal experience. The works of Mr. Joseph Conrad are a case in point.'

to the public,[1] very characteristic of him and of special interest as he gives in many of them the genesis of the books, the history of initial suggestions. But all his stories expand far beyond their frame and appeal to no special public – looking for exoti[ci]sm, or adventure, or the sea – but to all of us who etc. etc." . . . All this of course short, and even crude if you like. You do know how to write pregnant sentences. Then the rest of the article a little shortened, say, for instance, by cutting out all mention of stories of which I say distinctly that I have no comment to make. Thus Richmond will get what he wants and you may save my hide from being permanently tarred.

Here both the readers and the press are more intelligent and will take the literary point at the beginning, but America is hopeless. There, the article being reproduced their silly brains will fasten on every geographical or ship's name connected with "Captain" Conrad, and the end of it as it stands now they will not only fail to understand, but they won't *see* at all. For it isn't a "story." This damned sea business keeps off as many people as it gathers in. It may have been otherwise twenty-five years ago. Now the glamour is worn off; and even twenty-five years ago the sea-glamour did not do much for the "Nigger".

But I daresay I am making all this fuss for nothing, and besides, no man can escape his fate.

Miss H. heard from T. J. Wise, who is at home now. Certainly, my dear, dispose of the stuff to him as soon as you like. It isn't anything of importance and I hope some other order of the kind will turn up, something better, which I would do in pen and ink and let you have.

A. Page is coming tomorrow, lunch, in a party of four. Business civilities. Damn expensive. Must be done.

Jessie sends her love

Ever Yours

J. Conrad.

To Eric S. Pinker
Text MS Berg; Unpublished

18.7.23
[letterhead: Oswalds]

Dearest Eric.

Thank[s] for your letter of this morning.

B and his wife were here for Sunday, bringing with them John who got a day's leave from school.

---

[1] In England they had appeared in Heinemann's limited collected edition, available only by subscription.

As far as this sort of thing can be satisfactory it was satisfactory. I was glad to have it over. We must now hope for the best.

I enclose here the two doctor's bills as you have agreed I should do.

A. Page & wife[1] left ½ an hour ago after a pleasant visit.

Ever affctly Yours

J. Conrad

To Eric S. Pinker
Text MS Berg; Unpublished

[Oswalds]
20. 7. '23

Dearest Eric.

I snatch this scrap of paper to say that Your view is right. I too had my doubts about the get up. This plan is better and we may be sure that there is no one in Garden City in the least inclined to ride for a fall.

Certainly my dear fellow. We'll be equally glad to see you and your Wife at any time when you can and feel like coming here.

No more at present. Our love to you both

Yrs

J. Conrad.

To Lewis Rose Macleod
Text MS Lubbock; Rude (1986) (in part)

[letterhead: Oswalds]
21. 7. '23

My dear Sir.[2]

Thanks for your good letter. Of course I'll be delighted to "foregather" when you return from your holiday, and – yes – we will let Curle come too though he may be a little young for the strong meat of our mature conversation. It will develop his mind. He's a promising boy.

I just had a note from him; from which I infer that it is about time he had a holiday. I hope both you and he will have a good and refreshing time while away from your Carmelite Convent.[3] Let me entreat you both to leave your

---

[1] Mollie Page (née Hall, 1896–1964) was active in charity work, gardening, and the Girl Scouts.

[2] Born in New Zealand to Scottish parents, Lewis Rose Macleod (1875–1941) began his journalistic career in New South Wales. In 1905 he moved to South Africa, where he became editor of the *Johannesburg Sunday Times*. From 1916 to 1924 he was literary editor of the London *Daily Mail*, where several of Conrad's essays first appeared. Macleod returned to Johannesburg in 1924 to edit the *Rand Daily Mail*.

[3] The *Daily Mail*'s offices were at New Carmelite House, Fleet Street, built on the site of a Carmelite (or White Friars) cloister. Conrad was baptised at the Carmelite monastery in

"cowls and habits" behind and be th[o]roughly "secular" in Your holiday proceedings into which I promise not to inquire too closely when we meet.

I was laid up and generally bothered with a lot of silly worries since my return from U.S.A. – else we would have asked you and Mrs Macleod to give us the pleasure of coming here for the day. Is it too late now? A Saturday. All we can offer is a sort of sit-in-the-garden and dream (if not exactly doze) day. And the journey *is* a grind. But the peace of this does not "pass understanding"[1] and you might find it useful if only for a few hours.

Very sincerely Yours
Joseph Conrad.

PS Text duly broken wherever I could crack it.

To Wilfred G. Partington

Text MS Williams; Unpublished[2]

[letterhead: Oswalds]
21. 7. '23

Dear Mr Partington

Many thanks for your letter and the copy of the Bookman's Journal. A very interesting number in every way.

My wife sends you her kind regards and thanks for the notice which is very much to her liking.[3]

My trip to the US was very pleasurable and in a way instructive. The weather was as admirable as the celebrated American hospitality. Praise can no further go.

I return the proof with a few corrections. I like the type very much and I know that the booklet will be a fine production.[4]

With our united regards, believe me

sincerely Yours
Joseph Conrad.

Berdyczów (Berdichiv, Ukraine) and claimed to have had Borys baptised at a convent of the order in London (*Letters*, 2, p. 23).
[1] Cf. 'The peace of God, which passeth all understanding' (Philippians 4.7 and the post-communion blessing in the *Book of Common Prayer*).
[2] Partington quotes the third paragraph in 'The Correspondence of Joseph Conrad', *Bookman's Journal*, 11.38 (November 1924), 86.
[3] Partington had reviewed *A Handbook of Cookery for a Small House* in the *Bookman's Journal*, 8.20 (May 1923), 48.
[4] Of *Laughing Anne*, which Partington was printing in a limited edition.

To [?]
Text BL RP 1873[1]

[letterhead: Oswalds]
21. 7. 23.

My dear Sir.[2]

Just a word to thank you for your book received yesterday. I am looking [forward] to reading it the very first day I can get a free moment to give myself up to it.

Yours faithfully

J. Conrad

To Richard Curle
Text MS Indiana; J-A, 2, 321; Curle 120 (in part)[3]

[Oswalds]
Monday
22. 7. 23

Dearest Dick.

The article as amended and added to by You is first rate.

I have ventured to compose the pars relating to M[irror] of the S[ea] and P[ersonal] R[ecord].[4] If your conviction will let them stand I would be glad. In a few other places I ventured a line or two in pen and ink.

As to *No[stromo]*. If I ever mentioned 12 hours it must relate to P[uerto] Cabello where I was ashore about that time. In LaGuayra as I went up the hill and had a distant view of Caracas I must have been $2\frac{1}{2}$ to 3 days. It's such a long time ago! And there were a few hours in a few other places on this dreary coast of Ven[ezue]la.[5]

Thanks a thousand times my dear fellow for Your work and thought and your inexhaustible patience. We are looking forward to your arrival on Sat. – or will it be Friday? Please drop me a line.

Would you mind to have the article typed in 2 cop: at my expense? I feel very depressed about the new edition for typographical reasons. In the

---

[1] Photocopy of unlocated MS.   [2] Unidentified.
[3] In the final paragraph, Curle omits all but the first sentence.
[4] For Conrad's contributions to the published text, see *Documents*, pp. 194, 196.
[5] In August and September 1876, Conrad sailed from Saint-Pierre, Martinique, to Cartagena (Colombia), Puerto Cabello and La Guaira (Venezuela), and back to Saint-Pierre. La Guaira is about 30 kilometres from Caracas, but the latter is between 900 and 1,000 metres higher, and thus visible on a clear day. Conrad was serving at the time as a steward in the *Saint-Antoine*, but she remained in port while Conrad was making his mysterious voyage. It may have involved smuggling weapons to the conservative Catholic faction in the Colombian civil war of 1876–7.

"double" vols the 2^d work has no title page.[1] My annoyance is extreme. The thing was understood.

Ever affectly Yours

J. Conrad.

To F. Warrington Dawson
Text TS/MS Duke; Randall 213[2]

[letterhead: Oswalds]
July 29th. 1923.

My dear Warrington.[3]

I met John Powell in New York and we talked of old times, mostly in affectionate reference to yourself, and with genuine sorrow at the heavy trial that fell to your lot. You were very much in my thoughts over there. From that land of novel experience and generous kindness I turned my eyes more than once towards Versailles where my second American friend (Crane was the first in time) gave us all – as I told J. P. – a great object lesson in serenity, courage, and undaunted fortitude.

My greatest regret was not to be able to visit the South. The time was short and the health too uncertain for that. So at least it seemed to me. Perhaps if you had been by my side – who knows! But this doesn't bear thinking about.

Certainly, my dear Warrington! You may do exactly what you like, and what you think best, for the object in view. Though, of course, I can not remember what I may have said in our many and intimate conversations, I can raise no objections to the text of the type-written pages you have sent me, and I sincerely rejoice that there is a publisher who seems to be taking the matter up properly. It appears, then, that good things can come even out

---

[1] The Dent Uniform Edition, which began to appear in 1923, has several such pairings, for example *Almayer's Folly* with *Tales of Unrest*, *The Mirror of the Sea* with *A Personal Record*.

[2] After wanting for many years to publish his letters from Conrad, Dawson worked fragments of this one into the Foreword to *The Crimson Pall* (Chicago: Bernard, 1927) alongside extracts from a critique of Dawson's work that Conrad had dictated to him in the summer of 1913; see Randall, pp. 63, 109, 212.

[3] (Francis) Warrington Dawson (1878–1962) came from a family of former plantation owners in Charleston, South Carolina. He wrote prolifically – fiction, essays, newspaper stories – and covered strikes, wars, peace conferences, and French politics. To quote Randall, 'he had a special taste and talent for conversing with the great and near-great' (p. 4). In 1909, while on a safari in East Africa with Theodore Roosevelt, he met Conrad's old friends the Sandersons, and when Dawson came to England in May 1910 to report the funeral of Edward VII, he carried an introduction to Conrad, to whom he introduced his fellow Southerner, the composer John Powell, in 1912. Subject after 1915 to attacks of psychosomatic blindness and paralysis, Dawson became increasingly confined to his apartment in Versailles.

of Chicago!¹ Does the "Virgin of Ivory" (très bien, ce titre) enter into the scheme of the contemplated publication?²

You are mistaken in thinking that you are no longer a memory for the boys. Even to John who was a very small boy when he saw you,³ you are a very living personality, as is evident from his talk. They both inquire after you constantly. I am living in hopes of coming over to France, (I mean Paris) in a not distant future; but there are many things in the way. You will be, of course, the first to hear of it directly the way is clear.

Jessie joins me in the expression of warm sympathy and love. She will be writing to you herself before long. She is still very crippled and often in pain – but there is some improvement.

Ever Yours

J. Conrad.

To Gordon Gardiner
Text TS Harvard; Unpublished

[letterhead: Oswalds]
July 29th. 1923.
(missed post 30ᵗʰ 7.23)

My dear Gardiner⁴

Curle has gone this morning after a short visit. He told me he had lunched with you; and said something about an operation being impending, which of course is disquieting. But being further questioned he also said you were looking well and seemed to have enjoyed your cruise.

Perhaps you will drop us a line to tell us something definite.

Curle is full of admiration for those personal pages of yours. The man is genuinely capable of judging, and so I rejoiced. I was delighted. But I was not surprised. The gift of narrative and characterisation seemed to me

---

¹ A play on the sceptical question from the Bible: 'Can anything good come out of Nazareth?' (John 1.46). The publisher was Bernard Bernard.

² Writing on the 20th, Dawson had told Conrad that he was just finishing a novel with this title set in France (Randall, p. 212).

³ In June 1914, when John was nearly eight.

⁴ An Aberdonian, Major Theodore James Gordon Gardiner (1874–1937), though troubled by ill health, had been a civil servant in South Africa, a tea planter in Ceylon, and a student at Harvard. After the First World War, in which he was involved in spy-hunting and the surveillance of enemy aliens, he worked as an arbitrator of industrial disputes and as Secretary of the National Club, London, a Christian society dedicated to improving 'the moral and social condition of the people'. His posthumous *Notes of a Prison Visitor* (1938) records his experiences of befriending convicts; he also published novels, and at his death was at work on a study of Napoleon. The friendship with Conrad began during the latter's visits to Scotland in 1916 and strengthened over the years.

your distinct gift, and I often thought of talking to you about it.[1] But you know I am always reluctant to urge a man to write; and I must say that your obstinate modesty about your powers made it seem indiscreet to insist. I have heard something about an arrangement having been arrived at with "Blue Peter".[2] The more obscure the periodical (providing it can pay something worth while) the better it is, in a way, from the point of view of eventual publication in book form. Am I right in thinking that this form of literary production comes easier to you than any other? In any case let me just drop a word as to husbanding your material. Don't think that talking to you like this I am like unto a scoundrel who adviseth the virtuous publican to put water in his beer.[3] No, it is the pronouncement of one who talks plain horse sense in a world in which the prodigal never gets the fatted calf.[4]

Jessie sends her love.

Yours ever

J. Conrad.

To Richard Curle

Text MS Indiana; Curle 121

[letterhead: Oswalds]
30. 7. 23

Dearest Dick

Ever so many thanks for your letter & enclosure.

It had been nice to have You here if only for a few hours.

M^r & Mrs A[lfred] B[orys] Conrad turned up suddenly in the afternoon – in quite good spirits but still homeless.

AB most appreciative of your friendliness. As he can get away for five days, they are coming here on Friday to stay with us (instead of B[road]stairs[5]) on their own as it were, with perfect liberty of movement –. They seem to like the idea – which was Jessie's.

She sends you her love.

Ever Yours

J. Conrad

Don't forget to present my duty.

---

[1] So far, Gardiner had published one novel, *The Reconnaissance* (1914). In 1928, he published a second, the Buchanesque *At the House of Dree*.

[2] *Blue Peter. The Magazine of the Sea, Travel and Adventure.* It took its name from the blue and white flag flown when a ship is about to sail.

[3] Despite the mock archaic language, not an allusion to the biblical publican (a collector of taxes for the Roman occupation) but the modern, inn-keeping kind, allegedly given to making his resources go further.

[4] As he does in the biblical parable of the Prodigal Son (Luke 15.11–32).

[5] A Kentish seaside resort.

To Florence Doubleday

Text MS Princeton; Unpublished

[letterhead: Oswalds]
30. 7. 23
6. pm.

Dearest Florence.

I hoped to send you an instalment of the serial[1] but a lot of things got in the way of literary composition, last week. So nothing but our love goes to you to-day.

F. N. D's letter just arrived. Will you O Gracious Lady of the Hill tell the Powerful Lord, Your husband that this toothless and insignificant person – he who writes these words – can not possibly object to his hideous countenance (limned by an Incomparable Artist) being imprinted on various books as suggested.

But Oh! I am grieved that the I. A.[?].[2] has failed with Effendi.

The sands are running out – the post is going – the fleet messenger waits.

Ever affectionately Yours

in haste

J. Conrad.

To F. N. Doubleday

Text MS Princeton; Unpublished

[letterhead: Oswalds]
[30 July 1923][3]

My dear Effendi.

Your good letter has just arrived, in time for me to acknowledge it by the Wednesday Packet.[4]

You have by this Pinker's cable and my week end letter expressing high approval of the changes, in the scheme of the Concord edition, you propose to make. The merit from every point of view being beyond question let us hope for just that grain of luck which tips the balance of success.

I tried last week to palm off on poor Florence a new serial "The Oswaldians". It is a worthless production and anyhow the 2^d instal^t is not ready. I do not know whether she will rejoice at that respite – but don't let her hope to escape the insipid tale.

---

[1] 'The Oswaldians'.

[2] The first initial could be read as 'I', 'J', or even 'S', but in the context, 'I[ncomparable] A[rtist]' makes most sense.

[3] The 'good letter' would be the one that arrived just as Conrad was writing to Mrs Doubleday.

[4] Transatlantic letters had to be posted on Mondays to catch the Wednesday packet service.

Our love to you both. We commend ourselves to Your memories.

Ever Your

J. Conrad

To Eric S. Pinker

Text MS Berg; Unpublished

[Oswalds]

31. 7. 23

Dearest Eric.

I hope You and your wife will enjoy your voyage of discovery in Wales and will manage to keep on good terms with these fierce mountaineers.

Thanks for communicating to me good Brand[t]'s letter.[1] I have not a distinct recollection of the conclusion we arrived at. On the face of it his letter shows that the stipulation of showing nothing but 100% MS to Editors was agreed to. But it is possible that in view of precedent action we took with the "Suspense", (and also of his strong wish to keep in with Lorimer[2]) I may have left in his mind a doubt whether that work was included. I am sure however that I made no definite promise.

It may turn out to be *inadvisable* from every point of view to impart fragments of 20.000 words.

I don't *feel* myself bound to do so.

Those people don't understand how my mind works in composition; and of course it is not a matter that can be explained to any one. We must take our own way – but we will do what we can for him. The most I have* could have said was "that I would see". A point may be reached when it could be done. I think that no painter could paint a historical composition (let us say) if every few days people (buyers?) came to look at it bringing into his studio an atmosphere of criticism and anticipation friendly no doubt, but profoundly disturbing by the very nature of things.

Give my love to your wife.

Ever affctly Yours

J Conrad.

---

[1] Carl Brandt's letter of 13 July (TS Berg; Stape and Knowles, pp. 213–14 [as 12 July]) reminds Conrad of his 'promise' to write a little note for his copy of *Nostromo*, and asks that their 'little agreement' to let 'Eric and myself have portions of anything new' apply 'to the book to follow the Mediterranean novel'. Conrad returned Brandt's letter to Pinker with a note on the verso: 'He's muddled. I believe he means the Rover by "The Med. Novel." I may have promised (perhaps!) to see what I could do towards letting him see the next 20000 of Suspense. That's what he means (?) Why! The next book after Suspense would be short stories. He apparently understood that. We, as it were, settled it. It seems he has tangled everything up. Yet he was calm – and I was too. These Americans are marvellous muddlers.'

[2] George Horace Lorimer (1867–1937), the editor of the *Saturday Evening Post*.

To Thomas J. Wise

Text MS BL Ashley 2953; Unpublished

[letterhead: Oswalds]

31. 7. 23.

My dear Mʳ Wise.

Thanks for your letter. I am not so indifferent to the fate of these pieces of paper which Quinn wants to sell now as not to prefer them to pass into your possession. But they have been out of my mind for a long time. Frankly I have had many other things to think about. I do not know how far I may trust my memory; but as far as my recollection goes I am fairly certain that: *Chance* – *Victory* – *Shadow-Line* – are complete, of the *novels*. And perhaps *Western Eyes*. Possibly *Secret Agent* (early form). Of the early books *The Outcast* is complete. *Al's Folly* all but Chapter X. *L. Jim. Nostromo* are mere fragments.

Pers. Record. is probably complete.[1] He has got a number of Short Stories belonging to that period too. But I can make no statement as to those (up to the Set of Six).

I believe he has all *Twixt Land & Sea* and *Within the Tides*.

But surely he can have no objection to giving all particulars to your agent – that is if [he] is disposed to sell privately. I fancy however he will put them up for auction.[2]

We are looking forward to Your visit with Mrs Wise.[3] Kindest regards.

Sincerely Yours

J. Conrad

Miss H. has volunteered to prepare you a list with particulars as far as our recollections go.

To Sir Sidney Colvin

Text MS Yale; Keating 360 (in part)[4]

[letterhead: Oswalds]

4. 8. 23.

My dear Colvin.[5]

I was more than glad to see your handwriting. I am touched by the thought and the time you have given to one who (whatever he may have

---

[1] Only one MS leaf of *A Personal Record* has survived (MS Syracuse); it never belonged to Quinn, and no TS is known.

[2] Quinn put his collection up for auction in New York three months later, in November 1923.

[3] Frances Louise ('Louie') Wise (née Greenhalgh, 1875–1939).

[4] Keating gives the bulk of the letter, but often resorts to paraphrase.

[5] Sir Sidney Colvin (1845–1927; knighted 1911) was among Conrad's closest literary friends. Conrad loved to read English poetry with him. Colvin had been Slade Professor of Fine Arts

been at one time) wears now the aspect (but not the heart) of a "graceless wretch".[1]

On my return from America I went home at once. We had to entertain in a small way my American hosts who had come over with me. I fully hoped to be in town again in a few days. Instead of which I had to go to bed with what seemed but a slight attack of gout yet made me feel uncommonly ill for days. That over I thought I would try to get hold of my work after that thoroughly disturbing interruption. (By this I do not mean the gout but the view of the "American Scene," as poor Henry James called it[2]). I found the job so difficult that I remained at it ever since holding on with clenched teeth. Bulldoggedly, as it were.

In all that time I was only in town once – on no pleasant errand. That being settled I felt so lame and impotent all round and *durch und durch*[3] (temp: 90° in shade) that I just crawled into the first South Eastern & Chatham train I could see (it happened to be the 4.20). I recovered sufficiently on my way home to have a bad time meditating on my total loss of all manly virtues. For indeed I had intended to present myself at the Residenz (in Palace Gardens) to kiss hands on my return and give a verbal report to both Your Serene Highnesses.[4] Of course I have no right to ask you to believe me. I have no rights – except such as mere compassion will accord to the most discredited of mankind.

But as your letter holds out a gracious promise of an audience (at any time) at the present Summer Palace[5] I will not give way to despair about myself.

The fact is that I must push on with my novel for the next 3 months. I can only do that to some purpose by segregating myself from my kind and cudgeling my wretched brains from morning to night. A dismal prospect. But it may come easier than I expect. It may! And then I will be able to allow myself a little latitude. Till then I trust the generosity and the affection of you

at Cambridge and Director of the Fitzwilliam Museum; from 1884 to 1912, he was Keeper of Prints and Drawings at the British Museum. Among his literary works were editions of Stevenson's letters and biographies of Walter Savage Landor and John Keats.

[1] These words have gone together since the seventeenth century, when they were linked in works by Bunyan, Congreve, and Dryden. Conrad, however, may have been quoting himself. Miss Jacobus uses the phrase in 'A Smile of Fortune', Ch. 4, p. 49.

[2] James's *The American Scene* (1907) renders his often unhappy impressions of the USA after almost thirty years of absence. He found the go-getting rowdiness of New York City particularly distasteful.

[3] 'Through and through'.

[4] As if at the palace of German princelings or grand dukes. The Colvins lived in Palace Gardens, the quietest and grandest street in Kensington.

[5] Probably E. V. Lucas's house at Tillington, near Petworth, West Sussex.

both not to cast out of your hearts one not easily forgetful but being wrought perplex'd in the extreme.[1]

Ever Yours

J. Conrad.

I kiss dear Lady Colvin's hands.[2] Both boys send their love. Jessie will be writing in a day or two.

To Gordon Gardiner
Text MS Harvard; Unpublished

[letterhead: Oswalds]

4. 8. 23

My dear Gardiner.

Thanks for your letter which, tho' it did not allay my concern, brought the relief, at least, of a definite statement. I understand your dislike and mistrust of surgical action. But my heart is heavy at the alternative of periodic pain which you are facing with such serenity!

In regard to the other matter (in which your pessimism is so uncalled-for as to be amusing) the exhortation I permitted myself in my last letter has also another bearing, which, I confess, was mainly in my mind. Though I am glad you don't mean to neglect the American field, I am afraid you will find it a most complicated affair – on account of copyright-securing regulations and of the "simultaneous pub^{on}" business. What I had in my mind however when writing was the economical use of "material", of your experience, of facts, sensations, impressions stored in your mind. It would be advisable often, to keep things, already at the tip of the pen, back for future use. Verb. sap.[3]

I hope you won't think me a "base, mercenary"[4] fellow, and break off relations after this. And *do*, when you come, bring some MS with you. I promise not to gush.

Ever Yours

J. Conrad

---

[1] In his final speech, Othello presents himself as 'one not easily jealous, but, being wrought / Perplex'd in the extreme' (5.2.345–6).

[2] Lady Colvin (née Frances Fetherstonhaugh, 1839–1924) had married Sidney Colvin in 1903; an essayist with a gift for literary friendship, she had been a second mother to Stevenson. See also the letter to her of 8 July 1924.

[3] *Verbum sapienti (sat est)*: 'A word to the wise is sufficient.'

[4] A commonplace found from the anonymous *Arden of Feversham* to Anthony Trollope's *The Eustace Diamonds*.

To G. Jean-Aubry
Text MS Yale; *L. fr.* 185[1]

[Oswalds]
5. Août. '23

Mon très cher.

Merci de Votre bonne lettre. On dirait – votre amitié ne dort jamais. J'ai été on ne peut plus intéressé par les détail[s] de vos activités que vous me donnez.

J'espère que le séjour dans Votre famille Vous fera du bien. Moi j'ai toujours l'impression que VS ne vous ménagez pas assez. Are you not overdoing it a little – mon cher Jean?

Jessie and the boys send their love. Nous avons ici Borys et sa femme pour quelques jours. Il fallait bien attendre cette assez sotte situation. Les deux personnes que ça regarde principalement ont l'air de se convenir parfaitement. Jessie en a pris son parti gracieusement. Moi aussi – a ma manière. Cet interlude e[s]t clos – et tout le monde en ressent un soulagement considérable.

J'ai le regret de Vous dire que *The Suspense* ne va pas. Ce livre m'a donné des mauvais moments. Enfin!

Oui mon cher. Je tiens beaucoup a mener Jean en France pendant Votre séjour près du Havre. J'ai fermement cette intention. Mais je n'en ai pas la certitude. Je vais vous écrire dans une dizaine de jours et alors, peut-être, Vous donner une date.[2] En ce moment j'attends la visite de Hugh Clifford. L'heure en a sonné. Donc je ferme ce petit [mot] pour ne pas perdre la poste.

Toujours votre vieux

J. Conrad

PS Rappelez moi au bon souvenir de M. et Mme Aubry.

My very dear fellow,

Thank you for your good letter. One would say – your friendship never sleeps. I have been most interested in the details of your activities.

I hope the time spent with your family will do you good. I've always had the impression that you don't take proper care of yourself. Aren't you overdoing it a little, my dear Jean?

Jessie and the boys send their love. Borys and his wife are here for a few days. This rather foolish situation was only to be expected. The two persons

---

[1] Jean-Aubry replaced the reference to Borys and his wife with 'B . . . et X . . .'.
[2] See Conrad's letter of 17 August.

chiefly concerned seem perfectly matched. Jessie has accepted the situation graciously. Me too – in my way. That episode is closed – to everyone's great relief.

I am sorry to tell you that *The Suspense* is not going well. That book has given me some bad moments. Well, enough of that!

Yes, my dear fellow, I very much want to bring John to France during your stay near Le Havre. It is my firm intention. But I am not sure of realising it. I shall write to you in a fortnight and then, perhaps, give you a date. At the moment I'm waiting for Hugh Clifford to arrive. The hour has struck. So I close this note in order to catch the post.

Ever your old

J. Conrad

PS Please remember me to M. and Mme Aubry.

To F. N. Doubleday

Text TS/MS Princeton; Unpublished

[letterhead: Oswalds]
Aug. 8th. 1923.

Dear Effendi,

Thank you for yours of July 27th. I am sorry I seemed to you in a muddle about the various issues of "The Rover". Your categoric statement makes it all extremely clear and I was very pleased to read it. You are very good and patient with me.

The fact is that the only edition I was in doubt of was the "blue cloth" (at two dollars). But that was before the modification in the get-up of the "Concord" had been adopted, and I may be excused for being momentarily in doubt on that point.

Now everything is clear and the whole scheme looks "perfectly lovely".

I have written to Florence last mail and I hope in time to prevent me being renounced, excommunicated, cast out into the outer darkness,[1] and generally annihilated. I am glad to hear that the Lady Commandant is well and cheerful.

Things here are settling down and humdrum life goes on undisturbed by any new hurricane.

---

[1] An echo of Matthew 8.12: 'But the children of the kingdom shall be cast out into outer darkness: there shall be weeping and gnashing of teeth.'

Curle's article for the "Times"[1] is quite a good thing from the publicity point of view and I hope you will find it suitable for America too. Curle himself has been staying with the Ranee of Sarawak[2] in the West and now is gone to Holland. He asked me to remember him to you both.

Beso las manos de la Excellentissima Señora and am always most
affectionately Yours
J. Conrad.

Love to Patty and Nelson.[3]

To Edward Garnett
Text TS/MS Indiana; G. 324

[letterhead: Oswalds]
Aug. 8th. 1923.

Dearest Edward.

I am sorry I put in an, apparently, unlucky form what I had to say about the two pieces of prose which you sent me. Don't forget, my dear, that I wrote to you, not to the young man;[4] therefore there could not be any question of putting the matter in a form which would spare his feelings. Neither did I wish for a moment to influence your opinion or your helpful attitude towards his work.[5] I repeat again that I may be utterly wrong as against your general judgment which was formed, also, on, no doubt correct, personal impression of a temperament (such as you describe it) attempting to express itself in terms of art.

It was that attempt alone on which I concentrated – on the actual pages before me, which, ex-hypothesi, ought to have been revelatory. I mean the

---

[1] It would appear in the *TLS* on 30 August.

[2] Lady Margaret Alice Lily Brooke, Dowager Ranee of Sarawak (née de Windt, 1849–1936), the estranged wife of Rajah Charles Brooke of Sarawak, was a well-known figure in London literary and artistic circles; Conrad, Henry James, Edmund Gosse, and R. B. Cunninghame Graham ranked among her many correspondents or frequented her salon.

[3] Doubleday's daughter-in-law and son.

[4] This letter has not survived, and was not in the sale of Garnett's letters from Conrad and Hudson (New York: American Art Association, 24 and 25 April, 1928).

[5] The 'young man' was the Irish fiction writer Liam O'Flaherty (1897–1984), one of Garnett's protégés, a son of the Aran Isles. In the summer of 1923, O'Flaherty was working on what became his best-known novel, *The Informer*, which deals with such Conradian topics as loyalty, conspiracy, and betrayal. For samples of the intense correspondence between him and his mentor, see George Jefferson, *Edward Garnett* (Cape, 1982), pp. 206–18. Around 1930, O'Flaherty published the pamphlet *Joseph Conrad: An Appreciation* (E. Lahr, n.d., Blue Moon Booklets, no. 1).

pages, not the subjects. Subjects in themselves never appear revelatory to me, if only because subjects are, so to speak, common property, lying about on the ground for one man after another to pick up and handle. That is what makes a subject such an insignificant thing, and also invests it with the potentiality of almost infinite suggestion. It depends really on him who picks it up.

The possession of a special temperament ought to make itself felt in the expression. I quite believe that his temperament is such as you describe it to me; but the fact is, my dear Edward, that somehow or other The Cow, as you told it to me, in say, about a hundred words, impressed me much more than the column of print which I read.[1] You don't know how good you were in your extremely simple resumé. And that not by any means as a result of some trick of a born raconteur. You certainly haven't got them. You displayed neither animation, nor conventional fluency; yet, as I often remarked when talking with you, your personality came through somehow, made the thing significant and distinctly worth hearing.

I felt nothing of the kind when reading the article. That's what it all amounts to. I will not for a moment suppose that you are wrong in your opinion as to the possibilities of future productions from that pen. But he, obviously, should be warned against a careless use of words and a too close contemplation of his subject. That of course doesn't mean that he should be told to *strive* for a personal expression. No! It is either in him or it is not in him. But a certain fastidiousness which would prevent him from putting down the first words that came into his mind ought to be cultivated, or else both his sympathies and his indignations will lose much of their force.

But who am I to lecture anybody, who have reasoned out and meditated so many pages of my own only to give them up in despair! My feelings ought to have nothing to do with this letter, or perhaps with any letter. These are matters more fit for intimate speech; and I am conscious of having talked with you so openly all my life that you have nothing more about me to learn.

Jessie sends her dear love

Ever affectly Yours

J. Conrad.

---

[1] O'Flaherty's story 'The Cow's Death', told from the cow's point of view, was published in the *New Statesman*, 21 (30 June 1923), 364, and in *Spring Sowing* (Cape, 1924; New York: Knopf, 1926). In both the English (Nonesuch) and American (Bobbs-Merrill) editions of Conrad's letters to him, Garnett has Conrad referring to 'the story' rather than 'The Cow'.

1 Conrad on arrival in New York

New York Tribune

Copyright, 1923,
New York Tribune Inc.

First to Last—the Truth: News—Editorials—Advertisements

Vol. LXXXIII No. 27,926   WEDNESDAY, MAY 2, 1923

Berlin Sends Out Plea for Ruhr Peace

30 Billion Gold Marks, Promises of Guaranty and Steps for Mutual Security Offered Allies

Seeks Moratorium Over Four Years

Bonar Law Plan Supported; To Be Explained to Reichstag To-day

By Joseph Shaplen
By Wireless to The Tribune

Copyright, 1923, New York Tribune Inc.

BERLIN, May 1.—Germany's note containing its definite proposals for settlement of the Ruhr and reparation problems was sent forth to-night. The note is addressed to the powers who were signatories to the Treaty of Versailles. It will be officially brought to the attention of the Allied governments by the German Ambassadors at Washington.

As foreshadowed in dispatches to The Tribune, the sum offered by Germany is 30,000,000,000 gold marks, although the note leaves the final total to the determination of a commission of international experts.

The substance of the note is as follows:

Germany offers the Allies a basic sum of 30,000,000,000 gold marks, payable. She would deposit by an international loan, the interest on which Germany ... amount of the loan itself ...

Joseph Conrad Comes to See Us, Not to Chide or "Uplift"

Great Chronicler of Tropical Seas and the Regions of Man's Spirit Holds Shy and Modest Court on Tuscania's Bridge Entering Port

By Burton Rascoe

Joseph Conrad, who shares with Thomas Hardy the distinction of being generally considered one of the two greatest of living English novelists, arrived in New York yesterday on his first visit to America. He made the trip over from Glasgow on the Tuscania, which is commanded by his friend, Captain David W. Boon, author of two books of the sea "Adventa," "The Blunderbuss" and ...

"Broken Stowage."

During his stay here the author of "Youth," "Chance," "Victory" and "Lord Jim" will be the guest of F. N. Doubleday at Oyster Bay, L. I. He is not to make any public addresses or gather material for a book. The only wish he expressed yesterday concerning New York ... was that of viewing New York and its environs from the top of its cravitt skyline. Another concern ambitious of his was to see New York's skyline from the harbor—he realized yesterday morning while mists blurred the sharp outlines of the buildings and moved him to re-... magnificent exclamations such as "Magnificent!" "Lovely!" "Incredibly beautiful!" "Marvelous!"

In this aesthetic opinion he had the concurrence of another distinguished artist aboard the Tuscania, Meldrum Brown, the elder brother of Captain Boon. "John Masefield once magnificent sight in the world than the view of Lower Manhattan rising in incoming steamship," said Mr. Boon, as in feverish haste he sought to catch in crayon what he thought so magnificent. ... have not seen all the sights in the world that I've wanted to ... The newspaper man who clambered ...

News Summary

The Tribune's
New Telephone Number
At 225 West 40th Street
Pennsylvania 4000

WASHINGTON

Science of ships authorized under quart ruling, says Attorney General Daugherty, and so he will begin enforcing new liquor ruling after thirty-days' grace period.

Democratic Presidential boom for Carter Glass under way, says Mark Sullivan.

FOREIGN

Germany's reparations offer of 30,000,000,000 gold marks sent to Allies and United States.

Scores hurt in May Day riots in France. Two killed in Milan, Italy. Little disorder elsewhere in Europe.

British government triumphs, 252 to 94, over combined Laborite and Liberal vote on Singapore naval base.

LOCAL

Building Men Give Boom 3 Years to Run

Hint of Buyers' Strike Is Being Used to "Slow Up" Activities, Survey by The Tribune Shows

Shortage of Labor Charged to Unions

Said To Be Keeping Number of Apprentices Low; Work Far Exceeds Need

A survey of the building trades in this vicinity by The Tribune, made by a nation-wide telegraphic inquiry, has made clear that there is a general agreement on the following facts about the causes, scope and probable duration of the unprecedented activity throughout the United States in construction work and of the abnormally high prices that now obtain:

1. The present boom in building springs from a shortage caused by the suspension of construction during the war, and from 1920 to 1922, when first high prices and then business depression caused necessary building to be postponed.

2. When the present program, arising from these causes is completed, which may take from three to five years, there will be a sharp drop in activity, as only a small percentage of the work now under way is due to normal industrial and population growth.

— Much Activity is Seasonal

Society Girl Who Is Missing

Miss Elizabeth Coit, of Montclair, sought by her parents since she disappeared last Monday en route to her summer home in Connecticut.

Police Search 3 States for Society Girl

Miss Elizabeth Coit, 22, of ...

Hoover Gives Sugar-Boycott His Approval

Wires Women Here They Are "On Right Track" in Cutting Down Use to Halt the Profiteers

Crusaders Vexed At Refinery Head

Warned Against Hoarding by E. D. Babst, Call Him "Eloquently Confusing"

Herbert Hoover sent his indorsement of the women's sugar crusade in a message from Washington yesterday afternoon to Mrs. Louis Reed Welzmiller, Deputy Commissioner of Markets and chairman of the women's sugar committee of greater New York.

"The women are on the right track. The way to control prices is by spontaneous control of consumption," he said.

This message and the news that President Harding had made a similar statement at the White House distinct to soothe the ruffled feelings of the crusaders after a conversation they had at 3 o'clock with Earl D. Babst, president of the American Sugar Refining Company.

"Eloquently Confusing"

"He told us we were rocking the boat!" cried Mrs. Welzmiller, bursting into her office in the afternoon.

"Eloquently confusing—that's what he was; but you saw right through it," another woman cried. "He doesn't want ...

U.S. to ... Violati... Daugh...

Barrooms on Exc... Boats Seem Sanct...

WASHINGTON, May ...
(The Associated Press)—American ships may run stations outside the three-mile obtain their liquor stocks and maintain their ... until they are ready to ... port, appears to have ... tioned by the United St... presume Court ruling on ... fic on the high seas. On ... of the decision, some off... lieve there would be no ... checking such a practice.

Illegal Loa...
$2,475,00...
Laid to B...

No Collateral Req... Motors Company of Estate's Fun... testing Heirs

From a Staff Correspondent

ALBANY, May 1—C...

3 Interior of the Curtiss James house at 69th Street and Park Avenue, scene of Conrad's lecture and reading

4a   F. N. Doubleday, *c.* 1917

4b   Jessie Conrad, 1923

5a   Miss Hallowes, Conrad's secretary

5b   The final words of *The Rescue*, inscribed for Miss Hallowes

6a   Richard Curle at Oswalds, 1923

6b   Jacob Epstein's bust of Conrad, March 1924

7   The funeral cortège at Canterbury Cemetery, 7 August 1924; from left to right: undertaker, John and Borys Conrad, their uncles Walter and Albert George, Richard Curle, G. Jean-Aubry, R. B. Cunninghame Graham, and, with a tribute from the Polish Legation, Count Edward Raczyński

which she did not raise at his entrance. He looked at her with a
serious and friendly expression before he sat down by her side. And
even then she did not move. He took her tragic immobility in silence
as a matter of course. His face which had never been very mobile had
acquired with years a sort of dignity.~~in its set expression~~. [blank] It had
been the work of years, of those married years which had crushed the last
vestiges of pertness out of the more emotional Aglae. When she whisper-
ed to him , "Bernard, this thing kill me a little every day" he felt
moved to put his arm round his wife's waist and made the mental remark
which always occurred to him poignantly on such occasions that she had
grown very thin. ~~He was, in the conditions of a life which did not~~
~~keep~~ its promise of contented bliss, most impressed by the loss of that
plumpness which years ago was so much appreciated by him. It seemed to
give to that ~~phrase~~ which he had heard before more than once an awful
sort of reality, a dreadful precision... A little... Every day.

He took his arm away brusquely and got up.

"I thought I would find you here," he remarked in an indifferent,
marital tone. "That man has gone now," he added.

With a deep sigh the maid of Madame de Montevesso ~~seemed to~~ made
~~an effort to come~~ out of the depths of despondency, only to ~~become~~ a
prey to anxiety.

"Oh, Bernard, what did that man want with Miss Adele?"

Bernard knew enough to have formed a conjecture that that English
fellow must have either left some papers or a message with Madame de

8　The last page of the last revised chapter of *Suspense*

To G. H. Clarke

Text MS Queen's; Unpublished

[letterhead: Oswalds]
9. Aug '23

Dear Mr Clarke[1]

Thank you for your letter. I am sorry to say I cannot just now spare any time for occasional work. Unfortunately I have no photograph to send you at this moment. Our best wishes for your prosperity.

Yours faithfully

J. Conrad.

To Eric S. Pinker

Text MS Berg; Unpublished

[Oswalds]
9. Aug 23.

My dear Eric.

I was very sorry to hear from Jessie this morning that your holiday was put off on account of your wife's health. I do hope she will mend soon and that you both will manage yet to have a good time.

Will you please my dear fellow pay in £15 to my acct out of the reserved fund. I had a heavy month what with taxes and other accts and have discovered this moment that I have only £4 to my credit. That will not carry me to the next 15th. And I must pay for a new tyre too!

Give my affect^te symapthy* to your wife.

Ever Yrs

J. Conrad

To F. N. Doubleday

Text MS Princeton; Unpublished

[letterhead: Oswalds]
Monday 13. Augt 1923

My very dear Effendi.

Thanks for the MS and a copy of Lord Jim in a case. Very nice.

Tell please the dear Lady Commandant that I am not able to answer her much prized letter by this mail.

---

[1] American-born, George Herbert Clarke (1873–1953) was educated in Canada and taught at various universities in the USA. From 1925 until his retirement in 1943, he was Professor of English and head of the English Department at Queen's University in Ontario. *The Sewanee Review*, which he edited from 1920 to 1925, featured his essay on Conrad in July 1922. He reviewed *The Rover* and *Suspense* for the same journal.

Mrs Porter's marriage has agitated me I mean the news of it. It seemed "so sudden!"[1] I hope she will find all possible happiness in the "rash step".

And since we are on the subject of "rash steps" I may tell you that we have had Borys and his wife here last week.

Details I keep for my next which will be for Florence. Jessie has written to her already. That woman is always showing off only to put me to shame.

Ever yours affectly

J. Conrad.

PS Borys has been appointed (3 weeks ago) manager of the London Depot of the Daimlers C[o]. Everybody is impressed by him getting that post after only a year's service with the Company.

Please dear Effendi send him the next quarterly draft direct: B. Conrad Esq[re] c/o Messrs. The Daimlers C[o]. Chapter St House. Vauxhall Bridge Road. London. SW.

He expects to remain 3 years there.

To J. M. Dent

Text TS/MS Berg; Unpublished

[letterhead: Oswalds]

Aug. 16th. 1923.

Dear M[r] Dent.

I am really sorry that you have been worried by this matter coming up for discussion. However I have had in a letter signed by Mr Hugh an offer to put those important details right so handsomely expressed that there is nothing more to be said. Perhaps I ought to have forwarded to you a short memorandum before leaving for America, if only for the guidance of third parties charged with the execution of the plan as agreed between us. My recollection is that there was never any difference between us two. My fault lies in taking too much for granted that the exact get-up of the American Limited publication would be followed.

I admit that when you were good enough to bring a bound copy (I think of the "Outcast") to the hotel, I did no more than look at the binding and the design on the flat, which I saw then for the first time, I think. It never occurred to me that changes might have been made in the title-page and I did not look at it at all.

---

[1] Mrs James Jackson Porter (née Margaret Kelly, 1893/4–1980), widowed since 1917, married John Chambers Hughes (1891–1971) on 27 July.

I trust that you will not feel too much annoyed with me for my share of the guilt – whatever it may be. Believe me with the kindest regards always
sincerely yours

Joseph Conrad.

To W. C. Wicken
Text TS/MS Berg; Unpublished

[letterhead: Oswalds]
Aug. 16th. 1923.

Dear Mr Wicken.

So Mr Eric has got away at last! I hope he will enjoy what is left of the fine weather.

In the matter of application from Jonathan Cape: I feel inclined to grant the permission for the inclusion of two passages from the article entitled "Well Done"[1] in their Anthology of Remembrance to be published on Armistice Day.

I don't think Dents can have any objection.

In the matter of the payment into my account; I did not intend the £15 paid in a few days ago to be deducted, as it appears from my letter to Mr Eric. There is a balance of some money earned by occasional work on which I asked Mr Eric to draw for that purpose. I had some unforeseen expenses which caused me to be short at the end of last month. As the deduction would only perpetuate the shortage from month to month I should like the full amount to be completed. However, this matter is not absolutely pressing for a fortnight or so.

I hope you are well and flourishing and that you had your leave during the hot weather when it would do most good. Pray give my regards to Miss Allen.

Yours

J. Conrad

To G. Jean-Aubry
Text MS Yale; *L. fr.* 186

17. Août. 23.
Oswalds

Très cher Jean.

Je ne peux pas vous dire précisement quand il me sera possible de venir au Havre. Ce sera en Septb^r au commencement du mois si cela peut s'arranger. Mme C – s'est mis dans la tête de faire le voyage aussi! Vous voyez ça d'ici.

---

[1] "'Well Done!'", serialised in the *Daily Chronicle* in August 1918, was reprinted in *Notes on Life and Letters*.

L'idée est de montrer Jean au Rev M. Bost, et de voir un peu le pays et la demeure pour pouvoir "placer" l'enfant dans un "millieu"* connu, quand on pensera a lui. Jean viendrait s'installer definitivement seulement a la fin Sept^{re}.

Ce serait pour une année scolaire (anglaise) c'est a dire commençant le 1er Oct^{re} 1923 et finissant le 1er Août 1924. avec vacances (une quinzaine) a la Noël et a Pâques.

L'idée est que Jean apprenne le français colloquial, comme commensal de la famille, et prenne quelques leçons de grammaire – juste assez pour pouvoir écrire une lettre d'affaires ordinaire de façon a être compris.

Comme je sais qu'il y a une école des Mecaniciens (de Marine) au Havre je pense qu'il sera facile de trouver pour Jean un professeur de mathema^{ques} (calculus, statique, dynamique) appliqués. Je veux dire leçons privées 3 ou 4 fois par semaine.

Voulez-vous cher Jean nous rendre le service de communiquer ce plan a M. Bost et le prier de Vous dire ce qu'il en pense? Peut-être voudra-t-il vous communiquer les conditions pour le séjour du garçon dans sa famille. Je voudrai savoir a quoi m'en tenir avant d'entreprendre le voyage. Peut-être il voudra voir Jean avant de se décider?

Pardonnez nous l'embarras que nous vous donnons.

Je travaille dur – mais ça va très doucement. Enfin!

Je vous embrasse. Jessie sends her love

Toujours Votre de cœur

Conrad.

My very dear Jean,

I can not tell you exactly when I can come to Le Havre. It will be in September, at the beginning of the month if that can be arranged. Mrs C– has taken it into her head to make the journey too! As you will see.

The idea is to introduce John to the Revd Monsieur Bost, and see a little of the house and its setting so as to be able to "place" the child in a familiar "milieu" when we think of him. John would actually move in only at the end of September.

It would be for one (English) school year, starting, that is, 1 Oct. 1923 and ending 1 August 1924, with a fortnight's holiday at Christmas and Easter.

The idea is that John should learn colloquial French as a member of the family, and should take a few grammar lessons – just enough to be able to write an ordinary intelligible business letter.

Since I know there is a school for engineers (marine) at Le Havre, I think it will be easy to find John a teacher for applied mathematics (calculus, statistics, dynamics). I mean private lessons three or four times a week.

Dear Jean, would you do me the favour of conveying this plan to Monsieur Bost and ask him what he thinks of it? Perhaps he will explain the conditions for the boy's stay with his family. I would like to know what to expect before undertaking the trip. Perhaps he would like to meet John before making a decision?

Excuse us for the trouble we are giving you.

I am working hard, but it goes very slowly. Enough of this!

I embrace you. Jessie sends her love.

Always yours affectionately

Conrad.

To F. N. Doubleday

Text MS/TS Princeton; Unpublished

[letterhead: Oswalds]

[20 August 1923][1]

Dearest Effendi.

I send You here my modifications and suggestions in the matter of
Frontispi[e]ces
for the Concord Ed:[2]

I hope you will find them useful and even interesting. If any of *my* frontis*ces* are adopted I beg the letter-press under them be printed as written by me.

I strongly dislike the photo of *Conrad at the Wheel*.[3] Please eliminate it!

Bone's etching must go in the *Mirror of the Sea* my *own* book. Couldn't have it in front of a novel.

Love to You all

Ever Yrs

J. C.

Rush to catch mail!!!

---

[1] Probably written on the same day as the enclosure, dated in Conrad's hand '20 Aug. 1923'.

[2] The enclosure is a three-page typed list of 'FRONTISPIECES SUGGESTED' compiled in Doubleday's office by Culbreth Sudler, and annotated by Conrad. Some of these handwritten annotations simply key photographs to books, e.g. 'photo Z', 'photo marked A at back'. The substantive ones are as follows: (*Almayer's Folly*) 'Will be forwarded by the boat sailing on the 25th inst'; (*Lord Jim*) 'Photo of the house where that book was written.'; (*Set of Six*) 'snapshot of Mrs Conrad and the children in the garden on the day "The Duel" was finished.'; (*The Shadow-Line*) 'photo of Mr Conrad on board the Special Service ship Ready (*not* at the wheel) 1916 on return from that cruise he wrote the Shadow Line'; (*Notes on Life and Letters*) 'The Library Quadrangle. University of Cracow where the MSS left by Mr Conrad's father are deposited'. On the Doubleday list, *The Shadow-Line* went with a photograph of the *Otago*; Conrad has transferred this photograph to *Within the Tides* – incorrectly, as he realised before sending Doubleday some 'Further remarks' on the 27th.

[3] One of the illustrations from Captain J. G. Sutherland's *At Sea with Joseph Conrad* (Richards, 1922), a book Conrad regarded as 'preposterous bosh' (*Letters*, 7, p. 484).

To Sir Hugh Clifford
Text MS Clifford; Hunter

[letterhead: Oswalds]
22.8.23

Très cher Ami.[1]

It has been a joy to see You here, and it is a comfort to think that you will be coming back in six months' time. I shall try to keep above earth till then if only to foregather with You at the Athenaeum. As to lunching that is another matter. I've lunched there a few times and it was dreadful. But perhaps since then the Kitchen-maid has died or has left to get married. Of course in that house one looks for the feast of reason and the flow of soul for which it is justly renowned.[2] I have written to Doubleday to get me a set of the Ltd Edition from which I could complete yours. (Vols 10 to 18). I have also written to our post-office, but as the parcels (there were two of 4 vols each) were not registered the outlook is hopeless, rather.

Au revoir then my dear friend. I hope kind Heaven will look after you – I mean our Heaven which knows not the Gods of the Wilderness.[3]

Ever your affectionate

Joseph Conrad

PS Jessie's love.

---

[1] Born into an aristocratic West Country family, the Cliffords of Chudleigh, Sir Hugh Charles Clifford (1866–1941; knighted 1909) went out to Singapore in 1883 to begin a career as a colonial administrator. He was serving as British Resident in Pahang, Malaya, when he wrote one of the earliest general appreciations of Conrad's work for the *Singapore Free Press*. Later, he was appointed to the governorships of Labuan and North Borneo, the Gold Coast, Nigeria, Ceylon, and the Straits Settlements. He published many volumes of short stories and sketches set chiefly in East Asia, and the novel *The Downfall of the Gods* (1911), whose background is the decline of the Khmer empire; collaborated on a Malay dictionary; and produced a Malay translation of the colonial penal code. His restless energy and independent mind were a frequent irritation to the Colonial Office.

[2] Conrad had been a member of the Athenaeum, a club often regarded as the preserve of bishops and professors, since 1918. 'The feast of reason and the flow of soul' is a line from Alexander Pope's 'To Mr. Fortescue' (128), *Epistles and Satires of Horace Imitated* (1733).

[3] In the Hebrew narrative of the Israelites' journey through the wilderness, Moses climbs Mount Sinai and comes into the presence of the All-Highest while his apostate followers cavort around the golden calf. In the usage of Conrad's day, allusions to 'the Gods of the Wilderness' sometimes signify the pagan, sometimes the commercial. Although by birth and by conviction a Roman Catholic, Clifford had a reputation for religious tolerance, shown for instance in his sympathies with Malay and African Muslims, but this tolerance did not necessarily extend to polytheism. His beliefs and his position as a colonial governor often put him at odds with both 'paganism' or 'fetish worship' and the 'material interests' of business people (see the notes to the letter to Curle of 4 March 1924 for the latter). Like Conrad (and Karl Marx), he may have seen some family resemblances between the two.

ps My duty and respects to Lady Clifford. Pray remember us to Your charming daughter to whom hearts have been lost here.[1]

To Thomas J. Wise

Text MS BL Ashley 2953; Unpublished

[letterhead: Oswalds]

22. 8. 23

Dear Wise.

Thank you for your friendly letter and interesting enclosure.

We had a great time on our visit to you and Mrs Wise and are looking forward very much to the pleasure of seeing you here according to plan.

With our united kind regards

Ever sincerely yours

J. Conrad

To Richard Curle

Text MS Lubbock; Rude and Neeper

[letterhead: Oswalds]

23. 8. 23

My dear Curle,

With the greatest pleasure. As I was writing to Clifford I announced to him your project to visit Nigeria within the next month or two.

Of course he is familiar with your name. Had you written before we would have given ourselves the pleasure to ask you to come down and meet him here. I told him also that you are thinking of sailing by one of the Sept^{er} packet-boats, and that he may meet you on board.

I don't think a letter of introduction is necessary after this. But if you prefer to have one drop me a word and I will send you the formal thing.

Jessie joins me in these friendly regards. She's delighted with the effect her cookery-book has produced on your salivary glands. Bon voyage and all possible luck in that part of the *Shadow Show*.[2]

Cordially Yours

Joseph Conrad.

---

[1] Sir Hugh had two daughters by his first marriage, Mary (born 1898) and Monica (born 1903). After their mother died in Tobago in 1908, they were brought up in England. Mary was now married, and Monica was soon to become Mrs Cecil Trafford. Sir Hugh's second wife, Elizabeth Lydia Rosabelle (née Bonham, 1866–1945), wrote novels and plays under her previous married name, Mrs Henry de la Pasture. Her daughter, Elizabeth Monica de la Pasture (1890–1943), became the novelist E. M. Delafield.

[2] A book of reminiscence and opinion by Richard's brother, J(ames) H(erbert) Curle, published in 1912. Curle draws on memories of almost every continent, but, given his own experiences, Conrad would have found the title peculiarly appropriate to colonial Africa. Chapter 3 gives an eye-witness account of the Jameson Raid, one of the great political contretemps of the 1890s, and a telling moment in the imperial history of southern Africa.

To F. N. Doubleday

Text TS/MS Princeton; Unpublished

[letterhead: Oswalds]

[27 August 1923][1]

My dear Effendi.

By this time you will have received the amended list of Frontispieces for the Concord Edition.

That list is based on the one relating to fourteen books you sent me in your last letter. I have made in it some changes which I would be glad if you accepted. But the only one on which I would insist is the placing of the Muirhead Bone etching as Frontispiece to the *Mirror of the Sea*. I want that book to have the advantage of Muirhead Bone's distinguished art.

I enclose here some further photographs and remarks connected with the Frontispieces.

R. Curle has been here for the weekend at the end of his month's holiday and has returned to his post at Carmelite House. He sends his regards to both of you. His article on my books, which, honestly, I think extremely good from every point of view (and especially that of publicity), is due to appear in the "Times Literary Supplement" this week. I have no doubt that it will be useful to Dents who are steadily publishing two volumes a month of the English Uniform.[2] Curle was very interested to hear from me about the altered scheme of the Concord Edition, and to see the provisional list of Frontispieces. In the course of conversation he suggested that his article, of which a copy has been sent to you, would possibly be a good thing for the Concord if reprinted by you next year in the form of a "prospectus-pamphlet." He points out that every book is mentioned in it, with more or less comment, and that it lays stress on the fact (is indeed written round the fact) that this edition is the first offered to the general public as containing all the Prefaces and Authors Notes. There is no doubt that from the literary point of view it is *the* feature, and also from the publishing point of view, since there are at least 60,000 words of new matter that the general public could not buy before. Therefore in that Edition they obtain about 3000 words of formerly inaccessible text and a significant Frontispiece (apart from a new and attractive get-up) for the extra 50 cents – which looks a good proposition from the buyer's point of view.

Thank you for all your nice letters. I hope I am not making myself a nuisance to you and partners with my comments, questions, and suggestions.

---

[1] Presumably written on the same date as the enclosed 'remarks', dated '27. 8. 23' in Conrad's hand.

[2] Telegrams exchanged between Conrad or his secretary and J. M. Dent (UNC) confirm that, by the end of July, Conrad had received copies of the first four volumes of the Uniform Edition: first *The Nigger of the 'Narcissus'* and *Lord Jim*, then *Romance* and *Youth* (see Moore, p. 439).

Don't imagine I am *insisting* on anything I may propose. The decision rests with the House. But I am too strongly interested to hold my tongue always. Pray give my affectionate regards to Mr Everitt and my friendly greetings to all the Loyal Band of workers.

Ever Yours

J. Conrad.

I have begun a letter to dear Florence which I won't be able to finish for this mail. Our dear love to You both.

27. 8. 23

In re Frontispieces.

Further remarks.

The "Mr Conrad at the Wheel" photo which your list allot[t]ed to the *Nigger* I do not want used at all in the Edition. I do not like it, and, in any case, it is not suitable for that book. We shall have to think of something for the *Nigger*.

The photo of "Conrad sitting on the deck of the Ready" is to be used for *Shadow Line*, as explained in my list.

The picture of the barque "Otago" should go for Frontispiece to *'Twixt Land and Sea* (<u>not</u> to *Within the Tides* as I placed it by mistake in my list).

My list suggested for *Arrow of Gold* a photo of the Cannebière, Marseilles, which is the town where I began my independent life. It occurs to me now that Muirhead Bone has done a lot of drawings in Marseilles and that perhaps (if not too expensive) you could get from him the right of reproducing one of them.

Enclosed here photo of the ship "Loch Etive" in harbour, which I propose for Frontispiece to *Chance*. It was my first ship as an officer.[1] A very young officer. The novel *Chance*, from a certain point of view, deals with a remarkable incident in the life of a young ship's officer.

The picture of the "Duke of Sutherland" which your plan allotted to the *Mirror of the Sea* is a very poor thing and it would be better not to use it at all.

If the photo of me as a boy which I sent to you in my last letter does not commend itself to you as a Frontispiece to *A Personal Record*, the reproduction of a MS page of the Author's Note will have to do.

For *Within the Tides* your suggestion for a MS page of the Author's Note is most suitable.

I am forwarding now one print and two negatives of the photo of my uncle's lithographic portrait which you must have seen in my study. It would

---

[1] He joined the ship as third mate in August 1880.

be a great pleasure to me if it could be used for frontispiece to *Almayer's Folly*, with letterpress below as suggested in my last letter.

For *The Rescue* I would suggest a very fine portrait of me taken last April by T. & R. Annan & Sons, 518 Sauchiehall Street, Glasgow, Negative No. 1.[1] I suppose he won't make any great charge for the right of reproduction.

Tales of Unrest ⎫   I have no suggestion to make, and unless the
Outcast of the Islands ⎬   Garden City has something to offer a reproduced
Nostromo ⎬   page from the respective Author's Notes will
Victory ⎭   have to do. As I imagine Mr Wise holds them
there would be no difficulty in obtaining them.

J. C.

PS (brain waves). 1$\underline{°}$ Why not use Saxton's map[2] enlarged as frontispi[e]ce for the Nigger? 2$\underline{°}$ Would you care to have photo of Capel House for *Victory*? Contemp^{y} photo with myself and John outside. Taken by the Cadbys 1914.[3] with whom I could arrange.

JC.

This would include in Edition all the homes we've lived in except this one (Oswalds) which might be eventually used for *Suspense*

To Richard Curle

Text TS Indiana; Curle 122

[letterhead: Oswalds]
28. 8. 23.
6.30 pm.

My dear Dick.

I had a letter from the editor of B[lue] P[eter]. He will want the MS by the 15th next, and that will be all right. I will have the thing done by to-morrow,

---

[1] According to Curle (*The Last Twelve Years of Joseph Conrad*, p. 162), Annan photographed Conrad in his bedroom at the St Enoch Hotel on the day he sailed for America. One of the photographs taken at this session features on the jackets of the present edition.

[2] Drawn in 1915 for the end papers of the first US edition of *Victory*, this map was a collaboration between Eugene F. Saxton, of Doubleday's, and his wife, Martha Plaisted Saxton (*Letters*, 5, p. 433).

[3] Will and Carine Cadby made studio portraits of Conrad in September 1913 and came out to the house in February 1915: see *Letters*, 5, pp. 284, 444. See also Carine Cadby, 'Conrad's Dislike of the Camera and How It Was Overcome', *Graphic*, 110 (1 November 1924), 728. They lived in Borough Green, Kent, professing both photography and cobbling.

I suppose.[1] His letter has been acknowledged and the little photograph of the hole in the bow of the "Torrens" enclosed.

He didn't mention in his letter anything about reproducing the MS or about a photograph of myself, but I certainly have no objection. He must however get the photograph from Annan himself, as the man took those negatives for nothing and ought to have his fee. There are several of them, but the one from No. 1 negative is the best.

Will you, my dear fellow, tell Hook that on the telephone, as my answer has gone.

Thank you very much for putting this affair through with such speed and efficiency. And of course the revelation of his readiness to jump at an occasional contribution from me is extremely valuable. I hope you have got into the shafts of the Carmelite cart and that the harness doesn't gall.

Jessie sends her love.

Yours ever

J. Conrad.

PS Partington's agreement is in the shape of a stamped letter.[2] I have issued directions and he will be looked after by the office.

To W. C. Wicken

Text TS Berg; Unpublished

[letterhead: Oswalds]
Aug. 28th. 1923.

Dear Mr Wicken.

I return to you Partington's letter. I don't remember how many sheets I have signed, but of course you will see that I get my royalties according to the number published.[3]

I suppose you have good news of Mr Eric. I intend to run up and see him on his return, on some day convenient to him. Perhaps he would drop me a line.

Yours faithfully

J. Conrad.

---

[1] F. A. Hook, the owner and editor of *Blue Peter*, wanted an article to go with a colour picture of the *Torrens*. The MS is dated 29 August. Published as 'A Clipper Ship I Knew' in the October issue, it was reprinted in *Last Essays* under the title 'The *Torrens*: A Personal Tribute'.

[2] Of 26 February 1923, to publish a limited edition of *Laughing Anne*; see *Documents*, pp. 228–9.

[3] Conrad's agreement with Partington was for 175 numbered and signed copies.

To Eric S. Pinker

Text MS Berg; Unpublished

[letterhead: Oswalds]

Thursday [30 August 1923][1]

My dear Eric.

Hail! I hope you have both returned much the better for your travels.

I have received the enclosed noted from the "decent" Vance and I must confess that I am very pleased at the good reception of *The Rover* as serial.[2] It must have been somewhat out of the ordinary for him to write in this strain. I presume they began pub[on] in their Aug[st] Number. I hope my dear it will come to us patting each other on the back over The Rover.

If you drop me a word to-morrow (Friday) I will come up on Monday – about 12.30. If I don't hear I'll refrain. But perhaps You will suggest a day if Monday isn't suitable?

I don't know whether M[r] Wicken told you of my request to have the monthly money completed. Any way please pay in £15.[3] What with guests and ever-present "unexpected" I can't stand a deduction – however righteous.

                                          Ever Yours

                                                    J Conrad.

---

[1] Vance wrote from New York on the 20th; given the timing of the mails, the 30th is the earliest possible Thursday; the reference to asking Wicken for the 'monthly money' makes a later date unlikely.

[2] Conrad enclosed a letter from Arthur T. Vance (TS Berg), who was going to send the September issue of the *Pictorial Review* under separate cover. This issue included the first serial instalment of *The Rover*, which was 'being very warmly received' in the USA, and a 'little appreciation of you by Mary Austin', the American writer, literary journalist, and feminist (1868–1934). 'Joseph Conrad Tells What Women Don't Know about Men' (*Pictorial Review*, 24.12, pp. 17, 28, 30–1), was her second article on Conrad; the first, 'A Sermon in One Man', was published in *Harper's Weekly*, 16 May 1914, p. 20. In 1929, she contributed the essay on 'Typhoon' to Keating's *A Conrad Memorial Library*, pp. 103–10. For Conrad's estimation of her publicity work for Vance's magazine, see *Letters*, 7, p. 346.

[3] On the 16th, Conrad had told Wicken that the payment would not be urgent for 'a fortnight or so'.

To Ambrose G. Barker
Text TS Pforzheimer; J-A, 2, 322

[letterhead: Oswalds]
Sept. 1st. 1923.

Dear Mr Barker,[1]

Thank you very much for your letter and the pamphlet in which I was very much interested.[2]

As a matter of fact I never knew anything of what was called, if I remember rightly, the "Greenwich Bomb Outrage". I was out of England when it happened and thus I never read what was printed in the newspapers at the time.[3] All I was aware of was the mere fact – my novel being, in intention, the history of Winnie Verloc. I hope you have seen that the purpose of the book was *not* to attack any doctrine or even the men holding that doctrine. My object, apart from the aim of telling a story, was to hold up the worthlessness of certain individuals and the baseness of some others. It was a matter of great interest to me to see how near actuality I managed to come in a work of imagination.

I hope you will do me the pleasure to accept the book[4] I am sending you – which is also a work of pure imagination though very different in subject and treatment from the "Secret Agent".

Yours faithfully

J. Conrad.

P.S. I suppose you meant me to keep the pamphlet, which I would like to paste into my own copy of the novel.

---

[1] An anarchist and secularist, Ambrose G(eorge) Barker (1862–1932) was keenly interested in the history of English dissidence. He wrote a history of the Walthamstow Working Men's Club and Institute, and built up a notable collection of works by and about Tom Paine; in 1938, he published a biography of Henry Hetherington, a leading Chartist, publisher of radical newspapers, and opponent of censorship.

[2] Identified by Norman Sherry as *The Greenwich Mystery*, by David John Nicoll (Sheffield, 1897): see *Conrad's Western World* (Cambridge University Press, 1971), pp. 379–94. As Jean-Aubry noted, Nicoll's description of the bomber resembles Stevie in *The Secret Agent*: 'He could hardly have been more than twenty-two. The hair and moustache were silky and fair, he had no beard, his eyes were blue.' As editor of *Commonweal*, Nicoll had been convicted of incitement to murder in the cause of anarchism and sentenced to eighteen months in prison (*The Times*, 7 May 1892, p. 13).

[3] Conrad signed off from the *Adowa*, the last of his ships, on 17 January 1894. At the time of the Greenwich bombing on 15 February, he was living near Victoria Station and finishing *Almayer's Folly*.

[4] *The Rover*, according to Jean-Aubry, but the novel was not yet serialised and would not be published as a book until December.

To Richard Curle

Text TS Indiana; Curle 123

Oswalds.

Sept. 1st. 1923.

Dearest Dick.

You must be surprised not to have heard from me before about the "Times" article. As a matter of fact I was working at the B[lue] P[eter] article and would not look at the Supplement till I had finished – which was done last night.

Many thanks, my dear fellow. Your historic survey of Mr C's books looks and reads magnificently. Your view as to what it should have been is gorgeously vindicated by the execution. I can't imagine anything that could have been better for its purpose. And I must say that Richmond has been most generous with his space. The display is distinctly impressive, and the "head" and "tail" pieces of writing are done in your best manner both as to sobriety and eloquence of expression. I can not thank you sufficiently.

I have written to-day to Hook to tell him that he will have the article on the 10th. It is absolutely ready now, but he must not be led to think that I do those things too easily. It took just three days from the first inception to the completing a copy fit for the printer. Easy money you may think. But the trouble is that it is all, as it were, expended before I even get hold of it. A damnable coil to be tangled in.

Our Wise friend is coming to-morrow, bringing his wife with him.[1] I intend of course to do a stroke of business if he is at all disposed for it, treating the thirteen pages of MS and the eight pages of heavily corrected TS as one item, for which I propose to ask not thirty pieces of silver but thirty-five pieces of paper.[2] Such is my rapacity! It is too late to hear your opinion about it, but my view is that I simply can not afford to be generous. I have besides a lot of small bills the damned journey to Havre before me.

As Mrs C. insists on going over too, the programme will be: arriving in London on the 10th, leaving for Havre by the night service on the 11th, returning from Havre by the night service on the 15th – in which case I will have the company of Aubry who returns to London for a month or two on that date. To tell you the truth I dread the enterprise, for I get very nervous and tired when I have to look after anybody. We take John with us of course, but we won't leave him in France because the Rev. Bost and his family don't return to their house in Havre till the end of Sept. They will come up for the day on the 12th, from their country house to see us in Havre.

---

[1] She was Frances Louis ('Louie') Wise (née Greenhalgh, 1875–1939).

[2] Wise paid Conrad £35 for the MS and TS of 'The *Torrens*: A Personal Tribute'.

Eric is back and I have arranged to see him on Monday to talk over various business matters, (damn them), while we lunch together, probably at one. But I will be at the R.A.C. before 12, and if this reaches you in time I hope you will step in and cheer me up by some optimistic talk. I will have with me a clean copy of: /THE TORRENS/ A Personal Tribute / By Joseph Conrad./ – so that you may read it at your leisure. And I would like to consult you in that connection on a matter I need not state here.

Jessie sends her love

Ever Yours

J. Conrad

To Edward Garnett
Text MS Virginia; G. 326

[Oswalds]
[1 September 1923]¹

Dearest Edward.

You must pardon this scrawl in answer to your good letter. I was touched by your memory of old times. If I said anything as what you quote it was sheer impertinence. I did not know then what style was; and if I have any conception of it now it cannot be other than very primitive. But – as I said in one of my prefaces – you were "always very patient with me at that time."²

And you are that now. Your dear and touching letter proves it.

My dear, in your feelings, in your judgements, your enthusiasms and criticisms, in all your fine reactions to that "best" which not every eye can see, You have been beautifully consistent, both in your subtle and your peremptory moods. It is thirty years now (almost to a day) since I came ashore for good. And the very next year our friendship began!³ Straight from the sea into your arms, as it were. How much you have done to pull me together intellectually only the Gods that brought us together know. For I myself don't. All I had in my hand was some little creative gift – but not even one single piece of "cultural" luggage. I am proud after all these years to have understood You from the first.

Ever yours

J. Conrad

PS Jessie sends her love.

¹ Date from postmark; Garnett has [August 1923].
² In the 'Author's Note' to *An Outcast of the Islands*, Conrad writes: 'At that time, and I may say, ever afterwards, he was always very patient and gentle with me' (p. x).
³ Without realising that he had made his last voyage as a sailor, he left the *Adowa* in January and met Garnett in November 1894.

To G. Jean-Aubry

Text MS Yale; *L. fr.* 188

[letterhead: Oswalds]
1er Sept. '23

Mon cher Jean.

Merci mille fois.[1] A moins de maladie, ou autre catastrophe, le programme est: depart pour Londres le 10. Depart pour Havre le 11 – service de nuit. Arrivée au Havre le 12 – je suppose de très bonne heure. Retour a Londres le 15 en compagnie je l'espère – de M. G. Jean Aubry. Ça Vous va-t-il?

Voudrez-vous très cher engager pour nous une niche composée d'une chambre double et d'une autre a un lit pour le "petit enfant". En 1875 il y avait un hotel sur une grande place avec des arcades – mais peut-être ça n'existe plus.[2] Croyez-vous qu'il y aura des voitures au debarcadère du paquebot? Je crois que nous serons arrivés a 7 h! du matin. Quel temps! Quelles mœurs![3]

Ever yours

J. Conrad

Mme C sends her love. Notre Jean a trouvé une traité de Géometrie en français et s'exerce avec. Il me prie de le rappeler a Votre bon souvenir.

My dear Jean.

A thousand thanks. Barring illness or other catastrophe, the plan is: leave for London the 10th. Leave for Le Havre the 11th – overnight service. Arriving in Le Havre the 12th – very early, I suppose. Return to London the 15th in the company, I hope – of Monsieur G. Jean Aubry. What do you say to that?

Would you, my dear fellow, reserve us a corner with one double room and another, single, for the 'small boy'? In 1875 there was a hotel on a large arcaded square – but perhaps that no longer exists. Do you think there will be taxis at the ferry landing? I think we shall arrive at 7! in the morning. What times! What customs!

Ever yours

J. Conrad

---

[1] Jean-Aubry had written on 25 August, estimating the costs of John's stay in Le Havre, suggesting the 12th or 13th as the best days for the visit, and noting his own intention of travelling to London on the 15th (TS Yale).

[2] An eighteen-year-old ship's boy, he arrived in Le Havre two days before Christmas 1875, after a rough passage from Cap Haïtien, thus ending his second voyage to the Caribbean in the *Mont-Blanc*.

[3] '*O tempora, O mores!*' Cicero, *In Catilinam*, 1.1.

Mrs C sends her love. Our John has found a French treatise on geometry and is working at it. He asks me to give you his greetings.

To Thomas J. Wise

Text MS BL Ashley 2953; Unpublished

[letterhead: Oswalds]

4. 9. 23.

Dear Mr Wise.

I was away yesterday when Your letter and cheque arrived.[1] Many thanks.

The Editor of the *Blue Peter* wants very much to reproduce a page of the MS in the Oct^er Number of the magazine.

Will you kindly permit him to do so? I would suggest the first page of the *MS – not* of type. He will approach you (most likely through our friend R. C.) on that matter in a few days.

It was a great pleasure to see you both here. I trust you had a good run back to the sea.[2] My wife joins me in Kindest regards to Mrs Wise and Yourself.

Sincerely Yours

Joseph Conrad

PS We are off to France for a week next Monday.

To D. C. Leech

Text MS Lubbock; Unpublished

[letterhead: Oswalds]

5. 9. 23.

My dear Sir.[3]

The obvious answer to your letter is that the view of an English master as a purveyor of personal details about a man whose work he does not know is new to me.[4] 40 pages out of 24 vols is not enough for even a superficial

---

[1] Wise paid £35 for the MS and TS of Conrad's *Torrens* article, as noted by Miss Hallowes on 4 September (*Documents*, p. 217).

[2] They were staying in Broadstairs.

[3] Donald Collins Leech (1899–1961) took a BA (Hons) at King's College, London, in 1921 and taught English at the King George V School, Southport. He eventually published five books on secondary-school English and preparing for the GCE (General Certificate of Education).

[4] A note by Leech of 6 February 1926 (MS Lubbock) explains the circumstances. He had written to Conrad asking if he could provide 'any details in connection' with 'Typhoon', a set book for the Northern Matriculation Examination in 1924, 'in order to make that book more personal & real in its appeal'.

judgment. Pray don't believe that I would urge you to read even one of them; I would only suggest that there is nothing easier in the world than leaving Joseph Conrad alone. Your boys' ignorance of that author can not possibly affect the success of their exams. Unless there is a "set book" (which I take leave to doubt) in which case *that* book is *the* thing, and the rest does not matter.

All I can do for You is to enclose this little pamp[h]let (a publisher's ad[v]ertis^t of my new edition) which contains a few facts and a bibliography. There was an article on "Mr Conrad's Books" in last week's issue (30 Aug.) of the *Times Litter^{ry}** Supplement.*

Yours faithfully

Joseph Conrad.

To Richard Curle

Text MS Indiana; Curle 124

[Oswalds]
7. 9. 23.

My dear Dick.

I have your letter & cheque. Many thanks.

We'll arrive at the Curzon for lunch and hope you will share the "modest repast" (vin ordinaire)

I have given up the idea of writing to the Suppl^t about Sir F[rank]'s communication, since you are willing to say something.[1] I have no locus standi in this affair, really.

Ever Yours

J. Conrad

---

[1] Sir Frank Swettenham's letter 'The Story of Lord Jim', in the *TLS* of 6 September, provoked Curle's reply of the 13th, Swettenham's riposte on the 20th, and a final detailed account on 11 October by Alfred Holt, managing partner of the Ocean Steam Ship Company of Liverpool, whose steamship *Antenor* had rescued the *Jeddah*. Sir Frank Swettenham (1850–1946) finished his long career in the Malay Archipelago as High Commissioner for the Malay States and Governor of the Straits Settlements; his experiences led to the writing of many books, including *Malay Sketches* (1895) and *British Malaya* (1907). In 'The History of Mr. Conrad's Books' (*TLS*, 30 August, p. 570), Curle links Conrad's own experiences and the anecdotes he had heard with episodes in his fiction, observing that 'It is this sense of contact with life that gives to his pages the feeling that things happened so and not otherwise.' Sir Frank took issue with this claim in a letter to the *TLS* (6 September, p. 588), pointing to some differences between the events of *Lord Jim* and his own recollection of the 'far from pretty' scandal of the pilgrim ship *Jeddah*. Unfortunately for his argument, his memory let him down, prompting him to claim that the original of Jim stayed on board. For Curle's response, see his letter to Conrad of 20 September. The first person to record the connection between the *Jeddah* and *Lord Jim* had been the sailor and writer William McFee, in March 1921; see *The Conradian*, 26.1 (2001), 91.

We are coming up on sunday only because Mama Piper[1] has collapsed with a bad throat. I will be awfully bored unless You bring me an interesting book or two (on loan I mean).

To G. Jean-Aubry

Text MS Yale; *L. fr.* 188

[Oswalds]
7. 9. 23.

Très cher.

Merci de Votre bonne lettre.[2]

Trouve-t-on du Bordeaux a l'Hotel de Bordeaux?

Voulez-Vous dejeuner avec nous le 12. Disons a midi. Avec du Bordeaux.

M et Mme Bost ne trouveront pas mauvais que ma femme vienne les voir avec moi? Elle veut voir où son oisillon sera niché. C'est excusable.

Du reste nous aurons une petite consultation la-dessus. Il faudra arranger une petite promenade pour elle et ainsi de suite. Elle tient a faire sa visite a Vos parents a sa première sortie – si ce ne serait que pour laisser des cartes.

Je Vous embrasse

Votre

Conrad.

My very dear fellow,

Thanks for your good letter.

Do they have Bordeaux at the Hotel de Bordeaux?

Would you lunch with us on the 12th? Let's say at noon. With some Bordeaux.

Will Monsieur and Madame Bost not mind my wife's coming with me to see them? She wants to see where her little chick will be nested. It's excusable.

Besides, we'll have a little consultation about all that. We will need to arrange a short walk for her and so forth. She insists on calling on your parents at the first opportunity, if only to leave a card.

I embrace you.

Your

Conrad.

---

[1] The Conrads' cook.

[2] Of the 3rd (TS Yale), telling Conrad that the local arrangements had been made.

To the Revd H. S. McClelland
Text TS/MS Mitchell; Unpublished

[letterhead: Oswalds]
Sept. 7th. 1923.

My dear Sir.[1]

Let me begin by thanking you for the offer of your generous hospitality in case I should come to Glasgow to lecture before the Trinity Literary Society. To my great regret however I can not accept it. Lecturing is not in my way. I have never done anything of the kind and as a matter of fact I do not consider myself fit for it. My voice, too, is an insuperable obstacle. I could not keep on talking for an hour.[2]

I am however very sensible of the compliment implied in your invitation.
Believe me

Very faithfully yours

Joseph Conrad.

To Bruno Winawer
Text TS/MS copies Yale;[3] Najder 292

[Oswalds]
9.9.23.

My dear Winawer,

My apologies for my long silence. I have always been slow to write letters. It's a strange kind of laziness, or perhaps a disease of the will which doubtless only death can cure.

I am pleased that the Czechs (whom I dislike without knowing why) are interested in your work. I liked "Engineer"[4] very much, very much indeed! The idea, the execution, the style. There are deep affinities between us – in our manner of thought and the nature of our feelings.

---

[1] The Revd Henry Simpson McClelland (1882–1961) was Rector of Trinity Congregational Church in Glasgow from 1915 until his retirement in 1956. During his ministry he invited many well-known figures, chiefly authors, to address the Trinity Literary Society, and sometimes also to take part in one of the Sunday services. He gave his recreation in *Who's Who* as 'travel in search of trouble', and at times lived as a tramp in London and Glasgow to learn the needs of the destitute. He described what he saw in 'I Became Down and Out That I Might Know the Brethren', *Nash's and Pall Mall Magazine* (October 1926).

[2] On 10 May, Conrad had lectured and read for an hour and a quarter in New York, but the experience could only have confirmed his longstanding conviction that he was not a public speaker, even when not confronted with a 400-mile railway journey to meet his audience. Quite apart from any struggles with pronunciation (as recalled somewhat sternly by William Lyon Phelps; see Phelps, p. 753), his grave illness in 1910 had weakened his vocal cords.

[3] Yale has two: a transcription of the Polish original, and a French translation, not by Jean-Aubry, but in his hand. The text given here was translated from the Polish by Dr Olga Amsterdamska.

[4] In April, Conrad had asked Winawer for a copy of his comedy *R. H., Inżynier* (*R. H., Engineer*) to take with him on his voyage to New York.

Shall I return the MS to you? I congratulate you on your Italian excursion. It was clearly a success. About my own ocean voyage I prefer not to speak. Entre nous, I felt the whole time like a man sitting dans un avion, in the fog, in a cloud of idealistic phrases; lost, surprised, amused – but terrified too. Nothing to grasp with either the eye or the hand! Obviously there is a force hidden behind it – a great force indeed – and certainly a talkative one. But it chatters like a well-trained parrot. It gives me the shivers! Tout cela est confié a Votre discretion,[1] 1° since I may be wrong and 2° I feel a great friendship towards many people there. Tout le monde a été charmant pour moi là bas.[2] Indeed one month is not enough to comprehend such a complicated machine. Perhaps a whole lifetime would not suffice.

Your "chronique"[3] is very amusing. Thank you for sending it. I agree that the situation is funny without being gay. A heartfelt handshake.

Ever yours

Joseph Conrad.

P.S. The translation of the Nigger is épatant![4] Where did they get that vocabulary?

To Eric S. Pinker
Text MS Berg; Unpublished

[Curzon Hotel]
[c. 10 September 1923][5]

Dearest Eric.

I send you this to look at, as I know you are interested in the details of the Concord E^d.

You will note FND's optimism – on the increase.

---

[1] 'I entrust all this to your discretion.'
[2] 'Everyone there was most charming to me.'   [3] A chronicle of current events in Poland?
[4] Najder describes Jan Lemanski's translation of *The Nigger of the 'Narcissus'* as 'done in an artificially "poetic", neo-romantic language' (p. 293, n. 1).
[5] This note was written on the last page of a list of frontispieces for the Concord Edition sent with Doubleday's letter of 31 August (TSS Berg). The references to Oswalds make it clear that the Conrads were already on their way to Le Havre. They spent the nights of 9 and 10 September at the Hotel Curzon and would have taken the boat-train to Southampton on the afternoon of the 11th, so a date around the 10th seems certain. Conrad forwarded Doubleday's list but not his letter of 31 August, which Miss Hallowes sent on to Pinker with the following note: 'Mr Conrad has gone up & wanted me to mention to you that he wrote an American letter settling last details on Monday of Concord Ed: get-up & frontispieces, and this fuss may be considered as over & done with! L. H. I enclose FND's last letter for your information.' Since Doubleday had asked for a letter as well as a telegram, it is likely that Conrad wrote to Garden City on Monday the 10th, but this 'American letter' has not survived. The note from Hallowes may date from the 16th, when Conrad took to his bed on returning from France, or earlier in the week, after Conrad had gone up to London.

Will you (as he asks) send him reply "night-letter",[1] I suggest as follows Frontispi[e]ces OK. House wrong for Nostromo.[2] For Unrest select photo b. Will send Oswalds for Rescue and suggestion for Nostromo soon.

Conrad.

I have had this moment wire from our gardener to say stove not arrived yet. Will you please ask the bank to wire me a credit for £10 to their agent in Havre. Or if not post a note to Grand Hotel, place Gambetta. This in case the stove is delayed and we elect to stay a couple of days over there instead of London. It would be cheaper. We can't go back to a house without a stove.

Ever Yours

J. C.

To Thérèse Aubry
Text MS Yale; *L. fr.* 189

[letterhead: Oswalds]

19. Sept 23.

Chère Madame[3]

Pardonnez-moi de ne pas Vous avoir écrit (au nom de la communauté) aussitôt notre arrivée. Le fait est qu'un tiers de la communauté s'est mis au lit en sortant de l'auto. Vous avez deviné que c'était moi. Il parait que je ne suis pas fait pour voyager. Ce n'est qu'aujourdhui que je suis entré dans mon cabinet ou j'ai trouvé sur ma table un monticule des lettres et paquets – qui pourront bien attendre un jour ou deux encore. Mais je veux sans perdre un moment de plus Vous remercier (au nom de la communauté) de la bienveillante réception que Vous et M. Aubry avez bien voulu accorder aux amis de votre fils, de votre charmante hospitalité et de Votre sympathie avec l'objet de notre voyage au Hâvre*. Nous en avons été vivement touché et nous en garderons toujour[s] un chaleureux souvenir – avec l'espoir de vous revoir avant bien longtemps soit ici soit en France.

Nous nous sommes quittés avec Jean sur le quai de la gare. Il a été un charmant compagnon de voyage. C'était un grand réconfort de l'avoir là car

---

[1] A cheap-rate cable or wireless message for delivery next day.

[2] Doubleday's staff proposed using a frontispiece previously meant for *Under Western Eyes*: 'Photo of house in which the book was written, with Mr. Conrad's eldest son, then a boy of twelve, and the dog Escamillo'. In other words, they had chosen a picture of Capel House instead of Pent Farm, where *Nostromo* was actually written.

[3] Thérèse Aubry (née Contant) and her husband, Frédéric-Ferdinand Aubry, were Jean-Aubry's parents. They lived at various addresses in Le Havre and had a country house at nearby Fontenay (Montivilliers).

je ne me sentai[s] pas bien du tout. Nous l'attendons la semaine prochaine ici pour une visite de deux ou trois jours, je l'espère. Avec lui on ne sait jamais. Il est tellement pris!

Ma femme et moi nous Vous prions chère Madame et cher Monsieur de croire a nos sentiments de la plus affectueuse reconnaissance.

> Toujours Votre dévoué serviteur
> Joseph Conrad.

PS. John presente ses respects et prie M. Aubry d'accepter les 3 photos du "Ping[o]uin", le bateau de son ami. Elles ne sont pas très bonnes. Au point de vue "voilure" celle ou il fait son abattée après avoir viré du bord est encore la meilleure.

Pardonnez ce gribouillage. J'ai encore un petit restant de fièvre.

Dear Madame,

Pray forgive me for not having written to you (in the name of the community) as soon as we arrived. The fact is that a third of the community went straight to bed on leaving the car. You have guessed correctly that it was me. It seems I was not made for travel. Not until to-day did I enter my study to find on my table a small mound of letters and packages – which can easily wait another day or two. But I would like without a moment's delay to thank you (in the name of the community) for the kind reception you and M. Aubry have given to your son's friends, for your charming hospitality and your sympathy for the purpose of our journey to Le Havre. We have been deeply touched and will always cherish a fond memory – with the hope of seeing you again before very long either here or in France.

We said good-bye to John on the station platform. He was a charming travelling companion. It was a great comfort to have him there, since I was not feeling well at all. We are expecting him here next week for a visit of two or three days, I hope. With John one never knows. He is so busy!

My wife and I beg you, dear Madam and dear Sir, to accept our most affectionate gratitude.

> Ever your devoted servant
> Joseph Conrad.

PS. John sends his greetings and asks M. Aubry to accept three photos of the "Penguin," his friend's boat. They are not very good. From the sailing point of view, the one where he falls off after changing tack is still the best.

Pray forgive this scrawl. I am still a bit feverish.

To Richard Curle

Text MS Indiana; Curle 125

[letterhead: Oswalds]

20. 9. 23

My dearest Dick.

Jessie and I are grieved and ashamed. But most of all we are thunderstruck. Why! of course we did *not* see you in town when on our way home. But by a strange aberration of thought we were under the impression that we had! Its too absurd for words, and I hope You will keep it quiet or else the world will say that both Jessie and I are in an advanced stage of senile decay. The delusion was so complete that when I saw the 1ˢᵗ domesᶜ servants article I wondered why you did not tell me that they were coming. Quite good stuff.[1]

We passed through town on Sunday arriving home at 4.30 pm; and at 5.30 I was in bed with a temperature and that dreadful asthma cough which reduces me to despair. It was beginning before we went over. I am downstairs now and was going to drop you a line today but I don't feel well.

Our love and regrets.

Ever Yours

J. C.

PS Let us know the earliest day You can run over. Sir Frank acts like an ass rather.[2] I am going early to bed to day.

Jessie stood the trip well. Enjoyed it. Arrangements are made. Serious, spartan French family. I am quite pleased but Mʳ John is pulling a long face rather.

---

[1] On 19 and 20 September Curle returned to the 'Servant Scandal', on which he had already published at least six articles; on this occasion, he wrote as the 'Special Correspondent' responsible for the April series on the failings of the Dole rather than as 'John Blunt'. The new pieces were 'Scaring Servants from Jobs' and 'False Advice to Girls. Faddist Influence on Servants'. Curle's bugbears were women who had done other kinds of work during the war and preferred going on the Dole to becoming servants, and teachers who advised their students to look for better opportunities. 'To make a girl discontented with the idea of domestic service is not a kindness but a cruelty' (20 September, p. 6).

[2] Curle made his riposte to Sir Frank Swettenham in the *TLS* of the 13th. Because the piece that started the correspondence was anonymous, the letter is signed 'The Writer of the Article' (p. 604). Curle points out that demanding strict fidelity to a chain of actual events misses the point of Conrad's work: 'I never argued that he followed history; indeed, I expressly stated that he has often built up a whole story from one incident.' Answering Curle on the 20th (p. 620), Swettenham continued to trust his memory: 'I feel sure that the real Jim felt he had been badly treated in being left on the Jeddah to drown with the pilgrims while his friends got away to report the disaster.' On 11 October, a letter from Alfred Holt & Co., the owners of the *Antenor*, which had towed the *Jeddah* to the port of Aden, at last set Sir Frank straight on the facts of the affair (p. 670). Curle's defence of artistic licence, meanwhile, had gone by the board.

To Edward Garnett

Text MS Private collection; G. 327

[letterhead: Oswalds]
20. 9. 23

Dearest Edward.

I was over in Havre arranging for John's stay in France ("to acquire the language") when your dear letter and your introduction to Hudson's corresp^{dce} arrived.[1]

Those pages are first rate and I am glad You have been moved to write them. Thanks my dearest fellow for the inscribed copy. It is the most touching and penetrating appreciation of a personality that I have ever read.

On our return last Sunday (for Jessie went over with me) I developed a temperature, (God knows why!) which kept me in bed till today: or else You would have heard from me before.

Jessie sends her dear love.

Ever Yours

J.Conrad.

To Eric S. Pinker

Text MS Berg; Unpublished

[letterhead: Oswalds]
20. 9. 23.

Dearest Eric.

I have still a little temp: today and am returning to bed early – but not bright.

I won't attempt more than this word of greeting. I can tell you all about the arrang^{ts} for John next week. Impression favourable. Thanks for attending to my request.[2] As a matter of fact it was not necessary and I have returned the unused credit note to the bank.

Ever Yours

J. Conrad.

Thanks for written cheque.

---

[1] The Introduction to Garnett's *Letters from W. H. Hudson, 1901–1922* (Nonesuch Press, 1923); see Conrad's letter to Garnett of 30 November 1923.

[2] See Conrad's letter to Pinker of [10 September].

To Hugh Dent

Text MS Lubbock; Rude (1988)

[letterhead: Oswalds]

22. 9. 23.

Dear Mr Hugh.

I return the pre[li]ms of the *M. of the Sea* and *P[ersonal] R[ecord]*. Thanks.

Yes. I wished to have the *M of the S* first. I consider it the more important work of the two.

Kindest regards from us both

Yrs

J. Conrad.

To Florence and F. N. Doubleday

Text MS Princeton; Unpublished

[letterhead: Oswalds]

22. 9. 23.

My dear Florence and Effendi.

Thanks for the delightful series of p-cards and other good news of you. It is but sober truth to say that ever since we parted I have been missing you both. It is a fact that I have left a considerable part of my heart in Long Island – I leave the exact locality for you to guess – and that, whenever I hear from you there is the feeling of a distinct "pull at the string".

I am sorry dear F. that the serial has fizzled out.[1] One makes plans in perfect good faith and then . . . But whatever fails you may be sure it will never be the affection.

I regret to say that my health has been disappointing. The horrible cough returns – and I have had just now a pretty bad time with it for a fortnight or so. It stopped the work too. Still I will admit that it may have been worse, and now I am improving rapidly. But it is very disturbing and depressing while it lasts.

After the A. Pages' visit[2] there were no Americans here – and indeed very few visitors of any kind. The faithful Dick turns up at intervals – one or two others – and of course Mr & Mrs B. C. are added to the "permanent" list. They are here now. There is no doubt that B. is a "Daimler success". In two months' time he has tripled the sales of the Chapter Street House and got rid of all the undesirables on his staff, without – as he says – making any dangerous enemies for himself. Which is just as well! John is going to France

---

[1] 'The Oswaldians', begun in July.
[2] On 18 July.

in a fortnight for his first term of residence in the Rev. Bost's house. I hope he won't shock them all by the levity of his outlook and the unceremoniousness of his manners. It will be an experience for him!

Poor Jessie is much the same. She sends you both her dear love. You are turning up every day in our marital conversations. She envies you the fate that permits of fishing expeditions, but without bitterness, and she hopes that you are having the best of time[s].

Pardon this inane letter. I wish I could convey to you half the warm feeling with which I turn to you across these thousands of miles – we all once traversed together.

Ever my dear Florence your most devoted friend and servant

Joseph Conrad.

To John Galsworthy

Text Marrot 536 (in part)

Oswalds
23.9.23.

My dearest Jack,

The vol. of your stories[1] arrived while we were over in Havre arranging for John's stay with the family of the Rev. Mr. Bost to learn French by "forced practice." This explains why I didn't write before.

Thanks, my dear fellow. It is a jolly good handful. Some of them I've seen before in Mags. – but not many. For instance the *Late – 299* was quite new to me. And so was *Feud*. The one I like best is *Philanthropy*. Terrific! Indeed the little sheaf of pages 176–216 is my favourite of the shorter pieces; of the longer I fancy most all from p. 235 to the end. I see *The Times Supplt.* reviewer selected *The Hedonist* to hang some rather inane verbiage on [. . .] [2]

---

[1] *Captures* had been published by Heinemann on 15 September.

[2] Pp. 176–216 contain four stories, 'Virtue', 'Conscience', 'Salta Pro Nobis', and 'Philanthropy', the last describing a writer's efforts to be rid of a destitute stranger with a wife and dog. The longer pieces that Conrad fancied are 'Late – 299' and 'Had a Horse'. 'A Hedonist' is set in South Carolina and contrasts the hedonism of a 'New Yorker addicted to Italy' with the stereotypical fidelity of a former slave. The *TLS* reviewer began by observing that these stories were 'neither unworthy' of the author 'nor yet on a level with his best work'; citing a passage from 'The Hedonist', the reviewer noted that by comparison with *The Forsyte Saga*, 'here the detachment is rather that of a certain fatigue' (13 Sept. 1923, p. 602).

To William Rothenstein
Text MS Harvard; Unpublished

[letterhead: Oswalds]

23. 9. 23

My dearest Will.[1]

Warmest thanks for the vol and the inscription.[2] Oh my dear how good – how profoundly appealing all this is – this little selection. And how it marks the march of inexorable time! Do you remember me coming to your studio in the East End. Even so! I had that privilege. The Quarry I saw the first time I came to your house in London – on the easel – and have kept it [in] my eye, so to speak, ever since.[3]

This Lawrence is magnificent![4]

Pardon this scrap. We must see each other soon. Give my dear love to Alice.[5] You two dears must have had a bitterly anxious time.[6] May it all pass away.

Give my love to all your children

Ever your

JC

To F. N. Doubleday
Text TS/MS Princeton; Unpublished

[letterhead: Oswalds]

Sept. 24th. 1923.

My dear Effendi

I kept business out of the letter intended for both of you, jointly, and addressed to Florence.

---

[1] The son of a Yorkshire wool merchant, William Rothenstein (1872–1945; knighted 1931) studied art under Degas and Whistler, and held his first exhibition in Paris at the age of nineteen. During the First World War he was the official artist of the British Fifth Army and the Canadian Army of Occupation. He was admired above all for his portraits, whether graphics, paintings, or drawings. Thanks to an introduction from Cunninghame Graham, the Conrads had been friendly with him, his wife Alice, and their family since 1903, when Conrad sat for the first of several portraits. They now lived in the Cotswolds.

[2] *William Rothenstein* (Ernest Benn, 1923), an essay on his work by Hubert Wellington accompanied by thirty-three plates. It belonged to the Contemporary British Art Series, whose general editor was Rothenstein's brother Albert Rutherston.

[3] Painted in 1903–4, *The Old Quarry, Hawkworth* now hangs in the Cartwright Memorial Gallery, Bradford.

[4] One of several portraits of T. E. Lawrence.

[5] Before her marriage, Alice Rothenstein (née Knewstub, 1867–1957) had been an actress; her stage name was Alice Kingsley.

[6] Rachel, the Rothensteins' eldest daughter (1903–89, Mrs Alan Ward), had won a scholarship to the Royal College of Music in 1922, but fell severely ill soon after. She suffered several relapses and did not fully recover until 1930.

By the time you read this you will have seen the scheme of Frontispieces which Mr Sudler[1] has sent me and which I have returned to him annotated, by way of the clearest possible answer.

The state of affairs is that everything is settled except the Frontispiece of the "Nigger".

When I got Mr Sudler's list I was in bed with a beastly cough and temperature, and was unable to write myself. But on returning him the list Miss Hallowes wrote expressing my view that the inscription which you want to reproduce (the one in which are the words "By this book I stand or fall") is not perhaps of the kind which would be advisable to broadcast in an edition, which, we both hope, will be selling in tens of thousands.

What is your view? It may be that I am exaggerating to myself the importance of the whole thing. But still, as Miss H. has expressed my feeling that this was a pronouncement more fit for a copy presented privately to a friend[2] than for a public declaration, please consider it from *that* point of view; and if you conclude that there is no harm in doing it then let it go in – for better or worse.

Otherwise I must confess I have no suggestion to offer; unless you could find an artist, either known or obscure, who could draw a head of a West Indian negro that would have a suitable character. This, however, might be inadvisable from another point of view.

I did not forget Mrs. Curtiss James' copy. I thought perhaps you would send me a pre[li]ms sheet for signature, but I think that what I am sending you now may do just as well – being a half sheet with enough paper left on it to have it bound-in with the volume. This is the best I can think of to avoid a long delay in the presentation copy. I suppose you will be having your binders at work on the de luxe "Rover" before very long.

I quite understand how the Newport festivities must have offended what you call, yourself, your "New England soul".[3] How blasé all those people must be! I can't really understand what gratification those people do get. I suspect just none at all. For the sweetness and charm and the humanity of social intercourse do not depend on expenditure. And even the splendour

[1] Culbreth ('Cully') Sudler (1898–1975), one of Doubleday's employees, and a collector of Conrad's work. Preparing the ground for his arrival, Sudler had written 'Joseph Conrad Comes to America' for the *New York Herald, Books*, 29 April, pp. 1–2.

[2] In a letter to Quinn, 8 December 1912, Conrad called *The Nigger* 'the story by which, as creative artist, I stand or fall' (*Letters*, 5, p. 145).

[3] Lavish entertainments marked the end of the social season in Newport, RI. Rhode Island is itself a part of New England, but many of Newport's most ostentatious habitués came from farther south or west. Doubleday traced his ancestry to the austerer setting of mid-eighteenth-century Connecticut.

of it does not exactly depend on that. It's a matter of taste, of tact, of kindly desire to please, much more than of brute lavishness.

Be sure dear Effendi that I am most grateful to you for your labours, and profoundly touched by the friendship that prompts you in the task. Please give my love to Patty and Nelson who are much in my thoughts

Ever Your old

Conrad.

To Richard Curle
Text MS Indiana; Curle 126

[Oswalds]
Wed^y [26 September 1923]

Dearest Dick.

The water being cut off for 3 days at the main on account of the pipe-connections which must be renewed, we are migrating to the Curzon to-morrow.

Jessie is coming by road. I'll be at the RAC about 12 for $^1/_2$ an hour on my way to Pinker with whom I'll lunch. I hope I'll see you or have a message from you there.

Our love

Yours

J. C.

To G. Jean-Aubry
Text MS Yale; Unpublished

Mercredi
[26 September 1923][1]

Très cher Jean

Nous sommes expulsés d'ici par le sacré poêle – et ça jusqu'au Lundi prochain!!

Nous serons a l'hotel demain (Jeudi) dans l'après midi. Moi je serai avec Pinker jusqu'a 3^h probablement. Mais a 4^h je serai là. Viendrez Vous prendre une tasse de thé avec nous? Sinon envoyez moi un petit mot ou un message par phone pour prendre rendez-vous car j'ai a vs causer. J'ai travaillé sur La Flèche.[2] C'est étonnant ce que vs avez fait! Nous sommes desolés tous deux de ne pouvoir pas vs avoir chez nous ce week-end.

Votre tout dévoué

Conrad.

---

[1] Date added by Jean-Aubry, probably from the postmark, and confirmed by the tale of the faulty stove.
[2] *La Flèche d'or*, Jean-Aubry's French translation of *The Arrow of Gold*, published by Gallimard in 1929.

PS J'ai écrit et j'ai reçu une lettre de M. Aubry tout ce qu'il y a de plus amicale.

Very dear Jean

We are evicted from here by the dam' stove – and until next Monday!!

We will arrive at the hotel tomorrow (Thursday) in the afternoon. I will be with Pinker until about 3.00 probably. But at 4.00 I will be there. Will you take a cup of tea with us? If not, send me word or a message by phone with a meeting time, since I need to have a chat with you. I've been working on the Arrow. What you've done is amazing! We are both so sorry we can't have you with us this week-end.

Yours most devotedly

Conrad.

PS I wrote, and have had a most friendly letter from M. Aubry.

To Eric S. Pinker

Text MS Berg; Unpublished

[Oswalds]

Wednesday. [26 September 1923][1]

Dearest Eric.

I am a victim of mishaps. It appears that we must clear out of the house, as on account of that dam' stove the water will have to be turned off at the main from to-morrow evening till (I fear) Monday morning!

Therefore Jessie is coming by road to the usual refuge to-morrow afternoon. I will be with you as planned in the morning, as she will give a passage to Miss H in the car.

The whole thing is damnable. But I don't think it is my fault as I had every reason to believe that the thing would have been done while we were away in France. Perhaps I ought not to have gone till the stove was here – but then I wanted to be in France while Aubry was in Havre to put me in touch with Bost.

In view of the expense of this complication I send you a letter which I had a few days ago, and intended to answer by a curt refusal. But as it is I held my hand. It may be worth Appletons while to pay me a 50 for that introduction.[2] If so then you would perhaps negotiate the affair with this man who is coming over here next week, it seems. I am worried more than I can tell you – also perhaps more than is reasonable on my part.

Au revoir.

Ever Yours

J. Conrad.

---

[1] The stove's malfunction gives the date.   [2] See the letter to Pinker of 14 October.

To Eric S. Pinker

Text MS Berg; Unpublished

[letterhead: Hotel Curzon]

[28 September 1923][1]

Dearest Eric.

Sir Robert Jones came here at 9 and stayed on for nearly an hour and a half observing Jessie's jumping muscle. He says it must be stopped or it will bring on a nervous breakdown. The leg will have to go into a splint again – electric treatment must go on – other things will be done too. But no operation of course or anything like that. I will tell you more when I see you on Monday – if I may. About noon.

Meantime I send you my thanks for the extra cheque, Jessie received today, and I put down here what I must ask you to do for me.

I will send you the doctors bill for the last quarter. But that is a *foreseen* expense. It will be something between 40–50. If App[let]on shies off perhaps some other occasion for an article may arise. It will not delay the novel – not 24 hours.[2]

I'll ask you to let me have a cheque I can give on acc^t to Jessie['s] dressmakers. Say £30. You may make it to Messrs Lewis & Hylands[3] and she will (or I will) send it direct.

To bring that advance within the budget I propose you should deduct £5 every month from my cheque and make it 175 instead of the present 180. That adv^{ce} then will [be] repaid by March next. I can't make a better offer. You see my dear fellow when we made the first reduction of income I gave up £29.15 per month (180 instead of 209.15) practically 300 a year and then took on myself both Karola and ex-Miss Seale^{*4} = to another 240. And of course I contemplated a complete change in the style of living to be brought about say in June. All that did not come off. I only mention these things you know because I want to set out the difficulties of my position. No margin at all. You see why this absurd stove business has crippled me so completely.

I don't want you to look on me as untrustworthy in my plans and resolutions. I have all these things before me all the time.

---

[1] The day of Sir Robert's morning visit, which must have taken place on the 28th. The Conrads arrived on the afternoon of the 27th; since many London offices, including Pinker's, opened on Saturday mornings, Borys could have picked up his allowance 'tomorrow', i.e. on the 29th.

[2] After his American tour, Conrad found it difficult to resume work on *Suspense*.

[3] Of Hythe, Kent.

[4] On 24 September, Jessie Conrad's nurse–companion Audrey Seal had married 'Long Charlie' Vinten, the Conrads' chauffeur.

Now as to John. His budget is £160 for 3 school terms. The last in Tonb[rid]ge has been settled. If you send me £45 by 10th Oct. it will carry him till Jany 15 1924 when he will be going to France again after a fortnights holiday. It's usual to pay in advance and I will also get him a return ticket (good for 3 months) which is a saving.

It would be kind of you to phone me a message in the course of the day that it will be all right – for I am worrying stupidly, no end. I would be glad too if you would let B have his all^ce tomorrow so that I can get from him the £14 or 15 (I advanced) on Monday to help clear me here.

Ever yours

J. C.

To Eric S. Pinker

Text MS Berg; Unpublished

[letterhead: Oswalds]
1. Oct. 23

My dear Eric

I had paid my hotel bill just before I went out to lunch with you, but strange as it may seem to you forgot to ask you to pay into my acc^t £10. as I think I havent quite enough to meet the cheque I had to draw. Or only *just enough*.

Those things always cost more than one allows for. If you make it a personal loan I will repay you in a few days.

Ever Yours

J. C.

To Richard Curle

Text TS/MS Indiana; Curle 127

[Oswalds]
Wednesday.
3. 10. '23

Dearest Dick.

I have been in an awful quandary about the frontispiece for the *Nigg^r of the N* in the Concord edition.

The latest brain wave is to get a photo on Tower Hill which would include part at least of the front of the Mint – where the crew part from each other.[1]

---

[1] 'And to the right of the dark group the stained front of the Mint, cleansed by the flood of light, stood out for a moment dazzling and white like a marble palace in a fairy tale' (p. 172). On Conrad's voyage in the *Narcissus*, the crew signed off in Dunkirk.

It seems impossible to find such a thing in photo shops. We are trying still. But in case we fail do you think you could get the D^y Mail photographer to take for me such a picture with a view to reproduction in US. I am prepared of course to pay a fee.

I am bothering simply because I feel that it ought to be done by a skilled person. I hope you won't mind. They are in a hurry over there and I should like to catch next *Wednesday* packet. Our love.

Ever Yours

J. Conrad

To Eric S. Pinker

Text MS Berg; Unpublished

[Oswalds]
Wed^y 6 pm. [3 October 1923][1]

Dearest Eric.

Your wire just to hand I am acting on your valuable suggestion, a letter to Curle leaving by the same post.

Thank you for your letter of this morning with its good news as to Torrens paper,[2] and everything else. You are a good fellow! Am fairly well. Stove in hot action this afternoon.

Ever Yours

J. Conrad.

To F. N. Doubleday

Text TS/MS Princeton; Unpublished

[letterhead: Oswalds]
Oct. 4th. 1923.

My dear Effendi.

You will have found on your return from the forest-life a letter to you and another to Florence meant jointly for you both. I am delighted to infer from the general tone of your remarks that you have had a good time and perhaps also good fishing. Did Florence fish too? Did you have any adventures with the Redskins? And did your guide wear leather stockings?[3] I love to imagine to myself you two trailing wearily home, loaded with fish, and then setting to cooking your spoil by the camp fire in a primitive fashion, as though the

---

[1] If the 'valuable suggestion' was the idea of the frontispiece photograph for *The Nigger of the 'Narcissus'*, the letter to Curle of 3 October dates this one as well.

[2] Its American publication would be in *Collier's Weekly*, where it came out on 27 October. See also the letter to Doubleday of 7 November.

[3] As in James Fenimore Cooper's *Leatherstocking Tales*, which Conrad read as a boy.

comforts and refinements of "The Settlements" were unknown to you and such a place as Effendi Hill did not exist. I wish I had been around and shared your feasts. You would have had a piece of fish to spare for me, I feel sure.

I have done no fishing – not even in troubled waters. I would not have been above doing that, but there have been no opportunities. So I have remained poor though not conspicuously honest and so far there is no occasion for you to congratulate me on the use of my time. I coughed a little (but that was too much), and worked a little (and that was not enough), and worried a good deal, such being my nature. Jessie and I went over to Havre to arrange for John's stay with the Rev. Mr Bost, in a house where there are eight young people and no carpets on the stairs, and the atmosphere is intellectually severe and domestic – of the high thinking and plain living sort.[1] If in those surroundings he doesn't pick up French of the best sort then there is no hope for him in this world. Jessie rather enjoyed the excursion. I did not so much – but that's my own fault probably.

All this is private history. In a more public capacity I have really enjoyed myself, only in connection with the arrangements for the Concord Edition. You must have had to-day my night letter in answer to your Marconi, calling upon final settlement of the Narcissus Frontispiece.[2] My proposal of getting for it a Tower Hill photograph was the outcome of a sudden brain-wave and I did take steps immediately to obtain something that would do. I am sorry to report that so far we have failed. I have, as a last resource, wired last night to Curle asking him whether he could get one of the Daily Mail photographers to take his engine up there and obtain something suitable for reproduction. But of course, my dear Effendi, you can not expect anything by the mail leaving next Saturday (6th). That would be impossible. We may however obtain a couple of photos in time for the next Wednesday packet. (10th) If we fail in this attempt then I would have to leave the matter to you; and I suppose the facsimile of that inscription of which you have spoken will have to do. My objections to it were raised only on the ground of expediency. The idea is not bad in itself, and, anyhow, I feel that the matter must be settled. I remain, however, in hopes that Curle will do his best.

[1] 'Plain living and high thinking are no more' – a line from Wordsworth's sonnet 'O Friend! I know not which way I must look.'
[2] Conrad's Western Union 'cable letter' (private collection) reached Garden City on the morning of the 3rd.

And apropos of Curle. It appears, my dear Effendi, that so far the New York Times has not paid him for his article,[1] and as that paper is not a young struggling periodical, Curle expected certainly some honorarium. I suppose it will be all right. His standing as a journalist is good here and he by no means regards himself as an amateur who does those things for the sake of seeing himself in print. I asked him to do that article on my books in order mainly to prevent some inadequate person stepping in and doing it for the Times Supplement. He took some pains about it and made alterations in deference to my suggestions, and, generally, put into it some of his spare time. So, frankly, knowing my man, I feel a bit uncomfortable about it. Could it be that the New York Times accepted that article under some misapprehension? Or perhaps by special request from you? In that case, my dear Effendi, there would be nothing to say; but I feel that it would be advisable to make some acknowledgment to Curle – say $50, or $75, which would be exactly what the Times Supplement did pay. You could send it to him without any explanation and debit my account with it. All this in confidence between us two. But probably there will be no need, and the N.Y.T. will do the right thing presently.

You would already have seen the half sheet with the inscription for Mr and Mrs Curtiss James. Do you think it will do? As the moment approaches I am growing more and more impatient to see "The Rover" launched on the (may Heaven grant it) wave of public favour that would sweep your Continent from East to West and leave a deposit of gold dust in our pockets. And what a balm for the soul a real big success must be! Do not think, my dear Effendi, that I am indulging in day-dreams. Neither am I ungrateful for such success as I have had, with the help of good friends at the head of which you stand. But I know you won't misunderstand me.

The other day I went to see John Galsworthy, who had not been well lately in consequence of an accident with a cricket ball, which started some internal trouble. He is better, and spoke appreciatively of you – which pleased me. I also called on Mr Evans, who was very nice and friendly, and most obliging in a small request I had to make. Everybody speaks very well of him. Eric Pinker's deliberate opinion is that taking London publishers as a whole Evans is as able as any. I was sorry to hear that Mr Byard was not well.[2] I was

---

[1] Excerpts from Curle's essay 'The History of Mr. Conrad's Books' had appeared in the *New York Times Book Review* on 26 August.

[2] Charles ('Charlie') Seddon Evans (1883–1944) and Theodore Byard (1871?–1931) were the London managers of William Heinemann & Co; Doubleday had acquired a controlling interest upon the death of its founder in 1921.

shown the Galsworthy leather edition (red) which pleased me greatly.[1] There was some initial conversation about a leather edition for me, which seemed to open good possibilities at, say, 5/– per vol. But it is not my affair to talk of these matters. You will be probably hearing of them from the proper quarter.

Am I right, my dear Effendi, in my impression that you said that the Concord Edition will follow the text of the Heinemann Limited Edition. That would please me vastly. I have also an impression of you having planned that in the Concord Edition each work will form a separate volume, exactly as in the Blue Cloth Edition. I hate to have two of them crammed together in one binding. It was positive pain to me . . . Now don't say: "He's a funny fellow", my dear Effendi.

Our love to Florence and to you. Remember me affectionately to your children. I hope the baby is thriving.

Ever Your faithful

J. Conrad

PS Thanks for returned photographs received this week OK.

To Richard Curle

Text MS Indiana; Curle 128

[letterhead: Oswalds]

5. 10. 23

Dearest Dick

Many thanks for your unwearied kindness in this as in other matters. I suppose I can't hope to have the print in time for the next Wed[y] packet?

Should it reach your hands on Tuesday pray my dear fellow post it straight to Garden City. Just write on back *Nigger front[ce] from J.C.* Blunt is great. Really you are very good in that column.[2]

Our love.

Yours

J. C.

---

[1] The Manaton Edition of Galsworthy's works, published by Heinemann, comprised 530 sets of 30 volumes, some bound in vellum, some in red morocco.

[2] The most recent 'John Blunt' column, 'False Ideas. The Loud-Spoken People', was printed in the *Daily Mail* on the 3rd. According to Curle, who was writing for a paper that made no secret of its proprietor's opinions: 'The poisonous propaganda which is so busy teaching an idiotic class-hatred is profoundly un-English, appealing neither to the English kindliness nor to the English commonsense, but it has spread simply because the majority, being frightened of voicing their true opinions, allow a crack-brained minority to sway their emotions rather than their intellects' (p. 8).

PS. So sorry Your last Vailimas have been delayed.[1] They came yesterday. Going to night.

To Gordon Gardiner

Text TS Harvard; *Listy* 456; Najder (1970), 44

[letterhead: Oswalds]
Oct. 8th. 1923.

Dear friend

I won't delay answering your good letter, though I am in bed for a day or so and can not write conveniently with the pen.

I am sending back the pamphlet of the rules of the Club.[2] It is very interesting, but it occurs to me, my dear Gardiner, unless all these words are printed for nothing and the scheme of it has no meaning – mere verbiage as it were – I can not very well belong to this Club by the mere fact that I was born a R[oman] C[atholic], and though dogma sits lightly on me I have never renounced that form of Christian religion. The booklet of rules is so, I may say, theological that it would be like renouncing the faith of my fathers.

Of course you will understand, my dear, that it is not with me any question of the principles but merely a matter of correct conduct. I do not think it would be correct for me to ask you to put my name down, and indeed I do not think it could be done since one of the conditions of membership is to be a Protestant.

This is my inner feeling, but as a matter of fact I perceive that I simply could not be elected since election to the Club is based not on any assurance of sentiment but on a clear matter of fact – member of the Church of England, for which in truth I have a great regard and sympathy. I think that you will agree with the reflections that prompt me in what I have said.

---

[1] The Vailima Edition of *The Works of Robert Louis Stevenson* was published in twenty-six volumes by Heinemann and Scribner's in 1922–3. In a letter of 26 April, Jessie Conrad told her husband that 'Two more of Dick's Stevenson volumes came and I sent them on' (MS Yale). As a Heinemann author, Conrad was perhaps entitled to the volumes or could buy them at an author's discount; in any case, he was passing them over to Curle.

[2] Gardiner was Secretary of the National Club in Whitehall Gardens. Its founding principles were: '1. That it is essential to the due administration of public affairs throughout the empire, that the Protestant principles of the Constitution, the Protestant reformed faith, as established by law, shall be maintained. 2. That the authority of Holy Scripture ought to be recognised in any system of national education, as the only infallible standard of faith and morals. 3. That it is the duty of all persons to endeavour to improve the moral and social condition of the people.' The Club offered reduced subscriptions for Anglican clergymen (Charles Dickens, Jr, *Dickens's Dictionary of London*, 1879 edition, under 'National Club').

I am afraid I am a lost soul. Some years ago I received an invitation to join a R. C. Association, presided [over] by the Duke of Norfolk,[1] the secretary of which at the time was W. S. Lilly,[2] for whose writings I had always a certain sympathy. The proposal itself was in a sense complimentary. We exchanged several letters but when the articles of the Association were sent to me in due course I discovered that the members engaged themselves with all their might and power to work for the restoration of the temporal power of the Pope. Conceive you that imbecility! Of course I pointed out that this was a political object, that the accomplished fact[3] had all my sympathy and that I certainly would not lift a finger to re-establish temporal power; upon which Lilly lectured me with great severity and that was the end of it. So you see now I have got to stand between the two, a prey to the first inferior devil that may come along. My only hope of escaping the eternal fires is my utter insignificance. I shall lie low on the Judgment Day, and will probably be overlooked.

Do not forget your promise to come here whenever you can. I shall be looking forward to seeing you. Jessie sends her love.

Your old

Conrad

To Richard Curle

Text MS Indiana; Unpublished

[Oswalds]

[8–12 October 1923][4]

Dearest Dick

We are so truly sorry. I don't know whether *all* children are to go through a tubercular trouble but I know that one of Jessie's sisters had at the age of 7 to go through a period of invalidism of that kind (more than a year). She became a fine healthy girl (under very adverse circumstances for they were

---

[1] Henry Fitzalan-Howard (1847–1917; 15th Duke of Norfolk 1860) hereditary Earl Marshal of England, and, by tradition, the senior Roman Catholic layman.

[2] William Samuel Lilly (1840–1919) was a barrister by profession and a Catholic apologist by conviction. In 1875 he published a popular selection of Cardinal Newman's writings. He also wrote on legal and literary topics.

[3] Accomplished by the schism between the English Crown and the Church of Rome in the sixteenth century.

[4] On 9 October Miss Hallowes reported to Jean-Aubry (MS Yale) that Conrad had been 'laid up for the last two days, & is still very unwell'; on the [17th] he told Curle that he had left his bed on Saturday the 13th. By the time of this letter the frontispiece photograph had been taken, but the *Daily Mail* photographer had not yet been paid (see the letters to Curle of 5 and 17 October; Conrad hoped that the prints would be ready for the 8th or 9th, to catch the Wednesday sailing).

poor) and is now a strong woman of 40.[1] So keep a good heart. The boy has every possible advantage and will get over it all right.[2]

Many thanks for the photos. Pray give the man 30/ and I will send you a cheque.

Am writing this in bed

Ever Yours

J. Conrad

To Eric S. Pinker
Text TS Berg; Unpublished

[letterhead: Oswalds]
Oct. 11th. 1923.

Dearest Eric

I must draw the line somewhere. I really can not write Fisher Unwin's advertisements for him, and especially about myself. And on reflection you will see the actual difficulty of such a thing. What can I write to that man who edits the prospectus? That I think "The Rover" is the best novel ever written? I am not going to write that. And even if I, so to speak, bargain my soul away for an advertisement and give him the material for a Preface that will be some day written for "The Rover" it would not be the stuff he wants.

Of course there are obvious things that could be said about it, but not by me: That in Peyrol I have a creation that resembles neither Lingard nor Dominique nor Nostromo and yet belongs to the same family;[3] or that I have invested with a sustained life an action which turns on a very narrow pivot – and so on and so on.

I know perfectly well what I have done, but let others find it out. And I can not throw my soul into the street, as it were, by saying how I managed to finish that book in circumstances of personal sorrow and great mental distress.

---

[1] Jessie Conrad's sister Ethel Foulds (née Rachel Ethel George, 1881–1931).
[2] Curle's son Charles, always known as Adam (after L'Isle-Adam, France, where he was born in 1916), came to the end of an eventful, sometimes dangerous life in 2006. He taught psychology and education at Oxford, Exeter, Harvard, and the University of Ghana. Inspired by Quaker and Buddhist teaching and example, he served as a mediator in many conflicts around the globe, including the Biafran and Indo-Pakistani wars and the fragmentation of Yugoslavia. From 1973 to 1978, he held the Chair of Peace Studies at Bradford University, the first such chair in the UK, and he won the Gandhi International Peace Award in 2000.
[3] Jean-Aubry had just told Conrad exactly that in a letter of 7 October (MS Yale): 'Vous avez réussi à faire un Peyrol qui ne ressemble ni à Lingard, ni à Dominic, ni à Nostromo, tout en appartenant à la même famille.' Lingard, Nostromo, and Peyrol are all to some extent modelled upon Dominique Cervoni, the Corsican who was Conrad's mentor and shipmate in Marseilles.

You know I do not like to dismiss any of your suggestions without the profoundest consideration; but I have been writing for nearly thirty years now and I consider that such a request is a proof of gross ignorance or immense cheek. You may think that I am missing altogether the nature of the request – that it is something very remote from the considerations I have put before you. Well, my dear, can you suggest the sort of thing that I could write over my signature for an advertising pamphlet? If you can I will consider it.

In haste

Ever affec^{ly} Yours

J. Conrad

To Eric S. Pinker

Text TS/MS Berg; Unpublished

[letterhead: Oswalds]
Oct. 12th. 1923.

Dearest Eric

I don't know what has happened. Yesterday I received Dr Reid's bill from which it appears as if his account rendered in July had not been settled.

That was the account which together with Dr Fox's[1] was sent to you, by arrangement, on July 18th, and was acknowledged as received for settlement. I had neither doctor's receipt but I surmised that they might have been sent to you. That is why I did not bother.

Perhaps the office has overlooked it, or may be the doctor has made a mistake. Anyway, my dear fellow, look into this matter and settle it for me. As you see, the account here inclosed (of Reid's) includes both quarters.[2]

The more I think of Mr F[isher] U[nwin]'s request the less I see how I could do anything of the kind over my signature.

This is my last day in bed.

Ever Yours

J Conrad

Pardon the blot. This damnable pen.

---

[1] Dr Campbell Tilbury Fox (1872–1949), MRCS, LRCP, the son of a specialist in fungal dermatology, completed his medical training at University College, London, in 1901, and was Medical Officer at the Cottage Hospital, Ashford, Kent. During the First World War, he served as a surgeon-captain.

[2] For Mr Reid, the surgeon and radiologist, see the letter to Jessie Conrad of 22 April.

To Ford Madox Ford

Text TS Yale; J-A, 2, 323 (in part); *Listy* 457[1]

[letterhead: Oswalds]
Oct. 13th. 1923.[2]

My dear Ford,[3]

Forgive me for answering your interesting holograph letter[4] on the machine. I don't like to delay any longer telling you how pleased I am to know you have got hold of such interesting work, in conditions which will permit you to concentrate your mind on it in peace and comfort. My warmest wishes for its success. I won't tell you that I will be "honoured" or "flattered" by having my name included amongst your contributors, but I will tell you that I consider it a very friendly thing on your part to wish to do so.

I don't think your memory renders me justice as to my attitude to the early E[nglish] R[eview]. The early E. R. is the only one I ever cared for.[5] The mere fact that it was the occasion of you putting on me that gentle but persistent pressure which extracted, from the depths of my then despondency, the stuff of the Personal Record,[6] would be enough to make its memory dear. My only grievance against the early E. R. is that it didn't last long

---

[1] Jean-Aubry prints only the first paragraph and gives the date as the 23rd. Morey's unpublished dissertation was the first to reproduce the whole letter. The first full publication was in *Listy*.

[2] Morey, pp. 221–7, gives a detailed account of the confusion surrounding the dating of Conrad's and Ford's correspondence in October and November 1923.

[3] Ford Madox Ford (né Hueffer, 1873–1939) wrote some eighty novels and memoirs in the course of a long and varied career in England, France, and the United States. He was also a poet and an inspired editor, who created two remarkable magazines, the *English Review* and the *transatlantic review*. His collaborations with Conrad included *The Inheritors* (1901), *Romance* (1903), and *The Nature of a Crime* (1909). Conrad and Ford quarrelled in 1909; by the end of 1911, a rapprochement had begun, but the friendship never regained its earlier closeness. After serving in the First World War, Ford changed his surname from Hueffer and, after a brief period as a smallholder in the south of England, settled in France, where he divided his time between Paris and Provence. It was in Paris that he founded and edited the *transatlantic review*; though it only ran from January 1924 to January 1925, it is one of the most significant of all Modernist periodicals in English. In his later years, he taught at Olivet College, Michigan, and became the mentor of such American writers as Robert Lowell, Peter Taylor, and Robie Macauley.

[4] Ford had written to Conrad on 7 October, inviting him to contribute to the *transatlantic review* (Stape and Knowles, p. 216).

[5] In his letter of the 7th, Ford had written: 'I remember you did not like the original *English Review* much.' Conrad's profession of fondness notwithstanding, *Under Western Eyes* and his articles on the sinking of the *Titanic* were serialised in the *Review* after its editorship had passed from Ford to Austin Harrison. In general, however, Harrison's list of contributors was much duller than Ford's.

[6] Under the title *Some Reminiscences*, it began in the inaugural issue, December 1908, and ran until June 1909; illness stoppped him from sending copy for the July number.

enough.[1] If I say that I am curious to see what you will make of the venture it isn't because I have the slightest doubts of your consistency. You have a perfect right to say that you are "rather unchangeable". Unlike the Serpent (which is Wise) you will die in your original skin. So I have no doubt that the Review will be truly Fordian – at all costs! But it will be interesting to see what men you will find and what you will get out of them in these changed times.[2]

I won't say anything about myself for it wouldn't be amusing and not even interesting. We are still sticking in this house till next year. A novel of sorts will appear at the end of this year. Another, half written, has been stewing in its own juice for months and months. I suppose I may take it that B^d Arago is a permanent address where you can be found from now on.

Yours

J. Conrad.

To John Galsworthy

Text MS Forbes; Unpublished

[Oswalds]
14.10.23

Dearest Jack

I am glad you are nearly over your trouble; but we are much concerned at the news about dear Ada.

Of course the journey to Montpellier is rather long.[3] But not so long as to Cannes for instance.

Is M'llier out of [the] question? Apart from its Faculty men there are, I hear, English doctors there. I do believe the climate would do. No mistral, no deadly chill breezes in the evenings.

I shudder to think how this cyclonic type of weather must have made her suffer.[4] It laid me up for 5 days. I only crawled down yesterday, and

---

[1] Conrad's attitude at the time had been deeply affected by Ford's tumultuous relationships, both personal and professional, and the ruin of what had been a warm and creative friendship. In 1909, Conrad complained of 'His furies, his agonies, his visits to various people of distinguished quality and his general carryings on like a spoiled kid' (*Letters*, 4, p. 253).

[2] Among them were Joyce, part of whose 'Work in Progress' *Finnegans Wake* appeared there, and Hemingway, who succeeded Basil Bunting as assistant editor. Among the women were Selma Lagerlöf, Jean Rhys, and Gertrude Stein.

[3] As Conrad well knew, having travelled there with his family in February, and again in December 1906. One of the city's great attractions, however, for those who wintered there, was the high quality of its long-established medical school.

[4] Heavy rain and gale-force westerlies had set in around the eighth.

had my first look at Your Lt^d Edition.[1] I like its get-up immensely including the type with the exception perhaps of the initial letters which look a little commonplace in comparison with the distinguished aspect of all the other features. And, my word! I am glad to have the reproduction of Rudo's portrait of you[2] for which I have a particular affection as a rendering, a likeness and a most distinguished piece of work. Thanks my dearest Jack.

John left home on Friday for Havre. It will be an experience for him. We shall see. Meantime we feel bereaved. No child in the house. Poor Jessie has rushed off to her mother to stand by while the news of the death of her youngest child is broken to her. She's 74 so I fancy she will take it quietly but Jessie is awfully upset herself.[3]

My dear love to You both

Yrs

J. C.

To Eric S. Pinker

Text MS Berg; Unpublished

[Oswalds]
14. 10. 23.

Dearest Eric

Thanks for your two letters. Your handling of the Jewett affair is quite right.[4] Anything above 50 would be welcome of course.

I am afraid my dear I must have expressed myself with undue warmth about the F[isher] U[nwin] suggestion. It was made to you and of course you very properly passed it on. I never associated you with the idea except as channel of communication. But I am glad you agree that nothing over the signature is possible. It is true that I have been asked once or twice by

---

[1] A presentation set of the Manaton Edition inscribed 'Joseph Conrad, affectionately, John Galsworthy, October 1923'; it featured in the Hodgson sale of Conrad books and MSS, 13 March 1925.

[2] The painter and illustrator Rudolf Helmut Sauter (1895–1977) was John Galsworthy's nephew.

[3] Herbert Frank George (born 1890) had died of influenza in East London, South Africa, on 12 October. He had been Chief Steward in the Union Castle Line's *York Castle*. His mother was seventy-six. Jessie Conrad wrote to Józef Retinger on 6 December: 'I think J. C. is feeling the shock of my young brother's death very much. He was like another son and as a boy spent much of his time in our home' (MS Biblioteka PAN, Cracow).

[4] See the letter to Pinker of [26 September]. The request from the D. Appleton Co. to write an introduction for a book is grounds for identifying the instigator of the 'affair' as Rutger B(leecker) Jewett (1867–1935), one of their senior editors. Earlier in his career, he had been John Lane's New York manager. Jewett was known as a publisher who admired and encouraged serious fiction. He was, for example, among the first to recognise the promise of Edith Wharton and was still editing her books. Before Jewett's time there, Appleton had published the US edition of *An Outcast of the Islands*.

publishers for a descriptive par. It was a fact that they did not know what to say. In each case I wrote a few lines which I handed to your father. I believe they were used by the publicity man. But truly I would not even like to do that.

I am afraid you had a dreadful day for your shoot.

Ever Yours

J. C.

To Thomas J. Wise

Text MS Dartmouth; Unpublished

[letterhead: Oswalds]
14. 10. 23.

Dear Wise.

Thanks very much for the cheque.[1] With that MS you have now all I have written (3 pieces) about Stephen Crane.

I do hope You will be able to acquire one of those MS of mine which Quinn is about to sell.[2] If fate had brought us together at or about 1911 it is certainly You who would have had them all!

My wife joins me in kindest regards to You both

Yours

J. Conrad

To [?]

Text MS Berg; Unpublished

[letterhead: Oswalds]
14. 10. 23

Madame.[3]

Je suis touché de Votre bonté. Le petit volume des vignettes pleines de charme et de cœur que Vous avez eu l'idée de m'envoyer a été reçu avec la plus grande appréciation, d'abord comme preuve de Votre bienveillance et puis comme une remarquable expression d'une rare person[n]alité pour qui j'ai eprouvé depuis longtemps déjà une sincère et respectueuse sympathie. Comme notre pauvre ami avait raison de Vous presser de le publier! Je regrette Votre characteristique* hésitation. Il aurait été si heureux de le recevoir de Vos mains.

---

[1] For Conrad's Preface to Crane's *The Red Badge of Courage* ('His War Book'), sold to Wise on 12 October for £35 (see *Documents*, p. 217).

[2] John Quinn's nearly complete collection of pre-1917 Conrad MSS, begun in 1911, was to be auctioned in New York.

[3] She is unidentified; perhaps her 'vignettes' were visual, perhaps verbal.

Je me suis permis de sourire doucement à Votre inscription. Hélas Madame je ne suis ni maître ni grand. Votre injustice envers Vous-même est trop évidente pour que j'en ose parler. Tant des généreuses sympathies pour les beautés et les souffrances de la terre ne pourraient exister sans cette grandeur d'âme que Vous Vous refusez.

Je suis Madame toujours Votre très fidèle et très obéissant serviteur

Joseph Conrad.

Dear Madame,

I am touched by your kindness. This little book of charming and heartfelt vignettes, which you were thoughtful enough to send me, was received with the greatest appreciation, first as a proof of your goodwill and also as a remarkable expression of a rare personality for whom I have long felt a sincere and respectful fondness. How right our poor friend was to urge you to publish it! I regret your characteristic hesitation. He would have been so happy to receive it from your hands.

I allowed myself a gentle smile at your inscription. Alas, Madame, I am neither a master nor great. Your injustice to yourself is too apparent for me to speak of it. So much generous understanding of the beauties and the sorrows of the earth could not exist without that grandeur of spirit which you deny in yourself.

I am, Madame, ever your most faithful and most obedient servant

Joseph Conrad.

To André Gide

Text MS Doucet; *L. fr.* 190

[letterhead: Oswalds]
16 Oct. 23.

Très cher ami,[1]

Merci de Votre bonne lettre.[2] Nous fîmes une visite au Havre seulement pour faire la connaissance de M. le Pasteur Bost et de sa famille. Il reçoit des jeunes étrangers qui veulent apprendre le Français. L'impression étant favorable nous avons envoyé notre Jean là bas il y a trois jours.

---

[1] Of all the literary friends of Conrad's later years, the French writer André-Paul-Guillaume Gide (1869–1951) was among the most distinguished and artistically remarkable. A born-again pagan and a recidivist puritan, his strengths lay in intimate autobiography and ironic fiction. Among his works are *Les Nourritures terrestres* (1897), *L'Immoraliste* (1902), *La Porte étroite* (1909), *Les Caves du Vatican* (1914), and *Les Faux-monnayeurs* (1926). He first met Conrad in July 1911, translated *Typhoon*, directed the other translations of Conrad's work into French, and dedicated *Voyage au Congo* (1928) to Conrad's memory.

[2] Of 8 October (Stape and Knowles, p. 219).

Nous ne fimes qu'aller et revenir. Mais étant au Havre il etait impossible de ne pas essayer de vous voir – même au risque de Vous déranger un peu. Nous avons regardé "la vieille maison."¹ Quel charme. Quel caractère! Mais il se faisait tard. Il fallait rentrer. Nous regrettament* infiniment de ne pouvoir attendre le retour de Mme Votre femme.² J'aurai[s] été si heureux de la saluer et de lui presenter Jessie, qui est fort touchée du message amical que Vous lui transmettez. She sends her love en retour et a l'espoir de faire la connaissance de Mme Gide avant bien longtemps. Exprimez je [vous] prie à ces Messieurs mes regrets de les avoir manqué[s].

Moi aussi mon cher Gide j'ai l'intention de finir quelque chose cet hiver. Je savais que vous étiez en train de préparer une nouvelle édition du Typhoon.³ J'attends mon exemplaire avec impatience. Je suis heureux de savoir que mon œuvre a des amis en France – et c'est a Vous et la [Nouvelle] Revue Française que je dois cette joie. Il n y a que la nrf pour publier les livres d'une façon attrayante, vraiment c'est parfait! Je viens de recevoir de la part de Mme Rivière et de Ph. Neel un exemplaire d'Une Victoire.⁴ Traduction tout-a-fait remarquable.

Pas de danger que Jean Vous oublie. Au printemps quand il aura appris un peu le Français peut-être Vous lui permettrez de Vous faire une petite visite. Amitiés de ma femme. Affectueuse poignée de main.

> Votre vieux
>
> Conrad.

My very dear friend,

Thanks for your good letter. We only visited Le Havre to make the acquaintance of Pastor Bost and his family. He takes in young foreigners who want to learn French. The impression being favourable, we sent John to him three days ago.

We did nothing but go and return. But being in Le Havre it was impossible not to try to see you – even at the risk of disturbing you a little. We have seen

---

¹ The Gides' country house in Cuverville, on the Seine, not far from Rouen. Gide was desolated not to have been there: 'et je n'étais pas là! Et vous n'avez trouvé personne! Et la vieille maison qui vous souhaitait depuis si longtemps n'a su s'ouvrir . . . Et sur votre carte aucune adresse, aucune indication qui permît de vous ratrapper, de vous rejoindre!'

² Madeleine Gide (née Rondeaux, 1867–1938).

³ Gide's translation originally appeared in the *Revue de Paris* in March 1918, shortly before its publication as a book by the Nouvelle Revue Française.

⁴ Translated by Isabelle Rivière and Philippe Neel, *Une Victoire* was serialised in *Le Temps* from 4 April to 11 June 1922 before its book publication in two volumes (Paris: Nouvelle Revue Française, 1923); see J. H. Stape, 'The Art of Translation: Conrad, Gide, and the Translation of *Victory*', *Journal of Modern Literature*, 17.1 (Summer 1990), 155–65.

"the old house." What charm. What character! But it was getting late. We had to return. We regretted immensely not being able to wait for your wife's return. I would have been so happy to greet her and introduce her to Jessie, who is touched by your friendly message. She sends her love likewise and hopes to make the acquaintance of Madame Gide before very long. Please convey to those gentlemen my regrets at having missed them.

My dear Gide, I am also trying to finish something this winter. I knew you were preparing a new edition of Typhoon. I await my copy impatiently. I am happy to know that my work has friends in France – and I owe this pleasure to you and the NRF. There's nothing like the NRF for publishing such attractive books, really it's perfect! I have just received a copy of Une Victoire from Mme Rivière and Ph. Neel. An altogether remarkable translation.

No danger of John's forgetting you. In the spring, when he will have learned a bit of French, perhaps you will allow him to pay you a visit. Greetings from my wife. With a friendly handshake.

Your old

Conrad.

To Richard Curle

Text MS Indiana; Curle 129

[Oswalds]
Wed^y [17 October 1923][1]

Dearest Dick.

Herewith 30/– for the camera man.

Jessie says she wrote to you yesterday. Do drop us a line about the boy and Yourself.

I got up last Sat after 4 days in bed and have [been] at work since Monday. Very slow though.

We heard from John who arrived safely.

Ever Yours

J. C.

To Eric S. Pinker

Text MS Berg; Unpublished

[Oswalds]
17. 10. 23

Dearest Eric.

Thanks for your letters received yesterday. I missed the post somehow last evening.

---

[1] Dated by Conrad's recovery from his illness and John's arrival in Le Havre.

I have received Dr Fox's receipt to-day. Thanks.

Mrs C has been much moved and interested.[1] I do not know how philosophical you can be, but I know that Borys' announced arrival (he was born in Jan:) spoiled my Xmas for me.

Anyway it's a great experience – I mean for the man. My old friend Hope always maintained that he lost a tooth for every one of his children. There were five of them.[2]

I had more fortitude but I *was* glad when it was over.

Affectly Yours

J. C.

Give my love to your wife.

To G. Jean-Aubry
Text MS Yale; Unpublished

18. 10. 23
[letterhead: Oswalds]

Très Cher,

Pourrez VS venir Dim^che pour lunch et rester jusqu'au jour ou Mme Alvar pourra venir vous chercher?[3]

Walpole[4] partira Lundi matin. Nous pourrons donc travailler ensemble un peu. Jessie sends her love

Ever yours

J. Conrad.

My very dear fellow,

Can you come to lunch on Sunday and stay until the day Madame Alvar can come to fetch you?

Walpole leaves on Monday morning. So we can work together a little. Jessie sends her love.

Ever yours

J. Conrad.

---

[1] Pinker's wife was pregnant.

[2] Four of the Hopes' children have been identified: Muriel (1881–1960), Fountaine (1882–99), Herford (1884–1941), and Conrad (1890–1963).

[3] On the 19th, Conrad wired Mme Alvar: 'Mrs Harding 14 Holland Park London Please let Jean know we will meet him 3.58 tomorrow delighted to see you and your party for lunch on Sunday regards Conrad'. Sunday was the 21st.

[4] The novelist Hugh Walpole: see the letter to him of 18 November.

To George Mansfield
Text MS Indiana; Unpublished

[letterhead: Oswalds]

19. 10. 23.

Dear Mʳ Mansfield.[1]

I remember You quite well and I was glad to hear from an old shipmate. The fact of me writing to you to rejoin the ship had escaped my memory till your letter recalled it.[2] All this is very far away now; but I have not forgotten that pleasant voyage and the excellent ship's company we had that time. The next was not so good,[3] and after that I left the sea. The dear old Torrens was my last ship.[4] With kind regards

Yours truly

Joseph Conrad.

To Eric S. Pinker
Text TS/MS Berg; Unpublished

Oswalds.

Oct. 20th. 1923.

Dearest Eric

Herewith a letter received to-day from A. S. Watt.[5] I answered by a few lines asking him to communicate with you direct.

I suppose you have no objection to negotiate with Watt. I have an impression you told me you were on friendly terms, and in any case this is a matter essentially for you. I admit, however, I am curious to know what is behind this, and I hope you will assuage my curiosity. But I don't intend to lose any sleep about this matter!

I will take this opportunity to expose to you my view of the attitude which it would be perhaps advantageous to take. Generally, it is governed by the immediate future, not by any remote considerations, and it is this:

---

[1] George Mansfield (b. 1869), from Essex, made his first voyage as assistant butcher in the *Torrens* from London to Adelaide in 1891–2. At the request of Captain W. H. Cope, Conrad, who was first mate, wrote to Mansfield offering him a berth for the return voyage as an ordinary seaman at £1 per month.

[2] See *Letters*, 1, p. 108.   [3] In 1892–3.

[4] Conrad made his last major voyages in the *Torrens*, but his final vessel was the *Adowa*, which was supposed to carry French emigrants to Canada in 1893. She got no farther than Rouen before returning to London.

[5] Alexander Strahan Watt (1880–1948) was the second son and successor to Alexander Pollock Watt (1838–1914), who in 1881 founded the world's first literary agency, A. P. Watt and Company. The firm's clients included G. K. Chesterton, Robert Graves, W. Somerset Maugham, William Butler Yeats, and H. G. Wells.

We may assume that "The Rover" is a factor of the situation as a potential success, perhaps of an exceptional sort. If that happens it would affect the whole market. If that hope is not realised then we may safely say that the position would be no worse than before. On these grounds I think that in another four or five months we may be approached on better terms than we can expect to get now. I think that the attitude towards my work in the film world has been undergoing a certain change in a favourable sense. Therefore, delay can not possibly hurt us. I mean "diplomatic procrastination", which I am sure you will know how to make inoffensive.

Supposing then that the above view is justified I feel that I would like you to have as great a body of my work to deal with as possible. I am bound to communicate to you all the proposals that come in my way, (like that French one about a fortnight ago, or this one) but I am seriously considering whether it would not be better to abstain from dealing with these things piecemeal till, at any rate, we find out whether a general offer may not be made to us under the influence of the stimulus given to my market by a new book. It is possible that next spring a treaty for the whole could be made on advantageous terms. From this point of view I ask whether it is worth while meantime to let people pick and choose what would be naturally regarded as the "best bits" by the other party simply because they had been already disposed of.

I have the less scruple in putting it before you because your own interest in a deal of that sort is to be considered. A thousand pounds in a lump, out of say a payment of five thousand for the whole, is obviously better than a hundred or two hundred now and again for detailed transactions, leaving a residue which may be branded as "unsaleable". The proverb of "a bird in the hand" comes in here, I admit, but I do not contemplate a very distant future. Right or wrong, I feel that the next five months may make a great difference for the better without endangering such prospects as we may have at the present time to any serious extent.

These are my reflections. Nothing in the above is meant to trammel your action in any particular instance. You obviously must have a clearer sense of the general situation. My point really is that the film world won't collapse for the next year certainly; and that there is a chance of my market position being improved within say five months.

I leave it to your mature consideration.

Ever Yours

J. Conrad.

I hope Your wife is going on well.

PS Don't think I am out to worry you about these d—d Doctors. I have Dr Fox's bill duly receipted. As to Read* (two quarters) did I understand correctly that you were going to pay one quarter now and the other next month? I have had no acknowledgment from him yet.

J. C.

To Lt-Colonel Matthew Bell
Text TS Texas; Unpublished

[letterhead: Oswalds]
Oct. 22nd. 1923.

Dear Col. Bell[1]

I hope you will not think us officious but my wife and myself think we ought to let you know of a possible tenant. It is an old acquaintance of ours, a Mrs Harding, who was here yesterday. She confessed to my wife that ever since she knew this house she wanted very much to get it, but did not like to say anything before being absolutely certain that we were leaving. In fact the house has pleased her so much that she would like to buy it. Should you not desire to sell, however, she would like to take it on a long repairing lease.[2] She asked us to ascertain your views before approaching you directly.

It can not be a sudden fancy because she has seen this house many times and appreciates the grounds very much, which she said she would like to keep just as they are. I need not tell you that if anything comes of it we will do our best to meet her wishes as to dates and so on.

Pray give my regards to Mrs Bell.[3] Jessie sends her love. Believe me

Sincerely yours

J. Conrad

P.S. It strikes me I ought to tell you that there is a Mr Harding, whose real calling is to be a devoted husband; but the world knows him as a wealthy solicitor with offices in Birmingham and London. Their town address is: 14 Holland Park, W. However, if you will let us know whether you will entertain either of those two proposals we will write to her and she will then approach you directly.

---

[1] Lt-Col. Matthew Gerald Edward Bell (1871–1927) was the owner of Bourne Park, Bishops-bourne, and thus the Conrads' landlord at Oswalds. He had served in India and Somalia.
[2] A lease in which the tenant assumes responsibility for maintenance and repairs.
[3] Mary Bell (born 1875) married the then Captain Matthew Bell in 1905 after four years of service as maid of honour to Queen Alexandra.

To Ford Madox Ford

Text TS/MS Virginia; TS draft Yale; *t. r.* (in part) and facsimile; J-A, 2, 323[1]

[Oswalds]

[23 October 1923][2]

Dear Ford.

Since you wish to quote I have expanded a little the passage in my letter. Of course you will use what you think fit.[3]

The early E[nglish] R[eview] is the only literary business that, in Bacon's phraseology, "came home to my bosom". [4] The mere fact that it was the occasion of you putting on me that gentle but persistent pressure which extracted from the depths of my then despondency the stuff of the "Personal Record" would be enough to make its memory dear. Do you care to be reminded that the editing of the first number was finished in that farmhouse we occupied near Luton?[5] You arrived one evening with your amiable myrmidons and parcels of copy. I shall never forget the cold of that night, the black grates, the guttering candles, the dimmed lamps and the desperate stillness of that house, where women and children were innocently sleeping, when you sought me out at 2 a.m. in my dismal study to make me concentrate suddenly on a two-page notice of the "Ile des Ping[o]uins". [6] A marvellously successful instance of editorial tyranny! I suppose you were justified. The Number One of the E. R. could not have come out with two blank pages in it. It would have been too sensational. I have forgiven you long ago.

---

[1] In the first number of the *transatlantic review* (January 1924), pp. 98–9, Ford quoted the second and third paragraphs of this letter and the fourth paragraph from Conrad's letter of 10 November. A facsimile appeared in Volume 2, no. 2, p. 326. Yale holds a TS draft of the two paragraphs with Conrad's holograph corrections which Ford has dated '18/11/23'. On a sheet accompanying this draft, Ford noted that this was the only Conrad letter he had ever sold, the sale being to benefit the magazine.

[2] Dated by Morey, p. 221.

[3] The following two paragraphs are a revised and expanded version of the second paragraph in Conrad's letter to Ford of 13 October. After Conrad's death, Ford included a facsimile in the memorial 'Conrad Supplement' to vol. 2 no. 2 (September 1924, p. 326), and again in *Joseph Conrad: A Personal Remembrance*. The letter to which Conrad is evidently replying is typed and dated '13/X/23', and enclosed two undated pages written earlier by hand in which Ford also asked for a contribution along the lines of *A Personal Record*, which Ford had commissioned for the *English Review* (Stape and Knowles, p. 221).

[4] From the dedication to the Duke of Buckingham in *The Essays or Counsels, Civill and Morall* (1597): 'I doe now publish my *Essayes*; which, of all my other workes, have beene most Currant: For that, as it seemes, they come home, to Mens Businesse, and Bosomes.'

[5] Someries. See *Letters*, 4, p. 146.

[6] *Penguin Island* (1908), a satirical novel by Anatole France (1844–1924, Nobel Prize 1921). Conrad's review appeared in the first number of the *English Review*, and was reprinted in *Notes on Life and Letters*.

My only grievance against the early E. R. is that it didn't last long enough. If I say that I am curious to see what you will make of this venture it isn't because I have the slightest doubts of your consistency. You have a perfect right to say that you are "rather unchangeable". Unlike the Serpent (which is Wise) you will die in your original skin. So I have no doubt that the Review will be truly Fordian – at all costs. But for one of your early men it will be interesting to see what men you will find now and what you will get out of them in these changed times.

I am afraid the source of the Personal Record fount is dried up. No longer the same man. Thanks for your proposal. I'd like to do something for the sake of old times – but I daresay I am not worth having now. I'll drop you a line in a day or two. My mind is a blank at this moment.

Your

J. Conrad.

To Eric S. Pinker
Text TS Berg; Unpublished

Oswalds.

Oct. 23rd. 1923.

Dearest Eric

I have your letter of the 22nd. and I hasten to assure you that as a matter of fact we agree completely in our view of the film matters. To take up a definite point first, I certainly agree with your advice to accept £1000 for "Typhoon"; if £1000 is to be got, for those sixty pages of print and for a story which I should have thought in my ignorance to be the least adaptable perhaps of the whole volume – the volume itself being about the least adaptable, I fancy, for film purposes of all the books I have written. The producers being English (Stoll's[1] is an English concern, isn't it?) is a point in its favour in my mind, so much so that we could take a little less even?

The idea at the back of my mind is to put myself right with you with those small transactions, leaving a certain body of work to negotiate with, later, if the conditions are favourable.

In connection with that I would mention to you that "Gaspar Ruiz" could be used in that way by itself, either dealing with the scenario done in collaboration with dear J. B.[2] or only as a story. In the first case your father's

---

[1] The Australian-born theatrical impresario Sir Oswald Stoll (1867–1942; knighted 1919) created an empire of music halls and theatres that included the London Coliseum. In 1918 he founded a film company, Stoll Picture Productions, involved in both production and distribution.

[2] For the collaboration with J. B. Pinker, see the letter to Eric Pinker of 31 January 1923.

participation is clearly defined; in the second case that story would have to be the subject of special arrangement between you and me. Should you ever get a "general" inquiry you could put Ruiz forward in preference to any other short piece.

I shouldn't like you to think that I am forming fantastic notions about "The Rover". I do not; though, naturally, I hope for the best. "Rescue" having touched 50,000 in the U. S. all I expect from the "Rover" is to get up to 60,000 (or a couple of thousand more) and give a healthy filip to all the previous books for the next twelve months or so. That isn't being intoxicated with hope – is it?

To resume my view of the film policy for the next four months or so: Any small deals which would help to put my account with you right, should not be missed if they come in our way; and for the rest give ourselves a chance to profit by any improvement that may take place in the nearest future. If we are going ever to get a share of that repulsive cinema-swindle which is being rammed down the public throat, let us at least make it as big as possible. I hardly need say that any negotiation you may conclude will not be objected to by me under any circumstances.

Always affct^{ly} Yours

J. Conrad.

To Richard Curle

Text MS Indiana; Curle 130

[Oswalds]

25 Oct. 23

Dearest Dick

Thanks for Your note. I'll await H[ammerton]'s communication[1] before thinking of the subject in the hope of receiving a helpful hint from him.

We were delighted by the good news of the boy.[2] Yes my dear, You made a very good thing of the Simple Life.[3]

Ever Yours

J. Conrad

Jessie's love.

---

[1] See Conrad's reply to J. A. Hammerton of 31 October.
[2] See the letter of [8–12 October].
[3] According to Curle's notes at Indiana, this 'refers to an ironical article' he had written. It was not among the recent 'John Blunt' columns. The title had also been used by Ford Madox Ford for *The Simple Life Limited* (1911), a satirical novel that caricatured Conrad and Garnett.

To Grace Willard
Text MS Berg;[1] Unpublished

[letterhead: Oswalds]
25. Oct. 23

Dear Mama Grace.[2]

It was great news of you and Catherine coming to New York. All our little circle here is very much interested and full of good wishes and of good hopes for her success. Last Sunday we had quite a lot of people here, Mrs Harding with a party, Jean Aubry, a few others, including Hugh Walpole – all friends of Catherine all people able to form a judgment; and we agreed that the best she can get would be no more than *her* gifts and her devotion to her art deserve. Of all that group of people who have been moved and delighted with her acting I am perhaps the one who had seen the least of her on the stage. Still I have seen her in Ibsen, in 18th Century comedy, in her Shakesperian creations.[3] But our close friendship had given me opportunities of closer appreciation of her capacities – which seemed to me even then marvellous. I have heard her talk about her exacting art, I have seen her study many of her parts, (some that seemed quite overwhelming for one so young) with a courage and an intuitive grasp of character which aroused my admiration. Une artiste des grands moyens[4] – without the slightest doubt – taking instinctively the best way to prepare herself for the opportunity which I trust will be given her before long. That is all she wants now: anything – from comedie de salon to problem-play (if such still exist)[5] her charm, her force and her inborn gift will make themselves felt. You know that I had made up my mind early to move heaven and earth to get her for the part of Mrs Verloc if ever the Secret Agent was put on the stage. However you had left London by then. I am glad now that she was not associated with that failure though I am certain that she would have had a personal success.

---

[1] Tipped into a copy of the first English edition of *The Secret Agent*.
[2] Grace Robinson Willard (1879–1933) was Catherine Willard's mother. A clergyman's daughter, she grew up in Cincinnati, Ohio. Her first métier was that of journalist and book-reviewer. While working in Europe as a foreign correspondent, her interests turned to interior design; she was a frequent visitor at Capel House and advised the Conrads on the furnishings and décor at Oswalds.
[3] See *Letters*, 6, p. 213, where Conrad is about to see her in Congreve's *The Way of the World*, and p. 534, where he discusses her performances in *Macbeth* and *Ghosts* and suggests she would make an excellent Winnie Verloc.
[4] 'An artist of great resources'.
[5] Plays inspired by Ibsen's social dramas were often produced in Edwardian London, but because of the theatrical censorship, many of these could only be given as 'private performances' arranged by organisations such as the Stage Society. One of the leading writers of 'problem plays' was Conrad's friend John Galsworthy.

I must close this to catch the mail. Things here are going very much as *usual.* John is in France to learn the language and Borys now the Daimler C°'s representative in London. We feel somewhat lonely.

Jessie and my love to you both. Our thoughts are with you often.

> Always yours and Catherine's most faithful and affectᵉ friend
>
> Joseph Conrad.

To J. A. Hammerton

Text TS/MS Private collection; Unpublished

> [letterhead: Oswalds]
> Oct. 31st. 1923.

Dear Mʳ Hammerton.[1]

Thank you very much for your letter and specimens of your instructions. I regret to say I have never seen a specimen of "Peoples of All Nations" but I fancy I understand pretty near the character of the publication which is a sequel to it, and I was very glad to hear you yourself are writing an editorial preface on definite lines. I also venture to think that I have an idea of what you want me to write. If I may say so, you want a bit of Conradese. I will do my best to furnish it to you, and I only hope you will not be disappointed when you see it.

Thanks for suggestions of titles. I will leave the final decision to you, but meantime I have put "Geography and Exploration" as a heading to the MS.[2] I begin by saying that Geography is a much more fascinating science than geometry because maps, which are its graphic aspect; are much more amusing than the figures in geometry books, and go on to say that, though study-geographers are making it a very exact science, it is still the one whose research is carried on under the open sky and amongst wide horizons. I intend to talk about old maps and new maps, their imaginative suggestions, and of the fascination they had for me as a boy, and so on and so on. The adventures of exploration will be mentioned, together with a few out-standing names – for, as a matter of fact, I have not much erudition in this or any other subject.

---

[1] John Alexander Hammerton (1871–1949; knighted 1932) was the editor and publisher of *Geography*. An energetic and prolific editor, Hammerton specialised in the subject of war: from 1914 to 1919 he edited *The War Illustrated*, a lavishly pictorial weekly, and later produced other popular and encyclopaedic works, among them the *Harmsworth History of the World* (8 vols., 1907–9), *The Great War* (13 vols., 1914–19), *Peoples of All Nations* (7 vols., 1922), *Wonders of the Past* (4 vols., 1923), *The Masterpiece Library of Short Stories* (20 vols., c. 1925), and *Outline of Great Books* (1936).

[2] The article appeared as a general preface to Hammerton's lavishly illustrated serial *Countries of the World* under the title 'The Romance of Travel', and was reprinted in *National Geographic*. It was included in *Last Essays* as 'Geography and Some Explorers'.

I have a little doubt whether I can spin out 5000 words of that desultory talk. I suppose you would not think 4000 too short and would accept it, of course with a proportional reduction of the fee. I mention this because I see from your letter that the time is short.

Believe me faithfully yours

J. Conrad

To Thomas J. Wise

Text MS BL Ashley 2953; Fletcher facsimile 107

[letterhead: Oswalds]
31. 10. 23

My dear Wise.

Thanks for the catalogue.[1] I had forgotten by this [time] what I had sent to Quinn. I wish to goodness we had been in touch in 1910–11 when those transactions began – for the collection looks interesting and I would have loved to see it housed in the Ashley Library.[2]

Cordial regards in haste

Yours

J. Conrad

To Richard Curle

Text TS Indiana; Curle 131

[letterhead: Oswalds]
Nov. 2nd. 1923.

Dearest Dick.

In the words of the parrot after the monkey pulled all the feathers out of its tail I have had "a hell of a time". I am dictating this from bed. The pain is less to-day, but I am not fit for much and I am very anxious about things.

I had a letter from Hammerton, which I have answered at once. From what he says the time is rather short and I haven't more than 1200 words of the article written. I shall try to work a little to-day. What it will be like God only knows. I am rather glad in answering H. I suggested that 4000 words might be enough for that introduction and that he could proportionately reduce the fee.

---

[1] For Part I of the sale of John Quinn's library, held at the Anderson Galleries, New York, in six sessions from 12 to 14 November.

[2] Despite Conrad's wish, Wise eventually sold at least eight of his Conrad items before the Ashley Library was acquired by the British Museum Library in 1937.

Herewith the 20 signed copies.¹ I have kept No. 3 for myself, as I like to have it here. I did not inscribe No. 1. specially to you; I just signed it like the others, but if you want me to make some addition it can be done later. I know that you will see to it that Wise gets his copy, and Hook also. Perhaps you would like to give No. 5 to somebody you know. Of the remaining 15 the proceeds of 10 would be for me. It is only fair that you should participate in things which are put in my way by you, especially this windfall for which certainly I have not done a stroke of work.

I hope you continue to receive good news of the boy.

Jessie sends her love.

Yours ever

J. Conrad

P.S. "S. Agent" will be performed at the Leeds Art Theatre next Monday week, under the direction of Laurie Ramsden, to whom I gave permission a few months ago.² I hear that there is much curiosity awakened there. I only wish I had somebody who could give me a trustworthy report of the performance. There will be, I believe, six of them.

To Richard Curle

Text MS Indiana; Curle 132 (in part)³

[Oswalds]

5. 11. 23⁴

Dearest Dick.

Many thanks. You really can't (and *ought not*) object to the enclosed. Had I been able to move I would have gone miles to find some object I could have presented to you in memory of the Torrens transaction which was a pleasant affair altogether. It would have been prettier no doubt, but when I reflect that if I had made an early marriage⁵ I could have been (easily) father of a man of your age this way seems permissible between you and me.

I am getting into a funk about Ham[m]erton. I'll see how much I will do by to-morrow evenᵍ for I am going to start work today. If I don't get on and do not feel fit it would be only decent to tell him. However I hope that etc. etc. Bain's infᵒⁿ is interesting.⁶ But the matter is not so simple. There is

¹ Of 'A Clipper Ship I Knew', published in *Blue Peter* in September; the editor, F. A. Hook, reprinted it as a pamphlet. Curle had arranged for the commission.
² See Conrad's letter to Pinker of 7 March. The production ran for four nights.
³ Curle omits the PS and the last five sentences of the second paragraph.
⁴ Conrad initially wrote '12' instead of '23'.
⁵ Conrad married in March 1896 at the age of thirty-eight.
⁶ James Bain of 14 King William Street, Strand, dealt in books and manuscripts.

Thomas J. to consider. I am in doubt about his state of mind. Hasn't Bain any idea how much the Am. client would pay for say 4000 of MS and the corr^d TS text?

Jessie sends her love

Ever Yours

J. C.

PS I am glad D. has sent the (I must say) beggarly fee . . . ¹

To F. N. Doubleday
Text TS/MS Indiana; Unpublished

[letterhead: Oswalds]
Nov. 7th. 1923.

My dear Effendi

An hour or so after despatching my evening cable to you your letter arrived, together with another from Garden City containing some more frontispieces for the Concord Edition.

I am glad to hear from Mr Sudler, that the photograph of the Tower Gardens is going to be used for the "Narcissus". He also speaks of using one of the Cadby photographs (the first one in the album which we sent and which has been returned to us) for publicity purposes. I beg that it should *not* be done. I do not want any *of the Cadby photos* to be used for the future, for reasons which I will not explain just now.

The reproductions of the frontispieces look extremely well. Will you convey my acknowledgments to all the workers connected with the getting up of that edition. To yourself, my dear Effendi, the originator and director of the whole plan, I send here my most affectionate thanks. You and yours are hardly ever out of my thoughts.

I note that the Concord Edition is to be printed from plates corrected by the Heinemann text of the English de luxe edition. This is most satisfactory. The Heinemann text is as correct as such things can ever be.²

The dummy copy of "The Rover" has arrived, and I am struck by the ingenuity of the idea of having them sent round to the book-shops. I am impressed by the figure of the subscriptions, and of course very delighted to know that the book is making such a good start.³ You did always believe in it from the

---

¹ For passages from 'The History of Mr. Conrad's Books' published in the *New York Times*; see Conrad's letters to Doubleday of 4 October and 7 November.
² Although relatively free from misprints, the Heinemann edition is marked by heavy-handed house-styling and other non-authorial alterations; in modern scholarship, it carries little textual authority.
³ In a letter to Conrad dated 24 October (TS Berg), Doubleday had reported 'real progress with all the Conrad enterprises', with advance sales of 19,408 copies of *The Rescue* and anticipating

first sight of the MS, my dear Effendi, and your personal impression gave me very great encouragement at the moment when I certainly wanted a moral tonic. I am pleased to be able to tell you that I have heard that here too the outlook is good. F. U. has the reputation of a man who *can* sell books, but his methods are more secretive than ever. It appears that on this side the subscription is about 20,000, which for England is remarkable. This, my dear Effendi, is between us strictly, as my informant begged me to be as discreet about it as the grave; and of course I haven't mentioned it to anybody in this country.

Now as to the "Mentor" article.[1] It is all right. I have made two or three corrections, which please have attended to, and for the rest we may let it go. Of course all these are my words, and the only objection I could have made is that the prose which I write avowedly for myself is mixed with the prose of my imaginative productions – that is of the stories and novels. Obviously what I write as coming from my young man of the "Youth" short story is different in tone from what I write in the "Personal Record" where I am speaking direct to the public about myself. Perhaps that could be acknowledged in such a manner as the following:-

. . . As Mr Conrad says in his story "Youth" which is admittedly autobiographical etc. etc. . . .

And before the quotation which is the last paragraph of "The Nigger of the 'Narcissus'" a line could be inserted saying:–

. . . And this is the manner in which Mr Conrad at the end of the "Nigger of the 'Narcissus'" addresses the companions of his sea-life in a farewell passage . . . etc. etc.

I have marked the place with an X on the copy.

I do not add that myself to the MS. The whole article is arranged with such great judgment and appreciative feeling that I am sure that the compiler will take my point at once and will know perfectly well how to mark tactfully the places where he passes from the "Personal Record" to extracts from other books.

advance sales of 25,000 for *The Rover*. Conrad forwarded the letter to Eric Pinker with a marginal note in a tone of guarded optimism: 'have expressed my satisfaction in a way which is expected and indeed there is reason to be satisfied. But that does not do away with my worry for the thing is now to "work the vein" and I have been hindered. However there's no reason for despondency.'

[1] In his letter of 24 October, Doubleday had enclosed a promotional article and requested Conrad's consent to publish it, describing *The Mentor* as 'a periodical which circulates 150,000 a month and goes to very good readers'. Conrad added a marginal note to Pinker: 'I have given consent after suggesting slight alterations. Quite good.' For more on this piece and its author, Harry E. Maule, see the letter to Doubleday of 20 November.

Of course my consent is given unconditionally, but I could not help point-ing out what jarred a little, not so much upon my feelings as upon my ear.

I am glad you like the article in Colliers Weekly.[1] Why is it, Effendi, that your magazine editors seem to be constitutionally unable to refrain from cutting out lines and even paragraphs? I suppose from considerations of space – but I am accustomed to be printed fully by our periodicals here, who also have their considerations of space. I admit that your editors do it quite well in a way; but has it never occurred to them that when a production is a matter of taste – either literary or culinary – it is very often the trimmings that make the dish palatable.

I knew very well, my dear friend, that you would not be angry with me for dunning you for Curle's fee. Don't imagine that the man himself had anything to do with it. He wrote to me to say he had heard from you; and he seemed very pleased. He is coming out stronger and stronger as a journalist, of the kind that writes special articles which cause a multitude of letters from all parts of the country to tumble into the office. I shall suggest to him to ask the Postmaster General for a commission on the great increase of business which his articles bring to the department.

I have been up today and intend to get down tomorrow. Those attacks coming one after another make life a wearisome, hindered sort of business. Anyway this child does not mean to get crushed. It intends to keep its boots on to the last.

My dear love to Florence.

Always your affectionate

J. Conrad

To Eric S. Pinker

Text MS Berg; Unpublished

[Oswalds]
8. Nov 23.

Dearest Eric

Thanks for your p-card. I did not realise I had been remiss in giving news of myself. I *crawled* down yesterday. I *came* down again to-day. I won't say I will run down tomorrow. I don't think it would be advisable tho' I am convinced it would not be dangerous. And moreover I have not been for a long time in a running mood. Want of "tone" my dear fellow – that's what it is. I had Fox here yesterday to try to account for it. He finds a pronounced flabbiness of

---

[1] The essay about the *Torrens*, 'A Clipper Ship I Knew' (27 October 1923). A PS to Doubleday's letter of 24 October (TS Berg) reads: 'That was a very delightful article in *Collier's*. I am sending you a copy, as you may have missed it. I picked it up on the railroad train this morning.'

heart, which ugly expression means simply that it is tired, misses a beat now
and then and generally behaves in a languid and if I may express myself so a
disheartened manner. All the other powers of my ego are similarly affected –
intellect, the power of kicking – of getting into a rage – of making jokes (not
that there is anything to joke about in general). My very worrying is of a,
technically, flabby character. But that, Fox says, I mustn't do. The only thing
that remains energetic is the power of digestion: the appetite which is quite
expensive. That being so it is a matter of recuperation and Fox does not make
much of that state of flabbiness which is bound to pass away (with the help
of a little medicine) in a very short time.

Neither do I make much of it. Frankly I am not very much surprised at
it. It's nearly 2 years since fate has given me a little breathing time and the
chance of an easy mind.[1]

This I take it is the explanation of that absurd depression of which I think
I spoke to you once, some little time ago. Otherwise I am recovering from
this bout in the usual manner – that is rather quickly. I will drop You a few
lines in a day or two. Thanks my dearest Eric for your inquiry. Really I had
nothing to write till to day, and this is it. I do hope your wife is going on well.
Pray give her my love.

Ever affc^{ly} yours

J. Conrad.

To Ford Madox Ford

Text TS/MS Yale; *t. r.* (in part);[2] *Listy* 458

[letterhead: Oswalds]
Nov. 10th. 1923.

Dear Ford.

I am going to write to you briefly in answer to your good letter[3] because
I have been laid up all last week and part of this, and feel abominably shaky
and not good for much.

Imprimis: as to Dent's people – envoyez promener ces gens-là.[4] Fancy
trying to turn the *Transatlantic* into an advertising pamphlet!

Next. *The Nature of a Crime.* I forgot all about it so completely that I mis-
trusted your statement till I turned up the old E[nglish] R[eview]s and discovered it in the first No. of the second Vol. There is also a batch of mixed MS

---

[1] Conrad was bedridden for the last week of 1921 and most of January 1922 with gout and
influenza (*Letters*, 7, pp. 399, 411, and *passim*). The virulent strains of influenza current at
the time meant that, even for someone much healthier than Conrad, recovery was far from
certain.

[2] Only the fourth paragraph.   [3] Of 8 November (Stape and Knowles, p. 222).

[4] 'Send those people packing.' Dent's had asked Ford to print in the *review* 'a sort of Conrad
supplement of appreciations and the like' (*ibid.*)

and typescript about that man Burden, of which a very insignificant part, a few pages at most, are in my handwriting right enough. Why on earth did we select a German pseudonym for that?[1] Is it because the stuff is introspective and somewhat redolent of weltschmerz? If you think advisable to dig up this affair, well, I don't see how I can object. I looked at it and it seemed to me somewhat amateurish; which is strange, because that is not *our* failing either separately or together.

Lastly. The paragraphs about *Romance* which you plan to include in your chronique need not be sent to me.[2] I suppose you will send me your No. 1 and I will see them there. I suppose our recollections agree. Mine, in their simplest form, are: First part yours; Second part mainly yours, with a little by me, on points of seamanship and suchlike small matters; Third part about 60% mine, with important touches by you; Fourth part mine, with here and there and* important sentence by you; Fifth part practically all yours, including the famous sentence at which we both exclaimed "This is genius," (Do you remember what it is?)[3] with perhaps half a dozen lines by me. I think that, en gros, this is absolutely correct. Intellectually and artistically it is of course, right through, a *joint production*.

Thank you for the promised book.[4] A vol. of mine is coming out in December (*The Rover*) and I will send you a copy of the first English edition.[5]

I hope you are making a good recovery. I am as limp as a rag.[6]

                                             Yours

                                                        J. Conrad.

---

[1] More Ford's than Conrad's, this story appeared in the *English Review*, April and May 1909, under the pseudonym 'Baron Ignatz von Aschendrof'. According to Ford's letter, they took this course 'principally because as we were both writing in that number it would have seemed as it were tautological to publish a collaboration'. The name combines Ford's name backwards with the German word for *ashes*. In the pre-war years, he made much of his German connections. Burden is the name of the crooked businessman at the story's centre.

[2] Ford's 'A Note on *Romance*' appeared in the second issue of the *transatlantic review* in February 1924 and was reprinted as an appendix to *The Nature of a Crime* (Duckworth, 1924; the Doubleday edition, also 1924, lacks the appendix). He had told Conrad that Dent's had 'asked me if I could not print a page or two of ROMANCE with indications of which passages were your[s] and which were my writing. They said they have received thousands of requests for this.'

[3] 'Excellency – a few goats . . .', spoken by a witness in the trial at the beginning of Part 5, in answer to the judge's question: 'Of what occupation?'

[4] *Mister Bosphorus and the Muses* (Duckworth, 1923), which Ford had promised in his letter of 8 November.

[5] Ford wrote to Conrad on 18 January 1924 (TS Yale) to thank him for this copy, which had gone astray in the *review*'s office.

[6] Ford had been 'laid up . . . with an attack of something resembling influenza'.

Am afraid I won't be able to do anything for your No 2. I haven't got two ideas in my head. Times are changed and I have changed with them.

To Richard Curle

Text TS Indiana; Curle 134

Oswalds.
Nov. 12th. 1923.

Dearest Dick.

I am sure you will be fraternally pleased to hear that I have this moment – 4.20 p.m. – finished my "Geographical" introduction, the light of day dying out of the window as line succeeded line on the last page.

You know I always turn to you to make life easy for me in certain ways, so perhaps you won't be surprised if I ask you to give Hammerton to understand that I should like to be paid on the delivery of the MS, I mean of course within the week or something of that kind. I have done it in full as agreed, 5000 words and perhaps 100 over, and I assure you I earned the money by the effort I had to put into it, both before I was laid up and during that time, and afterwards too. For my convalescence was by no means good and to-day is the first day on which I do not feel absolutely ill, though I have been actually at work ever since last Thursday.

I had Fox to come and see me, and the fact of the matter is that the action of the heart is not satisfactory. "Flabby heart," he calls it in his horrid way. As a matter of fact the organ is tired, and must have been growing so for the last 18 months perhaps, with the strain and worry of one thing after another – but you know the history of the last 18 months as well as I do – and now it betrays its condition by fluttering and missing about every fourth beat. This accounts for that unshakeable despondency of which I complained to you more than once; for there is nothing organically wrong to account for it. However I repeat that I am better to-day, and the only thing I dread is the persistence of the cough which has played a considerable part in bringing me low.

I can do no more to-day and I will take a full two days to revise the article, of which Miss H. will make a clean copy. We expect to send it off to Hammerton on Thursday.[1] You may communicate to him the good news, for I imagine he may be wondering at the delay.

And now it's done let me thank you, my dear fellow, for shoving the thing in my way. It's obvious that for some time I have not been fit to grapple with the novel, and it was a great moral comfort to have some work to do

---

[1] If the date on the letter to Hammerton is correct, it did not go off until the 20th; the revisions were delayed by another attack of gout.

which I was capable of doing; not to speak of the material convenience of having the extra money which was very much needed and would have had to be obtained outside the provision of the normal budget. A necessity which worried me exceedingly.

I trust you were not annoyed with us for putting off your visit here with Sartoris.[1] You see what was behind it. A really rather low physical state, with unpleasant sensations, coupled with a desperate resolve to get the Hammerton thing through. S. would have had a dismal time and I simply did not feel equal to seeing a comparative stranger, who, as a matter of fact, I like very much. We should be glad if you found an early opportunity of bringing him down here, and in any case we hope to see you here before Dec. 15th. Jessie may have to run up to London to see Sir Robert. She looks well but I am rather worried about the constant exasperating twitching of the great muscle which is the sort of thing that may bring on a nervous breakdown. She sends you her love.

Yours ever

J. Conrad.

To Gordon Gardiner

Text MS Harvard; Unpublished

[letterhead: Oswalds]
[mid-November 1923?][2]

My dear Gardiner.

Jessie has written to you by this morning's post; and I send these few lines to thank you for your letter to me. I feel remorseful when I think of the effort You had to make to give me this great and exquisite pleasure. Your message is characteristic of that grace, humanity, that generous kindliness which are the invulnerable part of You; the precious possession of those who have the good fortune to be your friends on this earth where it has been your lot to suffer so much to our grief and for our admiration.[3] My dear Gardiner I can't tell you how much I appreciate your feelings towards me. Do please travel in the morning if you can manage to get away. The car will meet the 12.30 in Canterbury.

Ever Yours in heart and mind

Joseph Conrad

---

[1] Curle's good friend George L. Sartoris, the dedicatee of his story collection *The Echo of Voices* (1917). Sartoris was a great-nephew of Fanny Kemble and her sister, the singer Adelaide Sartoris.

[2] Dated by Gardiner's visit; see the letter to Walpole of 18 November.

[3] Gardiner had been suffering from recurrent illness since his youth.

To Eric S. Pinker

Text MS Berg; Unpublished

[Oswalds]
[18–22 November 1923][1]

Dearest Eric.

Many thanks for your letter of advice.

I am certainly improving. The cough tho' is not gone yet. Have you seen the fuss over the MS prices in N.Y.? Absurd. Lots of people here have been impressed and I suppose the publicity of the thing has some trade value.

You'll hear from me again in a few day[s].

Yours ever

J. C.

To Hugh Walpole

Text MS Texas; *Listy* 460

[letterhead: Oswalds]
18. Nov. 23

My dear Hugh.[2]

Thanks for yours of congratulation and condolence (nicely dosed) upon the N York sale stunt. It's puffectly ridic'lous. But – I didn't laugh. On the other hand I didn't curse. I lay low and did nuffink.[3]

I am recovering slowly from a bad shake-up. Am taking a heart tonic. Gardiner arrived. Congratulated each other on our healthy appearance. He is taking injections. Cheered each other up immensely.

---

[1] The first section of the Quinn sale (items A–C) was held on 12–14 November, and prices for the Conrad items were reported in *The Times* of 15 November and the *TLS* of 22 November. Conrad's gout accounts for the fact that no letters can be dated with certainty between 12 and 18 November. The gout returned after the 22nd: see the letter to Pinker of the 26th.

[2] Hugh Seymour Walpole (1884–1942; knighted 1937) was born in New Zealand, but his parents soon returned to England, where his father became Bishop of Durham. As a young man, he admired and was admired by Henry James. As a novelist, Walpole first met recognition with *Mr Perrin and Mr Traill* (1911) and *The Duchess of Wrexe* (1914). In *The Dark Forest* (1916), he drew on his experience of working as an orderly with the Russian Red Cross, for which he was invested with the Order of Saint George for bravery under fire. Before meeting Conrad, who was to treat him as a protégé, Walpole had already published his critical appreciation, *Joseph Conrad* (1916; revised edition, 1924). Among his more recent novels were *Jeremy* (1919) and *The Cathedral* (1922).

[3] About the sale of Quinn's Conrad MSS, see the letter to Jean-Aubry of the 20th. Conrad may be echoing Twain, an author he enjoyed: 'Who ever heard of a state prisoner escaping by a hickry bark ladder? Why, it's perfectly ridiculous' (*Adventures of Huckleberry Finn*, 35). 'Puffectly' and its variants are common in the nineteenth-century fiction of the American South, but they also show up in comic renderings of south-east English speech, and 'nuffink', as in 'I didn't do nuffink, guv', is pure stage Cockney.

Borys arrived unexpectedly (after delivering a car in Margate) about 10:30 pm. I sat up rather late tête-a-tête with him. After an exhaustive inquiry into his position and prospects which are quite good (considering all the circumstances) I have consented to guarantee his acc^t so that he could face the prem^{ry} expenses of getting into the new flat and beginning life on a decent footing.[1] And here comes a request to you to help me in this. Perhaps You will be shocked (or amused) when I tell you that is no difficulty of finance at all but of moral cowardice. If I come forward in the usual way my bank manager is bound to know what is being done and of course E. P. too. I have nothing against them (and E. P. has always been very friendly and decent). But not a long time ago I had [been] made to hear – or feel rather – that I was a weak person and exploited at that. Now I never did think so. I did not like it. I shrink from the repetition of the experience. I would look upon it as an immensely friendly act if you would step forward and guarantee for B £100 overdraft for a year. Should you be called upon I would of course repay you at once. He is confident he will be able to put right his acct in another 8–10 months,. He has asked me only for 75 but I think he had better have £100 because of certain expenses hanging over his head (in the near future). I hope you will neither laugh nor cry over me but take an indulgent view.

Jessie sends no message because she does not know I am writing to you.

Ever Yours

J. Conrad

To Hugh Walpole
Text MS Texas; Unpublished

[letterhead: Oswalds]
19. Nov 23

Dearest Walpole.

Thanks very much for Your prompt and hearty action.

B. is laid up here with a severe chill or else downright "flu". His wife arrived this morning – and the whole performance will last I hope no longer than a week. Jessie came out strong a[s] usual. I remained crocky, groggy tottery, staggery, shuddery shivery, seedy, gouty, sorry wretch that I am.

What is the most terrible is that the animal still keeps going and even cuts small jokes and expects his family to laugh at them.

Do try dear H to see us before Xmas. "en passant".

---

[1] Conrad's son Borys had just been appointed to a new job at the London depot of the Daimler Company.

Photo arrived this morning and we like it much. Jessie wants to hang it up in her room. I said in French that it was "pas convenable".[1] She, in Polish, called me a donkey. The prospect is good for a first rate squabble. In haste to catch post. Bon voyage to you[2] and our best love and thanks.

Ever yours

J. Conrad.

To G. Jean-Aubry

Text MS Yale; *NRF* 115–16; *L. fr.* 192

[letterhead: Oswalds]
20. Nov. 23

Très cher Jean.

Je suis un misérable de ne pas avoir donné signe de vie si longtemps. Merci de vos Cartes postales.

J'ai eu une mauvaise attaque de goutte qui m'a laissé un peu plus abimé que de coutume. Le cœur commence a s'en ressentir. J'ai fait venir Fox. Ça va mieux à présant*.

Comme vous voyez rien de bien neuf.

Je suppose que l'écho du vacarme fait par la presse au sujet de la vente par enchères de mes MS en Amerique ne vous est pas arrivé. La chose est innouie* pour un écrivain vivant. La somme totale est de £22 000. Le MS de *Victoire* a atteint £1600. Western Eyes £1.360. etc etc. Un article de 33pp. a été payé £300.[3] C'est idiot, mais – Quinn a fait une jolie affaire. Il a gagné 1000% (je dis mille) car il m'a payé a peu près £2000 depuis 1911 ou 1912. Quand a moi je suis tout simplement devenu un personage. Des gens qui n'aurait pas pu lire une page de moi sans tomber de haut mal me proclament grand écrivain. Mais rassurez Vous! Je suis bon prince. Je suis prêt a vous accorder une audience aussitot votre retour. De même veuillez dire a Mme Alvar que quand j'aurais l'honneur de venir la saluer chez elle, je la prie de ne pas faire derouler un tapis rouge ni allumer d[e]s flambeaux a la porte de sa maison. En attendant je lui baise la main et je me reccomande a son bon souvenir.

Yeats a eu la Nobel Prize. Mon opinion la-dessus est que si c'est une reconnaissance literaire du nouveau Etat Libre Irlandais (et ca m'en a tout l'air) ca n'a pas détruit complètement ma chance (ou la chance de Galsworthy)

---

[1] 'Not proper'. [2] Walpole would be spending Christmas in Edinburgh.
[3] The thirty-page MS of Conrad's 'Admiralty Paper' was acquired by the songwriter Jerome D. Kern for $1,750; it is now in a private collection in California. The text was published posthumously and reprinted in *Last Essays* as 'The Unlighted Coast'.

de le décrocher dans un ou deux ans. Et puis Yeats est un poète et le choix n'est pas mauvais.[1]

Je Vous embrasse de tout mon cœur. Jessie sends her love.

Votre vieux

Conrad

Very dear Jean,

I am a wretch for not giving any sign of life for so long. Thanks for your postcards.

I've had a bad attack of gout which left me rather more crushed than usual. The heart begins to feel the effects. I've had Fox come. It's better for now.

As you see, nothing terribly new.

I suppose the echo of the row made by the press over the auction of my MS in America hasn't reached you. Such a thing is unheard-of for a living author. The sum total is £22,000. The MS of *Victory* reached £1,600. Western Eyes £1,360. etc. etc. An article of 33 pages fetched £300. It's idiotic, but – Quinn has turned it into a good thing. He made 1000% (one thousand, I'm saying) because he has paid me £2,000 since 1911 or 1912. As for me, I have simply become a personality. People who would not have been able to read a page of my work without falling seriously ill proclaim me a great writer. But be reassured! I am a good prince. I am ready to grant you an audience immediately upon your return. Please tell Mme Alvar that when I have the honour to come and pay my respects, I beg her not to have the red carpet rolled out or flaming torches posted at her front door. In the meantime I kiss her hand and commend myself to her good wishes.

Yeats has had the Nobel Prize. My opinion about that is that if it's a literary recognition of the new Irish Free State (which looks to be the case) it has not completely destroyed my own chances (nor those of Galsworthy) of landing it in a year or two. And then Yeats is a poet and the choice is not bad.

I embrace you with all my heart. Jessie sends her love.

Your old

Conrad

---

[1] The Irish Free State came into existence on 6 December 1922. Although its autonomy was compromised by stipulations in the peace treaty of 1921, the new state was no longer part of the United Kingdom, and thus an award to an Irish writer might not be an obstacle to honouring a British writer, particularly a novelist rather than a poet, in the near future. Conrad was never officially nominated for the prize, but Galsworthy became a Nobel laureate in 1932.

To F. N. Doubleday

Text TS Indiana; J-A, 2, 324

[letterhead: Oswalds]
Nov. 20th. 1923.

Dear Effendi

All of you who went must have had a tense sort of evening at that sale. Was the atmosphere vibrating with excitement, or, on the contrary, still with awe? Did any of the bidders faint? Did the auctioneer's head swell visibly? Did Quinn enjoy his triumph lying low like Brer Rabbit,[1] or did he enjoy his glory in public and give graciously his hand to kiss to the multitude of inferior collectors who never, never, never, dreamt of such a coup? Well, it is a wonderful adventure to happen to a still-living (or at any rate half-alive) author.

The reverberation in the press here was very great indeed; and the result is that lots of people, who never heard of me before, now know my name, and thousands of others, who could not have read through a page of mine without falling into convulsions, are proclaiming me a very great author. And there are a good many also whom nothing will persuade that the whole thing was not a put up job and that I haven't got my share of the plunder.

However I must say that I have received many letters of condolence and sympathy. Altogether I have had an amusing time, while Jessie, without loss of time, sent a 500 word article on the preservation of those manuscripts to the Daily Mail.[2] The editor wrote to congratulate her on her journalistic instinct. The cheque for it will come in due course, and ought to keep her in chocolates for a long time.

I have been downstairs for more than ten days and am beginning to feel better. Your letters containing good news and evidencing your more than friendly care for my reputation and fortune in America helped to carry me over the bad time. Amongst the correspondence received I have had also a letter from Sudler with the proof of the drawing for "Nostromo" frontispiece

---

[1] In Joel Chandler Harris's *Uncle Remus Stories*, Br'er Rabbit finds sanctuary by lying low in his briar patch.

[2] 'The Romance of the Conrad MSS.', *Daily Mail*, 17 November 1923, p. 8. The article was posted the day before (Jessie Conrad to L. R. Macleod, 16 November, MS Lubbock). In it, she describes her prudent habit of stowing the MSS away in 'a couple of deep drawers in an old yellow press . . . Often my husband would insist that they should be burnt. Although a fairly dutiful wife, I managed, however, to avoid their destruction.'

according to my suggestion.[1] I have also had a few other frontispieces, very good reproductions of various photographs. Would you, dear Effendi, send me two complete sets, as each of my boys clamours for one. Borys wants to frame them and hang them up in his new home, and John declares that he will want them to decorate his "diggings" when he settles in Coventry as a pupil of the Daimler Co.

We had the pleasure of receiving here Mr Maule, whom all of us like. I did not talk much business with him, as we both agreed that all the material points have been settled, and he had to catch an early afternoon train back to town. I told him however that I had sent back the "Monitor"* article[2] to you with a few minor suggestions. He seemed pleased to hear it.

The day approaches for "The Rover" to look the public in the eye, and, if possible, to hit it in the most sensitive spot. Tell me, dear Effendi, if I am entitled to any copies of the limited edition? If so I would be glad to have them for there are one or two persons whose sensibilities I should like to hit by a presentation copy of a special kind.

On this side what is annoying is the confounded general election which will get in the way of everything for a week or two. We have given permission to put off publication to the 2nd Jan. 1924. I don't know what F. U. will decide to do.[3]

I perceive I must stop this talking if I want to catch the Friday boat. It is only since my visit to you, my dear friends, that I have realised how far America is from Bishopsbourne – so much of my heart has been left there!

Ever Your affectionate

Conrad.

---

[1] He had proposed his own drawing of the Great Isabel lighthouse. Conrad sent this drawing to Culbreth Sudler some time between mid-September and mid-November. He wrote: 'I suggest that you should get an artist who would draw the greater Isabel with the lighthouse on it. Island in the shape of a wedge with the lighthouse above the cliff and the low horizon occupied by a silver white cloud with the full moon above it.' Then comes Conrad's sketch: 'Something like this. I never could draw. JC.' Lower down, he wrote: 'Remote suggestion for the great Isabel. & the legend below could be "The Great Isabel." If the artist reads the last two pages of the first chapter, it would give him all three islands as far as I judge it necessary to describe them. J. C.' (MS Private collection).

[2] This was the article for *The Mentor*; in the end, it did not appear there, but may have been used for Doubleday's own publicity. Its author was Harry E. Maule (1886–1971), a Doubleday employee and editor of *Short Story* magazine. A versatile writer, his publications ranged from *The Boy's Book of New Inventions* (1912) to *Selma Lagerlöf* (1926).

[3] The election would be held on Thursday, 6 December. Doubleday published the limited edition on 30 November and the trade edition on 1 December; deciding against a postponement, Unwin published on the 3rd.

PS Tell H. H. the Ranee of Effendi Hill that her faithful servant was immensely impressed by her get up on the photograph taken at the Readery. Does she put it on to read? . . . But I will restrain my impudence till next time. My love to her.

To J. A. Hammerton

Text MS Berg; Unpublished

[letterhead: Oswalds]
20. Nov 23

Dear Mr Hammerton.

I am sending a copy which cannot be called "clean" but ought to be plain enough for the printers.[1]

I feel so much behind time that I won't delay a day to have the thing re-typed again. This is not the first draft.

I have given you full measure. You will cut out what you like – or rather what you do not like.

I should like of course to see a proof. One makes sometimes stupid mistakes of fact which of course are not the reader's affair.

Believe me

very faithfully yours

J. Conrad

To Bruno Winawer

Text TS copy Yale; *Głos*; Najder 293

[Oswalds]
20 Nov. 23

Dear Winawer,

Heartfelt thanks for your letter and the pamphlet about Einstein[2] which for me is a small masterpiece of its kind.

Acceptez, o! homme versatile, ma poignée de main.[3]

Bien à Vous

J. Conrad.

---

[1] 'The Romance of Travel' (later 'Geography and Some Explorers') appeared in the first issue of Hammerton's *Countries of the World* (February 1924).
[2] *Jeszcze o Einsteinie: teoria względności z lotu ptaka* (Warsaw, 1924, trans. as *More about Einstein: A Bird's-eye View of the Theory of Relativity*).
[3] 'Allow me, o! many-sided man, to shake your hand.'

To Edmund Candler

Text MS Morgan; Candler xli

[letterhead: Oswalds]
21. Nov. 23

My dear Candler,[1]

If I only knew you consent to take me on the terms of "a hopeless brute" I would be able to compose my mind. But I suspect that you still persist in taking me for a "decent person" and its perfectly agonising. For in that character I feel obliged to (and I do) burn with remorse and shame whenever I think of you. A cruel if deserved fate. And we all here think often of you – and say: We must go and see them down South there.[2] But for poor Jessie travelling is no small matter and I am getting less and less fit for it.

We were very very sorry to have missed you when over here. I had taken her to see the surgeon and it is always a matter of 3–4 days. Since our return home I have been laid-up three times. That sort of thing cuts life into little bits and is exceedingly monotonous. My fate will be to die not from the disease but from the boredom at its dilatory and stereotyped processess*. An ignoble fate. And when I think of the fine occasions I had of being knocked off the topsail yard or washed overboard and drowned off Cape Horn!

But I don't repine. As a dear old lady said: We must be brave.

We were glad to hear something of you from Miss H. We haven't given up all hope of going south – your way. "Hope dies hard", you know.

Jessie sends you her most friendly greetings. Believe in my, now old, affection for you.

Yours

Joseph Conrad.

My regards to Miss H if still with you.

---

[1] A teacher, traveller, and author, Edmund Candler (1874–1926) read classics at Cambridge, then taught in Indian schools and colleges from 1896 to 1903. From 1906 to 1914 he was Principal of Mohindra College in Patiala. He was for many years a prolific correspondent and travel writer for *Outlook*, *Blackwood's*, and the *Allahabad Pioneer*. Grievously wounded in Tibet in 1904, he recovered to become the official correspondent with the Indian Expeditionary Force in Mesopotamia in 1917, recording his experiences in *The Long Road to Baghdad* (2 vols., 1919). He was also a roving reporter for *The Times* in the Transcaucasian republics in 1918–19.

[2] The Candlers were now living near Hendaye, in the French Basque country.

To Emilio Cecchi

Text MS Vieusseux; Curreli 18 with facsimile

[letterhead: Oswalds]
21. Nov 23

Dear Mr Checchi*,[1]

Pray accept my warm thanks for the kind thought of sending me your admirably sympathetic article[2] – as it has been defined to me by one of my friends a lover of Italy and quite a competent judge.

Pray believe me
Very faithfully yours
Joseph Conrad.

To Sydney Cockerell

Text MS Texas; Meynell 325 (in part)[3]

[letterhead: Oswalds]
21. Nov 23

My dear Cockerell.[4]

Thanks for Your letter of condolence a propos of the Quinn scandal. For it really is scandalous for people to pay such prices for mere pieces of paper. However I have nothing to complain of. Quinn paid me the prices I asked – altogether about £2000 since 1912 or a little more and the money came very conveniently then.

Truly I've never had such a success. People who had never heard of me before are now aware of my name, and others quite incapable of reading a page of mine to the end have become convinced that I am a great writer.

---

[1] The attempt at a phonetic spelling might be the result of talking about Cecchi with the 'lover of Italy'. A Florentine living in Rome, the scholar and critic Emilio Martino Gaetano Cecchi (1884–1966) was instrumental in introducing the works of Conrad and other English and American authors to Italian readers; a particularly influential work was his *Storia della letteratura inglese nel secolo XIX* (1915). A prolific author of essays, travel narratives, and studies in art history, and co-founder of the Roman literary review *La Ronda*, Cecchi became one of the foremost Italian critics of the first half of the twentieth century. Most of his essays on Conrad were reprinted in *Scrittori inglesi e americani* (Lanciano: Carabba, 1935).

[2] Cecchi's article 'Joseph Conrad', from the Roman daily *La Tribuna* of 20 October; for a full and valuable account of the background to this letter and the article, see Mario Curreli, 'Cecchi, Critico Conradiano', *Italianistica*, 28.2 (May-August 1999), 251–64.

[3] Without the third paragraph.

[4] After a brief career as a coal merchant, Sydney Carlyle Cockerell (1867–1962; knighted 1934) became secretary to William Morris and the Kelmscott Press. Director of the Fitzwilliam Museum, Cambridge, from 1908 to 1937, he was widely connected in artistic circles and counted among his literary friends not only Conrad but Wilfrid Scawen Blunt and Thomas Hardy.

Sorry I didn't thank you before for the very interesting account of the earthquake.[1]

I have been laid up lately again. The monotony of that thing is intolerable. The same odious sensations, in the same order and ending in the same period of depression!

It won't be disease but the awful boredom of it that will end by killing me. Our warmest regards.

Yours

J. Conrad.

To Richard Curle
Text MS Indiana; Curle 135

[letterhead: Oswalds]
[21 November 1923][2]

Dearest Dick.

Thanks for yours. Of course Jessie and I will be delighted if you can come with Sartoris as you suggest.

The after-effects of my last fit of gout were more pronounced than usual. I had Fox over to see me. Nothing fundamentally serious. I am much better.

We dispatched the article of full length (5.500w. about) yesterday to Hammerton. I hope he will find it suitable. It was rather a grind – yet, in a sense I was glad I had something to do when obviously not fit to work at the novel.

The Times has given all the principal figures reached at that idiotic sale.[3] What it has done for me is that I have suddenly become known to lots of people who had never heard of me before. Yes. I agree with you that the price of future MS. will be affected favourably. But there are no MS! I haven't heard from Wise. I don't think he expected such an enormous boost.[4]

All luck to you in the campai[g]n.[5]

Ever yours

J. C.

Jessie sends her love.

---

[1] Among the major earthquakes that year were those on the Sino-Tibetan border (March), in southern California (July), and in Bengal (11 September), but the most frightful was one in Japan (1 September) that caused many thousands of deaths, practically levelled Yokohama, and left a million and a half people in Tokyo homeless.

[2] Conrad's cover letter to Hammerton sent with 'The Romance of Travel' is dated 20 November. A report of better health went to Jean-Aubry on the same date; there was another relapse around the 23rd.

[3] *The Times*, 15 November 1923, p. 8.

[4] To the market value of his own collection.

[5] The campaign to advance Conrad's interests or the imminent general election? Curle was neither covering the election nor standing himself, but perhaps he was working for a candidate.

To Edward Garnett
Text MS Berg; G. 328

[Oswalds]
21 Nov. 23

Dearest Edward.

Yes Quinn promised to keep the MSS together – but the mood passes and the promise goes with it.[1] But did you ever hear of anything so idiotic as this sale? But it is my greatest success! People who never heard of me before will now know my name. Others who had never been able to read through a page of mine are convinced that I am a great writer. If I could let it get about (discreetly) that the whole thing was a put up job between Quinn and me and that I got my share of the plunder I believe I would become "universally respected." But that is too much to hope for.

The Rover my dear Edward is not what you have seen. It's a 80000 w. thing I finished in July 1922. Since it had no wealthy young squires and French Countesses in it I did not intrude it on your notice.[2] It is Revolutionary and you are an Aristocrat. I know you well.[3] But I did mention it to you slightly – once. However you will soon have your copy and be able to jump on it with both feet. I won't mind as long as it does not make you sick. A thing of sentiment – of many sentiments.

Ever yours

J. C.

Will be looking impatiently for H[udson]'s letters.[4]

To Christopher Morley
Text MS Haverford; Unpublished

[letterhead: Oswalds]
22. Nov. 23

My very dear Christopher.

Thanks for your little book of innermost thoughts[5] and even more for Your dear long letter written it seems at the turn of life's way. I am deeply touched that your thought has turned in my direction – but what I feel most is

---

[1] In his letter of the 15th (Stape and Knowles, p. 224), Garnett had written: 'I thought you told me that he was going to present them to some Public Library. Was he, then, just the ordinary astute American? or was he forced by necessity to make a profit of how many hundred percent?'

[2] Garnett had read the first three chapters of *Suspense* in 1921 and made suggestions (Stape and Knowles, p. 183, and *Letters*, 7, p. 335). The squire and the French Countess are Cosmo Latham and Adèle de Montevesso, the hero and heroine of *Suspense*.

[3] A tease – Garnett saw himself as an enemy of privilege.

[4] See the letter to Garnett of the 30th.

[5] *Inward Ho!* (Garden City: Doubleday, Page, 1923), a collection of fifteen short essays originally published in the *New York Evening Post*.

my unworthiness before your attitude. It is recognition of the sort you give me that makes one feel humble and doubtful. Yet I would not have missed it for all the diamonds of Golconda[1] for "something human is dearer to me than the wealth of all the world".[2] And You have proved Your excellent humanity by the manner and matter of your essays on Daily Life (not daily trifles which to some are so lifelike) and by Your firm hold of those hopes that mark a man who faithful to our common earth yet would build his fortunes on those treasures which are not found underground.

No more to-night as want to catch Friday's ship. I was laid up when You[r] letter and your gift arrived to cheer me up. Jessie sends you her most friendly thanks and regards. Love to you both dear people and to your precious chicks who someday will give you yet the word of life's riddle.

Affectly Yours

J. Conrad

To Eric S. Pinker
Text TS Berg; Unpublished

[letterhead: Oswalds]
Nov. 26th. 1923.

Dearest Eric.

I will spare you a recital of the horrible time I have had since I wrote to you last. As a matter of fact that sort of thing can be borne but it [is] almost unfit to talk about. I am still in bed and quite unable to write with my own hand.

Before this relapse I managed to finish a piece of work for a man called Hammerton. It is an introduction to some sort of Geography book, to appear in monthly parts; one of the Harmsworth publications. I am not quite fit to explain how it came in my way, or say much about it, but herewith enclosed is the payment. As I was quite unfit to work at the novel I thought I could do something, and this is the result. Please, my dear fellow, deduct the commission due and pay in £180 to my account.[3] I will tell you the whole tale of it afterwards. Now I am simply not fit.

Jessie is going to town by rail on Wednesday, having an appointment with Sir R. Jones on Thursday morning. It would be very friendly and nice of you to give her a look-in at the Curzon where she has wired for a room. Perhaps you would lunch with her on Wednesday about one or half past, or drop in

---

[1] Until the eighteenth century, the mines of Golconda, near Hyderabad in south central India, were the world's only source of rough diamonds.

[2] Conrad had used these words of Rumpelstiltskin in the Grimm fairy tale as the epigraph to *Youth*.

[3] Pinker's standard commission was 10 per cent.

to see her on Thursday afternoon. It would be a comfort to me to know you had seen her. The trouble with that limb is growing quite serious, and Reid has confessed that he has not got the slightest idea how it can be met. We shall see what Sir Robert will say.

No more now because I am not equal to dictating yet.

My love to you both,

J. Conrad

To Eric S. Pinker

Text TS Berg; Unpublished

[letterhead: Oswalds]
Nov. 28th. 1923.

My dear Eric

I am so pleased you are going to lunch with Jessie. Though she does not show it she is not easy in her mind about what may have to be done with her limb; for something will have to be done; and if all those kinds of outside treatment are found powerless then . . .

The latest Beer development would be perfectly easy to deal with except for the fact that it is you who have had all the worry connected with this business, had to advance the money to me, enter into correspondence, etc. etc. At any rate you had all the inconvenience and worry in whatever degree, whereas it is to me that Beer offers compensation. I do not feel that I have to be compensated for anything; but I do feel (or at any rate I hope) that if I had had to put up with inconveniences arising from what was certainly a failure to perform the contract, I would have written to him that there could be no question of anything of the kind; I mean of accepting the voluntarily proffered damages.[1]

I believe the fellow is straight. I liked him well enough; and this insistence in shoving money on to me under these distressing circumstances has something touchingly comic about it. I still think I haven't skinned him by accepting the terms he offered, but I feel inclined to believe that his intentions were generous enough.

I won't touch on any other point in this letter, my dear fellow. I am still on my back to-day and trying to keep off worrying thoughts at arm's length. Very poor fun that. I will just say like poor crazy Miss Flite in Dickens' "Bleak House" "Pray accept my blessing."[2]

Ever Yours

J Conrad

[1] Whatever the nature of the problem, by 6 December Conrad had received two copies of the Crane biography; see the letter to Knopf of that date.
[2] She blesses Esther and Ada in Chapter 3.

To F. N. Doubleday
Text TS Indiana; Unpublished

[letterhead: Oswalds]
Nov. 29th. 1923.

My dear Effendi

I am sorry to say I am back again in bed and not quite fit yet to sit up to write a letter; so I dictate this for the purpose of acknowledging the receipt of the six copies of "The Rover", very glorious and magnificent in its white and gold get-up. I am only afraid that with this magnificent envelope people may be disappointed in the humble text. It is really more fit for a novel about queens and princes, warriors and statesmen, than for a tale about an old rover and a half-crazy farm girl. Nevertheless I consider myself lucky to have such a splendid limited Edition for my latest prose. My warmest thanks to all concerned.

You tell me to be careful of my gifts. I will be, and I will take particular care to make no mistakes in the inscriptions. Two of these will make my name fragrant in the nostrils of two great ladies and I shall expect most effusive letters from them. But as I go down the list of names I hardly see anybody worthy amongst the inferior mob. I shall weigh every claim nicely. Such a chance does not come twice in a lifetime.

Your communications ease the hours of pain which have fallen to my lot lately. As a matter of fact I am not very fit even to dictate just now, though I must say that I am again on the mend. I hope there will not be another relapse. My stock of resistance has run very low.

Jessie has gone to London to see Sir Robert Jones or else she would have sent her love. She is immensely impressed with the books.

Ever dear Florence and Effendi

Your affectionate

J. Conrad

To Edward Garnett
Text G. 329

[letterhead: Oswalds]
Nov. 30th. 1923.

Dearest Edward,

I have been laid up for days and days and your volume of H[udson]'s letters was most welcome alleviation to the worry and general horror of the situation.[1] I think that your little introduction at the beginning is the most charming and touching thing that I ever remember having read. The Letters

---

[1] Garnett's *153 Letters from W. H. Hudson* (Nonesuch Press, 1923). Garnett had been a close friend of W(illiam) H(enry) Hudson (1841–1922), the Argentine-born naturalist and novelist. Hudson,

themselves of course are particularly interesting. It is extraordinary how his correspondence reproduces the accent of his talk. But I was glad to have the man brought close to me once more, and, as it were, led up and commented upon in your friendly voice.

I dictate this because I am not fit to sit up long enough to write a whole letter in pen and ink. In fact I don't feel very fit even for dictation. The Patron of Letters[1] has "delivered the goods" in his own inimitable style, and here is your own copy – the first to leave the house. I would have sent it two days before only I wanted to be able to scrawl the inscription.

Ever your own

J. Conrad

To Allan Wade
Text TS Lubbock; Unpublished

[letterhead: Oswalds]
Nov. 30th. 1923.

My dear Wade,[2]

I have been laid up and not even fit to do any dictation; but I am better now and hasten to thank you for the more than generous sample of the "Criterion"[3] which is really very good and did help me through some pretty bad, sleepless hours of more than one night.

You will get in due course your and Claudine's copy of "The Rover".[4] I have certain difficulty in getting extra copies from my publisher, so, I fear, there will be some delay in my friends coming by their own.

Give my love to Your wife.

Affect^{ly} Yrs

J. Conrad

---

a reclusive man, saw little of Conrad, but many of the writers in Conrad's circle, above all Garnett, Ford, and Cunninghame Graham, looked on Hudson as a great master of English prose. When Hudson died, Conrad told Garnett: 'there was nothing more *real* in letters – nothing less tainted with the conventions of art . . . He was a nature production himself and had something of its fascinating mysteriousness' (*Letters*, 7, p. 513; see also pp. 514–15, 519).

[1] One of several ironic names for Garnett's former employer T. Fisher Unwin, who was bringing out *The Rover* on the 3rd.

[2] An actor, director, bibliophile, and scholar, Allan Wade (1881–1958) made his début in 1904 and worked for Harley Granville-Barker from 1906 to 1915. A producer for the Stage Society and a founder of the Phoenix Society (1919), he also assembled a large library of Modernist writers. His numerous publications include a bibliography of W. B. Yeats (1951) and editions of Henry James's dramatic criticism (1948) and Yeats's letters (1954), along with translations of plays by Jean Giraudoux and Jean Cocteau.

[3] The literary quarterly founded by T. S. Eliot in 1922.

[4] Claudine Wade was French; the Conrads liked her, and she gave the script of *The Secret Agent* an attentive reading (*Letters*, 7, pp. 451, 579).

To Richard Curle

Text MS Indiana; Curle 133

[Oswalds]
Monday. [3 December 1923][1]

Dearest Dick.

Thanks for the send-off in the D[aily] M[ail] to-day.[2]

I do want you to come this weekend but I don't think I am equal to "company." I am by no means well yet. So perhaps we will put off Sartoris' visit to better times. It could be no pleasure to see a man groaning in a dressing gown.

I wonder what the fate of The R. will be? Your copy Ed. de Luxe is waiting for you here

Ever Yours

J. C.

To T. Fisher Unwin

Text TS Colgate; Unpublished

[letterhead: Oswalds]
Dec. 3rd. 1923.

T. Fisher Unwin, Esq.
Dear Sir,[3]

I beg to thank you for a copy of the very attractive Blue Cloth edition received to-day. It was in a sense a surprise, because somehow I did not know that there were two different editions to be published simultaneously.[4] But no doubt all this has been arranged with Mr Eric Pinker. I suppose I may take it that the Green Cloth edition is really the First English edition. I ask because, as you know, some people are very anxious to have the first edition, and any confusion on that point is very undesirable.

---

[1] The date of the *Daily Mail*'s review. Curle gives [November].

[2] Curle's signed review of *The Rover* appeared on p. 8, under the heading 'Conrad Looks at Nelson'. After praising the depiction of Nelson, Curle turns to the novel's ending, claiming that 'it is relieved from final tragedy by the magnificent sacrifice of old Peyrol, and by the supreme happiness of its finish . . . Its epic spirit draws to a triumphant conclusion and its whole air of strangled passion fades into the sunlight of lasting peace.' Curle also reviewed the novel for *Blue Peter* (January 1924, p. 434).

[3] T(homas) Fisher Unwin (1848–1935) published *Almayer's Folly*, *An Outcast of the Islands*, and *Tales of Unrest* at the beginning of Conrad's career, *The Arrow of Gold* and *The Rover* towards its end, and *Tales of Hearsay* posthumously. Neither his business practices nor his adherence to the Liberal party endeared him to Conrad.

[4] There were three: the green cloth, the slightly smaller blue cloth (18 rather than 20cm tall, uniform with *The Arrow of Gold* in Unwin's Cabinet Library), and a red cloth overseas edition.

Thank you for your letter. Of course your use of the 1896 photo in the Cabinet Edition is justifiable as there is no other portrait of that time in existence.[1] As to the jacket of the Blue Cloth "Rover"[2] I regret I did not know that anything about it[*] before, because I could have suggested your using for it a photograph by Messrs. T. & R. Annan, 518 Sauchiehall Street, Glasgow. (Neg. No 1.). This is a very good likeness taken only last April. I regret not having a copy to send you from here.

Yours faithfully

J. Conrad

P.S. Cheque for £4.10– enclosed to cover account and another half dozen copies which you will be good enough to send.

To Eric S. Pinker

Text TS/MS Berg; Unpublished

[letterhead: Oswalds]
Dec. 3rd. 1923.

My dearest Eric

This morning I was greeted with the "Times" notice of "The Rover", and the half column in the middle page of the "Daily Mail", obviously Curle's work.[3]

No doubt there are other first day publication notices of this the first novel which comes out under your reign at Talbot House. I must thank you for your efforts on its behalf and for your unvaried friendliness in this and all other matters ever since you took my affairs in hand as part of your inheritance. My thoughts were very much with poor J. B. this morning. I used to drop him a line on the day of publication always; feeling how much of my successive achievements I owed to him. And I am touched to think that now he is gone from us the connection is not broken, since he left me on going away the friendship of his son which has been such a support to me both in my public work and in my private life, for nearly two years now.

---

[1] It was a wedding portrait: see *Letters*, 1, Plate 12.

[2] The jacket has a boldly coloured marine picture of waves breaking on a rocky coast, in the background a sailing ship, and on the clifftop, the whitewashed buildings of a farmstead.

[3] The review in *The Times* (p. 15) opened on a note that would recur in other periodicals: 'Mr. Conrad's new story . . . is one that everyone will read with an enjoyment unmitigated by any necessity for intellectual strivings. It is a romance of simple texture, and the threads of its incident[s] as well as those of its emotions are neither as mysterious or as complicated as some other of this author's weavings.' Among the literary virtues the anonymous reviewer found to admire were the 'exquisite and economical' treatment of the plot, the dramatic skill of the dialogue, the 'cunning touches' in the characterisation of Peyrol, and the 'epic quality of the final chapter'.

I could not help expressing to Fisher Unwin my satisfaction at the get up of both editions, both the Green Cloth and the other, practically a pocket size published simultaneously at the same price. They are really very attractive. Even the jacket of the Green Cloth is the best jacket I ever had since jackets came into fashion.[1] I don't want you to think that I gushed to F. U. I just, precisely, gave the devil his due. However he wrote to me to express his profound satisfaction at my approval.

I ought to have thanked you long before for your last letter to me. I have thought of what you say in it, but you will forgive me just now if I don't give you my point of view which is at least arguable. It would be nice if I could have a talk with you before the year is out, but I feel a scruple in asking you to take a journey down here; which is a beastly grind especially at this season. I am getting on slowly and I do not think it would be prudent for me to come up to town until after the New Year, perhaps. I hoped to run up on the 15th to meet John on his arrival from Havre, but the fellow can look after himself by now and I don't intend to take any risks. I would have also liked to have seen Borys in his new home. But that too will have to wait.

He is apparently going in on the 10th. He gets his furniture from Waring & Gillow.[2] Those people don't sell on the monthly payment system, but they made him a proposal to give him a trade discount on condition that he should pay £100 on delivery and the balance next June. This isn't what he expected to have to do. I have told him that I would see whether I could not advance to him the first £100 against his allowance of the 1st of Jan. and the 1st of March. I should like to help in that matter if you can arrange it for me. He has been advised of a rise of salary next January but I don't suppose he can pay £100 away now unless he is helped; and I should like to see him settled in a decent way.

It was kind of you to call on Jessie twice. She appreciated it greatly. She told me you looked well and that your home news was good.

Love to you both

Yours

J. C.

---

[1] It shows the tartane as it sinks, the flag of France still flying; around the vignette is an elaborate frame ornamented with sea shells. Dust-jackets became popular in the Edwardian period; several of the earlier Conrad jackets, such as those for *Under Western Eyes* (Methuen) and *Within the Tides* (Dent) are almost entirely filled with text or, like the one for *Some Reminiscences* (Eveleigh Nash), simply carry a picture of the author; others, such as *Chance* and *Victory* (Methuen), feature an alluring scene from the book's interior.

[2] On Oxford St.

I'll send Miss H to ring you up about the above transaction 10.30 to-morrow (Tuesday).

To Edward Garnett

Text TS Yale; J-A, 2, 325; G. 330

[letterhead: Oswalds]
Dec. 4th. 1923

My dearest Edward.

I am so sorry I can not answer you by hand. I have been flattened out more than I can remember by this last bout.

The generosity of your criticism,[1] my dear Edward, is great enough to put heart into a dead man. As I have not claimed to be more than only half-dead for the last month, I feel, after reading your letter, like a man with wings. Every word of your commendation has electrified the dulled fibres of my being. My absolute belief in your sincerity in questions of literary art has relieved me of that load of weary doubt which I have not been able to shake off before. It relieved me thoroughly, because the belief in the absolute unflawed honesty of your judgment has been one of the mainstays of my literary life. Even if led astray, even if apparently mistaken, there is that in you which remains impeccable in its essence. In all your literary judgments there is never anything suspect. Your very prejudices are genuinely personal and, in a manner of speaking, can be thoroughly trusted.

Therefore I gather like a real treasure all the words of commendation you give to Cath[erine], Arlette, and the doctrinaire Real. I gather them the more eagerly because what I most feared in the secret of my heart was an impression of sketchiness. This is perhaps my only work in which brevity was a conscious aim. I don't mean compression. I mean brevity ab initio, in the very conception, in the very manner of thinking about the people and the events. I am glad you find Peyrol captivating; and indeed I am made glad by all the appreciative remarks you make which are much, very much beyond my highest expectations; though of course, my dear, I won't pretend I did not know that you would be looking for good points and make the most of them; for nothing can be less doubtful to me than your affection and your amazing faculty of comprehension. What you say about the English side of the book – the fleet, the Vincent scenes etc. – shows how you do marvellously respond to the slightest shades, the faintest flavours, the simplest indications

---

[1] Of *The Rover*, see Stape and Knowles, pp. 225–6. Garnett found it 'simply admirable in *construction* & in *the harmony of its parts*' and heard an improvement in the quality of Conrad's dialogue: 'The talk in "The Rover" is extremely good, with no awkwardness' (p. 225).

of sentiment underlying the action. My dear Edward, it is good to write while there is a reader like you about.

And of course your critical ability, that very sensitiveness in response, has made you put your finger on the weak spot. I can honestly say that I did see it myself but not so clearly as since I have read your letter. You were not likely to miss Scevola, and, by Jove, now you have uttered the words he does look to me too like a bit of "a scarecrow of the Revolution."[1] Yet it was not my intention. It is not the fault of the original conception but the fault of presentation, of the literary treatment. But apart from that, to take him fundamentally – pray look at my difficulty! Postulating that Arlette had to remain untouched, the terrorist that brought her back could have been nothing else than what he is or the book would have had to be altogether different. To me S is not revolutionary, he is, to be frank about it, a pathological case more than anything else. I won't go into a deeper exposition. Your intelligence will take the hint at once. The situation at Escampobar could not have lasted seven or eight years if S had been formidable. But he was never formidable except as a creature of mob psychology. Away from the mob he is just a weak-minded creature. As you know there were many like that. I tried to give a hint of it in what Catherine says about him: "the butt of all the girls," "always mooning about," "Run away from his home to join the Revolution." He is weak-minded in a way as much as my poor Michel, the man with the dog, whose resigned philosophy was that "somebody must be last". Even amongst terrorists S was considered a poor creature. But his half-witted soul received the impress of the Revolution which has missed the simple minded Michel altogether. I never intended S to be a figure of the Revolution. As a matter of fact if there is a child of the Revolution there at all, it is Real, with his austere and pedantic turn of mind and conscience. The defect of Scevola, my dear Edward, is alas in the treatment, which instead of half-pathetic makes him half-grotesque; and no amount of wriggling and explaining will do away with the fact that so far he is a failure. A created figure that requires explaining to Edward Garnett *is* a failure. That is my sincere conviction. But as to a "formidable" Scevola . . .

Yes, my dear. I know you will believe me when I tell you that I had a momentary vision of quite a great figure worthy of Peyrol; the notion of a struggle between the two men. But I did deliberately shut my eyes to it. It would have required another canvas. No use talking about it. How long

---

[1] 'I don't question your reading of his nature or the justice of your verdict – but it seems to me that to show him only in profile – as it were – as *Citizen Scevola* – is what weakens the springs of the *drama*. For such a bloodthirsty ruffian should be formidable, in all his relations, – & he fades away steadily before our eyes, like a revolutionary scarecrow' (*ibid.*).

would I have had to wait for that mood? – and the mood of the other was there, more in accord with my temperament, more also with my secret desire to achieve a feat of artistic brevity, once at least, before I died. And on those grounds I believe you will forgive me for having rejected probably a greater thing – or perhaps only a different one.

What I regret now is the rejection of a half thought-out scene, four pages or so, between Catherine and Scevola. But when it came to me the development of the story was already marked and the person of Catherine established psychologically as she is now. That scene would have checked the movement and damaged the conception of Catherine. It would have been, and it would have looked, a thing "inserted". I was feeling a little bit heart-sick then, too, and anxious also to demonstrate to myself as soon as possible that I could finish a piece of work. So I let it go.

Here you have, my dear Edward, the confession of my weaknesses in connection with the secret history of "The Rover". Had I been writing with pen and ink I would probably come nearer to expressing myself. You can form no idea of how much your letter has eased and comforted me, even physically. It was good of you to have written at once and while (as you say) "heavy with a cold". I hope it isn't the beginning of anything. I hope too, my dear, that you will be able to let me have a look at you soon. As soon as you like. You know, it won't be really safe for me to come up to town for quite a long time.

My love to you.

Yours ever

J. Conrad

To Eric S. Pinker
Text MS Berg; Unpublished

[Oswalds]
Tuesday 4th
12. 23

Dearest Eric.

Herewith agreement duly signed.[1] I had a letter from B this morning telling me that the furniture people accepted his counter-proposal and that he can manage without an advance.

Awfully good of You to be so ready to come down to see me. It will cheer me up to see and hear you.

---

[1] Probably regarding Borys's allowance.

I've had an enthusiastic letter from E. Garnett about The Rover. He's no flatterer – so I am delighted to see him so impressed.

Ever Yours

J. C.

To Arnold Bennett
Text MS UCL; J-A, 2, 328

[letterhead: Oswalds]
5. Dec. 23

My dear Bennett[1]

This, my latest, is remarkable mainly for a howling anachronism in the first twenty lines;[2] but it is not on that ground that I "obtrude it on your notice" (pretty cliché, that)

No. It is because I feel (why conceal it?) that twilight lies already on these pages. Perhaps it is not unfitting that the man who for twenty years or more gave to my work so many proofs of his appreciation should now accept this book from my hand.

Yours

J. Conrad

To John C. Niven
Text J-A, 1, 99 (in part)[3]

[Oswalds]
[5 December 1923][4]

You could not really have believed that I had forgotten my[5] time in the *Vidar*. It is part of my sea life to which my memory returns most often, since there is nothing to remember but what is good and pleasant in my temporary

---

[1] (Enoch) Arnold Bennett (1867–1931) is best remembered for novels such as *The Old Wives' Tale* and the Clayhanger trilogy, set in the 'Five Towns' of Staffordshire where he spent his youth. After a decade in Paris, Bennett returned to England in 1912 and served during the First World War as Director of Propaganda for the War Ministry. In 1918 he refused a knighthood. He was a longstanding admirer of Conrad's work and reviewed it perceptively.

[2] In the opening paragraph of the British and American first editions, Peyrol drops anchor after a six-month voyage, showing no emotion when he hears 'the rumble of the chain', but anchors in the Napoleonic era were hauled by ropes. See the notes to Conrad's letter to Blanchenay of 8 April 1924. Later editions replace 'chain' with 'cable'.

[3] Excerpted by Jean-Aubry. The original was last seen on the wall of a pub in Troon, Scotland, in the 1950s. John Campbell Niven (1853–1926) was second engineer in the *Vidar* in 1887, when Conrad was serving as first mate. There is a lively fictional portrait of him as 'John Nieven', a 'sturdy young Scot' and a 'fierce misogynist' in *The Shadow-Line* (p. 6). For Niven's letter to Conrad, see Stape and Knowles, p. 226.

[4] Dated by Jean-Aubry; Niven had written from Woburn Sands, Buckinghamshire, on the 3rd.

[5] Emended from 'any' in J-A's reading of the now-missing holograph.

association with three men for whom, I assure you, I have preserved to this day a warm regard and sincere esteem.[1]

To F. N. Doubleday

Text TS/MS Indiana; J-A, 2, 328 with facsimile

[letterhead: Oswalds]

Dec. 6th. 1923.

Very dear Effendi

This is in answer to your letter of Nov. 22nd which reached me on the 3rd of this month. *Victory* (2 cops) and *Lord Jim* (2 cops), of the Concord Edition, arrived by the same mail but did not reach this house till the day after. I honestly think that it is a remarkable production and I must say that I am pleased with every feature: the cloth, the paper, the Minute Man under the title, the title-page itself, the fount, the spacing of the lines which is just right, and the proportions of the margins. The jacket too is nice with its simple landscape. I must also mention the back which avoids being dead flat in a very pleasing manner.[2] I am quite impressed by the consistent attention to detail which is visible in the finished product. Let me tell you, Effendi, that I feel I never had such a birthday present in my life.[3]

I was touched by the congratulatory wire from Florence and you. The day was not marked by any festivities. In fact I had managed to forget it. Jessie came into my room at seven o'clock (which is not her usual practice) and I just simply asked her what was the matter? She said "I thought I would be the first to see you to-day". The word birthday was not mentioned. It is forbidden in the family by a decree which I promulgated on my 50th birthday. Both boys, though, managed to get in a letter to me, apparently about nothing in particular, just expressing the hope that I was better.

As a matter of fact I was then getting better and I was well enough to-day to drive as far as the polling station and record my vote. The day is mild, luminously grey, with a pleasant temperature and no wind. The elements are favourable to this election. We shall see what will come of it. It is very obvious

---

[1] The signature of Niven's letter reads: 'John C. Niven, late 2nd Engineer / For Capt James Craig / James Allan (late) 1st Eng^r'. Conrad served in the *Vidar* from *c.* 19 August 1887 to 2 January 1888. For details of the ship and her voyages, see Norman Sherry, *Conrad's Eastern World* (Cambridge University Press, 1966), pp. 30–1, 89–118.

[2] The figure of the Minute Man, an icon of the War of Independence created for its centennial, appeared on the half-title page; the front of the jacket evokes rural New England; the rear has a medallion of a sailing ship in a storm, a list of the volumes, and a quotation by Christopher Morley: 'He speaks between the lines of his noble prose a language at once unbelievably more foreign and more familiarly intimate than any words actually written – the language of the human spirit, recognised by all and wholly understood by none.'

[3] Conrad had turned sixty-six on 3 December.

that 90% of the electors can not possibly form any reasoned judgment on the issue. There has been quite a lot of hearty and conscientious lying about it. And this is as it should be; for, in economical problems, what is true to-day may be quite untrue in another three months' time.[1]

The poor "Rover" came out in the middle of that scrimmage just as the old man himself returned right in the middle of a revolution. But I can't say he arrived unperceived. The daily press gave him the best send-off it could under the circumstances, half columns and three-quarter columns, and shorter notices – whatever space could be spared – on the day of publication. Criticism laudatory and benevolent, but (speaking in all humility) rather unintelligent.[2] From Edward Garnett I had a private letter which braced me up morally and physically; for Edward's sincerity is above suspicion. But it isn't so much the press, which had not yet the time to have its say, but the general impression that the name of the book is, as it were, vibrating in the air that is most cheering. There is also the valuable commercial fact of the heavy subscription in advance, amounting in itself, I believe, to more than six months' sales of "The Arrow of Gold". To give the devil his due I must admit that Fisher Unwin can turn out a decent book.

This, my dear Effendi, is all my news. I am now on the up grade and don't anticipate any set-back. Neither do I expect to do any work this month, because it must take some time to recover the creative tone. And you know that in many ways, pleasant and unpleasant, I have had a rather strenuous year.

It is settled that Epstein will come down to make my bust.[3] I couldn't resist Muirhead Bone's pleading. I shall see something of M. B. because the whole family is going to stay in Canterbury for the Christmas week.[4] I send you both here the season's conventional wishes for a Merry Christmas and

---

[1] One of the principal and most warmly debated issues was the future of tariffs. Baldwin, the Conservative leader, held doggedly to the protectionist line, while, as they always did, the Liberals stood for free trade; both these parties claimed that their policies would create more jobs. Campaigning as, to all intents and purposes, one party, the Conservatives and Ulster Unionists won more seats than any other group, but a less formal alliance of Liberal and Labour MPs had a combined majority of around ninety and was able to form a coalition government.

[2] Even the praise came qualified with unwelcome remarks. For example, 'J. B.' (James Bone?) in the *Manchester Guardian* (3 December, p. 5) applauded Conrad's sense of pace: 'the tale races to its close in as fine a piece of direct narrative as Mr. Conrad has ever written. Once again Mr. Conrad has forbidden the jog-trot of the casual reader; it is hard climbing until that noble summit has been reached. One moves with effort at first, with ease later, with delight increasing.' The reviewer then spoils the effect by claiming that the finale is worthy of G. A. Henty or the early Kipling – not to Conrad's eyes the most flattering of associations.

[3] In March 1924, the American-born sculptor Jacob Epstein (1880–1959; knighted 1954), who was now living in London, made a portrait head and a bust of Conrad. See the letters to Jean-Aubry, Curle, and Adams of 19, 25, and 26 March 1924.

[4] See the letter to Doubleday of 7 January.

a happy New Year, but you know that I am always with you both, in heart and mind, and shall always be "till death doth us part".

Ever Yours

J. Conrad.

PS My love and best wishes to Patty and Nelson and to Mr & Mrs Babcock. Jessie sends her warmest Greetings.

PPS It would be nice and kind of you to spare me a Concord set for Miss Hallowes. She has toiled with infinite devotion on preparing and correcting the text of all these editions. I was going to give her the Dents Set but she has fallen in love with the Concord.

To Fountaine Hope

Text Wright; Unpublished

[letterhead: Oswalds]

6. Dec 23

My dearest friend[1]

I am so sorry you should have troubled to write. I feel very remorseful towards your dear wife and you, for indeed I should have written when sending the book. But I was not very well and not quite fit to use the pen just then, and I wanted you to have your copy on the day of publication.

All through October I intended to propose myself for a visit to you in the first week of November. But just about the 1st I got a slight attack of gout which developed into something very nasty indeed. And so I was laid up all last month.

I will say no more now. It is late and I am very tired. In a few days I will be sending you a copy of the *Britain's Lifeboats*.[2] The N[ational] L[ife] B[oat] Institution asked me to give them a foreword. It is short, hardly a page.

Please give my love to the Conrads and to Herford and his wife from whom Jessie had a charming letter. May all happiness attend the youngest of the Hope family on his way through life.[3]

Ever yours

J. Conrad

---

[1] (George) Fountaine (Weare) Hope (né Hopps, 1854–1930) was one of the first friends Conrad made in England. A *Conway* boy who later served in the *Duke of Sutherland*, Hope became a 'Director of Companies' and invited Conrad to cruise the Thames estuary in his yawl, the *Nellie*; Conrad drew upon these cruises in *Chance* and *Heart of Darkness*. Hope left a memoir entitled 'Friend of Conrad' (see *Documents*, pp. 1–56).

[2] By A. J. Dawson (Hodder & Stoughton, 1923); as well as Conrad's Foreword, there was an Introduction by the Prince of Wales.

[3] Roger Paul Hope was born in 1923; his parents, Herford and 'Jean' (née Jenny Marjorie Woods), had married in 1919. Named in honour of his father's friend, Conrad Hope was Herford's brother.

To Alfred A. Knopf

Text TS Texas; Unpublished

[letterhead: Oswalds]
Dec. 6th. 1923.

My dear Mr Knopf.[1]

Many thanks for the two copies, especially the grand format, of Crane's biography.[2] Both sizes are very attractively got up. I like very well your fount and the spacing of the lines.

I am going to drop a few lines to Mr Beer to congratulate him on his achievement. It is a live book, more so than any biography I ever read. The manner and the tone are remarkably adapted to the personality. After reading it the most indifferent person can not doubt Crane's existence, personal and literary.

My wife joins me in kindest regards and best wishes to Mrs Knopf and yourself.

Very faithfully Yours

Joseph Conrad.

To T. Fisher Unwin

Text TS Colgate; Unpublished

[letterhead: Oswalds]

T. Fisher Unwin, Esq.
Dec. 7th. 1923.

Dear Sir,

Thank you for your letter. I quite understand now the state of affairs as to the First Edition.

I regret I have no photograph to send you. I have no copyright in Mr Annan's photographs, and I have no doubt a fee would have to be paid.

I enclose herewith the balance of 3/– on the receipted account received yesterday.

Yours faithfully

Joseph Conrad

---

[1] While still an undergraduate, Alfred Abraham Knopf (1892–1984) had corresponded with the Galsworthys and visited them in Devon. On graduating from Columbia University in 1912, he went to work at Doubleday, Page, where he was responsible for orchestrating the highly successful publicity campaign for *Chance*. In 1915, he began his own firm. With his wife, Blanche Wolf Knopf, he built up an extraordinary list that included, over the years, Wallace Stevens, Willa Cather, Dashiell Hammett, Langston Hughes, Thomas Mann, Jean-Paul Sartre, Simone de Beauvoir, Albert Camus, Yukio Mishima, Doris Lessing, and Toni Morrison.

[2] Thomas Beer's *Stephen Crane: A Study in American Letters*, with Conrad's Introduction.

To Christopher Ward

Text MS Delaware; Unpublished

7. 12. 23
[letterhead: Oswalds]

Dear Mr Ward.[1]

Sorry I am so late in thanking You for the little book and the friendly inscription.[2] I greatly enjoyed the parodies on those writers I have read, and I have no doubt those on the others have the same merit – which is considerable.

Sincerely Yours

Joseph Conrad

To Sydney Cockerell

Text MS Texas; Unpublished

[letterhead: Oswalds]
Dec 8 1923[3]

My dear Cockerell

My warm thanks to you and your dear wife[4] for your birthday letter.

I am sorry I did not write before, but I was not quite fit to hold the pen. I was laid up for nearly a month but am recovering now. Not very fast.

My love to you both.

Yours

J. Conrad.

PS As it looks as though you had bought the book I will hold back the copy destined to you and will in a few days send you a copy of the 1st Am^{can} edition.

---

[1] Christopher Lewis Ward (1868–1943) had been a successful Delaware lawyer and businessman before he took up literature at the urging of his cousin, Henry S(eidel) Canby, the editor of the *Saturday Review of Literature*. He published novels, plays, short stories, and poetry in addition to several historical works about the American Revolution.

[2] *The Triumph of the Nut and Other Parodies* (New York: Henry Holt, 1923), with parodies of Edith Wharton, Sinclair Lewis, F. Scott Fitzgerald, Willa Cather, T. S. Eliot, and others. Ward's parody of Conrad's *Victory* appeared in a second volume, *Twisted Tales*, published the following year.

[3] The date is not in Conrad's hand.

[4] The illustrator Florence Kate Cockerell (née Kingsford, 1892–1949).

To Eric S. Pinker

Text MS Berg; Unpublished

[Oswalds]
Sat. 8. 12. 23

Dearest Eric.

Delighted to hear You are coming next Wed^y for lunch.

Yes my dear. I have the Concord books; and truly for an U. S. prod^{on} they are got up well.

Ever Yours

J. C.

To Edward Garnett

Text MS Yale; G. 334

[letterhead: Oswalds]
[11 December 1923][1]

Dearest Edward

Thanks for your dear, friendly letter.[2]

Pray let me know how you are. I am better. But my dear fellow a gout (the most obscure of diseases) of 32 years' standing (and when the patient is 65 years old[3]) is not to be driven off by the Medicine-men incantations. My dear I consulted people in France (Montpellier) & in England in Switzerland.[4] I have tried all sorts of treatment and diet. Of course it will do me in the end – but one must go sometime. Don't be angry and let me know about yourself.

Ever yours

J. C.

To R. B. Cunninghame Graham

Text MS Dartmouth; J-A, 2, 329; Watts 198

[letterhead: Oswalds]
12. 12. '23

Très cher ami.

We are much relieved by your news. I curse myself for a dismal crock who can't go to see a friend in trouble.

---

[1] Dated from postmark.
[2] In his letter of 5 December (Stape and Knowles, p. 227), Garnett implored Conrad to place himself in the care of Sir Robert Jones. 'Dont you understand that the gouty poison in the body will do for your heart or your kidneys *soon*; – & that it *can* be got rid of.'
[3] Just turned sixty-six.
[4] Montpellier in 1906 and 1907; Champel in 1891, 1894, and 1895.

I assume that the horse actually went down and that you alighted "parado."[1]

I hope to goodness he didn't roll over you.

I shall hope for a line from you soon.

Mrs Dummett wrote me a most charming letter. So I see I am pardoned.

Epstein I believe is going to operate on me now. I have been told that Tittle's drawing of you is good.[2]

Jessie sends her love.

Ever Yours

J. Conrad

To Perriton Maxwell[3]

Text Maxwell (1923); Ray 69 (in part)

Bishopsbourne, Kent, England
[December? 1923]

I have been a stranger to Santa Claus all my life.[4] You'll understand how the Polish children did not need a Germanic fairy saint to give them the sense of sanctity and joy attached to the day of Nativity in the hearts of Roman Catholics.

But I have no feeling against him personally, and if American children want him – why should not they have him?

What's the objection? I don't know the case. And you want me to vote! Sir, I would perish rather! Why should I legislate – or attempt to – for American children and their parents – not to speak of Santa Claus himself?

---

[1] Cunninghame Graham had told Conrad, 'Yesterday my horse slipped sideways with me & strained my back & today I can only just walk with a stick' (Stape and Knowles, p. 229). 'Parado': equestrian Spanish for 'on your feet'. For a discussion of other recent letters from Graham in praise of *The Rover* (Stape and Knowles, pp. 227–9), see Eloise Knapp Hay and Cedric Watts, 'To Conrad from Cunninghame Graham: Reflections on Two Letters', *Conradiana*, 5.2 (1973), 5–19.

[2] Conrad had sat for the American artist Walter E(rnest) Tittle in 1922 (*Letters*, 7, p. 494); the results were two oils, two lithographs, and a dry-point.

[3] The editor and author Perriton Maxwell (1866–1947) worked for many New York newspapers and periodicals including the *World, Metropolitan Magazine, Cosmopolitan, Saturday Evening Post*, and *Vogue*. In April 1912, when Maxwell was editing *Nash's Magazine* in London, Conrad had offered him a commentary on the sinking of the *Titanic*; Maxwell's New York newspaper rejected the offer, and the essay appeared in the *English Review* (Ray, pp. 66–70).

[4] On behalf of *Collier's Weekly* (New York, 15 December 1923, pp. 10–11), Maxwell had asked a 'grand jury of 18 Famous Writers What They Thought of Santa Claus'. The other respondents included Galsworthy, Shaw ('Santa Claus be blowed!'), Hall Caine, Dorothy Canfield, Israel Zangwill ('Of prohibition, America has surely had enough'), and H. G. Wells ('I am disqualified to vote. I am over fourteen').

I want him free – free to come and go, to exist or vanish, to please or displease. I believe in freedom and in the pursuit of happiness – without legislation. And if I voted I would to a certain extent legislate. That never!

I want liberty for American men, women, children, for Santa Claus, and for myself. 'Give me liberty – or give me death!'[1]

With my love and Xmas wishes to all free Americans, I remain, faithfully yours (but still violently protesting as the curtain falls),

Joseph Conrad

To Eric S. Pinker
Text MS Berg; Unpublished

[Oswalds]
16. 12. 23

My dear Eric.

Thank you for your letter advising the payment of the extra £100 for which I asked you.

No doubt it will take me some time to recover. Fox was down here to-day to arrange the programme for a general treatment. He found that, notwithstanding the strain of two relapses, the heart has recovered its tone, quite. He took my blood pressure. My arteries are like those of a much younger man. I feel confident that the analysis of the urine will give a satisfactory result. The cough is the difficulty but as a matter of fact the lungs are clear.

I give you all these details because I feel sure of your interest.

My love to you

J. C.

To Richard Curle
Text MS Indiana; Curle 136

[Oswalds]
17. 12. 23

Dearest Dick

I havent yet shaken off the trouble – but the improvement if slow will be lasting.

Fox has been over and we have arranged a treatment to be followed for 4 or 6 weeks directly all the acute symptoms are gone. Of course I feel as tho' I had been ill. But as a matter of fact the heart-action is quite normal now, the lungs are clear, pulse and temp have been normal for some time already

---

[1] Having played to his American audience by quoting the preamble to the Constitution ('the pursuit of happiness'), Conrad now cites Patrick Henry's speech of 23 March 1775 to the Virginia Convention.

and my blood-pressure is quite satisfactory. In fact my arteries are younger than my age.

When can we expect You here? I have been wondering as to your health. Please let us know. Have you seen Gwatkin?[1] His novel is not bad and I can see now why it had that sale.[2] Shall I send it to you – or has he given you a copy?

Up to 10 Dec. F. U. disposed of 26000 cop of The R. 18000 in UK and 8.000 colonial – in round numbers. (1st imp) I have heard that the booksellers in this part of the country can no longer procure 1st impression copies.

Love

J. C.

To Arnold Bennett

Text MS UCL; J-A, 2, 330

[letterhead: Oswalds]
20. 12. 23

My dear Bennett,

Warmest thanks for the inscribed book – the first presentation copy since the treasured *Leonore*,* you gave me twenty two or three years ago![3]

We haven't been throwing our works at each other's heads! – yet no man's work has been more present to my thoughts. Only I am a dumb sort of beast; while you could always find time to speak of me in words which I'll never forget.[4]

Sorry to hear You have been seedy. I hope you are definitely on the mend.

I have had a beastly time of it for the last month. Too much pain to think, too much pain to read – and almost to care. However that is over apparently.

Affectly Yours

J. Conrad.

---

[1] Frank Trelawny Arthur Ashton-Gwatkin (1889–1976), the son of the Rector of Bishopsbourne, wrote novels about Japan under the pseudonym 'John Paris' while serving in the British Foreign Office as an economic adviser. The first of these, *Kimono* (Collins, 1921), dealt with prostitution and the ordeals of a Japanese heiress married to an aristocratic English diplomat against her family's wishes.

[2] *Kimono* had been reprinted seventeen times by 1923.

[3] The new book was *Riceyman Steps*, a powerful psychological study of loneliness and starvation, inscribed to 'Joseph Conrad from his faithful admirer, Arnold Bennett. Xmas 1923.' Bennett's *Leonora*, one of the Five Towns novels, set in the Potteries district of Staffordshire, was published in October 1903 (see *Letters*, 3, p. 80).

[4] Bennett had reviewed some of Conrad's early works anonymously, and praised *Nostromo* as 'the finest novel of this generation . . . It's the Higuerota among novels' (letter to Conrad, 22 November 1912; Stape and Knowles, p. 87). For Conrad's reaction to Bennett's unforgettable words about *The Rover*, see the PS to the letter to him of 2 January.

To Thomas J. Wise

Text MS BL Ashley 2953; Unpublished

[letterhead: Oswalds]

20. 12. 23

My dear Wise

I have not been able to write to you before. I have had a pretty bad time of it this month past – yet I managed to write an article of 5000 before the things got too bad.

I have had a few letters from US still harping on the sale. I can not believe that all these prices were fictitious. In fact I know that some of them were not. Then why the others? I do not see the object of such a conspiracy. However all that is without the slightest importance. But in any case the collection is scattered now and the sale has made you the largest holder of Conrad MS.

I hope you have been keeping well.

My wife joins me in Xmas greetings to Mrs Wise and yourself and warmest wishes for a happy New Year.

Very sincerely Yours

J. Conrad

To Louise Alvar Harding

Text MS NYU; Unpublished

[letterhead: Oswalds]

22. 12. 23

Dear Mrs Harding

Pray accept this copy which had been put apart for you on the day of publication. Had I known you were on a flying visit to London just then you would have had it on the 2^d of Dec^{er}

I learned with the greatest satisfaction of your successes during the tour. I wish I had been at some of these lectures (*not* about J. C.) to hear your fascinating singing and Jean's wise discourses.[1]

My wife joins me in affectionate good wishes to you all for the coming year. Please give my friendly greeting to Mr Harding and my love to the "Wonder-Children".[2]

Believe me always very gratefully and affectionately yours

Joseph Conrad.

---

[1] On 20 November, Jean-Aubry had written from Marseilles, where he had just lectured on Conrad to an audience of more than 700. He was leaving the next day for similar events in Chambéry and Geneva. Earlier, he had spoken in Roanne, Le Puy, St-Étienne, Nîmes, Montpellier, and Lyons (MS Yale). Mme Alvar and Valéry had joined him for part of the tour (25 October, TS Yale).

[2] Sigrid and Charlie Harding.

To J. M. Dent

Text MS Berg; Unpublished

[letterhead: Oswalds]

Xmas. 1923

Dear Chief.

Many thanks for your munificent present. Nothing could have given me greater pleasure than this beautifully bound copy of the *Mirror* and the expression of your appreciation of that book.

My thoughts are with you and yours today. Accept for yourself and them all my affectionate good wishes.

Always Yours

J. Conrad

I have been seedy for more than a month now.

To Bruno Winawer

Text TS copy Yale; *Głos*; Najder 293[1]

[letterhead: Oswalds]

Xmas Day 1923.

My dear Winawer!

In my thoughts I am with you today. I was unable to write sooner as I was in bed for about a month and am still not very well. Your letter arrived two days ago. Thank you very much. Please accept my best wishes for the coming year and for the whole of your (longest possible) life. Yes, my novel came out in December. In a few days I'll send you a copy of the American edition.

A hearty handshake,

Bien à Vous

J. Conrad.

To Aniela Zagórska

Text MS copy Yale;[2] Najder 294

Oswalds,

Xmas Day, 1923.

My dear Aniela,

I could not write sooner because I was in bed and even now I am not feeling entirely well. My thoughts join you today – but this is nothing extraordinary.

---

[1] Translation from Najder with minor alterations.

[2] When Aniela Zagórska translated this letter into French, she apparently omitted part of the now destroyed Polish original.

I think of you every day. I send you my wishes for happiness in the coming year and for all the rest of your life and I embrace you fraternally[. . .]

In a few days I shall send you a copy of the American edition of my novel *The Rover*. Everyone here sends you our affectionate wishes and kisses.

Always your

Konrad.

To Richard Curle
Text MS Indiana; Curle 137

27. Dec. 23.
[letterhead: Oswalds]

Dearest Dick.

I am awaiting with impatience the announcement of Your visit. Things are not so well here. Jessie is menaced with an ab[s]cess in the upper part of the leg – (deep in) but the doctor is not certain. If it isn't that then it must be something equally serious. Reid assured me there was no immediate cause for anxiety. He is coming to see her to-morrow and then will notify Sir R. Jones.

J. is, as usual, cheerfully facing it upstairs with fomentations on her leg. But I am sure that inwardly she is feeling a bitter disappointement* at what she calls "another set-back." I hope to goodness it won't turn out something worse.

Don't allude to the state of my mind when you answer this – as Mrs C expects to be shown Your letters.

Ever Yours

J. Conrad

There is a bottle of Tobermory whisky awaiting You here. Jessie would not send it for fear of breakage.

To Captain David Bone
Text MS Sprott; Knowles

[letterhead: Oswalds]
29.12. 23

My dear Captain.

Ever so many thanks for the book you have been good enough to inscribe for me.[1]

My wife begs leave to join me in most sincere and affectionate wishes of all possible happiness to you all for the coming year and the years to come.

I forward you a letter I had from the Sec^y of the Life-boats.[2] Perhaps you will see your way to do something for them.

---

[1] Bone's *The Lookoutman* (1923).   [2] George F. Shee, Secretary of the RNLI.

Muirhead and family are staying in C'bury. It is very delightful for us to be able to see them. Both Jessie and I are confined to the house by our respective infirmities.

Please remember me particularly to Mrs Bone, to Miss Bone and to your boy.[1]

May you all prosper in peace and contentment!

Ever Yours

J. Conrad

To the Hon. Michael Holland
Text MS Private collection; Unpublished

[letterhead: Oswalds]

29. 12. 23

My dear Holland.[2]

Confined to the house and at times to my room I have been struggling single-handed with an exceptional amount of correspondence. This is my only excuse for not answering before Your good and friendly letter. Pray forgive me and believe that nothing could have given me greater pleasure than your warm appreciation of *The Rover*.

I have been laid up more or less for the whole of the last month. My poor wife too has suffered a set back in the condition of the operated limb. This "festive" season has not been very cheerful for us.

I think that in the eyes of a boy of ten or eight the father still has a certain prestige. In the paternal relation one must not expect too much. Neither one's hopes nor one's fears (thank God) are ever fully realised, and natural affection helps to smooth the differences that may arise. Neither of my boys (26 and 18) can be called intellectual. But they both are straight-thinking creatures and though I have had moments of anxiety we are very good friends and I feel I have their confidence almost as fully as when they were little.

I was very much interested in what you say of your recent African journey. I think I understand your feelings perfectly. But of course my experience was very slight (only 2 years on the Congo)[3] and seems like a dream now.

---

[1] Freda, later Mrs Sprott, and David. When Conrad sailed with her father in the *Tuscania*, she had been allowed to accompany them as far as Moville (Knowles, note to the present letter).

[2] The Hon. Michael James Holland (1870–1956) was a Kentish neighbour and a keen book collector. Until the end of 1913, he lived at Smeeth Hill, near Aldington. In his earlier years he had travelled in South Africa and British Columbia; his experiences there were recollected in *Verse* (1937). During the First World War, he won the Military Cross while serving as a captain in King Edward's Horse.

[3] Although his contract was for three years, Conrad spent just over six months in the Congo, from 12 June 1890 until the end of the year.

Jessie joins me in affectionate wishes of peace and happiness for you and all yours

Yours ever

J. Conrad

To Ferdinand and Thérèse Aubry

Text MS Yale; *L. fr.* 193

[letterhead: Oswalds]
[30 December 1923][1]

Cher Monsieur et Madame[2]

Nous vous envoyons nos meilleurs vœux de nouvelle année. Quand je dis "nous" cela veut dire que notre Jean est inclus. Il est là dans mon meilleur fauteuil a me regarder écrire.

Nous ne savons comment Vous exprimer toute notre reconnaissance pour les bontés que Vous avez eu pour ce garçon. Mon cher monsieur j'aurais dû Vous écrire il y a longtemps pour Vous remercier de la lettre qu'il m'a remis. Pardonnez moi. Cette maudite goutte m'exténue et me rend incapable du moindre effort mental.

Votre Jean a passé la Noël ici. Il n'a pas du trouver ça très gai. Ma pauvre femme n'était pas bien et moi je ne faisais que geindre. Mais pour nous c'était un grand réconfort de l'avoir là. Quand il nous quitta il avait bonne mine, mais en arrivant (le 22) il avait l'air d'un homme qui ne s'est pas ménagé. Et c'est vrai qu'il a dit et fait un tas des choses pendant sa tournée.

Je vais confier a John un exemplaire de mon roman qui vient de paraître pour qu'il Vous le remette. Vous voudrez bien lui trouver un petit coin sur un rayon de Votre bibliot[h]èque. C'est la chose la plus "francaise" que j'ai jamais écrit et c'est dédié a Votre fils.

Veuillez croire cher Monsieur et Madame a nos sentiments d'amitié et de reconnaissance les plus sincères.

Joseph Conrad.

PS Vous me permettrez chère Madame de Vous baiser la main en remerciment pour le super-excellent pain d'épices que Vous avez eu la bonté de nous envoyer. J'en ai eu la plus grosse part. Je suis assez petit garçon encore pour m'être chamaillé avec John au sujet du dernier morceau.

---

[1] Date from postmark.
[2] Frédéric-Ferdinand Aubry, Jean-Aubry's father, was born in 1860; for Mme Aubry, see the letter of 19 September.

Dear Sir and Madam,

We send you our best wishes for the New Year. When I say 'we', that means our John is included. He is here in my best armchair watching me write.

We don't know how to express all our gratitude for the kindnesses you have shown this boy. My dear Sir, I should have written to you long ago to thank you for the letter he has given me. Pray forgive me. This cursed gout makes me weak and leaves me incapable of the least mental effort.

Your Jean spent Christmas here. He can't have found it very merry. My poor wife was unwell and I did nothing but groan. But for us it was a great comfort to have him here. He looked well when he left us, but upon arriving (on the 22nd) he seemed like a man who had not been taking good care of himself. And it's true that he said and did so many things during his tour.

I shall entrust John with a copy of my novel which has just been published, to give you. Please try to find a little corner for it on one of your library shelves. It's the most 'French' thing I have ever written, and it is dedicated to your son.

Pray believe, dear Sir and Madam, in our most sincere friendship and gratitude.

Joseph Conrad.

PS Allow me, dear Madam, to kiss your hand in thanks for the super-excellent gingerbread that you so kindly sent us. I had the largest portion. I am still enough of a little boy to have squabbled with John over the last bite.

To Townley Searle
Text MS Yale;[1] Keating 380

[Oswalds]
[late December 1923][2]

Dear Sir.[3]

Pray note that the copyright on the article is vested in Dly Mail and I *cannot* give you the authorisation to reprint.

J. Conrad

---

[1] Written on Searle's letter to Conrad of 24 December 1924 requesting permission to reprint 'Christmas Day at Sea', which had appeared in the *Daily Mail* on Christmas Eve.

[2] Dated by Searle's letter.

[3] (R.) Townley Searle owned the First Edition Bookshop at 99 Wardour Street, London. In 1923 Searle published *The Flying Horse* as a literary and book-collector's magazine edited (and largely written) by T. W. H. Crosland, who died the following year. Later, Searle wrote a book on Chinese cookery (1932), compiled a bibliography of Gilbert and Sullivan (1931), and edited and illustrated a selection of Gilbert's ballads and his farce *A Colossal Idea*.

To B. A. Levinson

Text TLS, 25 July 1958, p. 423

[Oswalds]

[1923]¹

I never supposed I would come upon the name of the old ship again. My contact with her was, as it were, only with my fingertips, but I have preserved a strong visual memory of her appearance. The vessel of that name however, which was sunk in 1911, could not have been the same. She must have been the other's successor, very likely the third of the name. The incident dated back to, I think, November, 1874, and that "James Westoll"² with her heavy rig and her engines probably of under a hundred horse-power would not have been afloat in 1911, unless as a haunting shadow of the sea. The advantage of the sailing ships was that, as long as they remained sound in body, they could earn their living at an advanced age. I myself have seen in our coasting trade a brig the age of which was something between ninety and a hundred years . . . but a steamship gets out of date quickly. . . . Probably the end of my "James Westoll" was the breaking-up yard some time in the eighties, though indubitably she was a very fine cargo boat of her time. [. . .] I hope that there is another James Westoll on the seas.

¹ Dated by the letter's owner, Bertram Arthur Levinson (*c.* 1877–1961), a lawyer who recalled that, while reading *A Personal Record* in 1923, he came upon a report of a current case involving the collision of the *James Westoll* with another ship in the Channel, and wrote to tell Conrad of this news.

² In fact, the relevant passage in Part 7 of *A Personal Record* (p. 135) misidentifies the ship Conrad touched in Marseilles in December 1874, which was not the *James Westoll* but the *James Mason*, an English steamer that entered the harbour on 10 December 1874; see Hans van Marle, 'An Ambassador of Conrad's Future: The *James Mason* in Marseilles, 1874', *L'Époque Conradienne*, 14 (1988), 63–7.

1924

To Arnold Bennett

Text MS UCL; J-A, 2, 330

[letterhead: Oswalds]
2 Jany 24

My dear Bennett

I am wholly delighted with your R. S.[1] Wholly. You will give me credit for not having missed any special gems but it is the whole achiev[e]ment as I went from page to page that secured my admiration.

As I closed the book at 7 in the morning after the shortest sleepless night of my experience a thought passed through my head that I knew pretty well my "Bennett militant" and that, not to be too complimentary, he was a pretty good hand at it; but that there I had "Bennett triumphant" without any doubt whatever.[2] A memorable night.

Don't imagine that this is the morbid receptivity of an invalid. In fact I have been captious and "grincheux" for days as is always the case when I am not well. *Entre-nous* I feel as if I were fighting my Verdun battle with my old enemy.[3] It isn't that the symptoms are unusually severe but it goes on and on . . . I begin to wonder whether I have sufficient reserves. But I am not hopeless. Only I feel unfit to talk to you about the book as it deserves and as I would like to talk of it. There is no doubt that there is something quintessential about it. They of that created group don't want any official papers pour se légitimer. Each and all are unquestionable and unanswerable.

Always with my real affection,

Yours

J. Conrad.

PS Did I thank you for your letter about the Rover? I[t] was the greatest comfort.[4]

[1] *Riceyman Steps* (1923), sent to Conrad on or before 20 December. Conrad lent this copy to Jean-Aubry; in a letter written on Conrad's behalf on 5 January (Yale), Miss Hallowes asked to have it back, 'as he has promised to lend it to someone else'.
[2] Echoing its antecedents in Roman Catholic liturgy, the Anglican *Book of Common Prayer* speaks of 'the whole state of Christ's church militant here in earth', battling the flesh and the devil in a 'spirit of truth, unity, and concord'; the Church triumphant is the muster of those promoted to glory in the next. Conrad neatly turns a metaphor of spiritual into a metaphor of artistic struggle – and achievement.
[3] Conrad's handwriting shows the effects of the chronic gout that was making him 'grincheux' ('grumpy'). The German offensive against Verdun in February 1916 was supposed to be the masterstroke in a war of attrition that would render the French army useless; although capturing all but one of the surrounding forts, the attackers failed to take the town itself. The fighting lasted eleven months and cost half a million French and German lives.
[4] Bennett's letter about *The Rover* of 17 December takes up Conrad's remark of the 5th that 'twilight lies already on these pages': 'There is no twilight in the beginning, nor in the end.'

To Borys Conrad

Text MS Boston; Unpublished

[letterhead: Oswalds]
2 Jan '24

Dearest Boy.

I surmise you sent the papers on to M[aid]stone – and that the engine was made before 1913.[1]

Herewith your copy of R[over].

We had no card from John this morning – as promised. Horrid kid.

Here everything much the same am sorry to say.

I understand you were flying about with Eric on N. Years eve and incidentally impressed Evans[2] immensely with your driving.

Our love to You both

Ever Your Father

JC

To Florence and F. N. Doubleday

Text J-A, 2, 331

Oswalds.
Jan. 7th, 1924.

Dear Florence and Effendi,

One is not naturally very eager to send cheerless accounts, but I suppose the truth must be told some time or other. After all it isn't so very bad; yet it's a fact that I have been more or less confined to my room for the last fortnight. Aubry arrived on the 22nd, to spend Christmas with us, and found me in bed; but on Xmas Day I came down to share in the Xmas middle-day dinner, the company being eight, including those two crocks the host and hostess, Aubry and our John, and the four Muirhead Bones,[3] who came over

---

There may be tinges of it in the middle, but twilight, whatever any of us may think concerning ourselves, is a natural and very beautiful thing, & personally I am quite reconciled to its reflections on my pages.' Because Bennett had been ill, he kept his praises short: 'I will say only that it perfectly held me, & that the hand of the master is everywhere in it' (Stape and Knowles, pp. 231–2).

[1] The Conrads' new purchase, a pre-war Daimler, had to be registered at the offices of the Kent County Council.

[2] Charlie Evans of Heinemann's?

[3] Muirhead's wife was Gertrude Helena (née Dodd, 1876–1962). Among other works, she had written *Women of the Country* (1913), *Furrowed Earth* (1921), and *Children's Children* (1909), one of several collaborations with her husband. Later, she also collaborated with her son, the artist,

from Canterbury, where they were staying in rooms over the Xmas week. It wasn't a rowdy revel, the major part of the company drinking water steadily, but there were mince pies and a certain affectation of cheerfulness. Your munificent presents were displayed, and John was playing tunes (whether sacred or profane, I am not sure) on the heavenly gong. Much talk about the Doubledays, with references to other inhabitants of the New World.

But next day Jessie had to remain upstairs with new and startling symptoms in the state of her limb. A distinct set-back. She has been able to come down for New Year's Day, when the whole tribe of M. Bones lunched with us and some other visitors called in the afternoon. As to myself, without entering into details, I will just tell you that I am now downstairs after another relapse which got hold of me on the 2nd of January and, judging by my feelings, I think will be definitely the last.

At any rate, I have been out to-day for a drive in the new car, a roomy, old-fashioned affair which I acquired from H. R. H. the Duke of Connaught through the Daimler Company (who were the makers). A great stroke of business, engineered by Borys.[1]

Dr. Fox, who has the most friendly remembrance of you both, has been looking after me with great devotion. You will be pleased to hear that all this long time of trouble doesn't mean anything in the way of a break-up. It is just a period of bad time to get over. As a matter of fact, my blood pressure has hardly altered for the last eight years, and as far as my arteries go I am much younger than my age. The worst, or at any rate the most worrying, feature is a spasmodic affection* of the small bronchial tubes, which, of course, causes a bad cough and a sort of semi-asthmatic condition. But even that will be alleviated in time. I confess that the periods of pain have been extremely severe, and only to be compared with a bad illness I had after finishing

writer, and broadcaster Stephen Bone (1904–58); in 1923–24, he was a student at the Slade. Gertrude Bone's reminiscences of the Christmas visit with her husband and their two sons can be found in the *Century Magazine*, 115 (1928), pp. 385–92.

[1] The Daimler Co. held the royal warrant as suppliers of motor-cars to the King and his family. Replaced by newer models, the old fleet, dating back to 1910, was brought in to Daimler's for resale; the royal insignia had to be removed from each vehicle, and any would-be buyer was vetted by the Lord Chamberlain. Because its body-work was designed for 'passengers . . . wearing ceremonial robes and head-dress', Borys realised that his mother would find such a car relatively comfortable. It would also be the first time the Conrads had owned a vehicle that gave them protection from the weather (*My Father: Joseph Conrad*, p. 159). The King's brother and Queen Victoria's third son, Prince Arthur William Patrick Albert (1850–1942) was named 1st Duke of Connaught and Strathearn in 1874. A graduate of the Royal Military College, Sandhurst, he was promoted to Field Marshal in 1902 after service in South Africa, Egypt, India, and Ireland. From 1911–16, he was Governor General of Canada.

Western Eyes and before I wrote *Chance*.[1] But at that time I was really in danger on account of high temperatures lasting for days. This time there was practically no temperature, and the whole thing has left after it a sense not of bodily exhaustion but of a certain mental languidness, which is passing away.

I have (under Fox's advice) resolved not to hurry and to give myself plenty of time for a thorough recuperation. Ideas and notions stir in my mind, as if that physical shaking had broken down some barrier which had been keeping them back for the last two or three years; but I have made up my mind not to give them their head till I feel confident of making good use of them.

The good news from America has been a great help all through, and I have to thank you all for it. The undoubted success of The Rover will I believe be the record for my work on this side.

Everybody who has seen the sample of the Concord Edition you sent me is very fascinated by it. M. Bone, who would not look twice at Dent's ed., has resolved to order one from you. Dick C, who, as a collector, has of course the Dent edition, would like very much to have this one too. Could we manage, dear Effendi, to present him with one jointly? You sign the first volume of the set and let me pay half the price and I will join my signature to yours. He has been most devoted all this time, even to the point of offering to resign his position in order to take me south. Of course one wouldn't dream of accepting such a suggestion. Going south is not necessary, though it might do good upon the whole. But taking Jessie away from the surgeons who know all about her is not to be thought of; and going away without her would do no good either to her or to me.

She has been as usual equably cheerful in regard to both my and her own troubles. She was immensely delighted with your munificent present. While confined upstairs she played various tunes on the musical instrument to let her orders be known in the kitchen. As to myself, I was moved profoundly by the sight of the thermos water-jug. It is exactly like the one I had by my bedside in your house, and brought the old days visibly home to my memory. I didn't actually kiss it (not being sure it was actually the same) but I did stroke it.

The conviction is growing very firm in my mind that those dear Doubledays are good friends to have; on which I end this, sending you our joint love; and shall now try to dictate a few lines before post time to two or three other kind Americans to whom they are due.

Love to dear Patty and no less dear Nelson.

---

[1] 'My last relapse had taken the form of gout in the abdominal muscle – an experience which I shall not forget if I live to a hundred' (*Letters*, 4, p. 322).

To Margaret Hughes

Text MS Morgan; Unpublished

[letterhead: Oswalds]
[7 January 1924][1]

Dear Mrs Hughes.[2]

To my great consternation the week end cable-letter send* to you at the end of the year has been returned to me as insufficiently addressed. As I was in bed with temperature when I dispatched I fear I omitted to wire the number.

My dear and charming friend (I call you that because you have done that for me which only a very sympathetic and understanding friend would have thought of doing) I am so sorry for this delay in thanking you for your charming present and still more for the friendly thought which prom[p]ted you. I call upon all the blessings to descend upon both your heads, with utmost sincerity and earnestness of which I am capable. Pray think of me ever as your most grateful friend and servant.

Joseph Conrad.

My admiring love to Miss Porter who is referred to here as "the wonder-child".[3]

To George T. Keating

Text TS Yale; Unpublished

[letterhead: Oswalds]
Jan. 7th. 1924.

My dear Keating[4]

Don't be shocked at my delay in thanking you for your weighty and ornate gift. Your kindness goes far beyond my deserts. Everybody pronounced the things beautiful. I was immensely interested to learn what particular MSS you bought, especially as to *The Shadow Line* which is dedicated to my boy,

---

[1] Date from postmark.
[2] For a letter written to her as the widow of Lt James Porter, see '1st May' [really 1 June] 1923.
[3] Jamie Porter, Mrs Hughes's daughter by her first husband. Conrad used the same phrase for Louise Harding's children.
[4] New York-born George Thomas Keating (1892–1976) amassed a rich collection of Conradiana from various sales as well as from Thomas J. Wise. He donated his collection, catalogued in *A Conrad Memorial Library: The Collection of George T. Keating* (1929), to Yale University in 1938. Keating worked his way up from errand-boy to the head of Moore and Munger, a New York firm dealing in paper and clay products, eventually retiring to California. He also collected operatic recordings and musical MSS, the American author James Branch Cabell, and materials about war, diplomacy, and the Spanish conquest of the New World.

who himself is very pleased to know that it found a home with such a good friend.[1]

I won't now you* give the history of the bad time I have had. But it was bad, and it accounts for my delay in thanking you for all the friendly thoughts you give to me.

I will say no more now (for the post time approaches) except to repeat my heartfelt good wishes to you both and to the children.[2]

Affectly Yours

J. Conrad.

To Richard Curle
Text Curle 138

[Oswalds.]
8. Jan. 24.

Dear Dick,

You shall have your Concord Set from me. The first 2 vols. (*Jim – Vic.*) have arrived this morning and I'll initial them for you. (thus R.C./J.C.)[3]

Ever yrs,

J. Conrad

To Eric S. Pinker
Text TS Berg; Unpublished

Oswalds.
Jan. 9th. 1924.

Dearest Eric.

Thank you for your letter. In regard to that rag-bag of a volume of short stories it seems to me to be purely a publisher's affair which can not be justified on any reasonable ground as far as the authors are concerned. Why do they come in? Unless it is as a kindness to Rhys I can not understand the object of such a publication, from their point of view.[4] As an advertisement it

---

[1] On Keating's behalf, the bookseller James F. Drake had paid $2,700 for the MS of *The Shadow-Line* at the Quinn collection sale. Conrad's dedication reads: 'To Borys and all others who like himself have crossed in early youth the Shadow-Line of their generation With Love.'

[2] The Keatings had two sons and a daughter.

[3] Curle notes that he and Conrad signed the first volume with their full names; the other volumes published before Conrad's death carried both sets of initials.

[4] Ernest Rhys (1859–1946), a Welsh poet, literary journalist, and publisher, had founded Dent's Everyman Library in 1906. With Catherine Dawson Scott, he was now assembling *Twenty and Three Stories by Twenty and Three Authors* (Thornton Butterworth, 1924). His memoir *Everyman Remembers* (1931) recalls his attempt to coax a story for this volume out of Conrad by bribing him with a Hogarth print (Ray, p. 134).

is worthless, I imagine. The financial side has nothing very fascinating about it. From a literary point of view I confess that I am not very much in love with "The Inn of the Two Witches" (which was written to order and is not a "representative" story) while on the other hand I confess that I would not like any of my other stories to go into the rag-bag. I seem to remember that last year I declined a similar proposal.[1] Any collection of that sort is apt to convey a false impression because the great public will attach to it the idea of "the best". Altogether a mere piece of book-making, mainly for the benefit of Dent because I have a notion that poor Rhys will get very few pence out of it.

Perhaps you would know how to gracefully decline in my name, if it can be done without giving offence.

John will be leaving for Havre on the 15th. Arrangements are being made for him to attend some lectures and to have also lessons in mathematics.

Out of his term allowance in the budget of £60 (£180 p.y.) will you please let me have £40 now to settle clothes bills etc. and I will take up the balance of £20 at Easter. What will happen afterwards I am not at all certain. If he derives any benefit in the next three months I should be inclined to let him go on for another term. If not then perhaps we will put him to Daimlers or other apprenticeship after Easter. You may be sure that that trouble will come before you in due time, like all the others with which I am apt to worry your head.

Yes, my dear Eric, I think I may say I am on the mend. But on that a lot could be said. I am pursuing Fox's treatment. I can assure you that Fox, for all his provincial jocosity,[2] is by no means a fool at his trade. He examined me last Sunday. Apart from the general improvement in the symptoms there is only the cough. This proceeds from a spasmodic contraction of the small air-vessels, a well-known (though not invariable) concomitant of the gout. This is being specially attended to. It looks at times like bronchitis and at times like asthma but it is neither. For instance for the last thirty hours or more I haven't coughed at all, and feel as if any suggestion as to me being afflicted with a cough would be the most absurd thing in the world. And yet a fit may come on before I have finished dictating this letter and almost reduce me to a rag. But even as to that the severity is distinctly diminishing. Of course I am not normal yet, but I don't feel hopeless by any means.

---

[1] In 1923, Conrad had consented to the Dent 'school-book' edition of 'Youth' and 'Gaspar Ruiz' and the Doubleday collection of shorter tales (which did not include 'The Inn of the Two Witches'). Both volumes appeared under Conrad's name.

[2] Since he grew up in Hendon, Middlesex, 'suburban' would be closer.

It is Jessie's state that really worries me, for the inflam[m]atory symptoms in the upper part of the leg are not gone yet, and there is a mystery about them which I don't like. I could not think of taking her away from her surgeons just now, and, as Fox remarked, it would do me no good whatever to go south by myself, because I would worry. It would certainly worry me enough to prevent me working and it is just that, in particular, that I can not afford. We had a vague idea of writing to Candler to ask whether one could get a modest little villa near Hendaye where we could really live cheaper than here, even including the rent.[1] Candler and his wife[2] know all about the place by now and would put us in the way of getting supplies and so on. If it ever comes to that this would be the best and cheapest way of getting a change of air. And perhaps it may come to pass. Anyhow Jessie will have to go up to London next week to be seen by Sir Robert Jones, and I begin to believe I will be able to come with her in the car.

I have got the Duke's machine, for which I have paid half the price so far. The proceeds of the old car nearly covered it and, really, the Cadillac was getting impossible, and I could not face the idea of being shut up here without any means of getting more than a few yards outside the gate.

With all affectionate sympathy for you both[3]

Ever Yours

J. Conrad

To Edmund Candler

Text TS Morgan; Unpublished

[letterhead: Oswalds]
Jan. 9th. 1924.

My dear Candler,

I beg and entreat you not to let this letter be a nuisance to you. Your presence down there seems to make Hendaye (or the immediate neighbourhood) the only possible place where one could seek refuge from the usual winter and spring horrors. The trouble is that I don't know whether I can take Jessie away from her surgeons. I myself have had a very horrid time for nearly two months, but I am on the mend.

---

[1] When the Candlers moved to the Basque country, settling just north of the frontier between France and Spain, Conrad told Edmund Candler that he had not been there since 1876 (*Letters*, 7, pp. 443–4).

[2] Olive Mary Candler (née Tooth, 1877–1950) was the fourth of eight children born to a sugar refiner and brewer in Brighton. She married Candler in 1902, and they had two children.

[3] Joan, their daughter, was born on 25 December and died on 5 January.

In case Jessie is mended sufficiently too, we would be infinitely grateful to you, and of course to Mrs Candler, if you would express your opinion as to the practicality of some such arrangement as a modest small villa in or within easy distance of Hendaye, with a native girl attached. You see, we two disgusting crocks would have to drive down in our old machine, with the faithful Charles to drive, and his wife who could attend on Jessie, and also watch the symptoms, as she is a qualified nurse and has a three years' knowledge of the case.

That is the idea. Is it too romantic to entertain? The only thing demanded from the villa would be to have a water-tight roof and some means of warming oneself indoors. Years ago, in Capri, we hired one from some peasants and it was delightful, but we nearly died of cold.[1]

The alternative would be some modest but clean hotel which could house us for, say, two or three months, with a possible sitting-room to work and live in. Would £60 a month about cover it.

Pray, my dear Candler, don't let this disturb you if you are not in the mood for domestic economy. Things are looking rather hopeless here just now.

Our warmest regards to you all

Affectly yours

J. Conrad.

To F. N. Doubleday

Text TS/MS Indiana; Unpublished

[letterhead: Oswalds]
Jan. 10th. 1924.

Dearest Effendi

I have received from Fisher Unwin a set of notices of the "Rover" which, after sifting, I am sending on to you to give you an idea of the sort of reception the book had. Of course this is only a selection. Hundredweights of those paper snips have come into the house (and in great part gone out of it up the chimney). Several virulent attacks have been made, and I was very pleased with some of them. One or two were merely stupid, but others were intelligent. They gave substance and reality, by contrast, to the avalanche of appreciations, while at the same time they could not affect the sales.[2] The

---

[1] They were there from January to May 1905.

[2] For an example of hostile judgment, see Raymond Mortimer's review for the *New Statesman*, 15 December, p. 306, reprinted in Sherry, pp. 358–60. Mortimer found the novel 'downright bad', sketchy yet overvarnished, the work of a novelist past his peak.

provincial press, with the exception of Glasgow,[1] spoke like one man in praise of the book; and that from the commercial point of view is a most important fact.

I have received the full three sets of Frontispieces for which I asked. They look extremely well. I feel like a horrid, spoilt, little boy, always asking for things and always getting them from inexcusably weak friends. I know it is very bad for me, but then it is very nice. You people are spoiling me. I am so demoralised that I have been actually thinking what more I could ask you for, and am unblushingly sorry to say that I can't think of anything, just now.

I have received parcels of books making up the copies of "Lord Jim" and "Victory" to five each – whence I conclude that I am going to have five sets of the Concord for myself. It is very good of Doubleday, Page & Co. to give them to me. It is very obvious that I am the spoilt child of the house. Please note that in consequence of that munificence I will be able to find a set for Dick Curle; so my suggestion regarding him in my last letter is cancelled. I intend one set for Muirhead Bone and his wife who have been fascinated by it and one will go to Miss Hallowes who, since she has seen the Concord, will have nothing to do with Dents' production which I intended to give her. That will leave me two, eventually for the boys, though Borys will probably get his at once to help furnish the new bookcase which he bought to furnish (with some other things) his first married home.

In this connection, he is certainly a success from a business point of view. Stratton and Instone, the great Daimler dealers in London (and indeed connected with the Daimler Co. in all sorts of ways)[2] have asked the Company to let them take over Borys for a year, mainly with a view to organise their wholesale trading department, which they are just opening. B. was very unwilling to leave Chapter St. House, which he had managed to pull in five months out of a slough of despond[3] into a very satisfactory position. However they bribed him by £250 down as a sort of premium, and the offer of a considerable commission, in addition, of course, to the salary which would be the same he had for managing the Chapter St. House. He came down here to talk it over with me, straight from Coventry (the Daimler headquarters) where he had been called to have this offer communicated to him. I advised him to accept, the more confidently because he has obtained a letter from the General Manager

[1] The anonymous reviewer for the *Glasgow Evening News* also praised the novel, but noted that for once Conrad 'appears to have been without a burning intensity of vision and conviction' (6 December 1923, p. 2; also available in Sherry, p. 357).

[2] Of 27 Pall Mall; they held the royal warrant as suppliers of luxury motors to the King's household.

[3] In John Bunyan's allegory *The Pilgrim's Progress* (1678), a bog where all but the most resolute give up hope: 'This miry slough . . . was-called the Slough of Despond'.

to the effect that his connection with the Daimlers will not be broken by his temporary acceptance of the new post. So upon the whole this new year opens for him with improved prospects, or at least with considerably more money than he expected. Anyway it is a testimony to his business abilities which coming to him, just eighteen months after he joined the company, is more than *I* expected. He will take over his new duties next Monday.

Next week Jessie will go up to see Sir Robert. There is a new reason for anxiety about that limb. I am recovering steadily. The weather is horrid, and I haven't been out for 2 months.

My best love to Florence. In haste to catch the village post.

Ever Yours

J. Conrad

To Ferdinand Aubry
Text MS Yale; *L. fr.* 194

[letterhead: Oswalds]
12 [13]. 1. 24.[1]

Cher Monsieur

Par le même courrier je vous envoie le vol du Rover. John n'arrivera au Havre que le 19, et je veux que le livre vous parvienne sans plus tarder. Je me permets de mettre dans l'enveloppe une lettre de M. Neel que j'ai reçue après le départ de Jean. Vous voudrez bien avoir la bonté de la lui remettre quand vous le verrez, le 18 de ce mois, je pense.[2]

Nous serons à Londres Mercredi prochain. Ma femme a un rendez-vous ce jour là avec so[n] chirurgien. Ma femme souffre beaucoup de sa malheureuse jambe. Je vous avoue que je commence à m'inquiéter sérieusement. Quand et comment ça finira – je me demande.

Nous voilà devenus grand[s]-parents depuis deux jours.[3] C'est un solide garçon. Mon fils et sa femme sont dans la joie! Tout ça c'est dans l'ordre.

Mes hommages à madame Aubry. *Jessie sends her love.*

Votre dévoué

J. Conrad.

---

[1] If Conrad had indeed been a grandfather for two days, this letter should be dated [13] January.
[2] In his letter of 7 January (MS Yale) Neel had offered to translate *The Rover* into French; Conrad's marginal note to Jean-Aubry reads: 'Cher J. J'ai répondu que je croyais que Vs aviez l'intention de traduire The R. Vous même, mais pas tout-de-suite, mais que Vs alliez lui écrire. Decidez. Votre JC'. Jean-Aubry's translation of *Le Frère-de-la-côte* was serialised in the *Revue de Paris* in the spring of 1927 and published as a book by Gallimard the following year.
[3] Borys's only child, Philip James Conrad (d. 2004), had been born on 11 January.

Dear Sir

By the same post I am sending you a copy of *The Rover*. John will not arrive in Le Havre until the 19th, and I want you to have the book without further delay. I have taken the liberty of enclosing a letter from Monsieur Neel which I received after Jean had left. Would you please be so kind as to give it to him when you see him, on the 18th of this month, I believe?

We will be in London this Wednesday. My wife has an appointment with her surgeon that day. My wife suffers greatly from her ill-fated leg. I admit that I am becoming seriously worried. When and how will it all end, I wonder?

As of two days ago, we are grandparents. It's a sturdy boy. My son and his wife are overjoyed! That is all as it should be.

My greetings to Madame Aubry. *Jessie sends her love.*

Your devoted

J. Conrad.

To Edith F. Crane

Text TS copy Virginia; Gullason 105

Oswalds,
Bishopsbourne,
Kent.
12. Jan. 24

Dear Miss Crane.[1]

A thousand thanks for your kind letter and the photographs. We are delighted with them. We had only one fairly good [one] taken in his study at Oxted, and one in a group taken on the occasion of our first visit to his house there.[2]

I am happy to know that Mrs. Crane approves of my preface.[3] Pray give her my respectful acknowledgments of her good opinion. We here had the greatest affection for Stephen and understood his fine character. For he was fine! A straight-thinking straight-acting man without guile. I will say nothing here of his great gifts.

---

[1] Edith F(leming) Crane (1886–1962) was Stephen Crane's niece, the daughter of his older brother Edmund Brian Crane (1857–1922) and Mary L. Fleming. She lived in Port Jervis, New York, where her grandfather had been a Methodist minister.

[2] In 1897–8, between stints of war-reporting in Greece and Cuba, Stephen and Cora Crane lived at Ravensbrook Cottage, near Oxted, Surrey. The Conrads stayed with them in February 1898.

[3] The Preface was either to Thomas Beer's biography of Crane or to a Heinemann edition of Crane's *The Red Badge of Courage*, both written in 1923 and included in *Last Essays*.

It was very kind of you to write me such a charming letter. My wife joins me in the expression of profound regard for Mrs. Crane and yourself.
Believe me always very faithfully yours

Joseph Conrad.

To Captain Arthur W. Phillips

Text TS Private collection; J-A, 2, 333

[letterhead: Oswalds]
Jan. 12th. 1924.

Dear Mr Phillips.[1]

I regret to have to dictate this letter to a fellow seaman, and an old "Torrens" boy at that, but my wrist just now cannot stand any prolonged pen-work.

It was very kind of you to write to me about your old days – even older than mine – in that ship.[2] I never served with Capt. Angell*, though I saw him two or three times on board while the ship was lying in London Dock. Captain Cope, an old friend of mine, commanded her then. It was the voyage after the famous dismasting, just to the N. of the Line.[3] The most absurd thing in the world by all accounts. I[t] was only a slight squall. The officer of the watch had just given the order "Stand by the royal halyards" when the outer jib-stay parted and, apparently with the jar of it others went and the foremast broke 8 feet above the deck going clean overboard without even touching the cow-stall, which, probably in your time too, was lashed close to it on the port side. With that everything went on the Main above the top, carrying with it the mizzen-topgallantmast. The puff of wind was gone as soon as the masts, and the water was perfectly smooth both before and after the accident.

Therefore I had the advantage on joining to find everything practically new – spars and rigging. All that was sent out to her to Pernambuco where she

---

[1] Captain Arthur Waller Phillips (1861 – *c.* 1932) was born in Kent and educated in Weimar (during the Franco-Prussian War) and at Tonbridge School. In 1877 he joined the training-ship HMS *Worcester* at Greenhithe, but was persuaded by his mother to enter a City office. He escaped after a couple of years and became apprenticed to Captain H. R. Angel, master and principal owner of the *Torrens*. Phillips later served as master of a steamer on the Great Salt Lake, Utah. He remained in America twenty-two years and was a pioneer in opening up Wyoming Territory.

[2] Conrad served as first mate in the *Torrens* under Captain Walter Henry Cope for two voyages to Australia in 1891–3.

[3] During her first voyage under Captain Cope, in November 1890, the *Torrens* lost her fore and main topmasts. Thanks to this misfortune and a fire in Pernambuco while refitting, the passage to Adelaide took 179 days, though the ship's average was 74. Captain Angel had remained the owner but no longer sailed with her: Basil Lubbock, *The Colonial Clippers* (3rd edition, Glasgow: James Brown, 1924), pp. 159–60.

was towed by a tramp steamer. I don't know for what reason they rove manila rope for fore and main rigging lanyards. I could never see the advantage of that. It gave me some trouble, especially my first voyage, after lying in Adelaide for a couple of months in perfectly dry, hot weather. The lower rigging hung in bights and I had to set up everything fore and aft before bending the sails for the homeward passage.[1]

Both voyages were uneventful and the passages not very good. From that point of view Capt. Cope was not a lucky man. I share to the full your sentiments about all kinds of mechanical propulsion. It changed the life entirely, and changed also the character of the men. There is not much difference now between a deck and a factory hand.

In the early part of last year I crossed to New York with my old friend Capt. David Bone commanding the "Tuscania". Of course I was made free of the bridge and the navigation room. I won't say I was not interested. I was, in a way, for about 30 hours till I went twice over all the switches working various gadgets. But I remained cold, completely cold before all those things which make the position of a ship's officer almost an indoor occupation. It is a fact that one can take a ship along now in white gloves and without, so to speak, opening one's mouth once. There were seven officers there and they were very charming to the old veteran; it was rather a special crowd since only two of them, juniors, had never set foot on the deck of a sailing vessel.

Capt. Bone, who had some ten years of sail, told me that they had wholly lost the "weather sense", that touch with the natural phenomena of wind and sea which was the very breath of our professional life. I was generally in his room when he was interviewing the heads of "departments", and I went also with him on his rounds. Once he made the remark to me that being a ship-master now was not like being in command of a ship but at the head of an administration. However, he told me also that in certain circumstances those big ferry boats required careful handling and that no two of them were alike.

I returned in the "Majestic". As to that all I can tell you is that on the $6\frac{1}{2}$ days' passage I hardly put my nose once on deck. It was really too dreary. I met the captain at a tea-party given by a fashionable lady passenger, but only exchanged a few words with him. He was in a hurry to get away, and what I

---

[1] Made from plantain skins, manila is stronger than hempen rope, and, thanks to its natural oils, does not need tarring. They 'rove manila rope for fore and main rigging lanyards': they used manila for the ropes that should hold fore and main riggings tightly to their blocks; 'hung in bights': drooped; 'set up ... fore and aft': set the spars along rather than across the length of the ship; 'before bending the sails': before attaching the sails.

remember best is him telling me that in one way or another "the command of a big ship like that was a pretty heavy load on a man's shoulders".[1]

Pardon this long screed. I hope you will have much success and pleasure in the coming yachting season.

Believe me very faithfully yours
Joseph Conrad.

To Eric S. Pinker

Text TS Berg; Unpublished

[letterhead: Oswalds]
Jan. 13th. 1924.

Dearest Eric.

Thank you very much for the letter and the £60 which you advised me had been paid to my account.[2]

I don't mean exactly to leave John to his own devices. I intend him to follow a Berlitz course of French three days a week and do mechanical drawing with a teacher on the other three.

I confess that Rhys has not secured my liking, either, on the few occasions I have seen him.[3] I am very glad to know that you share my views on those absurd anthologies thrown out on the market. A school-book of that kind is a different thing somewhat.

I will confess to you that I am quite anxious about Jessie. That deep-seated trouble somewhere among the muscles where there should be no trouble, points out to some undesirable complication. One doesn't see how and where it is going to end. And the pain is increasing.

The plan is for all of us to come up on Wednesday. In this connection it strikes me that I haven't communicated to you Borys's news. But I daresay he has done so himself. Mrs C. of course will be delighted to make the acquaintance of her grandson, but the trip to London is primarily to see Sir Robert. We expect a letter from him on Tuesday.

I don't look forward much to all this, but for the pleasure of seeing you and having a talk over many things. Last night I had by post inside a printed

---

[1] The RMS *Majestic* was then the largest ship in the world; see the letter to Curle of 18 May 1923. Her captain was Commodore Sir Bertram Fox Hayes (1864–1941), whose memoirs, *Hull Down*, were published in 1925.

[2] For John's expenses in France.

[3] Conrad first met Ernest Rhys during the war. For his visit to Oswalds in 1920, see *Letters*, 7, pp. 202–6. His account of this visit appeared in the New York *Bookman*, 56 (December 1922), pp. 402–8, as 'An Interview with Joseph Conrad'.

circular from Garden City a scrap of paper signed by Effendi stating "'Rover' sales up to Jan. 4th, 48,000 and going strong".

Nothing more, but that is satisfactory enough I think.

I will 'phone you on our arrival at the Curzon.[1] No use making arrangements beforehand. Our intercourse must be regulated by your convenience.

Give my love at home.

Ever affecly Yours

J. Conrad

To Richard Curle
Text TS Indiana; Curle 139

Oswalds.

Jan. 14th. 1924.

Dearest Dick.

I hasten to tell you I am very grateful for every tactful step you have taken in this matter.[2] I must confess I had some slight qualms about Wise. Your action has done away with them, and of course you can not doubt I am animated by the most friendly sentiments towards T. J. W. Of course I will sign and annotate his copy with pleasure.[3]

I can now tell you definitely that we are coming up on Wednesday, hour uncertain. But even if we were to arrive before lunch I would hesitate to ask you, as Jessie says the food is simply beastly. I could certainly take you out to the R. A. C., but then my dear I am not quite right yet, and I don't know whether I will be fit at the end of the journey. This is the hard truth. Naturally we expect you to drop in at any time and on any occasion when you feel like it; and we won't even object to your getting poisoned in our company.

Thanks once more

Love from us both.

Yrs

J. C.

PS Sir R. J. visit fixed for 11 o'clock Thursday.

---

[1] On Curzon Street, Mayfair, it was now the Conrads' hotel of choice – in spite of the 'beastly' cuisine deplored in the following letter.

[2] A disingenuous footnote by Curle suggests that Conrad, who normally offered his MSS to T. J. Wise, was arranging for the sale of the MS of 'Geography and Some Explorers' via J. E. Hodgson, although the sale was actually being negotiated by Curle (Curle to Hodgson, 14 January, MS Bodley).

[3] His copy of *The Rover*, as Curle notes.

To Nora Tattersall

Text MS Yenter; Unpublished

[letterhead: Oswalds]
15. Jan. '24

Dear Mrs Tattersall[1]

There must be some misunderstanding. I never talked with the Ashton-Gwatkins about my car. My chauffeur Charles Vinten may have been talking to Mrs Ashton-Gwatkin[2] about his own car – but of course of that I know nothing. As I have arranged with Charles Vinten (more than a week ago) to have the whole day to himself on the 17th my car can not go out on that day.

Yours faithfully

J. Conrad

To Richard Curle

Text MS Indiana; Curle 140

[letterhead: Hotel Curzon]
Wed^y 10.30. [16 January 1924][3]

Dearest Dick

Sir Robert appointed tomorrow Thursday 10.30 for his visit to Jessie.

We have been to see B[orys]'s home and child. The baby is really quite nice. Everything looks quite satisfactory there. Saw B for a moment about one o'clock. He is happy no doubt and looks less strained than ever I've seen him look for the last 4 years.

I hope you'll 'phone me a message early in the morning. After Sir R. J. has been my time is yours. Will you lunch?

Ever yours

J. C.

---

[1] Nora Mary Dorothea Tattersall (née Beatson, 1867–1942) and her husband Major John Cecil de Veel Tattersall, whom she married in 1909, were acquaintances of the Conrads living at Charlton Place, Bishopsbourne.

[2] For Mrs Ashton-Gwatkin, see the letter to Curle of 1 February.

[3] Dated by the visit to London.

To Messrs Hodgson & Co.

Text MS Bodley; Unpublished

[letterhead: Hotel Curzon]

17. Jan. 24.

Dear Sirs[1]

This is to acknowledge receipt of the sum of £155 (One hundred and fifty five pounds) by your cheque received to-day.[2]

Yours faithfully

Joseph Conrad

Messrs. Hodgson & C[o].

To Messrs Hodgson & Co.

Text MS Bodley;[3] Unpublished

[letterhead: Hotel Curzon]

17. I. 24

Dear Sirs

Will you please correct the error in the wording of the cheque.[4]

Yours faithfully

J. Conrad

To Edmund Candler

Text TS Morgan; Candler xli (in part)[5]

[letterhead: Oswalds]

Jan. 20th. 1924.

My dear Candler,

I thought it best to send a wire to tell you that for this winter, at any rate, the idea of taking Jessie away from the doctors is not to be thought of. With

---

[1] This long-established London auction house in Chancery Lane offered literary MSS and fine books. Conrad sold copies of the privately printed limited-edition pamphlets through the firm, and after his death they sold his library and papers for Jessie Conrad. Its principal was John Edmund Hodgson (1875–1952), an authority on the history of British aviation.

[2] For the MS and corrected TS of 'Geography and Some Explorers'.

[3] Enclosed in an unstamped envelope marked '*Personal*', this note was apparently either delivered by hand or enclosed with the previous letter.

[4] Perhaps two 'errors': 'There is a slight misunderstanding. I have, as I explained to you, a firm offer already of £150 unless I can get £155 from you. This I provisionally accepted. If you can give me £155 then the deal is settled' (Curle to J. E. Hodgson, 14 January, MS Bodley). Hodgson had apparently also written the cheque to Curle, who noted: 'On a previous occasion some charming person hinted that I was making a good thing out of it &, while such innuendos don't worry me much, I have no desire to give the slightest apparent handle to such people.' The MS and 'first copy' TS of 'Geography and Some Explorers' were eventually acquired by George T. Keating and are now at Yale.

[5] Without the second and third paragraphs.

the encouragement of your wife's charming letter we seized eagerly on the idea of staying with you, and the disappointment is severe.

The last words of Sir Robert Jones were that he would give her leave to travel abroad probably in May next. It is too late to go south at that time of the year. Very likely we will not go anywhere; but we are going to leave this house for good in September, and that would be the time, before we get into another, to take some months off. It is a long time to make plans in advance, but certainly there is the possibility and the desire to come over and stay with you, that is if on trial you don't find us too much of a handful – not because of our wildness but because of our comparative helplessness. If it is only half as exasperating to others as it is to us at times, then you won't want us very long with you.

We got home late last night, a good run from London over rather muddy roads, and in a high westerly wind. Jessie's treatment will begin to-morrow – doctor's motor at the door every second day; but I will not enter into the ensuing details of the procedure. It will be generally horrid, of that there can be no doubt.

Thank you for your good letter about "The Rover". The book had a good reception from every point of view; so good as to make my heart heavy when I think that "The Rescue" (a big try, anyhow) did not get half the attention, (or perhaps only it is half the chatter) that "The Rover" provoked. Of course I have no reason to be ashamed of the thing, and I am not even sorry I wrote it; but I do think that both praise and blame have been disproportionate and this causes me to feel that I don't care a hang for either.

Jessie sends her most friendly regards to you and hopes, as indeed I do too, that you are making a successful fight of it with your own private fiend.[1] Hers is very hard to exorcise. But she is pretty hard too. Six years of disappointed hopes have not robbed her of her serenity, but I suspect that she is growing a little heart-weary of all this.[2] She will be writing in a few days to Mrs Candler, to whom please convey my thanks and give my duty (as they used to say in the 18th century).

Always affecty yours

J. Conrad.

---

[1] Candler had been seriously wounded in Tibet in 1904, and his health had suffered generally from his years of hardship as a war correspondent and travel writer in the East.

[2] The first of Sir Robert Jones's operations on her knee was in 1917.

To Eric S. Pinker

Text MS/TS Berg; Unpublished

Oswalds.

Jan. 21st. 1924.

My dear Eric

I have been going into figures by my own unaided light, though I know very well that the thing is to produce, not to calculate, but one must count one's money sometimes and the prospect of the deal in films brings me to terms with this necessity.[1]

We will first deal with that assuming that the transaction will be completed at the end of the month. I put here my point of view thus:

Deal,	22,500	$18,000 @ $4.25 = £4235 net, of which, for option,
Com. 20% =	4,500	paid $5000 – equal to £1176, which I propose to
	$18,000 net.	throw into the general account with you against which I draw. This will leave at my disposal eventually, on completion, £3059 which I am proposing to invest in its entirety if the state of my account allows.

That is of course the question. I have not seen yet the account for the last six months; but I know that on June 30th I owed you £1400, which is the important fact. I estimate that I called on you in the course of six months, what with doctors' bills and other charges, for £2000. On the credit side all I know is that there have been three payments of £1000 each: that is, on July 1st. £1000 from D[oubleday] on account of old book royalties; on Nov. 1st. £1000 on account of "The Rover"; and £1000 from T. F[isher] U[nwin] for "The Rover". There would also have been royalties for the first six months on my Eng. editions, the figure of which I will not attempt to estimate, and £30 per vol. in agreement with Dent on the Collected Ed., 16 vols up to Dec. incl. equal £480; and some small payments, as for instance £400 from Beer.[2] Anyway I hope that altogether there was enough to meet the half year's tax, and leave £1000 against your debt of £1400 and int[erest] – or, at any rate, enough to pay off half of the above; and that the rest will be paid off in the course of the next three months, or at most in the course of the next half year.

---

[1] The nature of this uncompleted deal is unknown, but the amount exactly matches the payment by the Alice Kauser Agency in 1919 for world rights to *Chance*, *Victory*, *Lord Jim*, and Conrad's half share in *Romance* (*Letters*, 7, pp. 422, 434, 436).

[2] For the Preface to his biography of Crane.

As to the future, what I see is this. First, £350 roy[alty] on de luxe "Rover" less 10% = *£315*. Then taking F. N. D.'s report of 48000 copies "Rover" up the* Jan. 4th. this year at 40 cents per $2 copy = $19,200 = (at $4.25 to £1) £4517, less 10% com. = £451. leaves me net £4000, of which £1000 advanced already, leaving a net balance of *£3000* already earned.

As to the Eng. sales we have nothing to go by so far, but F. U. statement of subscription as 18,000 copies in England (@ 25% roy.) and 8000 colonial (@ 6d per copy): making gross roy. £1887, less 10% com. leaving £1699 net, of which an advance of £1000 has been paid, leaving a balance already earned of *£699*.

By adding all the amounts underlined in the preceding two paragraphs you will see, my dear Eric, that there is at the present moment actually a sum of £4014 already earned. I don't think you will find any mistakes in the arithmetic, though in working it out some odd dollars and shillings may have been neglected. It is this summary survey of the situation, my dear fellow, which makes me hope that I will be able to invest fully £3000 out of the Cinema deal which you have negotiated last week. I consider it as well as concluded, because I can't bring myself to believe that those people will let the option lapse.[1] $5000 for a month seems to me too considerable a sum to throw away like this. I imagine those people would be content to make a very small profit on the whole transaction rather than make us a present of it. But if they will do so, why, all I can say is it will be easy money in our pockets. Personally I would be ready to give any amount of options at that price.

In conclusion, reverting again to the year 1924, I see from your letter of June 12th. 1923, that there is a stipulated payment from F. N. D. for March 1st. for the "Rover" of £1400. On this I will only remark that the book has already earned more than twice that amount. (See the R. statement above). As to the other payment June 1924 of £1119 on account of Concord Edition, I will say nothing now, except that the Concord Ed. @ $2.50 per vol. on a 15% royalty will earn much more than that in the course of 1924, or will have to admit itself a dismal failure. But it won't be that. What I think it will do is to kill all the older editions in the course of time. Therefore what we call now ordinary royalties will no doubt dwindle. But that need not mean a loss. It will mean a lot of new negotiations for you.

Jessie says that I owe her about £20 borrowed on various occasions in the last six months. My recollections are vague, but I don't intend to make her swear to the correctness of her account; so please send her a cheque for that amount, and enable me to look her again in the face.

[1] In the event, the option did lapse; see the letter to Pinker of 30 January.

I am dictating those little jokes with an anxious heart. This morning Dr Reid came to administer the first injection of the new treatment, but could not do so, because when he put the needle in at the spot she has been pointing out for the last six weeks, there was an issue of fluid utterly unexpected and revealing a state of affairs which neither Sir Robert nor Reid had any suspicion of. About two cubic centimetres came out and are gone to London for immediate analysis. No perceptible relief was afforded, but she takes a very cheerful view; for there is a certain comfort in being able to say, "I told you so". Of course she is again confined to her bedroom, for the nth time since we came into this infernal house. She sends her love.

Always affec^{tly} Yours

J. Conrad

PS. The above rigmarole of figures points to a hopeful future. For I can't admit that the book will collapse all at once like an old donkey falling down in the shafts. It would be an ignoble fate.

To Messrs Henry Sotheran & Co.

Text TS NYU; Unpublished

[letterhead: Oswalds]

Jan. 22nd. 1924.

Dear Sirs,[1]

Will you kindly send me from your catalogue No. 80 the following works: 54, 618, 1274, 1290. for which cheque for £2. 0. 0. is enclosed.[2]

Yours faithfully,

Joseph Conrad.

Messrs. H. Sotheran & Co.

---

[1] Henry Sotheran & Co. can claim to be the oldest antiquarian bookshop in the world. Founded in York in 1761, the firm moved to London in 1815. In Conrad's day, the firm's premises were at 42 Piccadilly, dealing in books, literary MSS, and sometimes publishing titles under its own imprint.

[2] The catalogue describes these books as follows: No. 54: Barruel (Abbé Augustin), *Mémoires pour servir à l'histoire du Jacobinisme*, 4 vols. London, 1797 (offered as Lot 101 in the Hodgson sale of books and MSS from Conrad's library in 1925); No. 618: Prest, Thomas, *Gallant Tom, or The Perils of a Sailor Ashore and Afloat: an Original Nautical Romance of Deep and Pathetic Interest* (Lloyd, 1841); No. 1274: La Siboutie (Dr Poumiès de), *Recollections of a Parisian under Six Sovereigns, Two Revolutions, and a Republic, 1789–1863*, edited by his Daughters Mesdames Branche and L. Dagoury, translated by Lady Theodora Davidson, 2nd edn (New York: Putnam, 1911); and No. 1290: *Charles Stewart Parnell: His Love Story and Political Life*, by Katherine O'Shea. Barruel's work on the French Revolution has been nourishing conspiracy theorists ever since; Prest was one of the most popular authors of Victorian sensational fiction; Katherine, or Kitty, O'Shea was Parnell's lover.

To [?]
Text MS BU; *Unpublished*

[letterhead: Oswalds]

22. Jan. '24.

My dear friend.[1]

You may be sure I am in closest sympathy with your and your wife's feelings.

I am startled at the singularly short notice to join. Have you obtained the perfectly justifiable extension for which you have asked? No doubt it will be a great wrench for all of you. I do not think however that any army officer or Civil Serv[t] is called upon now to serve for seven years in India without at least one leave home.

That sort of separation is hard to bear. It leaves a sense of aching void for a long time. You do not tell us where Cyril's regiment is stationed. One would like him to make his first start in the best possible conditions. Give him my love and my wishes for the best possible luck professional and otherwise. As to merit that is his own affair and I know that he wont fail in that.

My warmest regards to You both.

Always Yours

J. Conrad.

To Eric S. Pinker
Text TS Berg; Unpublished

[letterhead: Oswalds]

Jan. 27th. 1924.

Very dear Eric

Thank you very much for your prompt answer to my letter which I really meant you to read at your leisure. I have also had your letter conveying to me Marks' statement about English sales.[2] All those really favourable news and good prospects ought to have been a greater help to my recovery than they have been. I am getting an impossible sort of person, I fear; and unless I join the Christian Scientists at once I am afraid I will have to regard myself as past praying for. The weather itself cannot be complained of very much, and yet I don't feel as if I were more than half way out of the hole.

The result of analysis of the fluid connected with Jessie's latest trouble has not come through yet. I hope the Official Analysts have not gone on strike too.[3] She looks rather better than she has done at the beginning of

---

[1] Unidentified. [2] Presumably, Marks worked for Unwin.

[3] On 21 January the Associated Society of Locomotive Engineers and Firemen had gone on strike over a wage dispute.

the week, but the pain is always there, and nothing can be done to relieve it immediately.

I see that she has finished the third and last part of that American article.[1] She will have to correct it however in a good many places. That brings the whole article to over 7000 words, which is much more than those people apparently asked for; yet I dont see how she could have made it shorter, the scheme of the whole thing being what it is. I was afraid that something of the kind would happen and advised her to select one single episode from each period; but she thought that it wasn't what was wanted, and I can't say I am displeased with what she has done. She will probably post it to you to-morrow.

An American has written to me asking me to sign and write a short note in a few of my first editions for which he offers to pay 1000 dollars.[2] I can't understand that frame of mind, but strictly speaking it is no business of mine, and I will drop him a line to send the vols: along. As to remorse for exploiting human folly I understand that Napoleon and several other great men upon whom I am anxious to model my conduct didn't know what remorse was.

Ever affectly yours

J. Conrad.

To F. N. Doubleday

Text TS/MS Princeton; *Listy* 462

[letterhead: Oswalds]
Jan. 28th. 1924.

Dearest F. N. D.

I cabled you my thanks for the smallest scrap of paper I ever received in my life, but which contained the biggest piece of good news that I ever had as an author. I am thinking seriously of having it framed as a memento of your and my success in the conquest of the public. The trouble is that I can't think of a frame splendid enough to be worthy of it. So I sent it (unframed as it was) to Jessie in the next room, and that woman concealed it somewhere in the depths of her P. P. B. (Precious Property Bag) and I haven't been able to dig it out yet.

All this about "The Rover" seems to me very dreamlike. Here too I have heard in strict confidence – I can't understand the reason of the mystery made of it – that the English Edition (*not* including Colonial) is approaching 30,000 and is expected to reach 40,000 by March. When I remember that it took a whole year to sell 22,000 or 23,000 of "The Rescue" I feel a little sad;

[1] Perhaps a first draft of Jessie Conrad's memoir 'Earlier and Later Days', which appeared in the *Saturday Evening Post* for 13 September 1924 (but not in three parts).
[2] See Conrad's letter to Keating of 28 January.

for it was rather a big thing, if I may dare to say so. However, I feel I have a fairly big thing up my sleeve. When it will at last come out of it, my dear Effendi, it is no use speculating. My brain is not becoming fibrous, my blood pressure is eminently all right – but a fellow must feel all right in *all* his body to do good work. It is clear also that I am improving; but it is damned slow (I beg Florence's pardon for using swear words), and all I can do is to try and not worry about it.

Last Saturday week we returned from a three days' visit to London, in our new and comfortable car (it dates from 1912 and costs me just £200, so there is no need to shout for the police) which carried us well. But our hearts were heavy. There is certainly some new trouble located deep in the leg, with which Sir Robert will have to deal. Therefore leaving England now for a "softer clime" is out of the question. So fate points to our staying in this house till next September, when we will leave it for good and perhaps then be able to treat ourselves to six or more months in the South of France.[1]

Yes my dear friends – hope deferred makes the heart sick![2] Jessie bears up very well. She puts in time, upstairs where she is confined, in making hats and coats for Mr Philip J. Conrad who, as far as I have been able to judge, seems a very decent sort of person indeed. I believe Jessie thinks so too – at any rate she has been talking of inviting him down here soon. She is, my dear Florence, answering to-day your charming and interesting letter about the farm and other things – while I, here, beg leave to kiss Your hands and commend myself to your kind thoughts. As to you dear F. N. D. all I'll say is th[at I]am

Always Yours

J. Conrad

To George T. Keating
Text TS Yale; Unpublished

[letterhead: Oswalds]
Jan. 28th. 1924.

My dear Keating

I am in receipt of your letter with all the interesting items of information.

Your project of a marvellous illustrated catalogue in which you intend to include the prose of Hergesheimer and Cabell is almost too much for my native modesty.[3] I am sure I must have blushed reading about it, but I am

---

[1] MS from this point.   [2] 'Hope deferred maketh the heart sick' (Proverbs 13.12).
[3] Keating's *A Conrad Memorial Library* (1929) catalogues the MSS and other materials in his collection with prefaces commissioned especially for the volume. Neither James Branch Cabell (1879–1958) nor Joseph Hergesheimer (1880–1954) was among the contributing authors. Both stood high in literary opinion of the time; for Conrad's favourable view of Hergesheimer, see *Letters*, 7, p. 106.

not sure, because there is no looking glass in my study. When I told Curle of it I imagined he would become very jealous. But on the contrary he seems to be friendly to you, and intends to send you a copy of the latest pamphlet which is called, not the "Spirit of Geography" but "Geography and some Explorers". Tell Gabriel[1] that nobody could possibly know anything about it since the MS and the corrected typescript, (which really amounts almost to another MS) were not finished till Nov. 15th last year.

You put forward the proposal of my annotating and signing a set of my American first editions for you, so that I can't but say: "Very well, it shall be done". But, if you want it done, please my dear fellow, let it be done at once. If you have not got yet all the items send me what you have now, and let the others follow. To wait till the end of this year will not do at all. First of all I don't know where I shall be at the end of this year. I propose to go to no warmer place than the South of France, and of course the books could not be sent on chasing me there. On the other hand we are bound to remain in this house till the month of May, and if I had the books here I would give them a little of my time every day and do the thing properly. In a matter of that kind putting off may end in a disappointment. Please let me know how you propose to send them: whether it will be through the firm in St. Mary Axe,[2] or direct here. Then, when the books are shipped, pray send me a weekend cable letter just to say that they have left your side and by what ship.

Our united kind regards to Mrs Keating, Yourself and the children.

Always Very cordially Yours

J. Conrad.

PS. Re "The Duel". From your description I can tell you that you have all there is of its first state, by which I mean the MS. The first pages in pen and ink having been lost in some way I had a clean copy in type made, which of course is not first state but has been sent simply to complete the story.

The MS of "The Return" is one of my very early ones. I had actually completed it a week or so before our eldest boy was born.[3]

J. C.

---

[1] Gabriel Wells (1862–1946), a New York bibliophile and dealer, was always keen to acquire Conrad MSS; see *Letters*, 7, p. 173, n. 3.

[2] Several forwarding agents had their offices on this street in the City. At No. 82, Neale & Wilkerson's Colonial & Foreign Shipping Agency offered through freight and express services worldwide.

[3] The MS of 'The Return' (Berg) is dated '24th Septer. 1897'. Corrected proofs of the story for *Tales of Unrest* were returned to Unwin on 11 December (*Letters*, 1, p. 422), just over a month before Borys's birth on 15 January 1898.

To J. A. Allen

Text TS Yale; Unpublished

[letterhead: Oswalds]
Jan. 29th. 1924.

Dear Sir,[1]

The story revived in the Transatlantic Review about which you inquire, under the name of "The Value of a Crime", obviously refers to the instalment in No. 1 of the Transatlantic under the title of "The Nature of a Crime".

I have no trace of it amongst my papers, but I have looked through my Nos. of the E[nglish] R[eview] and can tell you that there are two instalments which appeared in Nos. 1 and 2 of Vol. 2 of the E. R. The author's name is of course fictitious. It is such a long time ago that I do not remember whether there is any more of it written, or really anything about it. Of course I remember the mere fact of collaboration and of course there is some of my work in it. What appeared looks like a fragment. F. M. H. wrote to me lately as to his desire to reprint it in the T. R. to which I did not or indeed could not object. But I haven't got the slightest recollection of what it is all about or how much of it we have done. Perhaps F. M. H. could tell you more.

Yours faithfully,

J. Conrad.

To Eric S. Pinker

Text TS Berg; Unpublished

[letterhead: Oswalds]
Jan. 29th. 1924.

Dearest Eric

You will be glad to hear that my progress continues, 60% of cough having vanished to my great relief. If another 20% goes I will be able to manage the rest while standing on my head – as my early friends in the forecastle used to say.

Ford M. Ford (formerly Hueffer) wrote to me from Paris about a piece of work we began together in the dim past somewhere, called "The Nature of a Crime".[2] I had forgotten all about it. Some or all of it appeared in the early E[nglish] R[eview]. It is apparently extremely short and I suspect it isn't finished at all. My part is very small. Anyway he has an offer from

---

[1] J(ohn) A. Allen (b. 1855) was a London publisher with offices at 16 Grenville Street, near Russell Square, Bloomsbury. In 1925 Allen reprinted a series of articles by Lord Darling from the London *Evening News* on crime, insanity, and murder, and in 1926, Kipling's speech 'The Art of Fiction' from *The Times*. After 1926 the firm specialised in equestrian literature.

[2] See Ford's letter to Conrad of 8 November 1923 (Stape and Knowles, p. 222).

Duckworth[1] to publish in book-form £150 advance on 15% royalty. That is all he tells me, asking my consent.[2] I have given it, mainly for the reason that I could not very well refuse without entering into a useless argument. Perhaps if you ask Duckworth he will be able to tell you something as to The Nature of that Operation. Perhaps it is only a limited edition that is contemplated? I fancy it could not be a success in the open market. I don't mind getting my share, as my name is worth that and more, and the thing is not wholly contemptible. The fact of the matter is that I have some extra expenses connected with the house and some personal matters which I should like to meet from extraneous sources, for I hate to overstep the settled budget by any serious amount. Therefore I assented to this and also to the American's proposition mentioned in my last letter, which together is roughly a windfall of £275. I may want some of it before it falls due, but I intend to borrow it only from my growing wealth and intend to pay those windfall sums into the general account between you and me.

The items of the proposed expenditure are many and various, ranging from a new overcoat for Vinten and a pair of new tyres to a "grant in aid" to meet Philip's travelling expenses, or is it "establish in life" expenses? I promised it to the best of my ability some time ago, before B's prospects improved and I can't very well draw back now. I won't tell you any more about the items of expenditure, more from fear of boring you than scandalising you.

I hope your wife's "fatalism" is carrying her through as easily as may be. Give her my love.

Ever Your affec^{tte}

J. Conrad.

PS I suppose you've heard from Mrs C. This damned thing hanging on makes it pretty hard for both of us – just now.

---

[1] Gerald Duckworth (1870–1937) started the firm in 1898. Its list was always strong in literature and the other arts. Ford's books on the Pre-Raphaelites, Holbein, and Dante Gabriel Rossetti appeared there, and Duckworth's published the early numbers of the *English Review*. In 1922, Ford signed a contract with them to publish all his work, old and new: Max Saunders, *Ford Madox Ford: A Dual Life* (Oxford University Press, 2000), II, p. 127.

[2] Ford's telegram of 24 January (Berg) stated: 'Duckworth offers hundred and fifty bookrights nature crime royalty fifteen would like accept if you agree. FordmadoxofParis'.

To E. H. Visiak

Text TS Texas; Visiak (facsimile) 224

[letterhead: Oswalds]
Jan. 29th. 1924.

My dear Sir.[1]

Since you put it on those grounds I will answer you seriously by asking first what is it that you expect me to tell you? Story telling, at any rate for me, is a vehicle for artistic expression. The preferences of a man who has written a considerable number of pages of what, he ventures to think, personal prose, are not to be thrown out to the public;[2] for this reason amongst others, that the public would not understand them. A man may like one of his works specially on account of some peculiar associations of the time. He may like it because in his conscience he believes that *there* he has come the nearest to his artistic intention, or has conveyed his meaning with the greatest clearness, or has achieved the greatest emotional sincerity, or simply has been able to attain what he thinks his best in plasticity or colouring or atmosphere. And how can those things be made understandable to a public which often fails to perceive the whole point of a composition? I don't blame the public for that in the least; but I do say that a man is entitled to keep those feelings to himself, not only because they are nearest his heart but also because in the nature of things they could not be made clear without elaborate explanation, which the public neither wants nor would be interested in.

And then, let me put the point before you that this is a private matter. It is eminently and legitimately so. For why should a man, who looks upon his work as a whole, be asked to, publicly, pick out one part of it and thus in a certain sense reduce all the rest to a second rank in the eyes of the world; or else expose himself to the comment that the author does not know what he has done? It is like asking for a certificate of imbecility.

For you, yourself, I will say, what you will not, perhaps, be surprised to hear, that there are pages and shorter passages in all my work of which I think with particular affection and satisfaction and perhaps with some pride. But even to your obvious and intelligent sympathy I will refrain from pointing

---

[1] E. H. Visiak was the pseudonym of Edward Harold Physick (1878–1972), a poet, novelist, and Milton scholar. He worked as a telegraph office clerk and schoolteacher before winning a Civil List pension to pursue his scholarly interests, producing a series of notes on Conrad in *Notes & Queries* in 1939–40, followed by *The Mirror of Conrad* (1955).

[2] Valuing rhythm over syntax, Conrad added the commas after 'what', 'think', and 'prose' in his own hand.

them out specifically. I can only hope that you will not be angry with me for that reserve which is not a matter of prudence but of deeper feeling.

Believe me very sincerely

Yours

J. Conrad.

To Eric S. Pinker
Text TS Berg; Unpublished

Oswalds.

Jan. 30th. 1924.

Dearest Eric.

If I have given you the impression of being anxious about the immediate ill. ed. of M. of S. then it is quite unwittingly.[1] As a matter of fact all those considerations that Evans puts before us have occurred to me and I suggest that we should make very plain to the people on the other side that there is not the slightest intention on our part to press the matter. It must stand adjourned sine die.[2] I admit I should be sorry to lose Everett's illustrations, if that must be the consequence of the above decision, but if we must, why we must.

It would be interesting to know what new scheme Doubledays are going to add to this "intensive culture" of Conrad success. I can't imagine what it can be unless broadcasting readings of selected passages. If so I should like to know about the machinery for collecting fees. I must be very stupid, but broadcasting always has struck me as a sort of philanthropic undertaking and I don't want to be made a party to any philanthropy. However, I suppose I shall be hearing all about it from you very soon.

I guessed that the option money[3] had not come through because I knew that you would advise me. Of course it may yet, but if it never does I won't be so much disappointed as you fear I may be. I think I understood the position

---

[1] The idea of an illustrated edition of *The Mirror of the Sea* using paintings, drawings, and prints by John Everett first occurred to J. B. Pinker in November 1921, when Conrad took it up enthusiastically, having been introduced to the artist's work by Will Rothenstein (*Letters*, 7, pp. 372–3). The plan was still under discussion with Heinemann's in early 1923: see the letter to Eric Pinker written on a February 'Tuesday'. Evidently Doubleday's did not like the notion of a distinguished publication that might distract attention from the various collected editions.

[2] 'Indefinitely'.   [3] See Conrad's letter to Pinker of 21 January.

and I did not feel unduly optimistic. I did send you my scheme for dealing with the money, but the proviso: "if we get it" was always at the back of my head. Since we are on that subject, would you, my dear fellow, ascertain from the archives of the office precisely what books have been disposed of in the 1919 transaction negotiated by J. B., so that we may know exactly what material we can dispose of should another opening present itself.[1] I have a confident feeling that sooner or later it will present itself so strongly that I hope on some future occasion to talk over with you, with a list before us, a consistent scheme of dealing with the aforesaid material. This is where *I am* still an optimist.

I have had a letter from B. in which he tells me that it so happened that he had double payments of his allowance, one from you and one from Doubleday, and remarks that this about finishes the allowance due from America. I suppose it does. He is also worried about the repayment which he promised to make to you. He has also furnished me with documentary proof that he has paid off some old debts which he either had not confessed or took upon himself at the time when we regulated his affairs in 1922. Under those circumstances I intend to write to him that I take over his liability to you, and that he need not worry. Materially it makes no difference as to the amount which I promised to give him, it only anticipates it. So I am not out of pocket by that. What I promised to do to help him with the special expenses I will do, of course, but I will want first to see the doctor's bill and the nurse's account, when I will have probably to draw a cheque. But what I may do will be more than covered by the transaction Hueffer proposed and about which I wrote to you yesterday. I don't want all those extra beneficences to come out of the money which passes through your hands.

I have been for a drive to-day, not a very nice day, but I really begin to think that the cough is leaving me. I haven't had so little of it on any given three days, I verily believe, since 1922. However, I mustn't be too optimistic.

Our love.

Yours ever

J Conrad.

---

[1] Eric's father had arranged the sale of rights to *Chance*, *Victory*, *Lord Jim*, and *Romance* in 1919; half the proceeds from *Romance* went to Ford.

To Charles Chassé
Text J-A, 2, 336

Oswalds.
Jan. 31st, 1924.

My dear Sir,[1]

You must forgive me a dictated letter in English because I do not want to delay in acknowledging your friendly communication, and my wrist does not allow me to hold my pen for any length of time.

Please receive my warm thanks for your article in the *Figaro*.[2] Its sympathy and friendliness are very precious to me. As to the references to my Slavonism, I am certain you wrote in all sincerity, like many English critics who had been raising the same point some years ago, but not so much lately.[3]

For, indeed, talking to you with perfect frankness, as one would to a friend of many years' standing, I have asked myself more than once whether if I had preserved the secret of my origins under the neutral pseudonym of "Joseph Conrad" that temperamental similitude would have been put forward at all. As to myself, I have my doubt. I believe that, here at any rate, what is personal has been put to the account of racial affinities. The critics detected in me a new note and as, just when I began to write, they had discovered the

---

[1] Charles Chassé (1883–1965), a French writer on English literature and modern art, was particularly interested in the work of Gauguin and the Fauvists. He was Director of the Paris School of New York University, and in 1922 published *Les Sources d'Ubu roi*, a study of Alfred Jarry's iconoclastic play. He wrote two books on Brittany and studies of Mallarmé and the Nabis; among the authors he translated were Sir Thomas Browne, Izaak Walton, Sir Walter Scott, Gordon Craig, George Bernard Shaw, and H. G. Wells.

[2] 'L'aristocratisme slave de Conrad', *Le Figaro, Supplément littéraire*, 29 December 1923, p. 3. Although ranging widely, the essay starts and finishes with *The Rover*.

[3] Certain English critics had brought up the notion of Conrad's 'Slavic temperament' in response to *The Secret Agent* and *Under Western Eyes*; among them was Edward Garnett, whose obsession with all things Slavic irritated Conrad (e.g. *Letters*, 4, p. 469). He had objected to the 'harping on my Sclavonism' by an American critic, H. L. Mencken, as recently as December 1922 (*Letters*, 7, pp. 615–16). While Charles Chassé reiterates the 'biographie tourmentée' of Conrad, beginning with his Polish roots, he emphasises the astonishing variety of Conrad's experience. Moreover, he does not try to explain Conrad in terms of racial or mystical communion with the Slavic soul; indeed, he is struck by the large number of uprooted, isolated characters in his fiction, many of whom resort to suicide. Nevertheless, Chassé sees Conrad's fixation on suicide as part of a general fascination with extremes of impetuous behaviour, a fascination he associates with 'slavisme': 'De ce slavisme procède aussi son indulgence, parfois un peu méprisante[,] pour ses erreurs et les crimes des autres hommes.' His 'aristocratisme', on the other hand, is exemplified in the deeds of other characters, such as masters of ships, who are isolated but in control both of their emotions and of the 'plèbe internationale des matelots' around them, for 'un bon capitaine de la mer est toujours bon capitaine de son âme'. The essay concludes with the question of Peyrol's end: is it another case of a lonely man surrendering to 'ses mauvais instincts' or what Chassé has previously called 'une suicide héroïque et patriotique'?

existence of Russian authors,[1] they stuck that label on me under the name of Slavonism. What I venture to say is that it would have been more just to charge me at most with "Polonism." Polish temperament, at any rate, is far removed from Byzantine and Asiatic associations. Poland has absorbed Western ideas, adopted Western culture, sympathized with Western ideals and tendencies as much as it was possible, across the great distances and in the special conditions of its national and political life, whose main task was the struggle for life against Asiatic despotism at its door.

So much for my heredity. As to formulative* influences, I must point out that I do not know the Russian language, that I know next to nothing of Russian imaginative literature, except the little I have been able to read in translations; that the formative forces acting on me, at the most plastic and impressionable age, were purely Western: that is French and English: and that, as far as I can remember, those forces found in me no resistance, no vague, deep-seated antagonism, either racial or temperamental.

This is the truth as far as I know. *Mais après tout, vous pouvez avoir raison.*[2] Men have but very little self knowledge, and authors especially are victims of many illusions about themselves. I put before you my claim to Westernism for no other reason but because I feel myself profoundly in accord with it.

Let me thank you once more for the pleasure your sympathetic appreciation of my work has given me.

To Dolly Moor

Text MS Private collection; Carabine and Stape

[letterhead: Oswalds]
31 Jan 24

My dear Dolly.[3]

Thank you ever so much for your charming letter which shows that you keep green the memory of the old times. Neither have I forgotten them.

---

[1] Just as Conrad was finishing *Almayer's Folly*, Constance Garnett's first translations of Turgenev began to appear: *Rudin* in 1894, *Fathers and Children* and *A Sportsman's Sketches* in 1895, *Smoke* and *Virgin Soil* in 1896. In 1895, E. L. Voynich's *The Humour of Russia* included the first English version of Gogol's 'Diary of a Madman'. By this time several versions of Tolstoy were available, for example N. H. Dole's *Ivan Ilyich and Other Stories* (1885), Vizetelly's *War and Peace* (1886), both made from French translations, and various renderings of *Childhood, Boyhood, Youth* from the early 1890s, some made directly from the Russian. Before 1911, however, the year of *The House of the Dead* and Constance Garnett's *Crime and Punishment*, those who wanted to know Dostoevsky had to read him in the original or in French.

[2] 'But you may be right after all.'

[3] Alice Dora ('Dolly') Moor (née George, 1884–1949) was one of Jessie Conrad's younger sisters. Joseph Conrad helped to pay for her education at the Bernardine Convent in Slough, Middlesex. In 1910 she married John Harold Harwar (born 1882), who was killed in action near Cambrai on 23 November 1917. She then married (George) Harold Moor in London and emigrated to South Africa, where her husband worked as a sugar refiner. They lived in Zululand, not far from Durban.

Though far, far out of sight you never have been out of my mind. I remember perfectly the compromising occasions which you mention. Certainly I carried you to bed more than once. Generally you would be fast asleep and as insensible as a stone, but, of course much more pleasant to carry.

As I look at poor Jessie crippled and often in pain I cant help thinking that those were happy times. I am glad to know that for all its trials life has been good to you and that the child is a happy woman now.

I am sorry dear that your copy did not get sent off long before this. The Rover will be posted to you tomorrow.

Give my cordial regards to your husband and believe me ever

Your affectionate and faithful old friend

Joseph Conrad.

To Eric S. Pinker

Text TS/MS Berg; Unpublished

Oswalds.

Jan. 31st. 1924.

Dearest Eric.

I have received this account from Withers.[1] In May I was in America but we have looked over all my papers and we can't find the account here. I can't think what it is for, unless it would be for making my will;[2] but that seems a long time ago and I was under the impression it was settled by the office, as he knows that I am a client and much more immovable than the heaviest piece of furniture in it. Perhaps you would be good enough to make inquiries and of course settle the thing.

Yrs

J. C.

PS.[3] Have just had letter from the polish dramatist and critic B. Winawer. The "Book of Job" man. There is no doubt he *can construct* a play.

He writes about the R[over]. He says "as a theatre man I feel that there is in it magnificent material for a stage creation of a beautiful, serious almost symphonic drama" etc. etc.

It is a feeler I believe.

[1] Messrs Withers, Currie, Bensons and Williams, Conrad's solicitors.
[2] Conrad had signed his last will on 8 August 1922; see *Documents*, pp. 245–51.
[3] MS begins.

Well, suppose he did try his hand at it; and suppose I took up the Polish text and put it in Conradese – do you think there would be a chance for it to be tried here – or (more likely) in America?

J. C.

To Bruno Winawer

Text TS carbon Yale;[1] J-A, 2, 335; Najder 294–5

[Oswalds]
Jan. 31st, 1924.

My wrist prevents my using the pen, therefore you must accept this dictated letter.

I am delighted to know that my old Rover has appealed to you I conclude aesthetically as well as emotionally, and that my artistic purpose commends itself to your judgment.

As to its adaptability for the stage I was at first surprised. But on thinking it over I see the possibility, though of course I do not see the way in which it could be visibly presented and spiritually rendered in spoken words. But it is a fact that the book has got very little description, very few disquisitions, and is for the most part in dialogue – en forme parlée.[2]

I will tell you at once, however, that if it is to be done you are the man to do it. And I hope with all my heart that you will make the attempt, for Poland at any rate.

That would be a matter of arrangement with Angela,[3] whom probably you would find more than willing. But being much impressed by what you say as to the drama[tic] possibilities [of] Powrotu Korsarza,[4] I am led to think that if done within ten or eleven months there would be a great chance for it in America. The book there is an immense success, and generally J. C. is receiving immense publicity on account of that particular work. Mere curiosity as to the visual presentation of a novel so much read and talked about may create a theatrical success, and if you like to try I will do my part in putting the text of your play exactly as you make it, without the slightest change or alteration, back into English, accepting your construction and whatever spirit your creative instinct will put into it, without discussion. Of course the English will have to be my own.

---

[1] The uncorrected carbon of the letter as dictated in English to Miss Hallowes, with 'B. Winawer' added in her hand. The final sentence, missing from the Yale text, comes from J-A.

[2] 'In spoken form' rather than indirect discourse.

[3] Aniela Zagórska.   [4] *The Return of the Rover.*

I put forward this suggestion because I am interested in seeing what you will do. The American prospect may make it worth your while from a practical point of view.

As to England I admit that my failure with "The Secret Agent" would be very much against a play with which I had anything to do. Mais on ne sait jamais.[1]

But I do not think that the Labour Government would forbid the play on the ground that being both Poles we are "horrid aristocrats" and enemies of the virtuous Bolsheviks.[2]

To Richard Curle

Text MS Indiana; Curle 141

[Oswalds]
1st Febr[y] '24

My dear Dick.

My report is that I am better but poor Jessie has not improved much. She was pleased with Your S[ister]'s letters.[3] We enjoyed Your week end with us very much.

Mrs Gwatkin[4] called yesterday. Need I say more?

Perhaps Jessie has told You that your sister and Col. Ruston called on us on Sunday. We were very pleased to see them. R apparently is about to sail to Austr[ali][a] on business.

If you could my dear fellow sell for me the Hud: Coll. Ed[5] I will send it to you. Only please do not let me worry you with that.

---

[1] 'But one never knows.' Conrad's stage adaptation of *The Secret Agent* closed after eleven performances at the Ambassadors Theatre, London, in November 1922.

[2] Here the world of Citizen Scevola, the zealous villain of *The Rover*, and the world of contemporary politics overlap. Poland and the Russian Soviet Federated Socialist Republic were at war in 1919–20, and the Red Army had advanced nearly to Warsaw. During this war, Conrad saw in the reborn nation 'one indomitable will, from the poorest peasant to the highest magnate', united in hostility to 'moral and physical pestilence bred in Russia' (*Letters*, 7, p. 40). He wrote the present letter nine days after Ramsay MacDonald had taken office as the first ever Labour Prime Minister. Although far from revolutionary, the new government was willing to recognise the Soviet Union (at that stage thirteen months old), and some party members looked there for their inspiration. These factors were enough to exacerbate the belief that Bolshevism was now rampant in Britain.

[3] His sister Muriel Amy Curle had married Joseph Seward Ruston in 1909.

[4] Frances Lilian Ashton-Gwatkin (née Ashton, 1868–1955), wife of the then rector of Bishopsbourne, Walter Henry Trelawny Ashton-Gwatkin (1861–1945), who assumed his wife's maiden name.

[5] *The Collected Works of W. H. Hudson* (Dent, 1923), issued in 24 volumes and limited to 885 sets.

I have tackled the Novel to-day. What a lot of work there is to do yet! However I feel not so very much disgusted. 30 pp *will have to* come out. But that's my least trouble. I feel fairly hopeful.

Ever Your

J. C.

To E. H. Visiak
Text TS Private Collection; Unpublished

[letterhead: Oswalds]
Feb. 1st. 1924.

Dear Sir

Thank you very much for your Milton book arrived this morning.[1] I have opened it and I have no doubt it is very interesting.

If you want to print something of mine in answer to your query you may of course print my first letter, or perhaps you would prefer the following:

I spread my affection over all my books for different reasons. I like best one for one quality and another for a different quality which I perceive in it, or even, perhaps, for what a critic would call a defect but which does not strike me so. When it comes to their work authors are perverse creatures. I will tell you also that there are passages in almost all my books which "I like best". Under those circumstances to select one book for preference could not be done without pondering, balancing, weighing, testing, and a lot of other delicate operations for which time is growing short. So I think that the secret of "the book I like best" will have to go with me to my grave.

Yours faithfully

J. Conrad.

To G. Jean-Aubry
Text MS Yale; *L. fr.* 195

[Oswalds]
[3 February 1924][2]

Mon Vieux

Que devenez vous? Etes Vous enseveli sous une avalanche de lettres?

Faut il envoyer a Marlboro' St mon jardinier avec une pelle pour Vous dégager?[3]

---

[1] *Milton Agonistes: A Metaphysical Criticism* (A. M. Philpot, 1923).
[2] Jean-Aubry wrote the French date on the MS.
[3] Jean-Aubry edited *The Chesterian*, a magazine published by Chester's, a firm of musical instrument makers at 11 Great Marlborough St.

Nous attendons un mot de Vous.[1] M. et Mme. B. C. sont ici avec le bébé
pour deux jours.

Jessie sends her love.

Ever yours

J. Conrad.

My old friend,

What has become of you? Are you buried under an avalanche of letters?
Should I send my gardener to Marlboro' Street with a shovel to dig you
out?

We are waiting to hear from you. Mr and Mrs B. C. are here with the
baby for two days.

Jessie sends her love.

Ever yours

J. Conrad.

To Eric S. Pinker

Text TS Berg; J-A, 2, 337 (in part)[2]

Oswalds.
Feb. 3rd. 1924.

Dear Eric.

I am glad you like the idea of giving Winawer his head. I have done so,
but of course he may be very busy, because he is a hard-working man in
journalism and other things. In my letter I said that if it could be done within
eleven months it would not be too late to try for a success of curiosity[3] in
America, where the people who had read the book would probably go to the
theatre too.

I am concentrating all my thoughts on the Novel, which certainly by the
time it is done will be a biggish thing – I mean both in matter and size. I have
been reflecting on certain aspects of criticism provoked by "The Rover". It has
dawned upon me that the note of disappointment that has been perceptible,
simply means that many people, (indeed, I believe, the majority of the critics)
took that book for the long-talked-of Mediterranean novel.[4] And naturally

---

[1] Jean-Aubry replied on the 6th (TS Yale) with news of his lecturing activities in France, his
writings on Conrad for the *Revue Hebdomadaire* and the *Revue de Paris*, and his encounters with
Ravel, Valery Larbaud, and Gide, who all sent their greetings to the Conrads.

[2] Jean-Aubry only gives the first two paragraphs.

[3] A Gallicism: *succès de curiosité*.

[4] One example is J. B. Priestley's review for the *London Mercury*, 9 (January 1924), pp. 319–20:
'while it is a fine book, it is not *the* book, the story that we, in the half-impudent, half noble
fashion of admiring readers, have been expecting for so long' (p. 320).

some of them said: "And is that all what*¹ it is, then?" I have no doubt at all about it in my mind. "The Rover" suffered in a sense from the confounded pre-natal publicity that the "Suspense" has evoked simply by being shown about and talked about too much. I too have been guilty of throwing hints. I shouldn't wonder if on its publication there was not a certain amount of feeling that "Here we've got the right thing". The book may profit by it. I must admit that as the "Napoleonic novel", the great "Mediterranean novel", the "Rover" must have appeared to some people rather slight. Well, they will find weight and body enough in what's coming. I can safely promise that.

I had a sudden wire Saturday evening from F[ord] M[adox] F[ord] asking to see me "between two trains" to-morrow. Jessie answered, giving two late-in-the-day trains, and pretty close together also. So he may find them too inconvenient; but in any case, if you have anything to say in the way of warning or advice to me you will be in time to give it to me telegraphically for my guidance in the conversation. But it must be done before four o'clock.²

You may be sure I didn't want to get in personal touch; but it would have been too brutal to say "No, I won't see you at all." I hope to goodness he will find it too inconvenient to come.

I presume that you have been in touch with Duckworth and have got at the inwardness of that transaction. I am glad you took steps to placate F. M. F. I regret that Dents did not put his name on the outside of the collaborated books.³ But both "de luxe" editions⁴ have not got it either.

Please, my dear Eric, pay in £45 to the bank, in advance of my outside earnings of which I spoke in a previous letter.

Have you fixed the date for your wife's going abroad? I hope she is feeling stronger now. Give her our love

Affectly yours

J Conrad.

PS Mrs B C and the baby are here since yesterday.

¹ One of Conrad's several MS emendations of the TS.
² Pinker responded with a five-page telegram (Yale) reporting that Ford 'considers himself insulted by publication of book in England and America without full advertisement his collaboration'; Pinker advised 'gentle handling' but suggested 'you may find card to play in connection with nature of crime permission to republish which can be revoked'.
³ In their Uniform Editions.
⁴ There were two in England, the Dent de luxe and the Heinemann, and the Sun-Dial in the USA, where Doubleday also had plans for what became the Memorial Edition.

To Eric S. Pinker

Text TS Berg; Unpublished

Oswalds.
Feb. 4th. 1924.

Dearest Eric.

First of all, as to actual interview with Hueffer. We met as if we had seen each other every day for the last ten years, and talked about his Review[1] with which Frank Harris[2] has nothing to do except, as usual, in the way of blackmailing. I mean in the form of protesting against the title (same thing happened for the English Review). F. M. F. answered vaguely my question who was behind him in that affair, except as to one name – John Quinn. He has been seeing quite a lot of him in Paris apparently, and Q. spent a lot of money buying pictures there.[3]

As to the questions he raised he begged to assure me privately that he will do nothing whatever and doesn't want me to do anything. This he repeated twice, once in Jessie's presence. But he said he had his knife into Dent. There is a man there, he said, called Rhys, who had been writing him rude and contemptuous letters about a matter quite unconnected with my edition, and he meant to be as disagreeable as he could to those people. As far as his most friendly protestations go we may dismiss that matter from our minds.

As we talked pleasantly of old times I was asking myself, in my cynical way, when would the kink come and what would be its nature, for I was thinking mostly of Duckworth, the other thing being settled.

The subjoined documents disclose the nature of the kink, as to which of course F. M. F. may be perfectly innocent.

One of those documents is the telegram received from Hueffer, on the strength of which *in its entirety* I gave my consent to the publication, by telegraphic reply.[4]

The other document is the memorandum of agreement with Duckworth for "The Nature of the Crime" which F. M. F. pulled out of his pocket with the words "We might just as well sign this and be done with it." He signed first. As I took the pen I asked on purpose, What is the advance he is giving

---

[1] The *transatlantic review*. After the first (January) issue, the cover was redesigned and the title went into lower case.

[2] The Irish-American author Frank Harris (1856–1931) worked as editor of the London *Evening News*, the *Fortnightly Review*, and the *Saturday Review*. His notorious autobiography, *My Life and Loves*, began appearing in 1922.

[3] Quinn collected modern paintings on a grand scale, and the sale of his MS collection the previous year had increased his capacity to do so.

[4] For Ford's telegram, see the notes to the letter to Pinker of 29 January.

us? F. M. F. answered: A hundred and fifty pounds. Thereupon I read the agreement carefully and failed to detect any clause alluding to the advance, so I said "Of course I can't sign this."

Hueffer accepted my declaration without comment, but on the point of going away he said that he would leave it with me to deal with; to which I said "All right." In the very doorway F. M. F. repeated that Duckworth had offered £150 advance, to which I said "I quite understand" and on that F. M. F. went away.

In consequence of those developments I hereby issue instructions to my trusty and well-beloved Eric Pinker to declare to Duckworth that Mr J. C. will not sign the agreement without the advance clause.

Also that Mr J. C. can not accept the agency of Messrs. Duckworth and Co. in placing that work in America, his engagements under various contracts with his publisher preventing him from doing so.

I suppose you agree with me that I really *can not*, simply because it may hurt D[oubleday]'s sensibilities.

Of course if Doubleday does not care to take up the thing you would be at liberty to go to somebody else, (or even you would be at liberty *if* you wanted to be *nice* to Duckworth to let *him* act); but the proviso can not be left to stand as it does in the contract, now.

Ever affectly Yrs

J Conrad.

To Eric S. Pinker

Text MS Berg; Unpublished

[Oswalds]
[early February 1924][1]

Dear E.

I send this as I think You had better reply – if only to bring the firm's name forward. But I know that German rights are contracted for already.[2]

Yours

J. C.

---

[1] Written on a TS letter of 30 January, sent to Conrad c/o Fisher Unwin's London office by the Dreimasken Verlag, Munich, Karolinenplatz 3, enquiring about German translation rights to *The Rover* or any previous novels by Conrad.

[2] Miss Hallowes's notebook lists the Munich firm of A. Langen as Conrad's German publisher (*Documents*, p. 239); most of his works would eventually be published by S. Fischer in Berlin.

To F. N. Doubleday

Text TS/MS Princeton; J-A, 2, 337

[letterhead: Oswalds]
Feb. 7th. 1924.

My dear Effendi.

I am trying to imagine you two dear people in your Island home, but the difficulty is that I am not certain in my mind whether the house had managed to get itself finished before your migration. I remember the exasperating reports that used to come to Effendi Hill, hinting at discreditable proceedings, breaches of trust, embezzlement of funds, infidelity of stewardship, and low intrigues – which would have driven me perfectly frantic but which you, dear Effendi, received with an appearance of philosophical calm, which was one of the, morally, most beautiful sights I have ever seen. My private conviction was that the house would never get finished, or at any rate not for several years. And even now, though I know you are in the Bahamas by this time, I am not at all certain that you have a roof over your heads. The utmost my imagination can achieve are walls about half-way up. I would be very much obliged if you would drop me a line to say that there has been no rain since you arrived. However, you two dear people are accustomed to sleep practically out of doors. . . .

I find also that I can't imagine Effendi Hill House with the rites of hospitality interrupted, its Ministrants departed; like a deserted temple! However, I suppose you will both be back about the end of April for a stay before you move on to the farmhouse.

I expect to hear soon from Eric about the scheme for a book of collected short stories. I assure you, my dear Effendi, that even if I were not certain that in all your schemes you think of my welfare (more than I deserve to be thought of) I would still be most reluctant to negative any scheme of yours. But of course I will be sincere with you, even at the risk of being thought unreasonable and crochetty*. I think that once, in conversation, I told you that in my view every volume of my short stories has a unity of artistic purpose, a mood of feeling and expression, which makes it different from every other.

Authors have many strange illusions about themselves; but I think that what I say would be visible to critical judgment, and even could be felt as a mere impression. For instance (even on mere inspection) the volume of my "Tales of Unrest" is a totally different expression of my art from say, "A Set of Six". Or the whole of the "Typhoon" volume from "Within the Tides". Or take the volume of "Youth" which in its component parts presents the three ages of man, (for that is what it really is, and I knew very well what I was doing when I wrote "The End of the Tether" to be the last of that trio)[1] I can't somehow imagine any of those stories taken out of it and bound cheek and jowl with a story from another volume. It is in fact unthinkable.

Having said that much I will say no more because I don't know what you have exactly in your mind. Of course if you think of a selected volume, a selection of the least significant tales could be made and published, with a special preface where I would try to express plainly my point of view. After all I am old enough by now to be allowed to give a clue to the younger generation that may do me the honour of reading my works.

I am glad to be able to tell you that I have turned the corner as far as my health is concerned. I am going now to grapple with the novel in which those critics that found "The Rover" somewhat slight work will find size and weight enough I can promise them.

Last weekend the baby came in state to visit us here, bringing with it its parents and its nurse. No objection can be taken to it – I mean the baby. It is strong and has a voice which in babies may be compared to a baritone amongst grownups. It also looks remarkably like a human being already. I am not so satisfied with Borys's health, which presents some neurasthenic symptoms again. As a business man he is certainly successful and has made for himself already a reputation in the motor world. I hope however that those symptoms are temporary and that they won't interrupt his progress. He has however a very good doctor who has pulled him together most successfully before and is confident of doing it again.

Poor Mrs C. is very much crippled with the new development of the leg.

She sends you both her best love and her best wishes for health and good time in the sunny Bahamas. And I send mine ditto with dutiful respects to the Lady Commander (whose hands I beg leave to kiss).

Ever my dear Effendi your old
J. Conrad

To Eric S. Pinker
Text MS Berg; Unpublished

Oswalds
Feb. 7th. 1924.

Dearest Eric.

In reference to our conversation this morning I of course confirm my statement that whatever you conclude with Duckworth will be accepted by

---

[1] Conrad's 'Author's Note' to the *Youth* volume opens with the declaration: 'The three stories in this volume lay no claim to unity of artistic purpose.'

me. Your remark that Duckworth ought to pay more is to a certain extent justified by the price you tell me he is going to put on the book – of which I knew nothing. I will however offer for your consideration that: having given my consent to Hueffer's proposal on the terms stated in his wire (which you have) it would be rather difficult to go back on my word. Of course when I received Hueffer's wire I thought the terms were settled, but the omission of the "advance clause" throws a doubt on the whole transaction.

Still if Duckworth inserts the clause of advance (of £150) I fear we will have to accept, since it is a fact that I have incautiously given my consent.

In this connection it occurs to me whether you could not propose to Duckworth a limited edition instead (which would be bought by Conrad collectors for certain); and then of course you could suggest any modification of terms which would seem fair to you.

Naturally Hueffer would have to be informed of such a step (if we take it) and if he objects we will simply drop it.

The only thing on which we can be like adamant is the advance as stated in Hueffer's telegram, on the terms of which I have based my consent.

§[1] As to future inclusion in Collected Works: That fragment could go at the tail of a volume of collected stories when the time comes. But that is very far off yet, and I believe that Hueffer (who wants to be friendly personally with me) will probably accept a lump sum for his proportion of royalties.

§ As to the feelings of Unwin and Dent: The thing is a fragment, of rather under 15000 words than over, as Hueffer tells me. It was written years before I had anything to do with Dent. It has nothing to do with Unwin, with whom I had never a binding contract as to my early works, of which each was the subject of a separate agreement. The agreements I have now with those people can not bind my past activities with which they had nothing to do. And moreover all my agreements with Dent relate to work done by myself alone, not in collaboration, except as to two books of importance, publicly known as such, and already published in book form.

§ As to American rights those must be kept in our hands for disposal, for in America I have only one publisher to whom I am bound as to past and future work. This is a sine qua non. Hueffer will understand this and will raise no difficulties, I venture to say. He wants to be friendly in personal relations with me. In fact, entre nous, too friendly, but as to that I will say nothing more here.

I can't finish this without telling you how sorry I am for springing this matter on you. I didn't quite realise what was going to happen. You see, first of

---

[1] Conrad added these paragraph marks in ink.

all I had a letter from Hueffer asking me for my permission to reprint that thing in the International Review.[1] I had forgotten all about it; but Miss H. looked up the old numbers of the English Review and naturally found it there. So of course I said: Certainly, print it if you like; remarking at the same time that it was hardly worth while to drag it up to light again. The next thing was the damned telegram (which you have) on receiving which I thought that having already given permission to reprint I might just as well say yes. Of course having done that I at once advised you by letter. I thought all this of no importance, except as to a possible few pounds. But with that confounded F. M. H. one never knows what one may be led into. The only thing I can add is that *if* you should personally dislike to have anything to do with F. M. H. in your official capacity, I will write any letters which you may judge necessary to write. I know that J. B. did not like to have anything to do with Hueffer; but this of course belongs to my own affairs which are in your hands, and I am ready to do anything you would like me to do in order to avoid contact with a person disagreeable to you. But vis-a-vis Duckworth you must represent me with full powers.

Ever affectly yrs

J. Conrad.

To Allan Monkhouse

Text TS Rylands; Unpublished

[letterhead: Oswalds]

Feb. 8th. 1924.

My dear Sir.[2]

I have received to-day a press cutting of the Manchester Guardian's Book Notes of Feb. 1st. I feel I must thank you for the reference to my work with which it opens[3] – even if I must convey it to you by means of a machine. I am especially touched by your kindness to him of whom for many years I used to think as "my poor Nostromo". At his first appearance the public had no use for him. Some newspapers (but that may have been the publisher's

---

[1] I.e. the *translatlantic review*.

[2] Allan Noble Monkhouse (1858–1936) was the dramatic and literary critic of the *Manchester Guardian* from 1902 until his retirement in 1932. A dramatist and novelist in his own right, he developed extensive contacts in the literary and theatrical worlds, and several of his plays were produced at Annie Horniman's Gaiety Theatre. His works include *Books and Plays* (1894), *Four Tragedies* (1913), and *Essays of Today and Yesterday* (1926).

[3] This instalment of Monkhouse's regular column in the *Manchester Guardian Weekly*, 'A Bookman's Notes', was devoted chiefly to Anthony Trollope, but also mentioned Conrad, noting that 'Mr. Conrad is one of those who improve on a second reading, or a third; I reproach myself that on a first reading of "Nostromo" I didn't praise it eagerly and strongly enough' (p. 92).

fault) failed to notice him at all. He has come since into his own, and that wound – for I was really hurt – has been healed a long time ago.

But I am profoundly touched by the generosity of your expressed regret. That indeed is a high tribute, too great almost, perhaps, for any work of man in any art where achievement must always fall short of the intention.

I read with the greatest pleasure what you say of Trollope. I made his acquaintance full thirty years ago and made up my mind about his value then, as a writer of remarkable talent for imaginative rendering of the social life of his time, with its activities and interests and incipient thoughts. I watched him coming into his own again with very great pleasure, and I agree with you as to the merits of the Barsetshire novels. His gift of intimate communion with the reader is very remarkable there. It is hardly less so in the sphere of London parliamentary and social life which is the subject of another cycle, if I may call it, of his novels.[1] I was considerably impressed with them in the early eighties, when I chanced upon a novel entitled "Phineas Finn".[2] I haven't seen them since, to tell you the truth, but I have preserved a strong impression of a notable gallery of portraits rendered with that same intimacy of technique (if technique is the word) in which I believe the secret of his fascination lies.

I may be wrong however. I have neither the equipment nor the temperament of a literary critic; and, generally, my feelings of repulsion or sympathy are so strong and so "primitive" that I dare not venture on criticism. But in the case of Trollope my sympathy is not tempestuous. It is quiet and deep, like his view of life around him. I don't mean to say that Trollope was very deep; but I question whether in his time, in a highly organised, if not complex, society, there were any great depths for him to sound. Like the young men of the Georgian era he was very much a man of his time and with a personal, obviously sincere, liking for mankind.

Reverting for a moment to "Nostromo". Have you got a copy of the edition which contains the Preface?[3] If you have not please drop me a pc. with the word "no" on it, and it will be a great pleasure for me to send it to you. The Preface is not important – but it is intimate. The text is the same, except for a few corrections bearing on the mere phrasing; but I refrained scrupulously from all second thoughts, from all additions, from all "modifications" however slight. A paragraph of about ten lines has been

---

[1] The six-volume 'Palliser' or 'Parliamentary' novels.

[2] *Phineas Finn, The Irish Member* (serialised 1867–8; book 1869). In the fourth chapter of *A Personal Record*, Conrad remembers Trollope in connection with his own first literary attempts: 'I cannot say what I read on the evening before I began to write myself. I believe it was a novel, and it is quite possible that it was one of Anthony Trollope's novels' (p. 71).

[3] The second English edition of the novel, published by Dent in 1918.

taken bodily out, for the simple reason that reading it after ten or twelve years I could find no intelligible meaning in it.[1]

My over-anxiety, passing often into a weary restlessness, while writing that book, is responsible for a frequent clumsiness of expression. I can look back at that time now with a smile. Not only the youngsters have their illusions about the importance of their work, which are ridiculous and also a little touching. I was 46 – but as an author still young – and I thought N. a big undertaking.

With grateful regards

Very sincerely Yours

J. Conrad

To Jacques Copeau

Text MS Texas; Unpublished

[letterhead: Oswalds]
9. Febr. 1924

Cher Monsieur.[2]

Mille remerci[e]ments pour la *Maison Natale* que Vous avez eu la bonté de m'envoyer.[3]

Je viens d'en finir la lecture et je suis fortement impression[n]é par Votre manière si simple et si effective de traiter le sujet le plus difficile, je pense, dans la region spirituelle. Acceptez mes félicitations et mes remerci[e]ments pour l'exquis plaisir que j'ai trouvé dans la lecture de la pièce.

Votre fidèle admirateur

Joseph Conrad.

---

[1] Keith Carabine discusses the substantial cuts and other changes made for the second English edition in his World's Classics edition of *Nostromo* (Oxford University Press, 1984), pp. xxxiii–xxxiv and notes. By taking the first English edition as his copy-text, Cedric Watts (Dent Everyman, 1995) gives the opportunity to read the novel as early readers knew it.

[2] The actor, director, theorist, and playwright Jacques Copeau (1879–1949) was one of the most important figures in modern French theatre. Together with André Gide and others, he founded the *Nouvelle Revue Française* in 1909 and in 1913 launched the innovative Théâtre du Vieux-Colombier, whose acting school he directed from 1921 to 1925. He adapted Dostoevsky's *The Brothers Karamazov* for the stage, and played the part of Mikulin in Marc Allégret's 1936 film version of *Under Western Eyes*.

[3] One of the last pieces to be given there, Copeau's three-act play *La Maison natale* started its run at the Vieux-Colombier on 18 December 1923. It was published in English as *The House into Which We Are Born* (New York: Theatre Arts, 1924). The *Maison* of the title is both ancestral dwelling and family business; the senior member of the family is a visionary, locked in unwilling conflict with his son-in-law, a tyrannical and philistine manager, who, for all his claims to know how the world works, ruins both family and firm.

Dear Sir,

Many thanks for *La Maison natale,* which you have so kindly sent me.

I have just finished reading it and am greatly impressed by the simple and effective way you treat what I consider the most difficult subject in the realm of the spirit. Please accept my congratulations and my thanks for the exquisite pleasure I have found in reading the play.

Your faithful admirer,

Joseph Conrad.

To Alfred A. Knopf

Text MS Texas; Unpublished

[Oswalds]

9. Febry '24

My dear M[r] Knopf.

Pardon this scrap of paper – the belated answer to your request – and the perfectly sincere statement that I am quite unable to do what You ask me to do. I ought to have said unfit rather.

The fact is I do not understand G. wholly.[1] I could say nothing of value from "the public" point of view in a concise form – or, I fear, in any other form.

My wife joins me in kindest [regards] to Mrs Knopf[2] and Yourself

Yours faithfully

J. Conrad.

To Eric S. Pinker

Text TS/MS Berg; Unpublished

Oswalds.

Feb. 9th. 1924.

Dearest Eric.

You resume[3] the situation correctly in saying that we are "committed to Duckworth on terms mentioned, but that details of agreement remain matters of negotiation." I regret I let you in for the situation by my

---

[1] Galsworthy, who had been a Knopf author for many years? If so, Conrad may be assuming that friendship and comprehension do not always go together, or simply declining yet another demand on his time. In an essay on his friend first published in 1906, Conrad observes: 'one perceives how difficult it is to get hold of Mr. Galsworthy's work. He gives you no opening' (*Last Essays,* p. 125).

[2] Blanche Knopf (née Wolf, 1894–1966) married Knopf in 1916. Actively engaged as a publisher, she ran the European side of the business after the Second World War and in 1957 became its president.

[3] A Gallicism: *résumer* means 'to sum up'.

light-minded acceptance of Hueffer's telegram. The affair seemed to me trifling. Apparently nothing is.

Yes, decidedly F. N. D. ought to be consulted; for the truth is that, whether we like it or not, he is the principal element in the whole scheme of handling my works. He has the largest field, and I think the sincerest regard for my interests with due regard to his own business, which last is perfectly legitimate. There is also the "personal element" which has its value.

Things here are not really improved but they are, I may say, *stabilised* for the present.

I see F[isher] U[nwin] is apparently advertising now in the magazines, the daily press having a rest. Fourth Large Impression is the slogan.[1]

Last mail's letter from F. N. D. advertises his departure for the Bahamas. Mentions also speedy dispatch to you of the details of the new publication-scheme, which it seems is something in the nature of a volume of collected short stories. I should imagine he really means a volume of Selected S. S. I have my private views on that subject. But we shall see.

I hope you are all well at home and in the office. We must get a sight of each other before you depart abroad on your escort duty.[2]

Affectly Yrs

J. C.

To Eric S. Pinker
Text MS and TSS Berg;[3] Unpublished

[Oswalds]
12. 2. 24.

Dearest Eric.

You'll find enclosed here my letter to you in answer to D'y's scheme par. by par. *and* my counter-scheme for your information.

Together with duplicates of the above for transmission to G[arden] City. The triplicate I keep for myself.

Your covering letter need only say – "This is what C writes to me with the request to transmit this duplicate to you. I think he is right." As to their scheme it is definitely NO.

Even as to my own I am reluctant. And if they accept it I hope you will stick out for terms as full as possible for a $5 book. I am justifiable since I propose to give *unpublished text* to the amount of 5000 w. We know that I can get £250 any time for that text alone.

---

[1] For *The Rover.*
[2] He was accompanying his wife on a trip to the South of France for the sake of her health.
[3] The cover letter is MS, the enclosures are TSS.

My idea would be to have nothing of the sort in England.

Funny people. They objected to the ill[ustrate]d edition of M of the Sea on the ground that the market would be full of various Conrads – and now they want to sho[o]t out this sort of thing on it!

I feel that it may be dangerous for the Concord E^d but I daresay they thought it out.

Many thanks for your exposé of the F. M. H[ueffer][1] situation.

I am sorry I've saddled you with this silly situation. For it is silly. And I was too when I answered that cursed wire.[2]

Affectly Yrs

J. Conrad.

Oswalds,
Bishopsbourne.
Feb. 12th. 24

My dear Eric,

I am writing you without loss of time on the matter submitted by the Garden City in their letter of Feb. 1st. 1924: SHORT STORIES by JOSEPH CONRAD.

1. The first observation that I want to make is that reasoning from analogy is dangerous. What is successful with Stevenson may not be so successful with Joseph Conrad,[3] if only on the ground that Stevenson is a virtuoso of style in picturesque presentation, whereas Joseph Conrad is much less of a literary man and, in any case, is a very different person.

2. The volume as planned by the list is much too big in my opinion. Moreover the list is wrong since it includes, for a reason I can't understand, HEART OF DARKNESS, which is 42,000 words, while the basis of the list itself is that of stories under 20,000.

3. The principle of including all the stories under 20,000 words is incomprehensible to me. It is like hanging all the pictures of a certain size together. I definitely negative that sort of classification.

4. I will certainly not ask Mr Muirhead Bone to write any Preface. He has got his own work to do. And frankly I don't think that Mr J. C.'s work wants any sort of introduction, as literature. But I admit that if such a volume of short stories is collected an explanation of the principle of collection may be made in the form of a Preface. My counter-scheme provides for that.

---

[1] Ford's name in the days of their collaboration.

[2] See Conrad's letter to Pinker of 4 February.

[3] In 1923, the New York publishers C. Scribner's Sons had brought out *The Short Stories of Robert Louis Stevenson*, a volume of 540 pages. For Conrad's long-held conviction that Stevenson was 'super-literary', see, e.g., *Letters*, 5, p. 257.

5. On the advantage from a selling point of view of publishing a volume of selected stories I am not competent to form an opinion; but considering the issue of a book at $5 at Christmas time (for presentation purposes, I presume) I submit that my counter-scheme as enclosed here will be better value, as "sanctioned by the author" and with some five thousand words of unpublished text in the shape of a Preface, which I would then certainly write myself.

6. Not having seen the dummy I can express no opinion on it, but it seems to me all right from description, and this matter I would leave entirely to the years-long experience and the good taste of the firm.

Always faithfully yours,

J. Conrad.

PS. This letter is typed in triplicate, of which this is No. 1.[1]

In triplicate N° 1.

MR. CONRAD'S SCHEME.

It is founded on the following basic considerations:

a. That a volume of 500 pages of Short Stories written at different times, in different moods, in different styles, will look and feel unreadable, and like a jumble of things in a box – from a literary and artistic point of view.

b. That to tear such a mass of matter out of the solid body of work having its own character and purpose may not turn out a good commercial proposition, for by its very bulk it may destroy the curiosity as to the rest of his whole production, instead of whetting the curiosity and creating a desire for a better acquaintance.

c. That a certain if not very obvious unity of purpose while associated with variety of treatment and subject is likely to appeal to the taste and even the feelings of the readers better than a mere heap of sixteen or seventeen stories, (each fairly long) and liable to tire out an ordinary person by the change of mood and the point of view.

d. That a book meant, I take it, for a Christmas trade and for purposes of being giving* as a present to various kinds of people, can be made to look worth the money by a larger margin and general get-up in all its other details without containing upwards of 200,000 words.

---

[1] The top copy of the letter and second carbon (No. 3) are at the Berg; the first carbon (No. 2) was sent to Garden City and is now at Princeton. 'Mr. Conrad's Scheme', also typed in triplicate, begins on a separate page.

Guiding himself by the considerations c and d Mr Conrad proposes a volume of about 124,000 words, with the Preface of say 4000 more. He has selected therefore eight stories which all deal specifically with seamen in their various relations, professional and with people ashore.

The book is to be divided into two parts, each containing four stories as follows: —

SHORT STORIES BY JOSEPH CONRAD

Part I	Part II
YOUTH	TYPHOON
THE SECRET SHARER	BECAUSE OF THE DOLLARS
THE BRUTE	THE PARTNER
TO-MORROW	THE INN OF THE TWO WITCHES

The guiding idea of this division is: Part First deals with young men; the triumphant feeling in the struggle with the sea (Youth); the sense of comradeship of the sea between two young seamen (S. Sharer); the above strictly professional. The other two involve women and shore relations: a young seaman losing the girl to whom he was engaged (Brute); and "To-morrow" giving the strength of appeal of a roving life.

Of course those stories have more than that in them, but certainly they may be looked upon in the above light.

Part Two deals with mature men of the sea: Capt. McWhirr wrestling with the Typhoon, strictly professional; The Dollars, character study of a humane seaman; The Partner presents a seaman victim of a plot concocted by people ashore; and finally the Inn is based subtly on the fidelity of the old seaman Tom to his young officer, which seems even to endure after death.

The above ideas will be developed in a Preface of five or more pages which will be the new matter of the volume and will give it a certain authority and individual value.[1]

The volume *should not* be called STORIES OF THE SEA, for in truth those are studies of seamen.

---

[1] In his Preface to *The Shorter Tales of Joseph Conrad*, published posthumously in October and collected in *Last Essays*, Conrad recapitulates the arguments made in the correspondence, first insisting on the integrity of each collection, then offering a rationale for the selection he has made.

To Allan Monkhouse

Text MS Rylands; Unpublished

[Oswalds]

13. 2. 24.

Dear Mr Monkhouse

Here is the book.[1]

I was delighted to see your name at the end of Your friendly letter. One never knows what the next gift from the Gods may be.

I await with impatience the promised copy of your play.[2] How good of you to think of sending it to me.

In haste

Yours most coridially*

J. Conrad.

To Eric S. Pinker

Text TS Berg; Unpublished

Oswalds,

Feb. 14th. 1924.

Dearest Eric

Thank you for your letter in which you say you backed up my counter-scheme.

Your remark about reduction of bulk has caused me to write to Everitt[3] and say that should bulk be important *Falk* could be included in my list.

This would bring my scheme well over 170,000 words.

Garden City scheme was 205,000, but their list of "under 20,000 word stories" included, perhaps by mistake, *H. of Darkness* which is 42,000 words! Fancy making that mistake.

I suppose you have nothing against me writing a special preface?

Ever Yrs

J. C.

We return dummy.[4] I like the get-up very much and have said so in my short note to Sam.

---

[1] The promised second edition of *Nostromo*.
[2] Probably Monkhouse's war drama, *The Conquering Hero: A Play in Four Acts* (Ernest Benn, 1923).
[3] Sam Everitt, at Doubleday's.   [4] Of *The Shorter Tales of Joseph Conrad?*

To Ford Madox Ford

Text TS Yale; TS carbon Berg; Unpublished

[letterhead: Oswalds]
Feb. 15th. 1924.

My dear Ford,

I regret very much that I can not sign the proposed agreement as I am bound by a definite understanding with my American publishers.[1] The whole matter of this publishing contract must be revised and I have put it in the hands of J. B. Pinker & Son.

I assure you that I regret immensely if this gives you any annoyance, but your original wire on which I based my consent said nothing about American rights but only mentioned Duckworth.

Eric Pinker is now in negotiation with Duckworth, and you will be informed of every step taken, in due course.

Yours in haste

J. Conrad

P.S. I have sent the agreement on to J. B. Pinker & Son, together with a copy of this letter, as they must be advised of all that happens in order to straighten up this affair with advantage to us both.

To Eric S. Pinker

Text TS Berg; Unpublished

Oswalds.
Feb. 15th. 1924.

My dear (long suffering) Eric

This is a new development which I have met provisionally by a letter to F. M. F. a copy of which is enclosed.[2]

Perhaps you will communicate with him and tell him to suspend all his activities. I suggest you saying to him that "Conrad's affairs in America are too important to be disregarded." Likewise perhaps it would be good policy if you assured him "that though J. C. could not sign Duckworth's agreement as it stood (with the clause of American rights) and can not sign this one, any new arrangement arrived at will be on terms no less than those offered in his wire."

The idea at the back of my head is that if the terms are less we could always make up to him what he expected by diminishing my proportion. Of course

---

[1] On 13 February, Ford had sent Conrad an agreement with Henry Holt & Co. of New York for a deluxe limited edition of *The Nature of a Crime* (Stape and Knowles, p. 236).
[2] A carbon of the preceding letter.

you will consider the discretion of all this. In any case do please communicate with him with reasonable friendliness and conciliatory firmness.

Ever Yrs

J. C.

To Robert de Traz
Text MS Favre; Unpublished

[letterhead: Oswalds]
15.2.24

Cher Monsieur et Confrère[1]

Merci de Votre bonne lettre.

C'est avec le plus grand regret que j'ai a Vous dire que je suis obligé de renoncer au projet de venir a Genève. C'est impossible cette année-ci.

Je vous assure qu'il m'en coûte d'arriver a cette decision. Mais c'est un cas de force majeure.

Remerciez je Vous en prie tous les bons amis de Genève pour leur bien-veillantes intentions a mon égard. J'y suis très sensible.

Je vous assure qu'il m'est très penible de renoncer au plaisir de faire votre connaissance cette année. Mais ce n'est que partie remise j'espère.

Mes cordiales salutations.

Bien à Vous

J Conrad

Dear Sir and Colleague

Thank you for your good letter.

I deeply regret to say that I must give up the idea of coming to Geneva. It's impossible this year.

This is a difficult decision, rest assured, but a case of *force majeure*.

---

[1] This must be a writer from Geneva with a penchant for Conrad and a group of enthusiastic colleagues. Robert de Traz (1884–1951) matches the description well. Born in Paris to a family of Swiss hoteliers, he began his literary career with *L'Homme dans le rang* (1913), a memoir of his life in the Swiss army. A passionate francophile, he became a war correspondent for the *Journal de Genève*, reporting from Verdun and the Argonne. His novel *Fiançailles* (1922) was 'crowned' by *Le Figaro* and awarded the Schiller Prize in Switzerland; his short stories appeared in the *Revue de Paris* and the *Mercure de France*. He edited the *Revue de Genève*, a significant international journal, from 1920 to 1930 – the whole of its run. The *Revue* published translations of 'The Partner' (July 1920), 'The Tale' (March 1923), 'The Brute' (February 1924), and 'Freya of the Seven Isles' (October–November 1928). Traz contributed a 'compte-rendu' of *Within the Tides* to the June 1923 issue (p. 796). He was well known to Jean-Aubry, who stayed with him in November 1923 (Jean-Aubry to Conrad, 20 November, MS Yale).

Pray thank all the good friends in Geneva for their kind intentions on my behalf. I'm very grateful.

I assure you that it pains me greatly to give up the pleasure of making your acquaintance this year. But this, I hope, is only a pleasure postponed.

With my cordial greetings.

Ever yours

J Conrad

To Eric S. Pinker
Text TS/MS Berg; Unpublished

PLEASE READ THE OTHER LETTER FIRST[1]
most secret

Oswalds.

Feb. 17th. [1924]

My dear Eric.

After sending you the copy of the letter I wrote to Ford I received a further communication from the man, who seems to be suffering from the idea that everybody in the world has insulted him.[2] One would think it a mania if one did not suspect that there is a purpose in it. I regret I can not send the letter to you, because I can't find it. I am afraid it dropped into the waste-paper basket and got carried off, but I had made a note of the material points which, you will perceive from my enclosed answer to him I am sending it* for your perusal and opinion. If you agree with my point of view that a small sacrifice is worth getting rid of the damnable "incubus" of that rotten "Crime"-imbroglio, then you will just post it for me; and as I rather think that the second paragraph of my letter to him will really reach the root of all his "cussedness," you will admit that the concession is worth while. In fact it is cheap. And what a luxury it would be to get rid of his nonsense!

I presume I can allow myself that luxury. After all, my dear fellow, I make myself responsible only for your commission, or, to be precise, for half your commission.

Apart from that point if there is anything in the letter you do not like you will of course point it out to me and the letter could be amended.

Please note that the assumption must be that you have not seen it. You will admit that I have dissembled my rage successfully.[3] I can't bear the idea

---

[1] The one to Ford, a copy of which Conrad sent to Pinker. The heading '*PLEASE READ*' is typed; '*most secret*', written by hand.
[2] Ford's letter of 14 February (MS Yale).   [3] The rest of the letter to Pinker is in MS.

of you being plagued with that bosh by my fault. That however will end it. His oppressively silly letter has at the end a honeyed phrase "of course I will defer to your wishes whatever it may cost me" or something to that effect.

Ever affectly Yrs

J. C.

Copy

Oswalds,
Bishopsbourne,
Kent.
February 18, 1924.

Dear Ford,

I am in receipt of your letter of the 14th inst. As you say so definitely that you can have nothing to do either with Doubleday or apparently anybody connected with my affairs what am I to say to you? It looks as if we had got into a blind alley. Considering however that I accepted your suggestion of Duckworth telegraphically without the slightest delay (though I have two publishers now, in London, who are naturally jealous of their rights and will have to be pacified) I venture to hope that you will give effect rather to the kindly declaration at the close of your letter.

As to the point: "that Duckworth would pay us the money *at once* and without commission", I would suggest in all friendliness that in consideration of you putting up with the requirements of my position vis a vis my publishers and the delay of publication, I should pay you at the end of March, 1924, your proportion of Duckworth's *original* offer (£150) in full – that is, seventy-five pounds.

With the proviso that should J. B. Pinker & Son, who really must act as my agents (as they have had all my affairs for twenty years in hand) manage to make a better bargain than the above (£150) you should have your share of such a surplus paid to you, without any deduction whatever, on the day of publication.

Pray consider this suggestion in the same spirit of fairness which prompts me to make it.

This understanding may be strictly entre nous, if you prefer; but in any case if you think it at all acceptable it would be sufficient for you to write a formal letter to J. B. Pinker & Son simply saying that "I have had a letter from Conrad which has induced me to remove my objections." Just that and no more.

The only alternative I can suggest would be, perhaps, to drop the matter altogether for a time, out of regard for your feelings towards people concerned, which not being of the "material order" would have to be regarded as predominant. As I accepted the proposal simply out of regard for your expressed wish I am ready to let the matter drop if your feeling tends that way.

Yours,

(Signed) J. CONRAD.

To Allan Monkhouse
Text MS Rylands; Unpublished

[letterhead: Oswalds]
19. 2. 24

Dear Mr Monkhouse

The play arrived yesterday and I read it in the evening (proper time for plays) with the greatest appreciation. It is full of truth, dramatic and human, presented with a sympathy and with a remarkable "justness" of tone which has appealed to me strongly.

Some day soon – if you permit me – I'll send you the copy so that you may write your name and mine on the flyleaf.

Yours sincerely

J. Conrad

PS Did I say that I can have no possible objection to you printing what I said of Trollope if you think it worth while.

To Eric S. Pinker
Text MS Berg; Unpublished

[Oswalds]
19. 2. 24.

Dearest Eric.

Thanks for yours of yesterday. I am glad You approved my epistle to the Ananias of Our Age.[1]

We will be in town on Wed. the 27 inst. to keep an app^t with Sir Robert. The other doctor will attend too. I think Jessie would like to stay till Sat and see a few people.

---

[1] I.e., Ford. In the Biblical narrative, Ananias gives Christ's apostles only part of the proceeds from a sale of land but pretends to have given them everything. When Peter rebukes him for lying 'not . . . unto men, but unto God', Ananias falls down dead (Acts 5.1–6).

Perhaps you'll drop [by] to lunch on the 27. 1.30? Jessie would be amused to hear us curse FMF for a whole half-hour.[1]

Our love to your wife and wishes for a pleasant journey.

I am at work.[2]

Affectly Yrs

J. C.

Thanks for advice of pay[t] to bank.

To Roman Dyboski

Text MS Berg;[3] facsimile *Poland*, August 1926; Krzyżanowski 78; Najder 295

[letterhead: Oswalds]
22. Feby '24

My dear Sir.[4]

I am sorry I am so late in thanking You for the 2 vols of Polish Literature which I have read with the highest appreciation – and for the brochure on the Religious Element in Polish National Life which told me many things I did not know before.

I can hardly express my sense of the good and patriotic work your* are doing by your publications in English, so attractive in matter and style. People here know very little of Poland – and I am afraid that there is not much *general* sympathy for the new state. But all that arises from sheer ignorance which only concise and perspicuous expositions of historical truth, can gradually dispel. Pray accept my warm and most respectful regards and believe me

most sincerely yours

J. Conrad.

---

[1] As she makes clear in *Joseph Conrad and His Circle* (New York: Dutton, 1935), pp. 112–16, 131–2, 138–9, Jessie Conrad loathed him.

[2] On what was published as Part III, Chapter 3 of *Suspense*.

[3] The original is in English.

[4] The Polish literary historian Roman Dyboski (1883–1945) lectured at King's College, University of London, and helped to define the literary traditions of the reconstituted Polish state. His *Periods of Polish Literary History* (1923) and *Modern Polish Literature* (1924) were published by Oxford University Press. Dyboski also published studies of Shakespeare, Milton, and Byron, and became Professor of Comparative Literature at the Jagiellonian University, Cracow. His wartime experiences were recorded in *Seven Years in Russia and Siberia (1915–1921)*. For his account of meeting Conrad at the Polish Legation in June 1924, see Najder (1983), pp. 262–6.

To John Galsworthy

Text MS Forbes; J-A, 2, 339[1]

[letterhead: Oswalds]

22. 2. '24.

Dearest Jack

We are so glad of Dear Ada's recovery from her bronchial trouble.[2] I've heard so much of the perfections of the Portuguese climate that I thought colds were unknown there. You must have caught them from the English visitors. I won't have one of my last illusions destroyed.

Your joint copy of the Rover (1st ed^{on}) was awaiting you here. Somehow I could not get anything definite about your address from Eric. I'll send it now to Hampstead.[3]

I am glad you think well of *The Rover*. I have wanted for a long time to do a seaman's "return" (before my own departure) and this seemed a possible peg to hang it on. The reception was good – and so were the sales – but when the book came out I was too seedy to care. I had about 10 weeks of [a] pretty bad time. My recovery was swift – but my confidence has been badly shaken. However I have begun to work a little – on my runaway novel. I call it "runaway" because I've been after it for two years (The Rover is a mere interlude) without being able to overtake it.[4] The end seems as far as ever! It's like a chase in a nightmare – weird and exhausting.

Your news that you have finished a novel[5] brings me a bit of comfort. So there are novels that *can* be finished – then why not mine? Of course I see "fiction" advertised in the papers – heaps of it. But publisher's announcements seem to me mere phantasms of my own disordered brain. I don't believe in their reality – which of course proves that I am not hopelessly insane – yet.

My congratulations my dearest fellow. *And* a short story too![6] I'll have to write two presently (to complete a vol:)[7] and I am incapable of finding a subject – even for one. Not a shadow of a subject!

---

[1] In the final paragraph, Jean-Aubry omits 'But age is stealing on her too, and'.

[2] Ada Galsworthy's health was not robust; see J. H. Stape, 'From "The Most Sympathetic of Friends": John Galsworthy's Letters to Joseph Conrad, 1906–1923', *Conradiana*, 32.3 (Fall 2000), 228–45. The Galsworthys had been wintering in Estoril, on the Portuguese coast.

[3] Where they lived at Grove Lodge.

[4] Conrad began writing *Suspense* more than three years earlier, in the summer of 1920.

[5] *The White Monkey*, the first instalment of the second Forsyte trilogy. The serial ran in *Nash's Magazine* (UK) and *Scribner's Magazine* (USA) from April to December 1924.

[6] The only one Galsworthy wrote in 1924 was 'The Water', a story set in the American West and published by the *Strand Magazine* in October. He did not include it in *Caravan: The Assembled Tales of John Galsworthy* (1925).

[7] The collection published posthumously as *Tales of Hearsay*.

— Poor Jessie suffers from some more painful symptoms in the operated limb. She's very crippled – but still cheerful in her equable way. But age is stealing on her too, and I see now and then something like the shadow of mortal weariness on her face. As to John he wrote me a long letter in French the other day – quite good. He studies at the Berlitz Inst^e draws at the Ecole pratique des Beaux-Arts, and fences 3 times a week – not to speak of driving the Br Consul's car, having teas (and, no doubt, improving discourses) with the British Chaplain, and conversing with the Bost Family (eleven of them).[1] The recital of his activities has made me quite giddy – so I end with our dear love to you both.

Ever Yrs

J Conrad

To G. Jean-Aubry
Text MS Yale; Unpublished

[Oswalds]
24. 2. 24

Cher Jean.

J'espère que tout est bien avec vous.

Nous serons à Londres Mercredi. Mais Pinker déjeunera avec nous – donc je ne VS invite pas ce jour là. Il y aura du monde pour le thé et le soir Sir Robert viendra officiel[le]ment et peut-être restera pour diner.

Il nous tarde de VS voir – mais ce ne sera que Jeudi que NS pourrons VS avoir bien a nous. Venez déjeuner. 1.30. Faites nous savoir si ça VS va

Votre vieux

Conrad

Dear Jean,

I hope all is well with you.

We shall be in London on Wednesday. But Pinker will be lunching with us – so I won't be able to invite you for that day. There will be people to tea and in the evening Sir Robert is paying an official visit and may stay for dinner.

We are eager to see you – but we can't have you all to ourselves till Thursday. Come for lunch at 1:30. Let us know if that suits you.

Your old

Conrad

---

[1] The Bosts had seven daughters and three sons. Pierre (1901–75) was now living in Paris, where his play *L'Imbécile* had been staged at the Théâtre du Vieux-Colombier in October 1923; he later wrote novels, and scripts for the film-makers Autant-Lara, Marcel Camus, Clément, Pabst, and Tavernier. The youngest son, Jacques-Laurent (1916–90) became an intimate of Sartre and de Beauvoir.

To Eric S. Pinker

Text TS Berg; Unpublished

Oswalds.
Feb. 24th. 1924.

Dearest Eric

Thank you very much for the account so carefully brought to date. It has inspired in me several reflections, whether salutary or not I can not say.

I won't say any more here as we are going to meet soon. I shall probably come up in the car with Jessie unless the day is very cold, in which case I will come up by train.

Ever Your

J C

To Ford Madox Ford

Text TS Yale; Unpublished

[letterhead: Oswalds]
March 2nd. 1924.

Dear Ford

I am very appreciative of your falling in with the requirements of my position in the matter of publishing the collaborated fragment of "The Nature of a Crime;"[1] and it is understood that at the end of this month you will receive from me a cheque for £75 as your proportion of the terms offered originally by Duckworth. It is only just (as I introduced the agent into this transaction) that I should pay whatever commission there will be. If the proceeds on book publication exceed the original £150 mentioned in your telegram, the surplus shall be divided between us, your share being paid to you free of commission.

However, I do not anticipate that we shall get much more, if at all. The publication can not possibly take place before September.

I answer in type because your letter found me in bed too. I am very sorry to hear of all your worries in connection with the Transatlantic Review.[2] I hope that you will get over these difficulties and secure a prosperous future for the T. R.

Yours

J. Conrad

---

[1] Ford had accepted Conrad's terms in a letter of 22 February (TS Yale).

[2] In his letter, Ford complained chiefly of the 'gross insolence' with which Pinker had treated him when they met in London on 4 February, but exhorted Conrad to 'let it slide if it becomes troublesome to yourself . . . As long as I do not have to correspond with him I shall probably forget his existence.' Ford went on to describe his problems funding the *transatlantic review*, which he had been running 'out of [his] own pocket' and would lose by the end of the year.

To Richard Curle

Text MS Indiana; Curle 142

[Oswalds]
4 Mch. 24.

Dearest Dick.

I had a letter from Sir Hugh Clifford. He sends me six copies of his address to the Legislative Council.[1] One of them I retain and the other five I am sending to You as requested by H. C. *with his love*. He asks you to give one to your brother, one to Col Ingles[2] and the other two to any one you may know who is interested in African affairs – as a counterblast to the nasty fairy tales which my Lord of the Western Isles[3] has been uttering lately about the Colony.[4] H. C. will arrive about end March. The report is very interesting.

---

[1] *Address to the Legislative Council of Nigeria* (Lagos: Government Printer, 1923). Clifford was Governor of Nigeria from 1919 to 1925. This address was given at the council's inaugural meeting on 31 October 1923. The occasion was significant. This was a deliberative body that, unlike the old Nigerian Council, represented all three sections of the colony (Lagos, and the Protectorates of Northern and Southern Nigeria), and, although the franchise required a substantial income, some of its elected members were Africans from Lagos or Calabar. Clifford had strongly advocated these reforms (which in the case of the vote followed recent precedent in the Gold Coast and Sierra Leone). He offered his listeners a mixture of admonition and encouragement: 'In a country such as Nigeria, which in too many of its areas has not yet emerged from barbarism, a strong and within limits an autocratic Government is essential . . . the duty which before all others this Council owes to Nigeria and to its people is that of upholding the standards and principles upon which good and efficient government is based; of forming, educating and leading public opionion along sound and rational lines; of fearlessly condemning all that is lawless and dishonest; and of championing the thing that is right, no matter whether it chance to be popular or unpopular' (p. 4).

[2] 'My brother, J. H. Curle, and Colonel Ingles had travelled out to Nigeria in the same ship with Sir Hugh Clifford' (Curle's note). Curle's older brother James Herbert Curle (1870–1943) was a traveller and author of autobiographical works including *The Shadow-Show* (1912), *This World of Ours* (1921), and *To-day and To-morrow: The Testing Period of the White Race* (1926). For *The Shadow-Show*, see also the letter to Richard Curle of 23 August 1923. John Darnley Ingles (1872–1957) had served with the Devonshire Regiment in South Africa and Flanders.

[3] William Hesketh Lever (1851–1925; 1st Viscount Leverhulme), soap manufacturer and philanthropist, had extensive business interests in Africa and had recently visited Nigeria. Conrad's use of his title may allude to a controversy in 1923 about his being granted letters patent for the title Viscount Leverhulme of the Western Isles in the Counties of Inverness and Ross and Cromarty.

[4] Leverhulme, whose companies depended on supplies of Nigerian palm oil, denounced the administration of Nigeria at the AGM of Lever Brothers on 12 April 1923 and at the AGM of the Niger Company on 21 August; he returned to the attack in 1924 and 1925 (see, e.g., *The Times*, 24 April 1925, p. 20). He claimed that the colonial government (headed by Clifford) was as autocratic as that of British North America in the eighteenth century, insatiable in its desire to raise taxes and feckless in spending the proceeds. Another cause of his Lordship's libertarian wrath was the policy that allowed indigenous Nigerians to buy land, while white Britons could only acquire leases. Clifford devoted nine pages of his 1924 *Address to the Legislative Council*, delivered on 11 February, to rebutting Leverhulme's charges. He accused his assailant of taking statistics out of historical context and argued that, far from being irresponsible

He gives me Ap 25 or May 2 as dates for a week end visit. I suppose You will join us. No hurry to fix it yet.

Ever yours

J. Conrad.

PS If you have already a copy perhaps Wise would like this.

To Eric S. Pinker
Text MS Berg; Unpublished

[Oswalds]
Wedny [5 March 1924][1]

Dear E.

I return the Duck'th agreement.[2] I like the 7-years clause and the reservation as to coll^d editions.

Ever Your

J. C.

To G. Jean-Aubry
Text MS Yale; *L. fr.* 196

[Oswalds]
7. 3. 24.

Mon cher Jean.

Nous regrettons beaucoup![3] Enfin!

Je vais patienter jusqu'au weekend prochain. Mais la semaine prochaine Curle sera là tandis que cette semaine-ci nous aurons èté* seuls.

Il y a au Lond. Mercury un article sur l'ensemble de mon œuvre par E. Shanks.[4] Il est court mais très sympathique ou, du moins, appreciatif. Il m'a

---

extravagances, public works such as railways, improved roads, and new schools would benefit Nigeria – and thus the companies that operated there.

[1] Dated '3/24' in another hand. The text of the agreement with Duckworth is dated '*March: 1924*' in Miss Hallowes's notebook (*Documents*, p. 233), and the recent correspondence with Pinker shows that Conrad was eager to lay this matter to rest.

[2] For *The Nature of a Crime*.

[3] Jean-Aubry had written the day before to say that he was too busy to visit that week: 'je mène en ce moment une vie de chartreux n'allant nulle part et ne voyant que des livres, du papier et de l'encre' (MS Yale).

[4] Edward Buxton Shanks, 'Mr. Joseph Conrad', *London Mercury*, 9 (March 1924), 502–11. Shanks (1892–1953) was himself a novelist and poet. His essay insists on Conrad's distinctiveness; more akin to Shakespeare and the Greeks than to modern novelists, he is a writer of great dramatic power, 'the novelist of situation rather than of character' (p. 508), who 'has emphasised . . . the poetic, the visionary qualities of the novel' (p. 510) and ranks as the 'great poet among English novelists' (p. 511). Moreover, he is a thinker as well as a poet and visionary; he has brought 'the

fait plaisir. J'ai hâte de voir votre article dans la Hebdomadaire.[1] Pouvez Vous m'envoyer aussi la Re[vue] de Gen[è]ve. Je suis bien content que [vous] ayez écrit a Neel. Il a besoin d'être surveillé.[2]

Jessie sends her love.

> Toujours Votre vieux
>
> Conrad

My dear Jean,

We're very sorry! Ah well!

I shall be patient until next weekend. But the following week Curle will be here, while this week we would have been alone.

The *London Mercury* has a survey of my work by E. Shanks. It is brief but very kind, or at least complimentary. I enjoyed reading it. I am eager to see your article in the *Hebdomadaire*. Can you also send me the *Revue de Genève*? I am glad to hear you've written to Neel. One needs to keep an eye on him.

Jessie sends her love.

> Ever your old
>
> Conrad

To Bruno Winawer

Text TS copy Yale;[3] *Głos*; Najder 296

> Oswalds,
> Bishopsbourne,
> Kent.
> 7th March, 1924.

My dear Sir,

I hope that you have got over your influenza. Although I didn't have it myself I was plagued by my own particular misfortune which always produces an inability to make any mental effort. C'est plus fort que moi.[4] Naturally I should have answered your kind letter long ago. I was moved to see how you had taken my proposal to heart. I am in absolute agreement with your general opinion as to how this work should be done and as to the details of

---

novel back closer to its first source of inspiration, to the impassioned contemplation of ideas' (*ibid.*).

[1] 'Joseph Conrad', *Revue Hebdomadaire*, 33.2 (23 February 1924), 439–52.

[2] Jean-Aubry's letter of the 6th reported on the translation of 'The Brute' just published in the *Revue de Genève*: 'ce n'est pas mal, avec quelques inadvertances que je vais signaler à Neel'. Perhaps to avoid embarrassing Neel, J-A reads: 'J'ai besoin d'être surveillé'.

[3] In Polish. Translation from Najder with some alterations.   [4] 'I can't help myself'.

its execution.[1] There is no need for any discussion of it between us. I can also assure you that no one has asked me and probably no one will ask me to dramatise this novel. In any case pour moi vous êtes le seul homme possible.[2]

However, I implore you to approach this work with an easy mind – not thinking about me at all and not feeling bound by any time limit – and with the conviction that should you find this work tedious there will be absolutely nothing on my part against your putting it off either for a certain time – or forever. You for your part will not hold it against me should I write to you that I feel unable to translate your play[3] into English in a manner worthy of it.

What do you think about it?

Pardon my scrawl.

With a cordial handshake

J. Conrad.

PS. Just now I am unable to write more about *Inżynier* except that I read the play with the greatest pleasure. C'est tout à fait bien![4] Thank you for having sent it.

To Conrad Hope

Text MS Wright; Unpublished

[letterhead: Oswalds]

9. 3. 24

My dear Conrad.[5]

Many thanks for your good letter. I mean to enclose a few lines in the vol. but Miss Hallowes was too prompt for me.

I am immensely comforted by the good account you give me of your father. I was on the point of making a dash at the Dingle from London the week before last but felt suddenly so unwell that I had to give up the idea. I have had generally a bad time since last November. I am now better. On the other hand my poor wife is again suffering from painful symptoms in her operated limb.

---

[1] Dramatising *The Rover*, see Conrad's letter to Pinker of 31 January.

[2] 'For me, you're the only man possible.'

[3] *R. H.*, *Inżynier* (*R. H., Engineer*), as mentioned in the PS.   [4] 'It's altogether splendid!'

[5] Conrad Hope (1890–1963), named in honour of Conrad, was the youngest child of Fountaine Hope. A motor engineer, he was the director of Candor Motors in Colchester.

I will not fail my dear Conrad to let you know of her visit to town. It will be a great delight to see you; and if your wife should be in town and inclined to visit "The Two Crocks"[1] our delight will be doubled.

Jessie joins me in my love to you both.

Ever affct yours

J. Conrad.

To Richard Curle
Text MS Indiana; Curle 143

[letterhead: Oswalds]
[10 March 1924.][2]

Many happy returns my dearest Dick. We expect to see you next week end. Meantime we shall drink your health tomorrow in "good red wine".[3]

Yours with great affection

J. Conrad.

To Eric S. Pinker
Text MS Berg; Unpublished

[Oswalds]
10. 3. 24

Dearest Eric.

Just a word to let you know that I've had a letter from G. City agreeing to *my* scheme for the Vol of Short Stories.[4]

You have heard from them too no doubt.

I cabled the suggestion that *The Witches* should be thrown out and Falk substituted; and asked for the *latest* date they are likely to require the new preface.[5]

I feel very fairly well and have got a better grip on my work.

---

[1] A 'crock' is an old broken-down horse.

[2] Curle would turn forty-one on the 11th. On the 10th, Jessie Conrad sent him a silver box for his writing-table and a birthday letter. At Conrad's request, she left room at the end for him to add his good wishes.

[3] In some versions of the Scottish ballad 'Sir Patrick Spens', 'The King sits in Dunfermline toon / Drinking the guid red wine'; in others, the wine is 'blude-red'.

[4] See Conrad's letter to Pinker of 12 February.

[5] Conrad's undated MS draft of this telegram (Yale) reads: 'Delighted with letter accepting so heartily my plan for volume of stories and submit after earnest reflection that the Inn be thrown out altogether being obviously inferior and replaced by Falk as the last story of second part. Agree with your view of not referring stories to original vols. Pray advise me latest date for delivery new preface.'

Let me just remind you of that bill (for car) £100 which will be presented at my bank on the 15 inst.

In haste

Ever Yrs

J. Conrad.

To Eric S. Pinker

Text TS/MS Berg; Unpublished

[letterhead: Oswalds]
March 12th. 1924.

My dearest Eric

Thanks for your letter of this morning which crossed mine.

Re the vol. OF SHORT STORIES BY J. C. I see that Garden City's plan is to make it a $5 book. Having regard to the new stuff it will contain (which will make it necessary for every Conrad-collector to buy it) I suggest I should have 20% on it. That is one dollar per copy. Of course I don't want to squeeze D. P. & Co.

As to the *N. of the C.* (curses on it) the terms in Sam Everett's* letter (of which you sent me a copy) are all right. We must only pay the £75 I promised F. M. F. end of this month. You know all about it; and will agree with my feeling that in this promise I must not even *seem* to fail.

I mention this because you may be away then and I may forget to remind "the office". I suggest that the covering letter should say: . . . "the sum of £75 on Mr Conrad's instructions, in accordance with your arrangement with him in the matter of "The Nature of a Crime".

What news of Your wife? Yesterday on opening the paper I had a moment's scare till I remembered that she could not have been in that train.[1]

Always affectly yrs

Conrad.

PS. This moment received wire from Everett* asking for preface middle May at latest. *Falk* will be substituted for the *Inn of Witches*. All settled now.

---

[1] *The Times* of 11 March (p. 14) reported the derailment of a train en route from Calais to the Côte d'Azur. Three English passengers were killed and several injured.

To the Royal Literary Fund

Text TS RLF; Unpublished

[letterhead: Oswalds]
March 12th. 1924

Mr Joseph Conrad regrets infinitely that he can not attend the Anniversary Dinner of the Royal Literary Fund.

Encl. £5 5–0

To Gilbert Grosvenor

Text TS Congress; Stevens

[letterhead: Oswalds]
March 13th. 1924.

Dear Mʳ Grosvenor.[1]

I have to thank you for your extremely interesting and beautifully illustrated magazine. I am very flattered to appear in it, and your letter received this morning completes my satisfaction by the news that the article has been well received.[2]

It is very good of you to propose to me a series of papers on Seamen Explorers. Nothing would give me greater pleasure than to contribute them, if I were properly equipped for the task. But the fact of the matter is that I know very little of the historical aspect of exploration; and an article worthy of your publication (on any of the individuals you name) would require a certain amount of reading for which just now I have not sufficient leisure. A general article on a period of sea exploration, in its picturesque aspect, would be easier. At present however I am plunged up to the neck in other work (which is much overdue) and want to concentrate exclusively on it.

I am sure you will understand.

Believe me, with kind regards,

very faithfully yours

J. Conrad

[1] Gilbert Hovey Grosvenor (1875–1966) was born in Istanbul. Upon graduating from Amherst College, he was invited by his father-in-law, the inventor Alexander Graham Bell, to join the National Geographic Society as editor of its magazine. He held this post from 1899 to 1954.

[2] 'Geography and Some Explorers' had been reprinted in the March issue of *National Geographic Magazine* (45, pp. 239–74).

To Aniela Zagórska

Text MS copy Yale;[1] Najder 297

Oswalds,

16 3. 24.

My dear,

[. . . .]Thank you for the magazines and books. I haven't yet dipped into the novel. I am very touched by the favourable response of the critics to the translation.[2] The article in *Robotnik*[3] is very good and has greatly pleased me.

A thousand embraces

Yours

Konrad.

To G. Jean-Aubry

Text MS Yale; *L. fr.* 196

[Oswalds]

19. 3. 24.

Très cher Jean.

Laissez que je Vs embrasse pour l'article sur J. C.[4] Je Vs assure qu'il m'a rendu heureux; et tout ce que Vs avez dit là me touche profondement.

Nous Vs attendons pour le week-end prochain. N'est-ce pas?

Le buste d'Epstein avance.[5] Ça sera plus que très-bien il me semble; mais je suis curieux de savoir ce que Vs en penserez.

Our love to you

Toujours Votre

J. C.

My very dear Jean,

Allow me to embrace you for the article on J. C. I assure you that it has made me happy; and I am deeply touched by everything you have said.

We shall expect you for this coming weekend. Agreed?

---

[1] When Aniela Zagórska translated this letter into French, she apparently omitted part of the Polish original, destroyed in 1944.

[2] Of *A Set of Six* (*Sześć opowieści* (Warsaw: Ignis, 1924)).

[3] *The Worker*, the daily of the Polish Socialist Party.

[4] 'Joseph Conrad', *Revue Hebdomadaire*, 33.2 (23 February 1924), 439–52.

[5] The sittings for Epstein announced in the letter to Doubleday of 6 December were now in progress at Oswalds. Epstein recorded his memories of the three-week-long experience in *Let There Be Sculpture: An Autobiography* (Michael Joseph, 1940), pp. 89–94. Miss Hallowes wrote to Jean-Aubry on the 17th (TS Yale), explaining that these sessions had left Conrad no time for writing letters. Epstein, however, recalls that she was taking dictation while Conrad sat for him.

The bust of Epstein is coming along. I think it will be better than very good; but I'm curious to know what you will think of it.

Our love to you

Ever your

J. C.

To Alice Gachet

Text MS Torun; *L. fr.* 197

[letterhead: Oswalds]

24.3.24

Chère Alice (vous permettez?)[1]

Je viens de recevoir Votre lettre. Je suis désolé d'avoir a Vs dire qu'il me sera impossible d'accepter l'invitation du French Club. D'abord j'en ai refusé beaucoup trop (et à Oxford même) pour faire une exception – et puis avec ma toux affreuse dont je souffre depuis 10 mois je ne pourrai pas faire l'effort physique nécéssaire pour parler pendant une heure.

Je vous en prie veuillez remercier le secretaire du C[lub] F[rançais] pour l'invitation et lui exprimer mon profond regret. Ce serait gentil a Vous de Vs rappeler que Vs nous avez fait la promesse de nous faire une petite visite ici. Peut-être a Pâques? Jetez nous un petit mot. Ma femme me prie de Vous faire mille amitiés de sa part

Votre devoué

J. Conrad

Dear Alice (if I may),

I have just received your letter. I'm sorry to have to say that I cannot possibly accept the invitation from the French Club. First of all I have refused too many of them (and even at Oxford) to make an exception – and then with my frightful cough, from which I've been suffering for 10 months, I could not make the physical effort necessary to speak for an hour.

Pray thank the secretary of the French Club for the invitation and convey my profound regrets. Do please remember that you promised to pay us a short visit here. Perhaps at Easter? Drop us a line. My wife, for her part, asks me to send you many kind regards.

Your devoted

J. Conrad

---

[1] Alice-Maude-Marguerite Gachet, also known as Alice Mary Gachet de la Fournière (1884?–1960), was a niece of Conrad's 'aunt' Marguerite Poradowska (née Gachet). Her mother was English, and she made her début on the London stage in 1922. An actress and director, she was for many years on the staff of the Royal Academy of Dramatic Art.

To Commander F. G. Cooper

Text TS Melbourne; Unpublished

[letterhead: Oswalds]
March 25th. 1924.

Dear Sir.[1]

It would give us great pleasure certainly to see you here. Up to the 11th of April we shall be at home. Our friends very frequently come for the day, leaving Victoria at 10.40 a.m. and arriving in Canterbury at 12.30. There is a train up to London about 5 o'clock.

We regret not to be able to ask you for a weekend, but from now on [and] for some time, our son with his wife and child comes and we shall not have a spare room.

If you will drop us a line a couple of days before the date which you decide upon, the car will meet your train in Canterbury.

Believe me with kind regards

faithfully Yours

J. Conrad.

To Richard Curle

Text MS Indiana; Curle 144

[Oswalds]
25. 3. 24

Dearest Dick.

The Hudson Ed. went off last Sat. in four parcels. How good of You to let me unload this affair on Your overcharged shoulders.[2]

To-day's J. B.[3] was indeed good – for the subject was not easy to treat – being within the borders of psychology. – The bust of Ep[stein] has grown truly monumental. It is a marvellously effective piece of sculpture, with even something more than masterly interpretation in it.[4] The cast will be made probably on Friday. The Keating Collection will be held here for

---

[1] F(rederic) G(eorge) Cooper (1876–1966) served in the war as a transport officer and was appointed Lieutenant Commander in 1915, leaving the service as Commander in 1921. His articles on Conrad, whom he had met, appeared in the *Nautical Magazine* (1921), *Blue Peter* (1929), *Mariner's Mirror* (1940), and *Annual Dogwatch* (1953).

[2] See Conrad's letter of 1 February.

[3] A 'John Blunt' column. Taking up a reader's suggestion, Curle had written in praise of 'Bluntness' (p. 7).

[4] Epstein quotes the two sentences beginning 'The bust', but adds, as if from the same letter, a paraphrased sentence from the fourth paragraph of the letter to Elbridge L. Adams of the 26th (*Let There Be Sculpture*, p. 94). Five or six casts were made of the bust; one is now in the Conrad room at the Museum of Canterbury, another – despite the Gallery's initial reluctance to give it a home – is at the National Portrait Gallery, in London.

Your inspection.[1] You'll find the items in the study but each wrapped up on account of the dust. Come when you like (with notice) but in any case I don't intend to return it for a month – even if completed by signatures, etc. before that time.

Jessie sends her love.

Yours ever

J. C.

To Eric S. Pinker
Text TS/MS Berg; Unpublished

[letterhead: Oswalds]
March 25th. 1924.

My dear Eric

Yes, it is certain that the French translation matter can wait until your return[2] – which I suppose will be some time about April 10th. Am I to understand that you have already sent the letter of which a copy has been forwarded to me?[3] It is all right; only I regret that you stated definitely that Aubry was to be the translator. One can never tell what that gentleman[4] will take advantage of to worry and annoy one. There is a group of men and one or two women who are busy translating my works, and Aubry has his share which will keep him busy for some time. Moreover, "Romance" is as a matter of fact already translated – and very well too.[5]

I have not written to F. M. F. yet and I don't think I will write until we have seen each other. My idea would be, as far as I am concerned, for a simple "yes or no" whether he wishes those two books to be included, telling him at the same time plainly that there is very little money in it, without entering into details. As a matter of fact I don't remember the conditions of the French agreement. Our move will, I am afraid, open up the question of translation in all the languages. As far as I remember the wording of other agreements they seemed to embrace also collaborated works. We shall have to consult as to what we must say to F. M. F.

---

[1] The set of US first editions he had inscribed for Keating; see Conrad's letter to him of 28 January.

[2] From the Côte d'Azur.

[3] Pinker's letter to Ford of 21 March (Ford's copy at Yale) requested his permission to include *Romance* and *The Inheritors* in the collected edition to be published by Gallimard.

[4] Ford, not Aubry.

[5] By Marc Chadourne, commissioned by Gallimard but not published by them. See the letter to Ford of 11 April.

Give our love to your wife when you see her. We hope you will have a nice run across France. I suppose you will keep clear of Paris, passing to the south of it.

Always affectly Yrs

J. Conrad

Epstein['s] bust is a monumental piece of work. Nothing could be finer. He won't be done before Sat. next.

To Frank Swinnerton

Text MS Arkansas; J-A, 2, 340

[letterhead: Oswalds]
[25 March 1924][1]

My dear Mr Swinnerton[2]

I want to tell you without delay that I have just received, from an old friend in America, two pp torn out of Vanity Fair which gratified and touched me more than I thought anything in print could do.[3]

The vital warmth of your article, after so many years' acquaintance with my books, found its way straight into my heart. I had no idea that a work of mine had awakened such a response in a boy of 17 who was to mature into a fellow-writer with such a grasp on life and such a power of personal vision.[4] Your generous words will be added to the small, treasured hoard of few men's utterances – the clearest of my reward – which I cherish like a miser his gold. But unlike a miser I prize most the thought that when the hour strikes I'll have it to leave behind me – an undreamt-of fortune!

---

[1] Date from postmark. Swinnerton replied on 26 April (Stape and Knowles, pp. 239–40).

[2] Frank Arthur Swinnerton (1884–1982), a publisher's reader for Chatto & Windus, was a chronicler of English literary life, reviewer, and novelist; among the novels were *The Merry Heart* (1909) and *Nocturne* (1917). Though London-born, he felt a great affinity for the Kentish countryside and wrote on other authors who loved the land in *The Georgian Literary Scene* (1935). As 'Simon Pure', he had a regular column in the New York *Bookman*, bringing the latest news from literary London. He had sent Conrad his condolences after the ill-starred production of *The Secret Agent*.

[3] 'An Estimate of Joseph Conrad: A Critical Discussion of the Novels of This Living Master, with a Special Comment on "The Rover"', *Vanity Fair*, 22.1 (March 1924), 54, 100.

[4] The article opens: 'It is always with pride that I remember how, when I was sixteen, I read a book called *The Nigger of the Narcissus*, by an author unknown to me, and appreciated the fact that it was good.' Afterwards, he came to value other books even more highly: 'Mr. Conrad brought psychology into romance. He restored grandeur to the characters who play parts in his books. They were complex human creatures, such as few English writers since Shakespeare have successfully ventured to portray. This Mr. Conrad did in *Youth* . . . in *Lord Jim*, and in *Nostromo*.' When he read *The Nigger*, he was already two years out of school and working as an office-boy.

I must also thank you for putting The Rover into his proper place with the authority which appertains to your critical standing in literature. The way that book has been written about had made me uncomfortable. Of course you are right. I don't say "just" because you have been indulgent to the utmost limit.[1]

Yours cordially

J. Conrad.

To Elbridge L. Adams

Text Adams 35 (in part); J-A, 2, 341[2]

[Oswalds]
26. 3. '24.

My dear Adams,

I was startled by your account of the operation. It looks to me as tho' you had come back from very far away. Pray do not do anything of the kind again.

Pardon me all my shortcomings. I am about the most imperfect man on earth; and if it had not been for the indulgence of my friends I would not know where to hide my head.

The fact of the matter is, my dear friend, that all this year – up to 3 weeks ago – I have not been well at all. Now I am better and am doing some work, slowly. Mentally I feel still languid. But all this is improving.

Epstein has been here for the last week doing my bust: just head and shoulders. It is really a magnificent piece of work. He will be done modelling this week and there will be five bronze copies cast. Muirhead Bone has arranged this.[3] I was reluctant to sit, but I must say that now I am glad the thing has come off. It is nice to be passed to posterity in this monumental and impressive rendering.

---

[1] When Swinnerton turns to *The Rover*, he is disappointed: 'It is on a lower plane, if a more popular plane, of romance. It is more clear, more proficient, much less than these others were' (p. 54). Although 'readable, exciting, credible . . . not all Mr. Conrad's minor magic of presentment can quite atone for the *obvious* qualities of his theme and his dramatis personae. *Lord Jim* and *Nostromo* were absorbing mysteries of creation for us, because they had been absorbing mysteries of creation for Mr. Conrad. From Mr. Conrad, nothing less than the superb is tolerable . . . It is a hard lot; but in its true perspective, this dissatisfaction with *The Rover* is tribute to Mr. Conrad's place among the elect – among those (and they are very few) who have created life as gods. He is a god; and as coming from a god, *The Rover* by comparison is but a toy' (p. 100).

[2] Jean-Aubry omits the last five words and (as usual) the signature, Adams the salutation and first paragraph.

[3] See Bone's letter of 31 March (Stape and Knowles, p. 237).

Besides this there is not much news to tell you. Alas! There is no chance of us coming to Mass[achusetts] to take possession of the cottage. In September we will leave this house and go into winter quarters in the South of France – I hope. But Jessie is not getting on very well and we may have to stick somewhere near the surgeons for God knows how long.

She is writing to-day to Mrs. Adams, to whom please give my love, as well as to the chicks. Whatever happens keep me in your memory and believe me

always yours

Joseph Conrad.

To Archibald Marshall
Text MS Lubbock; Unpublished

[letterhead: Oswalds]
26.3.24

My dear Marshall[1]

Yes! It was many years ago. In the year of *Many Junes* – you remember.[2]

Thanks for your kind and warm appreciation of the Rover.[3] As coming from a fellow craftsman Your commendation gives me special pleasure not only by its generous terms but by the friendly feeling which prompted You to write them down for my eye.

I hope all is well with you and Yours.

Cordially yours

J. Conrad

To Walter B. Rodd
Text MS NLA; Unpublished

[letterhead: Oswalds]
26.3.24

My dear Sir.[4]

Thanks for your letter with the press-cuttings.

I was in Sydney for the first time in 1879 – then in 1880. I was appointed to the command of the barque "Otago" belonging to Messrs Henry Simpson

---

[1] As 'Archibald Marshall', Arthur Hammond Marshall (1866–1934) wrote a multitude of novels and critical essays. A partner in the short-lived publishing house of Alston Rivers, he had worked with Ford Madox Ford, and was employed for a time on the *Daily Mail*.

[2] Marshall had sent Conrad a copy of his novel *Many Junes* in 1908.

[3] Marshall had written to Conrad from Hyères on 9 March, saying that the novel 'has moved me profoundly' (Stape and Knowles, p. 237).

[4] Walter Barnstaple Rodd (1884–1965) lived in Roseville, New South Wales.

& Sons by the British minister in Ban[g]kok[1] her master having died on her passage out. This was in 1887. I left her in 1889 resigning my command in order to return home by Suez. I visited Australia again in the years 1892–3 as chief mate of the ship Torrens.

These are all the details bearing on my relations with Australia. To enter on a long narrative is impossible so I will only say that I met there with nothing but kindness from people in various social spheres and that I have acquired a great affection for that Young Continent which will endure as long as my faculty of memory itself endures.

Pardon this hurried scrawl.

Believe me with kind regards

very faithfully Yours

J. Conrad

To F. N. Doubleday
Text TS/MS Princeton; Unpublished

[letterhead: Oswalds]
March 27th. 1924.

My dear Effendi.

We were very glad to get your letters and Jessie answered at once addressing to the Garden City. I held my hand till now, thinking that there might be something more vital to say. But the only news of importance is that Epstein is finishing my bust.

Some time ago I paid a call at 21 Bedford St. and saw Mr Byard, from whom I heard to my great concern of Florence's loss[2] and of her subsequent illness. It was however too late then to write to you with any hope of catching you in New York and I must say that Mr Byard reassured me, partly, by stating definitely that Florence had made a recovery and that you were already on the way down South. Truth to say I did not know exactly how to address you down there. This checked me, and meantime your letter arrived. As the mails are running now I thought it was no use trying to catch you in Nassau. Give Florence my love and sincere sympathy and my hope that her long sun-bath in the Bahamas has done her good.

We were delighted with the photo postcards. The house is very much what I imagined from Florence's description of it, and I think that both your figures in the garden are very like. The man apparently hiding behind a tree

---

[1] In his letters, as in his fiction, Conrad used the nineteenth-century Polish spelling.

[2] Her brother, Stephen Van Wyck, a corporate lawyer, had died on 23 January at the age of sixty-six after a long illness (see the *New York Times*, 23 January 1924, p. 17).

is Evans, I suppose. I haven't been in town since his return, so I haven't seen him yet.

During your absence G[arden] C[ity] and I settled by correspondence the scheme of the volume of selected stories. I will send the Preface in time. I think that in republishing any of my former work it can not but do good to have some fresh matter included; if only for the reason that it would force every collector of Conrad items to buy the book, or his collection would not be complete. And of course it may, I suppose, have some effect also with the general public.

Friend Everitt will have communicated to you my grumbling letter about the "Rover" volume going into the "de luxe" edition without any notice to me and therefore without an Author's Note. You will be glad to hear that I got over the shock. But really, my dear Effendi, I ask myself what was the reason for such haste. The feature of the "de luxe" edition are the Author's Notes, and if I had been warned I would certainly not have delayed the appearance of the volume more than a month.

I must beg you, my dear Effendi, to put a stopper also on another matter which has been a source of some worry to me. Gallimard, of the Nouvelle Revue Française, got in a state of extreme excitement and exasperation on discovering that proposals offering the translation into French of "The Rover" had been made to one or two French papers; one of them being "L'Intransigeant". However they originated nobody was authorised to make them on my part, as you know, since the fact of my comprehensive agreement for all my works (*including serials*) in France has never been a secret. That agreement dates a good many years back, and I can not be a consenting party to anything being done otherwise than through the N. R. F. and *that* must be left to *me*. Gallimard has made up his plan of campaign and got together a body of distinguished translators under the direction of Monsieur André Gide, and I can not accept any translation by anybody outside that group. Such proposals are encroaching on the rights made over under contract with Gallimard. I assured him that I knew nothing about it and that I would give no authorisation to any outside translator whatever. The "Intransigeant" and other French papers have been warned.[1]

I am better as to the cough. Mentally I am picking up too and if this continues I hope to do good work yet. I have been sitting to Epstein for two weeks now. He will be done to-morrow. He has produced a wonderful piece of work of a somewhat monumental dignity, and yet – everybody says – the

---

[1] TS ends.

likeness is striking. I was very reluctant to sit but now I am glad I did. E, too, is pleased with himself.

I end in haste as this must be posted tonight (it is now 7 pm) as the cross-London traf[f]ic is dislocated.

My dear love to you both best of friends.

Ever affectly Yours

J. Conrad

To Eric S. Pinker
Text Telegram Berg; Unpublished

[Oswalds]
[27 March 1924][1]

Bookishly Strand London

Ford correct in what he says[2] Romance translation has been done long time ago and surely French agreement is on royalty basis not merely ten pounds a volume Please send me French agreement to ascertain terms I will not write Ford before you return Am inclined if collaborations not formally included in [. . .][3]

To Sir Hugh Clifford
Text MS Clifford; Hunter

[letterhead: Oswalds]
30.3.24[4]

My dear Clifford.

I did not expect to read of Your arrival till the 31.[5] That is why this letter was not awaiting You at your address. Your copy of *The Rover* (a novel of mine) was dispatched on Sat; but I managed to miss the post with this sweat, having been hindered by Epstein who was here doing my bust. A very fine piece of work which cost him twenty days of his life, and truth to say, of mine too.

Yes my dear friend! – I haven't missed either the romance or the spirituality of high endeavour in Your report.[6] A fine piece of work – Six years of Your

---

[1] Date-stamp.

[2] Pinker had written to Ford on 21 March (copy in Ford's hand at Yale), requesting his permission to include *Romance* and *The Inheritors* in a French edition of Conrad's works to be published by Gallimard, and offering Ford £10 for the rights to each volume.

[3] The rest is missing.

[4] Hunter gives the impossible date 30.2.24. Conrad's '2s' are often written with a backward flourish that can be mistaken for a '3'.

[5] Clifford arrived from Lagos on the 28th, landing at Plymouth.

[6] His *Address to the Legislative Council of Nigeria*; see the letter to Curle of 4 March.

life, and of other lives too, but if that was not worth it, then I don't know what could have been.

Jessie joins me in congratulations on your respectable status of a Grandfather. I too may count myself respectable in that way now, but do not feel particularly elated.

We will be delighted to see You here on the 25 Ap – unless You prefer your other date (5 May) – for as long a stay as possible. May we ask the two men who were here on the last occasion?[1] I don't like to do it till we hear from you. Jessie sends her kindest regards to Lady Clifford to whom please give *mes hommages les plus respectueux*

Ever with the greatest affection

yours

J. Conrad.

To Henry S. Canby

Text TS Yale; J-A, 2, 341–2

[letterhead: Oswalds]
April 7th. 1924.

Henry S. Canby Esq.

Dear Sir,[2]

Thank you for your friendly letter.

The truth is that I know nothing of the book of which you speak. My business is not the reading of books – at any rate not reading of fiction and I don't know that I am at all qualified to write introductions for other people's stories. I don't care for writing at all. What interests me is creative work. I hope you won't take it ill if I decline your suggestion. One does that sort of thing for a personal friend, of whom one thinks highly, or for some work of a remarkable artistic or intellectual character, or for some profound

---

[1] The previous August.
[2] A Yale graduate, Henry S(eidel) Canby (1878–1961) edited the *New York Evening Post Literary Review* before founding the *Saturday Review of Literature* in 1924 and organising the Book-of-the-Month Club two years later. A Yale professor after 1922, Canby influenced American literary tastes for decades. His many publications include an autobiography and studies in nineteenth-century American literature. Among the items in his collection *Definitions* (New York: Harcourt, 1922) is an article reprinted from the *Evening Post*, 'Conrad and Melville' (pp. 257–68), one of the first to bring these authors together. He wrote introductions to *Within the Tides* for Doubleday's Memorial Edition (1925) and *Under Western Eyes* for Keating's *A Conrad Memorial Library* (1929).

personal reason as, for instance, the introduction I wrote for a geographical publication in London.[1] But otherwise I am really not competent and, to speak the whole truth, not sufficiently interested.

It seems to me that people imagine I sit here and brood over sea stuff. That is quite a mistake. I brood certainly, but . . .

"Youth" has been called a fine sea-story. Is it? Well, I won't bore you with a discussion of fundamentals. But surely those stories of mine where the sea enters can be looked at from another angle. In the "Nigger" I give the psychology of a group of men and render certain aspects of nature. But the problem that faces them is not a problem of the sea, it is merely a problem that has arisen on board a ship where the conditions of complete isolation from all land entanglements make it stand out with a particular force and colouring. In other of my tales the principal point is the study of a particular man, or a particular event. My only sea-book, and the only tribute to a life which I have lived in my own particular way, is "The Mirror of the Sea."

I regret to say that I have not seen your article in the New York Evening Post on the occasion of the Limited Edition. I am very glad you are going to write on the pop. ed. Does that mean the "Concord" which Double-days are bringing out? Will you be kind enough to send it to me? I think we shook hands at Mrs Curtis[s] James's.[2] I was extremely tried, notwith-standing everybody's display of kindliness, by this new experience which will remain unique. I am truly glad to hear that the Literary Editor of the New York Evening Post was interested by my attempt to survey the genesis of "Victory", poor as it must have been. It is a book in which I have tried to grasp at more "life-stuff" than perhaps in any other of my works, and the one too, of which the appreciation of the public has given me the most pleasure.

Will you give our friend Chris[3] my love for himself and all the family?

Believe me, with great regard,

Always cordially yours,

Conrad

---

[1] 'The Romance of Travel', later known as 'Geography and Some Explorers'.

[2] On 10 May 1923, when Conrad read and lectured to some 200 guests at her Park Avenue mansion.

[3] Christopher Morley.

To Messrs Methuen & Co.
Text TS Colgate; Unpublished

[letterhead: Oswalds]
April 7th. 1924.

Messrs. Methuen & Co. Ltd.

Dear Sirs,[1]
    I am interested to hear that you are resetting "Victory"[2] and since you are
so good as to offer to send me the proofs I shall be glad to see them.

Yours faithfully,

J. Conrad

To Lieutenant Blanchenay
Text L. fr. 198–9[3]

[Oswalds]
April 8th 1924.

Mon cher Monsieur,[4]
    Je regrette d'avoir à vous répondre à la machine.[5] J'ai la goutte au poignet
droit. L'enflure de ma main la fait ressembler à un gant de boxe.
    Merci bien de votre bonne lettre à propos du *Rover*. Elle prouve surtout
l'humanité de votre caractère, car le premier paragraphe de ce livre contient
un anachronisme atroce pour lequel vous auriez pu me faire passer au conseil. Je veux dire le bruit de chaine quand Peyrol jette l'ancre dans l'avant-
port. Une chaîne en 1796![6] C'est inoui! Je n'avais pas pu lire les épreuves

---

[1] The London publishing house founded in 1889 by Algernon Methuen (1856–1924), brought
out *The Mirror of the Sea, The Secret Agent, A Set of Six, Under Western Eyes, Chance,* and *Victory*. Although text-books were the company's mainstay, its other authors included Kipling,
Stevenson, and Maeterlinck.

[2] For the third English edition, in a smaller format; making, as was the custom of the house, a
tactical confusion between impression and edition, Methuen's called this the 'tenth edition'
(William R. Cagle, 'A Conrad Bibliography' [unpublished TS Indiana], p. 220).

[3] Jean-Aubry notes that this draft was found among Conrad's papers.

[4] 'Lieutenant de vaisseau' Blanchenay, as Jean-Aubry calls him, was presumably the same
person as the more junior 'enseigne de vaisseau' who had translated Pietro Gribaudi's study
of Genoa as *Le Port de Gênes, les voies d'accès des Alpes*; later published in book form (Paris, n. d.),
it first appeared in the *Revue Maritime* for October 1910. In the French navy, *enseigne de vaisseau,
première classe* is the rank below *lieutenant*, and *lieutenant* is the rank below *capitaine*. Tentatively,
Conrad's correspondent may be identified as Pierre-Frédéric Blanchenay (1884–1958), born
in Tebessa, Algeria, to a military family with connections in Toulon.

[5] That is, dictated to Miss Hallowes for her to type up.

[6] Although the use of metal anchor chains goes back to the ancient Chinese and the Greeks,
it was not until 1808 that new methods of forging made production on a large scale possible.
In that year, Robert Flinn opened his factory in South Shields, on the north-east coast of
England, and Samuel Brown took out the first patents. In 1816, the Royal Navy began to fit
new vessels with chains rather than hemp ropes, and in 1830 this innovation became standard
for all naval ships. Similar developments were taking place in the French and American navies.

moi-même. Quinze jours après l'arrivée du premier exemplaire je l'ouvris d'une main distraite. Vous pouvez vous imaginer la secousse que ce bruit de chaîne m'a donné. J'ai commencé par le geste de m'arracher les cheveux; puis je me suis dit qu'à mon âge ça ne se faisait pas; qu'il fallait me résigner à porter cette chaîne à mon cou jusqu'à la fin de ma vie. En vérité il n'y avait rien à faire. Plus de cinquante mille exemplaires étaient en circulation ici et aux Etats-Unis sans compter le Canada et l'Australie qui avaient leurs éditions séparées. Les presses marchaient. Il faudra maintenant attendre le moment de préparer "The Rover" pour l'édition grand format (Limited Ed.), dont il fera le Vol. xx. Ce sera dans six mois. J'ai déclaré le texte de cette édition ètre le texte définitif (standard text). C'est alors, cher Monsieur, que je vais faire les corrections dans le sens des remarques que vous avez bien voulu me communiquer dans votre lettre. Je vous en suis infiniment reconnaissant. J'aurais dû me rappeler que dans la marine on ne disait pas "mon capitaine". Quand on se fait vieux on oublie. J'espère que si j'avais été dans la peau du vieux Peyrol j'aurais pris soin de carèner ma tartane de temps en temps. Mais voilà! Je n'ai pas pensé à l'écrire.

My dear Sir,

I regret having to answer you on the machine. I have gout in my right wrist. The swelling of my hand makes it look like a boxing glove.

Thank you for your kind letter about the *Rover*. It proves above all the humanity of your character, for the opening paragraph of this book contains an atrocious anachronism for which you could have taken me to court! I mean the noise of the chain when Peyrol lets go the anchor in the roadstead. A chain in 1796! It's unheard-of! I was not able to read the proofs myself. A fortnight after the arrival of the first copy I opened it casually. You may imagine the shock that the noise of this chain gave me. I began by tearing my hair; then I told myself that at my age that wasn't done; that I would have to resign myself to wear this chain around my neck for the rest of my life. Truly there was nothing to do. More than fifty thousand copies were in circulation here and in the United States, without counting Canada and Australia, which had their separate editions. The presses were rolling. It will now be necessary to prepare *The Rover* for the Limited Edition, where it will be vol. xx. This will be in six months. I've declared the text of this edition the standard text. It is at that time, dear Sir, that I shall make corrections along the lines of the remarks you were good enough to communicate to me in your letter. I am infinitely grateful to you. I should have remembered that in the navy one did not say "my captain". When one grows old one forgets. I hope that if I had been in the skin of old Peyrol I would have taken care to careen the keel of my tartane from time to time. But there we are! I didn't think to write it.

To W. C. Wicken

Text TS Berg; Unpublished

[letterhead: Oswalds]
April 8th. 1924.

Dear Mr Wicken,

Herewith I return the procuration[1] for Doubleday & Page. You will see from the signature that my wrist is better.

Can you drop me word as to when you expect Mr Eric. A nice cheap house is offered for two months in Biarritz and I am thinking perhaps it would do us both good to run over. In any case we could not leave here till May 6th.[2]

With kind regards,

Yours

J. Conrad

To Ford Madox Ford

Text TS carbon Yale; Unpublished

[Oswalds]
April 11th. 1924.

My dear Ford,

I wasn't really well enough to attend to your letter at once.[3]

The facts are as follows: collaborated works are not included in the agreement with Gallimard of Dec. 15th, 1915, which recites the titles of the works subject to negociation.

(b) In that agreement all works the publication of which dates back more than ten years are disposed of at the rate of £10 per volume.

(c) The ground of that small price is that such works have fallen dans les domaines publiques.

---

[1] A Gallicism for 'power of attorney'.

[2] Conrad's wrist having worsened, Miss Hallowes wrote to Mr Wicken on 13 April (TS Berg) to ask that £10 be paid into John Conrad's special account for his next term at school, and to say that the trip abroad was uncertain pending advice on Jessie Conrad's condition from her surgeon, Sir Robert Jones.

[3] Of 3 April (TS carbon Cornell); see Stape and Knowles, pp. 238–9, as '[early April]'. Ford had suggested buying the translation of *Romance* from Marc Chadourne and placing it with Simon Kra or another Parisian publisher. *L'Aventure* was eventually published by Kra in 1926.

Those are the points of the agreement which are material to the question raised in your letter.

In regard to the points touched in your letter I must first declare that I heard only quite lately that "Romance" had been translated. Of course the collaborated works can not be published without your consent. That is perfectly obvious.

For my part I can not accept your suggestion that we should buy jointly the translation of "Romance" from the translator. I am perfectly willing that you should make terms with Gallimard to the greatest advantage possible, promising to give my assent to them without any question, declaring that in that case I would make over to you the totality of the proceeds whatever their amount may be.

The above applies to both the collaborated works.

But I call your attention, entre nous, that already in 1915, when I was signing the contract with Gallimard for my works both those works books* were already in the domaine publique, having been published before 1904. Excuse me from writing any more just now. I am horribly seedy and can't think of anything that might meet your wishes better. My impression is that any firm, or any ten firms can publish those books now, since they have been out so long.

To G. Jean-Aubry
Text MS Yale; Unpublished

[letterhead: Oswalds]
23.Ap.24

Mon cher Jean.

Assurez je Vs prie pauvre Mme Alvar de la part que nous prenons dans la perte douloureuse qu'elle vient de faire.¹ Je comprend[s] parfaitement que Vs ne voulez pas quitter Londres en ce moment. Merci de Votre bonne lettre. Ce que Vs faites "mousser" Conrad. C'est innoui!

---

¹ Her father, Ernst Johan Beckman, had died in California on 16 April. He had emigrated to the USA in 1916, eventually settling in Santa Barbara. In his native Sweden he had been a writer and a Member of Parliament. Replying to this letter, Jean-Aubry wrote: 'il y avait entre ce père et cette fille une communauté de vision parfaitement exceptionelle' (24 April, MS Yale).

J'ai beaucoup de peine a manier la plume, et Miss H. n'est pas là. Je vais écrire plus longuement, dans un jour ou deux, a la machine.

Je Vous embrasse

Votre vieux

Conrad

Jessie sends her love to you.

My dear Jean,

Pray assure poor Mme Alvar of the share we take in the sad loss that she has just suffered. I understand perfectly well that you do not want to leave London at present. Thanks for your kind letter. How you do "puff" Conrad. It's unheard-of!

I find it very difficult to handle a pen, and Miss H. is not here. I will write at greater length in a day or two, on the machine.

I embrace you

Your old

Conrad

Jessie sends her love to you.

To G. Jean-Aubry
Text TS Yale; Unpublished

Oswalds.
27th April. 1924.

Cher Jean

I return to you the MS of your really most successful translation of that old Preface[1] which after all those years grates on my disillusioned point of view. Nevertheless I thank you warmly for your faithful labour which proves to me once more what a good friend you are.

The alterations which you have authorised me to make do not amount perhaps to a dozen lines altogether and, of course, they are just suggestions on which you will exercise your discretion.

To speak of Hueffer:

I will have nothing more to do with him or the collaborated works. They are not included in the contract with Gallimard and I have authorised Hueffer to come to terms with Gallimard or whoever else he likes, making over to him the complete proceeds of whatever arrangements he concludes. I had to

[1] To *The Nigger of the 'Narcissus'?*

do that because I can not be mixed up in any difficulties with that man, and I do not care to have collaborated books included in the French translations of my works.

I have asked Eric to write to Gallimard in that sense. I never intended to engage those two works and in that respect the agreement is perfectly clear.

We were in London for 36 hours, as Sir Robert Jones wanted to see Jessie. I did not phone to you because I knew how busy you must be and I am looking forward to long and satisfactory talks with you when you come down to see us.

I am sorry to say that there will have to be another operation, either at the end of May or in the first week of June. It is a horrible prospect for us both, but Jessie is ready for anything that may bring relief to the constant pain from which she suffers.

No more just now except our united love.

Votre

Conrad

To Eric S. Pinker

Text TS Berg; Unpublished

[letterhead: Oswalds]
April 27th. 1924.

Dearest Eric

I enclose the letter to Ford which is in the nature of an agreement. Will you please read it critically and if you agree that the terms are correct will you please post it on?

Thank you ever so much for your letter received on Saturday. I only hope that it will not be in vain.

Now I will give you the result of my meditation on Dent's proposal which amounts to this, that he can dispose of 5000 sets to the Enc[yc]l[opaedia] Britan[nica] people at 50% discount. This is a transaction involving cash payment to the amount of, roughly speaking, £25,000. The questions which arise are: the effect on the market; the effect on Dent's attitude towards the edition as a whole.

As to the first, the transaction will of course kill the bookselling market for two or three years. Whether it will upset the booksellers is hard to say, but their attitude to Dent is already so inimical that it can hardly make matters worse.

As to the second, I do not think that the fact of Dent getting his capital outlay back in this way will make him indifferent to the fate of the edition as one of the assets of his business. Personally I do not think it will be so, but I know that you fear there may be a danger of that.

Now there is a question of royalties raised by Dent. I think we may lay it as a principle that I can not contemplate reducing my royalty by 50% in order to have this transaction carried out.

The royalty under the contract for that edition is $1/8 = 20$ pence per vol. I think we may suggest giving up 6d, which is not quite 30%. But as a matter of bargaining we may go up to 8d which would be rather more than 30%. In other words we could accept a royalty of 1/- per vol. which would give me, as you mentioned yourself, the gross amount 100,000 shillings, equal to £5000. Out of that Hueffer will get sixpence on two separate vols, equal to £250.

That is unavoidable.

Then there is the advance of £30 per vol. which is equal to £600, and my question is whether that will be deducted. But frankly I don't think it would be quite just. What is your view as to the legal position? My impression was always that an advance is an advance, and considering that in this transaction with the Encl. Brit. Dent will get a lump sum of £20,000, I think he will be doing fairly well, even if the production of the edition has cost him 2/- per vol. or for that matter even 3/- per vol. Anyway it is a quick turnover.

Giving up 50% of my royalty, especially if the £600 have got to be returned, would from a certain point of view be not worth while. On the other hand I doubt if Dent could sell enough sets in the next three years to give me royalties to the amount of £4000 spread over that period.

I hope, my dear Eric, this long rigmarole will not give you a headache.

I have half a notion that this transaction may fail altogether unless it is carried out soon.

We arrived home after a good run, but Jessie suffered from the jolting. She remained in bed all yesterday but is down to-day. Now the thing is decided on the time will seem atrociously long; for one can not help thinking of it.

Our love to you

Yours

J Conrad

PS. Will you please write to Gallimard washing our hands of Ford and all his collaborated works altogether.

To Aniela Zagórska

Text MS copy Yale; Najder 297

Oswalds,
April 28th.1924.

Ma chère Angèle,

I am obliged to dictate this letter in English as I cannot use my right hand for writing in pen and ink for any length of time. I can just manage to sign my name.

I was very glad to hear from you that you are going to take the holiday on which you have set your heart. I am sorry to tell you that Sir Robert Jones has decided on another operation for Jessie, which he hopes will remove all the causes of those inflammatory troubles in the tissues from which she has been suffering so long. This operation will take place in Canterbury towards the end of May, and I hope to be able to transport Jessie back to Oswalds about the middle of June, where of course she will have to remain in bed some time longer.

The period of waiting will not be very pleasant. I will feel it more than Jessie herself who takes everything very quietly as you know. My health has been very wretched for a long time. I do not mean that I have been laid up much, but I have not been able to work, and this gives me considerable anxiety. However, I am feeling a little better just now, though my wrist is still very swollen and very painful.

There can be no question of us going abroad before the end of this year. We will be leaving this house in September, but we have not yet found another and our plans are very unsettled. Of course we will be delighted to have a visit from Miss Rakowska.[1] I remember her mother very well as a charming girl of 20. You do not give us her address in London, or else we might have written suggesting a day, but I hope that she will drop us a line.

Our dear love to you and best wishes for a pleasant journey. You may take it for certain that we will be in this house up to September 1st unless something utterly unexpected happens to call us away.

Your faithful

Konrad.

---

[1] Irena Rakowska was the daughter of Maria Rakowska (née Oldakowska), mentioned in Tadeusz Bobrowski's letters to Conrad (Najder, p. 167); she visited Oswalds with a friend in July; see Conrad's letter to Jean-Aubry of 22 July, and Ray, pp. 268–73.

To Richard Curle

Text MS Indiana; Curle 145 (in part)[1]

[Oswalds]
Thursday. [1 May 1924][2]

Dearest Dick.

Delighted to hear You are coming for lunch on Sat.

I am very glad You have asked E[ric] P[inker] and his wife to lunch next Thursday.[3] It's very kind of you as they don't know many (if any) interesting people.

Jessie sends her love. She has been upstairs for 3 days so as to rest her leg which is giving her a lot of pain when she moves. I am improving slowly. What news there are I am keeping for your ear when you come.

Ever yours

J. C.

PS Never supposed *you* wrote the par: about the "I say –" book. Of course not. Todays J[ohn] B[lunt] particularly good.[4]

To Eric S. Pinker

Text TS Berg; Unpublished

Private

Oswalds.
May 1st. 1924.

My dear Eric

On receipt of your letter of the 29th April I was about to alter my letter to Ford in the sense of your remarks when the man himself walked into this house, being on his way to London. It seems he had written to me he was coming; but that announcement didn't reach me till after he had arrived. I have no doubt he posted it late on purpose.

---

[1] Curle omitted the comment in the second paragraph about the Pinkers' lack of interesting acquaintances.

[2] Curle's dating.   [3] To dinner, Curle notes.

[4] Curle's columns for the *Daily Mail* appeared under the heading 'I Say'; the *Mail* was publishing a collection under that title. On 1 May, 'Blunt' challenged the assertion by the President of the Wesleyan Conference, the Revd T. Ferrier Hulme, that 'never was there such a depraved manhood as today'. Curle deplored the 'unphilosophic' tendency to see nothing but bad in the present and nothing but good in the past: 'Humanity has many faults, but one does not know humanity only by knowing its faults. Above all, one does not know it unless one is able to perceive that people may have a totally different point of view from oneself without being worse than oneself' (p. 7).

Having him there I thought I would just talk to him. The result of our conversation is embodied in the letter which I composed after he had left me.[1] I send it here to you for your inspection and forwarding to Paris where F.M.F. returns on Sunday. In the enclosed letter the paragraph beginning with the words *This stipulation* . . . is inserted in order to conciliate the swelled-headed creature who seems to imagine that he will sweep all Europe and devastate Great Britain with an eventual collected edition of his own works. I humour that strange illusion being anxious to have the matter settled on definite lines for good.

Answering now your letter of the 30th Ap. bearing on Dent's proposed deal with the Encycl. Brit. I wish first to say that, as it presents itself now, it loses much of its special character, and the possible objections to it (which we have discussed together) lose much of their force, since you have settled in principle the reduction of royalty on such advantageous terms. Giving up twopence is giving up really very little; and, no doubt, it may be true that the transaction with the Encycl. Brit. will not affect the bookselling trade. I am very certain that in the matter of eventual payments you will be successful in making the best possible arrangement. Old Dent has written to me a letter expressing most friendly and disinterested sentiments. So, I think, we may just simply let him go on and conclude the deal *if he can.* I quite understand that there is a chance that it may fall through. In any case thank you, my dear fellow, for putting it on what I consider an advantageous basis for me. The only drop of gall in this sweetness is the £312. 10. 0 which will have to go to F[isher] U[nwin].[2] It's horrible!

As to the "Trevessa" business. Hopkinson & Co.[3] did write to me direct shortly after you left for the continent, offering me £50. I was very seedy and wrote definitely declining to have anything to do with it. Mr Wicken's letter was received here soon after. It stated that Mr W. had informed those people that I was not likely to do it under £100; but I regarded the matter as closed.

---

[1] See the following letter.
[2] Under a previous contract, Fisher Unwin still held the rights to some of Conrad's works.
[3] In June 1923 the merchant freighter SS *Trevessa*, loaded with 6,564 tons of zinc concentrate, sank in the Indian Ocean when the constant battering of severe weather opened a seam in her shell. The crew managed to sail 1,700 miles in two open lifeboats to land on Rodrigues Island, northwest of Mauritius; 11 men died on the 23-day voyage. The London publishers Martin Hopkinson & Co brought out Cecil Foster's *The Loss of the Trevessa* in 1926.

Please tell Mr W. that I am very sorry for not having acknowledged his letter. I thought I had done so.

I think we will let it rest. I know nothing of the "Trevessa" affair except several short pars in the newspapers. I have seen no report of the official inquiry, neither did Hopkinson send me the proof of the Captain's narrative. There are features in the story of that ship's loss and of the boats' journey which did not strike me very favourably as a man who has envisaged professionally the possibility of such an eventuality in his own case; and had given much thought (as a matter of duty) to all the possible contingencies of such an event. And, anyhow, I think that such a story, if well told, may be left to speak for itself.[1]

———————

I have sent a cable letter to Doubleday to say that owing to their own precipitancy "The Rover" must go into all the editions without a preface. If Gabriel Wells[2] was in such an infernal hurry they might have warned me (at the cost of a couple of dollars) of the situation, and I would have done my best. I haven't yet got over my intense vexation with their casualness on a matter which, literarily, has its importance.

I am now working at the Preface for the vol. of Selected Tales, and expect to have it ready in a few days. I will be delayed by a visit from Sir Hugh Clifford, who is coming on Sat. and will stay till Tuesday morning.

Our love to you both.

Affctly Yrs

J. Conrad.

To Ford Madox Ford
Text TS Yale;[3] Unpublished

[letterhead: Oswalds]
May 2nd. 1924.

Dear Ford,

In the matter of our collaborated works what I propose is this:

You, F. M. F., will give me the right of dealing with the collaborated books "Inheritors" and "Romance" as far as inclusion in *any* English and American

---

[1] 'Youth', which Conrad based on his experiences in the *Palestine*, tells a rather similar story of a dangerous cargo and escape by open boat. The chairman of the Board of Trade inquiry had told the captain and crew of the *Trevessa*: 'We are proud of you and your comrades for the extraordinary gallantry of your conduct' (*The Times*, 17 November 1923, p. 9), and the City of Liverpool presented the captain with a commendatory plaque.

[2] Wells had commissioned Doubleday to produce the Sun-Dial Edition, limited to 735 sets, and must have been over-eager to see *The Rover* join the series.

[3] Ford's retyped copy, now at Indiana, was notarised on 2 August 1929 by John C. McGrath in Kings County, New York.

edition, past or future, is concerned; subject to you receiving one half of the proportion of royalties falling to the share of those two books to be paid to you whenever they fall due in the terms of any agreement they may be subject to.[1] This would apply also to any reprints of those books by themselves, either under the terms of the original agreements for their publication or any new arrangement I may make for our mutual benefit.

This stipulation is not meant to prevent you from including those two books in any edition of *your* complete works which you may arrange for in England, I receiving my proportion (one half) of the royalties earned by these books.

In consideration of the above, I, J. C. make over to you completely all the rights of translation of "Inheritors" and "Romance" into French or any other European language, and renounce my share of any proceeds thereof; even in the case of you finding it convenient to negotiate their inclusion in any complete edition of *my* translated works which I may have contracted for abroad.

If you agree please drop me a line stating formally that you accept this arrangement.

Yours

J. Conrad

To George T. Keating
Text TS Yale; Unpublished

[letterhead: Oswalds]
May 6th. 1924.

My dear Keating.

Thank you for your friendly letters which, I am afraid, I have not all acknowledged. I hope you will carry through the matter of business which has called you to Portage,[2] and that success, you so well deserve by your courage, industry and talents, will attend you through a long and, in every way, happy life.

I have this moment (the clock has just struck 12 noon) written the inscription on the last item, which has happened to be "Tradition".[3] The cases will be nailed down this afternoon and dispatched to London as soon as we

---

[1] Conrad was replying to Ford's proposals in two recent letters; see Stape and Knowles, pp. 238–9.

[2] A township in the forests of north central Pennsylvania where the Keating family had been early settlers, giving their name to various landmarks. Keating worked in the paper industry, and perhaps was inspecting logging jobs or pulp mills.

[3] Keating had offered Conrad $1,000 for a set of his works with inscriptions (see Conrad to Pinker, 27 January 1924). The inscriptions are recorded in Keating's *A Conrad Memorial Library*, and the original copies are in the Keating Collection at Yale.

hear from Messrs Turner Davies.[1] Miss Hallowes will write to them by this evening's mail.

I am glad my dear Keating, that, (with the exception of some "extra books" which have not arrived yet) your wishes have been completely carried out. In certain of the items you will find the handwriting rather shaky and unattractive, but my wrist went bad about the end of March and stopped me for a time. It was getting better so very slowly that I began to fear an unconscionable delay; so I went on as soon as I could use the pen for ten or fifteen minutes at a time – which is about my limit even yet. I am anxious to get your collection back to you, and I hope that you will not be disappointed with the general effect of that "body of inscriptions".

You need not fear that I would consecrate my remaining days to the writing of film plays. The play of which you speak I did in collaboration with a friend in the year 1920.[2] There are a good many of my works which I would be glad to see disposed of to some film people, but I haven't the slightest intention of working at them myself. As you know my selling success came to me late and was never really very great. It would be pleasant, and would ease my mind too, if I had some actual cash to leave behind me, to secure a comfortable existence for my wife. Royalties on copyrights is not much to depend on. In any case it is a precarious sort of property. Nothing however would induce me to work at film plays myself.

I hope that Mrs Keating and the children are well and flourishing in every way. My wife sends her love. I am sorry to say there will have to be another operation on her knee some time towards the end of this month.

Believe me

Yours always

J. Conrad

To Eric S. Pinker

Text MS Berg; Unpublished

[Oswalds]
Tuesday [6 May 1924][3]

Dearest Eric.

I 'phoned the office asking that John when he calls about noon tomorrow should be given £10 in treasury notes to take him over.[4]

---

[1] A London firm of freight forwarders.
[2] The collaboration with J. B. Pinker on *Gaspar the Strong Man* was in 1921.
[3] The reference to the *Shorter Tales* Preface fixes the date; see Conrad to Doubleday, 8 May.
[4] To France, where he would carry on with his studies.

I don't want to keep him any longer as the date of the operation is very uncertain. But I'll have him over here for a week while Jessie is in the nursing home. She will expect it rather, and I too will be glad of the company. Col Ruston of Ruston and Hornby (he married R[ichard] C[urle]'s sister) offered to take John into their engineering works. We left it open.

The preface for the "Shorter Tales" (about 2000 w) was posted yesterday to catch the *Majestic* tomorrow (Wed^y). I suppose you'll me[e]t today Sir H. Clifford. Dick told me you are dining with him this evening.

I am improving and feel quite hopeful. Of course I am not fit to run races – or even to look at one perhaps – but my plodding days are not over yet.

Our love

Yours

J. C.

To Eric S. Pinker

Text MS Berg; Unpublished

[letterhead: Oswalds]
[6 or 7 May 1924][1]

Dearest Eric

I have sent on the S[uper]-tax statement duly signed to the Sp[ecial] Comm[ission]ers.[2]

Have you noticed in my last my request for £10 on John's acc't

Love from us both

Yrs.

JC

To F. N. Doubleday

Text TS/MS Princeton; Unpublished

[letterhead: Oswalds]
May 8th. 1924.

Very dear Effendi.

I feel I have delayed an answer to your last good letter too long. But really there was nothing very good to tell you; and I am beginning to feel ashamed of seeming to groan and grumble interminably every time I open my mouth.

---

[1] To reach Pinker in time to give the money to John, this reminder would have to go out by the last post of the 6th or the first of the 7th; Conrad's shaky handwriting accords with the gout mentioned in Miss Hallowes's letter to Culbreth Sudler of 10 May (Lubbock).

[2] Of Inland Revenue. For super tax, a levy on incomes over £2,000 p.a., see the notes to the lettter of 11 June 1923.

On our last visit to London, after much hesitation and a lot of consideration, Sir Robert Jones has surrendered to the inevitable and has decided to operate on Jessie once more, as the limb can not be left in the condition in which it is now; especially as the strain and pain begin to affect her general health. The date is not fixed yet but it will be the end of May. It will be done in a Canterbury nursing-home, so that she will be taken home to complete her recovery directly she can be moved safely in an ambulance. I will get John back from France to keep me company for the first week or so, and Borys will come down from London for the day. He and everybody connected with the motor trade are much disturbed by the prospect of the abolition of the protective tax.[1] He has got on very well, (since after not quite two years with the Daimlers he is in receipt of £600 a year) and before the budget was introduced he had a prospect of a considerable rise next August; for the trade was flourishing and Stratton & Instone to whom he had been lent by the Daimler Co. to help in developing their business, were doing extremely well. Well, we shall see, but I admit that I too feel uneasy on his account.

John will stay in France till the end of August. There are three firms now ready to accept him as a pupil, and I think that when the moment comes to take a decision he will incline towards shipbuilding after all. Whatever he chooses I will be glad to see him start on his way to earn an independent existence.

Hugh Clifford was here last weekend for a couple of days and I had to relate to him the history of my American journey. How far away already it seems! Yet nothing can dim the recollection of Effendi Hill and the dear friends who made my every day there a precious memory.

I was delighted to hear the good news in your letter as to the prosperity of the business. Evviva!. Hoch!. Hip-hip-hip hurrah!. Garden City for ever!

My joy at the good report of Florence's and your health, if not so noisy, is even more intense. I don't know what sort of weather you are having on Long Island. Here, at this moment, it is raining. I am sitting by the fire and looking at the young leaves shaking and shivering outside in the cold wind.

---

[1] In his 1924–5 Budget, the Chancellor of the Exchequer, Philip Snowden, had announced that various tariffs, including those on imported vehicles, would be abolished in August. The result was a slump in business. In the words of *The Garage and Motor Agent*: 'the postponement of the abolition of duty on imported cars is another example of misplaced kindness. The public have, of course, stopped buying until August to see what can be saved by waiting, and both British manufacturers and importers of cars may be faced with immense stocks at the end of the season' (10 May 1924, p. 95).

Just now Jessie and I have nobody here but we expect the Borys' baby with all his attendants and escort down for the weekend. That won't break the peace. That baby is the quietest I have ever known. He seems to thrive exceedingly. I wonder how the world will look in twenty years' time when he will have to find his own little place in it.

You will have seen from my cable that I take the same view you do as to the missing preface. Obviously the other editions can not have it. We must let it go at that. The preface for the "Shorter Tales" was posted in time to catch the "Majestic" on Wednesday last. I did not think it was advisable to make it very long. I just said what I felt I had to say and that is all. I hope you will approve. There is a reference to you in it which does not express *all* my feelings, but in matters of sentiment a man ought to be reserved.[1] Anyway if you don't like it you may strike[2] the par: out.

Beso las manos de la Illustrissima* Señora[3] and commend myself to her gracious memory. I am haunted by the ghosts of those days when I had the honor[4] to live under her benevolent and fascinating rule as if "in a corner of Paradise" (as they say in Poland). Now the world seems flat and stale[5] – but I have not given it up. I've given up nothing, but what the brutal years have robbed me of. But time is an enemy that cannot be resisted.

Our dear love to you both.

Ever yours

Joseph Conrad

PS Affectionate remembrances to Patty and Nelson. Greetings to all friends.

To Edward Garnett

Text MS Boston; G. 334

[letterhead: Oswalds]
[May 11, 1924][6]

Dearest Edward,

I can hold a pen yet. For weeks I've had a bad wrist; or I would have thanked you before for the *M[an] at the Z[oo]*.[7] D[avid] may be congratulated

---

[1] For the reference, see the letter to Doubleday of 2 June.   [2] MS begins here.

[3] 'I kiss the hands of the most illustrious lady'.   [4] Conrad uses the American spelling.

[5] Cf. Hamlet's first soliloquy: 'How weary, stale, flat, and unprofitable / Seem to me all the uses of this world' (1.2.133–4).

[6] Dated by Garnett, who noted that this was 'Conrad's last letter to me'.

[7] The novel by Garnett's son David, just published by Chatto and Windus. Upset by a quarrel with his lover, a misanthropic Scot decides he would be happier living in the London Zoo. The authorities let him try the experiment, and thousands come to see him.

in pulling off this piece with great tact and subtlety. I think that, upon the whole, he has done well *not* to emphasise the irony more, against his Father's advice. It was undutiful, of course; but it was wise. My view is that the initial quarrel of the lovers (deliciously absurd) gave the note – and the whole thing is perfectly in tune as it stands. I think he would be capable, if he let himself go, of a very pleasant ferocity. The *Twilight of the Gods* had more than a whiff of it in its gentle playfulness[1] —

Old days!

From a purely "worldly" point of view I regret that this is "the second". Not that I think one better than the other – but the L[ady] into F[ox][2] was more "intimate" (no doubt about it) and had a note of anxious pathetic earnestness in the narrative which I believe accounted for some fashionable tears which, I am assured, were shed over it. This one is a trifle harder. What will the public say?

And now – what next? The fount could not have been dried by these two dips.[3] I am very interested. Give D. my affectionate greeting.

Jessie sends her love.

Ever yours

J. Conrad

To G. Jean-Aubry
Text MS Yale; Unpublished

12. Mai 24
le soir.

Très cher.

Certainement. On sera heureux de VS voir arriver le Samedi par le train que VS dites.

Je n'ai pas encore ouvert *l'adversaire*.[4] La pièce n'est pas encore arrivée.[5] La terminaison du Pers: Rec^d est une grande nouvelle.[6]

---

[1] A collection of fantastic and satirical tales by Richard Garnett, Edward's father, published in 1888.

[2] David Garnett's tale of metamorphosis, published in November 1922. Conrad congratulated Edward Garnett on its success in a letter of 10 March 1923.

[3] It flowed into such novels as *The Sailor's Return* (1925), *Aspects of Love* (1955), and *The Sons of the Falcon* (1972).

[4] The translation of 'The Brute' in the February issue of the *Revue de Genève*.

[5] In his letter of 11 May (MS Yale), Jean-Aubry told Conrad that he would send him a dramatisation of 'The Inn of the Two Witches'. Jean-Aubry forwarded a letter from its 'jeune adapteur' with his own letter of 31 May (MS Yale).

[6] As *Des souvenirs*, Jean-Aubry's translation was published by Gallimard in 1924 in an edition of 780 numbered copies. He wanted to bring a substantial portion of the MS on the visit proposed for Saturday. Another recent translation, the 'Character of the Foe' section from *The Mirror of the Sea*, accompanied the letter of 11 May.

Jessie sends her love.

En toute hate pour ne pas manquer la poste.

Toujours votre vieux

Conrad.

Evening

My very dear fellow,

Certainly. We will be happy to see you arrive on Saturday by the train you mention.

I haven't opened 'L'adversaire' yet. The play hasn't arrived yet. The completion of *A Personal Record* is great news.

Jessie sends her love.

In great haste so as not to miss the post.

Ever your old

Conrad.

To Ford Madox Ford

Text TS copy Yale;[1] Unpublished

Oswalds.

May 13th. 1924

Dear Ford,

Will you drop me a word, as you said you would, stating that you agree with the contents of my letter of May 2nd.

Yours,

J. C.

To Eric S. Pinker

Text TS Berg; Unpublished

Oswalds.

May 13th. [1924]

My dear Eric,

Very sorry. The thing slipped my memory. Of course I am not very anxious to write any sort of foreword[2] but if it is only a question of copyright perhaps the other author would be inclined to do it.

Always yrs

J Conrad

---

[1] A typed copy made for Conrad and bearing his initials; in his correspondence with Ford, he was unusually formal and legalistic.

[2] To *The Nature of a Crime*.

To Ford Madox Ford
Text TS Yale; Unpublished

[letterhead: Oswalds]
May 17th. 1924.

Dear Ford,

Thank you very much for your letter conveying your agreement with mine of May 2nd.

I have looked at the proofs and made a few corrections which escaped you. I have also considered your proposal of writing a preface and I forward you here the outcome of it, with the hope that you will act in the spirit of the last paragraph.[1] It seemed to me that in the collaborated work neither of us could write a preface with propriety.

Yet from the point of view of the book's future and also from consideration of copyright in U.S. I think each of us may contribute a few words of introduction over our own separate signatures.[2] The enclosed is my contribution. I hope it will meet with your approval, (I mean as to it being suitable from the point of view of the public) and that you will find time to say something, in that or any other vein.

If you are too full of work, or do not want the bother from any other reason, you may delete the last paragraph and move my initials up accordingly.

But I hope you will not. For your contribution of an introduction will be not only valuable, per se, but may influence the fortunes of the book in a considerable way. After all, this is the last piece of our joint work that is likely to appear and it seems to me becoming that we both should be heard on such an occasion.

Yours

J. Conrad

---

[1] Conrad's Foreword to *The Nature of a Crime* is dated 14 May 1924, as is Ford's cover letter to Conrad accompanying the proofs (TS Yale). At the end of his Preface, Conrad writes that he will 'pass the pen' to Ford 'in the hope that he may be moved to contradict me on every point of fact, impression, and appreciation . . . For it would be delightful to catch the echo of the desperate, earnest and funny quarrels which enlivened those old days. The pity of it is that there comes a time when all the fun of one's life must be looked for in the past!' (Duckworth, 1924, p. 7).
[2] The new material would extend the copyright of the whole.

To Eric S. Pinker
Text TS Berg; Unpublished

Oswalds.
May 18th. 1924.

Dearest Eric.

Thank you very much for letter advising payment.

You will see from the enclosures what has been done in the last three days. One of the enclosures consists of Ford's letter acknowledging the arrangement as to collaborated works. You have got the copy of that. Whether Ford will have it properly stamped I don't know, but I daresay he will. At any rate this will be the basis of all future intercourse with that gentleman.

I also have had from him the proofs of the *N. of the* C.*, and in view of your note suggesting the same thing I composed the Preface, (enclosure A) which I hope will meet with your approval, and have written him the letter, (enclosure B[1]) stroking him the right way so that he should do his part. I think it is a good way out; for, you understand how I shrank from appearing to take the production under my wing by letting it go out with a preface only by myself. I won't say any more on that point. I hope he will fall in with my suggestion. Whatever happens you may let D.P.[2] know that there is a preface; enough for copyright purposes. I posted the letter with preface and corrected proofs last Saturday to Paris, and they will be in his possession by the time you read this. I leave it to him to forward everything to Duckworth.

I am relieved to think this episode is over.

No news yet from Sir Robert. Jessie doesn't look very well, and the pain increases. I am just fighting on, and that is all I can say.

I have had a satisfactory letter from Nelson and I am thankful that something is going on well. I suppose Dent's negotiation has not fallen through so far.

Ever affect[ly] Yours

J. Conrad

PS Was Dick's entertainment a success? he seems to think so. I hope both of you are well and cheery. Our love to Margot.[3]

---

[1] A copy of the letter of the 17th (TS carbon Berg).
[2] Doubleday, Page would be publishing the book in the USA.   [3] Margit, Pinker's wife.

To Eric S. Pinker

Text TS/MS Berg; Unpublished

Oswalds.

May 22nd. 1924.

Dearest Eric.

I enclose for your inspection the contents of the envelope received from Hueffer this moment. Three pages of Preface and the covering letter.[1]

On the Preface there is nothing to say; but the letter, which suggests that I should suppress it, requires a little consideration. His warning, (however well meant) of some forthcoming scandal I am inclined to disregard.[2] What scandal there was is an old story, and other considerations make me suspect that the supposed resuscitation of it is a figment of F. M. F's imagination. He seems to be in a curious state of mind, not altogether new to me, and I reckon there is not very much in it.

His other suggestion: to include in the vol. a sort of "analysis of collaboration" applied to some parts of "Romance" need not be negatived; at any rate as far as I am concerned.[3] It is fairly correct. Therefore the matter might be left to Duckworth and the Garden City. The analysis in question is a matter of a few pages of the "transatlantic review". The most that can be said for it is that it will add a little to the bulk of the volume. This may be the publisher's point of view. Hueffer's remark that it will provoke a certain amount of special notice from the critics, is, I believe, just.

These are my thoughts and conclusions. If you agree with them will you please take such action with the publishers as is necessary for the inclusion of preface and analysis, both, or either of them.[4]

Ever affec^ly Yours

J. C.

PS Do you know Watts* is sending out a new ed (1924) of Letters to Watts.[5] That's all right – but why should he send a copy to *me*? Never done it before!

---

[1] Ford to Conrad, 21 May, headed 'Private' (TS Yale).

[2] Because he was so muddied by scandal, Ford suggested dropping his own Preface, but keeping Conrad's. An old hostility had come to life. In 1912, Elsie Hueffer, who refused to grant him a divorce, had taken Ford's lover Violet Hunt to court to stop her calling herself Mrs Hueffer. Now, 'Mesdames Elsie and Violet H. Hueffer' were 'about to burst into even more violent litigation as to their right to use my abandoned patronymic'. Hence, Ford did not know 'whether you ought to associate your name so intimately with mine' (*ibid.*).

[3] According to Ford, Henry Holt 'was very anxious to include as an appendix the analysed version of passages from *Romance*' published in the second number of the *transatlantic review*.

[4] The British and American editions of *The Nature of a Crime*, published in September, included the two prefaces and "A Note on 'Romance'".

[5] A new edition of *Letters Addressed to A. P. Watt* (London: A. P. Watt and Son, 1893), which included letters and testimonials by Arthur Conan Doyle, Thomas Hardy, Rudyard Kipling,

Anyhow the collection reminds me of the bundle of testimonials the washermen used to bring on board ships arriving in Calcutta – quite as numerous and nearly as glowing.

To Ford Madox Ford
Text TS Yale; Unpublished

[letterhead: Oswalds]
May 22nd. 1924.

Dear Ford

I have just time before the evening post to acknowledge receipt of your letter covering the Preface.

I do not know what may be coming in the way of "unpleasantness" between women; but I am totally unaffected by your kind warning. The Preface is very nice and characteristic, and to tell you the truth very much something that I expected. I am not sure I did not mean "discussions" when I wrote "quarrels," but the last word was right, since it has provoked your friendly contradiction.

As to the analysis – if the two publishers consent (and I don't see why they shouldn't) it will, in my view, be an interesting addition. This opinion of mine will be conveyed to Duckworth and Doubleday without loss of time.

Am I to take it that you will send my Preface and a copy of yours to Duckworth, together with the proofs? Or do you want me to send my copy to Duckworth – I mean *my* copy of *your* Preface? Please drop me a postcard.

I am right sorry that you are abandoning the *t. r.* [1] As to the novel[2] I think that, between us two, if I tell you that I consider it "tout à fait chic" you will understand perfectly how much that "phrase d'atelier"[3] means to the initiated.

Yours

J. Conrad

---

and many other authors who had chosen Watt as their literary agent. An expanded edition came out in 1894.
[1] Comparing himself with a dung beetle rolling goat droppings up a hill, Ford had announced that he was giving up the *transatlantic review*, with no successor in view (Ford to Conrad, 21 May). The *review* brought out a Conrad memorial supplement in October (2, pp. 325–50) and lasted till January 1925.
[2] *Some Do Not*, recently published by Duckworth, the first volume of the 'Tietjens tetralogy' now known as *Parade's End*.
[3] 'Altogether chic' . . . 'workshop phrase'. Cf. the letter to Winawer of 9 April 1923, where, Conrad writes: '"Très chic" – as French painters used to say of their pictures. This formula expressed the highest praise.'

To Ford Madox Ford

Text TS and carbon Yale;[1] Unpublished

[Oswalds]
May 24th. 1924.

Dear Ford.

I return to you the Agreement (triplicate) with Kra for "Romance".[2] In the terms of the agreement into which we entered on May 2nd, I have nothing to do with it. All the rights for translations being transferred to you in consideration of my having a free hand in dealing with our col[l]aborated works in English speaking countries.

This being so my signature is unnecessary. I take this opportunity to state clearly again that you have the sole and absolute right to dispose of them in French translation, all the proceeds arising from that source ("Inheritors" and "Romance") being made over to you in their entirety.

J. C.

I am interested in your visit to the U.S. and I hope it will be both entertaining and profitable.[3]

You must have by this time my letter written on the 22nd in re Preface and Analysis of collaboration. Drop me a word on a postcard what I am to do with your Preface and whether you have sent mine to Duckworth with the proofs.

J. C.

To J. St Loe Strachey

Text TS Lords;[4] J-A, 2, 343; Stape (1989)

[letterhead: Oswalds]
May 24th. 1924.

Dear Mr Strachey.

Thank you very much for your letter.[5] I am very sensible to the compliment of being asked to contribute to the Spectator.

---

[1] The typed PS appears only on the carbon.

[2] On 22 May, following instructions from his agent Victor Llara, Ford had asked Conrad to sign and return copies of the contract (dated 26 March) with Simon and Lucien Kra of Éditions du Sagittaire for the French translation of *Romance* (MS Yale).

[3] This was Conrad's last letter to Ford, who replied from Plymouth on 31 May aboard the *Paris* en route to New York (MS Yale; printed in Saunders, 2, p. 158).

[4] And a carbon copy at Yale.

[5] Of 23 May (Stape and Knowles, p. 240), inviting Conrad to address the question, 'Is Europe dead?' See the letter to Strachey of 27 May.

I think you will agree that living as I do out of the world (too much so, alas! – but it's too late to repine now) and not even reading the papers with any regularity, I am not competent to deal with the subject. Speaking entre nous, Europe collectively may be dead but the nations composing it don't give me that impression. France is working hard from end to end. Italy has given us a marvellous example of vitality quite lately.[1] Germany is very much alive internally in her own characteristic way. The newly created states do, at any rate, struggle for life as if they believed in their future. No. Europe is very far from being a graveyard. One need not be very optimistic to see that. So it seems to me. But it may be the illusion of a solitary man. I do not know what may happen to-morrow, but I hope I will be allowed to keep that illusion to the end of my life.

Believe me, with the greatest regard,

Sincerely yours

J. Conrad

To Amelia Ward

Text MS copy Yale;[2] Unpublished

[letterhead: Oswalds]

24 / 5 / 24

My dear Amelia[3]

I was delighted to hear from you. I assure you my dear friend of old days that I have no recollection of receiving a letter from poor Herbert.[4] It cannot have reached me. I am truly sorry to hear you have lost him and your dear Mother[5] for whom I had a great affection and regard as you know. I am

---

[1] Benito Mussolini's National Fascist party took over the government in the autumn of 1922 and had just won a large majority in the parliamentary election of 6 April 1924. The party made much of such catchwords as 'youth', 'vigour', and 'renewal'. Its rhetoric was taken seriously by the British press, not least in some of the newspapers irregularly read at Oswalds. The *Daily Mail* in particular was given to extravagant praises of the man its proprietor, Lord Rothermere, repeatedly hailed as 'The Saviour of Western Civilisation'.

[2] A copy in Amelia Ward's hand, indicating that Conrad's original was on Oswalds stationery.

[3] Amelia Ward (1862–1929) was one of the eight children (four sons and four daughters) of William Ward, Conrad's landlord at 6 Dynevor Road, Stoke Newington. When Conrad and his friend Adolf Krieger were lodging with the family, she was nineteen and working as a machinist. Her younger brother William worked as an assistant storekeeper at the London Sailors' Home, where Conrad had often stayed between voyages. The Wards had lived in Gibraltar and South Africa, and after some years in England emigrated to Australia.

[4] Herbert F. Ward (1869–1922), who was born in Cape Town, died in Sydney. There is no record of a letter from him, but among the volumes from Conrad's library sold by W. Heffer & Sons in 1925 was a copy of Ward's *A Voice from the Congo* (New York: Scribner's, 1910) inscribed by his son: 'To Joseph Conrad, from the Author's Son, in sincere admiration, Rodney S. Ward, Christ Church, Oxford, May, 1922' (Heffer catalogue 251, item 2902).

[5] Dolores Mary Ward (born in Gibraltar about 1839) died in Australia in 1914.

touched by the terms of your letter. I am not conscious of having deserved all the kind things you say. But I remember how good you all were to me, and how on my voyage, I looked forward to the unfailing warm welcome awaiting me in your home. Thanks for all your news, so interesting and so difficult to believe. I can't imagine Lilly the mother of eight children. I still see her as a dear little girl, as she was in Dynevor R^{d}.[1] Strangely enough, I don't remember her so much in Sydney whereas all the rest of you live in my memory as I saw [you] last there – on board the "Otago."

I have been married 28 yrs now. We have two sons. One 25 and married, the other 18. I will collect a few photos and send them to you soon. Give my affectionate remembrance to everybody and my best wishes for all possible happiness. To you and Lizzie[2] I send my love, which you will accept for the sake of old days when we were young together.

Always yours

J Conrad

To Richard Curle

Text MS Indiana; Curle 146 (in part)[3]

[Oswalds]

[late May 1924][4]

Dearest Dick.

Here everything is much the same. No date yet. It is very good and dear of you to promise to stand by me in the coming trial (and it will be that for me) in this more than brotherly fashion. I am very touched and very grateful.

On the actual day B. promised to come down early. John will be wired for in time too to see her just before the operation. It is Jessie's own wish. She is much comforted by the thought of your unfailing friendship towards us all. I am looking forward to a visit from you while she is in the Nurs: Home. I can't shake off a sort of vague dread tho' I agree with you that there's nothing

---

[1] Matilda R. Ward, aged six when Conrad knew her.

[2] Elizabeth, born in Gibraltar, was twenty when Conrad lodged with the family; like her younger sister Amelia, she was employed as a machinist.

[3] The third paragraph was omitted.

[4] Curle dated this [May 1924]. Conrad was working on the Preface to *The Shorter Tales* at the beginning of the month, and sent it to New York on the 7th (the 'Wednesday last' of the letter to F. N. Doubleday of 8 May). By the time Conrad wrote the present letter, he had had a reply from Nelson Doubleday; unless this reply arrived by cable, it could not have reached him any earlier than the 25th. On the 29th, Conrad told Aubry that the date of his wife's operation was now set.

else for it. The situation as it is cannot last. Neither am I without hope of complete success.

The 3 last "Blunts" were remarkably good. Also the other articles. Instone having been elected President of the Motor Ma[nu]f[acture]rs Association gave a dinner at which he placed B on his left hand; Stratton (the other partner) being on the right. He considers his position in the firm perfectly secure whatever happens. The question is – how the trade will stand the blow?[1]

Eric and his wife were delighted with your entertainement*. E. thinks you make a delightful host, while the company was pleasant beyond his expectations. Was *our* Gov: Gen: in good form?[2] E. was much struck by his amiability.

Jessie sends her love.

Ever Yrs

J. Conrad.

PS I had a satisfactory letter from Nelson Doubleday. I have sent them a preface for the Vol of Coll^d Stories.[3]

To the Rt. Hon. Ramsay MacDonald

Text MS copy Berg; Morley
Copy:

[letterhead: Oswalds]
27 May 1924.

Sir.[4]

It is with the deepest possible sense of the honour H. M. The King is graciously willing to confer on me on your recommendation, that I beg leave to decline the profferred* knighthood.

In conveying to you my sincere thanks I venture to add, that, as a man whose early years were closely associated in hard toil and unforgotten

---

[1] Instone was a pioneer racer and a founder of the RAC. No recent 'John Blunt' column had dealt with abolishing the tariffs on imported cars, but Curle may have written editorials against the government's proposal to do so. The *Daily Mail* regarded Free Trade as a Liberal folly.

[2] Sir Hugh Clifford.

[3] The preface had been sent on the packet of 7 May; see Conrad's letter to Doubleday of 8 May.

[4] The Right Honourable James Ramsay MacDonald (1866–1937), the illegitimate son of a Scottish farm labourer and a maid-servant, became the first Labour Prime Minister of the United Kingdom in 1924, after more than twenty years as a national official of the party. His first term lasted for only nine months, but he served again as Prime Minister from 1929 to 1935, this time as the head of a 'National' or coalition government.

friendships with British working men, I am specially touched at this offer being made to me during your premiership.

I have the honour to be, with the greatest regard

Your obedient servant

Joseph Conrad.

The Rt. Hon. Ramsay Macdonald M. P.

To J. St Loe Strachey

Text TS Lords;[1] J-A, 2, 343; Stape (1989)

[letterhead: Oswalds]
May 27th. 1924.

Dear Mr Strachey.

It is very good of you to write to me and, of course, I can have no objection to you quoting the passage you mention. But writing to you, in perfect confidence of being understood, I am afraid I did not watch the wording. It strikes me that for purposes of quotation the phrase "Europe collectively may be dead" is not very good as it stands.[2] Perhaps it would have been better if I had written: "Europe outwardly may look dead" (in the sense that its old watchwords and formulas of international intercourse are dead).

However, I will leave that to you, merely remarking that words that get into print become at once victims of that "uncomprehension" which is the characteristic of the bulk of reading mankind.

I shall look forward eagerly to your article[3] in which my words will have the honour to be embodied.

Kindest regards.

very faithfully Yours

J. Conrad

---

[1] And a carbon at Yale.

[2] These revisions are registered on Conrad's letter of 24 May in Strachey's hand.

[3] Strachey's article, 'Topics of the Day: Is Europe Dead?', appeared in *The Spectator* on 31 May (p. 868). Lightly edited by Strachey, Conrad's text reads: 'Europe outwardly may look dead, in the sense that its old watchwords and formulas of International intercourse are dead, but the nations composing it don't give me that impression. France is working hard from end to end. Italy has given us a marvellous example of vitality lately. Germany is very much alive internally in her own characteristic way. The newly-created States, at any rate, struggle for life as if they believed in their future. No. Europe is very far from being a graveyard. But it may be the illusion of a solitary man. I do not know what may happen to-morrow, but I hope I shall be allowed to keep that illusion to the end of my life.'

To G. Jean-Aubry

Text MS Yale; *L. fr.* 199

[letterhead: Oswalds]
29. 5. 24.

Cher Jean.

Merci de Votre lettre et l'intéréssante coupure.

L'operation aura lieu la semaine prochaine – mais Sir R ne peut pas accorde si* il pourra arriver ici pour la nuit de mardi ou de jeudi. Il operera dans la matinée.

Ce sera un grand reconfort de vous avoir ici; et si vous apportez le MS du Pers: Rec: nous pourrons travailler ensemble.

Je vais VS envoyer une depêche pour VS faire savoir le jour. Jean va arriver Samedi prochain pour 15 jours; et Borys a promis d'etre là aussi.

Faites nos amitiés a la chère Mme Alvar. Je vais lui envoyer un petit mot par la poste, aussitôt l'affaire finie.

Jessie sends her love.

Je VS embrasse

Votre

J. Conrad

Dear Jean.

Thank you for your letter and the interesting cutting.

The operation will take place next week – but Sir R can not yet decide if he will arrive here for Tuesday or for Thursday night. He will operate in the morning.

It will be a great comfort to have you here; and if you bring the MS of *Personal Record* we can work together.

I'll send you a telegram to let you know the day. John will arrive next Saturday for a fortnight; and Borys has also promised to be here.

Give our regards to dear Mme Alvar. I will send word to her by post, as soon as the business is finished.

Jessie sends her love.

I embrace you

Your

J. Conrad

To George T. Keating

Text TS/MS Yale; Unpublished

[letterhead: Oswalds]
May 29th. 1924.

My dear Keating

Here is the de luxe "Rover" vol. which, I presume, closes the series of notes and inscriptions for your Conrad collection. I hope you will find this last item satisfactory. I could not give you an extended bibliography, but I have written all I know; and, after all, those are the material points.

The transcription does not look very well but my wrist is still very weak and gets painful very soon after I begin to write. It is a horrible nuisance.

I am glad to hear that you have acquired the MS of the Preface for the volume of Collected Stories. The MS and the First Typed Copy are going to you by the same mail in a large envelope.

I have ventured to add to it four pages of another Preface for a little book called "The Nature of a Crime" (collaborated with Hueffer many years ago) which will appear at the end of this year. I hope you will put those very scratchy pages away with your other manuscripts as a memento of our friendship and the affectionate esteem in which I hold you. It is a very small item but it is unique as the only Preface I have written for any collaborated piece of work.

My wife is going to have another operation on her knee next week and I feel the strain of waiting till it is over. She joins me in warm regards to you both and the children.

Believe me always most sincerely yours

J. Conrad

PS Many thanks for letting me have a view of the Nelson letter which is most interesting.[1] I appreciate very much your taking the risk of loss in order to give me that great pleasure.

J. C.

---

[1] A four-page letter from Admiral Nelson, written on board the *Victory* on 6 April 1805, to report the escape of the French fleet from Toulon. It thus corresponds with the final scene of *The Rover*; see Keating, pp. 338–40. The MS is now at Yale.

To André Gide

Text MS Doucet; *L. fr.* 200[1]

[letterhead: Oswalds]
30. 5. 24.

Mon très cher Gide,

Pardonnez-moi de ne pas Vs avoir remercié pour le livre plus tôt.[2] C'est mon poignet gouteux. Je peux a peine tenir la plume. Ai-je besoin de Vous dire que Vos pages me sont toujours précieusement sympathiques. Dans le vol que Vs avez eu l'amitié de m'envoyer il y a des pages que je connais. Je ne connaissais pas les Prefaces. Je les ai lues avec délices – et aussi les cons[i]d[érati]ons sur la Mythologie.

Voilà bientôt quatre ans que je [n]'ai fait rien qui vaille. Je me demande si c'est la fin? Peut-être. En revanche je suis devenu asthmatique. C'est assez embêtant. Ce qui me console c'est le succès (modéré j'en conviens) des traductions françaises. Et cette consolation c'est a Vous que je la dois.

Ma femme, qui se recommande à Votre bon souvenir, n'en a pas fini avec les opérations. On va lui en faire une la semaine prochaine. La 5ème depuis 1917!

Pensez a moi comme Votre fidèle admirateur et ami.

J Conrad[3]

My very dear Gide,

Forgive me for not thanking you sooner for the book. It's my gouty wrist. I can barely hold a pen. But I don't need to tell you that I find your pages always congenial beyond measure. In the volume you so kindly sent to me there are some pages that I know. I did not know the Prefaces. I have read them with delight – and also the reflections on Mythology.

It will soon be four years since I have done anything of any merit. I ask myself if it's the end? Maybe. Moreover I've become asthmatic. It's a nuisance. What consoles me is the success (moderate, I admit) of the French translations. And this consolation I owe to you.

---

[1] Jean-Aubry corrected Conrad's French and replaced the last sentence in the third paragraph with 'Encore une!' ('Another one!').

[2] Gide's *Incidences* (Paris: Nouvelle Revue Française, 1924), a collection of essays, letters, travel journals, and prefaces to books. The items mentioned here are 'Considérations sur la mythologie grecque', pp. 125–30, and prefaces to Baudelaire's *Les Fleurs du mal*, Stendhal's *Armance*, and Pushkin's *La Dame de pique* (*The Queen of Spades*), pp. 159–87.

[3] For Gide's reply of 7 June, which begins: 'Votre exquise lettre rend un son si triste', see Stape and Knowles, p. 242.

My wife, who sends you her greetings, has not yet finished with operations.
She will undergo one next week. The 5th since 1917!
Think of me as your loyal admirer and friend.

J. Conrad

To Louis Roché
Text L. fr. 201

Oswalds
30. 5. 24.

Cher Monsieur,[1]
C'est mon poignet goutteux qui m'a empèché de vous remercier tout de
suite pour le volume de vers que vous avez eu la bonté de m'envoyer.[2] Ce
bon mouvement n'a pas été perdu. J'ai à vous remercier pour le réveil des
sympathies et des sensations que je n'espérais plus retrouver dans ma vie.
Que puis-je dire de plus, pour vous donner l'idée du plaisir (complet et sans
défaillance) que la lecture de vos vers m'a donné? Car voilà bientôt soixante-
cinq ans que mon nom a été inscrit sur le rôle d'équipage de ce vieux navire
enchanté qui roule sans timonier à travers l'inconnu,[3] et que vous avez si
bien regardé, dans sa magnificence et dans son ignominie, avec la noble
clairvoyance d'un poète.
Veuillez accepter une affectueuse poignée de mains.

Bien à vous.

Dear Sir,
My gouty wrist has kept me from thanking you immediately for the volume
of poems that you so kindly sent me. That good impulse has not been lost.
I have to thank you for reawakening sympathies and feelings that I had
given up hope of feeling again in my lifetime. What more can I say to give
you an idea of the pleasure (complete and faultless) that the reading of your

---

[1] Louis-Marie-Émile Roché (1903–89) was a minor French poet who later made a career as a
diplomat, serving as French attaché to Warsaw (1931), Brussels (1932), Vienna (1934), London
(1937), and Dublin (1940), and after the Second World War as Ambassador to Australia (1952–5)
and Lebanon (1956–60). He published two further volumes of poetry: *Si proche et si lointaine*
(1946) and *Le Solitaire de Castille* (1949).
[2] *Temps perdu* (Paris: Le Divan, 1924). Jean-Aubry noted that Conrad was especially fond of one
poem in this collection, 'Ciel de Nuit' ('Night Sky').
[3] Conrad refers here to a quatrain in 'Ciel de Nuit':

> Dans l'air froid, balisé par des feux innombrables,
> La terre, vaisseau triste aux vieux mâts pourrissants,
> Mène, sans timonier, vers des ports improbables,
> Son grand rêve de gloire obscur et impuissant.

verses has given me? Because it will soon be sixty-five years ago that my
name was written on the crew list of this old enchanted vessel that rolls
without a helmsman across the unknown and that you have seen so well, in
its magnificence and its ignominy, with the noble clairvoyance of a poet.

Please accept an affectionate handshake.

Yours truly.

To Captain Francis McCullagh
Text MS Klett; Stape (1988)

[letterhead: Oswalds]
31. 5. 24

Dear Sir.[1]

My warm thanks for the inscribed copy of "Bolshevik Persecution" You
have been kind enough to send me.[2]

I have read with interest this most remarkably able account of a significant
episode in the long tale of religious persecution. It reproduces (apart from its
actual subject) the whole atmosphere of the Russian revolution in its horror
and its stupidity in a most convincing manner.

Believe me, with very kind regards

faithfully Yours

J. Conrad

To Elbridge L. Adams
Text Adams 36, 44 (in part)

[Oswalds]
[early June 1924][3]

We were very glad to hear from you and to know that you are all well and
flourishing in the Green River Farm.

---

[1] An Irish-born author and adventurer, Captain Francis McCullagh (1874–1956) was fluent
in five languages. As a reporter for the *New York Herald*, he rode with the Cossacks in the
Russo-Japanese War of 1904–5 and was captured by the Japanese. During the First World
War he served in the Dardanelles campaign as a lieutenant in the Royal Irish Fusiliers, and
then involved himself with cloak-and-dagger intrigues in Serbia and Macedonia. Captured
in Siberia after the fall of Omsk, McCullagh spent two years as a prisoner of the Bolsheviks
in Moscow, an experience he described in *A Prisoner of the Reds* (1921). An ardent Catholic and
anti-Bolshevik, McCullagh later wrote books denouncing *Red Mexico* (1928) and praising the
Nationalist armies in *In Franco's Spain* (1937).
[2] *The Bolshevik Persecution of Christianity* (John Murray, 1924).
[3] Conrad learned of the new date set for Jessie Conrad's surgery after his letter to Gide of
30 May.

I return the fifteen pages typescript with some remarks and slight corrections on the margins. My having done so is a sufficient demonstration of my
attitude towards the proposed publication. The decision of course must rest
with you. I have the best recollection of the personality of the writer, but a
rather faint one of what was said on that particular evening.[1] This does not
mean that the memory of my visit to your home is a fading memory. That
will never fade; for it is based on the warm and abiding sense of your and
your wife's affectionate welcome and deep kindness, which surpassed my
confident expectation and secured my lifelong gratitude.

I suppose Jessie has written to your wife about the operation hanging over
her head. Its date has been now fixed for the 13th of this month. We all, here,
are hoping for the best; and indeed there are grounds to hope that it may
finally do away with those painful local troubles which have disabled her and
caused her so much suffering in the last two years. But of course one can't
help being anxious.

I haven't done much since you have seen me, and, truth to tell, I have not
been very well either. Our intention is to leave this house in September, but
I must confess that we have not yet found another. All this is very disturbing
mentally – and the sense of bodily discomfort of which I am almost never
free is not very helpful to literary composition. I will not deny that my spirits
suffer from this state of affairs. But I won't enlarge on that, which I regard as
a passing phase which must be faced with all the resolution one can muster.
We haven't had many visitors here lately and, truth to say, I don't feel very
sociably inclined.

To F. N. Doubleday

Text TS Princeton; J-A, 2, 344

Oswalds.
June 2nd. 1924.

Very dear Effendi

I am glad you accept the reference to you in my Preface[2] in the spirit in
which it was traced; which is that of affection. Florence's delightful letter

---

[1] As the Adamses' guest during his American tour, Conrad had met Dr John Sheridan Zelie
(1866–1942), whose draft account of the evening had been forwarded for Conrad's approval;
it was published in 1925 in Adams's *Joseph Conrad: The Man* and reprinted in Ray, pp. 191–7. A
Yale graduate and Presbyterian clergyman, Zelie served as a chaplain with the American Red
Cross in France in 1918–19 and thereafter with the First Presbyterian Church of New York.
During the Volga famine of 1922 he was active with the American Relief Administration. He
was among the mourners at Conrad's funeral.
[2] In his Preface to *The Shorter Tales of Joseph Conrad*, Conrad paid tribute to his 'old friend and
publisher . . . who is an idealist and who would simply hate to let anything "just happen" in
his business. His business, to my mind, consists, mainly, in being the intermediary between

arrived this morning and warmed up the cold air of a gloomy wet day. After reading it and taking it to my heart downstairs I sent it up to Jessie, who I think will not come down to-day.

All the family was here yesterday, John having arrived from France on a short visit, as we thought that the operation would take place this week. However it has been put off till the 13th, Sir Robert's engagements preventing him from coming down here before. He will arrive here on the 12th for the night. Jessie intends to give him his dinner and then at about 8.30 drive to the nursing-home in Canterbury. Sir Robert intends to operate very early next morning and then go on to London, after lunching with the local surgeon.

Both of them are hopeful that this will do away definitely with all those local troubles which have been such a source of pain and worry to us both. But that of course can not be ascertained for some time as such troubles have been known to recur even after a whole year.

I notice with a certain amount of satisfaction that "The Rover" is still an object of critical discussion. I have this morning received a two pages-and-a-half criticism from the editor of the "Dial" under the ominous caption "A Popular Novel".[1] And it was not meant ironically. I never dreamed that such a thing would happen to me. I must confess that I have been extremely interested by what the critic, (Gilbert Seldes) was moved to say.[2] I have seldom met two pages and a half of print that contained so much in the way of insight,

---

certain men's reveries and the wide-awake brain of the rest of the world . . . for reasons of a deeper personal kind, having nothing to do with business, his words have great weight with me' (*Last Essays*, p. 141).

[1] *Dial*, 76 (June 1924), 541–3.

[2] An essayist, novelist, playwright, and screenwriter, Gilbert Seldes (1893–1970) helped to define the role of American cultural critic. He was managing editor of the *Dial* and also New York correspondent for the *Criterion*, T. S. Eliot's journal of literature and ideas; although still a contributor, Seldes had just resigned the post of managing editor at the *Dial*. He writes of *The Rover*'s fortunes: 'it swept along, and the number of copies sold is large, surprisingly large for an author who only a few years ago was the property of the few' (p. 541). Recognising the novel's 'severity of style', Seldes ascribes its success to 'skilful promotion' rather than any submission to undiscriminating tastes: 'The popularity of The Rover is all the more interesting because it seems not deliberately designed by the author.' Nevertheless, 'one might say that it is a pity for Conrad to beome popular with a novel of his second order'. Conrad's strength is as 'a novelist distant in spirit from our direct contemporaries. He is a romancer, not a satirist, and his preoccupation is a moral, not a social, one. The two things go so seldom together; where the framework is melodrama, the moral tone is usually high, but the moral interest lacks intensity. In Conrad the drama moves magnificently; deep within it there is almost always a case of conscience . . . whenever the moral predicament has no great gravity, as in The Rover, the result is weak. For it is only when Conrad is engaged in a dilemma that he has the power of creation, which . . . means the power to create a separate world in which events and characters have life, almost without reference to the logic of our events and the limitations of our characters' (p. 542). His recent popularity is a belated recognition of his artistic seriousness. At a time when fiction's concerns have become more petty, his is the real thing: 'The creative capacity, in whatever degree it exists nowadays, tends to belittle itself, to attach itself to ideas, to criticize or satirize, to do anything in short but make the effort to

comprehension, and I may add also misunderstanding; in addition to subtle feeling (all of a most intelligent kind). I feel half inclined to write a letter to the editor, but I have never answered any criticism in my life, so far, and I am loth to break the rule. Moreover I think that an author who tries to "explain" is exposing himself to a very great risk – the risk of confessing himself a failure. For a work of art should speak for itself. Yet much could be said on the other side; for it is also clear that a work of art is not a logical demonstration carrying its intention on the face of it. I wish I had you within reach, so that I could take your advice from a certain point of view and dear Florence's from another.

But after all I suppose that silence is the most becoming.

Ever yours

J. Conrad.

To Florence Doubleday

Text MS Princeton;[1] J-A, 2, 345

[Oswalds]

[2 June 1924]

Dearest Florence.

I was delighted with your good and charming letter. Give my affectionate regards to the Saffords (not forgetting Cordelia) and express my high appreciation of Mr & Mrs Davies'*[2] friendly recollection of my unworthy self. To all American friends – greetings! with extended right arm a la "fascisti".[3]

The only news – strictly *entre nous trois* – which I have to send – is: that 3 days ago I had a letter from the Prime Minister (it came in a long envelope and I thought it was a supertax form) offering me a "birthday honour" in the shape of knighthood. I declined with deference and, I hope, in appropriate terms.[4]

Consider yourselves sworn to secrecy. The letter is marked "private & conf[identi]al" – and the news must not get [into] the papers either here or in America.

---

soar . . . And the duration and ease of his flight, however they vary from one book to another, are secondary considerations. He is still an eagle, and not a beast of burden' (p. 543).

[1] Written on the verso of the letter to Doubleday.

[2] Mr and Mrs John W. Davis; he was a former ambassador to the UK.

[3] The salute of Benito Mussolini's National Fascist party.

[4] See Conrad's reply to Ramsay MacDonald of 27 May, six days earlier.

Ever since this happened Jessie has been teasing me. I am glad she has something to amuse her – a good, old, domestic joke. She sends her best love to you both.

I am dear Florence

your most affect^te friend and servant.

J. Conrad

To Eric S. Pinker

Text MS Berg; Unpublished

[Oswalds]
2. June 24.

Dearest Eric

Sorry to say the operation has been put off till the 13th. Sir R. can not manage to come down here before the 12th. He will dine and sleep here and operate next morning in the St George Nursing Home in C'bury.

Of other news the best is only that the P. Minister has offered me a "birth-day honour"[1] of the usual kind which I have declined with proper deference.

Of course this is a "conf[identi]al" communication, so be on guard against anybody connected with the press – even remotely; as it would be most unpleasant for me if the refusal got into the newspapers.

Our love to yourself and your wife.

Alway[s] affect^y Yours

J. C.

To Aniela Zagórska

Text MS copy Yale;[2] Najder 298

[Oswalds]
2. VI. 24.

My dear Aniela,

I have just received your letter and am writing these few words to let you know that the operation will take place on the 13th of this month.

---

[1] Knighthoods are conferred twice annually, at the New Year and on the sovereign's official birthday, which for George V was 3 June.

[2] Zagórska's French translation.

Thank you for your letter and for the press-cuttings. I am delighted to know that I am touching hearts and souls – and that the *Set of Six* is so highly regarded from the artistic point of view.[1] Those stories had no success here.

I am not working; I can not work. This is quite worrisome. But let that remain strictly between us.

Both of us, Jessie and I, embrace you affectionately.

Always your

Konrad.

To Captain Francis McCullagh

Text TS carbon Yale;[2] Unpublished

[Oswalds]
June 5th. 1924.

I do not recollect very well what it is I have said when thanking you for the book you have been good enough to send me. The letter was simply a personal appreciation of your excellent work, and I would not like to be put forward as a man having any special knowledge of Bolsheviks or other Russians of any kind. I regard "Under Western Eyes" as a purely literary composition, without any other significance but that which attaches to an attempt at creative art;[3] but of course I authorise you to quote whatever you like out of my letter to you.[4]

To G. Jean-Aubry

Text MS Yale; *L. fr.* 202[5]

[6 June 1924][6]

Cher Jean.

Je pense que je pourrais venir mercredi prochain. Sir Robert arrivera ici Jeudi soir pour diner. L'operation (je viens de l'apprendre) aura lieu a 10.15. vendredi matin (a Canterbury).

Savez-vous ce que me veut le Ministre?[7] Ça ne peut être seulement l'envie de me donner a manger.

---

[1] *Sześć opowieści* (Warsaw: Ignis, 1924), translated by Wilam Horzyca, Leon Piwiński, and Tadeusz Puljanowski, was part of a planned eighteen-volume edition of Conrad's works, of which only six were completed.

[2] Lacking the salutation and farewell.

[3] On the 5th, McCullagh had written: 'As a matter of fact your own books "Under Western Eyes" and "The Secret Agent" gave me, long ago, a sure key to the psychology of the Russian revolutionary and of the Russian police-spy' (Stape and Knowles, p. 241).

[4] McCullagh replied on 6 June, citing the two sentences he wished to quote in advertisements for the second edition of his book (Stape and Knowles, p. 242).

[5] Jean-Aubry omits the PS.   [6] Date in Jean-Aubry's hand, confirmed by contents.

[7] Conrad had been invited to lunch at the Polish Legation with Konstanty Skirmunt (1866–1951), who served as Foreign Minister for several months in 1921–2; see the PS to Conrad's letter to Borys of 6 June. Jean-Aubry, who was in touch with the Polish military attaché, had

J'ai l'idée qu'on va me demander a écrire quelque chose. Mais que pourrai-je écrire?

Oui très cher. Revenez avec moi ici passer merc:, diner avec Sir R. J. et passer la nuit de Jeudi ici. Jessie ira au Nursing home après le diner. Nous pourrons travailler Jeudi matin.[1] Vous et Mrs C. ferez une partie de bézique[2] dans l'après-midi. Votre présence nous aidera a passer le temps d'attente. Voulez Vous?

Jessie sends her love.

Votre vieux

Conrad

Sneller[3] VS menèra a la station a 9.30. Sir R. et moi quitterons ici pour Canterbury a 10ʰ.

Dear Jean,

I think I could come up next Wednesday. Sir Robert will arrive here Thursday evening to dine. The operation (I've just learned) will take place at 10:15 Friday morning in Canterbury.

Do you know what the Minister wants with me? It can't be just a desire to feed me.

I suspect they are going to ask me to write something. But what could I write?

Yes, my dear fellow. Come back here with me to spend Wed:, dine with Sir R. J. and spend Thursday night here. Jessie will go to the nursing home after dinner. We can work Thursday morning. You and Mrs. C. will play a game of bézique in the afternoon. Your presence will help pass the time while we wait. Would you mind?

Jessie sends her love.

Your old

Conrad

Sneller will take you to the station at 9:30. Sir R. and I will leave for Canterbury at 10 o'clock.

---

written to tell Conrad about an earlier plan to have him meet the Queen of Roumania, but she had now left London (31 May, MS Yale). Najder (1983) gives two eye-witness accounts of the lunch (pp. 262–8).

[1] On Jean-Aubry's translation of *A Personal Record*.

[2] A two-handed card game invented in France, played with two or more 32-card packs.

[3] A venerable taxi-driver, once described by Conrad as looking like a Russian general (*Letters*, 7, p. 305).

To Borys Conrad
Text MS Wellington; Knowles and Miskin

[Oswalds]
6th June 1924.

Dearest Boy.

We have heard today that Sir R. will arrive for the night at 7.56 (Cant. W) and the operation is fixed for *10.15* Friday. Perhaps You could get here (Oswalds) by Nine to breakfast with us – I mean Sir R. and I? Mother will go to the nursing home on Thursday 8.30. pm.

Drop us a line. Mrs C. has been for a nice drive today. She looks fairly well. Our dear love to You three

Ever Your affct Father

J. C

PS. I am invited to lunch at Polish Lega*tn* on Wednesday. Think coming up in the car. I'll write again.

To Eric S. Pinker
Text TS Berg; Unpublished

Oswalds.
June 6th 1924.

Dearest Eric

Thank you very much for your letter. If your impression of Furst is favourable we had better go on with the affair; always excepting the two collaborated works in the terms of my agreement with Hueffer.[1]

---

[1] On 20 May 1924, Henry Furst followed up an earlier letter to Conrad which is now missing, as are Conrad's replies. Mario Curreli gives the text of the surviving letter (TS Berg) in 'Cecchi, Critico Conradiano', *Italianistica*, 28.2 (May–August 1999), 251–64. Furst had published an article on Conrad in the Italian periodical *L'Idea Nazionale*: 'L'Arte di Joseph Conrad' (19 April, p. 3); later in the year, he would add a memorial tribute, 'Il Poeta navigatore' (12 August, p. 3). The earlier article includes the final episode of *Lord Jim* in its first Italian translation. Furst (1893–1967) was born in New York, but often claimed that his life really began in 1912, when he went to Italy. Known there as 'Il Cardinale', he had an odd career, oscillating between support for Fascism and condemnation (the latter, particularly, in his columns for the *New York Times Book Review*), working as D'Annunzio's private secretary when the flamboyant man of letters captured Fiume and installed himself as dictator, ghostwriting Eugenio Montale's book reviews, writing poetry and fiction on his own account, and managing a boxing team. Often collaborating with his wife, 'Orsola Nemi' (Flora Vezzani), he translated Croce into English, and, among many others, Kafka, Henry Miller, Norman Douglas, Saki, Ernst Jünger, and R. L. Stevenson into Italian. In his letter of 20 May, Furst had proposed an Italian edition of Conrad's collected works, adding that he wanted to translate 'Youth' himself. He referred to 'a very important Italian firm of publishers' already interested in the edition; this was Alpes, the firm owned by Mussolini's brother Arnaldo, which published *Nostromo*, *Tales of Unrest*, *A Set of Six* (as *Gaspar Ruiz*), and *Victory* before abandoning the project in 1931.

The warning of that should be sent, I think, to the German and the Norwegian people, and also the Dutch, as I have given up all Europe to F. M. F.

By the way, F. M. F. has departed for America. I had a letter from him in which he says that the shareholders of the "Transatlantic Review" having gone on their knees (or words to that effect) to beg him not to resign the editorship of the T. R. he has graciously condescended to retain the post for some time longer.[1]

A propos of *the* novel.[2] The manuscript having been rearranged, new chapters written in, and so forth, it is very important, my dear Eric, that you should warn our agent in America that though there is a lot of typescript flying about, *only the one of which every single page will be marked by the letter "F" in red pencil* will be good for purposes of publication.[3] *When* that one will be delivered is another matter, on which I say nothing. The great thing is that when the time for printing comes, (either serial or book) there should be no doubt in their minds what copy to use. I consider that notification as very necessary.

Of course there may be more than one T.S. marked "F" (for final) on each page; but the point is that all the copies in existence now, must in effect be regarded as cancelled. That doesn't mean that all the text has been re-written. It has been only corrected afresh, re-arranged, interpolated, and so on. I have been at that unprofitable but very salutary work for a long time. The fact of the matter is, my dear Eric, that the showing about the MS in its early stages has hung like a fatal millstone round my neck (I mean my mental neck). It was a weakness of which dear J. B. and I have been guilty under justifiable circumstances, no doubt. But there can be no doubt also that it has affected me in a most surprising way, by trammelling the free exercise of my imagination, since I felt myself bound by what went before, simply because some people had seen it.[4] This has never happened to me with any other of

---

[1] An effect in the eye of the beholder: Ford had said only that 'at a shareholders meeting of the T. R. last week I was unanimously requested not to resign the editorship, so I shall not. It will be run while I'm away by young Hemingway who's the best boy that I know – with tastes astonishingly like my own' (letter of 31 May, in Saunders, 2, p. 158).

[2] Conrad had decided to precede the long account of Cosmo Latham's departure from Genoa that became Part IV of *Suspense* in the published version with a 'new' chapter, presenting various reactions to Cosmo's disappearance, that became Part III, Chapter 3.

[3] None of the surviving TSS is marked in this way.

[4] Samples of *Suspense* had been circulating since 1922 in the hope of finding a serial publisher, and by July 1923 some 331 pages of 'First Draft' TS had been delivered to T. J. Wise.

my works, because, even in the case of "Victory" (which Munsey's man was allowed to see before it was finished[1]) the whole thing was so far completed in my mind that there was nothing to do but the mere writing, and that, as a matter of fact, amounted only to three or four chapters. Now, you know that as to "Suspense" it was very different. It became, as it were, semi-public property, and the effect on me was at times simply paralysing.

Very absurd no doubt. But you will understand without explanation that it has been very horrible too; especially during the period of the after-the-war reaction which affected one's soul as much as one's body. I am feeling free now and hope to go on increasing the pace as the days go by.

Sir Robert will arrive here at 8 o'clock in the evening, to dine and sleep, on Thursday, and operate next day at 10 o'clock. The pain is growing more severe from day to day, and poor Mrs C. is positively looking forward to being carved, as it will certainly relieve her of that at once; and, let us hope, permanently.

As to me, there are moments when I do feel awful. It isn't that the operation is dangerous, but with her habit of body one can't help feeling anxious about the anaesthetics, which I understand last time caused them some concern – and she was three years younger then!

Well no more! It may be I'll see you before the day. Our love to you both.

Ever affectly Yrs

J. Conrad

To John Galsworthy
Text MS Forbes; Marrot 543

[letterhead: Oswalds]
8.6.24[2]

Dearest Jack.

I feel compunctions not having written before about *The Forest* – a piece of work to which I came with the greatest interest.[3] But for most of the time

---

[1] Conrad had thought it 'a good thing' to have his agent show Robert Hobart Davis of *Munsey's Magazine* 200 pages of TS; eventually, the magazine took *Victory* and published it in a single issue (*Letters*, 5, pp. 288–9, 342).

[2] A slip attached to the MS, probably by R. H. Mottram, misdates this as 8 July.

[3] Galsworthy's four-act drama started its run at the St Martin's Theatre on 6 March; it had a lukewarm reception there: see Marrot, pp. 541–2. The script had just been published by Duckworth in London, and Scribners in New York. Its presentation of brutality, corruption, and hypocrisy in an African context was bound to interest the author of *Heart of Darkness* and 'An Outpost of Progress'. The first and fourth acts are set in London, the second is set in Uganda, and the third in the Belgian Congo. A coalition of philanthropists and financiers are backing an anti-slavery campaign in central Africa: one of the money men aims to 'ramp' the market in

I was not able to hold a pen, and dictating is odious work. So I put it off –
waiting for better days.

Anyway it is a fine thing. Never since *Strife* had there been such a first act![1]
I can say no more! As to the audacity of any man attempting to put the*
Darkest Africa on the *stage*, the mere thought of it gave me a retrospective
shudder. The remoteness of the two [settings?] would have made me dizzy,
and I would have funked the mere sound of the names you use with such
impunity. In fact on reading all this seemed to me marvellously atmospheric;
an impression which was confirmed by Hugh Clifford who directly on his
arrival from Nigeria went to see the play.[2]

To Grace Willard

Text MS Yale; Unpublished

[Oswalds]
8. 6. 24.

My dear Mama Grace

I can't tell you how unhappy I feel at the horrible bad luck which is pursuing
you two dear women so relentlessly.

Jessie is writing by this post so I am sending only this scrap of paper to tell
you of my heartfelt sympathy. What with one thing or another I am half out
of my mind.

Please drop us a line as soon as you feel fit for the exertion.

Yours affectionate[ly]

J. Conrad

mining shares, another wants to replace African forced labour with indentured labourers from
China, while a rich Evangelical and a principled Liberal look on in well-meaning ignorance.
The leader of the expedition also has an agenda – to control the search for diamonds in
Kasai province. The African scenes feature an exotic half-Arab, half-Congolese woman, and
a great deal of offstage drumming and onstage double-crossing. On his return to London, the
expedition's doctor and one of its few survivors, ask the backers to 'Imagine the back of night,
the bottom of hell, and you'll have some conception of the conditions' (Duckworth edition,
p. 104).

[1] In *Strife* (1909) Galsworthy had brought to the stage a struggle between the owners and
managers of a tin-plate works and their employees; the anarchist Emma Goldman was among
the play's admirers.

[2] Here Conrad reached the end of a page, and the rest is missing. Clifford had arrived in
March. One of his duties was to appear as patron of the Nigerian pavilion at the British
Empire Exhibition, Wembley, a vast display of imperial variety and power.

To Eric S. Pinker

Text MS Berg; Unpublished

[Oswalds]
9. Jun 24

Dearest Eric.

In the matter of my American expenses:

I had from you (in one payment) £300 for that purpose. Then I drew from Doubleday $1000 – say £200 – when over there.

On arriving in London I had on me £15 at the most. But as I drew also a few small cheques on my current account, we may put the expenses of the trip at £500, for purposes of rebate on income-tax.

Kindest regards

Yours

J. Conrad

To Borys Conrad

Text MS Conrad; Unpublished

[Oswalds]
[10 June 1924][1]

Dearest Boy.

I am coming by car to-morrow (Wed:) and hope to be at the RAC by noon.

The real object of the visit is a lunch at the Polish Legation. I've been asked many times and there is a chance of it being useful (perhaps) to you in the way of business if I keep in touch with the people there.

Will you come over to R.A.C. for a social drink.[2]

Our dear love

Father

J. C.

John is coming up with me.

---

[1] Conrad's invitation for lunch the following day confirms the date.
[2] Borys's workplace was only a few doors away.

To Richard Curle

Text MS Indiana; Curle 147

[Oswalds]
[10 June 1924][1]

Dearest Dick.

Jessie was *so* pleased with Your encouraging letter!

I will be in London to morrow (Wed:) but will make no call on your time as I remember you telling me Wed: was a heavy day with you.

The object of my visit will be only to lunch at the Polish Legation (at 1.30). I will travel up by Car as I shirk the rail. I am certain to be [at] R.A.C. a little after 12 noon and if you can spare the time for a social drink it would be nice. Do you think You would be able to come down here next week end? But perhaps that would be too dismal. I'll send you word directly the oper'on is over.

Ever yrs

J Conrad.

To Sir Hugh Clifford

Text MS Clifford; Hunter

[Oswalds]
13. 6. 24.

My dear Clifford

Everything went off very well. Jessie stood the an[a]est[ic] perfectly, and Sir R. Jones hopes he's taken away everything that may have caused the trouble. He shaved the bone in two places and excised the old scar completely. –

We may now hope for the best; but whether the relief is permanent time only will show.

Last night just before leaving here for the Nursing Home she asked me to give you her love. I saw her today at noon, directly after she came to, for a moment, when she was pleased to see me but not inclined to talk. I will see her again at 6.

Ever Affect[ly] Yours

J. Conrad[2]

---

[1] Date in Curle's hand, confirmed by Conrad's social arrangements.

[2] Clifford replied on 16 June (Stape and Knowles, p. 243).

To G. Jean-Aubry
Text MS Yale; Unpublished

Oswalds.
13. 6. 24

Mon cher Jean

L'opération a été un grand succès. Sir Robert a l'éspoir d'une réussite complète – mais ça c'est une question a laquelle on ne pourra repondre définitivement avant un an au moins.

Jessie a supporté l'opération très bien. Je l'ai vue pour un moment a Midi. Je la reverrai a 6ʰ ce soir.

Je VS embrasse

Votre

J. C.

Mes hommages a Mme Alvar.

My dear Jean

The operation was a great success. Sir Robert hopes for a complete recovery – but that's a question that can't be answered definitely until at least a year has passed.

Jessie bore the operation very well. I saw her for a moment at noon. I will see her again at 6 this evening.

I embrace you

Your

J. C.

My regards to Mme Alvar.

To Lady Millais
Text MS Private collection; Unpublished

[letterhead: Oswalds]
14. 6. 24.
3. pm.

Dear Lady Millais.[1]

Thank you very much for your wire. I hope I addressed the reply properly.

I had just seen Jessie when it came. She looks uncommonly well. She took the anesthaetics* perfectly and the whole thing was over in one hour and a

---

[1] Mary St Lawrence, Lady Millais (née Hope-Vere of the Marquesses of Linlithgow, 1861–1948, widowed 1897), a Scotswoman, lived in Ashford with her son Sir John Everett Millais (the artist's grandson), Conrad's sometime chess partner. She was a close friend of Jessie Conrad, and served in her later years as a Justice of the Peace.

quarter. I am happy to be able to tell you that both surgeons believe that the cause of trouble had been removed at last, and that there are good grounds for the hope that the years of trouble are over at last for "the patient Jessie".

Both Sir Robert and Dr Reid were surprised at finding an unsuspected affection* of the bone, evidently of long standing. The affected portion has been removed and Sir Robert has also excised the old scar entirely so as to make sure that no nerve-ends may be involved and cause renewed suffering. I can hardly believe yet in this complete brightening of prospects. Sir Robert went away immensely pleased with his mornings work, and Dr Reid who always thought that there was something unaccounted for in Jessie's condition was wreathed in smiles as he met me at the door yesterday.

I can not tell you dear Lady Millais how much and how profoundly I appreciate Your sympathy and friendship.

Believe me always your most faithful friend and servant

J. Conrad

PS I am going to see Jessie at five o'clock. She will be writing to you soon.

To Ada and John Galsworthy

Text MS Forbes; Unpublished

[letterhead: Oswalds]
15.6.24.

Dearest Ada[1] and Jack.

I am very happy to be able to say that there is every reason to hope that this time the source of all the trouble has been found and removed. I won't enter into the complicated details more than to say that it was of an inflammatory nature and seated deeply in the bone (where its presence was unsuspected) and was probably of long standing. No wonder poor Jessie was always saying that her leg "felt sick" – apart from the pain. Sir R. marvels at her endurance. He went away feeling, as he said, immensely relieved and most hopeful. Dr Reid who has been looking after her for 2 years goes about wreathed in smiles. Mrs C herself has a good deal of pain just now but is positively cheerful. She sends her dear love, and will before long be writing to You herself. I am going

---

[1] Ada Nemesis Galsworthy (née Ada Pearson, 1864–1956) was adopted by Ernest Cooper, a Norwich doctor. As a teenager she studied the piano in Dresden; later, she composed songs. Conrad wrote a Preface for her translations from Maupassant, *Yvette and Other Stories* (1904). Although involved with John Galsworthy, she had been unhappily married to his cousin Arthur until 1904, when the death of John, Senior, eased the threat of family sanctions and she and John Galsworthy were able to marry. The Galsworthys had houses in Hampstead and Devonshire, but for the sake of her health, they often wintered overseas.

to see her now (10. am). I hope to have her home to finish her convalescence in about 3 weeks.

Ever your most affectionate and grateful

J Conrad

To Eric S. Pinker
Text MS Berg; Unpublished

[letterhead: Oswalds]
15. 6. 24.
10 p.m.[1]

Dearest Eric.

Jessie was very pleased to get your letter yesterday. She looked surprisingly well. The whole thing went off most successfully. Sir Robert told me that she lost hardly any blood and therefore there was no shock.

While driving with me from here to Canterbury of* Friday morning Sir R. confessed to me that he knew nothing – except that her sensations were perfectly genuine and that something *had* to be done. He hoped to God that he would *see* something; but that *in any case* there were things that he had made up his mind to do on general principles. I could see he was very concerned, tho' he spoke hopefully.

When I arrived at noon to the nursing home (after it was over) I could see the three of them Sir R. Dʳ Fox and Reid at the door wreathed in smiles. It appears that applying pressure to the bone, the surface of it gave way in one place (corresponding to the principal pain-spot on Dʳ Reid['s] diagram) disclosing a cavity caused by an internal inflam[m]ation of the bony tissue obviously of long standing – probably several years. But who could have suspected that! It was enough to account for 90% of the trouble. Sir Robert shaved off all the diseased parts, cut away the congested flesh tissues in the neighbourhood and excised entirely the old scar lest there should be any nerve-ends involved in it. The bone shavings have been sent away to the laboratory to be examined, but Sir R. assured me that he was convinced that there was nothing malignant in that affection*. It is rare in adults but not so in children, generally as a result of a blow or a fall on a sharp edge of a stone. No wonder poor Mrs C always complained that her leg "felt sick" – apart

---

[1] Writing to Lady Colvin from Oswalds at 10 a.m. the same day, Conrad had reported: 'I am happy to be able to say that the surgeons have found (and removed) what was probably the cause of 90% of the horrid trouble. There are good grounds to hope that the years of pain are at an end for that patient woman . . . I am going to see her now . . .' (unlocated letter sold as lot 172 at the Colvin sale, Anderson Galleries, New York, 7 May 1928; text from catalogue).

from the pain. I have just had a message from Canr^y. She had a better night and is looking cheerful. I am going there now.

Our love.

Yours affectly

J. Conrad.

To Eric S. Pinker
Text MS Berg; Unpublished

[Oswalds]
16. 6. 24.

Dearest Eric.

Everything here goes on well.

Jessie has begged me to ask you to pay £20 *extra* to her acc^t at her Bank. Will you please do that.

I am recovering my balance too. – I mean the mental – not banking.

Ever yours

J. C.

To Jessie Conrad
Text MS Yale; *JCLW* 115

[Oswalds]
17. [18] 6. 24[1]
Wed.^y

Dearest Chica.

There's nothing wrong really but I had a little temperature last night, and some severe coughing; so I have 'phoned for Fox to come and have a look at me. He will be here some time in the afternoon. I have decided to remain quietly in bed today.

I imagine you'd approve this resolution; but as a matter of fact I am feeling better now than I felt last morning.

I am anxious to hear how you are today and get a little message from you.

I am sending you all yesterday's and this mornings post. I send you also one great hug and several small ones with pats and kisses and all other long-established forms of endearments that pass between us in every day life.

You are a dear!

Ever Your own

J. Conrad

---

[1] The 17th was a Tuesday.

To Jessie Conrad
Text MS Yale; *JCLW* 119

[Oswalds]
[18–27? June 1924][1]

My dearest Chica.

I did not have a very good night – it could not have been expected but I am feeling no worse certainly. Got up to wash and found myself very shaky at first. I am taking medicine like a good boy and intend to be very careful of myself.

Thanks for your nice good-night note and the grapes.

I am going to wire Eric that I can not come. Will you write to him suggesting he should come down to see us both any convenient day?

I would like *you* to write that letter rather than write myself.

I want badly to *see* you. Hugs and kisses and no end of love.

Your own Boy

J C

To Jessie Conrad
Text MS Indiana; Unpublished

[Oswalds]
Friday [20? June 1924][2]

Dearest Chica.

Good morning. I am sore all over coughing but feel better in myself.

I hope you had a decent night.

There are no letters this morning.

You are a dear.

Your own

J. Conrad.

---

[1] Jessie Conrad dated this letter 'June 1924'; this and the following four letters seem to accord with the period of Conrad's own illness, when from *c.* 18 to 27 June he was unable to visit Jessie in the Nursing Home and sent her written notes at least once a day. Unless otherwise noted, undated letters are presented in the sequence established in *JCLW.*

[2] The reference to Conrad's cough makes Friday the 20th more likely than the 27th, since he reported feeling better by the 22nd.

To Jessie Conrad

Text MS Yale; Unpublished

[Oswalds]
Friday ev'g [20? June 1924][1]

My dearest Chica

I was most excited to hear that the stitches have been cut.[2]

I can't say I have had a delightful day. Too much cough. And I miss you awfully. Especially at night when from time to time I remember you are not in your room.

The rabbin[3] is very attentive and exasperating. Audrey directs the whole sick-bay business very well indeed.

They are all very good really.

Eric wired his visits for Tuesday.

Fox thinks my general state better.

You are the dearest and I love you all out-of-doors

Your very own

J C

To Jessie Conrad

Text MS Yale; *JCLW* 121

[Oswalds]
[20–27? June 1924]

My dearest Jess.

Am better this morning but feeling very tired. Cough easier.

I wonder what kind of night You had.

No letters this morning except just a line from Dick to say he's sorry.

I'll get up to have bed-sheets changed. I slept quite a bit last night but I am all sore from coughing.

Can't think of anything funny to say. I dread the coming of awful boredom. How weary you too my dearest will begin to feel presently.

Do tell me all about yourself.

You are a great dear.

Ever your very own

J C

---

[1] Conrad's reference to his cough accords with the previous letter.
[2] Stitches would normally be removed at the end of one week.
[3] A nickname for Dr Fox or Dr Reid?

To Jessie Conrad
Text MS Yale; *JCLW* 123

[Oswalds]
[20–27? June 1924]

My dearest Rita[1]

I had a tolerable night tho' I am still coughing in fits. Only they are shorter. My temp[re] still keeps up a little. My appetite is better this morning, tho' I am not wildly interested in food.

Audrey is very good. It is nice to have John drop in from time to time. But I feel depressed when I remember suddenly at night that you are four miles off.

Send me a report about Yourself if only verbal through John if you don't feel inclined to write.

You are a P. T.[2] and I am

Your own

Boy.

To Jessie Conrad
Text MS Yale; *JCLW* 125

[Oswalds]
22. 6. 24

Dearest Jessie.

Thanks for Your mornings note. It's a great comfort to know that you are going on so extremely well.

I am definitely better today. I assure you I am being very careful with myself and I don't propose to come out to see You till I get permission from my medical man. He has not been here yet but I think he is sure to come to-day.

I am anxious to know what you really think of the Illingworth's house of which B. spoke. I think it is a good chance to get relieved of this immediate anxiety at least.[3] We could look about from there. Your first drive must be that way.

Your very own

Boy.

---

[1] Rita de Lastaola was the heroine of Conrad's novel *The Arrow of Gold*.

[2] 'Perfect Treasure'?

[3] The Conrads hoped to leave Oswalds, which they found too expensive, in September. Mr and Mrs George Norton Illingworth lived at Great Baynden, Horsmonden, Kent, about fifty miles from Bishopsbourne. Other Illingworths lived in Herne Bay. Although, like Odysseus, Conrad preferred to live inland, Herne Bay's proximity to Canterbury (and a railway station of its own) makes it the likelier place. Moreover, some of the George family had settled there.

To Jessie Conrad
Text MS Yale; *JCLW* 127

[Oswalds]
[23–27? June 1924]¹

Dearest Chica

An evening hug and a loving good night to you
I am much the same with good hope of improvement for tomorrow
I am trying to be a model patient

Ever Your own

J C

To Perriton Maxwell
Text TS facsimile Maxwell (1924); Randall (1969)

[letterhead: Oswalds]
June 23rd. 1924.

Dear Sir,

First of all let me tell you that the Canadian Government is not subservient to the English Parliament which has nothing more to do with Canada than it has with China, as a Parliament.² The rule of the British Monarch is not theoretical, it is symbolical, no power whatever being attached to it. It is to a certain extent judicial, since there are still legal appeals to the Privy Council for a decision in certain Canadian suits.

I do not know enough of the United States to express an opinion, but it is very obvious that the United States in conjunction with the British Overseas Dominions, like Canada, would have been something utterly and completely different. For one thing, it is very doubtful if they would have had all the West Pacific slope; but as to imagining what that part of America would have been like is a vain enterprise. It certainly would have been something very fine and of great weight in the affairs of mankind generally and of the English race in particular. But of course that was impossible.

Yours sincerely,

Joseph Conrad

Perriton Maxwell Esq.

---

¹ Jessie Conrad placed this note just after the letter of 22 June announcing that Conrad's health was improving.
² Maxwell had invited Conrad to consider the 'probable present-day conditions had America remained under the political domination of Great Britain'.

To Jessie Conrad
Text MS Yale; *JCLW* 129

[Oswalds]
Tuesday [24? June 1924]¹

Dearest Jessie.

I have had a tolerable night. But even the wakeful hours would have been made happy by the good report from the laboratory on the samples of your bones.²

You are a marvellously *sound* person! Oh my dearest what a relief to know that everything is going on well with you.

I am impr[ov]ing but would like to see Fox once more about carrying on the treatment. Audrey has sent a 'phone mess[a]ge.

John will have to play host to Eric. I think he'll do it well.

All my love to you

Ever Yours

J C

To Jessie Conrad
Text MS Yale; *JCLW* 131

[Oswalds]
[Wednesday, 25? June 1924]³

My dearest Girl,

I've had a good night and feel much improved generally. I promised Fox not to go out before Friday when I will see You at last after this long separation.

Everything was satisfactory yesterday. Very!

I had a good talk with Eric and Fox about the future. All that will keep till we meet.

I send you Dick's letter.

Send me your good new[s].

Many hugs and love "all-out-of-doors."

Your own

J C

¹ Bone samples had been removed during Jessie Conrad's surgery on 13 June.
² Confirming the absence of cancer or tubercular infection.
³ Jessie Conrad dated this note as 'Wednesday June 1924'.

To Jessie Conrad

Text MS UCL; *JCLW* 127

[Oswalds]
[26 June 1924]¹

Dearest Girl

Improvement maintained. Am expecting decent night. Hope You will sleep restfully too.

Yes. Send weekly N Home acct straight to the office.

It's a great bore to [be] kept away altogether from all sight of you.

Deepest love from

Ever your own

J. C.

To Stefan Pomarański

Text MS copy Yale;² *Ruch*; Najder 299

[letterhead: Oswalds]
28th June, 1924.

Dear Sir,³

I have received your letter and your 'present' which is so precious to me & I thank you from all my heart.⁴ I will answer your letter in full when I recover my health which has lately been very unsatisfactory. At this moment I feel a little better & must tell you that the subject you touch upon in your letter lies particularly near my heart. It is not the first time similar reflections have reached me from Poland, sometimes from very distinguished compatriots. *Your letter will not remain unanswered.*

As regards my nomination as honorary member of the Polish Geographical Society, about which you wrote [to] me before,⁵ I fear that my merits do not deserve this action of yours. I should like also to ask you to write me down

---

¹ This is the first of the undated June notes in *JCLW*, but Conrad's continued improvement and the reference to long separation suggest placing it after the previous note of [25? June]. The nursing home bills may also have prompted Pinker to have £600 transferred the following day from the business account into Conrad's personal account (letter to Pinker of 27 June from Mr Lewis, Manager of the Westminster Bank Ltd, Charles Deering McCormick Collection, Northwestern University).

² Text from the Yale copy, an MS translation into English, with amendments from the Polish.

³ A Polish archivist and historian, Stefan Pomarański (1893–1944) was later an editor and biographer of Marshal Józef Piłsudski (1867–1935).

⁴ In his letter of 22 June (TS Berg, MS copy Yale), Pomarański announced that he was making Conrad a present of an original MS of 'some youthful poems' by Apollo Korzeniowski, with the request that it be returned some day to one of the Polish libraries. For the broader biographical significance of the Pomarański–Conrad correspondence, see Najder, p. 299, n. 3.

⁵ The Yale copy of Pomarański's letter makes no mention of this invitation.

as a member of the Mianowski Club about which I have received Żeromski's beautiful pamphlet.[1]

You may be at rest concerning my father's manuscript. Especially do I prize the little pencil portrait from those times. I shall try to show you my gratitude some day for this memory.

Accept meanwhile my hearty handshake.

Konrad Korzeniowski

To Jessie Conrad
Text MS Yale; Unpublished

[Oswalds]
Sunday [29? June 1924]

My dearest Chica

I have just had your message. No dear I'll not come out today [since] you think it will be more prudent not to do so. Anyway I have taken some fizzy medicine this morning and am expecting the usual consequences.

Young Gwatkin[2] called yesterday and proposed to visit me this afternoon. He has got his hen with him – but the Old Birds are away for the week end. It's funny.

Can't say I feel very bright. Still I have no particular pain [any]where today and I didn't have a bad night. I am horribly bored with the situation and I am unhappy at being separated from my Kitty. Bless you my dearest darling.

Ever Your own

J C

To Eric S. Pinker
Text TS Berg; Unpublished

[letterhead: Oswalds]
June 29th. 1924.

Dearest Eric.

I am returning to you the two American agreements.[3]

I must also thank you for your letter which I received on Saturday, advising me of the payment of the guaranteed overdraft and the extra £100 paid into my current account. You have made it perfectly clear; and by the same post

---

[1] In 1881 a foundation supporting research in science and the humanities was set up in memory of the physician and professor Józef Mianowski (1804–79).

[2] A novelist and diplomat, son of the Rector of Bishopsbourne; see the notes to the letter of 17 December 1923.

[3] With Doubleday, for *The Shorter Tales of Joseph Conrad* and *The Nature of a Crime*. Both agreements were signed on 27 June (*Documents*, p. 236).

I had a letter from the Bank advising me of the same and stating my credit on the current account to be £160, which is just about correct.

I wish I could tell you that I am getting on like a house on fire, but that would not be exactly true. I am however improving, and hope to become a fairly efficient human being in another fortnight or so – but not before.

Our love to you.

Yours

J Conrad

To Eric S. Pinker
Text MS Princeton; Unpublished

[Oswalds]
30. 6. 24
7pm.

Dearest Eric.

Very happy to get your wire. I'll communicate it to Mrs C this evening. Give our love to Margot*.

Ever affec^ly yours

J. C.

To Jessie Conrad
Text MS UCL; Unpublished

[Oswalds]
[June–July 1924]

Darling Kit

Just a word to say foot easier. Am rather cast down at not having seen you today but am in good hopes for tomorrow.

You are a very great Dear.

Your own boy

J. C.

To Jessie Conrad
Text UCL; Unpublished

[Oswalds]
[June–July 1924]

Dearest Jess.

Just a word to say I had a good night and to send you my dear love.

Your own

J. C.

To Jessie Conrad

Text MS Yale; *JCLW* 117[1]

[Oswalds]
Wed[y] [2 July 1924][2]

Dearest Jess.

I send you the Pinker old wire and letter. Also a letter from Mama Grace received this morning. I don't know if I'll feel equal to have her for the weekend. Moreover I want to ask Dick to come down. *That* will do me good whereas to see Grace will be fatiguing beyond anything. Think over what can be done and we will have a talk when I come to see you.

It is dear and sweet of You to have written entire letters and to have sent me that very welcome note of this morning. I am feeling rather shaken and lost without you near me; but I have not had a bad night and as far as bodily feelings go I am fairly comfortable this morning. It is the wrist that is restless and unable to steady itself. I am sorry to be so stupid. But that will soon pass when you come home.

Au revoir till 3 o'clock.

your very own

J C

I sent also F. N. D's letter.

To Richard Curle

Text MS Indiana; Curle 148

[letterhead: Oswalds]
Wed[y] 2 July. [1924]
6.30 pm.

Dearest Dick

Any chance of You coming down here on, say, Friday ev[g] for the week-end?

If you do bring me a couple of books – not novels. I have had a severe cold and sub-acute bronchitis which left me like a rag. Am trying to fight off a fit of severe depression which has taken me by the throat as it were. Hard luck.

Just came back from a visit to Mrs C. She is chirpy. Great luck.

Ever Yours

J. Conrad

---

[1] Omitting 'I don't know if I'll feel equal to have her for the weekend. Moreover' and 'whereas to see Grace will be fatiguing beyond anything'.

[2] Grace Willard visited Oswalds on Sunday 6 July.

To G. Jean-Aubry

Text MS Yale; Unpublished

Oswalds.

2. July. 24.

Très cher.

Je suis heureux de Vous savoir ici.[1] Moi j'ai eu une bronchite qui m'a tenu au lit plus d'une semaine.

Mrs C. va très bien mais je crois qu'elle ne pourra revenir a la maison avant au moins dix jours.

Cette bronchite m'a fatigué. Puis-je espérer VS voir ici la semaine prochaine?

Toujours Vtre vieux

J. Conrad.

Jessie's love.

My very dear fellow.

I am happy to know you are here. I've had bronchitis, which has kept me in bed for more than a week.

Mrs. C. is doing well, but I think she will not be able to return home for another ten days at least.

This cold has wearied me. Can I hope to see you here next week?

Ever yr old

J. Conrad.

Jessie's love.

To Eric S. Pinker

Text MS Berg; Unpublished

[Oswalds]

Wed. 2 July. 24.

Dearest Eric.

I hope your wife is going on as well as was expected. Give her my love & sympathy.

My bronchitis has shaken me a lot. But it is gone completely by now and after a week's course of a tonic I expect to be able to pull myself together to some purpose.

---

[1] Back in England after one of his many visits to the Continent.

John is leaving for France Sat: next.

Pardon this scrap of paper. Can't find anything else at hand.

Ever affect^{ly} Yours

J. Conrad

To Joan Conrad

Text MS Conrad; Unpublished

[letterhead: Oswalds]

Thursday.

4. [3] July 24.[1]

My dear Joan.[2]

Many thanks for Your good letter. I was very disappointed at not seeing You last Sunday, and distressed to know that You were temporarily laid up. I do hope You will be able to come down with B next Sunday.

I am sorry to say I still feel considerably shaken, after the bronchitis. Still my cough is nearly gone and my lungs have been pronounced quite clear by Dr Fox who was here yesterday.

Mrs C continues to look well and cheerful. Her wound however has been fomented and may have to be opened in one place so as to be thoroughly drained. Dr Reid seems satisfied with the way things are going so far.

My love to you three. It seems an awful long time since I saw Philip. I am looking forward to seeing you and B soon. It is a lonely life here with Mrs C away. John is leaving on Sat morn^g.

Ever affect^{ly} Yours

J Conrad

---

[1] Thursday was the 3rd; Conrad's mention of John's leaving 'Sat morn^g' rather than 'tomorrow' suggests that the date, not the day, is wrong. He made the same slip in the following letter.

[2] (Madeline) Joan Conrad (née King, 1894–1981) met Borys Conrad during the war. They married secretly in 1922, but Conrad knew nothing of the marriage until his return from America in June 1923. Jessie Conrad, in particular, was hostile to the marriage and her daughter-in-law: 'Apart from the secrecy, which was not necessary, it was a most disastrous marriage from every point. To begin with she is not even of a good working class, in fact she belongs nowhere. Both Conrad and and* I tried to make the best of it' (Jessie Conrad to Warrington Dawson, 18 May 1926, MS Duke). They were officially separated in 1933, after a three-year estrangement (Jessie Conrad to Walter Tittle [1935], MS Texas).

To Ernest Dawson

Text MS Yale; Unpublished

[letterhead: Oswalds]
Thursday. 4 [3] July '24

My dear Dawson.[1]

I sent your letter on to Jessie in her Nursing Home in Canterbury. I was under the impression she had written to you a few days ago. That you had no wire after the operation (quite successful) is Miss Hallowes' fault. She assured me that she had [your] name on the list of friends. I can't cut her head off because she is gone on leave to France. That You had not had a word from me since is simply because that* the day after the operation I was laid up with a severe chill and bronchitis. It is dreadful to be laid up here away from the Missus. She looks well and cheerful and may be back home in another fortnight.

I feel (and probably look) horribly limp and my spirits stand at about zero. Here you have the horrid truth. But I haven't been well for a long time and *strictly "entre nous"* I begin to feel like a cornered rat.

No more at present. Pray believe in my warm and constant affection.

Ever Yours

J. Conrad.

To Sir Sidney and Lady Colvin

Text MS Yale; J-A, 2, 345

[letterhead: Oswalds]
8 Jly 24

Dearest Friends.[2]

I've just come from Jessie who showed me Your letter. What adds to my desolation is the awful feeling of not being able to show in any way the profound affection I have for you both, dear Lady Colvin and for dear Colvin whose friendship is the greatest reward and the most precious gift that the gods have given me. My heart sinks while I write these words – mere words alas – like a vain cry of a man in a bottomless pit. I am the most useless of

---

[1] Major Ernest Dawson (1884–1960) was introduced to Conrad by W. H. Henley and H. G. Wells. He served in Burma as a magistrate and an officer in the Rangoon Volunteer Rifles, and contributed reminiscences and stories of Burma and Australia to *Blackwood's Magazine*. He lived in Rye, East Sussex, but he spent long periods of his retirement on the Continent. His brother A. J. Dawson was also among Conrad's friends.

[2] Frances, Lady Colvin (née Fetherstonhaugh, 1839–1924), made a living as an essayist after she separated from her first husband, the Revd A. H. Sitwell. She married Sidney Colvin in 1903, and they became close friends with Conrad, as they had been with Stevenson. She was now gravely ill. She died on 1 August, two days before Conrad.

men and apparently the most selfish. I feel and Jessie feels with me, that we ought to be nearer – to have always been nearer – to You both.

Please give Colvin my dear love, and accept this inarticulate attempt to express the concern and sympathy from your ever loving friend and devoted servant

J. Conrad

To Richard Curle
Text MS Indiana; Curle 149

[Oswalds]
8. July. [1924]
1. pm.

Dearest Dick

May I expect you on Friday ev^g? Please drop me a line so that I may warn Vinton* for "late duty".

Jessie goes on well, but her return home may be delayed beyond the first estimate for another week. I find life rather dismal now without John.

The article will be all right. It will have to do with Sailors Saints University Dons etc. Subjects of Legend.[1]

Ever Yours

J. Conrad

To G. Jean-Aubry
Text MS Yale; Unpublished

[Oswalds]
8 July. '24

Cher Jean

Jetez moi un petit mot pour me dire si [vous] venez samedi prochain. Aussi l'heure du train. J'aimerais bien vous voir arriver for lunch.

C'est triste ici John etant parti. Je passe mes après midis avec Mme Conrad – qui est plus Mme Conrad que jamais. Quand* a moi je suis loin de me sentir "moi-même" encore, mais je ne souffre pas et ma bronchite est partie completement.

Je Vous embrasse

Votre vieux

Conrad.[2]

Jessie told me to send you her love. Mrs Willard was here Sunday.

---

[1] 'Legends', unfinished at Conrad's death, was collected in *Last Essays* (1926).
[2] Conrad sent Jean-Aubry a telegram date-stamped on the 9th (Yale) which reads: 'So sorry no room tonight Do come tomorrow morning train our love'.

Dear Jean

Drop me a word to let me know if you can come this Saturday. Also the time of the train. I'd very much like to see you arrive for lunch.

It's dismal with John gone. I spend my afternoons with Mrs Conrad – who is more Mrs Conrad than ever. As for myself, I'm far from feeling 'myself' yet, but I'm not in pain and my bronchitis is completely gone.

I embrace you

Your old

Conrad.

Jessie told me to send you her love. Mrs Willard was here Sunday.

To Eric S. Pinker

Text MS Berg; Unpublished

Oswalds. 8. July '24

Dearest Eric.

Things are going on here in a normal way. Mrs C's wound is draining heavily (just as well) and that will put off for a week or so longer her return home. I have made a very good recovery, but am still feeling languid and depressed in a certain measure. I go to see Jessie every afternoon and devote the morning to pen and ink either upstairs or down here, in the study, where I am writing this (1 pm) just before sitting down to my solitary lunch. We both miss John of course; tho' I had Mrs Willard here for last Sunday (not very cheering) and may have somebody for the next week-end.

Please send me (or pay in) £20 on John's year's allowance. I am keeping within limits but I have his tayler's* bill etc. to meet and will have to pay for some coaching in mathematics he had from Goodburn while he was here. His travelling I paid for out of my own budget. I have also paid out of the £100 (you paid in extra) the local taxes up to Sept next. (£33. 10s). And that's the last here I hope. But this is a damnable month for unexpected bills. There will be Jessie's dressmaker presently too. In view of that I am writing the article about "Legends" (prov. title) of which we thought for the D[ai]ly Mail. Don't move yet in the matter as I would like to engineer it so that *I am asked* for it. I will see R. C. next Sunday and will find out.[1] Meantime I may finish it. And anyhow Roberts of the Work* To Day (ex-Worlds Work) has been asking me for copy.[2] So that it could be placed with him at need – say £80

---

[1] 'Legends' appeared posthumously in the *Daily Mail* on 15 August, with a prefatory note by Curle.

[2] *The World Today*, edited by Henry Roberts, was the English edition of *The World's Work*, a journal founded by Doubleday's partner Walter Hines Page. Conrad's 'Legends' was published only in the *Daily Mail* and *Last Essays*.

for here and US and perhaps £20 for the MS itself from some modest MS collector. I hope I am not overestimating my value, in both markets! Miss H being away on leave I'll send you the pages for typing. But I am not writing *only* that. I work at the novel too, every day, if only a page or so. Meantime if you have an inquiry or see a way to handle the thing to advantage pray do so. I make these plans personally sometimes because I really can't expect you to peddle my small wares; but you must not regard yourself as in the least tram[m]elled by my action on this or any other occasion.

Drop me a line about Margot and yourself. It would be cheering to hear from you.

Affect^{ly} Yours

J. Conrad.

To Sir Robert Jones

Text J-A, 2, 346

[Oswalds]
Thursday
10 July, '24.

Dearest Friend,

Perhaps your grateful patient has told you of my idiotic behaviour in going to bed with bronchitis. I am better now. Fox says the lungs are clear. But I feel languid. I have been to see Jessie three times this week but when I get home I get to bed and give myself up to passive contemplation of no very cheerful kind. It is 18 months since I have done any work that counts![1]

The only comfort (and it is enormous) I have is to feel that Mrs. C. (as we all call her) is going on splendidly. She looks altogether another person. The expression of her physiognomy is quite different. I noticed that the very day after the operation. It is as if, like a magician of old, you had exorcised a devil. Marvellous! I won't say anything of my relief. It is infinite.

Pardon this scrawl. I am writing in bed. I think it is still the best place for me; though for the last day or two I am feeling stronger. The cough has left me entirely – the first time for the last two years.

Pray give my dear love to Hilda and Fred.[2] I hope all is well there.

Always your most affectionate and grateful.

P.S. Please don't trouble to answer this.

---

[1] That is, since before his trip to America in May 1923.
[2] Sir Robert's daughter and his son-in-law, Frederick Watson (1885–1935).

To Auguste Gilbert de Voisins

Text *L. fr.* 202–3

[letterhead: Oswalds]
11. July 24.

Mon cher Monsieur,[1]

Merci mille fois de votre si amicale lettre. Je suis en convalescence d'une villaine bronchite. Ma femme est à six kilomètres d'ici, à Canterbury, dans un nursing home, après une sérieuse (mais pas dangereuse) opération. Miss Hallowes étant en congé, je suis seul à me morfondre, dans cette horrible boite que nous espérons quitter en septembre. Vous ne la connaissez pas; car c'est à Spring Grove, il y a bien cinq ans déjà, que nous avons eu votre très agréable et intéressante visite. J'espère que vous nous ferez le même plaisir – ici ou ailleurs – à votre prochain voyage en Angleterre.

Toujours bien cordialement votre.

My dear Sir,

Many thanks for your friendly letter. I am now recovering from a nasty attack of bronchitis. My wife is six kilometres from here, in Canterbury, in a nursing home, following a serious (but not dangerous) operation. Miss Hallowes being on holiday, I am languishing alone in this wretched hole which we hope to leave in September. You don't know it, since it was at Spring Grove that we had your very interesting and agreeable visit some five years ago. I hope you will give us the same pleasure – here or elsewhere – on your next visit to England.

Always most cordially yours.

To Hamlin Garland

Text MS USC; Knowles and Stape

[Oswalds]
15. 7. '24

Dear H. Garland.

Thanks for your note. My wife is still in the Nursing-Home. She sends her regards. We will be happy to see you here in August.

Yours

J. C.

---

[1] The son of a French officer and a Greek princess, Taglioni's grandson, and Hérédia's son-in-law, Comte Auguste Gilbert de Voisins (1877–1939) enjoyed a large fortune that enabled him to collect and travel as he pleased; he featured as a rider in Buffalo Bill's circus and made two expeditions to remote parts of China. He also wrote poetry and fiction, and translated some of Robert Browning's poems; Conrad owned four of his books, including *Le Bar de la Fourche* (1909), a novel about prospecting for gold in California.

To Eric S. Pinker

Text MS Berg; J-A, 2, 345

[Oswalds]
15. 7. '24.[1]
7. pm.

Dearest Eric.

You are right. I don't want to sign any copies of the N of the Crime, or make myself specially responsible for that idiotic publication.

Things here do not look so well just now. I won't enter into details – but there are one or two bad signs. Still – it may only be a passing trouble. She is in much pain just now. I've just come from the N^g Home. She sends you her love.

Ever affect^ly yours

J. C.

To Eric S. Pinker

Text MS Berg; Unpublished

[Oswalds]
16. 7. '24

Dearest Eric

The enclosed belongs to matters dealth* with by the office, so I send it at once.

I take it that the monthly was paid in. However I will not need to draw for a day or two.

We are awaiting a letter from Sir Robert.

Yrs affect^ly

J. C.

To Eric S. Pinker

Text Telegram Berg; Unpublished

[Oswalds]
[18 July 1924][2]

Bookishly London

Have not had usual notice of payment to bank yet Will you also tell me something of Partingtons Proposal re the two plays[3] as I don't like to answer his letter to me without hearing from you

Love to you both.

Conrad

---

[1] Jean-Aubry reads the date as 5 July.   [2] From date-stamp.
[3] To publish two of Conrad's adaptations for the stage, *Laughing Anne* and *One Day More*.

To Eric S. Pinker

Text MS Berg; J-A, 2, 347

[letterhead: Oswalds]
Sund: 20/7/24

Dearest Eric.

Thanks for your good letter. I am no end sorry to hear your wife is not so well. Drop us a word on a p.c.

It is extremely important that in conveying to O'Brien my refusal to let the *N[ature] of the* C[rime]* appear in the *Best Stories of 1924* you should point out with some emphasis that the *N of the C* is 18 years old and would be altogether out of place in such a vol.¹ There have been pars. in the press alluding to it as a fresh collaboration! My refusal is absolute. Partington's terms are acceptable and under the circumstances we had better accept them – I suppose.² Every little helps. But it's vexing a bit in view of the plan I had to have *all* my plays in one vol. to be included in both my L^{ted} and all the coll^{ed} editions (Eng. & Am.). It is a compl[icati]on too for P requires a preface – and that preface would not do if ever the 3 plays appeared together, say in the two *L^{td}* or in the *Coll^{ed}*. And then again I imagine FND will want to publish too. Have you any notion how is he likely to feel about it?

Ever Yrs.

J. C.

To Clare Ogden Davis

Text MS Texas; Unpublished

[letterhead: Oswalds]
21. 7. 24

Dear Mrs Davis.³

I will explain my delay in writing when we meet. The principal question is: Will you run down here on Wednesday by the morning train from Victoria 10.40 which arrives in Canterbury East at 12.30? I will meet you at the station. The saddest thing is that I will have to take you back there at 3.30 to catch

---

¹ Two Americans, John Coumos and Edward Joseph Harrington O'Brien (1890–1941) co-edited many volumes of the Best British Stories series. The volume for 1924, published by Small and Maynard of Boston, included stories by Somerset Maugham, T. F. Powys, and Edith Sitwell.

² See the previous telegram to Pinker.

³ The Texas-born journalist and author Clare Ogden Davis (1892–1970) was a police reporter before her marriage to John Burton Davis, with whom she collaborated on seven novels under the pen name Lawrence Saunders. Her interview on 24 July would have been the last granted by Conrad, but there is no record of its publication.

the train to London – as I must spend the rest of the afternoon with my wife who has been for some time in a nursing home after a severe operation.

Is it worth your while?

With best regards

Joseph Conrad.

PS Please say yes or no on the enclosed form.

To Richard Curle
Text MS Indiana; Curle 150

[Oswalds]
22. 7. '24.

Dearest Curle.

Thanks for your letter. Mrs C. is coming home on Thursday which is cheering tho' she will have to lay up for a week or two longer in her room upstairs.

I am not getting on very well with my paper, but it will be not very long now before it is finished. Do, dear Dick, send me that book of travels in Arabia I asked you for. I've nothing to read.[1]

Thanks for the return of the French book.[2] I am slightly gouty in one hand and the corresponding foot.

Ever affctly yours

J. C.

To G. Jean-Aubry
Text MS Yale; *L. fr.* 203

[Oswalds]
22. 7. '24

Très cher Jean

Comment ça va?

Mrs C revient le Jeudi mais seulement pour garder son lit a la maison pendant une semaine ou deux encore avant de s'essayer a marcher. Les deux jeunes filles[3] seront ici pour le week-end prochain. John revient le Samedi. Pourquoi ne viendriez VS pas? On pourra Vous caser. Envoyez nous donc un petit mot.

---

[1] Curle replied on 23 July (Stape and Knowles, pp. 243–4), sending the two-volume *Arabia: A Record of Travel and Exploration* (1922), by Harry St John Bridger Philby (1855–1960); from 1921 to 1924, he served as Chief British Representative in Transjordan.

[2] Curle denied any knowledge of this book.

[3] Irena Rakowska-Łuniewska (a distant cousin of Conrad's via Aleksander Poradowski) and her friend Miss Świeżawska; for her account of their visit, see Najder (1983), pp. 271–3.

Je VS envois le livre de don Roberto selon son desir.[1]
Our dear love.

Toujours Votre

Conrad

My very dear Jean,

How is everything?

Mrs C returns home on Thursday but only to keep to her bed for a week or two before trying to walk. The two girls will be here this week-end. John returns on Saturday. Why don't you come down? We could put you up. Drop us a line.

I send you Don Roberto's book according to his wishes.

Our dear love.

Ever Your

Conrad

To Eric S. Pinker

Text MS Berg; Unpublished

[Oswalds]
22. 7. 24
6.30 pm.

Dearest Eric.

Perhaps Mrs C has told you already that she is coming home on Thursday.

Of course she will have to lie-up still for a week or more. But it will be a great relief to have her out of that place which was depressing tho' she had the best of care there.

Reid will be coming out twice a week to attend her for some time yet. Audrey will do such nursing as may be required.

I hope I will get a word from you to-morrow morning's post with better news about your wife.

Ever affctly Yrs

J. C.

[1] *The Conquest of the River Plate*, by R. B. Cunninghame Graham (Heinemann, 1924).

To Borys Conrad

Text MS Conrad; Unpublished

[Oswalds]

Friday [25? July 1924][1]

Dear B.

As mother had written to Joan I refrained from answering your letter, for it is still a painful process.

I think there is no occasion to be uneasy about her general health, so far. But I'll be thankful when the waiting is over.

I am better, but what with occasional twinges and chokes I do not "feel safe" as it were.

I do hope You will have better weather when You come for the next week-end.

My love [to] you three.

Your father

J C

To Eric S. Pinker

Text MS Berg; J-A, 2, 347 (in part)[2]

[Oswalds]

Sunday. [27 July 1924][3]

My dear Eric.

Thank You for Your letter. I meditated over it a bit and I wonder whether you think an answer could be given Partington to the effect that: – Conrad says that he will write a preface[4] (anything from 3–6 pp) (I suppose it would be a small vol) if Mr Part^{on} will agree to make the advance on pub^{on} £120.

I think the preface is well worth the extra 20 in *advance* from his point of view. Its effect will be that every collector of Conrad will have to get the vol. if he wants his coll^{on} to be complete. And of course others too may be influenced to buy by the fact of there being a preface.

---

[1] Dated by the reference to Borys's visit a week later.

[2] Omitting the third and fourth paragraphs.

[3] The date '30/7/24' appears on the MS in another hand. J-A accepts this date, but 27 July was the only Sunday between John's return from France on 26 July and Miss Hallowes's expected return on 2 August.

[4] To *Laughing Anne & One Day More*, published posthumously by John Castle with an introduction by John Galsworthy dated 'September, 1924'.

I don't want to do it. But you see my dear E that £120 will go a long way to pay the doctor's bills now lying on my table: Fox's & Reid's for the past ½ year. R's includes the operation fee and Fox has been looking after me pretty closely ever since *Febʸ*. They amount together to £130. Yet I assure you that both these men are letting me off easily, as their fees go.

So you see that's why . . . And indeed I would have asked P. to make it 150 if I did not want to avoid the chaffering which such a demand might provoke.

I wait for Miss H's return (on the 2ᵈ) to send you my newspᵉʳ article.[1] No typist could make out that mess. But she will. So I will send a correctᵈ clean copy (duplᵗᵉ). You will pass on one of them to the Dʸ Mail directly you have settled the Am. pubᵒⁿ. Jessie has a long road before her yet. She sends her love in which I join to you and Margot.

Ever yours

J. C.

PS Please send me £10 *John's* on *acct* to pay his board & lodging in France. He is here now.

To Eric S. Pinker

Text MS Berg; Unpublished

[Oswalds]
29. 7. 24.

Dearest Eric.

Many thanks.

Please send L[aughing] Anne along. Miss H. will read it for corrᵒⁿˢ as soon as she returns.

Yrs

J. C.

---

[1] 'Legends', unfinished at Conrad's death, appeared posthumously in the *Daily Mail* on 15 August (p. 8) with a prefatory note by Richard Curle and a facsimile of 'The Last Written Page'.

To Richard Curle
Text Telegram Indiana; Curle 151

[Oswalds]

31 July 1924[1]

Delighted if you will put up with Johns Room Philip and Co will be here

Conrad[2]

---

[1] Date-stamp. Curle replied the same day confirming his arrival on 1 August (Stape and Knowles, p. 244).

[2] Joseph Teodor Conrad Korzeniowski died on the morning of 3 August and was buried under that name on the 7th. In his memorial essay '*Inveni Portam*', Cunninghame Graham wrote of the last moments at the graveside: 'The priest had left his Latin and said a prayer or two in English, and I was glad of it, for English surely was the speech the Master Mariner most loved, and honoured in the loving with new graces of his own.'

SILENT CORRECTIONS TO THE TEXT

The following slips have been silently corrected.

Missing full stop supplied
1923: 14 Jan. (to Pinker): after 'Friday'; 20 Feb.: after 'seulement'; 21 March (to Pinker): after 'visit'; 23 March: after 'Sweden'; 12 April (to Bone): after 'Sick of it'; 15 April: after 'times'; 22 July: after 'Ven[ezue]la'; 31 July (to Wise): after 'form)'; 19 Nov.: after 'them'; [3 Dec.]: after 'to-day'; 6 Dec. (to Doubleday), PPS: after 'Concord'.

1924: [7 Jan.]: after "wonder-child"; 31 Jan. (to Winawer): after 'what you will do'; [3 Feb.]: after 'love'; 12 Feb.: after 'right'; 17 Feb.: after 'effect'; 26 Mar. (to Marshall): after 'Yours'; 23 April: after 'you'; 8 May: after 'American journey'; [11 May]: after '*Z[oo]*'; 24 May (to Ward): after 'you' at end of first sentence; after 'believe'; after 'R*ᵈ*'; after 'Otago'; after 'together'; 29 May (to Keating): after 'pleasure'; 8 June (to G. Willard): after 'relentlessly'; [10 June] (to Borys Conrad): after 'Legation'; after 'R.A.C'; [20? June]: after 'dear'; Friday ev'g [20? June]: after 'cut'; [25? June]: after 'new[s]'; [26 June]: after 'maintained'; 28 June: after 'handshake'; 29 June: after 'you'; 2 July (to Curle): after 'Great luck'; 4 [3] July (to Dawson): after 'rat'; 8 July (to Curle): after 'all right'; 8 July (to Pinker): after 'etc'; 20 July: after '(Eng. & Am.)'; 22 July (to Jean-Aubry): after 'caser'; [25? July]: after 'three'; [27 July]: after 'Margot'; 29 July: after 'returns'.

Dittography
1923: [2 Feb.]: a second 'I' after 'and yet I'; 14 March: a second 'over' after 'I am going'; a second 'of' after 'Doubleday told me'; 11 May: a second 'after' after 'effect of reaction'; 7 July: first 'You' is doubled; 21 July (to Macleod): a second 'to' after 'Mrs Macleod'.

1924: 26 March (to Rodd): a second 'as' after 'as'; 15 June (to Pinker): a second 'he' after 'he' in 'he had made up'; [June–July] (to Jessie Conrad beginning 'Just a word'): a second 'in' before 'good hopes'; 15 July (to Pinker): a second 'have' after 'I've'.

Capital Letter supplied
[27 Aug. 1923]: before 'This'.

Comma supplied
1923: 6 May (to Jessie Conrad): after 'H.'; 11 May (to Jessie Conrad): after 'table'; 14 July: comma moved from before to after 'expression'; 4 Aug. (to Gardiner): after 'facts'; 19 Nov.: after 'gouty'.

Question mark supplied
6 Feb. 1923 (to Jean-Aubry): after 'venir nous voir'; 7 March 1923 (to Dent): after 'affair'; 10 April 1923: after 'dine'; [6 June 1924]: after 'Ministre'; 2 July 1924 (to Curle): after 'week-end'.

Quotation marks supplied
21 June 1923 (to Doubleday): after 'The Rover'; 3 Dec. 1923 (to Pinker): after 'Mail'; 7 April 1924 (to Canby): after 'Sea.'; 24 May 1924 (to Ward): after 'Otago.'.

Dash supplied
8 July 1924 (to the Colvins): after 'nearer'.

Bracket removed
8–12 Oct. 1923: after 'circumstances'.

Bracket supplied
[27 July 1924]: after '3–6 pp'.

Emendations to copied or dictated letters
1923: 9 March: '1923' for '1823'; 1 Sept. (to Curle): 'a month or two' for 'a month of two'; 20 Nov. (to Doubleday): 'hang them' for 'hang then'; 3 Dec. (to Unwin): 'English' for 'Emglish'; 4 Dec. (to Garnett): 'when I tell you' for 'whan I tell you'; 1924: 7 April (To Canby): 'psychology' for 'phycology'; 2 June (to F. N. Doubleday): 'Preface' for 'Preafce'.

INDEXES

In Index I, which identifies recipients, only the first page of each letter is cited. Letters to multiple recipients are indexed under each name and marked ^{††}. Tentative identifications are marked [†].

In Index II, an index of names, run-on pagination often covers more than one letter. References to British political institutions are consolidated under 'British (or UK) government and constitution'; to London and its localities, under 'London'; to New York and its environs, under 'New York'; to serial publications, under 'Periodicals'; to educational bodies, under 'Schools, colleges, and universities'; and to ships, under 'Ships'. References to works by Conrad, uniform editions, and selections from his writing appear under his name.

INDEX I. RECIPIENTS

Adams, Elbridge L., 12, 52, 106, 333, 371
Allen, J. A., 285
Alvar: *see* Harding, Louise Alvar
Aubry, Ferdinand, 254^{††}, 269
Aubry, Jean: *see* Jean-Aubry, G.
Aubry, Thérèse, 174, 254^{††}

Barker, Ambrose G., 165
Bell, Lt-Col. Matthew, 204
Bendz, Ernst P., 36
Bennett, Arnold, 240, 249, 259
Blanchenay, Lt Pierre-Frédéric†, 340
Blasco Ibáñez, Vicente, 53
Bone, Capt. David, 30, 50, 79, 252
Burleigh, Louise, 14

Canby, Henry S., 338
Candler, Edmund, 226, 266, 276
Cecchi, Emilio, 227
Chassé, Charles, 290
Chew, Samuel C., 107
Clarke, G. H., 153
Clarke, Harald Leofurn, 4
Clifford, Sir Hugh, 158, 337, 383
Cockerell, Sydney, 227, 245

Colvin, Lady, 399^{††}
Colvin, Sir Sidney, 146, 399^{††}
Conrad, Borys, 8, 89, 104, 260, 378, 382, 408
Conrad, Jessie, 84, 85, 87, 90, 93, 95, 100, 102, 104 (2), 387, 388(2), 389 (2), 390 (2), 391, 392 (2), 393, 394, 395 (2), 396
Conrad, Joan, 398
Conrad, John, 92
Cooper, Commander F. G., 330
Copeau, Jacques, 305
Crane, Edith F., 270
Curle, Richard, 5, 8, 18, 47, 77, 80, 87, 94, 100, 118, 129, 134, 140, 143, 159, 162, 166, 170, 176, 182, 185, 189, 191, 200, 207, 210, 211, 217, 228, 234, 248, 252, 264, 274, 275, 294, 321, 325, 330, 348, 364, 383, 396, 400, 406, 410

Davis, Clare Ogden, 405
Davray, Henry-Durand, 27
Dawson, Ernest, 399
Dawson, F. Warrington, 141
Dent, Hugh, 38, 178
Dent, J. M., 67, 154, 251

INDEX II. GENERAL